S0-ATB-644

History of Interpretation

San Jose Bible College
Memorial Library

Listha Robert's Sister

Presented by

M/M Porter Roberts

William Jessup University
Library
333 Sunset Blvd.
Rocklin, Ca 95765

3C111

History of Interpretation

Frederic W. Farrar

San Jose Bible College Library
790 S. 12th St., P.O. Box 1090
San Jose, California 95108

BAKER BOOK HOUSE
Grand Rapids, Michigan

Reprinted 1961 by
Baker Book House Company
from the 1886 edition
published by E. P. Dutton

Paperback edition issued 1979
ISBN: 0-8010-3489-2

Library of Congress Catalog Number: 61-10004

PHOTOLITHOPRINTED BY CUSHING - MALLOY, INC.
ANN ARBOR, MICHIGAN, UNITED STATES OF AMERICA
1979

PREFACE.

In publishing these Lectures there are two remarks which I ought at once to make, because they may serve to obviate much criticism which will have no relation to the objects which I have had in view.

1. By Exegesis I always mean the explanation of the immediate and primary sense of the sacred writings. If I were treating the subject from an entirely different point of view it would be easy to show that much of the material which has furnished forth many hundreds of commentaries remains practically unchanged from early days. But this material is mainly homiletic. It aims almost exclusively at moral and spiritual edification. In such practical instruction the writings of the Fathers and the Schoolmen abound, and it is often of the highest intrinsic value even when it has but a slender connexion with the text on which it is founded. When I speak of Scriptural interpretation I am using the phrase in its narrower and more limited meaning.

2. It is obvious that within the compass of Eight Lectures an exhaustive treatment of so wide a subject would be impossible. To write a full history of Exegesis would require a space of many volumes. I here only profess to deal

with the chief *epochs* in the progress of Biblical science, and my endeavour has been to give some account, however brief, of those who caused the chief moments of fresh impulse to the methods of interpretation. Hence, there have been many eminent commentators whose names do not occur in the following pages because their writings produced no change in the dominant conceptions. The remark applies especially to the great Romanist commentators since the Reformation, such as Vatablus († 1547), Maldonatus († 1583), Estius († 1613), Cornelius à Lapide († 1657), Martianay († 1717), Calmet († 1757), and others. I should be the last person to depreciate their conspicuous merits.[1] In any complete History of Exegesis the names of these great and learned writers would of course find an honoured place. I have not been able to touch upon their labours partly from want of space, but chiefly because I only profess to furnish some outline of the epoch-making events of Scriptural study.

There does not exist in any language a complete History of Exegesis. Large materials for such a task are collected in such works as the *Isagoge of Buddeus* (1730), Schröck's *Kirchengeschichte* (1768—1812), Rosenmüller's *Historia Interpretationis* (1795—1814), Meyer's *Geschichte der Schrifterklärung* (1803), Klausen's *Hermeneutik des Neuen Testaments* (translated from the Danish 1841), Diestel's *Geschichte des Alten Testamentes* (1869), Reuss' *Die Geschichte der Heiligen Schriften* (1874), Merx's *Die Prophetie des Joel und ihre Ausleger* (1879),[2] and others which will be found mentioned in the appended Bibliography. Much information on parts of the subject may also be derived from the various Histories

---

[1] For some account of these Commentators, see Klausen, *Hermeneutik* (*Germ. Tr.* 1841), pp. 249-252. Werner, *Gesch. d. Kath. Theol.* 1866.

[2] I give the dates of the editions which I have myself used.

of Grätz, Jost, Neander, Gieseler, Böhringer, Dorner, Milman, and others. But the entire history has never been completely and satisfactorily written, and it would furnish worthy occupation for a lifetime of study. If I have sometimes wearied the reader with too many references I have done so in the hope that they might prove useful to some student who may hereafter undertake a task so interesting and so instructive.

In writing these sketches of the History of Biblical Interpretation I have never forgotten that the Bampton Lectures are meant to be apologetic. My sole desire has been to defend the cause of Christianity by furthering the interests of truth. So far as former methods of exegesis have been mistaken they have been also perilous. A recognition of past errors can hardly fail to help us in disencumbering from fatal impediments the religious progress of the future.

I have desired to carry out the purposes of the Founder in three ways.

First, by drawing attention to the inevitable change in the conditions of criticism which has been necessitated alike by the experience of the Christian Church and by that advance in knowledge which is nothing less than a new revelation of the ways and works of God.

Secondly, by showing that there is in the final and eternal teachings of Scripture a grandeur, which, in all ages, however learned or however ignorant, has secured for them a transcendent authority. A Book less sacred would have been discredited by the dangerous uses to which it has often been perverted; but no aberrations of interpreters have been suffered to weaken, much less to abrogate, the essential revelation which has exercised from the first, and will "to the last syllable of recorded time" continue to exercise a unique power over the hearts and consciences of men.

Thirdly, by robbing of all their force the objections of infidels and freethinkers to the historic details or moral imperfections of particular narratives of the Old Testament. This endeavour has an importance that those only will appreciate who have tried to understand the thoughts of many hearts. "There are things in the Old Testament," says Professor Drummond, "cast in the teeth of the apologist by sceptics, to which he has simply no answer. These are the things, the miserable things, the masses have laid hold of. They are the stock-in-trade of the freethought platform and the secularist pamphleteer. A new exegesis, a reconsideration of the historic setting, and a clearer view of the moral purposes of God, would change them from barriers into bulwarks of the faith."[1] But we cannot meet these objections by treating the Bible as a mere word-book, as a compendium of homogeneous doctrines, as "an even plane of proof texts without proportion, or emphasis, or light, or shade." The existence of moral and other difficulties in the Bible has been frankly recognised in all ages, and it is certain that they can no longer be met by such methods as were devised by Philo, or Origen, or Aquinas, or Calovius. But they vanish before the radical change of attitude which has taught us to regard the Bible as the record of a progressive revelation divinely adapted to the hard heart, the dull understanding, and the slow development of mankind. They are fatal to untenable theories of inspiration whether Rabbinic or Scholastic, but they are powerless against the clearer conceptions which we have neither invented nor discovered, but which have been opened to us by the teach-

---

[1] *Contributions of Science to Christianity,* Expositor, Feb. 1885.

ing of the Spirit of God in the domains of History and of Science. It may be said that the Bible is the same to-day as it was a thousand years ago. Yes, and Nature too is the same now as she was in the days of Pythagoras; but it is as impossible to interpret the Bible now by the methods of Aqiba or Hilary as it is to interpret Nature by the methods of Pythagoras. The History of Exegesis leads us to the complete transformation of a method, and leaves us with a Bible more precious than of old, because more comprehensible, while it is at the same time impregnable in every essential particular against any existing form of assault.

But instead of dogmatically propounding a scheme of interpretation, I have allowed the History of Interpretation to suggest to us its own scheme, and to deliver for our guidance its own lessons. We shall see system after system— the Halakhic, the Kabbalistic, the Traditional, the Hierarchic, the Inferential, the Allegorical, the Dogmatic, the Naturalistic—condemned and rejected, each in turn, by the experience and widening knowledge of mankind. These erroneous systems arose from many causes. The original Hebrew of the Old Testament was for many ages unknown to the Christian Church, and when Greek also became an unknown language to all except a few, the caprice of interpreters was freed from important checks. Religious controversy went to Scripture not to seek for dogmas but to find them. Mysticism interpreted it according to the mood of the moment and placed the interpreter above the text. A spurious and unenlightened idolatry for the letter of Scripture ignored its simplicity and universality, and sought for enigmas and mysteries in the plainest passages. A scholastic orthodoxy developed elaborate systems of theology out of imaginary emphases, and by the aid of exorbitant principles of inference. Some of these causes of error are removed, but we still meet the pale and feeble shadows of the old systems wandering here and there, unexorcised, in modern commentaries. They can, however, only be regarded with curiosity as anachronisms and survivals. It is perhaps inevitable that as each individual has his idols of the cavern, so each age should have its idols of the forum or the theatre, to which it offers a passionate yet half-unacknowledged worship. But the last word of the sacred Book was a word of infinite significance. It was, "Little children, keep yourselves from idols." Idols are always a fatal hindrance to the attainment of the truth. Sooner or later they that make them become like unto them, and so do all who put their trust in them. Such εἴδωλα—"ignorant well-meanings, credulous suspicions, and fond conceits"—these fleeting images born of confusions of language, false theories, and perverse demonstrations,[1]— only vanish when the light of God penetrates into the deep recesses of the shrine. HISTORY is a ray of that light of God. A great part of the Bible is History, and all History, rightly understood, is also a Bible. Its lessons are God's divine method of slowly exposing error and of guiding into truth. "*Facts* are God's words, and to be disloyal to God's facts is to dethrone Him from the world." Orosius began his summary of the *De Civitate Dei* with the memorable words, *Divinâ Providentiâ agitur mundus et homo.* It was from the same point of view that Bossuet composed his History. "History," said Vico, "is a Civil theology of the Divine Providence." "The History of the World," said Wilhelm von Humboldt, "is not intelligible apart from a

---

[1] "*Idola fori* omnium molestissima sunt ; quae ex foedere verborum et nominum se insinuarunt in intellectum." "*Idola theatri* innata non sunt . . . sed ex fabulis theoriarum et perversis legibus demonstrationum plane indita et recepta."—BACON, *Nov. Organum.* lib. i. lix. lx.

Government of the world." "Every step in advance in History," said Fichte, "every mental act which introduces into its chain of occurrences something absolutely new, is an inflowing of God. God alone makes History, but He does this by the agency of man."[1] "Great men," says Carlyle, "are the inspired texts of that divine book of Revelations whereof a chapter is completed from epoch to epoch, and by some named History."[2] And if we look for higher sanctions than those of Vico, or Humboldt, or Fichte, or Carlyle—higher too than those of Orosius, or Augustine, or Bossuet—we find them in St. Paul's Philosophy of History in his speech at Athens, that "God made of one every nation of men . . . . having determined their appointed seasons, that they should seek God if haply they might feel after Him and find Him;"[3]— or in the yet briefer testimony of St. John, that there is a true light, a constant, continuous revelation of the Word which lighteth every man, and is ever coming into the World;[4]—or once again in two pregnant passages of the Epistle to the Hebrews, "God who fragmentarily and multifariously spake unto the Fathers in the Prophets, hath in these last days spoken unto us in His Son;"[5] and "But now hath He promised, saying, 'Yet once more will I make to tremble not the earth only but also the heaven.' And this word 'Yet once more' signifieth the removing of those things that are shaken . . . . that those things which are not shaken may remain."[6]

But it may perhaps be asked, "How can the Bible have been liable to agelong misapprehensions if it be a Divine Revelation?"

---

[1] Fichte, *Spec. Theology*, p. 651.
[2] *Sartor Resartus*, p. 108.
[3] Acts xvii. 26-30.
[4] John i. 9.
[5] Heb. i. 1.
[6] Heb. xii. 27.

i. The answer is very simple : the Bible is not so much a revelation as the *record* of a revelation, and the inmost and most essential truths which it contains have happily been placed above the reach of Exegesis to injure, being written also in the Books of Nature and Experience, and on the tables, which cannot be broken, of the heart of Man. " Where the doctrine is necessary and important," there, says Whichcote, " the Scripture is clear and full."

ii. But, secondly, I borrow the method of Bishop Butler, and say that the agelong misinterpretations of the Bible are no more a disproof of its divine authority, than are the age-long misinterpretations of Nature any disproof of its Divine Creation. If the History of Exegesis involve a history of false suppositions slowly and progressively corrected, so, too, does the History of Science. Kepler was contented to wait a century for a reader, where God had waited six thousand years for an observer. God is patient because Eternal, and man who is slow to learn spiritual truths, is still slower to unlearn familiar errors. Being men and not angels, it is by a ladder that we must mount step by step towards that heaven which the mind of man can never reach by wings.

iii. And, thirdly, explain or illustrate the fact as we may, a fact it is. " Twenty doctors," said Tyndale, " expound one text twenty ways, and with an antitheme of half an inch some of them draw a thread of nine days long." [1] The last Revision of the Bible has once more reminded us that many passages and hundreds of expressions which have been implicitly accepted by generations, and quoted as the very word of God, were in fact the erroneous translations of imperfect readings. If the vast majority of Christians have always had to be content with a Bible which is in so many

[1] *Obedience of a Christian Man.*

instances inaccurately copied or wrongly translated, it is not astonishing that they should also have had to put up with a Bible which in many instances has been wrongly explained. Now if indeed every word of Scripture had been written "by the pen of the Triune God," we might have thought that these errors involved an irreparable loss. But the loss is in no sense irreparable. It affects no single essential truth. "If after using diligence to find truth we fall into error where the Scriptures are not plain, there is no danger in it. They that err, and they that do not err, shall both be saved."[1]

But it must not be supposed that the lessons which we may learn from the History of Exegesis are merely negative. It has positive truths to teach as well as errors to dispel. It may show us the stagnation which poisons the atmosphere of Theology when Progress is violently arrested, and Freedom authoritatively suppressed. It may show us the duty and the necessity of that tolerance against which, from the first century down to the present day, Churches and theologians have so deeply and so continuously sinned. It may show us above all that the strength of the Church is not to be identified with the continuance of methods which have been tried and found wanting, or with the preservation of systems which have been condemned by the long results of time. Truth rests on something far different. It depends upon faithfulness to the immediate teaching of Christ, and on obedience to the continual guidance of His ever-present Spirit. The authority of the Scripture can only be vindicated by the apprehension of its divinest elements. We cannot understand its final teaching except by recognising the co-ordinate authority of Faith, and by believing that to us, as to the holy

[1] Chillingworth, *Religion of Protestants.*

men of old, the Spirit still utters the living oracles of God. Many lessons have been derived from Scripture which are alien from the final teaching of the New Dispensation, but

> " One accent of the Holy Ghost
> The heedless world has never lost."

And is it a small lesson if we thus learn that we are not bound passively to abandon to others the exercise of our noblest faculties, nor to shut our eyes to the teachings of experience ; but that it is our duty with fearless freedom, though in deep humility and the sincerity of pure hearts, to follow in all things the guidance of Reason and of Conscience ?

" A man may be an heretic in the truth, and if he believe things only because his pastor says so, or the assembly so determines, without knowing other reason, though his belief be true, yet the very truth he holds becomes his heresy." So spake the lofty soul of John Milton.

" He who makes use of the light and faculties which God hath given him, and seeks sincerely to discover truth by those helps and abilities . . . . will not miss the reward of truth. He that doeth otherwise transgresses against his own light." So spake the serene wisdom of John Locke.

Could we listen to manlier voices ? But if we look rather for theological, for orthodox, for episcopal authority its best teaching will be of the same tenor. "For men to be tied and led by authority, as it were with a kind of captivity of judgment, and though there be reason to the contrary not to listen to it, but to follow like beasts the first in the herd, this were brutish." So spake one whom the Church of England once revered—Richard Hooker.[1]

" Reason," says Culverwell, "is the daughter of Eternity,

---

[1] *Eccl. Pol.* ii. 7, § 6.

and before Antiquity, which is the daughter of Time."[1] "Reason can, and it ought to judge, not only of the meaning, but also of the morality and evidence of revelation." So spake one whom we still profess to revere—Bishop Butler.[2]

"No apology can be required for applying to the Bible the principles of reason and learning; for if the Bible could not stand the test of reason and learning it could not be what it is—a work of divine wisdom. The Bible therefore must be examined by the same laws of criticism which are applied to other writings of antiquity." So wrote Bishop Herbert Marsh.

Do we need yet higher authority to show us that we are in the right when we scorn to register the decrees of human fallibility, or to float down the smooth current of religious opinions? If so we may find it abundantly in Scripture. "The spirit of man," says Solomon, "is the candle of the Lord."[3] "Brethren, believe not every spirit, but try the spirits whether they are of God."[4] So said St. John the Divine. "Prove all things; hold fast that which is good." So wrote St. Paul.[5]

Do we seek yet higher authority for this indefeasible right of private judgment? We have the authority of Christ Himself. "Why even of yourselves, judge ye not what is right?" So spake the Lord of Glory.[6]

But further, this history has taught us that with Freedom, and the fearless appeal to the reason and the conscience in judging the separate utterances of Scripture, so too there must be PROGRESS. "Truth," says Milton, "is compared in

---

[1] *Ductor Dubitantium*, I. ii. § 64.　　[2] *Light of Nature*, p. 136.
[3] Prov. xx. 27.　　[4] 1 John iv. 1.
[5] 1 Thess. v. 21.　　[6] Luke xii. 57.

Scripture to a streaming fountain; if her waters flow not in a perpetual progression they sicken into a muddy pool of conformity and tradition." A timid attitude, a passive attitude, a servile attitude belongs to the spirit of fear, not to that of a sound mind. It is nothing short of a sin against light and knowledge—yes, I will say it boldly, it is nothing short of a sin against the Holy Ghost—to stereotype, out of the pretence of reverence, the errors of men who were not more illuminated by God's Spirit than we may be, and who in knowledge were hundreds of years behind ourselves. Lactantius, on the authority of Scripture, denied that the earth was round; and Augustine that there could be men at the antipodes; and the Spanish theologians that there could be a western hemisphere. "Who," asks Calvin, "will venture to place the authority of Copernicus above that of the Holy Spirit?" "Newton's discoveries," said the Puritan John Owen, "are against evident testimonies of Scripture." With what outbursts of denunciation has almost every new science been received by narrow literalists! Surely such ignorant condemnations show us that the revision of the principles and methods of exegesis is rendered absolutely necessary by the ever-widening knowledge of modern days. Theology must reckon with this infinite desire of knowledge which has broken out all over the world, with this rapid and ever-rising tide of truth which she is impotent to stay. We may store the truth in our earthen vessels, but, as has been truly said, they must lie unstopped in the ocean, for if we take them out of it we shall only have "stagnant doctrines rotting in a dead theology."

I have, therefore, endeavoured as regards each of the seven epochs of exegesis to point out the causes and the origin of its special conceptions; to set the series of writers, and

movements, and views in their true historic horizon ; to see
the manifold influences which affected the schools of exegetes and were modified by them ; and to show how many
of these conceptions have been proved by the course of time
to be more or less untenable. We shall see exegesis fettered
under the sway of legalism; of Greek philosophy ; of allegory ;
of tradition ; of ecclesiastic system; of Aristotelian dialectics ;
of elaborate dogma. We shall observe the revival of the
methods of the School of Antioch in the emergence of
grammatical and literal interpretations at the Renaissance
and the Reformation, and shall see reviving energies strangled
for a time by the theological intolerance of a Protestant
scholasticism. We shall survey the influence upon exegesis
of a philosophic scepticism, and shall note the lines and
methods by which the attacks of that scepticism have been
rendered powerless. But in judging of *systems* there is
scarcely an instance in which I have failed to do justice to
the greatness and sincerity of *men.* Aqiba and Philo,
Origen and Augustine, Aquinas and De Lyra, Spener
and Calixt, Schleiermacher and Baur have severally received
the meed of acknowledgment due to their genius and their
integrity. We may say of them all, " Habeantur . . . . pro
luminibus, sed nobis sit unicum numen."[1] The rejection
of their methods no more involves injustice to them than
the rejection of the Ptolemaic system involves any contempt
for the genius of Ptolemy.

There are two tasks which I have not attempted to
perform :—

i. It has been no part of my duty to lay down any theory of
Inspiration. It has indeed been impossible to avoid frequent
references to one theory—that of verbal dictation—because

[1] Rivetus, *Isagoge*, cap. 18, § 11.

from it (as I have been obliged to show) every mistaken
method of interpretation, and many false views of morals and
sociology, have derived their disastrous origin. That theory
has never offered any valid proof for the immense demand
which it makes upon our credulity.[1] It confessedly traverses
all the *prima facie* phenomena of Scripture, and yet it finds
no support in the claims of Scripture for itself. It sprang
from heathenism, and it leads to infidelity. It has been
decisively rejected by many of the greatest Christian theologians, and—as I have had occasion to prove—is inconsistent
with the repeated expressions of many by whom it was
nominally accepted.[2] But while we shun the falsehood of

[1] Tholuck, in his admirable paper on "The Doctrine of Inspiration,"
translated in the *Journal of Sacred Literature*, vi. 331–369, thinks that the
view of inspiration which regarded Holy Scripture as the infallible production
of the Divine Spirit, not merely in its *religious*, but in its *entire*, contents,
and not merely in its *contents*, but in its very *form*, is not earlier, strictly speaking, than the seventeenth century. He refers to Quenstedt, *Theol. Didact.
Polem.* i. 55 ; Heidegger, *Corp. Theol.* ii. 34 ; Calovius, *Systema*, i. 484, &c.,
&c., and says that the Lutheran symbols contain no express definition of the
inspiration of the Scriptures. He was of course aware of the loose,
rhetorical, popular phrases used by many of the Fathers and Schoolmen, but
he points out that their modes of dealing with Scripture belie their verbal
theories, as in Papias, *ap.* Euseb. *H. E.* iii. 39 ; Orig. *in Joann.* tome i. p. 4
(ed. 1668) ; i. p. 383 (*id.*) ; Aug. *De Cons. Evang.* i. 35, ii. 12, 28 ; Junilius,
De partibus Div. Leg. i. 8, and to many passages of Jerome. He also
quotes Agobard, *adv. Fredegis*, c. 12, and St. Thomas Aquinas, *Summa*, i.
qu. 32, *art.* 4 ; Abelard, *Sic et Non*, p. 11 (ed. Cousin). Many Roman
Catholic theologians admit minor errors, discrepancies, &c., in the Bible, *e.g.*
Bellarmine, Bonfrère, Cornelius à Lapide, R. Simon, Antonius de Dominis,
Erasmus, Maldonatus. So also did Luther, Zwingli, Colet, Brenz, Bullinger,
Castellio, Grotius, Rivet, Calixt, Le Clerc, &c. Such views are inconsistent
with the Verbal Dictation Dogma of Calovius, Voetius, and the Formula
Consensus Helvetici. See Tholuck, *l.c.*

[2] Among theologians who have indirectly or explicitly rejected the theory
of verbal dictation and infallibility (though some of them at times used loose
popular and general language entirely inconsistent with their own admissions)
may be mentioned among English writers Hooker, Howe, Chillingworth,
Bishop Williams, Burnet, Baxter, Tillotson, Horsley, Doddridge, Warburton,
Paley, Lowth, Hey, Watson, Law, Tomline, Dr. J. Barrow, Dean Conybeare,
Bishop Hinds, Bishop Daniel Wilson, Bishops Van Mildert and Blomfield,
Archbishop Whately, Bishops Hampden, Thirlwall, and Heber, Dean Alford,

this extreme we equally shun the opposite falsehood of treating Scripture as though it did not contain a divine revelation. If we accept the Inspiration of Scripture, without attempting to define it, we only follow the example of the Universal Church. Neither the Catholic creeds, nor the Anglican articles, nor the Lutheran symbols, nor the Tridentine decrees define it. In modern times especially, bishops and theologians of every school have been singularly unanimous in repudiating every attempt to determine exactly what Inspiration means.[1] "It seems certain," said Bishop Thirlwall, "that there is no visible organ of our Church competent to define that which has hitherto been left undetermined on this point," namely, what is the line to be drawn between

Thomas Scott, Dr. Pye Smith, and very many living or recent theologians. See for references Dr. A. S. Farrar, *Bampton Lectures*, pp. 668-671 ; Pusey, *Historical Enquiry*, ch. v.

[1] "I was in nowise called upon to attempt any definition of Inspiration," says Archbishop Tait in his Pastoral Letter, "seeing that the Church has not thought fit to prescribe one."

"The Church has laid down," says the Archbishop of York in his Pastoral Letter, "no theory of Inspiration ; she has always had in her bosom teachers of at least two different theories."

"We heartily concur with the majority of our opponents," says the Bishop of Gloucester and Bristol in *Aids to Faith*, p. 404, "in rejecting all theories of Inspiration."

"Let us beware," says Dean Burgon (*Pastoral Office*, p. 58), "how we commit ourselves to any theories of Inspiration whatever."

"Our Church," says Bishop Thirlwall (*Charge for* 1863), "has never attempted to determine the nature of the Inspiration of Holy Scripture" (p. 107 ; see, too, *Charges*, i. p. 295).

"If you ask me," says Dr. Cotton, Bishop of Calcutta, "for a precise theory of Inspiration, I confess that I can only urge you to repudiate all theories, to apply to theology the maxim which guided Newton in philosophy, *hypotheses non fingo*, and to rest your teaching upon the facts which God has made known to us" (*Charge of* 1863, p. 69).

"It must be borne in mind," says the *Quarterly Review*, "that the Church Universal has never given any definition of Inspiration" (April, 1864, p. 560).

"It seems pretty generally agreed," says the Bishop of Winchester, "that definite theories of Inspiration are doubtful and dangerous" (*Aids to Faith*, p. 303).

the divine and the human elements in the Bible. Under
such circumstances we turn to the Old Testament Scriptures,
and there we find many instances to prove that "inspiration"
involves neither general perfection nor infallibility, nor any
perpetual immunity from imitations of intellect or errors
of practice.[1] If we endeavour to arrive at the meaning of
the word from its usage in our own formularies we there repeatedly find that the term "inspiration" is given to processes
of grace which never exclude the coexistence of ordinary
human imperfections.[2] And this is in exact accordance with
every indication which we derive from the New Testament, for
it shows us that inspired men, after the gift of Pentecost, in
nowise regarded themselves as being exempt from human
weaknesses, and indeed differed widely from each other in
matters of minor importance, while they were in absolute
agreement about essential truths. It is a mere *a priori*
theory to assume that in their written words their personality was obliterated by a supernatural ecstasy or all
their most trivial expressions invested with the dignity of an
utterance of God. The words of St. Chrysostom about St.
Paul—εἰ καὶ Παῦλος ἦν ἀλλ᾽ ἄνθρωπος ἦν, and of St.
Augustine about St. John—"*Inspiratus a Deo, sed tamen
homo*"—to say nothing of the example set by St. Jerome
and some of the greatest Fathers, show that there is no need

---

[1] "Inspiration" is attributed to Bezaleel, though art was in its merest
infancy (Ex. xxxi. 3–6) ; to men of ordinary skill in husbandry, though the
husbandry was quite rudimentary (Is. xxviii. 24–29) ; to Balaam, Gideon,
Othniel, Jephtha, Samson, David, Jonah, &c., though full of imperfections.

[2] "Works done before the grace of Christ and the *inspiration* of His
Spirit."—*Art.* xiii. "Cleanse the thoughts of our hearts by the *inspiration*
of thy Holy Spirit."—*Collect in the Communion Service.* "Beseeching Thee
to *inspire* continually the Universal Church."—*Prayer for the Church Militant.*
"Grant . . . that by Thy Holy *inspiration* we may think those things that
be good."—*Collect for Fifth Sunday after Easter.* "Come, Holy Ghost, our
souls *inspire.*"—*Veni Creator.* See, too, the Homilies for Whitsun Day and
for Rogation Week.

to deny the moral or other difficulties which allegory was invoked to explain away. Inspiration can only be confused with verbal infallibility by ignoring the most obvious facts of language and history. Christ only is the Truth. He alone is free from all error.

ii. Nor have I been called upon to lay down any formal system of Exegesis, though to a certain extent the germ of one comprehensive system is involved in the rejection of many which have hitherto been dominant. If, as the ancient interpreters constantly asserted, allegory is not valid for purposes of demonstration, and if nothing is revealed allegorically which is not elsewhere revealed unmistakably without allegory, it is clear that by abandoning the allegoric method we cannot lose anything essential. Bishop Marsh and Bishop Van Mildert laid down the rule that we need only accept those allegories which are sanctioned by the New Testament. But of allegories which in any way resemble those of Philo or of the Fathers and the Schoolmen, I can find in the New Testament but one.[1] It may be merely intended as an *argumentum ad hominem ;* it does not seem to be more than a passing illustration; it is not at all essential to the general argument; it has not a particle of *demonstrative* force; in any case it leaves untouched the actual history. But whatever view we take of it, the occurrence of one such allegory in the Epistle of St. Paul no more sanctions the universal application of the method than a few New Testament allusions to the Haggada compel us to accept the accumulations of the Midrashim ; or a few quotations from Greek poets prove the divine authority of all Pagan literature ; or a single specimen of the Athbash

---

[1] Gal. iv. 21- 27.

in Jeremiah authorises an unlimited application of the method of Notarikon.[1]

And as we have rejected the extravagances of the allegoric method, we similarly reject the exaggerated claims of the traditional and dogmatic Schools of Exegesis. As for tradition, we trace it back to its earliest extant sources, and find that even in Papias and Irenaeus, in Tertullian and Cyprian, it has been unanimously rejected by the Christian world both as to many matters of fact and many matters of opinion. And as for Church doctrine, we absolutely accept the guidance of those early and very simple creeds which are unambiguously deducible from the Scriptures themselves, but we refuse to make of Scripture the leaden rule[2] which must always, and at all hazards, be bent into accordance with the ecclesiastical confessions of a particular Church. Astronomers once interpreted the facts of the sidereal heavens by rules founded on the geocentric hypothesis. Infinite confusions and complications resulted from the attempt to force the actual stellar phenomena into agreement with that theory when men came to model heaven and calculate how they might—

> "Build, unbuild, contrive,
> *To save appearances,* how gird the sphere
> With centric and eccentric scribbled o'er,
> Cycle and epicycle, orb in orb."

Kepler himself lost years of labour by the *a priori* assumption that the circle was a perfect figure, and that, therefore, the stars could only revolve in circles. The mistake of the Schoolmen and the Post-Reformation dogmatists was analogous to this. They assumed that all Scripture must

---

[1] Jer. xxv. 26 ; li. 41. See *infra,* Lect. ii., where these allusions are fully explained.

[2] Ὥσπερ καὶ τῆς Λεσβίας οἰκοδομῆς ὁ μολύβδινος κανών. Πρὸς γὰρ τὸ σχῆμα τοῦ λίθου μετακινεῖται.—ARIST. *Eth. N.* v. 10.

be absolutely perfect down to its minutest details. They argued that the whole cause of religion was lost if it could be proved—as in course of time it was proved to their complete confusion—that the sacred text abounded in various readings due to the carelessness, the ignorance, or the bias of scribes, and that the Masoretic points, so far from being "inspired," were comparatively modern. They used the whole system of mediaeval Catholicism, or of Lutheran and Reformed confessions, not only to suggest, but to dictate the results of a nominally unfettered inquiry. In this way they strove, but happily in vain, to render impossible the growth and progress of religious thought. He who would study Scripture in its integrity and purity must approach the sacred page "with a mind washed clean from human opinions."

If the Bible as a whole possesses a divine authority that authority must rest on its inherent nature and its actual phenomena, not on the theories and inventions of men respecting it. "Whatever excellence there is in it," said a wise and holy modern philanthropist, "will be fireproof; and if any portion of it be obsolete or spurious, let that portion be treated accordingly." We may therefore assume that all Exegesis must be unsound which is not based on the literal, grammatical, historical contextual sense of the sacred writers. It is an exegetic fraud to invest with their authority the conclusions at which we only arrive by distorting the plain significance of their words. It is the duty of an Exegete to explain, and not to explain away. If the Revelation of God has come to us in great measure through a Book set in time, place, and human conditions, it is impossible that we should rightly apprehend the meaning of that Book otherwise than by linguistic and literary laws. Only by studying the temporary setting can we reach the eternal verity. And if it be objected that this is to interpret the Bible as we interpret any other book, we will not merely answer that the necessity for such a rule has been admitted by some of the wisest alike of the Rabbis, the Fathers, and the Reformers, but will say that from such a formula fairly apprehended there is no need to shrink. The Bible indeed is not a common book. It is a book supreme and unique, which will ever be reckoned among the divinest gifts of God to man. But yet, being a book, or rather a collection of books, it can only be interpreted as what it is. The ordinary methods of modern criticism, ratified as they are by the teaching of history, afford to us the best means of discovering, across the chasm of the Ages, both the original meaning of the sacred writers and whatever admissible indications of other and larger meanings may be involved in what they taught.

My main wish and object has been to show the true basis whereon rests the sacredness of Holy Scripture. So far from detracting from the infinite preciousness of the truths which we can learn from Scripture best—and often from Scripture only—I earnestly desire to rescue those truths from the confusions and perversions to which they are still subjected. It is because there is no Book and no Literature which can for a moment supply the place of the Bible in the moral and spiritual education of mankind that I would do my utmost to save it from the injury of false theories and impossible interpretations. But it is impossible not to see that they who have approached it in the spirit of freedom have served it best. How rich and varied are the testimonies which might be collected from every quarter to its potency of influence ! When Dean Stanley was visiting the foremost of modern exegetes, a New Testament which was lying on the table accidentally fell to the ground. " In this Book," said Heinrich von Ewald, as he stooped to pick it up, " in this Book is contained all the wisdom of the world." " That Book, sir," said the American President, Andrew Jackson, pointing to the family Bible during his last illness, " is the rock on which our Republic rests." " I fear you are ill," said Dr. Latham to Faraday whom he found in tears with his hand resting on an open book. " It is not that," said Faraday with a sob, " but *why* will people go astray when they have this blessed Book to guide them?" [1] " This collection of books," said Theodore Parker, " has taken such a hold on the world as no other. The literature of Greece, which goes up like incense from that land of temples and heroic deeds, has not half the influence of this book. It goes equally to the cottage of the plain man and the palace of the king. It is woven into the literature of the scholar and colours the talk of the streets." " How," asks Professor Huxley, " is the religious feeling, which is the essential basis of conduct, to be kept up in the present utterly chaotic state of opinion . . . without the use of the Bible? The pagan moralists lack life and colour, and even the noble Stoic, Marcus Antoninus, is too high and refined for an ordinary child. By the study of what other book could children be so much humanised and made to feel that each figure in the vast historical procession fills, like themselves, but a momentary space in the interval between two eternities, and earns the blessings or the curses of all time according to its efforts to do good and hate evil?" [2] These various voices do but repeat the calm judgment of Hooker, " There is scarcely any noble part of knowledge worthy the mind of man but

---

[1] The anecdote was told me by Professor Acland, who heard it from Dr. Latham.   [2] *The Contemp. Rev.* Dec. 1870.

from Scripture it may have some direction and light."[1] No man would endorse more heartily than I the words of our translators of 1611, " If we be ignorant, the Scriptures will instruct us ; if out of the way, they will bring us home; if out of order, they will reform us ; if in heaviness, comfort us ; if dull, quicken us; if cold, inflame us. *Tolle, lege. Tolle, lege.*" Yet, while we echo all these glowing eulogies and many more, we do not forget the warning of the great and pre-eminently "judicious" theologian whom I have just quoted, "Whatsoever is spoken cf God, or things pertaining to God, otherwise than as the truth is, though it seem an honour, it is an injury."[2]

Many readers, discouraged by the apparently negative character of much that is here dwelt upon, may perhaps desire a fuller development of the positive side of the truth respecting the Scriptures. In proof that I deeply sympathise with that desire, I may be surely allowed to appeal to a series of works, spread over a space of twenty years, in which I have devoted my best thoughts and most earnest labour to develop and elucidate the truths taught in the Book of Books. No generous mind will condemn me, if, in proof that no purely negative or destructive criticism would have my sympathy or express my feelings, I humbly venture to refer to my commentaries on St. Luke and the Epistle to the Hebrews, to the *Life of Christ*, the *Life of St. Paul*, the *Early Days of Christianity*, and the *Messages of the Books*.

There only remains the pleasant duty of offering my best thanks to those who have so kindly helped me by their suggestions or in other ways during the preparation of these Lectures. To my kind and learned friend Prof. A. S. Farrar, D.D., Canon of Durham, I am peculiarly indebted for valuable advice and assistance, of which I shall always retain a

[1] *Eccl. Pol.* III. iv. 1. [2] *Eccl. Pol.* II. viii. 7.

very grateful remembrance. I have also to tender my sincere acknowledgments—of which they will forgive the very inadequate expression—to the Dean of Wells, the Dean of Westminster, the Rev. Dr. Wace, Mr. W. Aldis Wright, the Rev. J. Lupton, the Rev. Dr. Stanley Leathes, the Rev. J. Ll. Davies, the Ven. Archdeacon Norris, Mr. P. J. Hershon, and other friends who have given me the advantage of their criticisms or suggestions. No part of my labour has caused me more pleasure than the fact that it should call forth the kind interest of those whom I have long honoured and esteemed.

In a work which covers such vast periods of time and which involves so many hundreds of references it would be absurd to suppose that I have escaped from errors. All that I can say is that in this, as in my other works, I have done—not perhaps the best that I might have done under more favourable conditions of leisure and opportunity—but the best that was possible to me under such circumstances as I could command. If in the following pages I shall have offended any, I am heartily sorry for every ground of offence which may have been caused by my own defective modes of statement or expression, and I beg the indulgent consideration of all who believe that I am actuated solely by the desire to do nothing against the truth, but for the truth. I cannot, indeed, regret a single word which has been spoken under the strong conviction that it *ought* to be spoken. I have never sought to please men : but to the Lord of the Church, to Him who standeth in the midst of the seven golden candlesticks, I cry in deep humility : "Coram te est scientia et ignorantia mea ; ubi mihi aperuisti suscipe intrantem ; ubi clausisti aperi pulsanti."

FREDERIC W. FARRAR.

CHRONOLOGY

RELATING TO BIBLICAL INTERPRETATION.

Ezra, B.C. 457
The Septuagint, 277.
Aristobulus about 100.

Hillel, d. A.D. 8
Philo, d. 40.
Aqiba, d. 135.
Clement of Rome, about 95 A.D.
Pseudo-Barnabas, about 100.
Josephus, d. 100.
Justin Martyr, 164.
"Rabbi," d. 200.
Irenaeus, d. 202.
Clement of Alexandria, d. about 216.
Tertullian, d. about 220.
Origen, d. 254.
Cyprian, d. 258.
Eusebius of Caesarea, d. 340.
Athanasius, d. 373.
Ephraem Syrus, d. 378.
Basil, d. 379.
Ambrose, d. 397.
Chrysostom, d. 407.
Jerome, d. 420.
Rabbi Ashi, d. 427.
Theodore of Mopsuestia, d. 429.
Augustine, d. 430.
Theodoret, d. 457.
Talmud & Targums, 4th and 5th Cent.
Pseudo-Dionysius, c. 500.
Gregory I. d. 604.
Bede, d. 735.
John Damascenus, about 756.
Walafrid Strabo, 849.   (*Glossa Ordinaria*, abridged from Rabanus
J. Scotus Erigena, d. 875.   Maurus.)

Anselm, d. 1109.
Theophylact, about 1112.
Anselm of Laon (*Glossa Interlinearis*), d. 1117.
Rupert of Deutz, d. 1135.
Hugo de S. Victore, d. 1141.
Abelard, d. 1142.
Bernard, d. 1153.
Peter Lombard, d. 1164.
Richard de S. Victore, d. 1173.
Euthymius Zigabenus, 12th Cent.
Spanish school of Jews—Rashi, Abenezra, Kimchi, 12th Cent.
Maimonides, d. 1204.
Aquinas' *Catenae*, 1250.
Hugo de St. Caro (*Postilla*), d. 1263.
Thomas Aquinas, d. 1274.
Bonaventura, d. 1274.
Albertus Magnus, d. 1280.
Nicolas de Lyra, d. 1340.
William of Occam, d. 1347.
Wiclif, d. 1384.
Hus, d. 1415.
Valla, d. 1465.
Ximenes, d. 1517.
Reuchlin, d. 1522.
Tyndale's New Testament, 1526.
Zwingli, d. 1531.
Cajetan, d. 1534.
Erasmus, d. 1536.
The Great Bible, 1539.
Council of Trent, 1545.
Luther, d. 1546.
Calvin, d. 1564.
Maldonatus, d. 1583.
Sixtus Senensis, about 1560.
Geneva Bible, 1560.
Cornelius à Lapide, d. 1657.
Douai Bible, 1609.
Authorised Version, 1611.
Estius, d. 1613.
Mede, d. 1638.
Grotius, d. 1645.
S. Glass, d. 1656.
Calixt, d. 1656.
Hammond, d. 1660.
Critici Sacri, 1661. Edited by Pearson.
Poole's Synopsis *Criticorum*, 1669-1676.
Cocceius, d. 1669.
Lightfoot, d. 1675.
Calovius, d. 1686.

L. Cappell, d. 1658.
Spinoza, d. 1677.
Spener, d. 1705.
Patrick, d. 1707.
R. Simon, d. 1712.
Vitringa, d. 1722.
Rambach, d. about 1730.
Clericus, d. 1736.
Schœttgen, about 1750.
Ugolini's Theasurus, 1743-1745.
Bengel, d. 1752.
Wetstein, d. 1754.
Calmet, d. 1757.
Carpzov, d. 1767.
Ernesti, d. 1781.
Lessing, d. 1781.
Moses Mendelssohn, d. 1786.
Michaelis, d. 1791.
Bp. Lowth, d. 1787.
Semler, d. 1791.
Rosenmüller, J. G. 1815.
Herder, d. 1803.
Kant, d. 1804.
Horsley, d. 1806.
Jahn, d. 1816.
De Wette, 1830.
Hegel, d. 1831.
Schleiermacher, d. 1834.
S. T. Coleridge, d. 1834.
E. F. C. Rosenmüller, 1835.
Neander, d. 1850.
Ferd. Chr. Baur, d. 1861.
Strauss, d. 1874.
Ewald, d. 1875.

TABLE OF CONTENTS.

LECTURE I.

SUCCESS AND FAILURE OF EXEGESIS, pp. 1—43.

LECTURE II.

RABBINIC EXEGESIS, pp. 47—107.

LECTURE V.

SCHOLASTIC EXEGESIS, pp. 245—303.

LECTURE VI.

THE REFORMERS, pp. 307—354.

LECTURE VII.

POST-REFORMATION EPOCH, pp. 357—394.

LECTURE VIII.

MODERN EXEGESIS, pp. 397—437.

xlvi   *Table of Contents.*

NOTES.

NOTES TO LECTURE VI.

NOTE TO LECTURE VIII.

EXTRACT

FROM THE LAST WILL AND TESTAMENT

OF THE LATE

REV. JOHN BAMPTON,

CANON OF SALISBURY.

———

———" I give and bequeath my Lands and Estates to the
" Chancellor, Masters, and Scholars of the University of
" Oxford for ever, to have and to hold all and singular
" the said Lands or Estates upon trust, and to the intents
" and purposes hereinafter mentioned; that is to say, I
" will and appoint that the Vice-Chancellor of the Uni-
" versity of Oxford for the time being shall take and
" receive all the rents, issues, and profits thereof, and (after
" all taxes, reparations, and necessary deductions made)
" that he pay all the remainder to the endowment of eight
" Divinity Lecture Sermons, to be established for ever in
" the said University, and to be performed in the manner
" following:

" I direct and appoint, that, upon the first Tuesday in
" Easter Term, a Lecturer be yearly chosen by the Heads

" of Colleges only, and by no others, in the room ad-
" joining to the Printing-House, between the hours of ten
" in the morning and two in the afternoon, to preach eight
" Divinity Lecture Sermons, the year following, at St.
" Mary's in Oxford, between the commencement of the last
" month in Lent Term, and the end of the third week
" in Act Term.

  " Also I direct and appoint, that the eight Divinity
" Lecture Sermons shall be preached upon either of the
" following Subjects—to confirm and establish the Christian
" Faith, and to confute all heretics and schismatics—upon
" the divine authority of the Holy Scriptures—upon the
" authority of the writings of the primitive Fathers, as
" to the faith and practice of the primitive Church—upon
" the Divinity of our Lord and Saviour Jesus Christ—upon
" the Divinity of the Holy Ghost—upon the Articles of
" the Christian Faith, as comprehended in the Apostles'
" and Nicene Creeds.

  " Also I direct, that thirty copies of the eight Divinity
" Lecture Sermons shall be always printed within two
" months after they are preached ; and one copy shall
" be given to the Chancellor of the University, and one
" copy to the Head of every College, and one copy to
" the Mayor of the city of Oxford, and one copy to be
" put into the Bodleian Library ; and the expense of print-
" ing them shall be paid out of the revenue of the Land
" or Estates given for establishing the Divinity Lecture

" Sermons; and the Preacher shall not be paid, nor be
" entitled to the revenue, before they are printed.

" Also I direct and appoint, that no person shall be
" qualified to preach the Divinity Lecture Sermons, unless
" he hath taken the degree of Master of Arts at least,
" in one of the two Universities of Oxford or Cambridge;
" and that the same person shall never preach the Divinity
" Lecture Sermons twice."

" Tractatio Scripturae a primis saeculis Novi Testamenti ad hodiernum usque diem diversas habuit aetates. Prima possit dici *nativa ;* secunda *moralis ;* tertia, *arida ;* quarta, *rediviva ;* quinta, *polemica, dogmatica, topica ;* sexta, *critica, polyglotta, antiquaria, homiletica.* Adhuc igitur non ea Scripturae viguit experientia et intelligentia in Ecclesia, quae in ipsa Scriptura offertur. Evincunt hoc opinionum luxuriantes discrepantiae et caligantes in prophetis oculi nostri. Plus ultra vocamur ad eam in Scripturis facultatem quae est *virilis* et *regalis,* perfectionique Scripturae satis prope respondeat. Sed *per adversa excoquendi* erunt homines prius. Earum aetatum historia et descriptio justum atque utilem tractatum daret."—Bengel, *Praefatio Gnomonis,* § v.

"Ye search the Scriptures, because ye think that in them ye have eternal life ; and these are they which bear witness of Me ; and ye will not come to Me that ye may have life."—John v. 39, 40.

HISTORY OF INTERPRETATION.

LECTURE I.

SUCCESS AND FAILURE OF EXEGESIS.

" Break up your fallow ground, and sow not among thorns." [1]—Jer. iv. 3.

THERE is not one of the sacred books which have been called " the Bibles of Humanity " which has not in the lapse of years become the subject of endless comment and explanation. As centuries advance, there is an inevitable change in modes of thought and forms of expression. Words and phrases become obsolete or acquire a wholly new connotation. The writings which nations accept as their chief guide in matters of religion derive their authority partly from the ascendency of master minds, partly from their own intrinsic depth, force, or beauty. Books which have once been acknowledged as sacred, become the centres of thousands of hallowed associations, and the reverence in which they are held grows deeper as age after age passes by. But the words of one age and nation can never be the exact and complete expression of the thoughts of another, and for books immortalised by the accumulated reverence of generations, Exegesis becomes a matter of necessity. It is required for the explanation of a significance which time has obscured, and for the co-ordination of ancient thoughts with the discoveries, the experiences, the philosophical inquiries of later periods.

[1] Lit. " Fallow for you a fallow ground." LXX. νεώσατε ἑαυτοῖς νεώματα. Comp. Hos. x. 12 · Matt. xiii. 7.

The Bible furnishes no exception to this universal law; but it stands alone among sacred books in that it is avowedly the record of a *progressive* revelation, of a revelation not homogeneous throughout in value and importance, but given fragmentarily and multifariously in many portions and many ways.[1] Holy men of old spake as they were moved by the Holy Ghost, but their language was subject to all the ordinary conditions and limitations of human speech. To quote the profound maxim of Rabbi Ishmael, which was so often on the lips of Maimonides, *the Law speaks in the tongue of the sons of men.*[2] Hence the one aim of the interpreter should be to ascertain the specific meaning of the inspired teacher, and to clothe it in the forms which will best convey that meaning to the minds of his contemporaries.[3] The task is far from easy. It may try the strength of hosts of labourers, and it requires a lifelong devotion to many branches of criticism, literature, archaeology, language, and history. But more is required than even this inexhaustible capacity for labour. The perfect Expositor needs further to be endowed with a genius cognate with that of the sacred writer.[4] He must above all be a man of dauntless independence and perfect candour. In the course of our inquiry we shall see again and again that even a translator has need of invincible honesty if he would avoid the misleading influences of his own

---

[1] πολυμερῶς καὶ πολυτρόπως. Heb. i. 1.

[2] דיברה תורה כלשון בני אדם. See Hirschfeld, *Halachische Exegese,* p. 142 ; Derenbourg, *Palestine,* p. 392.

> " The myths and parables of the primal years,
> Whose letter kills, by Thee interpreted,
> Take healthful meanings fitted to our needs ;
> And *in the soul's vernacular* express
> The common law of simple righteousness."—WHITTIER.

[3] Aug. *De Doctr. Christ.* i. 1. *" Duae res quibus nititur omnis tractatio Scripturae, modus inveniendi quae intelligenda sunt, et modus proferendi quae intellecta sunt."* Ernesti, *Inst. Interpr. " Est interpretatio facultas docendi quae cujusque orationi subjecta sit,* seu efficiendi ut alter cogitet eadem cum scriptore quoque."

[4] " Willst den Dichter Du verstehen ?
Musst in Dichter's Lande gehen."—GOETHE.

"Intelligere scriptorem is dicendus est qui idem quod ille dum scribebat cogitavit, legens cogitat."—KUENEN, *Critica Lineamenta.*

a priori convictions. The legend which tells us how Luther hurled his inkstand at the Spirit of Evil in his Patmos at the Wartburg indicates the fierce temptations which the faith of the Interpreter must be strong enough to resist. But it would seem to require a greatness more than human to attain to the full measure of this absolute honesty. Not only in the Septuagint and in the Vulgate, but even in Luther's version, and in the English Bible, there are admitted errors which indicate the theological bias of the translators and not the unmodified thoughts of the sacred text.[1] Few are the translators, fewer still the Exegetes, who have been so free from various idols of the cave, the forum, and the theatre as to abstain from finding in the Bible thoughts which it does not contain, and rejecting or unjustly modifying the thoughts which indeed are there.

The founder of the Bampton Lectures placed "the divine authority of the Holy Scriptures" in the forefront of the truths on which he wished these sermons to be preached. To maintain that authority will be my one object in the large and difficult task which I have undertaken. Of late years the Bible has been assailed by many critics, and we may fear that the minds of thousands have been disquieted. It is but too probable that such assaults will increase in number and in violence. The Voice that once shook the earth " hath promised, saying, Yet once more will I make to tremble not the earth only, but also the heaven. And this word, 'Yet once more,' signifieth the removing of those things that are shaken, as of things that have been made, that those things which are not shaken may remain." [2] Many beliefs have been shaken to the very dust which were once erroneously deemed essential to the

---

[1] Of the LXX. I shall speak *infra*. The most striking instance of supposed bias in Luther's version is in Rom. iii. 28 ("vox 'SOLA' tot clamoribus lapidata"), but "*alone*" had appeared in the Genoese Bible (1476), and the Nuremberg Bible (1483). For the English version, see among other passages, 1 Sam. iii. 15 ; 2 Sam. viii. 18 ; Acts ii. 47 ; 1 Cor. xi. 27 ; Gal. i. 18 ; Heb. vi. 6 ; x. 38, although there is not in any single passage any intentional *mala fides*.

[2] Heb. xii. 25, 26.

maintenance of our belief in Scripture. With the defence of these *débris*, with the reconstruction of these ruins, we are not concerned. They were but untenable additions, fantastic human superstructures, weak outworks, unauthorised priestly chambers, the clustering cells of idols innumerable, which had been built round the inviolable shrine. They were the additions made thereto, sometimes by usurping self-interest, sometimes by ignorant superstition. They did but weaken the building, and deform the original design. They have crumbled under the hands of time, or have been demolished by hostile forces, often amid the anathemas of those who erected them. But as they have been swept away we have seen more clearly the beauty of the Temple, bright with the Glory of the Presence, built after the pattern given in the Mount.

If the Scriptures be holy and of divine authority, no deadlier disservice can be inflicted on them than the casuistical defence of conventional apology. On the altar of Truth I will offer no such strange fire, I will burn no such unhallowed incense. The Bible would have no claim to sacredness if it needed any apology beyond the simplest statement of plain facts. Even when the Ark seems to totter it is more really profaned by the Uzzah-hands of officious reverence than by the rudeness of the Philistines themselves. The divine authority which I would maintain is that of Scripture in its simple meaning, in its native majesty; of Scripture as the manifold record of a progressive revelation. The Bible forms an organic whole, but it is composed of many parts of unequal value. It consists of no less than sixty-six books in different languages, in different styles, of different ages.[1] It is not a book but a library. It contains the fragments of a national literature, and the fragments only. Many books which have now perished are quoted in its pages. No less than *ten* such works—by Nathan, Shemaiah, Gad,

---

[1] The word Bible represents not τὸ βιβλίον but τὰ βιβλία, a term which began to be used in the fifth century. The Scriptures were also called *Bibliotheca*. Jer. *Ep.* 6 ; Durandus, *Rational.* i. 27 ; Du Cange, s.v.

Iddo, Ahijah, Hosai, Jehu son of Hanani, Isaiah, and others who are unnamed—are referred to in the Books of Chronicles alone. It was written by kings and peasants, by priests and prophets, by warriors and husbandmen, by Jews, by Christians, and in parts even by Gentiles; by poets and chroniclers; by passionate enthusiasts and calm reasoners; by unlearned fishermen and Alexandrian students; by exclusive patriots and liberal humanitarians; by philosophers who knew from reasoning, and mystics who saw by intuition, and practical men who had learnt by experience the lessons which they recognised to be eternal and divine. He who would truly reverence Scripture must reverence it as it is. He must judge of it in its totality, and by its actual phenomena. Its authority is derived from its final and genuine teaching. If our faith in it be strong and living we must estimate it, book by book, and utterance after utterance, by its own claims, and by the manner in which it justifies them, without the invention of mechanical theories, or the adoption of arbitrary interpretations. We shall not, indeed, for one moment, deny to Scripture that prerogative of all inspired language by which its meaning is not always exhausted by a single aspect of truth. Where it is dealing with spiritual facts or expressing unfathomable mysteries, the letter of it should be to us as the Urim of Aaron, while the revealing light of the Spirit within us steals over the oracular gems. Simplicity of interpretation does not exclude the many-sidedness of truth which suggested to St. Paul the epithet "richly variegated,"[1] and which made Erigena compare the meanings of Scripture to the glancing hues on a peacock's feather.[2] But "the revelation of God's words giveth understanding to the simple."[3] The humblest Christian may claim his share in the illumination promised to all God's children, and

---

[1] Eph. iii. 10. ἡ πολυποίκιλος σοφία τοῦ Θεοῦ. Vulg. *Multiformis*, comp. Eur. *Iph. T.* 1150.

[2] *De Div. Nat.* iv. 5. "Est enim multiplex et infinitus divinorum eloquiorum intellectus. Siquidem in pennâ pavonis una eademque mirabilis ac pulchra innumerabilium colorum varietas conspicitur in uno eodemque loco ejusdem pennae portiunculae." [3] Ps. cxix. 130.

may therefore refuse to resign into the hands of usurpers, however venerable, the indefeasible rights of the human Reason and the indefeasible duty of the human Conscience. He must not confuse revealed facts with theological notions.[1] He must not permit long-tolerated errors to put on the air of abstract truths. He will interpret language by the only laws whereby it can be judged. He will sweep aside all arbitrary glosses of which he can trace the genesis and divine the object. He will do this all the more in proportion to his conviction that the Holy Scriptures contain the Word of God, which it is of infinite importance that he should not confuse with the teaching of ignorant and imperfect men. When Alexander was besieging Tyre, the worshippers of Apollo chained their idol-palladium with golden fetters to the altar of Melkarth, because they feared that he was about to abandon their city.[2] If they had been capable of truly honouring him they would have known that the Divine is of its very nature free. Scripture must neither be made into such an idol, nor treated with such misgiving. It will need no defence if it be left to the power of its inherent greatness; it will be overthrown or taken captive if it be trammelled by the vain theories of idolatrous worshippers.

I. The task before us is in some respects a melancholy one. We shall pass in swift review many centuries of exegesis, and shall be compelled to see that they were, in the main, centuries during which the interpretation of Scripture has been dominated by unproven theories, and overladen by untenable results. We shall see that these theories have often been affiliated to each other, and aug-

---

[1] "This presumptuous imposing of the senses of men upon the words of God, the special senses of men upon the general words of God; this deifying our own opinions and tyrannous enforcing them upon others; this restraining of the Word of God from that latitude and generality, and the understandings of men from that liberty in which Christ and the Apostles left them, is, and hath been, the only fountain of all the schisms and that which maketh them immortal. . . . Let those leave claiming Infallibility that have no title to it, and let them that in their words disclaim it, disclaim it also in their actions."—Chillingworth, *Rel. of Protestants,* iv. 16.

[2] See Q. Curtius, iv. 14; Diod. Sic. xvii. 41. "Hinc Tyrii, superstitione inducti, catenis aureis simulacrum Apollinis in basi devinxere, impedituri, ut persuasum habebant, Dei ex urbe migrationem."

mented at each stage by the superaddition of fresh theories
no less mistaken. Exegesis has often darkened the true
meaning of Scripture, not evolved or elucidated it. This is
no mere assertion. If we test its truth by the Darwinian
principle of "the survival of the fittest," we shall see that, as
a matter of fact, the vast mass of what has passed for Scriptural interpretation is no longer deemed tenable, and has now
been condemned and rejected by the wider knowledge and
deeper insight of mankind. If we judge of it by the Hegelian
principle that History is the objective development of the Idea,[1]
and that mankind is perfectible by passing through certain
phases of thought, which are in themselves only moments of
transition, then we shall see that past methods of interpretation were erroneous, and how they originated, and why they
were erroneous, because the course of History has stripped
off the accidents which pertained to the enunciation of truth,
and given us a nearer insight into the truth itself. And to
the limited application of such a method to the phenomena
of exegesis we are invited by the phenomena of Scripture
itself. It was an ever-advancing revelation. The gradual
development of the canon of interpretation is just what we
should have expected from the gradually developed conditions
under which the revelation is presented to us. We make
use of relative truth as a means of getting ever nearer to
the absolute. But, without any appeal either to Science
or Philosophy, we may simply point to the fact which will
become clear in the course of these Lectures, that the
fuller acquaintance with the original languages, the development of criticism, the profounder study of History, Psychology, Archæology, and comparative Religion, have resulted in
the indefinite limitation, if not the complete abandonment,
of principles which prevailed for many hundreds of years in
the exegesis of Scripture, and in the consignment to oblivion
—for every purpose except that of curiosity—of the special

---

[1] It is a significant and beautiful fact that the Hebrew canon places
the historical books of Joshua, Judges, Samuel, and Kings among the
Prophets.

meanings assigned by these methods to book after book and verse after verse of the sacred writings.

✢ If this be the lesson of History, as I believe it is, then to reject it is to reject the testimony of the Holy Spirit of God. For secular History too is a revelation. It is, as Vico called it, " a civil Theology of Divine Providence." To refuse the plain teaching of advancing experience may be a more essential blasphemy than to reject humanly-invented theories of Inspiration, or methods of explaining Scripture —whether Rabbinic, Alexandrian, Patristic, Scholastic, or Reformed.

Take by way of instance the entire Talmud. It includes the discussions, thoughts, inferences of well-nigh a thousand years, and it makes every verse and letter of Scripture "a golden nail on which to hang its gorgeous tapestries." But it may be said, without fear of refutation, that, apart from a few moral applications and ritual inferences in matters absolutely unimportant, for every one text on which it throws the smallest glimmer of light, there are hundreds which it inexcusably perverts and misapplies.[1] The remark applies with scarcely less force to the comments of the Schoolmen. In these too we find the same intensity of investigation, the same futility of result. They idolised the outward Book, but giving themselves up to vain fancies and superstitious theories, did not penetrate to the inmost life.[2] If men have built good materials on the foundation of Scripture, they have also built masses of wood, hay, stubble, of which no small portion has been reduced to ashes by the consuming test of Truth. But while this fire has burned up the scaffoldings with which they have concealed and injured the Temple, the inner Shrine has been protected by its own Shekinah, and the probatory

[1] The only excuse that can be made for the Talmudists is that their quotations were often *avowedly allusive rather than exegetical*. Hence the old rule אם אין ראיה לדבר זכר לדבר, which Wogue renders, "Si (cet passage) ne prouve pas la chose *il peut servir du moins à la rappeler.*" *Hist. de la Bible*, p. 168. See Yoma, f. 83, 2 ; Yebamoth, f. 64, 1, quoted by Mr. Hershon, *Genesis*, pp. 131, 293.

[2] See John v. 36-40, with the remarkable comment of Canon West-cott.

flames have not melted its gold and silver, or scathed so much as one of its precious stones.

We may at once note two reasons why exegesis tends to become non-natural.

The one is the growth of religious practices and rites of worship which have their root in conceptions of life unknown to the sacred books. Pharisaism, for instance, in the days of the Second Temple was guided by a number of "counsels of perfection," [1] which had partly arisen from contact with thoughts outside the range of Judaism, and were partly due to custom and the Oral Law. In their arguments with the Sadducees it was useless for "the Chasidim" [2] to appeal to the *Oral* Law which their opponents rejected. They thus felt themselves compelled so to explain the *Written* Law as to extort from it the sanctions which it did not really contain.

The other misleading tendency is the growth of religious opinions which are developed by the natural progress of the intellect or by intercourse with other nations. The Jews learnt much from their contact with Chaldaeans, Persians, Greeks, Egyptians, Romans. But they did not understand that God was also the God and Father of the Gentiles, and, being misled by *a priori* theories, they would not believe that views which they embraced with enthusiasm were not contained, at least implicitly, in their own sacred books.[3]

It is to the union of these causes that we owe a large part of the Rabbinic and Alexandrian exegesis. It was an exegesis *ad hoc,* rendered necessary in Palestine by Pharisaism, in Alexandria by enthusiasm for Greek Philosophy.

The Christian expositors inherited the fatal legacy of Palestinian and Alexandrian methods. There is hardly an error in their pages which cannot be traced back in principle to the Rabbis or to Philo. But besides this they were them-

---

[1] תִּקֻּנוֹת, of which seven are attributed to Ezra. See on the subject, Wogue, *Hist. de Bible,* p. 170.

[2] This was the original name of the party which developed into Pharisaism. 1 Macc. ii. 42, vii. 13 17 ; 2 Macc. xiv. 6. The word is rendered "*saints*" in Ps. lxxix 2, xlvii. 10, &c.

[3] The Rabbis said, "Turn the law again and again, *for everything is in it.*" Aboth, v. 22.

selves swayed by analogous influences. The doctrines of
monastic asceticism and the claims of the mediaeval Papacy,
as well as various Aristotelian and Platonic views among the
Schoolmen, were as remote as possible from anything which
could be found in Scripture; yet they had to be tortured
out of the sacred page. The process is constantly going
on. To this day men of all schools unconsciously deceive
themselves and others by a liberal adoption of the words of
Scripture in meanings inconceivably remote from those which
they really imply. But the practice, whether resorted to by
the orthodox or the unorthodox, is in reality a violation of the
majesty of Scripture—an intrusion of the subjective into the
sphere of revelation.[1]

II. There are seven main periods and systems of Biblical
interpretation. The *Rabbinic*, lasting, roughly speaking, for
1000 years, from the days of Ezra (B.C. 457) to those of Rab
Abina († A.D. 498);[2] the *Alexandrian*, which flourished from
the epoch of Aristobulus (B.C. 180) to the death of Philo,
and which was practically continued in the Christian Schools
of Alexandria, from Pantaenus (A.D. 200) down to Pierius;
the *Patristic*, which in various channels prevailed from the
days of Clement of Rome (A.D. 95) through the Dark Ages
to the *Glossa Interlinearis* of Anselm of Laon († 1117); the
Scholastic, from the days of Abelard († 1142) to the Reformation; the exegesis of the *Reformation Era* in the sixteenth
century ; the *Post-Reformation* exegesis which continued to
the middle of the eighteenth ; and lastly the Modern Epoch,
which seemed for a time to culminate in widespread atheism,
but after a period of " dispersive analysis " has ended in
establishing more securely, not indeed the fictitious theories
of a mechanical inspiration, but the true sacredness and
eternal significance of Holy Writ.

[1] Among the Jews this misinterpretation was elevated into a sacred principle. They quoted Ps. cxix. 26, and explained it to mean, "If it is opportune
to act for Jehovah, one may violate the Law." Berakhoth, *ad fin.* ; Gittin,
f. 60. The rule admits of a true though very limited application (Matt. xii.
4), but is wholly inconsistent with the Inspiration dogmas of the Rabbis
and of Protestant scholasticism.

[2] Rab Abina was the last of the Amoraim, and completed the Babylonian
Gemara at Sora, A.D. 498.

Of the methods adopted in these epochs some had their roots in Judaism, which led to the worst developments of a fantastic letter worship ; others in a Pagan gnosticism, which revelled in the extravagances of allegorical perversion ; others again in the one-sided abuse of principles in themselves admissible. In the Patristic and Scholastic epochs respect for a supposed tradition was made the basis for ecclesiastical usurpation, and the symbolism of parts of Scripture served as a pretext for spiritualising the whole. In the Post-Reformation epoch the misapplied expression " analogy of faith " was used as an engine of slavery to Confessions and Articles. Happily, however, in the Providence of God, the knowledge of Scripture was advanced not only in spite of these aberrations but even by means of them. The disputes with heretics in the first four centuries secured the authority of a pure canon. The attention paid to separate phrases led to textual criticism. The arbitrariness of allegory served to establish the importance of the historic sense. The tyranny of hierarchic tradition necessitated the Reformation. The half-Pagan Renaissance brought in its train the thorough mastery of the original languages. The unprogressive deadness of Protestant Scholasticism ended in the overthrow of an unnatural hypothesis of verbal dictation. And when the reaction had gone too far—when nothing was left but a cold and unspiritual rationalism to meet the unbelief caused by idealising philosophies—there occurred the great revivals of deep faith and spiritual feeling, of Christian philanthropy and evangelic truth.[1]

And thus it has come to pass that after the errors no less than after the assaults of so many hundred years, surviving the misrepresentations of its enemies, and the more dangerous perversions of its friends, the Bible still maintains its unique power and grandeur ; is still the sole Book for all the world ; is still profitable beyond all other books for doctrine, for reproof, for correction, for instruction in righteousness ; is still found worthy to be called a Book of

[1] See Lange, *Grundriss d. bibl. Herm.* xxi.-xxiv.

God, written for our learning that we through endurance and through comfort of the Scriptures might have our hope. Its lessons are interwoven with all that is noblest in the life of nations : "the sun never sets upon its gleaming page." "What a Book!" exclaimed the brilliant and sceptical Heine, after a day spent in the unwonted task of reading it. "Vast and wide as the world, rooted in the abysses of creation, and towering up beyond the blue secrets of Heaven. Sunrise and sunset, promise and fulfilment, life and death, the whole drama of Humanity, are all in this Book!" "Its light is like the body of the Heavens in its clearness; its vastness like the bosom of the sea; its variety like scenes of nature."[1]

It will not, I trust, be supposed, that the object of this survey of the History of Interpretation is nothing but the sterile and self-glorifying contemplation of abandoned errors. "Do we condemn the ancients?" asks St. Jerome. "By no means; but after the studies of our predecessors we toil to the best of our power in the House of the Lord."[2] We study the past not to denounce it, not to set ourselves above it, not to dissever ourselves from its continuity, but to learn from it, and to avoid its failures. It has much to teach us by way of precious instruction, as well as by way of solemn warning. If we shall have to dwell upon its mistakes it is only that we may have grace to avoid them, and to be on our guard against similar tendencies. For error strikes deep into the human mind. It has never been easy to pluck it forth by the roots. Unless we constantly break up our fallow ground, the scattered seeds and fibres of bitterness will germinate again and again in the teeming soil.

And though we shall be compelled to notice the many aberrations of exegetical theology, we shall also see that scarcely in any age has it been absolutely fruitless. So far as Homiletics may be allowed to play a part, however humble, in the region of Interpretation, every age has added something to the knowledge of Scripture, because every age has added

---

[1] Dr. Newman, *Tracts for the Times*, No. 87.
[2] Jer. *Apol. in Rufin.* ii. 25.

something to its profitable and moral application. In one sense, and that a most important one, it may be said of Scripture as of Nature that—

> " There is a book who runs may read,
> Which heavenly truth imparts ;
> And all the lore its scholars need
> Pure eyes and Christian hearts."

In much that belongs to the region of theology, in almost every question which pertains to history, literature, and the real significance of language, the holiest may go astray from inevitable ignorance ; but never has there been a period in which the Bible, or such part of it as has been suffered to filter its way to the multitude between the inclosing rocks of authority or through the choking sands of tradition, has not been a well-spring of salvation. Its most primary, its most essential truths, which are so few and simple that they might be written upon the palm of the hand, have always been sufficient for the saving of the soul.

Nor is it only the few ultimate and essential truths of Scripture which the mists of interpretation have been unable wholly to obscure. Devious as has been the path of exegesis, it has gathered multitudes of treasures in the course of its wanderings. There is scarcely a sincere commentary, scarcely even a compilation written in any period, from which something may not be learnt. Each age, however mistaken in its hermeneutic conceptions, has contributed some element of elucidation, some fragment of knowledge, some flash of insight. The age of the Rabbis lost itself in worthless trivialities, and suffocated the warmth and light of Scripture under the white ashes of ceremonial discussion, yet in preserving the text of the Old Testament it rendered services of inestimable value. The age of the Fathers, though its exegesis was ruined by the license of allegory, yet in the works of Origen, Theodore of Mopsuestia, Jerome, and Augustine, produced commentaries which will never lose their importance. The age of the Schoolmen, amid its masses of unprofitable subtlety and endless systematisation, left its legacy of exhaustive and philosophic thought. The age of the Reformation revived

the studies which alone render possible a sound interpretation, and shook itself free—if not completely yet to a great
extent—from the errors of tradition, and the trammels of
bondage. The Post-Reformation exegesis retrograded into a
new form of that scholastic despotism, which seems congenial
to the servile intellect of the majority; yet it enriched
the treasures of an immense erudition, and struck out new
and fruitful principles of illustration and research. And
though in modern times Biblical interpretation has often
been too weak and too biassed to defeat the powerful
attacks of enemies, yet the Church of God has learnt
many a valuable—many an absolutely needful—lesson even
from those who would fain have destroyed for ever the
authority of her sacred books. Science after science has
been invoked, method after method of philosophical inquiry
has been applied, to dethrone from their supremacy the
Jewish and Christian Scriptures; yet they remain supreme.
There never, perhaps, was any period in the world's history
in which, throughout every region of the globe, those Scriptures exercised a more powerful sway over the minds of men.
They are the one Book which is found alike in the hut of
the barbarian and the closet of the thinker; the one Book
which is equally precious to the pauper and to the king. The
solvents of modern criticism have but brightened the truths
which had been soiled by the accretion of ages, and they who
used them have unwittingly beautified what they intended
to destroy. We may well take courage when we consider
how many have been the enemies of Scripture, and how
impotent has been their hatred. In vain did Antiochus
Epiphanes rend, profane, and destroy the Books of the
Law;[1] in vain did Diocletian endeavour to suppress the New
Testament;[2] in vain did the English priesthood make it excommunication to read and heresy to possess the Bible of
Wiclif; in vain did the inquisitors of Philip burn those
who dared to study for themselves the sacred words;[3] in vain

---

[1] 1 Macc. i. 54-57.　　　　　　　[2] Euseb. *H. E.* viii. 2.
[3] Motley, *Rise of the Dutch Republic,* i. 73, 228.

did Tunstall buy up and burn the editions of Tyndale's translation.[1] The keen wit of the Greek, the haughty scorn of the Roman, the glancing fence of the sophist have been in vain. Celsus and Porphyry, Marcion and Lucian, Julian the Emperor and Libanius the rhetorician, heretics and humanists, Bolingbroke and Paine, and Voltaire, the French encyclopaedists, the English deists, the German philosophers, the keen Neologians, the subtle Materialists, the eloquent literary men—what have they effected? Some of them have been men of far more splendid genius than all but a few of the professed defenders of Christianity. No one would think of comparing the writings of the early Fathers with those of Tacitus or Juvenal, and few Christian apologists have been comparable for intellectual power to Spinoza, or Lessing, or Voltaire. And yet, because it has been allied with innocence and spiritual insight, " the irresistible might of weakness has shaken the world." The assailants of Christianity have cleared away some of our errors; they have exposed some of our perversions; but they have not overthrown a single essential truth. Like Asa of old, the Church has built the outposts of Judah out of the ruined fortresses of Ephraim.[2]

III. But while history has shown that we have nothing to fear for the sacredness of the Scriptures, it has taught us also that this sacredness has often been discredited, and that religion itself has been weakened in the minds of men, by the prevalence of perilous misinterpretations. And how often has the Bible thus been wronged! It has been imprisoned in the cells of alien dogma; it has been bound hand and foot in the graveclothes of human tradition; it has been entombed as in a sepulchre by systems of theology, and the stone of human power has been rolled up to close its door.[3] But now the stone has been rolled away from the door of the sepulchre, and the enemies of the Bible can never shake its divine

---

[1] See his monition in Collier, *Eccl. Hist.* iv. 61 ; ix. 84.
[2] Bossuet.
[3] " The Church is safer and the Faith healthier when it is not bound by the fetters of a too curiously-articulated creed."—Bishop Jeremy Taylor (*Dissuasive from Popery*, bk. 1, § 4, *passim*).

C

authority unless they be fatally strengthened by our hypo-
crisies, our errors, and our sins.

I repeat, then, no defence of that divine authority can be
more directly serviceable than the removal of the false methods
of interpretation by which it has been impaired. We can
judge of those methods, not only from the vast folios in which
their application has been illustrated, but also from the rules in
which they have been summarised. The rules might be correct,
and yet their application might be extravagant; but if the
rules themselves be valueless, or liable to the most facile
misapplication, the systems based upon them cannot be
otherwise than erroneous or unsatisfactory.

Now it happens that most of the seven epochs which I
have mentioned have left us their rules either as a definite
exegetic compendium, or in the form of a pregnant principle ;—
and there is not one such scheme which has not been proved
to be imperfect or mistaken, by that light of God which
shines on so steadily and impartially, and "shows all things
in the slow history of their ripening."

1. The Rabbinic age has left us the principles of its exegesis in the seven rules of Hillel.[1] That great and estimable
Rabbi—one perhaps of the doctors who as they sat in the
temple were astonished by the understanding and the answers
of the youthful Jesus—may be regarded as the founder of
the Rabbinic system. He was not the inventor of the Oral
Law, and he added very little to the vast number of "decisions"
(*Halakhoth*), which form the staple of Jewish tradition; but
he introduced order and system into a chaotic confusion, and
he devised a method by which the results of tradition could
at least in appearance, be deduced from the data of the
Written Law. The gigantic edifice of the Talmud really rests
on the hermeneutic rules of Hillel as upon its most solid
base.[2]

---

[1] These rules (מידות) are found in Tosefta Sanhedrin, c. 7, at the end of
Sifra ; and in Aboth of Rabbi Nathan, c. xxxvii. See Derenbourg, *Palestine*,
p. 187 ; Hamburger, *Talm. Wörterb.* ii. s.vv. *Exegese* and *Hillel* (pp. 209,
405).

[2] These rules in their briefest form are : 1. " Light and heavy " (קל וחומר),
i.e. a minori ad majus and *vice versa.* 2. "Equivalence " 3. Deduction

At first sight they wear an aspect of the most innocent simplicity. The first of them, known as the rule of "light and heavy," is simply an application of the ordinary argument "from less to greater."[1] The second, the rule of " equivalence," infers a relation between two subjects from the occurrence of identical expressions. Thus it is said both of the Sabbath and the Paschal sacrifice that each must be " *at its due season*," and if this means that the *daily* sacrifice must be offered on the Sabbath, then the Paschal sacrifice may also be offered on the Sabbath. The third rule was " extension from the special to the general." Thus since work might be done on the Sabbath for necessary food, necessary food might also be prepared on the other festivals. The fourth rule was the explanation of two passages by a third.[2] The fifth rule was inference from general to special cases. The sixth was explanation from the analogy of other passages.[3] The seventh was the application of inferences which were self-evident. Some of these rules are as old as the unconscious logic of the human mind ; some of them are exemplified even in the Law of Moses. The rule of " analogy," and the rule of " light and heavy," were used by our Lord Himself in His arguments with the Pharisees, and in His teaching of the multitude.[4] And yet in the hands of a casuist these

from special to general. 4. An inference from *several* passages. 5. Inference from the general to the special. 6. Analogy of another passage. 7. An inference from· the context. For these seven rules, developed by Rabbi Ishmael into thirteen, and by R. Eleazar into thirty-two, and subsequently to forty-nine, see Trénel, *Vie de Hillel*, p. 34 ; Crenius, *Fascic. Theol.* iv. ; Jost, *Judenthum*, i. 257 ; Derenbourg, p. 384-401 ; Merx, *Eine Rede vom Auslegen*, pp. 44, 45 ; Barclay, *Talmud*, 40-44 ; Ginsburg, s.vv. *Midrash, Hillel*, and *Ishmael ben Elisha* in Kitto's Cyclopaedia ; Weber, *Altsyn. Theol.* 106-113 ; Chiarini, *Théorie du Judaïsme*, i. 64-68. On the relation between Hillel's and Ishmael's rules, see Grätz, iv. 429. The thirteen rules (*Shelosh Esreh Middoth ha-Thorah*) are found in the Jewish Prayer-book. The additions of R. Eleazar were chiefly Haggadistic. See Schwab, *Berakhoth*, Introd. p. liii.
[1] The Jews observed that this rule is found in Num. xii. 14.
[2] The relation established between two passages was called *semukin* (סמוכין). For specimens see *Berakhoth*, f. 10, 1 ; Weber, *Altsyn. Theol.* 120.
[3] It had been applied long before Hillel by Simeon ben Shetach in a question relating to the punishment of false witnesses. See Derenbourg, p. 106.
[4] *Analogy ;* of David and the Shewbread, Matt. xii. 5. *A fortiori* (πόσῳ μᾶλλον) ; of the sparrows and man, Matt. x. 29. The whole Epistle to the Hebrews is an *a fortiori* argument.

harmless-looking principles might be used, and were used, to give plausibility to the most unwarrantable conclusions. Thus Rabbi Eleazar, the teacher of Aqiba, used the first rule—the common argument *a fortiori*—to prove that the fire of Gehenna had no power over Rabbinic scholars. Since (he said) fire has no power over a man who smears himself with the blood of a salamander, which is only a product of fire, how much less will it prevail over a pupil of the wise whose body is altogether fire, because of his study of the Word of God, which in Jer. xxiii. 29 is said to be as fire?[1] R. Simon ben Lakish used the same rule to prove that no Israelite could suffer the penalty of Gehenna. The gold plate on the altar resisted fire, how much more even a transgressor of Israel?[2] But worse than this, these rules might be so applied as to subvert the very foundations of all that was tenderest and most eternally moral in the Mosaic Law. The second and fourth rules, for instance, which only profess to explain passages by the recurrence of phrases, or to remove contradictions between two passages by reference to a third, sound perfectly reasonable, and yet were made responsible for many perversions. Thus, since in Ex. xix. 26, we find " the Lord *came down upon Mount Sinai*," and in Deut. iv. 36, " *Out of heaven* He made thee to hear His voice," the verbal contradiction is reconciled by Ex. xx. 22, " *Ye have seen* that I have talked with you from heaven," and by the inference that God bowed down the highest heaven upon the top of Mount Sinai. Frivolities of this kind do no great harm ; but the second rule, which deduced inferences from " equivalence " of expression, furnished an excuse for masses of the most absurd conclusions.[3] Thus it is argued that Job married Dinah because the word " *a foolish woman* " is applied alike to the daughter of Jacob

---

[1] Chagiga, f. 27, 1.

[2] *Id. ib.* In Sanhedrin, f. 106, 2, the word "weigher" (A. V. "receiver") in Is. xxxiii. 18, is explained to mean " one who weighed all the *a fortiori* arguments of the Law."

[3] The technical name of this rule is גזרה שוה. Thus it was inferred that the brother-in-law's *right* shoe was to be pulled off by a widow, from a comparison of Deut. xxv. 9, with Lev. xiv. 25. It is inferred that Samuel was a Nazarite from the comparison of 1. Sam. i. 11, with Judg. xiii. 5.

and the wife of Job ; and Lot, contrary to the express testimony of Scripture, is represented as a monster of iniquity,[1]
because it is said that " Lot lifted up his eyes and saw all the
plain of Jordan that it was well watered," and the separate
phrases of this sentence are elsewhere used of Potiphar's
wife, of Samson, of the son of Hamor, and of other offenders.[2]
It was a still more serious mischief that this rule led to one
of the many ways in which Rabbinism, professing to adore
the very letter of the Law, sapped its most fundamental
principles. In Ex. xxi. 5 a Hebrew servant is not to be
dismissed if he says, " I love my master, my wife, and my
children; I will not go out free." The merciful object of
the Lawgiver was to obviate the worst curse of slavery—
the forcible severance of the nearest relations. In Deut. xv.
16, however, the word " wife " is not mentioned, but the
slave is to stay with his master if he says that he loves
his master and his house " because it is well with him."
Whereupon, since it was often burdensome to retain a
Hebrew slave in the sabbatical year, the Mekhilta thus
applies Hillel's second and fourth rules. The slave need not
be kept (1) unless he has a wife and children, and (2) his
master also has wife and children ; nor (3) need he be kept
unless the master loves him, as well as he the master ; and
(4) if the slave be lame or ill he need not be kept, because
then it cannot be said that " it is well with him." [3] What is the
result of this unworthy casuistry ? The object of Moses had
been to provide at least one safeguard against the abuse of
a bad but tolerated institution ; the object of the Rabbinic
logician is to substitute naked formalism for a merciful law.
By mishandling the letter he purposely and for his own
benefit destroys the spirit. Instead of a noble and religious
explanation of the intention of the Lawgiver, he supplies us
with an excuse for cruel and selfish convenience. This rule

---

[1] Rabbi Jochanan (Nazir. f. 23, 1), Hershon, *Genesis*, p. 264.
[2] Namely, in Gen. xxxix. 7 ; Judg. xiv. 3 ; Gen. xxxiv. 2 ; Hos. ii. 5.
Also the same word (כבר) is used of " the plain " of Jordan, and " a piece "
of bread in Prov. vi. 26.
[3] Qiddushin, f. 22, 1. Merx, *Eine Rede vom Auslegen*, p. 46.

of "equivalence" has always been prevalent in scholastic systems.   It means the isolation of phrases, the misapplication of parallel passages, the false emphasising of accidental words, the total neglect of the context, "the ever-widening spiral *ergo* from the narrow aperture of single texts." It is just as prominent, and quite as mischievous, in Hilary and Augustine, in Albert and Aquinas, in Gerhard and Calovius, as in Hillel or Ishmael.   Hillel was personally a noble Rabbi; yet by his seven rules he became the founder of Talmudism, with all its pettiness, its perversion of the letter of the Scripture which it professed to worship, and its ignorance of the spirit, of which no breath seemed to breathe over its valley of dry bones.   And yet—let me say in passing —Jews have been found to assert, and nominal Christians to repeat, that Jesus was a disciple of Hillel, and borrowed from Hillel the truths which He revealed ![1]

2. We pass to the second epoch, and find that *Alexandrianism* also has left us its hermeneutic principles.   Those principles are given by Philo in his books on dreams, and on the unchangeableness of God,[2] and the details of their application are scattered throughout his numerous writings. *Negatively* he says that the literal sense must be excluded when anything is stated which is unworthy of God;—when otherwise a contradiction would be involved;—and when Scripture itself allegorises.   *Positively* the text is to be allegorised when expressions are doubled; when superfluous words are used; when there is a repetition of facts already known; when an expression is varied; when synonyms are employed; when a play of words is possible in any of its varieties; when words admit of a slight alteration; when the expression is unusual; when there is anything abnormal in the number or tense.   Many of these rules are not peculiar

---

[1] So first of all Geiger, followed by Friedländer, Löw, Renan, and many others.   See further in Lect. II. Hillel's rule, " The more law the more life " (Aboth, ii. 8), is so direct an antithesis to John v. 39, 40, that our Lord might almost seem to have been formally repudiating it.

[2] *Quod Deus Immutabilis,* 11 ; *De Somniis,* i. 40.   For the details as found in the book, *De Legis Allegoriis,* and Philo's other treatises, see Siegfried Philo, pp. 160-197.   Some illustrations are given *infra,* Lect. III.

to Philo, but are found no less in the Midrashim, and were adopted by Origen. They point to methods which have been applied to thousands of passages during entire centuries, and it is not too much to say that for the most part they do but systematise the art of misinterpretation. They have furnished volumes of baseless application without shedding upon the significance of Scripture one ray of genuine light. The rules become still more futile when they are only applied as Philo applied them, to a translation abounding with errors; but in any case they have scarcely a particle of validity. The repetition "Abraham Abraham" does *not* imply that Abraham will also live in the life to come;[1] nor does "Let him die the death" mean "Let him die in the next world as well as in this." The Septuagint word, ἐγκρυφίας, for "cakes" in Gen. xviii. 6 does not imply the duty of esoteric teaching;[2] nor because the word κόσμος means both "universe" and "adornment," does it follow that the dress of the high priest is (as the Book of Wisdom tells us) a symbol of the world.[3] Such explanations, or applications, or half-applications, often deduced from the falsest etymologies,[4] may be found in thousands in exegetical literature, from the days of Philo down to those of the Reformation, and even much later. Must we not deplore so fruitless an exercise of fancy, so sterile a manipulation of the Sacred Book?

3. Let us pass from Philo to the third epoch.[5] No interpreter except Origen and Jerome has ever exercised so deep

---

[1] Gen. xxii. 11; Lev. xviii. 6.   Bereshith rabba, § 39, 56.   Philo, *De Gigant.* 8.   [2] *De Sacrif. Ab. et Cain.* 15.
[3] Wisd. xviii. 24.   Philo, *De Vit. Mos.* iii. 14.   *De profug.* 20.   *De Migr. Abr.* 18.
[4] The identification of Rachel with contemplative, Leah with practical virtue, adopted by Gregory (*Homil. in Ezech.* ii. 2), and immortalised by Dante (*Purgat.* xxvii. 101-105), partly depends on the derivation of Rachel from רָאָה חֹל ὄρασις βεβηλώσεως (*De congr. erud. grat.* § 6); though, in another aspect Rachel stands for things wholly different—*e.g.* the source of temptations (*De poster. Cain.* 40) and of earthly hopes (*Leg. Albegg.* ii. 13).
[5] The chief hermeneutic manuals in the Patristic epoch are—
Diodorus, τίς διοφορὰ θεωρίας καὶ ἀλληγορίας (no longer extant).
Adrianus, Εἰσαγωγή (A.D. 433). It is printed in the *Critici Sacri*. vol. ix., 1660, and was edited by D. Hoeschel, 1602.

[Eucherius

an influence on the modes of exegesis as Augustine. His comments are sometimes painfully beside the mark, but we get an insight into the erroneous methods by which he was led astray when we find him endorsing with warm praise the seven rules of Tichonius.[1] Those rules are as baseless as Philo's, and even more so than those of Hillel. A book written by Eucherius, Bishop of Trèves about the year 450, called *Liber Formularum Spiritalis Intelligentiae*, shows the lengths to which allegory had been developed before the fifth century. In this dull and desultory dictionary of metaphors everything is reduced to generalities and abstractions.[2] It is argued that all Scripture must be allegorically interpreted because David says, "I will open my mouth in parables, *loquar in aenigmate antiqua.*"[3] The argument which does not hesitate to apply to the whole literature of a millennium and a-half the misinterpreted expression which the Psalmist used of a single psalm, is a fair specimen of the futility of the proofs offered in defence of these bad methods.[4] The rules of Tichonius had apparently been

---

Eucherius Lugdunensis, *Liber formularum spiritalis intelligentiae* (A.D. 440 ; *Bibl. Patr.* Colon. vol. v. 1 ; Migne vol. 50).
Tichonius, *De Septem Regulis* (*Bibl. Max. Patr.* Lugdun. vol. vi. p. 839).
Hieronymus, *De optimo genere interpretandi* (*Ep. ad Pammachium*).
id. *De studio scripturarum* (*Ep. ad Paulinum Presbyterum*).
Junilius, *De partibus legis divinae* (circ. A.D. 550, *Bibl. Max. Patr.* Lugdun. vol. x. p. 340).
Cassiodorus, *Institutiones* (circ. A.D. 560). (*Opp.* ed. Garet., 1679, Migne, vol. 69.)
I do not add the so-called *Clavis* of Melito, because it is not a translation of the Κλείς of Melito of Sardis, but, as Steitz has proved, a mediaeval Latin work (*Stud. u. Krit.* 1857).

[1] *De doctr. Christ.* iii. 30-37.

[2] Thus the "head of God" is the essential divinity; the "hair" the Holy Angels or the elect; the "eyelids" His incomprehensible judgments; His "mouth" is Christ; His "lips" the agreement of the Old and New Testament, &c., &c. This book, which occupies seventeen folio pages, is a melancholy proof of the depths to which exegesis had sunk. Eucherius is the first to use the word ἀναγωγὴ, to imply the reference of Scriptural passages to the New Jerusalem. The *Libellus de formulis* has been edited by Franc Pauly.

[3] The remark is borrowed from Clem. Alex., *Strom.* v. 12, § 81. περὶ πάσης γραφῆς . . . ἐν τοῖς ψαλμοῖς γέγραπται ὡς ἐν παραβολῇ εἰρημένοις. He proves his point from isolated passages like Ps. lxxviii. 2 ; 1. Cor. ii. 6 ; Matt. x. 27 ; Mark iv. 34, &c. (*Strom.* vi. 15, § 125.)

[4] The Psalm itself (Ps. lxxviii.) bears no resemblance to what we call "a parable," nor does it contain anything enigmatic.

designed to bring some sort of method into this vast region of Phantasy, which existed long before the days of Eucherius. He thought so highly of them as "*claves et luminaria*" to the law and the prophets, as to assert that they furnish a secure protection against the possibility of error.[1] The first is "About the Lord and His mystic body," namely the Church. Thus in the same passage one clause, such as, *dolores nostros ipse portavit*, applies to Christ, but following clauses, such as *Deus vult, ostendere illi lucem et formare illum in prudentia*,[2] apply not to Christ but to the Church. And in Is. lxi. 10, *Sicut sponso imposuit mihi mitram*, applies to Christ, but the following clause, *et sicut sponsam donavit me amictu*, applies only to the Church.[3] The second rule was "about the Lord's bipartite body," or about true and false Christians. Thus, in Cant. i. 5, "I am black but comely," the first epithet refers to false Christians; the second to true Christians. The third rule "about the Promises and the Law," is theological.[4] The fourth rule is "about Genus and Species," or whole and part. According to this, all nations mentioned in Scripture are types of Churches and may represent either the good or the bad side of the Church, and the words of the Scripture may with constant arbitrary variation, refer sometimes to the whole Church, sometimes to a part of it. The fifth rule suggests a sort of kabbalism of numbers. The sixth rule "About Recapitulation," professes to account harmonistically for events which are related out of order, and supposes a sort of vague analogy between different cycles of generations. The last rule "about the devil and his body," is the counterpart of the first and proposes to teach us how we are to apply some passages to the devil and some to wicked men.[5] These

---

[1] Gennadius cites them as being meant "*ad investigandam et inveniendam intelligentiam scripturarum.*"

[2] Is. liii. 4.

[3] Is. lxi. 16. Vulg. "Induit me vestimentis salutis . . . quasi sponsum decoratum coronâ, et quasi sponsam ornatam monilibus suis."

[4] It is also called "*De spiritu et literâ,*" "*De gratiâ et mandato.*"

[5] *E.g.* in Is. xiv. 3. *Quomodo cecidisti de coelo* applies to the devil ; *corruisti in terram* to the ungodly.

rules are perfectly arbitrary ; but Augustine in three different
passages, and after him Cassiodorus[1] and Isidore of Seville
refer to them with marked praise, and consider that they
throw no small light on the hidden senses of Scripture.[2]
Partly owing to Augustine's approval they became for a
thousand years the fountain-head of unnumbered misinterpretations.[3]

4. It will not be needful here to do more than allude to
the erroneous principles of the other epochs. Throughout the
whole of the scholastic epoch (4) dominated the pure fiction
of the *multiplex intelligentia,* or " fourfold sense," which fills
volumes of elaborate commentary,[4] and which, together with
the unquestioned acceptance of false traditions and usurped
authority, vitiates the popular compendiums of five hundred
years. The Reformation (5) witnessed an immense advance ;
but (6) in the epoch which succeeded it, the mediaeval subordination of Scriptural study to Papal authority was succeeded by
another subordination of it, nominally to a so-called " Analogy
of Scripture," really to the current Confessions of the various
Churches. The whole Bible from Genesis downwards was forced
to speak the language of the accepted formulae, and the " perspicuity of Scripture " was identified with the facility with which
it could be forced into semblable accordance with dogmatic

---

[1] Cassiodorus, *Institt.* i. 10. On Tichonius see Gennadius, *De Script. Eccl.*
18 ; Trithemius, *De Script. Eccl.* 92. Cave, *Hist. Lit.* p. 275 ; Migne, *Patrolog.*
vol. 50 ; Tillemont, vi. 81 ; Neander, iii. 280 ; Klausen, *Hermen,* p. 133 ;
Semler, *Diss. Hist. de vii. regulis Tichonii,* Halae, 1756 ; A. Vogel in *Herzog.*
vol. xvi.

[2] Tichonius said, "Quarum si ratio . . . accepta fuerit, clausa quaeque
patefient et obscura dilucidabuntur." Augustine says, "Non parum adjuvant
ad penetranda quae tecta sunt." *De Doctr. Christ.* iii. 4, § 30. *Retractt.* ii.
18. *Contra Epist. Parmeniani,* i. See too Jer. *De virr. illustr.* 18.

[3] Augustine vaguely saw in them a Donatist taint : " quae *sicut Donatista*
loquitur," *De Doctr. Christ.* iii. § 43. They are still referred to by Hugo of
St. Victor (*Erud. Did.* v. 4) ; and Perez of Valentia († 1490). Incomparably
superior was the Εἰσαγωγὴ εἰς τὰς θείας γραφὰς of Adrianus. He says that
three things are to be considered, the διάνοια, the λέξις, and the σύνθεσις,
through which we arrive at θεωρία. His book belongs to the school of
Antioch, and aims at edification not by allegory but by facts, and by the doctrine of types. Till the days of Nicolas of Lyra it had little influence.
Among the Roman Catholics Santes Pagninus (1540) still holds to Tichonius.

[4] The first traces of the *fourfold* sense occur in Eucherius († 450) ; of the
threefold sense in Origen.

systems. To this day men repeat the vague and extravagant
assertions of seventeenth century divines, which furnish no
assistance and solve no difficulty, and which can only be maintained in detail by an accumulation of special pleas.[1] They
confidently take the words they find in use among their
neighbours, without much troubling their heads about a
certain fixed meaning; "whereby," says Locke, "besides the
ease of it, they obtain this advantage, that as in such discourses they seldom are in the right, so they are as seldom
to be convinced that they are in the wrong; it being all one
to go about to draw men out of their mistakes who have no
settled notions, as to dispossess a vagrant of his habitation
who has no settled abode."

IV. Many of these unfounded principles still exercise a pernicious influence. In the past they have introduced an
incredible amount of confusion and darkness. The task of
the expositor cannot be expedited by rules so mechanical. It
requires wide knowledge, it requires the still rarer gift of a
fine sympathy. To interpret aright the lyric cry of the
poet, the passion of the prophet, the rushing vehemence of
the orator, demands something of the poet's, the prophet's,
the orator's emotion. Quite apart from all need for spiritual
vision, a sense of style, a psychological insight, an exquisite
literary tact, a capacity to appreciate the varying shades of
thought which may lie hidden behind the same words, a
power of realising and reproducing the thoughts of men

---

[1] Thus they repeat Hollaz and Quenstedt in calling Scripture a *perpetua
norma fidei ac vitae in universâ ecclesiâ* without explaining the wide difference
between the spirit of Judaism and that of Christianity, and although we
set aside a host of positive regulations, and some even of those which are
found in the New Testament (Acts xv. 20; Jas. v. 14). They go on speaking
of the *"Perspicuity and self-interpreting faculty"* of Scripture, though
the strife of interpretations cries to heaven even in passages of the utmost
importance. The Church of Rome forbids us to interpret *"contra unanimem
consensum Patrum,"* though exegetically there is no such thing; and the
dogmas of verbal dictation and infallibility still find defenders in spite of the
facts that (1) they must be useless to millions who cannot read the original;
that (2) the Vulgate of the Latin Church, the Septuagint of the Greek Church,
and the various Protestant versions teem with errors; that (3) alike the
original text and its true meaning are in many passages entirely uncertain;
and that (4) the hermeneutic rules adopted by different branches of the
Church are widely different.

who lived in other lands and in ages far away, are gifts
which are none so common as to render it likely that the
work of Scriptural Interpretation will soon be exhausted. But
so long as we are entangled in *a priori* conceptions—while
we treat as though it were one continuous and coaeval book
the scattered literature of fifteen hundred years—while we
attach the same value to the rudimentary religious conceptions
of a nomad warrior and the deepest thoughts of a great
philosophical Apostle,—while we deal with the Old Testament
as if it stood on the same level of revelation as the New—
while, in defiance of the whole history of the canon we give
the title of " Word of God " as indiscriminately to the Books
of Chronicles or Ecclesiastes, or to books in which, as in
Esther or Canticles, the name of God does not so much as
once occur, as we do to the Gospel of St. John—while we
speak of God as the *auctor primarius* not only of the deepest,
sweetest, purest, noblest thoughts which have ever been
uttered by human lips, but no less of the savage imprecations of Jewish exiles against their enemies and of terrible
narratives which only prove the imperfect morality of times
of ignorance :—so long as we do this we cannot take one
step farther in the right direction. A dogma which
attaches to the crudest and least spiritual narrative of
Genesis or Judges the same ethical value and supernatural
infallibility as to the words of Christ, is the deathblow to all
sane, all manly, all honest interpretation.[1] Yet this dogma
prevailed for ages. If such a view of inspiration were
alone orthodox or admissible no man of unwarped intelligence would have any refuge save in heterodoxy. So far
as this age has advanced beyond the exegetic principles
of the Talmud or the Schoolmen, it has been by
naturalness, by independence, by fearless allegiance to
truth, by searching Scripture not merely to " improve " it
into moral commonplaces, or to torture it into the utterance

---

[1] " It is impossible rightly to comprehend Scripture if we read it as we read
the Koran, as though it were in all its parts of equal authority, all composed
at one time, and all addressed to persons similarly situated."—DR. ARNOLD.

of sectarian shibboleths but to discover what the writers really meant and really said. The Rabbis, the Alexandrians, the Fathers, the Schoolmen, the Protestant dogmatists all assure us, and that repeatedly, that the words of the Old Testament are, in their literal sense and their obvious meaning, sometimes trivial, sometimes imperfect, sometimes morally erroneous. In such cases they got rid of the letter by distorting it into the expression of some sentiment of their own by the aid of allegory. What we should rather do is always to accept the clear meaning of Scripture, but always to judge it by the clear light of Christ.[1]

But we cannot yet be said to have learnt the lessons of the past in all their fulness, while so many of the proof texts in common use are mistaken accommodations; and while we follow the strange practice of establishing disputed doctrines by a mosaic of passages taken out of authors who not only differed from each other, but who may even —like St. James, for instance, and St. Paul, or like St. Paul and the author of the Epistle to the Hebrews—use the same technical words in different meanings. Better even the antitheses of Marcion, and *sic et non* of Abelard, than much of the casuistry which has passed for the orthodox reconciliation of apparent contradictions. Till we cease to palter and juggle with the words of Scripture in a double sense; till we cease to assume that the Trinity is revealed in the beginning of Genesis, and that Canticles furnishes a proof of the duty of Mariolatry; till we abandon our 'atomistic' method of dealing with Scripture and the treatment of its sentences as though they were magic formulae; till we repent of the fetish-worship

---

[1] Is. viii. 20 : "To the law and the testimony. If they speak not according to this word it is because there is no light in them." John vi. 39. The Jewish Midrash was very elaborate, but it did not lead to Christ. A Scotch divine has wisely said, "If we find even in the Bible anything which confuses our sense of right and wrong, that seems to us less exalted and pure than the character of God should be ; if after the most patient thought and prayerful pondering it still retains this aspect, *then we are not to bow down to it as God's revelation to us* since it does not meet the need of the earlier and more sacred revelation He has given us in our own spirit and conscience, which testify of Him."

which made some of the Jewish theologians say that all the
law was of equal importance from "God is one God" to
"Timna was the concubine of Eliphaz;"[1] till we give up the
late and humanly invented theories which with a blasphemy
only pardonable because it was unconscious, treated the voices of
human anger and human imperfection as the articulate Voice
of God; till we admit that the Bible cannot and may not be
dealt with by methods of which it gives no indication, and
of which we see the absurdity when they are applied to every
other form of literature whether sacred or profane—we may
produce improved forms of Rabbinism or Scholasticism, at
our pleasure and at our peril, but we shall never clearly
understand what is, and what is not, the purport of the
revelation contained in Scripture. There was bitter truth
in the reproach of St. Augustine to the Donatists, *Quod
volumus sanctum est;*[2] and in the sarcasm of St. Jerome,
Quicquid dixerint hoc legem Dei putant;[3] and in the famous
epigram of Werenfels—

> "Hic liber est in quo quaerit sua dogmata quisque
> Invenit et pariter dogmata quisque sua."

V. It would be easy to furnish still further proof of the
position that in every age since the days of the Apostles
there have been false methods of exegesis, and that these
false methods have led to false results. It is startlingly
illustrated by the fact that the very word by which we
designate the two divisions of the Bible as the Old and New
Testament is a mistranslation and a mistake.[4] It might be

---

[1] Lekach Tob. (quoted in Ersch und Grüber, *s.v.* Inspiration).
[2] Aug. *c. Ep. Parmeniani,* ii. § 31.
[3] Ep. ad Paulin. 7.
[4] The word "Testament" is derived from Matt. xxvi. 28. 2 Cor. iii.
14, &c. (comp. Jer. xxxi. 31.) St. Jerome rendered בְּרִית, "covenant," by
foedus or *pactum,* but it had been rendered *testamentum* in older Latin versions.
Tertullian prefers *instrumentum,* but adopts *testamentum* as being in common
use (*c. Marc.* iv. 1, 2 ; *De Pudic.* 12). Augustine also uses both words (*De
Civ. Dei.* xx. 4). Luther adopted *Testament* in preference to *Bund,* and since
his time the usage has been fixed. But the Jews knew nothing of *wills* till
they became acquainted with Roman customs. בְּרִית never means anything
but *covenant;* and in the New Testament διαθήκη only has the meaning of
"a will" by a sort of play upon words in Heb. ix. 17. Neither division of
the Bible has the smallest analogy to "a will," so that the explanation offered
by Lactantius (*Instt. Div.* iv. 20) is quite inadequate.

shown by taking any single book and proving, chapter by chapter, the impossibility and often even the absurdity of the many divergent interpretations of its salient passages. It might be shown again by a catena, from almost any part of Scripture, of passages which have for centuries together been explained in a manner now abandoned as entirely untenable. We may illustrate it still more decisively by showing the hopeless confusion which has reigned among commentators about the general drift and significance of whole books of Scripture. For instance, is it no opprobrium to Christian scholarship that for seventeen centuries no Christian scholar before Joachim Oporin had discovered the continuous design and central conception of the First Epistle of St. John, of which St. Augustine had nothing better to say than *Locuturus est multa et prope omnia de caritate ;* and Calvin nothing better than *Sparsim docendo et exhortando varius est ?* Let us, however, take the more striking case of one of the Books of the Old Testament, the Book of Ecclesiastes. Even the name of it, both in Greek and Hebrew, is of disputed meaning; and, difficult as the book is, Luther said that it is almost more difficult to clear the author from the fancies palmed upon him than to develop his meaning. Some of the Rabbis attacked it as being not only apocryphal in authorship, but heretical in tendency. [1] These conclusions were only escaped by a liberal use of allegory. Even in the fifteenth century R. Isaac ben Aramah complains that some expounded it with far-fetched literalism, others philosophically, others traditionally, and that all alike had altered its meaning into palatable sentiments, while none of them had " drawn sweetness from this flint." [2]   St. Jerome and St. Augustine by extreme applications of the allegoric

---

[1] Megilla, f. 7, 1 ; Shabbath, f. 30, 2.   "O Solomon, where is thy wisdom ? . . . Thy words not only contradict those of David thy father ; but they contradict themselves." Vayikra Rabba. f. 161, 2. Jer. in Eccl. xii. 13. See Ginsburg, *Coheleth*, p. 15. Wogue, *Hist. de la Bible*, p. 61. It narrowly escaped ejection from the canon by the school of Shammai because of (1) its contradictions and (2) its supposed epicureanism (Midrash Koheleth on Eccl. xi. 9).

[2] See Ginsburg, p. 66.

method explain it as alluding to Christ and the sacraments, and are followed by the Schoolmen. [1] Olympiodorus declared that it is a treatise of natural philosophy ; Hugo of St. Victor that it is meant to teach us to despise the world ; Brentius and Luther, reversing the judgment of the Mystics, said that it was meant to teach not the contempt but the enjoyment of the blessings of life. Melanchthon supposed that it was designed to prove an overruling Providence and a future judgment. De Wette, on the other hand, thought that the writer inclined to fatalism, scepticism, and epicureanism, and gave no hope of a future life. Heine calls it "the Song of Scepticism," and Delitzsch "the Song of the Fear of God." [2] Surely if it be so difficult for students to grasp the drift and meaning of an entire book, their views as to the meaning of separate passages must often be extremely fallible.

Many other instances might be furnished, *e.g.* the Book of Esther,[3] the Prophecy of Hosea, the Apocalypse, the Song of Solomon. Can anything be more grotesque and more melancholy than the vast mass of hypotheses about the latter—hypotheses which can make anything of anything ? Like Esther it never mentions the name of God and it narrowly escaped exclusion from the canon. [4] It re-

---

[1] *e.g.* Ch. iv. 8. " *The eye is not satisfied with seeing.*" " Christ is always desiring and seeking our salvation." ii. 24. " *There is nothing better for a man than that he should eat and drink.*" It is good to partake of the Lord's Supper. Jer. x. 16, " *Woe to thee, O land, when thy king is a child.*" Ecclesiastes calls the devil a child because of his foolishness. Aug. i. 7, " *All the rivers flow into the sea.*" Joys end in sorrow. (R. of St. Victor), xii. 5, " *The almond tree shall flourish* " " The almond tree is Christ—the rind, the shell, and the kernel correspond to the flesh, the mind, and His Divinity."— Peter Lombard.

[2] Delitzsch, Eccl. p. 183 (E. Tr.)

[3] " The Book of Esther is not once quoted in the New Testament. It was not considered canonical by two considerable Fathers, Melito and Gregory Nazianzen. It contains no prophecy, it has nothing on the surface to distinguish it from a mere ordinary history ; nay, it has no mark on the surface of being a religious history, not once does it mention the name of God, or Lord." *Tracts for the Times*, vol. v. " Creed and Canon compared." The name of the King of Persia occurs in Esther 187 times.

[4] See Shabbath, f. 30. 2 ; Aboth of Rabbi Nathan ; Yadaim, iii. 2, and Maimonides, *ad loc.* Wogue, *Hist. de la Bible* pp. 56, 65. It owed its admission to the mystic interpretation. Munk, *Palestine*, p. 450. The Jews forbade any one to read it before the age of thirty, and anathematised its literal interpretation. *Sanhedrin*, iii. 1.

presents, say the Commentators, the love of the Lord for the congregation of Israel;[1] it relates the history of the Jews from the Exodus to the Messiah;[2] it is a consolation to afflicted Israel;[3] it is an occult history;[4] it represents the union of the divine soul with the earthly body;[5] or of the material with the active intellect;[6] it is the conversation of Solomon and Wisdom;[7] it describes the love of Christ to His Church;[8] it is historico-prophetical;[9] it is Solomon's thanksgiving for a happy reign;[10] it is a love-song unworthy of any place in the sacred canon;[11] it treats of man's reconciliation to God;[12] it is a prophecy of the Church from the Crucifixion till after the Reformation;[13] it is an anticipation of the Apocalypse;[14] it is the seven days *epithalamium* on the marriage of Solomon with the daughter of Pharaoh;[15] it is a magazine for direction and consolation under every condition;[16] it treats in hieroglyphics of the sepulchre of the Saviour, His death, and the Old Testament saints;[17] it refers to Hezekiah and the ten tribes;[18] it is written in glorification of the Virgin Mary.[19] Such were the impossible and divergent interpretations of what many regarded as the very Word of God![20] A few only till the beginning of this century saw the clear truth—which is so obvious to all who go to the Bible with the humble desire to read what it says and not to import into it their own baseless fancies—that it is the exquisite celebration of a pure love in humble life ; of a love which no splendour can dazzle and no flattery seduce.[21]

---

[1] The Targum.   [2] R. Saadia Gaon.   [3] Rashi.   [4] Ibn Ezra. [5] Joseph Ibn Caspe.   [6] Ibn Tibbon.   [7] Abravanel.   [8] Origen, and the mass of Christian expositors, except Theodore of Mopsuestia, the school of Antioch, and most modern scholars.   [9] Nicolas of Lyra.   [10] Luther, Brenz. [11] Castellio, Dr. Noyes.   [12] Ainsworth.   [13] Cocceius. [14] Hennischius.   [15] Bossuet.   [16] Durham.   [17] Puffendorf. [18] Hug.   [19] Many Roman Catholic Commentators.

[20] It was the favourite theme of mediaeval exegesis. The eighty-six sermons of St. Bernard only come down to the end of the second chapter.

[21] To this view the way was led by Grotius, Bossuet, Lowth, Herder, Jacobi, &c. It is adopted by Ewald, Hirzel, Umbreit, Meier, Friederich, Hitzig, and most of the best modern commentators. See the admirable summary given by Dr. Ginsburg, and by Zöckler in Lange's *Bibelwerk.* Luther might well say, "Quodsi erro veniam meretur primus labor, *nam aliorum cogitationes longe plus absurditatis habent.*"

D

When, however, we leave the consideration of whole books we need not go farther than the interpretation of the first chapter, and even the first verse of the Bible without being forced to confess that exegesis has stamped even its initial labours with the impress of its own incompetency. Surely if ever a revelation was clear, simple, majestic, of infinite importance, it is the verse : *In the beginning God created the heaven and the earth.* It is the basis of all Monotheism ; the eternal protest of the human heart enlightened by the Spirit of God, against every prominent form of error respecting His Being. It corrects, as with one stroke of the pen, the aberrations of millions of mankind ; of the few Atheists who have said there is no God ; of the numberless Polytheists, belonging alike to the most refined and to the most degraded races, who have worshipped many gods ; of the philosophic dreamers to whom God has only been a name for the soul of the universe ; of the whole heathen races and the Manichean heretics who believed in two gods ; of the moderns who, whether within or without the Church's fold, deny that we can know anything about God ; even of the Alexandrians and others who borrowed from Greek philosophy the notion that Matter was coeval with God. These truths at least are of unspeakable importance to the human race ;—and now what has exegesis to say on this simple verse ?

i. We turn to the Talmud, and it tells us, in accordance with Hillel's rule of " equivalence " that " *in the beginning* " occurs also in Jer. xxvi. 1, and that we must therefore infer that at that period, " *in the beginning* of the reign of Jehoiakim," Jehovah intended to reduce the world to chaos but relented.[1] It also tells us [2] that the Septuagint translators, apparently in copying out the law in Greek letters for Ptolemy, transposed the words, and put *Elohim* before *Bereshîth*, lest the Greeks should make the mistake of supposing that *Bereshîth* was the name of a God who created Elohim ! Further, the Rabbis dwell on the dispute between the scholars of Shammai, who maintained from this verse that the heavens were created first,

---

[1] Sanhedrin, f. 103, 1. [2] Megilla, f. 9, 1.

and the scholars of Hillel, who from Gen. ii. 4, declared
that the earth was created first; and they tell us how after
endless discussion and quotings of counter-texts, the Mishnic
Rabbis decided that the heaven and the earth were both
created at the same time.[1] They tell us, moreover, that
Shamayim, "heaven," is derived from *eesh-mayim,* "fire-water,"
because in the firmament, God mingled those two elements.[2]
This however does not nearly exhaust the spurious inferences deduced by various. forms of Kabbalism from the
first word of Scripture. Since by anagram [3] *Bereshith*
can be read *Bethishri,* it was inferred that the world was
created in September (Tisri); since, acrostically,[4] the letters
of the word give the initials of the Hebrew sentence, "God
saw that Israel would accept the Law," the world was created
for the sake of the Law. Since the Hebrew words, "in the
beginning God created," can be transposed by anagram
אלהים יתברא בראש, therefore the Pentateuch is to be regarded
as an allegory. Turning to the Zohar we find that, by further
methods of Kabbalism, the words are supposed to indicate
that a luminous point of fire created a temple, of which the
name was Elohim. We come down to Rashi, so great an interpreter in the eyes of his countrymen, that he was called
emphatically *Parshandatha,* or the "Exegete of the Law," [5]
and we are told that (by Hillel's rule of " equivalence ")
the Torah begins with this text, and not with the precepts
of the Law, to show that God had given the earth to the
Israelites; since in Jer. ii. 3, Israel is called "the *beginning*
(ראשית) of His increase." Continuing the traditions of
Kabbalism we find that even in the epoch of the Renaissance
Reuchlin tried to prove the doctrine of the Trinity
from Gen. i. 1, because acrostically the word בָּרָא "He
created" involves the initial letters of Father, Son, and

---

[1] Chagiga, f. 12, 1.
[2] Chiarini, *Théorie du Judaïsme,* ii. 216.
[3] Known to the Jews by the name Themoorah. See Lect. II.
[4] This process was known as Notarikon. See Lect. II.
[5] See Geiger, פרשנדתה, *Ein Beitrag zur Gesch. der Bibel-Exegese.*

Spirit (אב, בן רוח);[1] and Pico of Mirandola (who is quoted with rapturous approval by Sixtus Senensis even as late as 1593)[2] gets by various permutations of the letters of the words the meaning that "the Father, in the Son, and through the Son, created the beginning and the end or peace, the head, fire, and foundation, by the good covenant of a great man."[3] Pico thus persuaded himself that in the Qabbala, there was more Christianity than Judaism. Lastly, if we might have hoped that these fantastic vanities could not possibly have survived the Middle Ages we are undeceived by opening one of the most popular of modern Jewish commentaries, the Tseénnah Ureénnah, or "Go ye and see," compiled by the Rabbi Jacob at Frankfort in 1693, but reprinted at Wilna as recently as 1877, and in daily use among the Polish Jews.[4] It opens with the remark that the Torah begins with the letter *Beth* because that is the first letter of *Berakhah* "Blessing"; then that the letter *Aleph* flew before the Holy One with the complaint that it had not been chosen; and was consoled by being told that the Decalogue should begin with Aleph. It proceeds to inform us that by Hillel's second rule, the world was created for the sake of the Law because that is called *the beginning of* His way;[5] for the sake of the sacrifices which were offered in the Temple, which is called "*Beginning*" and was created before the world;[6] and for the sake of tithes which are also called "*Beginning* (i e. first fruits) of corn."[7] You will perhaps wonder that I should

---

[1] So in "the stone (אבן) which the builders rejected" he saw the Father and the Son (אב בן), and out of "Righteousness" (צדק אלהים, Dan. ix. 24) he gets by Gematria, Messiah Jehovah (משה יהוה). See Ginsburg, *The Kabala*, p. 62; Wolf, *Bibl. Hebr*. i. 9.

[2] See Sixt. Senens. *Bibl. Sanct.* p. 173. He calls this hermeneutic folly "*luculentissimum exemplum.*"

[3] Among Christian Kabbalists, all of whom more or less approved of such methods, may be mentioned, besides Picus of Mirandola († 1494), Raymond Lully († 1522); Cornelius Agrippa († 1535); Van Helmont († 1464); Fludd († 1637); Henry More († 1687); and others. See Ginsburg, *The Kabbala*, p. 124.

[4] צְאֶינָה וּרְאֶינָה. The title is taken from Cant. iii. 11. A translation of the Comment on Genesis by Mr. P. J. Hershon is now in the press.

[5] Prov. viii. 22.

[6] Jer. xvii. 12. See Hershon's *Talmudic Miscellany*, 104, 4.

[7] Deut. xviii. 4.

waste your time by such inconceivable puerilities. Puerilities, yes! but by referring to the beginning of the Midrash you will see that they are but a few specimens out of many ; [1] and they are the direct result of an extravagantly superstitious estimate of the letter of Scripture. They neglect the essential truth and majesty of the revelation and substitute for it a mass of ineptitude ;—and yet they depend on rules which have been accepted among generations of mankind for two thousand years, and which are still regarded by many as constituting the exegesis of the Sacred Book !

ii. But this is not all. The interpretation of this verse is responsible not only for triviality but for positive heresy. We turn to Philo, and we find that he can extort from it the deadly error of philosophic dualism.[2] Nothing can be clearer than the meaning of Genesis, that God created *all things.* It has not a word to say about the eternity of matter, as though matter were the source of evil, and of opposition to the divine activity. Philo, without the least scruple, perhaps with no suspicion that he was mistaken, makes Moses speak the language of Plato, and Genesis express the thoughts of the Timaeus.[3] It is needless to dwell on the astonishing methods by which he extracts from the Bible the views of the Stoic cosmogony ; [4] but he was partly influenced by the LXX., which translates "The earth was without form," by " The earth was *unseen.*"[5] This gave room for the pretence that

---

[1] Midrash Bereschit Rabba, Parascha. i. (Wünsche, *Bibl. Rabbinica*).

[2] He derives this view from Gen. i. 31. God praises all that He has made (τὰ ἑαυτοῦ τεχνικὰ ἔργα), but He does not praise matter (τὴν δημιουργηθεῖσαν ὕλην), which is lifeless, corruptible, heterogeneous, discordant. *Quis Rer. Div. Haer.* 32.

[3] Siegfried, *Philo*, pp. 230-235. Philo gives the same epithet, ἄποιος, alike to chaos and to God. See Ewald, *Die Lehre der Bibel von Gott*, pp. 238-241. Philo's Scriptural proofs (?) of the ἄποιος καὶ ἄμορφος ὕλη are very characteristic. They are derived (1) from the fact that in Gen. xxxi. 32-42 Laban (λευκασμὸς) has the unmarked cattle, which shows that matter has no properties (*De Profug.* 2), and acquires its seal, or stamp, from the Logos (*De Somn.* ii. 6) ; (2) from Deut. xxiii. 1, because the τεθλασμένος is excluded from the Church of God ; and (3) from Gen. xv. 10, which is applied to "the cutter-word" dividing material and immaterial things !

[4] There are similar speculations in that part of the Qabbala which deals with the work of creation (מעשה בראשית).

[5] ἡ δὲ γῆ ἦν ἀόρατος καὶ ἀκατασκεύαστος.

the creation primarily intended was that of an immaterial heaven and an invisible earth—a creation ideal and not material.[1]

iii. Once more, when we look to the Fathers we find that some of them, in that fatal ignorance of the original languages of Scripture which rendered so many of their speculations abortive at the outset, had the impression that the first verse of Genesis in the Hebrew ran "*In the Son* God made the world."[2] Here indeed there was no heresy, for so we are expressly taught in other parts of Scripture.[3] But the critical mistake as to the reading, and the exegetical mistake as to the interpretation, tended from the first to confirm views which were radically untenable as to the nature and relation of the two covenants.

iv. It would not be difficult to pursue the subject and to show the wild speculations of cosmogony which have been foisted into the very opening accents of revelation. But enough has been already said to show how small is the title of Exegesis to that infallibility either as to principles or details which it has so often been fain to claim, not only for Scripture but for itself. It has largely misinterpreted its own oracles and, for century after century, stumbled hopelessly upon the very threshold of the Sacred Book.

v. In conclusion, let us not fall into the common error of fancying that such mistaken inferences are of little practical importance. If they be harmless in some instances, they may be very fatal in others. " The true sense of Scripture is Scripture ; "[4] but " by giving it a wrong sense," says Bishop

---

[1] Philo, *De Opif. Mundi*, 7. Philo's favourite comparisons for creation are drawn from *building* and *planting*. Philo seems to contradict these his normal views in *De Somn.* i. 13, where he says, ὁ θεὸς τὰ πάντα γεννήσας οὐ μόνον εἰς τὸ ἐμφανὲς ἤγαγεν ἀλλὰ καὶ ἃ πρότερον οὐκ ἦν ἐποίησεν, οὐ δημιουργὸς μόνον ἀλλὰ καὶ κτίστης αὐτὸς ὤν. On the self-contradictions of Philo, see Gfrörer, *Philo*, ii. 2. Apparent contradiction rises from his use of τὰ μὴ ὄντα to imply the chaos. Gfrörer, i. 330.
[2] Aristo Pellaeus (*ap.* Routh, *Rel. Sacr.* i. 91). "Plerique existimant," says Jerome (referring also to Tertullian and Hilary) . . . "in Hebraeo haberi *In Filio Deus coelum et terram :* quod falsum esse ipsius rei veritas comprobat." See Ambrose, *Hexaem.* i. 4. Basil, *Hexaem.* Hom. i. Tertullian, *C. Praxeam.* Petavius, *De Off. Sex. Dierum.* i. § 16.
[3] Heb. i. 2 ; John i. 3 ; Col. i. 16 ; 1 Cor. viii. 6.   [4] St. Augustine.

Wordsworth, " men make God's word become their non-word, or even the Tempter's word, and then Scripture is used for our destruction, instead of making us wise unto Salvation." [1] The misinterpretation of Scripture must be reckoned among the gravest calamities of Christendom. It has been the source of crimes and errors which have tended to loosen the hold of the sacred writings upon the affection and veneration of mankind. Recall but for a moment the extent and the deadliness of the evils for which texts of the Bible have been made the command and the excuse. Wild fanaticism, dark superstition, abject bondage, anti-nomian license, the burning hatred and unbending obstinacy of party spirit—have they not each in turn perverted the Scriptures to which they appealed ? It is grievous to recall how many a bloodstained period of history might have been redeemed from its agony and desolation if men had only remembered what Christ so plainly taught—that the Law of the Old Testament was as yet an imperfect law, and the morality of the Old Testament as yet an imperfect and un-developed morality.[2] How often have the sanguinary sup-porters of mistaken shibboleths defended their outrages by the injunctions of the Pentateuch ? The infamous assassina-tions of princes, or murderous plots against them, by a Ravaillac, a Jacques Clement, a Balthazar Gérard, an Antony Babington, an Everard Digby, were preposterously justified by the examples of Ehud and Jael.[3] The Crusaders, thinking that they did God service by wading bridle- deep in the blood of infidels who were often morally superior to themselves, justified

---

[1] *Miscellanies*, ii. 17.

[2] Matt. v. 21–43 (comp. xv. 1–9 ; xxiii. 1–23) ; Mark ii. 18–28 ; vii. 2–23 ; x. 2–12 ; Luke ix. 51–56 ; xiii. 11–17 ; John viii. 1–11.

[3] See Suarez, *De Fide*, vi. 4 ; Mariana, *De Rege*, p. 69. There can be little doubt, if any, that Pius V. sanctioned attempts on the life of Elizabeth. For the blasphemies of Pope Sixtus V. after the murder of Henry III. by Clement, see De Thou as quoted by Lecky, *Rationalism*, ii. 178 ; Hallam, *Hist. of Europ. Lit.* ii. 39–46. The impudent claim to a right of deposition led naturally to tyrannicide, and Suarez says that when St. Paul wrote, " Let every soul be subject to the higher powers," he did not include the excommunicated ! The last attempt to murder the Emperor of Germany (1884) was calmly defended by the murderer from Old Testament examples ! See Oxenham, *Ethical Studies*, pp. 406-413.

their massacres by the exterminating wars in the Book of Judges, which Bishop Ulfila wisely delayed to translate into Gothic because he feared the effects they would produce upon the minds of his wild converts. Thousands of poor harmless women, maddened by torture into false self-accusations, were burnt to death by Sprenger as witches, on the supposed authority of a text in Leviticus.[1] A crime so atrocious as the massacre of St. Bartholomew was hailed by Pope Gregory XIII. with acclamation, and paralleled by the zeal for God of ancient heroes. Texts were used to crush the efforts of national liberty, and to buttress the tyrannies of immoral despotism.[2] The murder of kings and passive obedience to them were alike defended by texts.[3] The colossal usurpations of the Papacy in the days of its haughtiest audacity were maintained not only by spurious donations and forged decretals, but by Boniface VIII. on the ground that the two swords of Peter meant the possession by Popes of temporal and spiritual dominion ;[4] and a century earlier, by Innocent III., on the ground that the Pope was intended by the sun to rule the day, and the Emperor only by the moon to rule the night.[5] When Innocent III. was giving to the Abbot of Citeaux his infamous advice to entrap the Count of Toulouse to his ruin, he wrote, "We advise you, *according to the precepts of the Apostle*, to use cunning in your dealings with the Count of Toulouse,

---

[1] Sprenger, author of the *Malleus Maleficarum*, was appointed Inquisitor by Innocent VIII. in 1484. Sir Matthew Hale, as every one knows, in 1665 sent two witches to be executed on Scripture authority ; and five are said to have been hanged at Northampton as late as 1712 (Parr's *Works*, iv. 182) ; and in Spain as late as 1781 (Buckle, *Hist. of Civilis.* i. 334) ; and in Switzerland in 1782 (Michelet's *La Sorcière*, p. 425). Even Wesley said, "The giving up witchcraft is giving up the Bible." So absurd a statement would practically bind us to everything which was ignorantly believed 3,500 years ago. See Lecky, *Hist. of Rationalism*, i. 1–150.

[2] Passive obedience was taught by theologians for centuries from the days of the early Fathers down to the seventeenth century. Grotius, *De Jure Belle et Pacis*, i. 4. A contemporary tells us that in the English Church after the Restoration the name of Charles I. was referred to ten times more often than that of Christ.

[3] See especially Mariana, *De Rege et Regis Institutione*, 1599.

[4] See the authorities quoted in Hallam, *Middle Ages*, ii. 26, 29. Wordsworth, *Miscellanies*, ii. 18.

[5] Muratori, *Script. Rer. Ital.* iii. 448. Decret. Greg. ix. lib. i. tit. 33.

treating him with a wise dissimulation, that the other heretics may be more easily destroyed."[1] Even the Spanish Inquisition—that infamy of Christendom—appealed to Scriptural warrant for the right to immolate its holocausts of victims,[2] and the blood-stained Alva received from the Pope a jewelled sword with the inscription, *Accipe sanctum gladium, munus a Deo.* In the days of her persecution the Fathers of the Church had taught mankind that "force is hateful to God;"[3] but, in the days of her despotism, not only cursings and anathemas, but the axes, the stakes, the gibbets, the thumbscrews, the racks, and all the instruments of torture kept in the dungeons of priests to deprave the heart of nations, and to horrify the world, were defended by scraps of texts and shreds of metaphor from the mercy-breathing parables of Christ. Texts have been used a thousand times to bar the progress of science, to beat down the sword of freedom, to destroy the benefactors of humanity, to silence the voice of truth. The gospel of peace, the gospel of knowledge, the gospel of progress, has been desecrated into the armoury of fanaticism, and the stumbling-block of philosophy. The gospel of light and love has been used to glorify the madness of the self-torturer, to kindle the faggot of the inquisitor, and to rivet the fetters of the slave. Who can deny these things unless he thinks to please God by going before Him with a lie in his right hand ? Even the poets of the world—poets the clearest in universal insight, and the deepest in spiritual emotion—have noticed and deplored them. Who does not feel the force of the

---

[1] "It is remarkable that when the Roman pontiffs, especially Gregory VII. and Innocent III., had any pernicious design to recommend, they were lavish in their appeals to Scripture."—TAYLOR.

[2] "In conclusion the Emperor ordered the Inquisition to make it known that they were not doing their own work, but the work of Christ." What nameless horror this "work of Christ" involved may be read in Motley's *Dutch Republic,* i. 288.

[3] "*Nec religionis est cogere religionem.*" Tertullian (*Ad Scapulam,* 2), *Religio cogi non potest.* Lactantius (*Div. Inst.* vi. 19). The old rule was Βιὰ ἐχθρὸν Θεῷ.

[4] Lord Bacon attributes the paralysis of science chiefly to the incubus of the theological system. See *Novum Organum,* i. § lxv., and there is a similar remark by Kepler in *De Martis Stellâ.*

hackneyed lines — hackneyed from their fatal truthfulness—

> "The devil can quote Scripture for his purpose"?

or,

> " In religion
> What damned error but some sober brow
> Will bless it and approve it with a text,
> Hiding the grossness with fair ornament?"

or,

> " Having waste ground enough,
> Shall we desire to raze the sanctuary,
> And pitch our evils there?"

or

> "Crime was ne'er so black
> As ghostly cheer and pious thanks to lack.
> Satan is modest. At Heaven's door he lays
> His evil offspring, and in Scripture phrases
> And saintly posture gives to God the praise
> And honour of his monstrous progeny"?

How then is it possible better to maintain the divine authority of the Holy Scriptures than by pointing out, and by forsaking, the errors whereby men have so often wrested them alike to their own destruction and to the ruin and misery of their fellow men? How can we better prove their sacredness and majesty than by showing that in spite of such long centuries of grievous misinterpretation they still remain when rightly used, a light unto our feet and a lamp unto our paths? How can we render them a loftier service than by endeavouring to set them free from false dogmas which have corrupted their whole interpretation with dishonest casuistry, and have thereby shaken to its very centre the religious faith of thousands alike of the most ignorant and of the most cultivated of mankind? And think not that I am pointing some mere conventional moral when I add that there is one way in which the very humblest of us may prove how inviolable is the truth, how infinite the preciousness of the lessons which we can learn from Scripture. It is by living in simple and faithful obedience to its highest and its final teaching. On that point at least, amid multitudes of imperfections, the greatest and holiest interpreters have ever been at one. "*Scripturae scopus est,*" says St. Augustine, "*dilectio Dei et in ordine ad Deum aliorum hominum.*"[1] "The fruit of sacred Scripture," said Bonaventura, " is fulness of felicity."[2] "Do not hear or read it," says Bishop Jeremy Taylor, "for any other end but to become better in your daily walk, and to be instructed in every good work, and to increase in the love and service of God."[3]—And this may God grant us all for His Son's sake !

[1] Aug. *De Gen. ad Literam.*
[2] Bonaventura, *Breviloq. Prooem.* So Abelard says that the object of the study of Scripture is "morum instructio ;" and John of Salisbury, "ut homo seipso melior jugiter fiat." (*Polycrat.* vii. 10.)
[3] Jer. Taylor, *Holy Living,* iv.

Διατί καὶ ὑμεῖς παραβαίνετε τὴν ἐντολὴν τοῦ Θεοῦ διὰ τὴν παράδοσιν ὑμῶν ; Ὁ γὰρ Θεὸς ἐνετείλατο λέγων . . . Ὑμεῖς δὲ λέγετε . . . Καὶ ἠκυρώσατε τὴν ἐντολὴν τοῦ Θεοῦ διὰ τὴν παράδοσιν ὑμῶν.—Matt. xv. 3—6.

Βλέπετε μή τις ὑμᾶς ἔσται ὁ συλαγωγῶν διὰ . . . κενῆς ἀπάτης κατὰ τὴν παράδοσιν τῶν ἀνθρώπων.—Col. ii. 8.

LECTURE II.

"Not giving heed to Jewish fables, and commandments of men who turn
away from the truth." [1]—TIT. i. 14.

A BOOK needs for the most part but little explanation in the age to which it is addressed. It may be
assumed as a fundamental principle that an author writes
for the purpose of being understood. His thoughts, his
allusions, his special opinions are influenced by the times
in which he lives, and are clearer to his contemporaries than
they can be to men of other epochs. But as the centuries
advance books require an interpreter in proportion to their
depth and sacredness. Schools of expositors were soon needed
to explain the Vedas [2] and the Koran. [3] Chairs were founded
to comment upon the *Divina Commedia* of Dante as early as
fifty years after his death, [4] and the existing commentaries on
that immortal vision are now nearly thirteen hundred in
number.

The interpretation of Scripture can hardly be said to have
begun before the days of Ezra. Indeed up to his days we

---

[1] οὐ προσέχοντες Ἰουδαικοῖς μύθοις καὶ ἐντολαῖς ἀνθρώπων ἀποστρεφομένων τὴν
ἀλήθειαν. Comp. verse 10. Εἰσὶ γὰρ πολλοὶ . . . ματαιολόγοι καὶ φρεναπάται,
μάλιστα οἱ ἐκ περιτομῆς.

[2] See Muir, *Sanscrit Texts*, iii. pp. 138-179.

[3] The Koran has its schools of expositors. The mystics (*Karmathai*) ; the
Rationalists (*Muatasiliten*) ; the scholastic students (*Mutekellemûn*). Like the
Sopherim, the Sunnites maintain the existence of Tradition (*Sunna*) ; and,
like the Karaites, the Schiites deny it. See Etheridge, *Hebr. Lit.* p. 295.

[4] The republic of Florence endowed a Lectureship in 1373.

are unable to say how much of the Old Testament in its
present form was known to the mass of the Jewish people.
The Mosaic system from a very early period seems not only to
have fallen into desuetude, but even to have been so utterly
forgotten that the discovery of the " Book of the Law " by the
high priest Hilkiah in the reign of Josiah produced a burst
of astonishment.[1] During the Exile it again fell into complete abeyance. In the days of Nehemiah its main provisions
were so little observed that their simple rehearsal woke
mingled feelings of amazement and remorse.[2]

Yet though we do not find in the Old Testament anything
which can be strictly called commentary, we do find, both
in the Psalms and in the Prophets, the enunciation of
principles so rich and broad that, had they been duly taken
to heart, nine-tenths of the labours of the national teachers
might have been saved from abortiveness. For those labours
were based on the two assumptions that every word in the
Five Books of Moses was supernaturally communicated,
and that every tittle of Levitical formalism was of infinite
importance. Nothing can be clearer than that the free
attitude of the earlier Prophets towards the Law would have
been impossible if they had accepted either hypothesis.
Had they done so, they too might have sunk to the level of
Priests and Scribes, and could never have been the inspired
teachers of mankind. Moses is only mentioned three times
in all the Prophets.[3] The word Sinai does not once occur
in them, nor the word High Priest. They scarcely show
a trace of any influence from the Levitic system. To the
official Priesthood their general attitude is one of strong
antagonism, and so far from bowing to sacerdotal authority
they rebuke these Temple ministers with scathing satire

---

[1] 2 Kings xxii. 8–15 ; xxiii. 1–3.
[2] Nehem. viii. ix. xiii.
[3] Is. lxiii. 12 ; Jer. xv. 1 ; Mal. iv. 4. It is only in the third passage that
" the law of Moses " is mentioned. Other allusions to " the law of the Lord "
are general, as Amos ii. 4, Hos. iv. 6, viii. 1 ; Jer. ix. 13, &c., Zeph. iii. 4.
A written law is referred to in Hos. viii. 12, Jer. viii. 8. See on the whole
subject Smend, *Ueber die Genesis d. Judenthums* (*Zeitschr. f. alttest. Wissensh.*
1882).

and unmeasured invective.[1] But what is most remarkable
is their varied and magnificent protest against the spirit of
legalism, which substitutes outward ordinances for genuine
holiness. In urging this theme Samuel, David, Isaiah,
Jeremiah, Amos, Micah, Hosea, Habakkuk, use language
so sweeping in its universality, that they might have seemed
to be filled with a spirit not only of indifference, but even of
contempt for that yoke of ritual bondage which it required a
courage as high as that of St. Peter, so many centuries afterwards, to declare that neither they nor their fathers had been
able to bear.[2] "Behold to obey," said Samuel, "is better
than sacrifice, and to hearken than the fat of rams."[3] "Thou
desirest not sacrifice," says David, "else would I give it thee;
but thou delightest not in burnt offerings."[4] "To what purpose is the multitude of your sacrifices unto me? saith the
Lord," is the message of Isaiah.[5] "I hate, I despise your feast-
days," is the word of the Lord through Amos.[6] "I spake
not unto your fathers concerning burnt offerings and
sacrifices," says the word of the Lord in Jeremiah; "but
this thing I commanded them, saying, Obey my voice."[7]
"What doth the Lord require of thee," asks Micah, "but
to do justice, and to love mercy, and to walk humbly with
thy God?"[8] "I desired mercy and not sacrifice," is the
terse message of Hosea. "I gave them also statutes that
were not good, and judgments whereby they should not
live,"[9] was the bold utterance which, however interpreted,
almost cost the prophet Ezekiel his place in the Jewish
canon.[10] Such thoughts were the most direct antithesis to
the views and methods of the Scribes.

---

[1] See Is. xxviii. 7, 8 ; lvi. 10, 11 ; Jer. iii. 16 ; v. 13 ; vi. 13 ; vii. 21, 22 ;
viii. 10 ; xii. 10 ; xxiii. 11 ; Ezek. xxii. 25, 26 ; Hos. vi. 9 ; Zeph. iii.
3, 4 ; Mal. ii. 1-10, &c.

[2] Acts xv. 10. [3] 1 Sam. xv. 22. [4] Ps. li. 16.
[5] Is. i. 11. [6] Amos v. 21, 22. [7] Jer. vii. 22, 23.
[8] Mic. vi. 6-9. [9] Ezek. xx. 25.

[10] See Jer. *Ep. ad Paulin.* Zunz, *Gottesd. Vortr.* c. ix. L. Wogue, *Hist.
de la Bible*, p. 34. "Revere the memory of Chananiah ben Chizkiyah, for
had it not been for him the book of Ezekiel would have been suppressed
because of the contradictions it offers to the word of the law. By the help of
300 bottles of oil . . . he prolonged his studies till he succeeded in reconciling
all the discrepancies."—SHABBATH, f. 13, 2. See too Menachoth, f. 45, and

E

Theoretically indeed these Prophetic teachings were always admitted. They were recognised in the Pentateuch itself.[1] When our Lord answered the question of the Scribes by summing up the Law in two great commandments, some of them at least were able to appreciate the glorious truth and insight of the answer.[2] Nay, if there be not a wilful falsification in the Talmudic records—if the later Rabbis did not in this instance as in many others light their torches at the sun which yet they cursed—Hillel himself had in a mutilated form given half of the same answer. Shammai drove away with a builder's rod the rude Gentile who promised to become a proselyte if he would teach him the whole Law while he stood on one leg, but Hillel converted him by answering, "What is hateful to thyself do not to thy neighbour. This is the whole law; all the rest is but comment and fringe."[3]

But if Hillel ever used those words it was one of the many proofs that he could breathe in a purer atmosphere than had been reached by his brother Rabbis. They had proclaimed that there were 613 precepts, of which some were "light" and some were "heavy."[4] It therefore became a frequent question among them, "which was the first and great commandment?" In the tract *Shabbath* we are told that the most important law was the one about fringes, so that, on one occasion, R. Rabba, having accidentally stepped on and torn his fringe while mounting a ladder, would not move until it had been mended. How little the Jews are ashamed of a judgment so diametrically opposed to the opinions of their mightiest Prophets is shown by the fact that no less a person than Rashi, even in the twelfth century, is still bold enough to repeat that the Law about fringes is the first and great

other passages of the Talmud cited by Hamburger *s.v.* Jechezkel; Hershon, *Talm. Miscell.* p. 226. The difficult verse, Ez. xx. 25, is alluded to in *Megilla* f. 32. 1.

[1] Deut. x. 12.

[2] Mark xii. 32–34. καὶ εἶπεν αὐτῷ ὁ γραμματεὺς Καλῶς, διδάσκαλε, κ.τ.λ.

[3] Shabbath, f. 31, 1. It must be borne in mind that "neighbour" usually meant "Jew." Baba Qamma. f. 38, 1, Amsterd. ed. Hershon, *Genesis*, p. 370.

[4] This was deduced from Gematria, because תורה = 611, which with "I am" and "thou shalt have no other" = 613. Makkoth, f. 23, 2.

commandment.[1] Such was the difference between the spirit of the Prophets and that of the Rabbis, in whose days " there was no Prophet more ! "

I. The question may well be asked. how a change so immense was effected, and to whose influence it was due. Vast revolutions are usually brought about by the genius of one man who concentrates in his own person the energy of some new impulse, and, for good or for evil, pours its tidal wave over coming generations with a force which, centuries afterwards, is still unspent.

The founder of Judaism as distinct from Mosaism;[2] he who transformed the theocracy into a nomocracy;[3] he who changed Israel from a people into a church, and from a political power into an international sect; he who established a system under which Prophecy ceased because it was no longer esteemed a necessity;[4] he who based the influence of the Scribe[5] on so strong a foundation that it

[1] Rashi on Num. xv. 39 (following the Talmud, Shevuoth, f. 29, 1) proved his point by Gematria (see *infra*, p. 98), because the numerical value of *Tsitsith* ("fringes") is 600, and this with the eight threads and the five knots = 613, the number of "all the commandments of the Lord." Num. xv. 39. A Jew who neglected to wear the *Tsitsith* was excommunicated (Pesachim, f. 113, 2) and regarded as a churl (*am ha-arets*, Berakhoth, f. 47, 2), since he transgressed five positive commands (Menachoth, f. 44, 1). Any one who wore them would have 2,800 slaves to wait on him (Shabbath, f. 32, 2). Rashi proves this from Zech. viii. 23, because there are four fringes, and if 10 men of the 70 nations seize hold of them, 70 × 10 × 4 = 2,800. See Hershon, *Talm. Miscellany*, p. 260.

[2] Weill, *Le Judaïsme*, i. 58.

[3] Weber, *Altsyn. Theol.* i. Hence it is Hillel's highest honour to be called a "scholar of Ezra," who revived the law. Sanhedrin, f. 11, 1. See Ezra, x. 7–8. Jost, *Gesch. d. Israeliten*, iii. Ewald (*Hist. of Isr.* v. 53) prefers the term Hagiocracy, *i.e.* the belief in a Holy Land, a Holy People, &c.

[4] See Ezra vii. 10 ; Ecclus. xxxix. 1. "Dignity" is the special prerogative of the Scribe. *Id.* x. 5 ; Matt. xxiii. 7, 8 ; Mark x. 51 ; John xx. 16. Weber, 4, 122. "The wise man (*i.e.* the Rabbi) is greater than the Prophet " (חכם עדיף מנביא, Baba Bathra, f. 12, 1). In Sanhedrin, 11, the Shekhinah, after the last prophet had died, rested on Hillel, and then on Samuel the Little. It is said that at the destruction of the Temple Prophecy was taken from the Prophets and given to the Wise. Baba Bathra, 18 c. After the death of Malachi the Jews had only the rare and dubious " Daughter of a Voice" (Bath Qol), on which see Jos. *Antt.* xii. 10, 3. ; Yoma, f. 9, 2 ; Jer. Sota, ix. 16. It is mentioned in the Jerusalem Targum on Deut. xxviii. 15.

[5] See the Talmudic references in Herzfeld, *Gesch. d. V. Isr.* i. 126. The Rabbis derived *sopherim* from *sophar*, " to number," because they numbered the letters of the sacred books. *Qiddushin*, f. 30, 1. This is a mistake (Jost, *Gesch. d. Isr.* iii. 119), though stated by Elias Levita. The Scribes did, however, number the letters, and found that the ו in Lev. ix. 42 is the middle

overshadowed the authority of Princes,[1] and caused even the
influence of Priests to dwindle into gradual insignificance;[2]
he who was the first to inaugurate the Midrash,[3] and the
Targum;[4] he who was the traditional propounder of the
decisions which form the earliest nucleus of the Mishna;[5]
the first author of liturgical forms;[6] the first authoriser
of local synagogues;[7] the first collector and editor of the
Canon;[8] the initiator of the long subsequent toil of the
Massorets; the historic originator of the ORAL LAW—that
man was EZRA, the priestly Scribe. He carried on the silent
revolution in Jewish conceptions of which the last eight
chapters of the book of Ezekiel are the indication, and which
find expression also in the Books of Chronicles.[9] In Ezekiel
we see the gradual passing of the Prophet into the Scribe, in
whom Prophecy finds it necessary to take the form of Law,
and who for glowing ideal visions furnishes a legislative
code.[10] The *Sopherim,* or Scribes, lasted for 138 years,
and were succeeded by the *Chakamim,* or the Wise

letter of the Pentateuch, and the י in Ps. lxxx. 11 the middle letter of the
Psalms.

[1] Hillel was the first Rabbi to be called a Prince (Nasî); Shabbath, f. 34,
1. Comp. Berakhoth, f. 28, 1; Schürer, *Neut. Zeitgesch.* 464; Weber, 122.

[2] "The wise" are called "Priests," though most of them were laymen, in
Nedarim, 40. See Shemoth Rabba. c. 34, and Sifra. f. 13, 2, where "Blessing" is specially declared to be apart from the Priests. See too Jos. *Antt.*
iv. 8, § 14; Jost. *Judenthum,* i. 37. Even Ezra is called "the Scribe" as a
title of more honour than "the Priest." Ezra vii. 11; Neh. viii. 4, 9, &c.

[3] Nehem. viii. 7; Ezra vii. 6, 25. The verb *darash,* in the sense of "to
explain," is first found in Ezra vii. 10; Nederam, f. ii. 37; Weill, i. 69.

[4] Nehem. viii. 8; xiii. 24.

[5] Ten ordinances of a trivial nature are attributed to Ezra in Baba
Qamma, f. 82, 1. See Waehner, *Antiq. Ebr.* ii. 689. Some of the so-called
Halakoth le-Mosheh mi-Sinai certainly came from the school of Ezra.
Herzfeld, i. 3.

[6] Berakhoth, f. 33; Megilla, f. 10; Maimonides, *Yad Hachazaka,* L. i. art.
iv.; Weill (i. 69) mentions the actual prayers.

[7] See Herzfeld, i. 127.

[8] Baba Bathra, f. 15; Megilla, f. 3; Weill, i. 71. The language used about
Ezra's share in the Canon is startling. We are told that he and his five companions *re-wrote* the Law (2 Esdras, xiv. 21-46), and the Talmud says that he
and the men of the Great Synagogue "wrote" the Old Testament.

[9] It will be seen at a glance that the Books of Chronicles are more an
ecclesiastical than a national history, and that they adopt the standard of
the Levitic Law. It has been thought that 1 Kings, viii. 1-4, compared with
the LXX., shows traces of Levitic glosses.

[10] See Prof. J. E. Carpenter, *Mod. Review,* Jan. 1884.

and they by the *Tanaim*, or "Teachers." After the lapse of another 500 years the Tanaim were succeeded by the *Amoraim*, or Discoursers, for 300 years; and they by the *Seboraim*, or Investigators, and *Gaonim*, or "Excellent," for another 400 years, down to the thirteenth century of our era.[1] Throughout every one of these Rabbinic bodies, from the foundation of legalism to the close of the schools of the East and West,[2] and indeed for twenty-two centuries the impulse given by Ezra continued to sway the course of Jewish thought. He was looked upon as a second Moses. "He would have been worthy," said Rabbi Jose, "to become the legislator of Israel had not Moses anticipated him."[3] Legends soon began to cling about his name like clouds about a mountain peak,[4] and even in the Koran he appears as Ozair, clothed with immortal youth.

And yet by what a gulf of inferiority is Ezra separated from the mighty Prophets of his race! It is a gulf like that which separates the Bible from the Talmud; the Decalogue

---

[1] See Etheridge, Hebrew Lit. *passim* ; Otho, *Historia Doctorum Mithnicorum*, pp. 13–32 ; Herzog, *s.v.* Rabbinismus. Grätz divides the epochs somewhat differently (*Gesch. d. Juden*, iv. 9):

The SOPHERIM, B.C. 458 to B.C. 320. From Ezra to the death of Simon the Just.

The CHAKHAMIM, B.C. 323 to A.D. 13. From Simon to the death of Hillel.

The TANAIM, A.D. 13 to A.D. 190. From Hillel to the death of Rabbi.

The AMORAIM, A.D. 190 to A.D. 498. From Rabbi to R. Ashî.

The SEBORAIM, A.D. 498 to A.D. 689. From Jose to Rav Shishana.

THE GAONIN, A.D. 689 to A.D. 900.

The Gaonim of Sora were contemporary with the Rabbanim of Pumbaditha. The most celebrated Gaon was R. Saadiah, A.D. 928.

[2] The Rabbinic schools in the East were closed in 1040. Under the Sopherim Mosaism was renewed ; schools were founded ; Targums began ; the scholar became powerful. Under the Chakhamim tradition was developed, and there grew up the rival schools of Pharisees and Sadducees. The Tanaim ended their labours by the publication of the Mishna. The Amoraim completed the Gemara.

[3] Sanhedrin, f. 22 ; Tosefta, 4, *ib.* ; Jer. Megilla, i. 9 ; Weill, *Le Judaïsme*, i. The proof itself depends on the futile Hillelite methods of "equivalence." Moses "*ascended*" to receive the law (Ex. xiv. 3) ; Ezra "*ascended*" from Babylon (Ezra vii. 6). Therefore the one was as worthy as the other.

[4] In the Targum, on Mal. i. 1, and in Megilla, f. 15, 1, he is identified with Malachi. For other legends, see the books of Esdras ; 4 Esdras viii. 20 ; x. 57–59 ; xiv. 9 ; Koran, *Sura.* ix. 31 ; Ewald, *Hist. of Isr.* vi. 164 ; D'Herbelot, *Bibl. Orient. s.v.* Ozair, iii. 89.

from the Halakha; the religion of righteousness from the religiosity of Tradition; the freedom of spiritual enlightenment from the pettiness of ceremonialism ; the holiness of the heart from the outward holiness of Levitic purifications.

But if a man is to be counted great from the extent and vitality of his influence then Ezra was great indeed. The restoration of the Law,[1] and the terrible sternness of the day on which, in inferential accordance with its precepts, one hundred and thirteen marriages were ruthlessly annulled, perhaps saved the Jewish nationality from extinction.[2] That tremendous measure inaugurated an era of legal strictness such as had never before been known. The establishment of synagogues trained the people in a worship largely independent of a centralised hierarchy.[3] It taught them how they might draw near to God in prayer without the incessant intervention of sacerdotal functions. It secured the reading of Moses every Sabbath day.[4] It necessitated the explanation of Scripture in a tongue understanded of the people. It extinguished for ever the temptation to Polytheism. In crisis after crisis, in struggle after struggle, it was sufficiently potent to save the Jews from national obliteration. Their love for the Oral Law strengthened them to withstand the hatred and intrigues of Samaritans and Ammonites. It enabled them to pacify the wrath of Alexander. It inspired them with an indomitable pride in their own destinies [5] amid the rivalries of Seleucids and

---

[1] Circumstances like that mentioned in Ezra iii. 4, can only be accounted for by the fact that Hebrew had practically become a dead language.

[2] Ezra ix. x. ; 1 Esdras viii. ix. Among those whose marriages were thus annulled were four of the highest priests, thirteen other priests, ten Levites, and eighty-six laymen. How little strictness had been attached to the rule is shown by the Ethiopian wife of Moses, the marriage of Salmon with Rahab, of Boaz with Ruth, of Solomon with Pharaoh's daughter, &c. David the darling hero of the nation was the near descendant of a Moabitess, and the marriage from which he sprang is made the subject of a tender and laudatory idyl.

[3] Jost, *Gesch. d. Israel.*, iii. 51.

[4] Acts xv. 28. Philo speaks in terms of warm praise of the synagogues and proseuchae. *Vit. Mos.* p. 168 (ed. Mangey). "When the Law had been forgotten by Israel, Ezra came from Babylon, and re-established it." Sukka, f. 20, 1–4 ; Esdras. xiv. 21–27.

[5] Weill, i. 97. In Megilla, f. 12, the words of Moses (Lev. xxvi. 44) are thus explained : "*I will not reject them* in the Babylonish captivity, when

Ptolemies.[1] It defied the bloody persecution of Antiochus. It prevented the Maccabees from overshadowing the Pharisees by a secular dynasty.[2] It resisted the subtle fascination of Greece, and could not be crushed even by the iron arm of Rome. It abased the pride of the Herods and the splendour of the Boethusîm.[3] It overawed the tyranny of greedy Procurators, aristocratic Sadducees, and murderous Zealots. It survived even the total ruin of Jerusalem, and was not quenched in the blood of martyrdom which followed the defeat of Barkokhba. It outlived the long persecutions of Roman and Byzantine emperors. It was not quenched amid the storms of Teutonic invasion. In vain were

> " The torture prolonged from age to age,
> The infamy Israel's heritage ;
> The Ghetto's plague, and the garb's disgrace,
> The badge of shame, and the felon's place ;
> The branding tool, and the bloody whip,
> And the summons to Christian fellowship ! "

The Jews were not exterminated by the fanaticism of the Crusades, nor by the proscriptions and massacres of the Inquisition. For 1700 years after the Third Captivity—the *Galuth Edom*[4]—they endured an almost unbroken martyrdom but again and again has Judaism emerged from the deluge of calamities, and again and again has the Oral Law been to them as their guide, their government, their country, their

God gave us Daniel, and the Three Children ; *nor will I abhor them* in Haman's day, when He gave us Mordecai and Esther ; *I will not annihilate them*, under Antiochus Epiphanes, when He gave the Maccabees ; *I will not break my covenant with them* in the captivity of Edom (*i.e.* Rome), when He gave us the house of Rabbi (*Judah ha-nasî*) and the wise of succeeding generations.

[1] The Maccabaean struggle was neither for political freedom, nor *pro aris et focis*, but for the Law. 1 Macc. ii. 27 ; iii. 21 ; vi. 59 ; 2 Macc. vii. 2, 23, 30, 37. Antiochus was especially eager to get the βιβλία τοῦ νόμου. 1 Macc. i. 56-58.

[2] See the story of Eleazar the Pharisee and John Hyrcanus, Jos. *Antt.* xiii. 10, § 5, and the quarrel of the Pharisees with Alexander Jannaeus, *Antt.* xiii. 13, § 5 ; and for this section of history, see Derenbourg, 70-205. The Sadducees rejected the Oral Law, and all traditional developments, but they were completely worsted in the contest. Jos. *Antt.* x. 22, 24 ; xviii. 1, 2 ; *B. J.* ii. 12.

[3] Herod married a daughter of Simon, son of Boethos, and was in close alliance with the hierarchic families. Jos. *Antt.* xv. 9, § 3.

[4] "Edom" was used in the Talmud as a cypher for Rome (אדום=רום).

pride, their consolation, the one anchor of safety to which
they trusted during the storms which, from the four winds
of heaven, were let loose upon them by the hatred of the
world.[1]

II. Yet inevitable and indispensable as was the work which
Ezra accomplished it is impossible not to feel that it was
work done in a decadent epoch, and for a degenerate people.
Ezra was like Ezekiel a Priest, and he was also a Scribe.
He could only be what he was; what God had made
him; what the times required him to be. If the
impulse which he gave to the national mind was in a poorer
direction than of old—if the Judaism which he established
was far inferior to the true Hebraic spirit—it is because such
was the will of Heaven. The truest and greatest Prophets
of Israel until the days of Ezekiel had treated the ceremonial
ordinances as infinitely unimportant in comparison with moral
purity. Ezra could not teach as they taught because his
age required a different spirit. It was God's will that
the Prophets whom this people had persecuted and slain
—the Prophets who had taught them truths which would
have made them free—should be followed by a lower order
of men; by Scribes, Pharisees, Rabbis, who would lay on
them heavy burdens, and whom, in the natural slavishness of
ignoble natures, on that very account they did not persecute
but adore.[2] Had Ezra been an Isaiah the history of the Jews
would have been different and nobler. They might have
accepted the Christ whom they crucified. Instead of filling
their dreary Talmud with the multiplication of meaningless
minutiæ, the Rabbis, like the Apostles and Evangelists, might
have been reckoned among the eternal teachers of the world.
For the good in the system of Oral Tradition was largely
mixed with evil. It produced nothing great in genius,
nothing intense in inspiration, nothing profound in thought,
nothing beautiful or noble in literature. One thrilling note

---

[1] See Weill, *Le Judaïsme*, i. 170 ; Grätz, iv. 1.
[2] See 2 Chr. xxxvi. 16 ; Hos. ix. 7 ; Matt. xiii. 57 ; Lk. iv. 24, xiii. 23,
xxiii. 36 ; John vii. 52 ; Acts xiii. 20, &c.

of David's harp, one passionate appeal of Isaiah's burning indignation, one eloquent homily of Hosea and Micah, even one last expiring gleam of nobleness flashed from the fading prophetic fire of Zechariah or Malachi, is as much better than folios full of inferential formalism as love is better than ritual and mercy than sacrifice. Tradition shifted the centre of gravity of the moral system. A minute ritual had become the sole possible fence of national holiness. The consequence was the gradual materialising of spiritual conceptions; the depreciation of righteousness in comparison with ceremonialism and theological opinion. Just as in the middle ages a suspicion of heresy was avenged by the stake, while heinous moral offences were easily condoned, so among the Rabbis, if a man were but an orthodox casuist his sins were recorded with unblushing indifference. The Talmud abounds in narratives which detail without the slightest blame the impurity of the Rabbis. Their hedge about the Law made no pretence of keeping out the wild boars of Pride and Lust, though it might exclude the little foxes of irregular ceremonial.[1] What else could be expected when "dazzling externalities" had once been substituted for eternal truths![2]

The so-called "Great Synagogue" which Ezra is said to have founded[3] slew Idolatry; but it substituted in its place a new idolatry. It was an idolatry more dangerous, more subtle, more delusive, more difficult to eradicate; an idolatry which ossified the very heart of religion. It assumed the most solemn sanctions only to thrust a Book, a Tradition, and a Ritual between the soul and God. "After the Feast of Tabernacles," says the Talmud,[4] "Ezra established a fast day

[1] Weber quotes Moed Qaton, f. 17, 1; Menachoth, f. 13; Berakhoth, f. 19, 1; 20, 1; Chagiga, f. 16; Avoda Zara, f. 17, 1; Sota, f. 7, 1, &c.
[2] See the weighty remarks of Ewald, *Hist. of Isr.* v. 63.
[3] Krochmal identifies the Great Synagogue with the Assembly of Notables in Neh. x. 1–27. See Aboth, i. 1; Aboth of R. Nathan, 1; Megilla, 17. Simon the Just was its last member (Aboth, i. 2; Jos. *Antt.* xii. 2, § 5). Jost defines them as "alle die bis zum Simon an der Spitze der Gesetzlehre in Judäa standen" (*Gesch.* i. 42). See the Excursus in Taylor, *Sayings of the Jewish Fathers*, pp. 124, 125.
[4] Yoma, f. 67; Weill, i. 72.

on which he and the Levites prayed to God with loud cries
to banish idolatry from the people. A billet fell from heaven
on which was written the word 'granted.' After three days
and nights of continued fasting the spirit of idolatry was delivered to them like a flaming lion which bounded out of the
Holy of Holies. By the advice of the Prophet Zechariah
they seized it, and flung it into a leaden coffin hermetically
sealed. They then prayed to God to annihilate also the Evil
Impulse, but they checked their prayer because they were
taught by a very short experience that its fulfilment would
involve the extinction of the human race.[1]

Alas! the Evil Impulse was so far from being exterminated
that it found its stronghold in the spirit of the Scribe. The
Law—not the Law in its simplicity but the Law modified,
transformed, distorted by Tradition—the Law robbed of its
essential significance by the blind zeal which professed to
defend it—became the centre of an abject servility.[2] It came
to be regarded as the only means of intercourse with God, and
almost as the substitute for God. Immeasurable evils ensued.
Piety dwindled into legalism. Salvation was identified with
outward conformity. A torturing scrupulosity was substituted
for a glad obedience. God's righteous faithfulness was treated
as a forensic covenant.[3] For prophecy there was only the miserable substitute of the "Daughter of a Voice;"[4] for faith the
sense of merit acquired by legal exactitude.[5] The "pious"
were hopelessly identified with the party of the Scribes.
The Synagogues became schools.[6] Ethics were sub-

---

[1] See another curious legend on the same page of Yoma.

[2] Their one professed object was μετὰ ἀκριβείας ἐξηγεῖσθαι τὰ νόμιμα. Jos.
Antt. xviii. 2, § 4 ; *B. J.* ii. 8, § 14.

[3] The אֱמוּנָה of God was looked upon only as an אֲמָנָה. In thus putting
the conception of a Covenant into the forefront, Ezra anticipated Cocceius
by 2,000 years. Ezra ix. 9, 19, 27, 28, 34.

[4] The Bath Qol.

[5] How unlike the general tone of the Psalms and Prophets is Nehemiah's
legalistic prayer that God would remember his good deeds ! "The last pure
glow of the long day of the Old Testament sun" died out in Malachi (Ewald,
v. 176), and with him perished "the loftiest and most characteristic activity
which the Law had permitted in ancient times."

[6] 1 Macc. vii. 12. συναγωγὴ γραμματέων. Comp. 1 Chron. ii. 55 ; Wellhausen, *Die Pharisäer u. Sadd.* 12.

ordinated to Liturgiology.[1] Messianism was debased
into an unmeaning phrase or a materialised fable.[2] The
pride of pedantry, despising moral nobleness, and revel-
ling in an hypocrisy so profound as hardly to recognise
that it was hypocritical,[3] wrapped itself in an esoteric
theology, and looked down on the children of a common Father
as an accursed multitude in whose very touch there was
ceremonial defilement.[4] This was the ultimate result of that
recrudescence of ceremonial, which was the special work of
the Scholars of Ezra. And of this work the basis was
a perverted Bibliolatry, and the instrument an elaborate
exegesis.

The new system had a success immense and fatal. In the
days of our Lord Pharisaism reigned supreme. " Why do ye
set at nought the commandment of God by your tradition? "
" In vain do they worship me, teaching for doctrines the commandments of men." Such had been the comment of Christ
Himself on the religionism which had not yet ripened in
its most unwholesome fruit. Thus early did the degradation
and annulment of everything which was precious in Holy
Writ begin with the system which professed to be founded
on its extravagant exaltation. Even in Ezra's days, though
the Books of Scripture were divided into what they called the

[1] Aboth, i. 2.
[2] See Talmudic quotations in Weber, 122, and in Weill, i. 95, fg.
[3] See Excursus I. Self-glorification of the Rabbis (Waehner, ii. 785, 786,
793; Hershon, Gen. 152, 439; Luke xi. 52; Matt. xxiii. 2; Weber, 126,
Miracles; Chiarini, i. 377).
[4] They spoke of these as "laymen," *Hediots* (ἰδιῶται) and "boors"
Amharatsim. The Hediot (הדיוט) is merely a man who has never become
one of " the Wise." He may become an Associate (*chaber*) but not a
Wise-man, because he does not devote his life exclusively to the Law.
Shabbath, f. 11, 1. The Ignoramus (Ecclus. xxxix. xxxviii. 24–34, "whose
talk is of bullocks"), or "people of the land," *am-ha-arets*, (עם הארץ)
was spoken of by the Rabbis with an almost inconceivable brutality,
of which a specimen may be seen in John vii. 49; Sota, f. 22, 1. The
resurrection was denied to them (Kethuboth, f. iii. 1) on the strength of Is.
xxvi. 14. "The dead live not, the shades (*Rephaim*) arise not." Rabbi
refused them corn in a famine (*Baba Bathra*, f. 8, 2). They are treated as
liars and rogues (*Pesachim*, f. 49, 2); and it was lawful to rend an Am-ha-arets
like a fish (*ib.*). They applied Jer. xxxi. 37, Prov. xxiv. 20, to *amharatsim*.
See Weber, 45–48; McCaul, *Old Paths*, pp. 458–464. Thus the Pharisees
were " Separatists " (*Perushim*) in the worst sense.

Tenakh,[1] that is the Torah, the Nebiîm, and the Khethubim, the Law was practically made to include all the rest.[2] It was regarded as eternal.[3] God himself was supposed to spend three hours daily in its study.[4] Its mere words and letters were potent as magic formulae. But it was at the same time pretended that the rule (*norma normans*) required the intervention of skilled interpreters without which it could not become the practice (*norma normata*). Thus on the one hand Rabbinism was founded upon bases as solid as that of the mediaeval Papacy, and on the other the plainest decisions of this deified Law were set aside with the most transparent effrontery.[5] Claiming too much for the Law the Rabbis left it too little. By adding to God's commandments so largely they also took from them. By imposing additional restrictions they broke down proper safeguards.

This tremendous tyranny of Rabbinism was built upon superstition and exclusiveness. The Scribes were declared to be the successors of Moses. The scholastic lecture-room was the heir of the political Sanhedrin. The Patriarchs of the House of Hillel combined for fourteen generations the powers of Davidic king and Aaronic pontiff. The casuists of Tradition completely superseded the Levitic Priests.[6] All liberty of thought was abrogated; all Gentile learning was forbidden; no communion was allowed with the human intellect outside the Pharisaic pale. Within the circle of Rabbinism the Jew was "the galley-slave of the most rigid orthodoxy." The yoke of the Romans was not so exacting as that of the Rabbis, which dominated over a man's whole

---

[1] Buxtorf, *De Abbrev. s.v.* תנך. See Bretschneider, *Dogmatik d. apocr. Schriften*, 64–67.

[2] See the Book of Baruch, ii. 27–34; iii. 37; iv. 1, and *passim*, 4; Macc. i. 16; Ecclus. xv. 1; xvii. 9.

[3] Wisd. xviii. 4; Tob. i. 6; 2 Macc. vi. 23; 3 Esd. ix. 39, &c. All sects alike claimed Scripture as their authority. Hamburger, *s.v.* Bibel.

[4] So Rabbi Juda asserted in the name of Rab. Avoda Zara, f. 3, 2.

[5] Weill (i. 62) says that the new exegesis which received its impulse from the days of Ezra established "liberty of interpretation," "qui modifie, qui transforme, qui tourne, qui retourne, qui remue le texte biblique."

[6] The Targum on Judg. v. 9 interpolates a pompous eulogy on the Scribes into the song of Deborah! The Scribes made it a high misdemeanour to reject their decisions.

existence and intruded itself into the most trivial actions of life. The weak were tortured by the knowledge that they could not so much as wash their hands or eat a meal without running the risk of deadly offences. The "ordination" [1] of the Rabbis made them oracles for every subject and every action, from the cleaning of the teeth to the last prayer in which the dying commended their souls to God. If any one gave a rule which he had not heard from *them* the Shekinah departed from Israel. [2] Their coercion was made yet more terrible by maledictions. "The whole range of action permitted to the Jewish mind was included in the mazes of a vaulted labyrinth from which there was no outlet but through the terrible gate of excommunication," of which the milder forms [3] blasted the reputation, and the sterner [4] shattered the temporal interests, and ruined the everlasting welfare. Rabbinism was nothing but a variety of sacerdotalism in which orthodox pedants, expounding a system of unconscious delusion, wielded all the authority of sacrificing Priests. [5]

It was the professed object of the Scribes to exalt and glorify the Law. [6] "The world," says Simon the Just, "stands on three things—the Law, Ritual, [7] and Well-doing," and the Law is significantly put first. "There are three crowns," says the Talmud, "the crown of Royalty, the crown of Priesthood, and the Crown of the Law, but the latter is of more worth than both the others, and he who has it is as good as if he had all three." "Be circumspect in justice," said the men of the Great Synagogue, "get many pupils, and make a

---

[1] סמיכה. See too Aboth, iii. 8 ; iv. 13.

[2] Berakhoth, f. 27, 2. See Etheridge, 56, 57 ; Jost, *Gesch. d. Israel.*, iii. 120.

[3] *Nesipha ; niddui.*

[4] *Cherem ; Shematta.*

[5] Scarcely had the Great Synagogue passed away when we find "the couples" (*Zougoth*) who succeeded to it leaving as the summary of their wisdom such rules as "Let thy house be a house of assembly for the wise, and dust thyself with the dust of their feet, and drink their words with thirst."

[6] See Ecclus. xxiv. ; Baruch iv. 1 ; *Bereshith Rabba*, c. 17. In Jalqut on Gen. i. 26, God says *to the Thora*, "We will make men." Aboth, vi. 10 ; viii. 22. For many passages of the Talmud see Weber, 16, 17. For a list of the terms of eulogy heaped on the Law—fire, light, dawn, milk, balm, pearls, &c., Waehner, *Antt. Ebr.* ii. 793 ; Weber, p. 55.

[7] עבודה, Temple-service. Aboth, i. 2.

hedge (סְיָג) about the Law." [1] The hedge was made; its construction was regarded as the main function of Rabbinism; [2] it excluded all light from without and all egress from within; but it was so carefully cultivated that the shrine itself was totally disregarded.[3] The Oral Law was first exalted as a necessary supplement to the Written Law; then substituted in the place of it; [4] and finally identified with the inferences of the Rabbis. The Pentateuch was disparaged in comparison with the Mishna, the Mishna in comparison with the voluminous expansions of the Gemara. Supported by the False Decretals of Judaism which asserted that the Oral Law had been handed down by Mosaic succession through a chain of recipients, the Scribes proceeded to make disobedience to their decisions more perilous than disobedience to a moral commandment.[5] "The voice of the Rabbi is as the voice of God." [6] "He who transgresses the words of the Scribes throws away his life." "Scripture is like water, the Mishna like wine; the Gemara like spiced wine."

[1] Siphri, 40, a. ; Aboth, iv. 17 ; Yoma, f. 72 ; Weber, *Alt. Theol.* 39 ; Weill, i. 96.

[2] Lev. xviii. 30. "Make a *mishmereth* to my *mishmereth.*" Yebamoth, f. 21 (Taylor on Aboth, i. 1). Yet the Rabbis pointed to Adam's "neither shall ye touch it" as an *addition* to God's command, and therefore a misapplication of the "hedge about the law."

[3] Similarly the very name Jehovah, in its true pronunciation, disappeared in consequence of the crude superstition with which it was nominally protected. It is now pronounced with the vowels of Adonai.

[4] The divinity of the Oral Law, or "Law upon the Mouth" (*Thora shebeal Pî*) was based on perversions of Deut. xvii. 8–12 ; xviii. 15–20, just as the Papal tyranny was based on a perversion of Matt. xvi. 19. See the preface to the *Yad Hachazaka* of Maimonides, and his comment on Sanhedrin, c. 10. The word "*mouth*" (A.V. "*tenor*") in Ex. xxxiv. 27 was explained to refer to the Oral Law. Aboth, i. 1; Weill. iii. 262–266. In Ex. xxiv. 12, they say that the five clauses refer to (1) The Decalogue, (2) The Thora, (3) The Mishna, (4) The Khethubin, (5) The Gemara, which were all taught to Moses on Sinai! The term, "Law on the Mouth," *i.e.* Oral Law, is found very early. Zunz, *Gottesd. Vorträge,* 45.

[5] To prove this they quoted Scripture for their purpose. Thus in Eccles. xii. 12 they altered סְפָרִים, "books," into סוֹפְרִים, "scribes," and להג, "study," into לַעַג, "derision." 'Erubin, f. 21, 2. In Eccl. x. 8, we find "whoso breaketh a hedge, a serpent shall bite him." Now the words of the wise are a hedge to the law, and the bite of a serpent is incurable. Shabbath, f. 110, 1. On the other hand, as Rashi says, the punishment of death is not threatened to many of the commands and prohibitions of the law. Comp. Berakhoth, f. 4, 1. Aqiba was ready to die of thirst rather than to neglect "the words of the wise" by not washing his hands before eating.

[6] 'Erubin, f. 21.

"The Scripture is as salt, the Mishna as pepper, the Gemara as spice."[1]   "There is no salvation," said Rab, "for the man who passes from the study of the Halakha to that of Scripture."[2]   "Men learned in Scripture are only as the tendrils of the vine; the Mishna students are the grapes; the students of the Gemara are the ripe clusters."[3]   "The study of Scripture is non-meritorious; the study of the Mishna deserves a reward; the study of the Gemara is an unapproachable virtue."   "He who only studies the Scriptures is but an 'empty cistern.'[4]   "Words of Scribes," said Rabbi Johanan, "are akin to words of the Law, and more beloved."[5]

It will be seen how easy was the step to the contemptuous setting aside of the whole meaning of Holy Writ.   For Scripture History we find the gross substitution of the fictions that Israel is sinless, and holy, and never committed idolatry; that Rebecca, and Rachel, and Leah were never actuated by any but the purest motives; that Reuben never committed incest; that Judah took the daughter of "a merchant," not of a "Canaanite;" that the Twelve Patriarchs were all immaculate; that they never meant to murder their brother Joseph until he tried to lead them into Baal-worship; that Tamar was a daughter of Shem, and was perfectly innocent; that it was only the Proselytes, not the Israelites, who worshipped the golden calf; that neither Aaron's sons, nor Samuel's sons, nor Eli's sons, were really guilty.   David, Bathsheba, Josiah, are all excused from blame, and so step by step by the aid of an exegesis which began in fetish worship and ended in casuistry, Scripture was first placed upon an idol's pedestal and then treated with contumely by its own familiar priests.[6]

---

[1] Sopherim, f. 15, 2.   Comp. Vayikra Rabba, c. 36.

[2] Chagiga, f. 10, 1.

[3] 'Erubin, f. 21, 2.   The very world would be in danger if the Mishnas only were consulted in legal decisions. Sota, f. 21, 1 ; Baba Metzia, f. 33, 1. See these and other quotations in Weber, *l. c.* 102–106 ; Weill, i. 91 ; Chiarini, *Théorie du Judaïsme*, i. 202–206.

[4] בור.   Sota, f. 22, 1.   [5] Berakhoth, f. i. 7.

[6] Sanhedrin, f. 55, 56.   "Whoever says that Reuben, the sons of Samuel, David, and Solomon, have sinned is decidedly in error." Sanhedrin, f. 55, 56.   See all the original passages of the Talmud quoted in Weber, *Altsyn. Theol.* 55, 56.

Nor is this all: the exegesis of the Scribes not only re-
versed the *history* of Scripture, but, as our Lord said, deliberately set aside the plain meaning of the laws which they
professed to deify. We have already noticed how they
abolished the humane provision of Moses for the slave who
did not wish to be separated from his family. In the same
way Hillel by his legal fiction of "the Prosbol," [1] found it easy
to nullify the fundamental Mosaic provision of the Sabbatic
year. "He did it," says the Talmud, "for the good order
of the world;" and by a still more transparent collusion he
set aside the Levitical law about the sale of houses. [2] The
Pharisees by their rule of "Mixtures" managed in a similar
way to get rid of everything which was inconvenient in the
Sabbath observances. These accommodations may have been
in themselves excusable; but thus to violate a Law which
they pretended all the while to regard as infinitely sacred, was
an encouragement to the grossest hypocrisy, and can only be
classed with the transparent frauds of an ignorant Paganism. [3]

Even where the Rabbinic misinterpretations were only
theoretical they were marked by the same sacrifice of the
spirit to the letter. In the treatise *Sanhedrin* it is argued
that the man who made *all* his children pass through the
fire to Moloch would be guilty of no sin, because Moses only
said "thy seed" and not "all thy seed." [4] "There was," says
the Talmud, "an unimpeachable disciple at Jabne who could
adduce a hundred and fifty arguments in favour of the clean-

---

[1] Gittin, v. 5. Derived from πρὸς βουλῇ (πρεσβυτέρων). In order to evade
the Mosaic law of the remission of debt in the Jubilee year the creditor
presented "before the council" a certified agreement that he would at any
time have the right to claim his debt. Sheb. x. 3, 4; Gittin, f. 36, 1, quoted by
Edersheim, *Prophecy and History*, p. 279. In earlier times according to Sheb.
x. 8, the creditor might remit the debt but *stand with his hand open to receive
it!* It utterly nullified Deut. xv. 2. Even the Rabbis were startled by this
sacrifice of the Mosaic law to convenience. Jost, *Judenth.* i. 266. See
Hamburger II. *s.v. Prosbul.* It was nothing more than *praevaricatio*—a
collusive agreement.

[2] Lev. xxv. 29, 30; Erachin. ix. 4. See Derenbourg, p. 189.

[3] Luzzato not only admits that the Rabbinic scholars did violence to the
natural sense, but even says that this was done on the principle of "preferring
general utility to exegetic verity." He quotes Cicero (*de Juvent.* i. 38),
"Omnes leges ad commodum reip. referri oportet, et eas ex utilitate communi,
non ex scriptione, quae in literis est, interpretari."

[4] Sanhedrin, f. 64, 2; Chiarini, ii. 229.

ness of creeping things." [1] "No one is appointed a member of the Sanhedrin who is not ingenious enough to prove from the Law that a creeping thing is ceremonially clean." [2] "God so gave the Law to Moses that a thing may be pronounced clean or unclean in forty-nine different ways." [3]

III. The builders of this vast inverted pyramid of exegesis, which so seldom explained and so often explained away, were many in number. The most eminent among them were Hillel; Shammai; Rabbi Johanan ben Zakkai; Rabbi Aqiba; and Rabbi Juda the Holy.

1. The Rabbis love to dwell on the life of "the sweet and noble HILLEL,"—his Babylonian extraction; his voluntary poverty; his life as a porter; his being found on a Sabbath morning by Shemaia and Abtalion half frozen in the window of their school; his varied learning; his whole day's argument with the Benî Bethyra, and the victory which he finally won by appealing to the "decision" of his teachers; his elevation to the post of President; [4] his imperturbable meekness; his profound and witty utterances; his humanism; his sacrifice even of the truth to avoid a quarrel with the school of Shammai; [5] his famous summary of the whole law under the rule of love to our neighbour.[6] His services were mainly two—namely, Classification and Hermeneutics. He reduced to Six Orders—the first oral basis of the future Mishna—the chaotic mass of rules which had gathered round the 613 Mosaic precepts. He also drew up the seven exegetic rules —perhaps due to the infiltration of Greek logic—which were the basis of all later developments of the Oral Law. Hence,

---

[1] 'Erubin, f. 13, 2.

[2] Sanhedrin, f. 17, 1. Quoted in Hershon's *Genesis*, p. 54.

[3] This latter quotation is from the post-Talmudic tract, Sopherim, c. 16 ; and it is proved (!) from Cant. ii. 4, because in that verse (by Gematria) the word וְדִבְלוֹ = 49. See Pesikhta Rabbathi, f. 23, 1 ; Eisenmenger, *Entd. Jud.* i. 454 ; Deyling, *Obs. Sacr.* iii. 140.

[4] נָשִׂיא (ἡγούμενος).

[5] Bîtsa, f. 20, 1. Hillel and Shammai were the last of the "couples" (*Zougoth*) who succeeded to the leadership of the schools after the death of Simon the Just. The previous couple, Shemaia and Abtalion, were the first to receive the title of "Exegete" (*Darshan*).

[6] On this see Tob. iv. 16 ; Jost, *Judenth.* i. 259.

F

like Ezra, he is called a restorer of the Law,[1] for his rules rendered it possible always to rediscover the Oral Law even if it was forgotten, and to maintain it against the Sadducees on grounds nominally scriptural. His extraordinary merits secured the Patriarchate to his descendants for four hundred and fifty years,[2] and he must be regarded as the earliest founder of the Talmudic system.[3] The Jews themselves deplored the bitter and sterile confusion which began in his school and that of Shammai.[4] The pupils of these schools were the first to display that fondness for pompous titles which is reprobated in the Gospels. A modern Jewish historian has had the extraordinary boldness to assert that Jesus " was a Rabbi of the school of Hillel."[5] The sentence has been seized with avidity by those who desired to diminish the greatness or depreciate the originality of Christ. Let it here suffice to say

---

[1] Sukka, f. 20, 1. In the wailing at his death they cried, " Oh, the pious ! oh, the scholar of Ezra ! " Sanhedrin, f. 11, 1. The very remarkable story of his elevation to the presidency of the schools is related in Pesachim, f. 66, 1 (Hershon, *Genesis*, p. 327). The Sanhedrin is first mentioned under Hyrcanus II. (Jos. *Antt.* xiv. 9), but may be referred to in 2 Macc. i. 8, 10 ; iv. 44 ; xi. 27.

[2] The patriarchs of the house of Hillel were, according to Hamburger (*s.v. Nassi*) : 1. Hillel. 2. Rabban Simeon. 3. Rabban Gamaliel I. 4. Rabban Simeon II. 5. Rabban Gamaliel II. of Jabne. 6. Rabban Simeon III. of Sepphoris. 7. Rabbi (Judah Hakkodesh). 8. R. Gamaliel III. 9. R. Judah II. 10. R. Gamaliel IV. 11. R. Judah III. 12. R. Hillel II. 13. R. Gamaliel V. 14. R. Judah IV. 15. Gamaliel VI. He is called *Batraa*, "the last." The office of Nasî was abolished by Theodosius (Cod. Theod. *de Jud.* i. 22) after a continuance of 446 years, A.D. 415. The people themselves were weary of the pride and exactions of the patriarchs.

[3] On the life and work of Hillel, see Budaeus, *Philos. Ebr.* 104–112 ; Grätz, iii. 172-178, 186-205 ; Derenbourg, 176-193 ; Jost, *Gesch. d. Isr.* iii. 112-118 ; Jost, *Judenthum*, 254-270 ; Weber, *Altsyn. Theol. passim* ; Friedländer, *Geschichtsbilder*, 19-29. The chief Talmudic passages about his life and doings are Berakhoth, f. 60 ; Joma, f. 35 ; Qiddushin, f. 71, 1 ; Sukka, f. 20, 1 ; Sota, f. 28, 2 ; Pesachim, f. 66, 2 ; Sanhedrin, ii. 1 ; Baba Bathra, f. 144, 1 ; Bereshith Rabba, c. 33, 98. See Fürst, *Kultur und Lit.* pp. 11-15. The schools of Hillel and Shammai only produced two books, the Megillath Taanith, and a book about the Maccabees (M. Beth Hasmonaim) no longer extant.

[4] The Nazarenes applied Is. viii. 14, "He shall be . . . for a stone of stumbling to *both the houses* of Israel," to the schools of Hillel and Shammai, "quod, per traditiones et δευτερώσεις suas, Legis praecepta dissipaverint atque mutaverint ; et has esse duas domos quae Salvatorem non receperint." Jer. *ad loc.*

[5] " Jesus . . . war ein Pharisäer der auch in den Wegen Hillel's ging."— Geiger, *Das Judenth.* i. 117. " Hillel scheint sein Vorbild und Musterbild gewesen zu seyn." — Friedländer, *Geschichtsbilder*, p. 32. " Hillel fut le vrai maître de Jésus."—Renan, *Vie de Jésus*, p. 35.

that no sentence can be imagined which, whether it be tested by principles or by details, is so utterly the reverse of truth. Our Lord taught with authority, and Hillel as one of the scribes. Christ appealed to the reason and to the conscience, Hillel to precedent and tradition. It was the object of Hillel to strengthen the hedge about the Law, and of Christ to break it completely down.[1] Hillel paid infinite regard to the Oral Law; Christ repudiated its validity with complete disparagement, and even with burning indignation. Hillel developed the Halakha and the Haggada; Christ never alluded to the one, nor uttered a single specimen of the other. Hillel was casuistic and particularist; Jesus universal and divinely spiritual.[2] Christ was the Messiah, and Hillel, sharing the deep religious decadence of his nation, declared that no such Messiah would ever come.[3]

2. SHAMMAI, the rival of Hillel, was a much less interesting person. He was a formalist of the narrowest school. In spite of his traditional rule—"make learning your business, speak little, do much, and receive every one kindly"—he is described as a man of sour manners and violent temper. The depth of his formalism may be estimated by the fact that he nearly starved his infant grandson in the attempt to make him fast on the Day of Atonement, and at the Feast of Tabernacles reared a booth over the bed where his daughter lay in the agony of childbirth. Unlike Hillel he has not left us a single ethical maxim of the smallest value. The Jewish proverb expressed the difference between them by saying that "Shammai bound and Hillel loosed;" in other words Shammai interpreted every legal maxim with the extremest rigidity, while Hillel allowed modifying circumstances. Their conclusions were often diametrically opposed to each other. Serious Jews complained that the

---

[1] See especially the right rendering of Mark vii. 19.

[2] On this question see Delitzsch, *Jesus und Hillel;* Ewald, *Gesch.* v. 12–48; Keim, *Jesu von Nazara,* i. 268–272.

[3] Sanhedrin, f. 96, 2, but see Jost, *Gesch. d. Isr.* iii. 150. So the mediaeval theologian, Joseph Albo, denies that Messianism is a Jewish dogma, otherwise the Soteriology of Law would be injured. Here we have the fundamental opposition between Judaism and Christianity.

Law became "two Laws." In consequence of this their
scholars even came to blows, so that the floor of the schools
was stained with blood; yet the Bath Qol declared that both
were right, only that Hillel won the palm by his superior
meekness.[1] The very principles at stake between the two
schools were a matter of dispute. With reference to Shammai's multiplication of details R. Eliezer approvingly said,
"When a cask is full of nuts you can still pour in mustard
seed without making it too full." "But," said R. Joshua, in
defence of Hillel, "when you pour water into a vessel already
filled with oil you lose in oil what you gain in water."

3. The services of JOHANAN BEN ZAKKAI were more
practical and real.[2] He was one of the greatest of the pupils of
Hillel, and the Talmud says that he burned with such ardour
while he studied the Law that the birds which flew over his
head were consumed. He opposed the Zealots, and resisted the
rebellion against the Romans. The legend of him relates
that, forty years before the Destruction of the Temple, when
the huge bronze doors had opened of themselves, Johanan
rebuked them with the words, "Why, oh sanctuary, dost thou
pretend to fear? I know that thou shalt be devastated.
Zachariah, son of Iddo, hath predicted, '*Open thy doors, oh
Lebanon, that the fire may devour thy cedars.*'"[3] Escaping
from the siege of Jerusalem by being carried on a bier as
one who had died, he was well received by the Romans, prophetically saluted Vespasian with the title of Emperor,
and after the fall of the city became a new Ezra to his
nation. How little did the Romans think when they granted
the humble request of the fugitive Rabbi to open a school at
Jabne,[4] that they were inaugurating a power which should

---

[1] On this paragraph see Jost, *Judenthum*, i. 260 ; *Gesch. d. Isr.* iii. 118 ;
Yom tob, f. 63 ; Jer. Shabbath, f. 61 ; f. 17, 1 ; f. 33 ; 'Erubin, f. 13, 2 ;
Sukka, f. 28, 1 : Maimonides on Aboth, v. 17 ; Grätz, iii. 178 ; Friedländer,
Geschichtsbilder, 26, sq.

[2] Sukka, f. 28,1 ; Baba Bathra, f. 134, 1 ; Tosefta Joma, 4 ; Derenbourg, p.
276 ; Friedländer, *Geschichtsbilder*, 28.

[3] Is. x. 34; Midrash Koheleth, 64 ; Gittin, f. 56 ; Aboth Rabbi Nathan, 4 ;
Grätz, iv. 13.

[4] Jabne, the ancient Jabneel, in the tribe of Judah, not far from Joppa,
was reconquered from the Philistines by Uzziah. It was six miles from
Jerusalem, and had a mixed population of Jews and Gentiles.

long outlive their own Empire, and should, sixty years
later, cost them a sea of blood to quench the flames of
another insurrection! Yet so it was! The fires that burnt
the Temple became the auroral glow of a new day for
Judaism.[1] Johanan, like Jeremiah after the destruction
of the First Temple, had the genius to see that religious
independence was a thing separable from, and even stronger
than, political existence. He strove to rescue what still
remained, and taught his people to take as their symbol
the Bush in the Wilderness, burning yet unconsumed.

The study of the Law became once more a rallying ground
for the race. Seated on his high chair with his " Associates "[2]
around him, and his pupils on low mats upon the floor, the
Head of the School might look with disdain and indifference
upon the agitations of the world. "Judaism found its last
asylum in its academies. A conquered nation changed its
military leaders into Rabbis, and its hosts into armies of pale-
cheeked students covered with the dust of the schools."[3] In-
flexible in the midst of crushing disaster, formed on the best
teachings of Hillel,[4] Johanan became the Gaius Terentius Varro
of Judaism. He did not despair of the Theocracy. Calm, resigned, sympathetic, nobly superior to the frantic spirit of
hatred which began to animate his race, his favourite quotation, like that of our Lord, was, "I will have mercy and not
sacrifice."[5] He said that the reason why no iron instrument

---

[1] Jost, *Judenth.* i. 6. Fürst says that the canon was developed between
B.C. 585–300 ; tradition and Jewish theology between B.C. 300–32. He placed
the most direct influence of Babylonish studies (Hillel, Chija, Nathan) between
B.C. 32 and A.D. 68.

[2] *Chaberim.*   [3] Isaac Disraeli.

[4] See Aboth, i. 12–14 ; ii. 5–7.

[5] Aboth of Rabbi Nathan, 4 ; *Gittin,* f. 56, 1. It was natural that from
this time should date the intense hatred of the Jews to heathendom, which
was repaid with a hatred equally intense. Henceforth the Jews and the
Pagans each acquired in the Jewish schools their *character indelibilis* as
respectively the friends and the enemies of God. The world becomes "the
kingdom of wickedness" (מלכות הרשעה), and every Pagan a "suspect"
(חשוד), mere straw and chaff. Samuel the Little introduced a curse against
heathens, Christians, &c. (Minim = heretics) into the "18 Benedictions"
(Shemone Esre). See *Jer. Berakhoth,* iv. 3 ; Weber, 148, 64–72 ; Zunz, *Gottesd.
Vorträge,* 367 ; Derenbourg, 345. The large-heartedness of R. Johanan to the
heathen appears from his explanation of Prov. xiv. 10 to mean that *mercy* is
the sacrifice which can be offered by the Gentiles (Baba Bathra, f. 10, 2).

might be used in building the altar, was because the altar is
the symbol of peace and iron of war. When the sanctuary
was desolate he taught his people to take refuge in the immaterial sanctuary of the Law. When their centre of unity
was destroyed he furnished them with " the impregnable
centre of the House of Interpretation ; "[1] when their walls
had been laid in ashes he taught them that in place of ram-
parts of marble the Lord would be "a wall of fire round
about."[2] By accommodating himself to the altered circumstances of his day he roused the Jews from the agonising
stupefaction of despair and made Jabne the heiress of
Jerusalem.[3] He largely developed a style of teaching which
was more adapted than the Halakha for the consolation
needed by such troublous days.[4] History presents no stranger
spectacle than that of a nation thus devoting itself to the
study of a Ritual of which much had been obsolete even in
the days of Ezra, but of which *every* essential particular
became, when Jerusalem was destroyed, impossible of per-
formance. The Jewish race has clung with desperate tenacity
to a religion local, priestly, and sacrificial, for nearly two
thousand years after the absolute destruction of its Temple,
its Priesthood, and its Altar ! For the Temple Johanan
substituted the Law ; for the Priesthood the Patriarchate ;
for the House of Aaron the House of Hillel. Shut out
from all political activity, robbed of all civil independence,
the Jews were content to spend centuries of wrangling discussion about Sabbatical minutiae and about the distinctions of
"clean " and "unclean" meats, while the nobler-minded of
them learnt Johanan's lesson that love and good works were
an atonement dearer to the Eternal than the sacrifices which
they could no longer offer.[5]

[1] Beth Hammidrash. Specimens of Johanan's exegesis are given in Qiddushin, p. 22, &c. See Friedländer, *Gesch.* p. 39.
[2] Zech. ii. 5.   [3] Jost, *Judenthum,* ii. 72.
[4] Grätz, iv. 19 ; R. Eliezer ben Jose developed the thirty-two rules for the
Haggada.
[5] On the great work of R. Johanan, see Grätz, iv. 10–27, 322–324 ; Derenbourg, 276–302 ; Etheridge, 55 ; Weill, i. 86–89 ; Jost, *Judenthum,* 13–25 ;
Hamburger II. *s.v.* Jochanan Sohn Sakai ; Friedländer, *Geschichtsbilder,* 36–
44. It is said that Titus spared the life of Gamaliel II. at his request. In

4. The greatest of the Tanaites [1] who carried on the work of Rabbi Johanan ben Zakkai, was the famous RABBI AQIBA the systematiser of Rabbinism, the Thomas Aquinas of the Oral Law. By a scheme of exorbitant interpretation he succeeded in making the Pentateuch responsible for the gigantic excrescences which had covered its decaying trunk. By a formalised method of combining possible inferences, and of drawing fresh inferences from inferences previously deduced, he founded a science of casuistry to which the plain meaning of the Written Law became of less and less importance. He treated the Oral Law, not as a body of fixed results, but as a living and multiplying material.[2] His chief master, Rabbi Eliezer, who had been a " closed cistern " of memorial traditionalism, and who always regarded a decision as impossible if he could say " That I have never heard "—naturally looked on him with suspicion. Many of the Rabbis indignantly opposed his subtle extravagances of fantastic exegesis. Applying Hillel's mischievous second rule that " identity of expression " always furnished a valid conclusion, he said that in Lev. vii. 12, " unleavened cakes *with oil* and unleavened wafers *with oil* " meant that half a log of oil was to be used with each. " Aqiba " said R. Eliezer " you may say ' with oil,' ' with oil,' all day, but I will not listen to you." " Expound and expound all day long " said R. Jose, the Galilean, " still thou canst neither add to, nor take from, the written word." " I can stand it no longer, Aqiba," cried R. Tarphon ; " how long will you patch things up in this arbitrary fashion ? " " Aqiba," exclaimed R. Jose with still more bitter severity,

---

the work of consolation he was aided by R. Joshua, who dissuaded his fellow Rabbis from giving up meat and wine, and devoted himself to raise their courage. " See," he said, " my brothers, Abel was persecuted by Cain, Noah by his contemporaries, Abraham by Nimrod, Isaac by the Philistines, Jacob by Esau, Joseph by his brethren, Moses by Pharaoh, David by Saul, Israel by many nations—and the Merciful God ever chose the persecuted ! "

[1] Learners. תנאים is the Chaldaic form of שונים.

[2] The Mishna of Rabbi Aqiba is no longer extant, though it was known to Epiphanius. The Jews distinguished it as a new Mishna (*M. acharona*) as distinguished from the older *Mishna rishona*. Among other helps to memory he arranged things in numbers. " Four sins deserve death ; " " Five classes of men cannot become priests," &c., &c. See Pirke Aboth v. and Aboth of R. Nathan, xviii.

"how long wilt thou make the face of the Shekhinah profane?"[1] R. Ishmael, especially, the author of the thirteen rules of interpretation, was firmly opposed to the method of Aqiba. He insisted on the rule "the Law speaks in human language," and that its terms are *not* to be literally pressed.[2]

For the most part, however, Aqiba received the boundless admiration of his countrymen. They wrapt in legend his romantic history. They told how he was a Proselyte, and a descendant of Sisera; how love for Rachel, the daughter of the wealthy Kalba Shebua, had transformed him from a shepherd and a churl (*am ha-arets*) into a Rabbi;[3] how, after twelve years of learned toil, he had returned to claim her, followed by 12,000 disciples, and though he found her in the abject poverty to which she had been condemned by her father, he had been content to wait for another twelve years before he finally returned with 24,000 students to show that he was worthy of her love. They told how, in requital for her pity in the days when she wept to pick the chaff from his hair after he had slept in the straw of the sheep-fold, he gave her a golden comb on which was engraved the city of Jerusalem. The wife of the Patriarch Gamaliel had been moved to envy by the splendour of the gift, but Gamaliel said to her, "Rachel has a right to it, for she once sold her hair to maintain her husband."[4]

When he died by heroic martyrdom, with the prolonged word *One* (אחד) from the Daily Prayer on his lips, a "Daughter

---

[1] Sanhedrin, f. 38, 2. The rebuke was given on a memorable occasion, when explaining the word "thrones" in Dan. vii. 9. Aqiba had ventured to say that one of the thrones was for the Messiah. According to R. Jose, to put the Messiah on a level with God was to render the Shekhinah profane. See Hershon, *Genesis*, p. 22.

[2] He recognised that the language of ,Scripture is sometimes hyperbolical (גוזמא), as in Deut. i. 28. He expressed the rule thus: דברה תורה לשון הבאי. The latter seems to be the Greek word ἡβαιά, and the rule means that sometimes a passage is not literally true.

[3] Aqiba confessed to his disciples that in his *am haarets* days he would gladly have torn a Rabbi with his teeth! That he was grateful to Rachel appears from his saying that "he is rich who has a wife full of good works." Shabbath, f. 25, 2.

[4] The Talmud abounds in references to Aqiba. Pesachim, f. 49, 2, &c., quoted by Grätz, Jost, &c. Hershon, *Genesis*, pp. 274, 275. The legends and facts of his life may be gathered from Nedarim, f. 50, 1; Aboth of R. Nathan, c. 6; Shabbath, f. 59, 2; Jer. Shabbath, f. 86.

of a Voice" was heard proclaiming his blessedness, and his
pupils bewailed his death with bitter cries.[1]

But they paid him the yet higher compliment of adopting
the whole of his amazing system.[2] He taught them, and
even Christians appear to have sanctioned his views,—that " as
a hammer divides fire into many sparks, so every verse of
Scripture has many explanations." [3] Now the saner exegesis
of the simpler days of the Sopherim had declared that "the
interpretation of the Law ought never to go beyond the
literal sense." [4] Aqiba, on the other hand, expounded the
Pentateuch on the hypothesis that it was an immense, intentional, and continuous enigma. His principle was that a
meaning was to be found in every monosyllable of Scripture.
If there is a superfluous " and " [5] or " also," [6] or sign of case,[7]
these are always to be specially interpreted.[8] If in 2 Kings,
ii. 14, it said of Elisha that " he *also* had smitten the waters,"
it means that Elisha did more wonders at the Jordan than
Elijah. If David says " Thy servant slew also [9] the lion, also [10]
the bear," the meaning (by the rule of " *inclusion after inclusion*)," [11] is that he slew three animals besides. If it is written

---

[1] They said that he was the only Rabbi who succeeded in entering Paradise
alive. Menachoth, f. 29, 2. On his martyrdom by having his flesh torn
away with iron, see Berakhoth, f. 61, 2 ; Grätz, iv. 177. According to Buxtorf (*Synag.* c. 5) this is why the Jews, in reciting the Shema, often dwell on
the last ד of אחד for half a minute.

[2] They combined it with the more logical system of his friendly rival, R.
Ishmael, who only allowed three passages in which *eth* was significant. Sanhedrin, f. 51, 1 ; Grätz, iv. 61 ; Jost, *Judenth.* ii. 74. Of the other Rabbis of
this period, Gamaliel II. was an organiser, Eliezer a pure traditionalist, and
R. Joshua a *via media* scholar.

[3] See Jer. xxiii. 29. This Rabbinic fiction of a *multiplex sensus* dominated
throughout the Middle Ages, and down to very recent times. It led, among
other mischievous results, to what was known in the Post-Reformation epoch
as the *emphatic* style of exegesis. Sanhedrin, f. 34, 1. In the tract Sopherim
it is said that with the Law God gave to Moses ninety-eight ways of explaining
it. (In the Machser for Pentecost, p. 69, *ap.* Hershon, *Talmudic Miscell.* 11.)
See Ecclus. xxiv. 29.

[4] אין המקרא יוצא מידי פשיטה. Shabbath, f. 63, 1. The Rabbis
maintain that the application of the thirteen rules does not make the Law go
"out of the grasp of simplicity " (see Chiarini, i. 54), though it could be
explained in forty-nine, or even seventy ways (צי פנים לתורה). Löw, p. 65.

[5] אף.   [6] גם.   [7] את.

[8] Megilla, f. 19, 2. This rule is called רבוי, or " *Inclusion.*" See Dr.
Ginsburg, *s.v.* Midrash in Kitto's *Cyclopædia.*

[9] גם את   [10] גם.   [11] רבוי אחר רבוי.

that God visited Sarah,[1] it means that with her He visited other barren women. Analogous explanations by the rule of "exclusion"[2] were attached to every superfluous "only"[3] and "from."[4] These might have been set aside as mere trivialities—the dust which gathers so thickly on the cerements of a dead religion—but Aqiba's methods, like the simpler ones of Hillel, were fraught with mischief. Rabbi Nehemiah of Emmaus, finding the case-sign *eth* in the verse "Thou shalt fear the Lord thy God,"[5] gave up Aqiba's theory, because in this phrase nothing else but God could be implied. But Aqiba, equal to the occasion, at once declared that in this instance the *eth* implied the fear due *also* to "the pupils of the wise"![6] Thus in the system of the Tanaites "nought is everything and everything is nought."

But Aqiba went still farther. He not only explained every particle and copula, but said that there was a mystic meaning in every letter of Scripture, and in every horn[7] and letter-flourish of every letter, "just as in every fibre of an ant's foot or a gnat's wing."[8] The Rabbis delighted to tell how

---

[1] אֶת־שָׂרָה.   [2] מִיעוּט.   [3] רַק or אַךְ.   [4] מִי.

[5] אֶת־ה'. Deut. x. 20. Mystic significance was attached to the particle את, because the two letters are the α and ω of the Hebrew alphabet. Dr. Ginsburg refers to Rashi on Num. vi. 13.

[6] Pesachim, f. 22, 1. For other instances, see Weber, *Altsyn. Theol.* 119. Aqiba is said to have borrowed the notion of this "emphatic" style of interpretation from his teacher, R. Nahum of Gimso. Jost, *Judenthum*, ii. 59. Practically the same rule is followed by Philo (περιττὸν ὄνομα οὐδέν, De Prof. 458), only he applied to ethics and philosophy what Aqiba applied to the Halakha. See Grätz, iv. 458 ; Hershon, *Genesis*, p. 280. When the pupils of R. Nehemiah asked what became of all his other explanations of the case-sign if the theory was to be abandoned, he said, "As I have secured a reward by the expositions, so shall I by their abandonment." The story is sometimes attributed to a R. Simon.

[7] These κεραίαι are such little horns and tips of letters as distinguish ד from ר, ב from כ, ה from ח. The Jews said, If any one, in Deut. vi. 4, changes ד into ר, he shakes the universe, for he makes God false (אחר) instead of One. If in Lev. xxii. 32 he changes ח into ה, he shakes the universe, for he says, "Ye shall not praise" (תההללו) for "Ye shall not profane" (תחללו) the name of the Lord." Vayyikra Rabba, f. 162, 1.

[8] These signs on letters are called "crowns" (כתרים, *apices*, virgulae supra literas notatae. Buxtorf, *Lex. Talm.* 1111) ; "points" (נקדות) and "thorns" (קוצים). These are purely graphic signs. Some words are "pointed" in the law (Aboth of R. Nathan, c. 33), and mystic meanings are attached to every one of them. Thus, in Gen. xxxiii. 4, we have וַיִּשָּׁקֵהוּ, "and he kissed him ;" the points are explained to mean that in kissing him he tried to bite him, but Jacob's neck was changed into marble, so that Esau's teeth were

"many rules unknown to Moses were declared by Aqiba."
In one Rabbinic legend Moses sees the Holy One attaching
crowns (כתרים) to the letters of the alphabet, and on asking
the reason is informed that many generations afterwards a
man, Aqiba, was to arise who would found on those tittles
innumerable decisions. Asking to see him in vision, Moses
is annoyed by total inability to understand him, and is only
consoled by hearing him remark, "This 'decision' was delivered orally to Moses on Sinai." [1] The Book of Canticles
was as favourite a field for mystical interpretation with the
Tanaim as with St. Bernard and the Victorines, and in the
verse "His locks are bushy" (Cant. v. 11) the words (תלתלים
קוצותיו) were explained to mean that from every "thorn" (קוץ),
or letter-point, whole "mountains" (תילין) of "decisions" can
be deduced ; and if the verse adds that they are "black as a
raven," the meaning is that these "decisions" will be developed
by him who is dark as a raven, because he studies them from
morning till evening ! [2] In this region of futile and fantastic
illusion Aqiba reigned supreme.[3]

Similarly, if in the sacred text a letter was larger or
smaller than the rest, or inverted, or suspended, or was
repeated, or omitted, or presented any other peculiarity, it
was seized upon by the Rabbis for mystic meanings.[4]
The two Yods [5] in וַיִּיצֶר ("and He formed," Gen. ii. 7)

blunted (Wünsche, *Bereschith Rabbi*, p. 383 ; Aboth of R. Nathan, c. 34).
In Gen. xix. 33, the ו in וּבְקוּמָהּ is pointed. In Nazir, f. 23, 1, this is taken
as indication that Lot was then aware of his sin. Jerome says, "appungunt
desuper *quasi incredibile*." See another instance in Gen. xviii. 9 (Hershon,
p. 309). See the introduction to Olshausen on the Psalms.
  [1] Menachoth, f. 29, 2. The story continues to say that Moses exclaimed,
"Lord of the Universe ! Thou hast such a man, and Thou deliverest the law
by me ! " and is bidden to be silent because such was God's will. Requesting
to see Aqiba's reward, he is shown his flesh weighed (after his martyrdom) in
the shambles. "Lord of the Universe ! " he cries, "such learning, and such
reward ! " "Be silent," is the answer : "it is my will." See Weil, iii. 268 ;
Hershon, *Genesis*, i.
  [2] Midrash, *Shir Hasshirim*, x. 11 (Wünsche, p. 139) ; 'Erubin, f. 21, 2.
  [3] Hirschfeld, *Halach. Exegese*, § 312 ; Weber, *Altsyn. Theol.* 117
  [4] Waehner, *Antiqq. Ebr.* i. 105.
  [5] Qiddushin, f. 30, 1 ; Buxtorf, *Tiberias*, i. 18, pp. 42–45. In Lev. xi. 42,
the larger ו in the word בחון indicates that it is the middle letter of the Pentateuch, and the suspended ע of מיער in Ps. lxxx. 14, that it is the middle
letter of the Psalms.

where one would have sufficed, indicate the two impulses
—the good and evil impulses in man.[1] The word "the increase," (מרבה), in Is. ix. 6, is, by the scribe's inadvertence,
written with a closed or final Mem, and this is explained to
mean that God meant to make Hezekiah into the Messiah, and
Sennacherib into Gog and Magog ; but the Attribute of Judgment pleaded that this would be unfair to David, and so the
counsel was closed.[2] In Haggai i. 8, "and I will be glorified "
(ואכבד), is written without the final ה, and since the numerical value of ה is 5, the omission is interpreted to mean
that five things—the Shekhinah, the Ark, the Urim and
Thummim, the sacred fire, and the Spirit of Prophecy—would
be wanting to the second Temple.[3] Similarly, if the article
(ה) is added to the *sixth* day only in Gen. i. 31, it is to show
that the world only existed conditionally on the obedience of
Israel to the Five Books of Moses. One more instance will
suffice.[4] The Rabbis are concerned to explain the fact that
in one of the alphabetic Psalms (Ps. cxlv.) there is no verse
which begins with the letter *n* (נ).[5] The reason is, said
Rabbi Johanan, because there is a verse in Amos (v. 2)
which begins with this letter, and predicts the irretrievable
fall of Israel ! Sometimes a fantastic change of reading was
made the basis of a mystic explanation. Thus, in Gen. ii. 4,
by a slight change, for "when they were created," the Talmud
gets "He created them with the letters ה and י " (the two

---

[1] *Yetser ha-râ* and *Yetser hattob*, Berachoth, f. 61, 1. Other Rabbis explained the two *yods* to refer to Adam and Eve ; to earth and heaven ; to this
world and the next. Bereshith Rabba on Gen. ii. 7 (Wünsche, p. 62). The
Yod which was taken from the name of Sarai was inconsolable till it was added
to the name of Joshua ! Sanhedrin, f. 107, 1.

[2] Sanhedrin, f. 94, 1. Probably the closed ם was due to a mere clerical
error.

[3] Yoma, f. 21, 2 ; Waehner, ii. 645 ; Prideaux, *Connection*, i. 162–178.

[4] *Shabbath*, f. 88, 1 ; *Aboda Zara*, f. 3, 1 ; Hershon, p. 77. For further
instances, see *Sanhedrin*, f. 103, 2 ; *Baba Bathra*, f. 109, 2 ; Döpke's *Hermeneutik.*

[5] Probably the verse is accidentally lost, for in the LXX. there is a verse
which would in Hebrew begin with נ. This verse in Amos was so disagreeable
to the Rabbis that in reciting it they substituted " the fall [*of the enemies*] of
Israel ; " or punctuated as follows : " The virgin of Israel is fallen : she shall
no more [fall] ; rise." R. Nachman bar Isaac thinks that in prophetic reference
to this verse, David wrote " The Lord upholdeth *all them that fall.*"

letters of His name, Jah), and proceeds to explain that the
reason for creating this world with ה was because that letter
resembles a porch, to indicate how easy it is to go out and
plunge into vice ; but there is an opening at the top of the
letter to show that repentance will readmit the wanderer from
above.[1] The world to come was formed with the little letter
to show how few should be saved.[2]

In exegesis of this kind indefinitely multiplied, the great
Rabbi spent his days.[3] The unhappy fate which fell upon
him, the ruin which he helped to precipitate upon his
country is a proof of the very small amount of insight which
such methods of handling Scripture were likely to produce.
In some of his decisions—for instance in the intense rigidity
of his rules about hand-washing, and the gross laxity of his
views about divorce—it is difficult to believe that he was not
actuated by a direct spirit of antagonism to Christianity.[4]
It may have been partly from this reason that he openly
adopted the claims to Messiahship put forth by the impostor
Barkokhba, and we can but hope that he did not inflame the
fanatical hatred which made that false Messiah the sanguinary
persecutor of the Christians. But in any case the Nemesis
of the outraged letter fell upon him. In the passionate
desire to protect Judaism from the new religion, he became

---

[1] Menachoth, f. 29, 2 ; Hershon, *Genesis*, p. 92.

[2] See Is. xxvi. 4, (rendered), " For with Jah Jehovah formed the world."
In the modern Jewish Liturgy the Ineffable Name is usually written
with two Yods (״) ; in the Liturgy of the Karaites it is written with three
letters (ייי).

[3] The five precepts which he gave to R. Simon ben Jochai in prison are
neither very valuable, nor very original, viz.—1. If you would hang yourself,
choose a high tree (*i.e.* appeal to high authorities for unpleasant decisions).
2. Teach your son from books which do not require correction. 3. Do not
marry a widow. 4. Unite good work with personal profit. 5. Combine grati-
fication with purity. *Pesachim*, f. 112, 1. For four of his sayings see *Aboth*,
iii. 10-13.

[4] He followed Hillel, for instance, into the extreme of laxity in interpreting
the famous *ervath dabar* ("matter of uncleanness," Deut. xxiv. 1). Hillel
had said that a man might divorce his wife if she burned his food ; Aqiba in
extreme antagonism to Christianity, said "even if he saw some woman who
pleased him better." *Gittin*, f. 90, 1. Modern Jews explain away this passage.
Jost, *Judenthum*, i. 264. Aqiba's scrupulosity about ablutions, and insistence
on the unity of God, even with his dying breath, probably had a polemical
significance. See Jost, *Judenthum*, ii. 62.

the strange Elias of a ferocious and nameless rebel.[1] He hailed Barkokhba as the Star of Balaam's vision, as the promised Deliverer of Israel; nor would he heed the warning of the less impetuous Rabbis, who said, "Aqiba, the grass shall grow out of thy jaws, and yet the Messiah will not have come." There was nothing which could save Aqiba or his nation, either morally or intellectually, amid their idolism of esoteric pedantry, which, passing itself off as a comment on the law, treated it practically as a field for the display of casuistry. Aqiba died at a very advanced age, the brave martyr of an ignoble cause, and in the blood-stained ruins of Bether[2] not only the schools of the Rabbis, but the Jewish race itself, seemed to be smitten once more into irretrievable ruin by the iron hand of Rome. Had Aqiba been trained in truer and nobler methods, he might not have committed the gross error of confusing a Barkoziba with a Barkokhba—the "son of a lie" with the "son of a star."[3]

5. Yet once more Judaism rose from the ashes in which it seemed to have been consumed. "On the day that R. Aqiba died," says Mar, "Rabbi was born; on the day when Rabbi died Rav was born; on the day when Rav died Rava was born; on the day when Rava died R. Ashi was born. The sun rises and the sun goes down."[4] Before the ten martyr Rabbis of the rebellion had died they had

---

[1] Jewish revolts of the most sanguinary character had broken out in Cyprus, Egypt, Cyrene, and Babylonia, and it has been conjectured that Aqiba's extensive travels may have had something to do with them. Jost, *Judenth.* ii. 66. On Barkokhba's rebellion see Dion Cass. lxix. 12-14; Grätz, iv. 157-197. His name was Simon, and if Bar Koziba was his real name it may mean that he was born at Kezib.

[2] Βίθθηρα, Euseb. *H. E.* iv. 6. Now *Beiter* six miles S.S.W. of Jerusalem. William's *Holy City,* i. 209.

[3] On Aqiba and his work, see Grätz, iv. 53–66, 148–166, 427–431; Jost, *Judenthum,* ii. 59–83; Derenbourg, c. xxiv.; Munk, *Palestine,* 605–606; Etheridge, *Hebr. Lit.* 66–76; Hamburger II. *s.v.* Bar Kochba; Milman, *Hist. of the Jews,* ii. bk. xviii.; Friedländer, *Geschichtsbilder,* pp. 68–81; Frankel, *Zeitschr.* iii. &c.; and the numerous interesting particulars of his life in Mr. Hershon's *Genesis,* and other Talmudic collections. His anticipation of the Mishna is mentioned by Epiphanius and he is alluded to by Jerome, *In Eccl.* iv. 13.

[4] Ecc. i. 5; Qiddushin, f. 72. 2. The assertion is not historically true, but represents the idea of the Rabbinic succession.

conferred ordination on successors who retired to Ussa.
Among these successors were men so eminent as Rabbi
Simeon ben Jochai, the master of the Qabbala, the legendary
author of the Zohar ; Rabbi Meir, the casuist,[1] who, re-
joicing in the Haggada, could tell no less than 300 stories
about foxes, and the touch of whose very staff was enough
to make a pupil wise ; and Rabbi Nathan, the author of the
celebrated "Sayings" which go by his name. They chose as
their Patriarch Simon, the son of Gamaliel II., who had been
saved as a schoolboy from the massacre of Bether. When
the schools of Jabne were finally broken up through the
passionate imprudence which led Simon ben Jochai to burst
into an invective against the Romans, the new Patriarch
removed about A.D. 166 to Tiberias, which became, for many
years, the metropolis of Rabbinism. He was succeeded by
his son, R. JUDA. A man often shows his true greatness by
recognising that the change of times requires the change of
institutions, and by rejecting restrictions which have ceased
to be tenable. This was the case with Rabbi Juda. Down
to his time the traditions of the Fathers had never been put
into writing.[2] A collection by Rabbi Chija was known as
Megillath Setharim, or "secret roll." [3] It had been a rule of
the Rabbis that what had been delivered orally was only to
be retained by the memory. That rule was founded on the
principle that circumstances change, and therefore that oral
decisions ought not to be regarded as final precedents.[4] By
this time, however, it had become an impossibility to retain
a mass of precedents so heterogeneous and so immense as
those which had been accumulated from the days of Ezra to
those of Aqiba. Accordingly RABBI JUDA, for the first time,
committed to writing the Oral Law, arranged under the six

---

[1] See Grätz, iv. 193, 195, 237, 470. Symmachos, the Greek translator, was
one of his pupils.

[2] Josephus and Philo refer to it as παράδοσις ἄγραφος, and τῶν πατέρων
διαδοχή. In Matt. xv. 2–6 the Oral Law is called παραδόσις τῶν πρεσβυτέρων
(comp. Mark vii. 3–13). St. Paul pointedly speaks of "the tradition of men,"
Col. ii. 8 (האבות מסורת).

[3] Gittin, f. 60, 2. These written notes were meant to be mere private
memoranda for the teacher's own use.

[4] Hurwitz. For the rule see Löw, p. 59.

orders of Hillel's classification. By this sensible innovation he earned such gratitude that he is always called "the Holy," or "the Prince," or "Our Master," or simply and emphatically by the mere title RABBI, as though no other were worthy to be compared with him.[1]

His compilation was called "The Mishna," "learning," or "Repetition," from *Shanah* (*tana*), "to learn," or "repeat." It acquired an influence truly secular. It summed up the labours of four centuries.[2] The Oral Law [3] had been recognised by Ezra; had become important in the days of the Maccabees; had been supported by Pharisaism; narrowed by the school of Shammai; codified by the school of Hillel; systematised by R. Aqiba; placed on a logical basis by R. Ishmael;[4] exegetically amplified by R. Eliezer; and constantly enriched by successive Rabbis and their schools. RABBI put the coping-stone to the immense structure. Thenceforth the Mishna moulded the entire theology and philosophy of Judaism. The publication of Tradition put an end to the independent energy of the Halakha, and closed the long succession of the Tanaim. They were followed by a new race, the Amoraim, who were rather commentators than originators. The Mishna became the bond of Jewish nationality. It put an end to the Patriarch-

[1] Hakkodesh, Hannasi, Rabbenu, Rabbi Rabba. Although Rabbi's violation of the accepted rule (*Gittin*, f. 60) is quite defensible, the same cannot be said of the distorted exegesis by which it was defended. This was by making Ps. cxix. 126 ("It is time for thee, Lord, to lay to thine hand, for they have destroyed thy law") mean "When we work for God we may break His law." See *Berakhoth*, f. 69, with Rashi's comment. Idols are subservient things, and when men make an idol of a dead letter, they are never at a loss to treat it as a thing subservient to themselves.

[2] Mishna (δευτέρωσις, Epiphan.) is derived from שְׁנִי, not from שָׁנָה, "the repeated." Thus Deuteronomy is called "*Mishnah Thorah*." The names Mikra (what is read) for scripture and Mishna for tradition are ancient. See Grätz, iv. 419–422; Deutsch, *Remains*, p. 17.

[3] First collected by R. Aqiba, enlarged by his pupil, R. Meir, and finally published by Rabbi (see Epiphan. *Haer.* i. 2, 9). It consists of Hillel's six orders (*Sedarim*), sixty-three tractates (*Massiktoth*), and 524 chapters. Rabbi unfairly suppressed the names of R. Nathan and R. Meir, because they once tried to undermine the haughty authority of Rabbi's father, R. Simeon III. R. Nathan is quoted by the formula "some say," and Meir's decisions are alluded to by the formula "*others* say" (אֹמְרִים אֲחֵרִים). See Waehner, i. 283. The additional collections of R. Chija, Bar Kappara, &c., were called *Tosefta*, which consists of fifty-two treatises and 383 chapters. Löw, p. 77.

[4] In his famous thirteen rules. See Friedländer, *l.c.* pp. 76–79.

ate, of which it was the child. It completed that "hedge around the law" which henceforth neither persecution nor dispersion could destroy, and through which neither Hellenism, nor Sadduceeism, nor Alexandrianism, nor Gnosticism, nor Christianity, nor the Renaissance, nor the Reformation, nor modern scepticism, down to the days of Moses Mendelssohn, could break their way. This strange collection of completed and dead "decisions," being treated as of divine authority, superseded, all but entirely, the Scriptures on which they professed to have been based.[1] The bold initiative of RABBI stamped on Judaism a character singularly dry and juristic, and laid upon the necks of all Talmudic Jews a yoke unspeakably more empty and indefinitely more galling than that of which St. Peter had complained even in days when the observance of Mosaism had not yet been rendered impossible by the fiat of History, which is the manifest will of God.[2]

6. Rabbi died A.D. 200.[3] The Talmudists tell endless stories of his wealth, his greatness, his friendship with the Roman Emperor whom they call Antoninus. But he left no adequate successor. With his death the splendour of the Patriarchate at once declined. The scholastic labours and discussions of Amoraim (A.D. 200–500) resulted in the Jerusalem Talmud, which discusses four only of the six Mishnaic orders.[4] The

---

[1] Pea, ii. 5 ; Yaddaim, iv. 3 ; Aboth, *ad init.*

[2] Thus there is an entire treatise of the Mishna about mingled seeds, with endless discussions about agriculture, which the Jews have ceased to practise for thousands of years ; and this is only one of many treatises which deal with details concerning sacrifices and Temple measurements which for ages have ceased to have the slightest meaning. It should, however, be said that Rabbi's innovations were all on the side of greater leniency. See Chulin, f. 6, 2 (quoted by Dr. Ginsburg, *s.v.* Jehudah, *Dict. of Christian Biogr.*). He there compares himself with Hezekiah, who broke in pieces the brazen serpent. For one of his noblest sayings, see Aboth, ii. 1.

[3] On the life and work of Rabbi, see Grätz, iv. 210 ; Friedländer, pp. 96–101. If he was friendly with any emperor, it may have been L. Verus Antoninus, or Caracalla. He had neither "speaker" (*chakam*) nor Deputy (*Ab Bîth Dîn*) under him, but was "the first spiritual autocrat."

[4] The Jerushalmi represents traditionalism rather than development, and hence is less valued. With the Targums of Onqelos and Ben Uzziel, the Mishna, Tosephta, Mekhiltha, Siphra, Siphrî, and Pesikhtha, together with traces in Ecclesiasticus, Wisdom, Tobit, and the books of Maccabees, it forms the Primary Tradition. The secondary strata of tradition are found in the Targ. of Ps. Jonathan, the Bablî, and the Midrashim.

G

GEMARA, or "completion," which, with the Mishna, makes up the Babylonian TALMUD [1] in its complete form—the Bablî of which the Jews speak with such enthusiastic affection—was completed and systematised mainly by RABBI ASHÎ, who died in A.D. 427.[2] The Talmud was finally closed in A.D. 490, by Rabbina Abina, the last of the Amoraim. It contains the long studies and discussions of the Jewish schools, "the fierce lightnings which shook the rafters" of Nehardea, Sora, and Pumbeditha.[3] In the work of the Palestinian and Babylonian academies, Edzard sees the fulfilment of Zechariah's vision of the flying roll.[4] The Gentiles possessed the Law in Greek, but in the Mishna and Gemara the Jews boasted that they possessed the secret, without which the Law was valueless. They openly made more use of the Talmud than of the Bible, preferring their broken cisterns to the waters that spring from the living rock.

7. It is no part of my purpose to glance at the farther labours of the Saboraim (A.D. 500-650), and the Gaonim ;[5] or to follow the devious stream of mediaeval Rabbinism.[6] Whatever may have been the special services to Jewish theology

[1] Talmud, "Learning," or "Teaching." See Bartolocci, *Bibl. Rabb.* iii. 359. The commonest edition of the Talmud is that of Bomberg (Venice, 1520) in twelve folio volumes, but the Amsterdam edition is of special importance because it is unexpurgated.

[2] The so-called Yerushalmi at present only has Gemara to less than two-thirds of the Mishna ; but Dr. Schiller-Szinessy has published some arguments to prove that it once extended over all the Six Sedarim. The Bablî has been the favourite of the Jews, owing perhaps to that fierceness with which it was persecuted, but scholars now generally incline to the view that the Yerushalmi is "in every way superior to it in age, in conciseness, in lucidity, in the value of its contents." See Dr. Schiller-Szinessy, *Occasional Notices,* i. p. i.

[3] Nehardea was on a canal (Nahar) which joined the Euphrates to the Tigris. Sora was on the Euphrates. The school there was founded by Rav (R. Abba Arekka), who wrote or edited the Siphra and Siphrî, and died in 243. Pumbeditha means "the mouth of the canal." On these schools and their teachers, see Fürst, *Kultur-gesch.* pp. 63-197.

[4] Zech. v. 1-4 ; Pref. to Berakhoth ; see Chiarini, ii. 41.

[5] Saboraim, "investigators," from *Sabar,* "to observe." Gaonim, "excellent," was the title taken by the heads of the college at Sora, and Rabbanim by those at Pumbeditha. See Maimonides, Pref. to Yad Hachazaka.

[6] Grätz divides this period into that of scientific Rabbinism in Spain (1040–1230), and one-sided Rabbinism down to Moses Mendelssohn (1230–1780). See the Excursus.

of RASHI the "Exegete;" of IBN EZRA;[1] of MAIMONIDES, "the Eagle of the Rabbis,"[2] and "the Light of the West;"[3] of SIMEON HADDARSHAN;[4] of the QIMCHIS, David and Moses;[5] of ABRABANEL;[6] and of others—these all of them continue the essential principles of Rabbinic exegesis, although in forms more scientific and philosophical. Maimonides may indeed be regarded as the founder of Jewish Rationalism, the first who strove to harmonise science with religion. As such he was anathematised by his stricter countrymen. But it is not till the days of Moses Mendelssohn that a breath of true renovation begins to pass over the valley in which for so long a period the bones had been so dry. Nor again will it be possible here to speak of the Karaites[7]—those Protestants of Judaism—who from the days of Anan ben David have exercised a powerful influence, but who, rejecting the Talmud, and maintaining the sole authority of Scripture, have worked for the most part outside the sphere of acknowledged Judaism.[8]

IV. But it is now time to ask, What is the main result of these many centuries of Rabbinic exegesis, beginning practically with the first prominence of the Oral Law in the age of Ezra (B.C. 457), and continuing almost unaltered to the days of Moses Mendelssohn (A.D. 1780)?

[1] See Buxtorf, *De Abbreviaturis*, p. 170. "Parshandatha," was explained to mean "interpreter of the law." He died A.D. 1102. He commented on the entire Old Testament. His comments on grammar, and the literal sense were full of value, but he follows the Talmud and the Midrashim.

[2] Ibn Ezra, born at Toledo, A.D. 1092, died in Rome, 1167. He is a Talmudist, but with some Karaite leanings.

[3] Rambam. R. Moses ben Maimon, born at Cordova, 1135, died in Palestine, 1204. "From Moses to Moses no one has risen like Moses." He was not a professed commentator, but his Moreh Nevochim and Yad Hachazaka are full of exegetical remarks. His comparatively free attitude towards the Talmud offended many Jews. "He was the speculative parent of Spinoza and of Mendelssohn." Milman, iii. 151.

[4] Author of the *Jalqut Shimeoni*, a Midrashic commentary on the Old Testament.

[5] David Qimchi's comments are chiefly grammatical. The grammar of Moses Qimchi (*Darki Leshon Hakkodesh*, Way to the Holy Language) was of great use to the early Humanists and Reformers. The Jews said of David's labours, "No law without the miller" (*quemach*), playing on the name Qimchi.   [6] Don Isaac Abrabanel, born 1436, died 1507.

[7] They are said to date from the days of Shemaia, the colleague of Abtalion. Grätz, iv. 5.   [8] See Excursus on the Karaites.

Setting aside the valuable services of the Massorets to textual criticism,[1] the main contributions of Rabbinism to the exegesis of the Old Testament are found in the Targums, in the Talmud, and in the Midrashim. These contain the sum total of Jewish enlightenment, on the subject of Scripture for hundreds of years, and though their authority is now more or less denied by the more liberal schools of Jewish thought, they still form the basis of interpretation among multitudes of foreign synagogues all over the world.

All that is exegetical in this immense cyclopædia of Jewish literature falls under the three heads of the Halakha, the Haggada, and the Qabbala.

i. The word HALAKHA means "Decision," norm, systematised legal precept. It is a Rabbinic word, derived from *halakh*, to walk. It is used to express the accepted conclusion arrived at after discussion, and to be followed in practice as a supplement to the provisions of the Written Law.[2]

The Mishna is all but exclusively composed of these decisions. It defines all matters of civil and religious interest for the Jews. It may be regarded as the *corpus juris* of Judaism. As exegesis it is nearly valueless. The very rules by which it was developed, the very principles on which it was founded, were, as we have partly seen, fantastic and untenable; nay, in many essential instances subversive of the most sacred principles of the Mosaic legislation. Nothing is more certain than that the mass

---

[1] On the Massorah, see Etheridge, 205 : Ginsburg, *Elias Levita*, pp. 101, 102, 120, 121. They applied to it Cant. iii. 8 (it was regarded as a sword to defend the law). Comp. Rashi, *ad loc.* and Aboth, iii. 13. For lists of the words written with majuscular letters, see Ginsburg's *Elias Levita*, p. 230. He does not admit Mr. Black's theory that they form a chronogram.

[2] In Ex. xxi. 1, the Targums, both of Onqelos and Jon. ben Uzziel, use the word *Halakha*, as the equivalent of מִשְׁפָּט. In Aramaic it is Hilkheta (הלכתא), which in Baal Aruc is defined as "*res quae it et venit ab initio usque ad finem.*" Buxtorf defines Halakha as "*constitutio juris, sententia, decisio, traduio decisa, . . . secundum quam incedendum et vivendum.*" *Lex. Talm. s.v.* הֲלָכָה, where he renders it *Ein Endurtheil*. For a classification of Halakhoth, see Maimonides, Pref. to the explanation of the Mishna ; Chiarini, i. 174 ; Etheridge, 178. The Mishna consists of : 1. Halakhoth. 2. Midrash—the development of Halakhoth by exegetic rules. 3. Talmud in narrower sense—fresh, argumentative applications. It has 525 chapters, 4,187 paragraphs.

of precepts in the Mosaic law are of obvious import, and
were intended to be understood in their plain and literal
sense.[1] The Rabbis themselves, in their more sober moods,
admitted this.[2] Yet such an admission was opposite to their
habitual practice. We find Rabbi Juda saying, " He that
renders a verse of Scripture as it appears (*i.e.* literally) says
what is not true." " He who adds to it," he continues, " is a
blasphemer." Yet the additions which the Rabbis made to
it multiplied its bulk a thousandfold, and that with the most
frivolous minutiae. Rabbi Eliezer glorified himself because
he could deliver 300 Halakhoth about Egyptian cucumbers,[3]
and there were 300 undisputed Halakhoth about " the tower
that floats in the air." [4] Nay, even Onqelos and the Septuagint translators are admitted to have made both additions
and alterations.[5] The Rabbis were not at a loss to account
for these facts. The Halakhoth, they said, were a part of the
Oral Law delivered to Moses on Sinai.[6] Like the ever-widening, yet ever-fainter, circle on the broken surface of a lake,
the ripples of an indefinitely expanded legalism spread long
after all trace of the first waves had died away.

Once in the school of Tiberias the pupils of Rabbi Eliezer
and of Rabbi Jose fell into a fierce quarrel about the lawful-
ness of using on the Sabbath a bolt with a knob. The
former said it might not be used ; the latter said it might be
used, since it was lawful on the Sabbath to use a bolt with a
knob to mash garlic. In their rage they actually tore asunder
a roll of the Law.[7] The roll of the Law was to all intents
and purposes torn asunder daily in the disputes of the
Rabbis. The foolish questionings, strifes, " legal battles,"
(μάχαι νομικαὶ, Tit. iii. 9), and " word-fightings " (λογομάχιαι,
1 Tim. vi. 4), about which St. Paul speaks, furnish us with

---

[1] Deut. xxv. 11–14.
[2] See Chiarini, i. 54, quoting Shabbath, f. 63, 1.
[3] Sanhedrin, f. 68, 1.
[4] See Sanhedrin, f. 106, 2, referring to Is. xxxiii. 18, " Where is he who
counted the towers ? " See Rashi, *ad loc.*
[5] Megilla, f. 3, 1 ; f. 9, 1.
[6] This was called the הלכה למשה מסיני, *Halakha le-Moshesh Missinai,*
Qiddushin, f. 49, 1.
[7] Yebamoth, f. 96, 2. See Rashi on Eccl. ix. 17.

the closest description of what went on in the Jewish schools.
For although the "decisions" were set even above Scripture;[1]
though God Himself is represented as repeating them in the
names of the Rabbis from whom they had emanated;[2]
though heaven is described as an academy in which the
angels play the part of the "associates;" though we are told
with frank blasphemy that the soul of a Rabbi was sum-
moned to decide when the Supreme and the Angels were
taking opposite sides in a question about leprosy; though
not even such miracles as the pillars of the room bending at
a word, and a caroub-tree plucked up by the roots, and water
running up hill, and even an utterance of the Bath Qol,
are sufficient to establish a "decision" against the majority
of the Rabbis;[3] though the most tremendous curses are pronounced against those who resist such a decision,[4] yet there
was scarcely a single Rabbinic precept about which there
were not eager and sometimes even savage dissensions.
There were, for instance, numberless disagreements between
the schools of Hillel and Shammai, and the Rabbis had to
come to the futile conclusion, that opposite decisions are
equally the word of God.[5] Yet the Talmudists themselves

---

[1] Baba Metsi'a, f. 331. In Gittin, f. 60, 2, this is argued from Ex. xxxiv.
27. "For after the tenor (lit. '*upon the mouth*') of these words have I made
a covenant with Israel." On Rabbinic modifications of special laws see
Castelli, *La Legge* (1884); Salschutz, *Der mosaische Recht*, and Edersheim,
Proph. and Hist. pp. 384-391.

[2] In Pesiktha of R. Kahana, f. 40, 1. Moses ascending heaven hears the
Holy One reading the Parasha about the Red Heifer, and repeating the Halakha
about it in the name of R. Eliezer. So too *Bammidbar Rabba*, c. 19. Stories
still more shocking to our views are found in *Shemoth Rabba*, cc. 30 and 43.
Vayyikra Rabba, c. 19 (Weber, 18, 19).

[3] See the remarkable story in Baba Metsia, f. 59, 2. The miracle worker
was the excommunicated R. Eliezer. An Halakha was sometimes left uncertain with the formula, תיק״ן, which is explained to be a mnemonic form for
"the Tishbite (Elijah) will settle doubts;"—and in other ways, for which see
Buxtorf, *Lex.* 2588.

[4] Megilla, f. 28, 2; Buxtorf, *Lex.* p. 612.

[5] In favour of this view they quoted Ex. xx. 1; Eccl. xii. 11; Chagigah,
f. 3, 2; Gittin, f. 6, 2; Yebamoth, f. 15, 2 (where R. Joshua thinks that to
decide between them would be like crushing his head between two great mountains). They dispute which was created first—earth or heaven, *Tamid.* f.
31, 2; about divorce (Gittin, f. 90, 1—a dispute of which we find traces even
in the Gospels, Matt. v. 31, 32; xix. 3-12); about the cleanness of wine and
oil (*Shabbath*, f. 17, 1); about the order in which blessings were to be given
(*Succah*, f. 56, 1); and about numberless other subjects. Sometimes the

confess that "as the disciples of Hillel and Shammai multiplied, who had not studied the Law thoroughly, contentions
increased in Israel to such an extent that the Law lost its
unity and became as two."[1] Having thrust a book between
men and God, and a tradition between men and the book
they thrust themselves between men and the tradition, and
so—once more like the mediaeval priesthood—built upon
ignorance and superstition a terrific usurpation.[2]

The object of the Halakha was the indefinite development
of rules to meet every conceivable case in which a legalist
might be supposed to be in doubt. "The real," says Göthe,
"is narrow; the possible is immense." The Halakhoth were
a system of scholasticism applied to ritual.[3] Take, by way of
illustration, the case of phylacteries. It must be regarded
as an open question whether the law about phylacteries was
ever intended to be taken literally.[4] The Karaites have
always rejected them.[5] Jerome comes to the conclusion
that the injunction on which they are founded merely meant
that the Law was to be carried into action, and to be
meditated day and night. But even if it be granted that the
use of phylacteries was intended, of what exegetical value are
the huge folio pages of minute discussion as to their shape,
size, and construction, as to the way in which the knot of them
was to be made, as to the question whether they are worn by
God Himself or not?[6] The same remark applies even more

---

scholars even came to blows and bloodshed (see the authorities quoted in Jost
Gesch. d. Isr. iii. 118).

[1] Sanhedrin, f. 88, 2. They applied the phrase "a rock of offence to both
the houses of Israel," to the schools of Hillel and Shammai. See Jer.
Comment. in Isaiam, ad loc.

[2] They openly declared that without their interpretations the Law was a
mass of unintelligible signs. Bammidbar Rabba, § 14. They first made the
Oral Law as sacred as the Written ; then "the Words of the Wise," and "of
the Scribes ;" and then made these last more sacred than all.

[3] There were *millions* of possible Halakhoth. "Every word of the Thora
can be explained in seventy ways." Bammidbar Rabba, § 13. R. Eliezer has
300 Halakhoth about one case of leprosy. Sanhedrin, f. 25, 2. 3,000 Halakhoth
were forgotten in the mourning for Moses. Temoorah, f. 15, 2.

[4] Or only figuratively, like Prov. iii. 3.

[5] Ex. xiii. 9.

[6] Berakheth (Schwab, p. 241).

forcibly to the elaborate regulations about fringes[1] and ablutions, and the endless disputations about the Sabbath and the major and minor prohibitions with which the Jews surrounded it.[2] One whole treatise of the Mishna, that known as "The Egg,"[3] derives its name from the question discussed in it as to whether an egg laid on the Sabbath or a festival may or may not be eaten—a question on which the great soul of Moses would have looked with infinite contempt.[4] The Rabbis themselves compared these masses of inferential precepts to a mountain dangling by a single hair.

In Rabbinic teaching precedent reigned supreme. Hillel, after arguing for a whole day in vain against the Benî Bethîra that the Paschal lamb must be offered on the Sabbath, not only wins his cause, but is made president of the schools, when he quotes the decision of Shemaia and Abtalion. The predominant formulae of the Talmud are appeals to the assertions of Rabbis.[5] And the Rabbis protected the whole system to the uttermost, just as clerical orders often defend the usurpations of priestcraft. Professional pedants felt the strong fascination of wielding despotic power over the souls of all who could be induced by terror, by custom, or by self-interest to accept their sway.

ii. The HAGGADA,[6] although it had its own feebleness and

---

[1] ציצית. One of the appendices to the Talmud is devoted to fringes. For an ingenious argument in favour of the necessity of the Halakha, see Grand-Rabbi Klein, *Le Judaïsme*, pp. 12-17.

[2] On Phylacteries, Fringes, Sabbath rules, see a paper by the present writer in the *Expositor*, v. 215, *sq.* The major and derivative prohibitions (*aboth* and *toldoth*) as regards the Sabbath are enumerated in Shabbath, f. 73, 1. See too the extracts from the Book of Jubilees, given by Hausrath, *New Test. Times* (E.T.), i. 95. On ablutions, see Mark vii. 1-4; Berakhoth, viii. 3, and the entire Mishnaic tract *Yadaim* (Hand-washings).

[3] *Bîtza.*

[4] Similarly a boundless extension was given to the humane precept not to seethe a kid in its mother's milk. Flesh and milk are not to be eaten together, otherwise the kid might be seethed in its mother's milk in the stomach of the eater!

[5] Such as *Tanu Rabbanan*, "our Rabbis have taught;" *Tani chada*, "a certain Rabbi has taught;" "Another has taught;" "We have a tradition;" "It is a Mishna," &c. "The scribes say," Mark ix. 11.

[6] אגדה is the Aramaic form for the Hebrew הגדה, and it is derived from נגד, *narravit*, of which Haggada is the Hiphel form (Hamburger, *s.v.*). Buxtorf defines it as "*Narratio, enarratio, historia jucunda et subtilis, discursus historicus aut theologicus de aliquo loco Scripturae jucundus, animum lectoris attrahens.*"

its own absurdities, was, on the whole, a nobler and more
human development of teaching. The word may be rendered
by "story" or legend. In its practical usage it corresponds
to our "homiletics," but its admonitions were mingled with
fables and apologues. It was never supposed to possess any
legal authority.[1] "If," says Dr. Deutsch, "the Halakha
was the iron bulwark around the nationality of Israel, the
Haggada was a maze of flowery walks within those fortress
walls."

Such teaching was obviously more attractive, and might be
made far more edifying than ritual decisions could ever be.[2]
"The words of the Haggada," said the Jewish proverb, "attract
the mind."[3] It dealt largely with moral theses, and the
wisest Rabbis felt that the Halakha and the Haggada should
be combined. "Whoever," says Rabbi Isaac ben Pinchas,
"has learnt Haggadoth without Halakhoth has not tasted
of wisdom, and is defenceless; if, on the other hand, he has
studied Halakhoth without Haggadoth he has not tasted
the fear of sin."[4] "Between the rugged boulders of the
Law," says Dr. Deutsch, "there grow the blue flowers of
romance and poetry—parable, gnome, tale, saga—its elements
are taken from heaven and earth; but chiefly and most
lovingly from Scripture and from the human heart."[5]

The Haggada sprung into importance in the days of
Rabbi Johanan ben Zakkai, when the stricken hearts of
the Jews were most in need of consolation. The stricter

---

[1] Schwab (Berakhoth, xv.) refers to Jer. *Ped.* ii. § 4 ; Shabbath, xvi. § 1 ;
and to the opinions of Maimonides, Juda Halevi, Ibn Ezra, &c. See too the
numerous quotations in Klein, *Le Judaisme* pp. 23—28.

[2] The Halakha, for instance, contains nothing so spiritual as R. Simlai's
reduction of the 613 precepts to one. Grätz, iv. 265.

[3] דברי אנדה מושכים הלב. Chiarini, i. 63. "Quaedam ex illis," says
Ibn Ezra, "sunt aenigmata, arcana, et parabolae sublimes usque ad aethera.
Aliae inserviunt ad refocillanda corda defatigata. Aliae . . . similes sunt corporibus ;
allegoriae autem sunt veluti vestimenta corpori adhaerentia. Aliae
sunt subtiles instar serici, aliae crassae veluti succus."

[4] Aboth of R. Nathan, c. 29. I have pointed out elsewhere that St. Paul
was an Haggadist, and treats the Halakha with marked indifference. But he
uses Rabbinic methods very rarely, and only by way of passing illustration,
and only for noble purposes.

[5] *Remains,* p. 145.

Talmudists professed to despise it. R. Joshua ben Levi said that he who wrote it down would have no portion in the world to come, and that he who explained it would be scorched.[1] R. Leiri, in the Maaseroth, curses all writings that contain the Haggada.[2] When the mass of the people deserted Rabbi Chija, who was lecturing on the Halakha, for Rabbi Abuhu, who was a Haggadist, the latter, in order to console the wounded jealousy of his rival, compared the Halakha to pearls which were too costly for the multitude who therefore deserted the merchant who sold them for the modest pedlar who sold only shells or sweetmeats. It was also compared to small coin.[3] But its value and necessity were more and more recognised as time went on. The people found in it more comfort and more reality than in the aridity of the Halakha. The Mishna has but few specimens of it; the Gemara abounds with it; the Midrashim have little else. The Halakha was compared to bread, the Haggada to water;[4] it is called one of the wonders of God, and the honour and glory of the wise.[5] In Siphrî it is compared to wine which gladdens the heart of man; and even though Maimonides never wrote his promised book on the Haggadoth, he compared them to baskets of silver which hide apples of gold.[6]

---

[1] Etheridge, *Hebr. Lit.* p. 183.

[2] Chiarini, ii. 44. "Rabbi ben Levi said, "He who writes an Haggada has no portion in the world to come. . . . In all my life I have never even looked at a book of the Haggada." Jer. Shabbath, c. xvi. On the other hand, R. Chaneenah bar Pappa taught (Deut. v. 4), "The Lord talked with you faces to faces (פנים בפנים). This must mean at least *four* faces; for Scripture a face for fear; for Mishna a moderate face; smiling for the Talmud, and friendly for the Haggada." Sopherim, c. xvi.

[3] Sota, f. 40; Weill, i. 126; Grätz, iv. 396. For a specimen see Weill, i. 154-162, and the Yalqut on Zechariah translated by Dr. King (Cambr. 1883).

[4] Chagiga, f. 14.

[5] Baba Bathra, f. 9; Midrash Tehillin, on Prov. 25; Weill, i. 125.

[6] Prov. xxx. 11. Maimonides, Pref. to Moreh Nevochim. Grätz compares the Halakha to the trunk of Judaism; the Midrash to the roots; the logical developments ("Talmud" in narrower sense) to the branches; and the Haggada to the flowers. iv. 19. The *close* translation of the lesson from the Law (the Parasha) by the Methurgerman, and the freer rendering of that from the Prophets (the Haphtara) is analogous to the use of the Halakha in developing the Law, and of the Haggada as applied to other parts of Scripture.

And thus the stream of the Haggada, long pent up, began to flow with full waters, bearing along a mingled mass of fables, apologues, appeals, similitudes, proverbs, quaint legends, moral applications, allegory, folk-lore, romance, and aphorism.[1] Its object was sometimes to arouse the attention fatigued by the dryness of ceremonial discussions; sometimes to thwart the curiosity of prying intruders by safe and convenient cryptographs; sometimes to lighten up an address by pleasant illustrations; sometimes to leave a mystery in its enigmatic shadows.[2] It played undisturbed over the surface of the Historic books. It is mainly due to the presence of some of the wildest Haggadoth in the Gemara, and in great measure to the misunderstanding of their real character, that the Talmud has acquired its common reputation for folly and perversity.

V. Since, then, the Mishna is mainly ritual, and the Gemara has a large infusion of legendary homiletics, and the two together make up the Talmud, let us ask, What is the Talmud?

The Babylonian Talmud fills 2,947 folio pages, and for many ages so completely overshadowed and superseded the Bible that it may be regarded as the sacred book of the orthodox Jews. Surely it is one of the strangest of the Bibles of humanity! It has been called "the Pandects of Judaism," but it is also the encyclopaedia of Jewish science, and the *Hansard* of nearly a thousand years of discussion in Jewish schools, and the *Rationale Officiorum* of all its ceremonial.[3]

---

[1] See Herder, *Briefe über das Studium der Theologie.*

[2] Maimonides, *l.c.* He quotes Ps. xxv. 14. It professedly abounds in the most monstrous exaggerations, which are sometimes not cryptographic, but sheer idle nonsense, as when R. Jose says that he saw in Sepphoris 180,000 streets of pastrycooks (Yalqut on Zech. ii. 2). Many such remarks were only meant to rouse the attention of somnolent hearers. The Rabbis sometimes expressed truth in a striking way. "Fear God even as ye fear men," said R. Jochanan ben Zakkai, on his deathbed. His disciples were astonished. "When you are going to do wrong," he said, "you look round to discover if any man sees you; take heed that God's all-seeing eye does not see your sinful thoughts." "Every man should repent," said R. Eliezer, "a day before his death." "But how does he know when he will die?" asked his disciples. "Then," said the Rabbi, "let him repent every day."

[3] See Zunz, p. 42; Deutsch, p. 17; Weber, p. 94. "On y rapporte, on y discute toutes les suppositions les moins pratiques, les moins imaginables." Schwab, Berakhoth, f. xvi.

It is a veritable *lanx satura*. It consists of disputes, decisions, stories, sermons, legends, Scripture comments, moral truths, prescriptions, observations, mazes of legal enactments, gorgeous day-dreams, masked history, ill-disguised rationalism. It is drawn from the promiscuous note-books of students of very diverse attainments and character in which they have scribbled down all the wisdom and all the unwisdom, all the sense and all the nonsense which was talked for centuries in the schools of all kinds of Rabbis.[1] The Jew might say of his beloved Babli,

> " Quicquid agunt homines, votum, timor, ira, voluptas, Gaudia, discursus, nostri est farrago libelli."

The work of hundreds of learned men of different ages, countries, and conditions, it forms a wonderful monument of human industry, human wisdom, and human folly.[2] Written in a style of lapidary brevity, it reads like a collection of telegraphic messages. It is also full of uncouth grammar, barbarous solecisms, and exotic words.[3] We can hardly wonder that it is difficult to discover the method of its apparently confused and desultory discussions, when we remember that it was developed amid conditions of peril and discouragement, amid endless disturbances of war and violences of persecution, under the jealous eye of Roman informers or the cruel greed and fanatical malice of Persian oppressors.[4] Such being its origin it naturally teems with errors, exaggerations,

---

[1] Rabbi Jehudi Hallévy makes some excellent remarks to this effect in Cusari pt. iii. 73, see Klein *Le Judaïsme* p. 40-46, who also quotes Ibn Ezra, R. Serira Gaon, Luzzatto and others, as well as such authorities as Buxtorf, Wagenseil, Selden, etc.

[2] Hurwitz ; Milman, *Hist. of the Jews*, iii. 5. The method of dispute in the Rabbinic schools was called " *Pilpul*," or " duel." There are four Schools of Talmudists : the Pilpulists, who almost ceased after the days of Mendelssohn ; the Casuists ; the Homilists ; and the Historic School, among whom may be reckoned writers like Rappoport, Zunz, Jost, Krochmal, Frankel, Geiger, Luzzato, Grätz, Steinschneider, &c. See Löw, *Praktische Einleit.* pp. 84–89.

[3] The language of the Talmud has been philologically handled by Geiger, Levisohn, Luzzato, L. Dukes, and others. The translation of the whole Talmud was begun by Chiarini (into French), and by Dr. Moses Pinner (into German), but in both cases proceeded no further than one volume. The translation by Dr. Moïse Schwab seems likely to become complete.

[4] See Etheridge, *Hebr. Lit.* 175.

and even obscenities; with strange superstitions of Eastern demonology; with wild Arabian tales about the freaks of Ashmodai; with childish extravagances of fancy about Behemoth and the bird Bar Juchne and the Shorhabor; with perverted logic; with confusions of genealogy chronology, and history; with exorcisms, incantations, and magic formulae; with profane and old wives' fables, of which some few may have had a hidden significance to those who had the key to their meaning,[1] but of which the majority were understood by the multitude in their literal absurdity.[2]

These " Jewish myths and genealogies," as St. Paul calls them, have their dark side. All that can be urged by way of excuse for their baser elements is that they were not always meant to be taken literally, or to be weighed in jeweller's scales. The Rabbi, talking familiarly in his lighter and unguarded moments, did not intend his eager pupils to retain and record his most rash and accidental utterances. Here, however, in this strange literary Herculaneum all things are swept together in wild confusion. Things grave and fantastic, great and small, valuable and worthless, Jewish and Pagan, the altar and its ashes are piled together in wild disorder. Amid the labyrinths of rubbish we require a torch to enable us to pick up an accidental gem.

Such gems, indeed, it contains. In this sea of the Talmud—"this strange wild weird ocean with its leviathans, and its wrecks of golden argosies, and its forlorn bells which send up their dreamy sounds ever and anon "—there are some treasures, which have frequently

---

[1] "Sed hoc interim etiam dicendum et sciendum, non omnia quae imperitis talia videntur, esse talia." Buxtorf.

[2] No one will take his estimate of the Talmud from such wholly uncritical collections as those of Raymond Martin's *Pugio Fidei*, or Eisenmenger's *Entdecktes Judenthum* (see Weber, xxxiii.). Even such valuable works as those of Lightfoot, Schöttgen, Meuschen, and Wetstein, are vitiated by the uncritical promiscuousness of the quotations collected. But after every allowance is made the Talmud is one of the dreariest of books.

[3] Deutsch, *Remains*, 1-58, 135-145. See Bartolocci, *Bibl. Rabb.* iii. 359 *sq.* Grätz, iv. 410-412; Etheridge, *Hebr. Lit.* 185. Buxtorf admits that there are in the Talmud " *inutiles quasi paleae et multi furfures* " but also " utilia quandoque esse grana et *puram similam.*"

been gathered, amid the froth and scum, the flotsam and jetsam of a thousand years. Exquisite parables and noble aphorisms are scattered in its pages here and there. The general darkness is sometimes broken by keen flashes of intellectual, and even of spiritual, light. But these are rare, and to speak of the Talmud in such terms of enthusiasm as those with which Dr. Deutsch charmed the unwary, or to say of it, with Professor Hurwitz, that no uninspired work contains more interesting, more varied, or more valuable information—is to be blinded by national prejudice to facts which any one can put to the test.

But the worst result of the influence exercised by the Talmud is the injury which it inflicted on the living oracles of God.

That injury was twofold.

On the one hand the Jews were taught to care more for it, and to devote more continued study to its masses of casuistry and extravagance than to the divine beauty of the Psalms and the noble moral teaching of the Prophets. Thus they were turned from the river of life to broken cisterns which would hold no water, or only the shallow and stagnant pools of a tradition polluted by a thousand strange and heterogeneous influxes. A " Biblical theologian " was as great an object of contempt to the Rabbis as he became to the Schoolmen in their worst epoch of decline.

On the other hand, the actual exegesis of Scripture in which the Talmud abounds is so arbitrary and so futile, so tasteless and so insincere, that it must have given to its students a radically false conception of their sacred books. It represented to them the Law of Moses as fragmentary without the supplement of tradition, and inexplicable without the intervention of Rabbinism. Let us, for instance, take the tracts Shabbath and Bîtza. The interminable discussions on Sabbath regulations which those treatises contain turn almost exclusively on false quotations or on inferences wholly without base.[1]

[1] For an instance see Chiarini, ii. 226.

VI. What has been said of the Talmud applies in general to all the Rabbinic writings and to the whole collection of Midrashim, of which the most celebrated are nothing but catenae of Talmudic passages.[1] The word Midrash means, in its strictest sense, the exposition of the Pentateuch and of the five rolls of Canticles, Ruth, Lamentations, Ecclesiastes, Esther, which is collected in the Midrash Rabba. Jewish exegesis, as applied in the Midrashim, was founded on the four methods mnemonically described as,

PaRDeS

or Paradise :—namely,

Peshat, or the literal sense ; the grammatico-historical meaning of words and sentences.[2]

Remez, or hint, the development of latent meanings.[3]

Darush, or homiletics,[4] including allegory and all kinds of illustration.

Sôd, or mystery.[5]

Exegetically the *Peshat* is alone of real value.[6] The *Remez* was chiefly devoted to the development of Halakha ; the *Darush* to the Haggada, and the *Sôd* to the Qabbala.

It was in the development of the *Sôd*, or mystery, that the Kabbalists found the chief sphere of their labours. The

[1] See Dr. Ginsburg in Kitto's *Cyclopaedia, s.v.* Midrashim ; and in Koheleth p. 30. It is a haggadistic collection, half homiletic, half exegetical in character.

[2] Compare the name of the Syriac version—Peshito, which implied that the version was simple and literal. Even some of the Sopherîm had laid down the rule that every interpretation was to accord with the literal (אין מקרא יוצא מידי פשיטו), but no one practically attended to it.

[3] An assonance, a change of letters, &c. " *Gott als Verfasser* könne mit einem Worte, mit der einfachen und natürlichen Bedeutung, noch eine andere verknüpft haben und Mehreres mit einem Male lehren. . . . Dieses heisst im Talmud תרתי שמעית מנה, Beides entnehme ich daraus." Hirschfeld, *Halach. Exegese,* § 104. See too § 112 ; Weber, 115.

[4] From דרש, " to search."

[5] The *Derek ha-kabbala.* See Etheridge, *Hebr. Lit.* p. 404.

[6] Critical Jews distinguish between popular commentaries like the Midrashim, and scientific commentaries (Perushim). The writers of the Midrash were neither Paraphrasts (*Targumists*), nor, properly speaking, commentators (*Hiphreshim*). The latter begin properly with Saadja in the tenth century, and include the great names of Rashi, Ibn Ezra, Maimonides, the Qimchis, and Abrabanel. Asaria di Rossi distinguishes between hyperbolical (*guzma*), haggadistic, and " exhaustive " Midrash. The latter, like what Sixtus Senensis calls the *Pandesiac* method, explained Scripture in all possible ways.

word Qabbala means "a thing received," but it was used for
"scholastic lore,"[1] and it was asserted that the Qabbala was
of equal sacredness with the Law, and had been received by
Moses on Sinai. The germs of the Qabbala, in some of its
branches, must be of early date, for it is referred to in the
Mishna.[2] Its two main divisions were the Real and the
Symbolical. The real Qabbala is more connected with
theosophy and thaumaturgy than with anything which could
be called exegesis. Its theoretical section comprised the
two great branches of inquiry, cosmogony and theosophy.
They were called the *Maaseh Bereshith*, or Work of the Creation, and the *Maaseh Merkaba*, or Work of the Chariot, which
derived its name from the Vision of Ezekiel. The *Maaseh
Bereshith* entered into endless speculations about the Creation,
the ten spheres, the four worlds, the *En Soph*, or "Infinite,"
Memra or the Word, Adam Kadmon the Primeval Man, the
mysteries of numbers, and so forth.[3] It sought to explain
the transition from the Infinite to the Finite, from Mind
to Matter. The *Maaseh Merkaba* plunged into inquiries
respecting the abstract nature of God, and was surrounded

---

[1] Ewald, *Hist. of Israel*, v. 190, E. Tr. Hence the word is even used for
"an amulet." See Buxtorf, *Lex.* p. 1953. Qabbala means the act of giving,
while Massora, from Masar, "to transmit," means the act of receiving. See
Ginsburg, *The Kabbala*, p. 4.

[2] The Qabbala, or "secret wisdom" (חכמה נסתרה),—called also from the
initials of these two words, חן, "grace,"—may be divided as follows :—

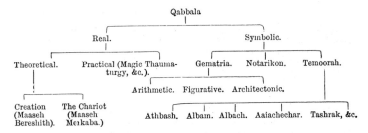

[3] The ten pure numbers (Sephiroth) represent the Being of God ; the
twenty-two which have letters as their signs are the creative word of God.
See the strange remarks of Philo on the number 7. *Vit. Mos.* iii. p. 156.
Kabbalism in general "bears about the same relation to Scripture that magic
does to nature." Reuss, *Gesch. der heiligen Schriften Neuen Testaments*,
p. 503.

with a veil of terror and mystery. Practical Kabbalism
instructed the neophyte in the manner in which the Incom-
municable name—the Shem Hammephorash—might be employed for magic purposes. The two chief books in which
these studies—if they may be dignified by such a name—
were developed, are the Zohar, attributed to Rabbi Simon
Ben Jochai, but in its present form not older than the thirteenth century; and the Jetsîrah, or Book of Splendour,
which Dr. Zunz assigns to the Gaonim in the eighth or ninth
century. The former is devoted to Creation, the latter to the
Chariot-throne.[1]

But if these branches of Kabbalistic lore, which were
largely influenced by Persian and other sources, touch even
the outer circumference of exegesis, on the other hand the
writings of the Rabbis abound in the symbolical Kabbalism
which proposed for the evolution of the supposed mystic
senses of Scripture thirteen methods, of which we can only
say that each is more impossible and arbitrary than the preceding. They are founded on the immense delusion that
the whole Massorah, even down to the verses, words, letters,
vowel-points, and accents, was delivered to Moses on Sinai,
and that "the numbers of the letters, every single letter, the
collocation of every letter, the transposition, the substitution,
had a special, even a supernatural power." These rules were
summed up under the three divisions of Gematria, Notarikon
and Themoorah, indicated, in the usual Rabbinic way, by the

---

[1] The earliest Kabbalistic book, Sepher ha Bahir, attributed to Nechonja
ben Hakana, a contemporary of Hillel, is no longer extant. It is mentioned
in the Chagiga, but the book published under that title in 1641 is a forgery.
Similarly a Sepher Jetsîra, touching apparently on thaumaturgist natural science,
is mentioned in Sanhedrin, c. 7 and f. 67. The extant Jetsîra does not properly belong to the Qabbala at all (Zunz, p. 165), and treats the first ten
numbers (*Seîroth*) and the twenty-two letters (*othîoth*) as "thirty-two wondrous
ways of wisdom," in which God created the universe. The Zohar ("splendour"), attributed to R. Simon Ben Jochai, but probably the work of a Spanish
Jew (Moses de Leon) in the thirteenth century (Grätz, vii. ; Ginsburg, pp.
78–89), is a mystic commentary on the Pentateuch. This branch of the
Qabbala lies wholly outside the region of exegesis. See Reuchlin, *De Arte
Cabbalistica;* Franck, *Système de la Kabbale ;* Dr. Ginsburg, *The Kabbala ;*
Jelinek, *Die Kabbala,* 1844; Etheridge, *Hebr. Lit.* pp. 297–353. Two important
Kabbalistic books are the "Lily of Secrets" (*Shoshan Sodoth*), by Ramban
(† 1260), and "Garden of Nuts" (*Genath Egoz*), by Jos. Karnitol (See
Etheridge, p. 359).

H

initial letters of the words, as GeNeTH.[1] These methods
play so large a part in Rabbinic exegesis that we must pause
to explain their character.

i. GEMATRIA is a corruption of *Geometria*, one of the many
Greek words which are naturalised in Talmudic Hebrew.[2] The
chief branch of this method resembled the Greek *isopse-*
phism and consisted in establishing mystic relations between
different conceptions, based on the numerical equivalence of
value in the letters by which they are expressed. Philologically
the Jews were "Analogists," *i.e.* they believed in the mystic
value and importance of names. Hence even as early as the
Pentateuch we find a sort of etymological comment, and in the
New Testament there are three instances of deep significance
attached to the sound of names.[3] To regard every name as
representing a number, and therefore as cognate to any other
name which yielded the same number, was a long step in
advance. Thus in Zechariah iii. 8 the promised Messiah is
spoken of as "my servant THE BRANCH." [4] Now the Hebrew
letters of *Tsemach*, "a sprout," are equivalent in value to 138;
and this is also the value of the letters of "Menahem," or
"Consoler" (Lam. i. 16), and consequently Menahem is
reckoned among the names of the Messiah.[5] In Gen. xlix.
10, "Shiloh come" (שילה יבא) is equivalent to 358, and that is
also the numerical value of Mashiach (משיח). Shiloh is therefore identified with the Messiah.[6] Again, because the letters
of *Mashiach* and of *Nachash*, "serpent," are isopsephic, they
said that it was the Messiah who would bruise the serpent's
head. Similar instances—of which some will be given in
the notes—may be counted by hundreds in the Rabbinic

[1] See Buxtorf, *De Abbreviaturis*, *s.v.* גנת. Klein, *Le Judaisme*, pp. 32-35.
[2] גמטריא, γεωμετρία. Dr. Ginsburg derives it from γραμματεία. The
actual numbering is called "reckoning" (חשבון). Bammidbar Rabba, c.
25. (Comp. Ecc. vii. 25, 27.) Weber, *Altsyn. Theol.* 118.
[3] "He shall be called a Nazarene," Matt. ii. 23. This is probably an allusion
to *Netser*, "a branch." Comp. Is. xi. 1. Sinai and Hagar, Gal. iv. 25.
Claudius = ὁ κατέχων, *qui Claudit*, 2 Thess. ii. 7.
[4] Rather "the sprout." Comp. Jer. xxiii. 5.
[5] Sanhedrin, f. 98, 2. צ = 90 ; מ = 40 ; ח = 8 = 138.
מ = 40 ; נ = 50 ; ח = 8 ; ם = 40 = 138.
This identification continues down to modern days.

writings.[1] We may here be content with one more specimen. In Gen. xxv. 21, the letters of the Hebrew word for
" his wife " (אִשְׁתּוֹ) have the value of 707, which is the
equivalent of the words אֵשׁ וָקַשׁ, " fire and straw," and is at once
mystically connected with Obadiah, verse 11, " the house of
Jacob shall be a fire . . . and the house of Esau of stubble." [2]
Of the applications of this method some are purely frivolous,
as when it is inferred that Eliezer was alone equal to
all the other 318 servants of Abraham because the letters
of his name have the value 318 ; or that there are never
less than 36 righteous in the world, because in Is. xxx.
18, " Blessed are all those that wait upon Him," the value
of the word " upon Him" (לוֹ) is 36 ; or that there are 70
nations of the world because " Gog and Magog " give the
number 70 ; or that there are 903 ways of dying because the
word for " *issues* of death," in Ps. lxviii. 21, gives the number
903 (תוצאות).[3] Some of the references, however, became
practically important, as when the length of a Nazarite's vow
might be limited to 30 days, because in Num. vi. 5, " he shall
be holy," the word " he shall be " (יהיה) gives the number 30 ;
or as when it was inferred that there might be 98 ways of
explaining the Law, because in Cant. ii. 4 the word for " and
his banner" gives the number 49 (ודגלו) ; or again, that the
Law had 613 precepts because the word for " incense " (קטרת)
gives 613.[4] Sometimes the inference even acquires for the

---

[1] In a curious passage of *De praescriptione haereticorum*, c. 50, Tertullian
speaks of Gematria. " Marcus quidam et Colarbasus *novam haeresim ex
Graecorum alphabeta componentes*. Negant enim veritatem sine istis posse
litteris inveniri, immo totam plenitudinem et perfectionem veritatis in istis
litteris esse dispositam." He says they founded the doctrine on "I am α
and ω." Thus because περιστερὰ = 801 = ΑΩ, they said that the Logos
was joined to Jesus at Baptism (Iren. *Haer.* i. 14, § 6). Going through
the alphabet in a reverse order, "Computant ogdoadas et decadas, ita ut
afferre illorum omnes vanitates et ineptum sit et otiosum." But it was not
only Gnosticism which eagerly availed itself of Kabbalistic exegesis. Thus we
find the mystic explanation of Abraham's 318 servants as a type of Christ,—
τ (= 300) being the Cross, and ιη (= 18) being the first letters of the name of
Jesus—as early as the Epistle of Barnabas (c. ix.).

[2] Sanhedrin, f. 97, 2.

[3] See Berakhoth, f. 8, 1.

[4] If by Athbash ב is changed into ק ! See Buxtorf, *De Abbreviaturis*,
p. 57. But *Thorah* gives the same result : ת = 400 ; ו = 6 ; ר = 200 ; ה =
5 = 611, which, with the Shema and the first commandment = 613.

Jewish mind a strong theological significance, as when they inferred that the Day of Atonement was the only day of the year on which Satan could bring no accusation, because the word Hassatan (השטן) gives only 364.[1] Sometimes also the method was used to explain away a plain fact of Scripture which militated with Jewish prejudices, as when it was asserted that Moses did not marry an Ethiopian woman (Kushith) but a "beautiful" woman, since Kushith yields the number 736 which is equivalent to "fair of form" (יפת־מראה). We find this kind of Gematria used cryptographically by St. John in the Apocalypse to indicate the name of Nero, as it is used in the Sibylline verses to indicate the name of Jesus.[2]

There were two other branches of Gematria, the *Architectonic*, which concerned itself with calculations respecting the Tabernacle, the Temple, and the ideal Temple of Ezekiel;[3] and the *Figurative*[4] (already alluded to), which speculated on the sizes and shapes of letters. Thus since the ד in the word אחד, and the ע in the word שמע, "Hear!" are lengthened in Deut. vi. 4, we are told that this is meant (i.) to show the greatness of the doctrine; (ii.) to show the power of God in the four quarters of the world (ד = 4); and (iii.) because ע and ד make up the word עד, "a witness." We find a curious instance of architectonic Gematria in Josephus, who, in referring to Dan. ix. 27, alludes to the Jewish belief that the Jewish Temple would be destroyed whenever it was made rectangular, because 4 being the signature of the world contradicts the idea of the sanctuary. Now the Temple became rectangular when the Zealots destroyed the tower of Antonia.[5]

---

[1] Yoma, f. 20, 1.

[2] Rev. xiii. 18. 666 = נרון קסר. Nero Caesar; Iren. *Haer.* v. 30; Sulp. Sev. *H. S.* ii. 29; Orac. Sibyll. i. 325. Ἰησοῦς = 888.

[3] Etheridge refers to Shichard's *Bechinath Happerushim*, p. 65, for some curious particulars. *Hebr. Lit.* p. 354.

[4] This figurative Gematria is called צריית. In their minute attentions to trivialities the Scribes registered the important fact that only two verses of the Law begin with ס (Ex. xxxii. 8; Num. xiv. 19).

[5] Jos. *B. J.* vi. 6, § 4. The "desolating *wing* (כנף) of abomination" was rendered "*corner* of abomination." Comp. Philo, *Vit. Mos.* p. 142; Hausrath, i. 123.

ii. NOTARIKON was another Kabbalistic method. The name
is borrowed from *Notarius,* " a shorthand writer," because
these writers used letters to stand for words.[1] It consisted in
forming words by the combination of initial and terminal
letters, or by regarding each letter of a word as the initial
letter of other words. The famous symbol $i\chi\theta\hat{v}s$ is an
instance of a word thus interpreted,[2] and it enabled Christians to recognise one another. Notarikon is mentioned in
the Mishna, and in Bereshith Rabba, § 46, it is discussed
whether it was known to Abraham.[3] A few specimens will
suffice. In Gen. ii. 3 the letters of *ElohiM LaasotH* are combined into *Emeth,* " Truth." The letters of Adam are made
to stand for Adam, David, Messiah, so that Adam's soul is
said to have passed into those of David and the Messiah.[4]
In Ps. lxxvii. 21, the word " Thou leddest " (נחית) is made
to stand for Wonder, Life, Sea, Law,[5] to imply that God
had wrought Wonders for His people, given them Life,
divided the Sea, and given the Law, through Moses and
Aaron. Some derived the name Maccabee from Mî
Kamoka Baelim Yehovah, " Who among the gods is
like unto thee, O Lord ? " (Ex. xv. 11).[6] These methods
remain in full force among the Talmudic Jews to this
day. Annually, on the day of Atonement, the Polish Jews
observe " the Atonement of the Cock," [7] and the head of

---

[1] See Buxtorf, *Lex. Talm. s.v.* נטריקון. Rabbi Nathan defines it as being
practised " when one letter is made to stand for an entire thing." The name
Naphtali is thus made to mean " My prayer is here accepted before the Lord,"
and *anoki,* " I " is made to stand for " I myself wrote and gave it."

[2] 'Ιησοῦς Χριστὸς Θεοῦ Υἱὸς Σωτήρ. The Greeks were, as Plutarch says,
familiar with these σημεῖα ἐν βραχέσι τύποις πολλῶν γραμμάτων δύναμιν
ἔχοντα.

[3] Shabbath, xii. 5.

[4] Nishmath Chajim, f. 152, 2. Similarly the soul of Cain passed into
those of Jethro (י), Korah (ק), and the Mizraim- ite (מ) whom Moses slew.
Yalqut Reubeni. Another *notarikon* applied to the name said that it stood for
Dust, Blood, Bitterness (מָרָה, דָם, אָפָר). The use of Notarikon continued,
even among the Fathers; as when 'Αδάμ is said to imply the four quarters of
the world, 'Αρκτός, δύσις, ἀνατολή, μεσημβρία.

[5] נסים, חיים, ים, תורה.

[6] For other instances, see Budaeus, *Philos. Ebraeorum,* p. 323 ; Buxtorf,
De Abbreviaturis, p. 58 ; Reuchlin, *De Cabbala,* iii. ; Chiarini, i. 57 ; Hamburger, *Realwört. s.v. Schrift.*

[7] Because in one passage of the Talmud נבר (" a man ") is used for " a
cock ".

the household, whirling a cock round his head, exclaims:
"Chalaphathi, Temarathi, Kapparathi," "This is my substitute, my commutation, my atonement." The initial letters of
these words make the word *Chathak*, "to cut," and consequently the Angel of Death is called Chatak (חתך). The
word is still more surrounded by mystic associations, because
by Gematria it yields the number 428, which is also furnished
by the Hebrew words, "This shall be an atonement for
thee." [1]

iii. The word TEMOORAH, or "change," [2] is used for an exegetical method which evolves new meanings by an interchange
of letters. Thus in Ps. xxi. 2, "The king shall rejoice in Thy
strength, O Lord," refers to "the Messiah" by transposing
יִשְׂמַח (shall rejoice) into *Mashiach*. In Ex. xxiii. 23, "my
angel" (מַלְאָכִי) is transposed into Michael, as also is the name
Malachi! [3] "*Cherem*," "a ban," becomes by Temoorah
racham, "pity," implying that there is always room for
repentance; or into *ramach*, of which the numerical equivalent is 248, showing that if a man do not repent the curse
will smite the 248 parts of the body. Reuchlin argued the
Divinity of Christ from the fact that Jesus (Joshua) in
Hebrew (יהשוה) gives the name Jehovah, and the letter שׁ,
which stands for "fire," and is a symbol of the Logos.[4] Often
the method becomes one of simple anagram, as when the
names Balaam Balak are turned into "Valley of Confusion."[5]
It is possible that the New Testament furnishes us with an
instance of Temoorah in Rev. xvi. 16, where the mysterious

---

[1] זה יהיו לך לכפרה. The name of this angel is also given by the *final*
letters of פותח את ידך, "Thou openest thine hand," Ps. clxv. 16. I take
this modern instance, which shows the extraordinary vitality of these methods,
from Hershon's *Treasures of the Talmud*, p. 107. It is a curious fact, which
may here be mentioned in passing, that many Kabbalists became Christians,
because the Trinity, the Atonement, &c., are supposed to be deducible by
these processes, but much more because they are said to be implied in the
Zohar. Among them were Ricci, Otto, Rittengal (a grandson of Abrabanel),
who translated the Jetsîra into Latin; and Jacob Frank, who took with him
some thousands of his followers. Beer, *Gesch. d. rel. Secten d. Juden*, ii. 309

[2] Called by some הפוך, "inversion."

[3] See Nachmanides in Kitto's *Cyclop.*

[4] The name Jesus is however ישוע in Hebrew.

[5] עֵמֶק בַּלְבֵּל.

word Armageddon may be meant for Harmagedol, *i.e.* Roma Haggedolah, Rome the Great. The names are also iso-psephic, for by Gematria they are both equivalent to 304.[1]

The commonest application of Temoorah consists, how-ever, in substituting for each letter in a word the letter which stands in an equivalent order in the other half of the alpha-bet.[2] This was called Athbash, Albam, and Atbach, &c. The chief interest of the method lies in the fact that there seem to be three instances of it in the Bible. Thus in Jer. xxv. 26, li. 41, the word Sheshach has always been understood to be a cypher for Babel, to which by Athbash it is equivalent. No Christian interpreter had any notion what it meant till Jerome learned the secret from his Jewish teacher. Again in Jer. li. 1, the meaningless expression, " *them that dwell in the midst* of them that rise up against me," becomes luminous if for *leb-kamai* we substitute by Athbash the word *Kasdim*, or Chaldeans (see *v.* 35).[3] Similarly an application of the cipher Albam explains an otherwise mysterious name in Is. vii. 6. Ephraim, Syria, and the son of Remaliah there take evil counsel to attack Judah and set up as king " *the son of Tabeal.*" Who was this Tabeal whose name never occurs elsewhere ? Mr. Cheyne says that " he was evidently a Syrian ; the name in Syriac means " God is good," just as Tav-Rimmon means " Rimmon is good." Dr. Kay even conjectures that he was a descendant of Naaman, and others that he was a powerful Ephraimite, perhaps Zichri (2 Chron. xxviii. 7). Apply the Albam, however, and for Tabeal (טאבל) we get רמלא, which may well be the same as Remaliah, either used by Isaiah as a scornful variation, or because it may

---

Hausrath, *New Test. Times*, i. 117.

[2] Thus in Athbash for A.B.G.D., &c., are substituted the corresponding letters at the opposite end of the alphabet, namely TH, SH, R, &c. In Albam, A.B.G.D., &c., are exchanged with L.M.N.S., &c. R. Chija, the Tanaite, is said to have invented the Athbash (Sukka, f. 52, 2), but probably it was much older. There are no fewer than twenty-four different kinds of this Themoorah.

[3] Ewald may be right in supposing that the use of these Kabbalistic methods in Jer. xxv. 26, li. 41, is due not to Jeremiah, but to the Babylonian editor of his book. *Propheten d. Alten Bundes*, ii. 247 ; iii. 141.

have originally been the secret watchword of the powerful conspiracy.

In these instances we have only the traces of a cypher suggested by policy or terror. In some cases, however, these anagrammatic alphabets have been used from time immemorial to explain certain passages of Scripture.[1] Thus, in Prov. xxix. 21, where it is said that "a petted slave will at last become a man's son," the word מָנוֹן, rendered "son," occurs here only. Some suppose it to mean "refractory," or "ungrateful," and Luther happily renders it "*so will er darnach ein Junker seyn.*" But by applying another Kabbalistic alphabet (*Atbach*)[2] we get for *mânôn* the word עֵהְדָה, *gnehdah,* "testimony," and the verse may be rendered "*He who satisfies his desire in this world against him it will testify at the end ;*" and this comment is as old as the Talmud.

Besides all these methods there was yet another which consisted in altering the words of the text into others which resembled them. It is strange that this absolutely arbitrary device for making the Scriptures say exactly what the interpreter wished to make them say was defended on the same principle of letter-worship as that which lay at the root of the whole system. The method was indefinitely facilitated by the plasticity of words in which the vowel-points could be altered in many ways. Thus the Bible was forced to imply thousands of things of which its writers never dreamed.[3] On the pretence that every word of it was supernaturally communicated by God, it was asserted that if words sounded at all like *other* words, that secondary meaning must also be implied! Hence the incessant Rabbinic formula, "*Read not so, but so.*"[4] Maimonides says that

---

[1] Sukka, 52, 2 ; Ginsburg, *Elias Levita,* p. 191, and *s.v.* Midrash in Kitto ; and Kabbalah, p. 54 ; Hamburger I. *s.v. Schrift.*

[2] For Atbach see Buxtorf, *De Abbreviaturis,* and Dr. Ginsburg in Kitto, *s.v.*

[3] As when the initial words of בָּרָא were made to stand for אָב, רוּחַ, בֵּן, (Father, Spirit, Son,) and so used as an argument in favour of the Trinity ; or as when the Jews said that the world was created on the first of Tisri, because the first word of Genesis, Bereshith, can be transposed into Bethisrî. See Glassius, *Philolog. Sacr.* 425, 438.

[4] אַל תִּקְרִי כֹּז אֶלָּא כֵן. Hirschfeld says, "Man konnte etwas *conjiciren und verändern,* indem man sagte, Wenn man die Worte verändert oder

the intention was not to destroy the Biblical reading, but to add to it a poetic (!) figure.[1] Thus, in Is. ii. 22, "for wherein is he to be accounted of," by reading בָּמָה, "a high place," for בַּמֶּה, "wherein," they get the deduction that whoever salutes his neighbour before prayer makes him as it were a high place![2] And if they desire to glorify the Sabbath they read, "Blessed is the man that keepeth the Sabbath, *and he shall be pardoned,*" instead of· "that keepeth the Sabbath *from polluting it.*"[3]

VII. The results of our long inquiry are very saddening. We have seen something alike of the methods and of the results of exegesis as practised for nearly 2,000 years by the very nation to which were entrusted "the oracles of God." We have been forced to the conclusion that the methods have been for the most part radically untenable, the results all but absolutely valueless.[4] The letter-worship and the traditionalism, which date their origin from the days of Ezra, the idolatry of the Law, the exaltation of ceremonial, the quenching of the living and mighty spirit of prophecy, the pedantry, the tyranny, the exclusiveness, the haughty self-exaltation of Rabbinism, the growth of an extravagant reverence for the oral rules which formed the "hedge about the Law," are results in themselves deplorable; but they become still more deplorable when we see that meanwhile all that was essential, divine, and spiritual in the Law was set at naught by human inventions. Exegesis became a mere art of leading astray. It ended in Pharisaism with all its fatal evils, substituting an empty externalism for the religion of the heart, making more of fringes and phylacteries than of justice, mercy, and truth. The profession of Bibliolatry slowly but surely undermined

---

umstellt so giebt es einem Sinn und eine Bedeutung ab, die genau überein, stimmt mit dem was man in der Bibel *erwartete!*" *Halach. Exegese,* 164.

[1] Moreh Nerochim, iii. 43. See Eisenmenger, *Entd. Judenth.* i. c. 8.

[2] Berakhoth, f. 14, 1.

[3] In Is. lvi. 2, by reading מחל לו for מהללו. In the same verse by reading Enos for "the man," they argue that even an idolater (Gen. iv. 26) shall be forgiven if he keeps the Sabbath.

[4] "The rules for this exegesis afforded as great a facility for introducing into the text, as for deducing from it, any and every imaginable conceit." Ginsburg, *Coheleth,* p 30.

the Bible which it nominally worshipped. The long
labours and discussions of Sopherim, Tanaim, Amoraim,
Saboraim, and Gaonim have left but a minimum of valuable
result. The Halakha was void of all spiritual significance.
Ceremonialism flourished under its auspices, but morality
decayed.[1] The sepulchre glistened white, but within it
was full of dead men's bones. The Haggada, though it
had nobler elements, lost itself in monstrous combinations,
and buried the natural simplicity of the Scripture narrative
under masses of legendary distortion. The Qabbala was
an arbitrary mysticism which led to nothing but delusion,
and was devoid of any foundation in any one of its
developments. It is true that we must not take literally all
that we find in the Rabbinic writings. They abound in
unsolved enigmas, and doubtless had many meanings to
which in the course of ages we have lost the key.[2] The
fact, however, remains—that volumes might be filled with
thousands of specimens of Rabbinic exegesis, of which it
would be difficult to say whether they be most baseless in
method, or most wide of all truth in the conclusions formed.
We should be paying to Talmudism too high a compliment,
were we to say that it is like

> "The pleached bower,
> Where honeysuckles ripened by the sun
> Forbid the sun to enter."

The most distinctive flowers of the Talmud are artificial
flowers—flowers by which we cannot for a moment be
deceived.

---

[1] See Psalm. Solomon, iv. 3, 4 ; viii. 9-11 (Hilgenfeld, *Messias Judaeorum.*
p. 12).

[2] Towards the close of the fifteenth century many Christians like Mirandola
and Reuchlin were eager to study the Qabbala, and Elias Levita was patron-
ised by Cardinal Egidius de Viterbo. Mirandola thought that he found
"more Christianity than Judaism in the Qabbala—the Trinity, Incarnation,
original sin, redemption, Angelology, Purgatory," &c., " in fact the same
gospel which we find in St. Paul, Dionysius, St. Jerome, and St. Augustine."
Pope Sixtus IV. wished the Kabbalistic writings to be rendered into Latin.
See Ginsburg, *The Massoreth Ha Massoreth* of Elias Levita, Introd. p. 12. If
there be anything distinctively Christian in Kabtalism, it is historically
derivable from Christianity itself.

To the Jewish scholars we owe indeed the boon of a text preserved to the utmost of their power: we owe the priceless labour of the earlier Massorets, and the philological knowledge of those mediaeval Rabbis who furnished the grammars and lexicons on which, after fifteen centuries of Christianity, a sounder exegetic method was gradually built. Indirectly too they have preserved for us in their writings many traditional facts of an interest and importance greater than have yet been fully understood. But even the most favourable estimate must reluctantly admit that their writings are principally valuable to the historian, the archaeologist, and the student of psychology, and that it is indirectly far more than directly that, from the days of Ezra to the days of Maimonides, they have furnished us with anything of intrinsic value for the right apprehension of Holy Writ.

Is that a harsh judgment? Nay, it is the judgment of Himself. Even in the days of the Son of Man the exegetic principles which find their full development in the Talmud and the Midrash formed the main elements of the popular religionism. And Christ's judgment of those principles was luminous and emphatic. It was " Why do ye transgress the commandment of God by your tradition ? " [1] It was " Ye have made void the Law of God because of your tradition." [2] It was " In vain do they worship Me, teaching as their doctrine the precepts of men." [3] It was " Ye read the Scriptures and ye will not come unto Me." [4]

[1] Matt. xv. 3.   [2] Matt. xv. 6.
[3] Matt. xv. 9.   [4] John v. 39, 40.

" There was a flute in the Temple preserved from the days of Moses, smooth, thin, formed of a reed. At the command of the king it was overlaid with gold, which made the sound less pleasant. There was also a cymbal and a mortar, preserved from the time of Moses which had become injured. Workmen of Alexandria were sent for by the wise men, who mended them ; but this so impaired their efficiency that they had to be restored to their former condition."—EIRECHIN, f. 10, 2.

" Lacte gypsum male miscetur."—IREN.

Ἐξ οὗ (Φιλῶνος) οἶμαι καὶ πᾶς ὁ ἀλληγορικὸς ἐν Ἐκκλησίᾳ λόγος ἔσχεν ἀρχὴν εἰσρυῆναι.—PHOTIUS, Cod. cv.

" τοῦτο σύμπαν τὸ ἐκλεκτικὸν . . . . φημί."—CLEM. ALEX. Strom. 1 c. 7, § 37.

Σχέδον γὰρ τὰ πάντα ἢ τὰ πλειστα τῆς νομοθεσίας ἀλληγορεῖται.—PHILO, De Josepho, § 6.

LECTURE III.

ALEXANDRIAN EXEGESIS.

"In that day shall there be an altar to the Lord in the midst of the land of Egypt, and a pillar at the border thereof to the Lord."—Is. xix. 19.

THE great secular tendencies of Exegesis among the Jews fall under two widely different divisions.

One of these, that of the Rabbis of Palestine and Babylon, was national, orthodox, indigenous, of which in the last Lecture we traced the growth and considered the methods. Their aim was, as we have seen, to interpret and to develop the sacred books by the methods of the Halakha, the Haggada, and the Qabbala, and the main monuments of their labours are the Talmud, the Targums, the Midrashim, and the beginnings of the Massora.

The other great stream of exegetic tendency was the Alexandrian. It represented the workings of the Jewish mind when it no longer maintained its rigid and exclusive jealousy of foreign influences, but had absorbed into its very life-blood the wisdom of the Greeks. It is of extreme interest and importance, because, even more than Palestinian exegesis, it left deep traces on the Biblical studies of the Christian Church. Its chief monument is the writings of Philo.

1. The Dispersion of the Chosen People, which familiarised the world with a purer morality and a monotheistic faith, was one of the methods of the divine economy for preparing

the way of the Lord and making straight in the desert a highway for our God. The political unity given to the government of many nations by the rise of the Roman Empire, and the unity of language created by the conquests of Alexander, helped to further the same great end. The letters of Hebrew, and Greek, and Latin above the Cross were a symbol of the testimony given to Christ by the three noblest languages of the ancient world.

But the great providential end—the spread of the Kingdom of God—could never have been achieved if the Jews of the Dispersion had retained that attitude of isolation which it had been the main object of Rabbinism to secure. If outside the range of Rabbinism "the hedge about the law" had not been broken into and trampled down in every direction, millions of Jews could never have adopted Greek customs and Greek conceptions, nor could they have facilitated the triumph of a world-religion over the superstitions of a decaying Paganism. In vain did the Rabbis of Jerusalem endeavour to stem the advancing tide of Hellenic influences among their countrymen. The memorable eighteen ordinances, discussed in the school of Rabbi Hananiah shortly before the fall of Jerusalem,[1] had been opposed by the milder Hillelites, but they had been passed amid blows and bloodshed, and their express object was to cleave a yet deeper rift of difference between the Jews and the heathen. But all such precautions were in vain. The drift of universal tendency was against them. The will of God, clearly manifested in the progress of events, and revealed yet more clearly by the teaching of the Holy Spirit, showed that the day was come when Mosaism was to be abrogated. We have already seen that the system so jealously maintained by the Rabbis was not Mosaism at all, but an immense superstructure of precedents per-

---

[1] The Shemoneh Esreh ; Shabbath, i. 7 ; Grätz, iii. 494 ; Derenbourg, 274. It was asserted that 120 elders, and among them several prophets, had a share in composing them. Megilla, f. 17, 2. Samuel the Little took special part in them. Berakhoth, f. 27, 2. These ordinances, to which the Mishna only alludes, are found in a *baraita* of R. Simeon ben Jochai in the second century. They consist of prohibitions which rendered all intercourse between Pagan and orthodox Jews impossible. See *Life of St. Paul*, i. 129.

vaded by a different and less noble spirit than that of Moses, and built only upon the drifting sand of fragments and inferences. Such a system was useless for mankind.

But meanwhile God became His own Interpreter. The little corner of the Mediterranean, bulwarked with sea, mountains, and deserts, in which for two thousand years He had kept alive some knowledge of His name, became the battle-field of heathen conquerors. The Chosen People were carried away captive, and the faith which had been cherished in their narrow borders went forth in its glory and its consummation to conquer the whole world.[1]

But long before the destruction of Jerusalem a complete change had come over the views, feelings, and habits of the most cultivated children of the Dispersion. Commerce had become universal among them, and commerce is the great disseminator of cosmopolitan ideas. It had for this very reason been discouraged by Moses in the days when the mission of Israel had been to retain and not to diffuse the revelation of the One True God. Of the Hellenists of the Dispersion, some, indeed, strove to keep alive among themselves the Hebraising views of the narrowest schools of Jerusalem, but the great majority learnt, even insensibly and unconsciously, the lessons of circumstance. They kept up respectful relations with the old hierarchy, but they moved in a different world. They could not sweep away the songs and philosophy of Hellas as mere " books of outsiders." [2] When once they had become familiar with the sunlight of Attic literature there could not but ensue some lifting of the heavy fogs of Rabbinic Scholasticism. They could not fail to unlearn the tenets of a narrow particularism, and to feel that—

> " All knowledge is not couched in Moses' law,
> The Pentateuch, or what the Prophets wrote.
> The Gentiles also know, and write, and teach,
> To admiration, taught by Nature's light."

It was only in virtue of this widened sympathy that the different-coloured streams of Judaism and Hellenism mingled

---

[1] Keim, *Jesu von Nazara*, i. 205.   [2] ספרים חיצונים.

I

their waters in a common lake. Alexandrian Judaism was Judaism tinged with Hellenic culture, and from Alexandrian Judaism were developed the learned schools of Alexandrian Christianity.

For it was almost exclusively in the splendid city of Alexandria that the fusion of Greek philosophy and Jewish religion took place. Egypt had been the House of Bondage for the fathers, but it became, as a Jewish historian has expressed it, a School of Wisdom for the children.[1]

The conquests of Alexander were not like those which merely disturbed for a moment the dreams of the brooding East.[2] They produced on the shores of the Mediterranean a cordial interchange of Greek and Eastern ideas.[3] By the founding of Alexandria, "the great Emathian Conqueror" left his deepest mark upon human history.[4] Its commodious harbour, its noble Pharos, its magnificent buildings, its regular structure, its healthy climate, its supply of pure water, its unrivalled position, made its market a rendezvous for the merchants of the world. The patronage of art and literature by the first Ptolemies, the magnificent encouragement of research by the Lectures and Libraries of the Serapeium, the Museum with its 400,000 volumes,[5] the free toleration accorded to Oriental theosophy, to Greek culture, to Jewish faith, made it a hotbed of intellectual excitement. In

---

[1] Grätz. Philo talks of ἡμετέρα ᾿Αλεξανδρεία. *Leg. ad Gaium*, § 22.

[2]   " The East bowed low before the blast,
            In patient, deep disdain ;
         She let the legions thunder past,
            Then plunged in thought again."
                       —MATTHEW ARNOLD.

[3] Many Greek words are transliterated in the Talmud, and it contains not a few purely Greek conceptions. See Löw, *Prakt. Einl.* 129. Many eminent Rabbis bore Greek names (Alexander, Antigonus, Trypho, Aristobulos, Euthunes, &c.). Three chests in Herod's temple were marked α, β, γ.

[4] On the civilising and cosmopolitan mission of Alexander, see Plutarch, *De Alex. Virt.* § 16 ; Oehler, *s.v. Volk. Gottes* (Herzog). On Alexandria generally, see Strabo, xvii. 1 ; Diodorus, xvii. 52 ; Pliny, *H. N.* v. 10, &c. All that is important as bearing on our subject may be seen in Hausrath, *Neut. Zeitg. Die Zeit d. Apostel*, i. 124, *sq.*

[5] For an amusing sketch of Alexandrian lecture-rooms, see Philo, *De Cong. Erud. Grat.* § 13 ; Dähne, i. 9.

Alexandria the people of Moses met the pupils of Aristotle and the followers of Zoroaster. The city became the common cradle of Poets and Geometricians, of Critics and Atheists, of Philonians and Neoplatonists, of Gnostics and of the scholars of Origen.[1]

To the Jews the city offered special attractions. Eight thousand of them had been settled in the Thebais by Alexander the Great.[2] The wise policy of the House of Lagos had given them a free citizenship and had protected them in their growing prosperity from the suspicion, rivalry, and hatred which it seems to be the destiny of the Jewish race to excite in all the peoples among whom they settle.[3] Before the Christian era they had increased to a million souls. They occupied two of the five districts of Alexandria,[4] and almost as a matter of course, they had absorbed the chief share in the traffic of the city. They had especially secured the pecuniary monopoly of the corn-ships which carried the harvests of Egypt to the granaries of Rome.[5] Their Alabarch became a person of great distinction,[6] and their Sanhedrin sat in an unequalled Synagogue " on golden seats frequent and full." [7]

---

[1] See the remarkable letter of the Emperor Adrian to Severianus, in which he says (with great exaggeration) that the Christians and the worshippers of Serapis were hardly to be distinguished from each other, and that alike these and the Jews were all *mathematici.* See too Matter, *Hist. de l'École d'Alex.* 15-23, and *passim ;* M. J. Denis, *La Philos. de Orig.* p. 2.

[2] B.C. 332 ; Jos. *C. Ap.* ii. 4 ; *B. J.* ii. 16, § 4 ; 18, § 7 ; Philo, *C. Flacc. passim ;* Herzfeld, iii. 436, *sq.* ; Grätz, iii. 256, *sq.* ; Jost, i. 351 *sq.* ; Ewald, iv. 308, *sq.* ; vi. 233, *sq.* Was this settlement of the nature of a "deportation" ? If so, it was very humanely carried out (Strabo, *ap.* Jos. *Antt.* xiv. 7, § 2).

[3] Jos. *Antt.* xii. 1. According to the highly exaggerated statement of Pseudo-Aristeas, Ptolemy Philadelphus (B.C. 285) released more than 100,000 Jewish slaves. It is certain that after the Battle of Ipsus (B.C. 301) thousands of Jews settled in Alexandria (Jos. *C. Apion,* i. 22), and Josephus said of Onias and Dositheus that Philometor intrusted to the Jews τὴν βασιλείαν ὅλην. *C. Ap.* iv. 5.

[4] Philo, *in Flacc.* § 8. [5] Philo. *in Flacc.* § 6.

[6] Jos. *Antt.* xiv. 4, §§ 1-4 ; vii. 2. On the ill-understood title, see Gesenius, *s.v.* in Ersch and Gruber, and Forcellini, *s.v.* Arabarches.

[7] Grätz, iii. 20. Of the Temple of Onias not much can be said. It never possessed any great importance. Kuenen, iii. 183. " Whoever has not seen the Great Synagogue of Alexandria has not seen the glory of Israel. Each of the seventy-one chairs was worth no less than twenty-one myriad talents of gold ! A flag had to be waved to show the people when to say Amen ! " Sukkah, f. 51, 2.

II. It was natural that this vast body of cultivated and prosperous Jews, who were equally ignorant of the Hebrew in which the Scripture lessons were read, and of the Aramaic into which they were translated by the Meturgemans of Palestine, should desire to possess their sacred books in the Greek language, which alone they understood. It is true that there was a strong feeling against the translation of the Law into an unhallowed tongue, and the strength of this feeling is shown even in the letter of the Pseudo-Aristeas. He makes Demetrius Phalereus tell Ptolemy that Theopompus had been smitten with madness for thirty days for introducing into his history some facts derived from an older translation of the Pentateuch ; and that the tragedian Theodektes had been struck blind for expressing Jewish truths in a Greek drama. But arbitrary religious convictions always give way to human convenience and necessity. Common sense prevailed over theological prejudice, and the Version for which the Rabbis kept an annual fast became the richest blessing of their fellow-countrymen throughout the world.

This is not the place to enter into the history of the Septuagint version. It is, however, certain that, whether it originated in the daily needs of worship among the Alexandrian Jews or was produced in obedience to the request of the Ptolemies who wished to add it to the treasures of their great Library, that famous translation became "the first Apostle of the Gentiles."[2] As regards Judaism, it kept millions in the faith of their fathers, so that they neither became Macedonians in Philippi nor Spaniards in Gades.[3] As regards Christianity, it exercised a powerful influence over the language, and therefore also inevitably over the thoughts, of the Apostles and the Evangelists.[4] Further than this its

---

[1] As regards the LXX. the Talmud is self-contradictory.   See Wogue, p. 136.

[2] See Philo, *Vit. Mos.* ii. § 7.

[3] Hausrath, *l.c.* p. 129.

[4] On the Septuagint, see Clem. *Strom.* 1, 9, § 45 ; Euseb. *Praep. Ev.* ix. 6, xiii. 12 ; Aristeae *Historia LXXII.* ; *Interpr.;* Philo, *Vit. Mos.* ii. §§ 5-8. Jos. *Antt. Prol.* § 3, xii. 2 ; *C. Ap.* ii. 4 ; Hody, *De Bibl. Text. Orientalibus,* Oxf. 1705; Frankel, *Vorstudien* ; Grätz, iii. 26-45, 429-446.   Herzfeld, *Gesch. d. Volkes Israels,* ii. 534-556 ; Dähne, *Religionsphil.* ii. 1-72 ; Stanley, *Jewish Church,*

effects upon the exegesis of Christendom can hardly be exaggerated. The universal acceptance of the fables about its origin narrated in the forged Epistle of Aristeas, the supernatural touches which from time to time were added to those fables by Philo and Josephus,[1] the credulity with which Justin Martyr, followed by many of the Fathers, accepted the inventions of the Alexandrian guides about the seventy cells,[2] all tended to deepen the disastrous superstition as to a mechanical and verbal dictation of the sacred books. The Greek version is quoted to a very large extent by the writers of the New Testament, even in passages where it diverges widely from the original,[3] and it furnished them with not a few of the technical terms of Christian Theology. It was partly on this account that the belief in its inspiration, asserted by Philo[4] and by the forged letter of Aristeas, was eagerly adopted by Irenaeus, Clemens of Alexandria, Epiphanius and Augustine, and opposed in vain by the better sense and more critical knowledge of Jerome.[5]

It is impossible that a translation should convey to any reader the exact sense of the original. Even where glaring errors are avoided, where the version is faithful, where the influence of religious or other bias is resisted, so great is the difference between the shades of thought conveyed by words in different languages, that even the Son of Sirach in translating the work of his grandfather had been forced to

iii. 255–262. The chief Talmudic passage about the LXX. is the curious one Megilla, f. 9, 1. For the bearing of the word γαῖσος (Josh. viii. 18) on the date see Hody, *De Bibl. Text;* Wogue, *Hist. de la Bible*, pp. 136–143 *ubi supra.*

[1] Jos. *Antt.* xii. 2, §§ 2–14 ; Philo, *Vit. Mos.* ii. § 7.

[2] Just. Mart. *Apol.* 13 ; Ambros. *in Ps.* 43. No. 74. See Klausen, *Augustinus,* pp. 74–79. The name Septuagint may, as Hitzig thinks (*Gesch. Volkes Isr.* 341), be due to the sanction of the version by the Alexandrian Sanhedrin. The date of its earlier portions is about B.C. 270–250. The work of some fifteen hands at least may be recognised in it, and the different translators were differently endowed.

[3] Out of 275 passages quoted from the O. T. in the New, there are 37 in which the LXX. differs materially from the Hebrew.

[4] Philo, *Vit. Mos.* ii. 6, 7, where he mentions the annual festival (ἑορτὴ καὶ πανήγυρις) in honour of the event in the island of Pharos.

[5] Iren. *Haer.* iii. 25 ; Clem. Alex. *Strom.* 1, 9, § 43; Epiphan. *De Pond.* iii. 6, 9–11 ; Aug. *De Doctr. Christ.* ii. 15 ; *De Civ. Dei,* xviii. 42 ; Jer. *Praef. in Pent.* "Nescio quis primus auctor cellulas Alexandriae mendacio suo exstruxerit." Cf. *Praef. in Paralip.*

remark that "the same things uttered in Hebrew and translated in another tongue have not the same force in them;[1]
and not only these things, but the Law itself, and the
prophets, and the rest of the books, have no small difference
when they are spoken in their own language."[2] St. Jerome,
for instance, had not been guilty of any intentional unfaith-
fulness in rendering μετανοεῖτε by "*poenitentiam agite*," but
those words, from the special connotation which they had
long received, conveyed to the minds of Luther and of his
contemporaries no other sense than the totally different
one " do penance." It came like a revelation to Luther's
mind when he found that the original word meant "*repent*,"
and this was one of the influences which led him to offer to
his native country the translation of Scripture which has
formed her language.

The Jews early learnt to dislike the Septuagint. The
Christians used it in their Messianic controversies, and even
accused the Jews—quite groundlessly—of having falsified
the original in passages which bore on Christian controversy. The Jews could easily justify themselves against
such a charge,[3] but their most orthodox Rabbis soon began
to declare that the translation of the sacred Law was a crime
and a misfortune as bad for Israel as the day on which the
golden calf was made.[4] Since the disaster was no longer
reparable, they entrenched themselves, on the one hand in
methods of interpretation which professed to preserve for
their own possession the true sense of Scripture, and, on the
other, threw the whole weight of their preference into the
scale of the versions of Aquila[5] and of the Judaising heretics,

---

[1] οὐ γὰρ ἰσοδυναμεῖ αὐτά.

[2] Prol. to Ecclus. οὐ μικρὰν ἔχει τὴν διαφοράν. Jesus Ben Sirach came to
Egypt in B.C. 132.

[3] The rendering ὤρυξαν, in Ps. xxi. 16 (Aquila, ᾔσχυναν), and the non-
acceptance of the Jewish reading *Kaarî*, "like a lion," is one striking disproof
of the charge.

[4] Sopherim, i. 7 ; Grätz, iii. 429 ; Zunz, *Gottesd. Vort.* 95.

[5] φιλοτιμότερον πεπιστευμένος παρὰ Ἰουδαίους ἡρμηνευκέναι τὴν γραφήν,
Orig. *Ep. ad African.* Aquilae secunda editio quam Hebraei κατ' ἀκρίβειαν
nominant, Jer. *ad Ezech.* c. 3. If the current of the times had not run too
strongly against them, Aqiba and other Rabbis would have refused the use of
any translation.

Theodotion and Symmachus. Aqiba, indeed, tried in vain
to forbid the use of *any* translation, and merely acquiesced in
the one which was most opposed to the Christians. His
pupil, Aquila, was so slavishly literal that, following the
exegesis of his teacher, he even rendered the case sign *eth*
by σύν.[1] His version was vaunted as the sole accurate
rendering of Holy Writ. All three translators are charged
with using their undoubted knowledge of Hebrew [2] to establish anti-Christian interpretations.[3] The Rabbis, however,
finally won their way still more completely. Since the days
of Justinian the Scriptures have been exclusively read in
Hebrew in their public worship, and the only version permitted
for private use is the Chaldee of Onqelos.

The Seventy had not realised that necessity for absolute
faithfulness which we now regard as the first duty of every
translator. Excellent as their version is, as a whole, it is in
many details faulty, and it is full of intentional as well as of
unintentional departures from the meaning of the original.
The Son of Sirach had observed that the culture of the Jews
in Alexandria differed in no small degree [4] from that of their
Palestinian brethren. This difference showed itself in many
ways. The Seventy do not scruple to prefer the current view
of their day to the literal and natural sense.[5] They show
repeated traces of the influence both of Jewish casuistry [6]

---

[1] *E.g.* in Gen. i. 1. Aquila has Ἐν κεφαλαίῳ ἔκποει ὁ θεὸς σὺν τὸν οὐρανὸν
καὶ σὺν τὴν γῆν. Origen naturally speaks of him as δουλεύων τῇ Ἑβραϊκῇ
λέξει (*Ad African.* § 2). So in India the Koran was regarded as too good
to be translated, and now the interlinear versions in Persian and Urdoo are
too literal to be intelligible. Muir, *The Corán*, p. 48.

[2] Ἑβραϊκὴν δὲ διάλεκτον ἀκριβῶς εἰσιν ἠσκημένοι, Epiphan. *Haer.* xxix. 7.

[3] "Qui scripturam nunc audent μεθερμηνεύειν, perperam interpretari."
Iren. *Haer.* iii. 24 ; Epiphan. *De Pond.* c. 13 ; Euseb. *H.E.* V. § 1. "Judaeus
et judaizantes haeretici qui multa mysteria salvatoris subdola interpretatione
celarunt ; " Jer. *Praef. in Job.* Aquila's translation, as a counterpoise to the
Septuagint, was so highly valued that R. Eliezer ben Hyrkanos applied to
him Ps. xlv. 2.

[4] εὗρον οὐ μικρᾶς παιδείας ἀφόμοιον, Prol.

[5] Cellarius, *De Septuag. Interpp.* § 20 ; *ap.* Hävernick, *Einleit.* § 70.

[6] Jewish casuistry ; the Halakha, Lev. xix. 19, τὸν ἀμπελῶνά σου ; xxiv. 7,
Frankincense *and salt;* Gen. ix. 4, κρέας ἐν αἵματι ψυχῆς ; xxxii. 32, οὐ μὴ
φάγωσι ; Deut. xxvi. 12, τὸ δεύτερον ἐπιδέκατον, &c. Herzfeld disputes many
of the references which Frankel regards as Halakhic (*Gesch. d. V. Isr.* ii.
542 fg.).

and Jewish legend.[1] They feel so philosophical a re-
pugnance to the simple anthropomorphism of the sacred
writers, that in the earlier books—before the age in which
such expressions no longer shocked a refined culture because
they were explained away by allegory—they deliberately
soften or alter the phrases of the original.[2] They occasionally suggest a parallel between Jewish and Pagan
ordinances with a spirit of tolerance which must have been
highly distasteful to the stricter Rabbis. Thus, when they
render Urim and Thummim by " Manifestation and Truth,"
they indicate a resemblance between the " Twelve Gems"
of Aaron's breast and the sapphire ornament called Thmei,
or " Truth," which was worn by the Egyptian priests.[3]
They introduce their Angelology where it has no sanction in
the existing text.[4] They call the Nethinim by the title
Hierodouloi.[5] They indulge freely in Egyptian technicalities.[6]
They do not abstain from many alterations—historical,
aesthetic, and even doctrinal—of which some are not a little
arbitrary. The Talmud, before the days when the Septuagint
had become entirely odious to the Jews, seems in one passage
to admit its inspiration, and yet at the same time confesses

---

[1] The Haggada, or Jewish legendary lore. Deut. xxxii. 8, guardian angels
of nations ; Josh. xxiv. 30, flint circumcision-knives buried in Joshua's grave ;
Ex. xiii. 18, "five abreast ; " Gen. iv. 4, Abel's sacrifice kindled by fire ; Josh.
xiii. 22, Balaam dashed down by Phinehas ; 1 Sam. xx. 30, Jonathan's mother
one of the maidens seized at Shiloh ; Numbers xxxii. 12, Caleb a Gentile by
birth. Many Haggadoth are introduced in the Book of Samuel.
[2] Ex. xxiv. 10, " They saw *the place where God stood. . . Of the Elders of
Israel not even one perished* (διεφώνησεν), and *they were seen in the place of God,*"
a singularly daring falsification. See Ex. iv. 16, 24, v. 3 ; Num. xii. 8 ;
xiv. 14 ; Job xix. 26, 27 ; xxxv. 14 ; Ps. xvii. 15 ; Is. xxxviii. 11. For a
fuller account of these passages see *Early Days of Christianity,* i. 261, fg.
Similar changes are found in the Targums. See Geiger, *Urschrift,* 318, fg.
Frankel, *Vorstudien, passim.* Siegfried, *Philo.* 18 ; Maqom, τόπος, "place,"
was a sort of recognised euphemism for God. Referring to Ps. xc. 1 ; xxxiii. 27,
Rabbi Isaac says that God is not in the Universe (Maqom), but the Universe is
in God. *Beresh. Rabba,* § 68 : Αὐτὸς ὁ Θεὸς καλεῖται τόπος. Philo, *De Somn.*
i. 575 ; Aboth, ii. 17 ; iii. 5, 6.
[3] Δήλωσις καὶ 'Αλήθεια. Aelian, *Var. Hist.* xiv. 34 : καὶ ἐκαλεῖτο τὸ ἄγαλμα
'Αλήθεια. Philo, *Vit. Mos.* iii. 11 ; Hengstenberg, *Egypt and the Five Books
of Moses,* c. vi.
[4] Deut. xxxii. 8 ; xxxiii. 2.
[5] 3 Esdr. viii. 5, &c.
[6] Such as ἀρτάβη, Is. v. 10 (Herod. i. 192) ; ἴβις, Lev. xii. 17 ; σχοῖνος, Jer.
xviii. 15 ; Orig. *ad loc.* and Herod. ii. 6 ; παστοφορεῖον, 1 Chron. ix. 26 ;
ψονθομφανήχ, Gen. xli. 45. See Hody, *De Bibl. Text.* p. 114.

that this inspiration led the " seventy-two elders " to make
thirteen deliberate changes. The passage is as blundering as
usual, and perhaps really applies to the version of Aquila or
to a copy of the Hebrew Scriptures in Greek letters, for the
changes alluded to do not exist in any text of the Septuagint.[1]
Five, however, of the alterations mentioned are *akin to*,
though not identical with, changes which the Greek translators actually made. Thus they seem to have been a little
shy of the word " ass." They make Moses put his wife and
children " upon the beasts of burden," [2] and instead of " I have
not taken one ass from them," they read " an object of desire." [3]
They translated " hare " by " shaggy-foot " ($\delta\alpha\sigma\acute{u}\pi o\nu s$) not by
$\lambda\alpha\gamma\acute{\omega}s$, and this is supposed to have been a delicate attention to
the House of Lagos, lest they should find the name of their
family among the unclean beasts.[4] More remarkable was the
interpolation of the word "*not*" to remove the apparent mistake of classing the hare among ruminants.[5] In Ex. xii. 40,
the words " and in the land of Canaan" seem to have been
inserted to get rid of a chronological difficulty. It is a far
more serious matter that in the very second verse of Genesis
the translators have rendered " *without form* " by " *unseen*,"
and have thus introduced the Platonic conception of a
distinction between the material ($\alpha i\sigma\theta\eta\tau\acute{o}s$) and the ideal
world ($\kappa\acute{o}\sigma\mu o s$ $\nu o\eta\tau\acute{o}s$) ; [6] and that in Is. ix. 6, in accord-

---

[1] Megilla, f. 9, i. On the traces of Alexandrian philosophy in the Septuagint,
see Dähne, ii. 1–72, who, however, makes the case appear much stronger than
it really is.
[2] Ex. ix. 20 : $\epsilon\pi\grave{\iota}$ $\tau\grave{\alpha}$ $\acute{\upsilon}\pi o\zeta\acute{\upsilon}\gamma\iota\alpha$.
[3] Num. xvi. 15 : $\epsilon\pi\iota\theta\acute{\upsilon}\mu\eta\mu\alpha$. In this passage they may have read חמד for
חמור. But we find the same tendency in Zech. ix. 9, where they use $\pi\hat{\omega}\lambda o s$;
this euphemism was suggested by the absurd rumours afloat among Gen-
tiles about the Jews as ass-worshippers ; as well as by the desire to escape the
ridicule of nations who were not aware that the ass is not in the East a
despised animal. Jos. *C. Apion.* ii. 10 ; Tac. *Hist.* v. 3. Comp. Minuc. Fel.
Oct. 9 ; Tert. *Apol.* 16, and the note in *Life of Christ*, ii. 197. So Josephus
substitutes $\kappa\tau\hat{\eta}\nu o s$ and $\emph{i}\pi\pi o s$ for "ass."
[4] Lev. xi. 6; Deut. xiv. 7. Cobet doubts this, and points out that Lagos
means not "hare," but "leader of the people," and that $\delta\alpha\sigma\acute{\upsilon}\pi o\nu s$ is a common
name for the hare. There must be some strange blunder in Megilla (f. 9, 1),
where it is said that they rendered *Arneveth*, "hare," by "short-footed,"
because *Arneveth* was the name of Ptolemy's mother. Arneveth bears no resemblance to Berenice, and she was Ptolemy's wife. Aquila uses $\lambda\alpha\gamma\acute{\omega}s$.
[5] See Stanley, *Jew. Ch.* iii. 261.
[6] $\grave{\alpha}\acute{o}\rho\alpha\tau o s$ $\kappa\alpha\grave{\iota}$ $\grave{\alpha}\kappa\alpha\tau\alpha\sigma\kappa\epsilon\acute{\upsilon}\alpha\sigma\tau o s$. See Philo, *De Opif. Mund.* § 10. Aquila

ance with the Alexandrian theosophy, they substitute " an Angel of mighty counsel " for " the mighty God."

The version of the Seventy must therefore be regarded not only as a translation, but as a corrected edition (διόρθωσις), almost as a running commentary, which freely manipulates the text in accordance with the exegetical traditions of the day.[1] The translators never scruple to introduce their favourite euphemisms,[2] or to indulge in their national susceptibilities.[3] They cannot be regarded as faithful or accurate, still less as inspired interpreters. Their intentional variations may be counted by scores, and their unintentional errors by hundreds ; and alike their errors and their variations were in a multitude of instances accepted by Christian interpreters as the infallible word of God.

The immense effect produced by this translation is shown by the comments of Philo and of the Fathers on mistakes of the Seventy which they accept as "inspired," but which sometimes completely misrepresent the meaning of the original. A few instances may suffice to illustrate this fatal magic and sorcery of mere words.

In Is. lx. 17 the Seventy render " I will give thy rulers in peace, and thine overseers in righteousness."[4] St. Clement of Rome, quoting from memory, gives the words Ἐπισκόπους and Διακόνους in this passage, and applies it as an ancient prophecy about the appointment of Bishops and Deacons.[5] Irenaeus also makes it a prophecy concerning Presbyters.[6]

rendered it κένωμα καὶ οὐθέν ; Symmachus, ἀργὸν καὶ ἀδιάκριτον ; Theodotion, κενὸν καὶ οὐθέν.

[1] Jerome, among other disparaging remarks, says, "Septuaginta quod nesciebant dubiis protulere sententiis," and "conjicio noluisse tunc temporis Septuaginta interpretes fidei suae sacramenta Ethnicis prodere " (*in Rufinum,* ii.). In Ep. 134, after a careful examination of the Psalter in the Septuagint he says, " Longum est revolvere quanta Septuaginta de suo addiderint, quanta dimiserunt quae in exemplaribus ecclesiae obelis asteriscisque distincta sint."

[2] Nah. iii. 5, τὰ ὀπίσω σου. Is. iii. 17, τὸ σχῆμα αὐτῶν. Job xxxi. 10, ταπεινωθείη, &c. 1 Sam. xxiv. 3, παρασκευάσασθαι. 1 Sam. xvi. 23 ; xix. 9, omission of Elohim and Jehovah.

[3] Ex. ii. 1, τῶν θυγατέρων Λευΐ (comp. Lev. xviii. 2) ; iv. 6, ὡσεὶ χιών ("leprous" omitted) ; vi. 12, ἄλογος (of uncircumcised lips) ; vi. 15, ὁ ἐκ τῆς Φοινίσσης, vi. 30 ; ἰσχνοφωνός ; 1 Sam. xv. 12, ἐπέστρεψε τὸ ἅρμα ; 1 Sam. i. 14, παιδάριον. They omit Ex. xxxii. 9.

[4] LXX, δώσω τοὺς ἄρχοντάς σου ἐν εἰρήνῃ καὶ τοὺς ἐπισκόπους σου ἐν δικαιοσύνῃ.

[5] Clem. Rom. *Ep. ad Cor.* § 42. [6] Iren. *Haer.* iv. 44.

Jerome does indeed alter the translation,[1] but in his usual timid and vacillating way talks of the admirable majesty of Holy Scripture in giving the name of " Bishops" to the future rulers of the Church![2]

In Jer. xi. 19, "Let us destroy the tree with the fruit thereof," the Seventy curiously read, " Let us cast the wood into his bread."[3] This was interpreted by the Fathers to mean, " Let us cast the Cross into the body of Christ," and Jerome says that this application is given by the consent of all the Church. Justin Martyr,[4] Tertullian,[5] Cyprian,[6] Lactantius,[7] even Origen[8] and Theodoret[9] all follow this impossible rendering and fanciful misapplication.

Again, in Jer. xvii. 9, "The heart is . . . desperately wicked; who can know it," the Seventy for *"anush,"* inscrutable," read *enosh,* "man"—*Homo est, quis cognoscet ipsum?*[10] It was nothing more than a mistake, yet the Fathers inferred from it the unknowable divine nature of Christ, and that He was both God and man.[11] In this instance, also, the better knowledge of Jerome pointed out that the argument was " *bono quidem voto sed non secundum scientiam.*"

A favourite quotation of the Fathers was " He reigned *from the wood*" which they applied to Christ. The words "from, the wood" are an addition found in some MSS. of the Seventy in Ps. xcvi. 10; and from the old Latin version the reading found its way into the pages of Tertullian.

In Hab. ii. 11, the Seventy render the word " *beam*" by the curious word κάνθαρος.[12] Some critics have altered the reading into κάνθον, κάναβον, κανθήριον, &c., but probably it merely

---

[1] Vulg., Ponam *visitationem tuam* pacem, et *praepositos tuos* justitiam.
[2] Jer. *ad loc.*
[3] Septuag., ἐμβάλωμεν ξύλον εἰς τὸν ἄρτον. v.l. τράχηλον. Vulg., *Mittamus lignum in panem ejus.*
[4] *Dial.* p. 298.
[5] *C. Jud.* 10 ; *C. Marc.* iii. 19.
[6] *Test. adv. Jud.* ii. 15.
[7] *Instt.* iv. 19.
[8] *Hom.* x. *in Jer.*
[9] Theodoret, *ad loc.*
[10] Jer. xvii. 9, βαθεῖα ἡ καρδία παρὰ πάντα καὶ ἄνθρωπός ἐστι (Vulg. *inscrutabile*) καὶ τίς γνώσεται αὐτόν ;
[11] Iren. *Haer.* iii. 20 ; iv. 66. Tert. *C. Jud.* 10. Cyprian *Test.* ii. 10. Lactant. *Instt.* iv. 13. Aug. *C. Faustum,* xiii. 8.
[12] Hab. ii. 11, καὶ κάνθαρος ἐκ ξύλου φθέγξεται αὐτά.

means a knot in the wood.[1] Some Latin versions rendered
it "*scarabaeus*," beetle, and this led to some singular comments.   Thus St. Ambrose (*De Obitu Theodosii*) speaks of
"Him who, *like a beetle*, called to his persecutors," and says
"He was the good beetle who called from the wood."[2]

Again, in Hab. iii. 2, the Seventy had "And thou shalt be
recognised in the midst of two animals," for "Thou shalt
revive thy work in the midst of the years."   This error led
to the most untenable inferences.[3]   In the two ζῶα Origen
sees the Son and the Spirit; Tertullian sees Moses and Elias;
other interpretations were Angels and men, Cherubim and
Seraphim, Jews and Babylonians, the Two Thieves, the Two
Testaments.   Augustine imagines an allusion to the ox and
the ass in the manger, and his view has exercised a deep
influence over the pictures of the Nativity in Christian Art.
The exegesis of the passage furnishes a good specimen of
fancy, working without restraint and without any guiding
principle on the material of pure mistake.[4]

The misinterpretation of a Greek word in Ps. xcii. 12,
"The righteous shall flourish as a palm-tree," led the Fathers
into an unfortunate argument.   They mistook the word
φοῖνιξ, "a palm-tree," to mean a Phoenix, and accepting all
the ancient fables about the Indian bird, they quote the
verse as a proof of the Resurrection and the Virgin-birth
of Christ.[5]

From Nah. i. 9, which the Seventy render "Thou wilt not
punish twice for it,"[6] the Fathers, and even St. Jerome, confidently maintain that the people of the cities of the plain,
and those drowned in the Deluge, will be saved hereafter;
and the Apostolical Canons laid down the rule that when a
priest had been punished for a grave crime (even, says the

---

[1] Vulg., *Lignum quod inter junctivas aedificiorum est* (tie-beam).
[2] On Luke xxiii.   We find elsewhere "*bonus scarabaeus*" applied to our
Lord.
[3] Irenaeus (*Haer.* iii. 10).   Eusebius (*Dem. Ev.* vi. 15) and Theodoret
read ζωῶν for ζώων, and interpreted it "two *lives*."
[4] Tert. *C. Marc.* iv. 22, &c.   See Whitby, *De S. Script. Interpret.* p. 137.
[5] See the passages quoted by Whitby, *l.c.* p. 85.
[6] Nah. i. 9, οὐκ ἐκδικήσεις δὶς εἰς αὐτό.   Cod. Al. οὐκ ἐκδικήσει δὶς ἐπὶ τὸ
αὐτό. Vulg., Non consurget duplex tribulatio.

Canon of [?] Basil, for a crime unto death), he was to be de-
posed but not excommunicated, " *non enim vindicabis bis in
id ipsum.*" Why the benefit of the verse was only extended
to priests does not appear.

St. Augustine, as is well known, being ignorant of Hebrew,
and finding in the Septuagint his nearest approach to the
original, had an exaggerated opinion of the sacredness of the
Greek version.[1] He seems to have doubted whether even
the errors were not of divine origin, and when in Jon. iii. 4
the Seventy read " Yet *three* days and Nineveh shall be destroyed,"[2] he argues as if the "three" were prophetically
significant of the time between the Death and the Resurrection of our Lord.[3]

We are surprised to find similar notions prevalent even in
the school of Antioch. Yet no less a commentator than
Theodore of Mopsuetia relies almost exclusively upon the
Septuagint, and not only does not consult the Hebrew, but
even fails to make use of the Syriac version, which would
have often thrown light upon the difficulties of the Greek.
It is astonishing that he should accept the unhappy rendering
" Amalthaea's horn " as an equivalent of Qeren Happuk,[4]
and argue from the allusion to Greek mythology that the
Book of Job was written by a heathen !

But while the Septuagint exercised so strong an influence,
and repeatedly betrays its Alexandrian origin,[5] it does not

---

[1] *De Doctr. Christ.* ii. 15 ; *Ep.* 28, c. 2 ; *Qu. in Gen.* 169 ; *De Civ. Dei*,
xviii. 42. Epiphanius regarded the Seventy translators as prophets *De mens.
et pond.* Justinian ordered the Jews to use the Septuagint προφητικῆς
ὥσπερ χάριτος περιλαμψάσης αὐτούς (*Novel. Diatax.* 146).

[2] LXX. ἔτι τρεῖς ἡμέραι, κ.τ.λ.

[3] *De Cons. Ev.* ii. 66 ; *De Doctr. Christ.* iv. 15. See Trench, *Sermon on
the Mount,* p. 18.

[4] " Horn of Stibium." Job xlii. 14. LXX., Ἀμαλθείας κέρας, Vulg.,
Cornu Stibii.

[5] The following instances are adduced by Franck, Frankel, Dähne, &c. :
Gen. i. 2, ἡ δὲ γῆ ἦν ἀόρατος : Gen. ii. 4, 5, ἐποίησε . . . πᾶν χλωρὸν ἀγροῦ πρὸ
τοῦ γενέσθαι ἐπὶ τῆς γῆς : Is. xl. 26, τίς κατέδειξε ταῦτα : Is. xlv. 18, ὁ καταδείξας
τὴν γῆν. These are supposed to bear on the Platonic idealism and the creation
of an ideal before the real world. Is. xl. 26, ἐκφέρων κατ᾽ ἀριθμὸν τὸν κόσμον
αὐτοῦ (Pythagorean notion of numbers) ; Is. xlii. 13, ὁ θεὸς τῶν δυνάμεων
(the *logoi* or intermediate potencies of Philo) ; Ps. cx. 3, πρὸ Ἑωσφόρου
ἐγέννησά σε (a Pre-existent Logos) ; Is. ix. 5, μεγάλης βουλῆς ἄγγελος (the
Logos), &c. Their views are combated by Herzfeld, *Gesch. des Volkes Israel*,
ii. 411-414.

show any symptoms of that which was the special tendency of Alexandrian exegesis, namely, the method of allegory. Its references to ritual and to legend, and its avoidance of anthropomorphism, are Palestinian no less than Hellenistic,[1] and too great stress has been laid on the supposed traces of conceptions derived from Greek philosophy. Greek influences produced far more decisive effects on the Book of Wisdom. In that book, side by side with traditions of the utmost extravagance, we have a direct incorporation of views borrowed from Plato and the Stoics. The unknown author who took the name of Solomon derives from Plato his doctrine of ideas, from the Stoics their systems of ethics. From Plato he had learnt the Immortality and prae-existence of souls;[2] the coeval existence of formless matter;[3] and the view that the body is the seat of all sin.[4] From the Stoics he had learnt about the Four Cardinal Virtues and the Intelligential Spirit which pervades the world.[5] The most remarkable instance of allegory in this book is the allusion to the High Priest's robes as an image of the whole world.[6]

In the semi-ethnic Jewish writings of this epoch we have another indication of the widespread desire on the part of cultivated Jews to share in the glories of Greek literature. The poet Ezekiel, who dramatised the Exodus, the elder Philo, who wrote an epic on Jerusalem, Theodotus, who related in verse the story of Dinah and Shechem, were all engaged in the then impossible attempt " to unite the *pallium* of Japheth with the *tallîth* of Shem."

Jason of Cyrene wrote in five books the story of the Syrian war, which is utilised in the Third and Fourth Books of the Maccabees. Apocryphal stories like "Bel and the Dragon" and the "Story of Susanna," as well as the legendary additions to Ezra, Esther, and other canonical books, show

---

[1] Dr. Deutsch has furnished many decisive proofs of this (*Lit. Remains,* pp. 348-356). Josephus was largely influenced by Philo, and occasionally refers to allegoric explanations. *Antt.* iii. 7. § 7. &c. See *Dict. of Christian Biogr.* ii. 452-458.

[2] Wisd. viii. 19.   [3] *Id.* xi. 17.

[4] *Id.* i. 4 ; viii. 20.   [5] *Id.* vii. 22-24.

[6] *Id.* xviii. 24.

that the Jews had felt the charm of Greek romance, and
desired that something which resembled it should exist among
themselves. But this whole style of literature was thoroughly
exotic. It has for the most part perished like a flower which
has no roots. The pseudepigraphy which was the favourite
literary form of these productions, and which led the writers
to borrow, on the one hand the names of Enoch, Solomon,
Jeremiah, and Baruch, and on the other to secure attention
for their thoughts under the name of Sibylline oracles or of
fragments from Orpheus and Linus, Homer and Hesiod,
Heraclitus and Xenophanes, indicated the artificial character
of the age. One Jewish poet succeeded in palming off his
versification of the Old Testament morality under the name
of the Ionian poet Phocylides. A literature which breathes
the very atmosphere of forgery and fiction is essentially a dead
literature. These Hellenists moved in an unwholesome atmosphere of exaggeration, unreality, and pious frauds, and
they naturally wrote " Musis et Apolline nullo." They were
trying to put old wine into fresh wine-skins, and to trans-
pose into Hellenic forms the wholly alien elements of Semitic
history. Josephus constantly shows the same desire. In his
suppressions and alterations he tries to throw the history
of the sacred books into a form which would most attract
the attention and least shock the prejudices of his Greek
and Roman readers. Doubtless Artapanus, Eupolemos, and
other Hellenistic historians were actuated by similar motives.
Many Greek and Egyptian writers, the priest Manetho, the
historians Agatharcides, Chaeremon, and Lysimachus, the
philosophers Apollonius Molo and Posidonius of Apamea at
different times attacked Judaism and its institutions, and
the Jews wished to defend themselves by every literary
method in their power.

III. But the most essential contribution of Alexandrian
Judaism to the history of exegesis is the allegorical method.
The first use of that method is seen in the fragments of
Aristobulus and the letter of Aristeas. It culminated in
Philo, and through Philo—mainly on the strength of a passing

instance in which it was used as an illustration by St. Paul—
it was transmitted to at least fifteen centuries of Christian
exegetes.[1]

i. Of the letter of the PSEUDO-ARISTEAS, we need say
but little. Though accepted by Josephus and Philo,[2] it
is an acknowledged forgery, teeming with deliberate fictions
and propped up with spurious documents. It had no
other object than the glorification of the Septuagint.[3] It
shows the allegorising tendency in its reference to ablutions and to the distinctions of clean and unclean animals,
but is probably of much later date than the writings of
Aristobulus.[4]

ii. ARISTOBULUS was an Alexandrian Jew and a Peripatetic
philosopher (B.C. 160) who, in 2 Macc. i. 10, is called "the
master," *i.e.* the tutor of Ptolemy Euergetes. He is the
reputed author of commentaries on the books of Moses
which were addressed to Ptolemy Philometor, and of which
fragments are preserved by Eusebius.[5] The genuineness of
these works was impugned by Hody and defended by
Valcknaer. Recently it has been impugned by Kuenen
though defended by Gfrörer.[6] In the sphere of Alexandrian

---

[1] See Müller, *Fragmenta Hist. Gr.* iii. 207–230 ; Euseb. *Praep. Evang.* ix.
17–39 ; Clem. Alex. *Strom.* i. c. 15 § 72 ; Jos. *Antt.* i. 15 ; *C. Ap.* i. 23 ; Grätz,
Gesch. d. Juden, iii. 483 ; Delitzsch, *Gesch. d. Jud. Poesie,* 211 ; Herzfeld,
iii. 517 ; Philippson, *Ezechiel und Philo.* 1836. The Palestinian Jews looked
very unfavourably on *all* authorship. Jost, *Judenth.* i. 367, 373.

[2] Jos. *Antt.* xii. 2 ; Philo *Vit. Mos.* ii. § 6, Fabric. *Bibl. Graec.* iii. 660.
Jost, *Judenth.* i. 372. Hody demonstrated the spuriousness of the letter. It
is printed in Gallandi, *Bibl. Patr.* ii. 771.

[3] The real Aristeas was an officer of Ptolemy Philadelphus.

[4] The High Priest Eleazar is made to say that the ritual of Levitism is
symbolic of higher truths ; that the eating of birds of prey is forbidden to
teach the wickedness of violence and injustice ; that animals which chew the
cud and divide the hoof are allowed for food to remind us of the duty of
thinking of God, and of the difference between right and wrong. These are
stated as additional reasons to the political and sanitary ones, and they are
followed by a special allegorical explanation of the prohibition to eat the
weasel and the mouse. Such commands were not merely given prohibitively
(ἀπαγορευτικῶς) but didactically (ἐνδεικτικῶς).

[5] See Clem. Alex. *Strom.* i. Euseb. *Praep. Ev.* vii. 13, viii. 9, ix. 6,
xiii. 12.

[6] Kuenen thinks that the real Aristobulus could never have ventured
to forge so many interpolations into the classical poems. On Aristobulus
see Valcknaer, *Diatribe de Aristobulo Judaeo,* 1806 ; Gfrörer, *Philo.* ii.
71-120.

literature we can rarely feel any certainty about such
questions. We are walking over

"Ignes
Suppositos cineri doloso."

Whether, however, we accept the fragments of Aristobulus
as genuine or not, his actual work was of very great importance for the History of Interpretation.[1] He is one of the
precursors whom Philo used though he did not name,[2] and he
is the first to enunciate two theses which were destined to find
wide acceptance, and to lead to many false conclusions in the
sphere of exegesis.

The first of these is the statement that Greek philosophy
is borrowed from the Old Testament, and especially from
the Law of Moses;[3] the other that all the tenets of the
Greek philosophers, and especially of Aristotle, are to be
found in Moses and the Prophets by those who use the right
method of inquiry.[4]

i. The first statement need not detain us long. Aristobulus
asserts that before the days of Alexander parts of the Law had
been translated into Greek, and that Plato, and even Pythagoras, to whom he afterwards adds Socrates, had largely
borrowed from them.[5] Similarly we find an attempt else-

---

[1] Eusebius (*H. E.* vii. 32) says that he wrote Βίβλους ἐξηγητικὰς τοῦ
Μωϋσέως νόμου. Fragments are preserved in Euseb. *Praep. Ev.* vii. 13, 14 ;
viii. 9, 10 ; xiii. 12, of which some are given by Clement in his *Stromateis*
(i. § 25 ; v. § 20 ; vi. § 37).

[2] *De Abrah.* ii. 15 ; *De Joseph.* ii. 63 ; *De Spec. Legg.* ii. § 2 (Mangey, ii.
329) ; *Leg. Allegg.* i. 55, and *De Decal.* 4. My references to Philo will almost
invariably be to the *sections*, which are numbered in all editions. I have chiefly
used Mangey and the Leipzig editions.

[3] See Justin Mart. *Apol.* i. 59 ; *Cohort.* 26, 30–33 ; Euseb. *Praep. Ev.* vii. 14 ;
Clem. Alex. *Strom.* i. c. 22. § 150. Ἀριστόβουλος δὲ . . . γράφει Κατηκολούθηκε
δὲ ὁ Πλάτων τῇ καθ' ἡμᾶς νομοθεσίᾳ . . . καθὼς καὶ Πυθαγόρας πολλὰ τῶν παρ'
ἡμῖν μετενέγκας εἰς τὴν ἑαυτοῦ δογματοποιίαν. Comp. *Strom.* v. c. 14. § 98 ;
Dähne, *De Clement. Alex.* γνώσει. Leips. 1831.

[4] See Clem. Alex. *Strom.* v. 20.

[5] Philo, in his dearth of the historic sense, borrows this thesis, and thinks
that Socrates and Heraclitus and Zeno either did borrow from Moses, or might
have done so. The same opinions lasted till the Middle Ages. Reuchlin
maintains the thesis in the second book of his *De Verbo Mirifico* (comp. *id.* i.
cap. 13, 14), asserting that Plato's Absolute Being (τὸ ὄντως ὄν) is borrowed
from "I am that I am," and the Tetraktys of Pythagoras from the Tetragrammaton. See Philo, *Quis rer. div. haer.* 43 ; *Quod omn. prob. liber.* 16 ; *De*

where to identify Gideon (Jerubbaal) with the priest
Hierombalos who furnished information to Sanchoniatho
the Berytian;[1] and the Prophet Ezekiel with Nazaratus
the Assyrian who is spoken of as one of the teachers of
Pythagoras.

Such statements are destitute of every particle of historical
foundation. They become doubly suspicious in the pages
of one whose national vanity has led him to the forgery of
impossible passages of Orpheus, Linus, Musaeus, and even of
Aratus, as well as to the falsification of Homer—passages
in which he makes the mythical Greek poets speak
familiarly of the history of Abraham and the legislation
of Moses. Hellenistic philosophy, like Palestinian Rabbinism,
attached boundless importance to precedent and authority;
and if such authority had no existence it was unscrupulously
invented.[2]

ii. As to the second point—the possibility of extorting
Greek philosophy out of the Pentateuch—it is maintained
partly by the modification of anthropomorphic expressions,
partly by reading new conceptions between the lines of the
ancient documents. In answer to a question of Ptolemy,
Aristobulus told him that Scripture was not to be literally
understood.[3] The "hand" of God means His might; the
"speech" of God implies only an influence on the soul of
man.[4] The "standing" of God means the organisation and
immovable stability of the world. The "coming down" of
God has nothing to do with time or space. The "fire" and
the "trumpet" of Sinai are pure metaphors corresponding to

---

provid. i. 77, 79; ii. 42, 48; *Vit. Mos.* i. 1; ii. 4; *De poster. Caini,* 39;
Quaestiones (Aucher, ii. 83, 178, 359, 373, 503); Jos. *C. Ap.* ii. 6; Franck,
Die Kabbala, pp. 8, 9.

[1] See Euseb, *Praep. Ev.* i. 10; Bochart, *Phaleg.* p. 776; Ewald, *Gesch.*
ii. 494.

[2] In quoting Homer, *Od.* v. 262, Aristobulus substituted ἕβδομον for
τέτρατον. Gratiger says outright "Judaeorum est mentiri," *Ad Chronol.
Euseb.* p. 405. On this subject of forgery see R. Simon, *Hist. crit. du V. T.* ii.
187; Dähne, i. 82; ii. 214-236. But we must not judge ancient pseudepigraphy
by the moral standard of the nineteenth century.

[3] Euseb. *Praep. Ev.* viii. 10.

[4] So too Philo. God does not speak—ἄπαγε, μήτ᾽ εἰς νοῦν ποτ᾽ ἔλθῃ τὸν
ἡμέτερον. Decal. § 9.

nothing external. The six days' creation merely implies continuous development. The seventh day indicates the cycle of hebdomads which prevails among all living things—whatever that piece of Pythagorean mysticism may chance to mean. Aristobulus, however, confined allegory within reasonable limits, and, as Dean Stanley has said, if he be held responsible for the extravagances of Philo, of Origen, or of the Schoolmen, he may also claim the glory of having led the way in the path trodden by all who have striven to discriminate between the eternal truths of Scripture and the framework, the imaginative vesture, in which those truths are set forth.[1]

IV. Here then we trace to its source one of the tiny rills of exegesis, which afterwards swelled the mighty stream of Philonian and Christian allegory. Before we notice the writings of Philo himself, it becomes a question of deep interest how this method arose. To what necessity did it owe its origin? Was it indigenous among the Jews of Alexandria, or did they derive it from other sources?

The study of history, of literature, and of comparative religion enables us to give to the first question a clear and decisive answer. Allegory arose from the deeply-felt necessity for finding some borderland for the harmonious junction of Greek philosophy with Jewish legislation. While the Rabbinic casuists were spinning cobwebs of ceremonial inferences out of the letter of the Law, allegory was used by the Hellenists for the totally different object of developing out of Moses the attenuated semblance of an alien philosophy. To the Rabbis the Pentateuch was the germ of all ritualism, to the Hellenists it was the veil of all gnosis.[2] Ezra and the Pharisees were the masters of the Rabbis; Plato and the philosophers of the Alexandrians. The Hellenists, however, were so far superior to the Rabbis that they set the spirit above the letter, and valued morality more than formalism. But both schools went widely astray. They lived in ages to which pure Mosaism, alike in its conceptions and its practices, had become impossible. The Scripture lessons—the Parashah

---

[1] *Jewish Church*, iii. 282.   [2] The LXX. use γνῶσις to render דַּעָה.

from the Law, the Haphtara from the Prophets—were read alike in the synagogues of Jerusalem and of Alexandria, but in both cities the exegesis was nothing but a travesty of the ancient documents—in Jerusalem a series of untenable inferences, in Alexandria an airy dream.

It was impossible for a cultivated Alexandrian, familiar with all the literary treasures of Greek thought, to live like a Palestinian Rabbi " within the four corners of the Halakha," or to think that life could be profitably spent in janglings over the microscopic details of an abrogated Levitism. We are not surprised to learn that the Rabbis of Jerusalem branded a man as " a genuine Alexandrian " [1] if he showed any of the independence which sprang from his superior education. A thoughtful Hellenist might indeed, like the author of the Book of Wisdom, find some outlet for the play of fancy in the fairyland of the Haggada ; but the Haggada was only applicable to questions of history and to illustrations of practical morals. It offered no answer to his deepest speculations.

Mingling daily with subtle thinkers of all schools from Egyptian priests to Greek atheists—talking one day on the mole or in the marketplace to some Eastern theosophist from the centre of Asia, and on the next to some bright Greek fresh from the Lyceum or the Academe, and trained in the encyclopaedic superficiality of that epoch [2]—no gifted Jew could remain spell-bound in the narrow self-assertion of his race. He might still retain his conviction that his own people had been exceptionally endowed with religious insight, but he could not remain ignorant of " the glory that was Greece, and the grandeur that was Rome." He could not fail to see that God had other sheep who were not of the fold of Israel, and that if He had given His law to the children of Shem, He had also endowed with infinite gifts of grace and culture, of art and science, of rule and dignity, the sons

---

[1] אלכסנדרי לאמיתי הוא. Rappoport, *Erech Millin.* p. 102, quoted by Siegfried, Philo, 6.

[2] Philo, *De Cherub.* 30 ; *De Agric.* 3, 4 ; *De Congress.* 34 ; *De Somn.* i. 35.

of Japhet. Brought into life-long contact with this brilliant
and fascinating world, how could a Jew any longer talk of
all countries except his own strip of seaboard as a mere
" without," or adopt the bigoted comment of R. Ishmael that
anything except the Mosaic Law could only be studied at an
hour which belonged neither to day nor night ? [1]

On the other hand an Alexandrian of the school of Philo
had no desire to apostatise.[2] He still felt the spiritual
superiority of Moses and the Prophets over Plato and the
philosophers. He regarded the Jews as priests of mankind,
and compared divine wisdom to Sarah the princess, and
human wisdom to Hagar the concubine.[3] He still reckoned
it among his deepest privileges that over his cradle he had,
as it were, heard the rustling of the oak of Mamre. The
Mosaic law was sacred and eternal; Greek philosophy was
inspiring, noble, irresistible. There must, he fancied, be some
middle term by which the two could be united.[4] Such a
middle term could not be found in the trivial and hairsplitting casuistry of the Palestinian schools. He felt himself
driven by an imperious necessity to show that nothing in his
ancestral faith shut him out from the charm of classical
antiquity and the splendour of philosophic truth. His object
was to defend the cause of Judaism alike against sneering
Greeks, wavering Jews, and narrow-minded Pharisees,[5] by
harmonising the dogmas of divine revelation with the
discoveries of speculative thought.[6]

A similar necessity has occurred again and again in the
religious history of mankind. It has driven the Brahmins to
provide a mystical interpretation for the Vedas. It has com-

---

[1] Menachoth, f. 99, 2 : Derenbourg, 361.
[2] Philo energetically repudiates all renegades from Judaism. He tells us
how one such "atheist" hung himself, "that the foul blasphemer might not
even end by a pure death" (*De Nom. mutat.* § 8), because he had sneered at
the splendid present of a single letter which God had made to Abraham and
Sarah.
[3] *De Abr.* 19 ; *De Congr. quaer.* 1-5.
[4] *De Migr. Abr.* § 16 ; *De Plant. Noe,* §§ 8, 17.
[5] See Neander, *Ch. Hist.* i. 72, 73 ; Herzfeld, ii. 515.
[6] "Ce qui soufflait dans Alexandrie c'était le vent de la conciliation, et s'il
y avait danger c'était moins d'être trop exclusif, que d'être tenté d'associer
ensemble des choses incompatibles." Denis, p. 7.

pelled the Sofi to find hidden senses in the Koran.[1] It furnishes us with an explanation of the fact that the Bible has met with an infinitude of varying and even opposite interpretations. Thinkers so different as Hillel and Shammai, as Aqiba and Philo, as Origen and Luther, have sought support in its pages, and maintained its unapproachable sacredness. In age after age it has been appealed to with confidence alike by Gnostics and Literalists, by Arians and Trinitarians, by Schoolmen and Reformers, by Lutherans and Zwinglians, by Calvinists and Arminians, by Catholics and Protestants, by Sacramentalists and Quakers, by Churchmen and Dissenters. It is only because of this elasticity and universality that the utterances of divine inspiration "pervade innumerable years because of God." There is in them a divine expansiveness, a many-sided significance. Men insist on harmonising them with current opinions. Now the only possible method for thus making ancient documents of felt authority express throughout their whole extent the thoughts of advancing ages is the method of finding in them a mystic sense which lies below the surface—in one word, the method of allegory. In the schools of Palestine the impulse of a patriotic particularism engrained the details of the law into the life of the people; in Alexandria by an exegetical art of turning everything into parable, the meaning of the Law was altogether volatilised in order to conceal an inward and unconscious apostasy from its menacing letter.[2]

V. The Alexandrian Jews were not, however, driven to invent this method for themselves. They found it ready to their hands. There is no more curious page in the history of exegesis than the undoubted fact—a fact recognised alike by Mangey one of the best early editors of Philo and by Siegfried the profoundest recent student of his writings—that the Apocryphal writers and Aristeas, and Aristobulus, and Philo, did but adapt to Scripture a method which had been developed by their heathen neighbours,—a method which had long been applied, and was under their own eyes being

---

[1] See Franck, *Die Kabbala*, 31.　　　[2] See Reuss, *Gesch.* § 503.

applied by contemporary thinkers to the poems of Homer.[1]
By a singular concurrence of circumstances the Homeric
studies of Pagan philosophers suggested first to Jews and
then, through them, to Christians, a method of Scriptural
interpretation before unheard of which remained unshaken
for more than fifteen hundred years.

The poems of Homer appealed so powerfully to the
Greek imagination, their felt charm and freshness was so inexhaustible, they were so rich in beautiful lessons of human
experience that they practically became to the Greeks a
sacred book. Plato was unable to harmonise Homeric crudi-
ties with philosophic convictions and therefore with daring
consistency he banished the poets from his ideal republic—
banished them with decision, though with all honourable
circumstance.[2] But in this the Stoics would not follow him.
They wished to bring their views into semblable accord with
the popular religion, and they accepted the method of
Theagenes, Metrodorus,[3] Stesimbrotus, Glaukon, and others
who had produced commentaries on Homer, and had explained away the many passages which came into collision
with the developed religious consciousness of their day. They
could claim a high and ancient authority for their views in
Anaxagoras, who, as well as Pythagoras, Democritus, and
Empedokles, is called " an allegorist."[4] Chrysippus, says
Cicero, wished to accommodate the fables of Orpheus,
Musaeus, Hesiod, and Homer to his own opinions of the
gods, and to make Stoics of the ancient poets. Diogenes
of Babylon in his book on Minerva allegorised physiologically
the story of her birth.[5] The best extant specimen of these

---

[1] Mangey in his Preface (*Philonis*, i. v.) says, "Magis interpretationem
Allegoricam invaluisse probabile est ex mythologicorum scriptorum inter
Ethnicos fama qui tunc temporis coeperant fabulas suas propudiosas et impias
mysticas umbris vel obducere vel defendere." On this subject see Lobeck,
Aglacphamus, 1829.

[2] *De Rep.* ii. *passim*. But Plato, too, allegorises Homer.

[3] See Tatian, *Or. ad Graecos*, 21 : "Metrodorus of Lampsacus, in his
treatise concerning Homer, has argued very foolishly, turning everything into
allegory."

[4] Diog. Laert. ii. 11, δοκεῖ πρῶτος τὴν Ὁμηρικὴν ποίησιν ἀποφήνασθαι περὶ
ἀρετῆς καὶ δικαιοσύνης.

[5] Cic. *De Nat. Deor.* i. 15. See Creuzer, *Symbolik*, i. ch. vi.

Stoic methods may be found in the *Homeric Allegories*, attributed to Herakleides of Pontus, a scholar of Plato. No book can prove more decisively how vapid those methods were, and how untenable were the results to which they led.[1]

Finding many lines in Homer which seemed to them unworthy, undignified, morally reprehensible, and even positively blasphemous, the Stoic Allegorists made no allowance for the differences of opinion and custom which separate earlier from later ages, but they set themselves to explain away all such passages as containing myths, and sacred enigmas, and adorable mysteries. In carrying out their object they had recourse to etymologies, to plays on words, to the juxtaposition of other passages, to physical allusions, to the symbolism of numbers, to the emphasising of separate expressions, to inordinate developments of metaphor, and interminable inferences from incidental phrases.[2] By these means there was no sort of difficulty in making Homer speak the language of Pythagoras, of Plato, of Anaxagoras, or of Zeno ; and borrowing from them the very same methods the Alexandrian Jews made the Bible express and anticipate the doctrines of the same philosophers.

But the Jews were driven to allegory by a far more imperious necessity than the Stoics, because their books were the constant butt for Gentile ridicule, and their persons for Gentile persecution.[3] And it was all the more easy for the Alexandrian Hellenists to adopt this method because, in Scripture itself, they found much importance attached to etymology and to symbolic numbers. They not only embraced the allegoric system, but they gave it an immense and wholly unwarrantable development.[4]

VI. In PHILO the Greek method is rigidly systematised and brought to its completion, though he was by no means

---

[1] The treatise of Herakleides Ponticus was printed by Heyne in his edition of the Iliad.

[2] See some excellent criticisms on this method in Cic. *De Nat. Deor.* ii. 18.

[3] Jos. *C. Ap.* i. 21 ; ii. 3, § 5 ; *B. J.* ii. 18, §§ 7, 8.

[4] It is in the fourth Book of Maccabees, erroneously ascribed to Josephus that we find the earliest meeting-point of Jewish and Greek methods.

the first Jew who adopted it.[1] He found three exegetic
schools existing among his countrymen. There were
Literalists, of whom he speaks with lofty superiority ;
Rationalists who apostatised from Judaism altogether and
whom he regards with sorrow and indignation ;[2] and
Allegorists, who had already learnt the secret how to
reconcile Judaic institutions with Hellenic culture.[3] Philo's
works are the epitome and the development of the principles
of the Allegorists.[4] To them—though not by name—he
constantly refers ; and on allegory the whole Philonian
philosophy entirely depends.[5] Eclecticism without originality
usually has a chilling influence upon belief, but by the aid
of allegory Philo was able to regard himself as a Stoic
philosopher and yet at the same time as a faithful Jew.[6]

He was very little imbued with Rabbinic culture.[7] Of the
Halakha he knew nothing. He makes little use of the
Haggada, though he was partially acquainted with it. Some
of his etymologies and a few details of his theological teach-
ing show an affinity to the Midrash. His chief culture was
Hellenic. He was deeply read in Greek literature, and

---

[1] Philo, *De Vit. Contempl.* § 3, ἔστι συγγράμματα παλαιῶν ἀνδρῶν οἱ . . .
πολλὰ μνημεῖα τῆς ἐν τοῖς ἀλληγορουμένοις ἰδέας ἀπέλιπον.

[2] *De Migr. Abrah.* § 39 ; *De Mut. Nom.* § 8.

[3] In practice, however, Philo was probably very free. He went to the
theatres of Alexandria (*De Ebriet.* § 43), and possibly even witnessed bull-fights
(*De Mut. Nom.* § 29).

[4] He expresses himself emphatically on the need of retaining Jewish institutions in *De Migr. Abr.* § 16, εἰσὶ γάρ τινες οἱ τοὺς ῥητοὺς νόμους σύμβολα
νοητῶν πραγμάτων ὑπολαμβάνοντες τὰ μὲν ἄγαν ἠκρίβωσαν τῶν δὲ ῥᾳθύμως
ὠλιγώρησαν, οὓς μεμψαίμην ἂν ἔγωγε τῆς εὐχερείας.

[5] Almost all that is personally known of Philo may be found in his *Leg. ad
Gaium*, 22–28 ; *C. Flaccum, passim ; De Spec. legg.* ii. § 1 ; *De Provid.*
(Aucher, ii. 187. Euseb. *Praep. Ev.* viii. 14 ; Mangey, ii. 646, 673) ; *De
Congr.* § 14 ; *Fragments* (Richter, vi. 200, 236) ; Jos. *Antt.* xviii. 8, § 1 ;
xx. 5, § 2 ; Euseb. *Praep. Ev.* viii. 13 ; *H. E.* ii. § 4 : and in the notices
of him by Jerome, Isidore Pelusiota, Photius (*Bibl. Cod.* cv.), and Suidas,
§ v., Φίλων. The date of his birth and death are unknown, but as he was an
old man (*i.e.* 56, see Aboth, v. 21) when he went as an ambassador to Gaius
(Caligula, A.D. 39), he may have been born B.C. 10–20. A good sketch is given
by Ewald, vii. 194 f.g., and I have collected the main facts in *Early Days of
Christianity*, i. 264-279.

[6] Euseb. *Praep. Ev.* viii. 14.

[7] He does however refer to "the tradition of the elders" *Fragm. ap.*
Euseb. *Praep. Ev.* viii. 7. See Bern. Ritter, *Philo und die Halacha*, Halle,
1879.

quotes from Homer, Hesiod, Theognis, Pindar, Solon, Aeschylus, Euripides, and Sophocles. It is an important confirmation of the source from which Jewish writers borrowed their allegorising method, that he quotes from a book otherwise so second rate as the Homeric allegories of Herakleides Ponticus.[1] He was particularly well read in the Greek philosophers and refers to " the great Plato," " the great and much-famed Heraklitus," Parmenides, Empedokles, Zeno, Kleanthes and the Pythagoreans. From the latter he borrows the symbolism of numbers, and from Aristotle the distinction between δύναμις and ἐντελέχεια.[2] If he remained a convinced and even a zealous Jew in spite of the Hellenic tendencies of his intellectual culture, it was because he believed in the strange methods which his predecessors had borrowed from the heathen. This belief enabled him to combine the mystic rationalism which he had learnt from Plato with the supernaturalism which he owed to his Jewish training. It was, however, impossible that the deep self-delusion thus induced could long continue. The " sophists of the literal sense," as Philo calls them, had good grounds for looking with suspicion on the religious philosophy which tried to turn Mosaism into a Platonic religion. Events proved that the God of Philo was but a vague abstraction, not the living God of Israel; that when the Law was explained away into vaporous commonplace it ceased to be a national power; that the history of Israel lost all its beauty and all its interest when it was turned into didactic allegory and poetic mist.[3] Philo could still visit Jerusalem and practise the precepts of the law,[4] but his powerful nephew, the Procurator Tiberius Alexander became an open apostate from the religion of his fathers.[5]

[1] *De Leg. Allegg.* i. § 33 ; *De Incorrupt. Mund.* § 61 ; see Siegfried, p. 138.
[2] *Quod Omn. prob. lib.* § 1 ; *De Incorrupt. Mundi*, § 3 ; *Quaest.* § 16 ; *De mund. opif.* § 4 ; *Leg. Allegg.* 1, 64 ; *De Nom. Mutat.* § 35.   See the quotations referred to in Siegfried, *Philo*, 138–140 ; Zeller, iii. 352, fg.
[3] See Siegfried, 156–159.
[4] Ap. Euseb. *Praep. Ev.* viii. 13.
[5] Jos. *Antt.* xviii., 8 § 4. xx. 5, § 2. Another of Philo's nephews (?) the Alabarch Alexander wrote a book to prove that animals are endowed with reason. Philo answered him in his *De Divinatione.* Aucher, i. 124-172.

Philo professes to respect the literal sense.[1] It is, however, clear from the tenor of his works, as well as from his special observations, that he regards the literal sense as a sort of concession to the weak and ignorant. To him the Bible furnished not so much a text for criticism as a pretext for theory. Instead of elucidating the literal sense he transforms it into a philosophic symbol. To him the literal compared with the allegorical sense is but as the body to the soul. The passages which he refracts through the distorting medium of his exegetic system may be counted by hundreds, whereas it is very rarely that he abides by the plain meaning of even the simplest narratives. Thus he cannot leave untouched even the humane command of Moses about the restoration at nightfall of a pledged garment, and the pledged garment is forced into a symbol of the gift of speech![2] "For," he says, "the whole, or the greatest part of the legislation is allegorical." "Most things in the law are manifest symbols of the unmanifest, and uttered symbols of things unutterable." Intercourse with alien races is a powerful solvent of fixed beliefs.[3] As the earlier contact of the Jews with Greek life had been the parent of Sadduceeism, so their later contact in Alexandria was the parent of an esoteric and mysticising allegory,[4] and finally Alexandrianism in its dazzling unreality was the precursor of the Gnostic systems which were the later offspring of a combination of Eastern with Western thought.[5]

The complete perversion of Scripture which results from Philo's method can only be adequately measured by those who are familiar with his writings. He was a good man, a man of fine genius and noble instincts. He was so sincere

---

[1] He generally rationalises it (see *Opp.* i. 146), but sometimes refers to it as ἡ ἐν φανερῷ καὶ πρὸς τοὺς πολλοὺς ἀπόδοσις ; *De Abr.* 29, ἡ ῥητὴ καὶ φανερὰ ἀπόδοσις or κατὰ λόγον (like the Midrashic פשיטו זה). For his other phrases see note. So the Mishnic doctors distinguished between the letter which they called the body (גופא), and the mystic sense which was as the soul (נשמתא).

[2] *De Somn.* i. § 16.

[3] *De Joseph.* § 6 ; *De Spec. legg.* § 32.

[4] See Vacherot, *Hist. de l'École d'Alex.* i. 165 ; Döllinger, *Judenth. u. Heiden.* x. iii. § 5. Philo's favourite mode of address to his reader is "Ye initiated" (ὦ μύσται).   [5] See Baur, *Die Christliche Gnosis*, 234-240.

that he even believed himself to be inspired.[1] The immeasurable differences which separate the views of one age from those of another can alone account for the fact that he, and his readers, and the school to which he belonged, should have preferred his cold abstractions to the living truths of Scripture. The Scripture narratives of early ages belong indeed to a partial revelation and betray an imperfect morality, but they are full of human tears and human laughter, and are enriched with some of the deepest lessons of experience. In the hands of Philo, the poetry, the prophecy, the narratives, even the simplest legal ordinances of Scripture are evaporated into commonplaces of philosophy, or turned into a vehicle for the rhetorical expansion of moral platitudes. Even where they have a value of their own, these teachings would have been far more valuable if they had been conveyed in a natural and straightforward way. Philo adopted the absurd thesis of Aristobulus, that Greek philosophy was a mere plagiarism from Moses and the Prophets.[2] But if the sacred writers had indeed intended to teach the tenets associated with the names of Plato and Chrysippus, all that could be said would be that their method was infinitely less suited to its purpose than that of the Greeks, and that it had so completely defeated its own object as to convey wholly different impressions to all but one in a million of those to whom the Scriptures were addressed.

In Philo's hands the Law becomes as different from its real self as, in the opposite direction, it did in the hands of the Halakhists; and the histories of Scripture are as completely set aside as they were by the Haggadists. Instead of the glorious story of Abram, the father of the faithful, we get a typical Stoic who departs from the Chaldaea of the sensual understanding to Haran, which means "holes," *i.e.*, the five senses which teach him that they are nothing without the soul! Finally he becomes "Abraham" that is "an elect

---

[1] He says that his soul was frequently filled with inspirations (θεοληπτεῖσθαι) and exercised divination (μαντεύεσθαι) *De Cherubim*, § 9 ; τὸ ἐμαυτοῦ πάθος ὃ μυριάκις παθὼν οἶδα. *De Migr. Abr.* §§ 7–35 ; See Gfrörer, *Philo*, i. 58.

[2] See *Quaestiones*. (Aucher, ii. pp. 83, 89, 359, 373, &c.)

father of sound;" in other words he attains to a knowledge of God and marries Sarah or abstract Wisdom. Jacob arriving at a certain place where the sun sets becomes Wisdom acquired by training, coming to the Divine Word when the perceptive faculty is found to be useless. When he says, " With my staff I passed over this Jordan," it would be abject (ταπεινὸν)—quite unworthy of the lofty understanding of a philosophic allegorist—to understand the statement literally. Jordan means " baseness; " the staff means "discipline; " and Jacob intends to say that by discipline he had risen above baseness. It is for such vapid teaching entangled in endless contradictions, and tedious with incessant tautologies, that the Philonian exegesis asks us to give up the simplest and most instructive of human histories ! Philo has no scruple in making the narratives entirely meaningless. Indeed he shows much contempt for mere narrative. In the literal sense Simeon is ferocious and vindictive; in the allegory he becomes the type of spiritual effort.[1] In Scripture Joseph is an innocent sufferer and the very type of youthful purity; but in allegory he becomes (in one aspect) the type of the sensual mind (φιλοσώματος καὶ φιλοπαθὴς νοῦς), and of one wise in his own conceit,[2] though in another aspect he is the victorious overcomer of pleasure ! The Patriarchs in Genesis are men of the lowest and coarsest character ; in allegory they become so many virtues. The indifference of Philo to the splendid records of his nation is shown by the fact that, after Joshua, he does not allude to a single king or hero of his race. Philo is concerned almost exclusively with the books of Moses.[3] In Mangey's index of the Scripture references to his works in one volume, there are about 1000 references to the Pentateuch, eighteen to the Psalms, eight to the Prophets, and only twelve to all

---

[1] *De Ebriet.* § 23.
[2] *De Somn.* ii. 14 ; *Quod Deus immut.* § 24 ; *Leg. Allegg.* i. § 63. I have given some specimens of Philo's allegories in *Early Days of Christianity*, i. 269.
[3] He calls him ὁσιώτατος καὶ θεοφιλέστατος τῶν πώποτε γενομένων. Ὁ ἱερώτατος, ὁ ἱεροφάντης ὀργίων, καὶ διδάσκαλος τῶν θείων (*Vit. Mos.* iii. § 24 ; *De Gig.* § 12).

the rest of the Old Testament. In the other volume there are only four references to Scripture passages outside the Pentateuch. His quotations are, for the most part, free reminiscences, and the Prophets are but rarely referred to—sometimes only vaguely, and without their names.[1]

We are not here concerned with Philo's theology. It was a mixture of elements which never coalesced sufficiently to make it an harmonious system. He derived it more from the Timaeus than from the Book of Genesis. The old proverb said rightly, "Either Plato philonises, or Philo platonises."[2] His dualism, his belief in the eternity of matter,[3] his assertion of the incognisable nature of God, his "intermediate Words," his Platonic idealism, his theory of the primeval androgyne,[4] his contempt for the body, were not learnt from Moses but from the Stoics, and "the holy Plato" and "the holy community of the Pythagoreans."[5] He only read his opinions into the Pentateuch [6] by impossible processes supported by the self-delusion of his own infallibility. His God is a philosophical abstraction—"a Place" rather than a Person—and the message of that God becomes in Philo's hands a tedious, vague, and ill-constructed enigma. His whole system is a frozen sea of generalities, a "death kingdom of abstract thought."

VII. Let us follow him from the beginning in his book " on the Allegories of the sacred Laws." " It would," he tells

---

[1] He uses the formula, εἶπέ τις τῶν πάλαι προφητῶν. He never mentions Ezekiel, or Daniel, or quotes as Scripture Esther, Ecclesiastes, or Canticles (see Frankel, *Vorstudien zu d. Septuaginta*, 29. De Wette, *Einleit.* 26). He acquired, however, a special predilection for Jeremiah, perhaps from traditions of his stay in Egypt. *De Cherub.* 14. Siegfried, p. 161. He makes very little use of Job.

[2] Suidas ; Jer. *Catal.* 11 ; *Ep.* 83.

[3] J. G. Müller, *Des Juden Philo Buch d. Weltschöpfung*, 1841 ; Dähne, i. 188, fg. Fragm. *ap.* Euseb. *Praep. Ev.* vii. 22 ; viii. 13. St. John emphatically repudiates the Philonian dualism. John i. 3.

[4] *De Opif. Mundi*, 24.

[5] *De Provid.* ii. 42 ; *Quis rer. div. haer.* 33. See a brief summary of his theological views in Zeller, iii. 214.

[6] מקום. *De Somn.* i. § 11. This term is also used by the Rabbis. Philo would not even speak of God's goodness, &c. since He is better than goodness. He can never be known in the *How*, only in the *That* (ὅτι ἐστι οὐχ ὅς or ποῖος). Hence he calls God ἄποιος. His whole being is in the four mysterious letters, the Tetragrammaton JHVH. *De proem. et poen.* § 7 ; Keim, *Jesu*, i. 286 (E. T.).

us, " be a sign of great simplicity to think that the world was
created in six days or indeed at all in time." Six, therefore,
is only mentioned because it is a perfect number, being the
first which is produced by the multiplication of two unequal
factors. On the seventh day God did not " rest," but, having
desisted from the creation of mortal creatures, began the
formation of more divine beings; and the word should be
rendered " He caused to rest." Nature delights in the
number seven.[1] There are seven stars in the Bear, seven
parts of the soul, seven viscera, seven limbs, seven secretions,
seven vowels, seven tones of the voice, seven strings to the
lyre;[2] and by God's " causing to rest " on the seventh day is
meant that when reason " which is holy according to the
number seven has entered into the soul, the number six is
then arrested, and all the mortal things which this number
appears to make." By " the green herb of the field " Moses
means " that portion of the mind which is perceptible only by
intellect." The verse " God did not rain upon the earth,"
means that God did not shed the perceptions of things
upon the senses. To take literally the words " God planted a
Paradise in Eden " is impiety; " let not such fabulous nonsense
ever enter our minds." [3] The meaning is that God implants
terrestrial virtue in the human race. The tree of life is that
most general virtue which some people call goodness. The
river that goes forth out of Eden is also generic goodness.
Its four heads are the cardinal virtues. Pheison is derived
from *pheidomai* " I spare," [4] and means prudence, and being

[1] Comp. Aristobulus (*ap.* Euseb. *Praep. Ev.* xiii. 12), δι᾽ ἑβδομάδων δὲ καὶ
πᾶς ὁ κόσμος κυκλεῖται.
[2] On Philo's fancies about masculine and feminine numbers, see *De Mut.
Nom.* § 35. *De Opif. Mund.* § 3. Jost, *Judenth.* i. 321. Clement of Alexandria
(*Strom.* i. 15, § 72) calls him a Pythagorean (τὴν παρ᾽ αὐτοῖς φιλοσοφίαν
ἔγγραπτον γενομένην προκατάρξαι τῆς παρ᾽ Ἕλλησι φιλοσοφίας διὰ πολλῶν ὁ
Πυθαγόρειος ὑποδείκνυσι Φίλων). His notions are half Pythagorean, half
Kabbalistic. Ewald thinks that the allusion of Clemens must be to the elder
Philo (vii. 206 E.T.). On his Stoic affinities see Zeller, *Phil. d. Griechen*,
iii. 346-352.
[3] He says that to understand literally the statements about Paradise is folly,
πολλὴ καὶ δυσθεράπευτος ἡ εὐήθεια (*De plant. Noe*, 8). For similar expressions
see *Leg. Allegg.* iii. 2 ; *De Mundi Opific.* 3, and note.
[4] It does not seem to strike Philo as strange that ancient Semitic names
should come from Greek roots. The whole allegoric system makes much use

an illustrious virtue it is said to compass the whole land of Evilat where there is gold. The name Gihon means " chest " or an animal which attacks with its horns, and therefore stands for courage, and it compasses Ethiopia or humiliation ; in other words, it makes hostile demonstrations against cowardice. Tigris is temperance ; the name is connected with a tiger because it resolutely opposes desire. Euphrates means fertility and stands for justice. Again, Pheison means " change of the mouth," and Evilat " bringing forth," which is an appropriate name for folly which always aims at the unattainable, and is destroyed by prudence manifested by speaking, *i.e.* by the changing of the mouth ! The carbuncle and emerald of the land of Evilat stand for Judah and Issachar. The Euphrates does not mean the river, but the correction of manners. The literal statement that God cast Adam into a deep sleep and made Eve of one of his ribs is fabulous ; the meaning is that God took the power which dwells in the outward senses, and led it to the mind. The serpent means pleasure, which leads Philo into a long disquisition about the rod of Moses, and the tribe of Dan. Dan means " temperance " though he is the son of Bilhah, which means imbibing ; he is a serpent in the path that is in the soul ; he bites the heels of the horse, because " passion has four legs as a horse has," and is an impetuous beast and full of insolence, and the soul which is the rider of this horse falls backwards, *i.e.* falls from the passions when they have been wounded.

Such explanations, with long digressions, strange etymologies, and imaginary parallels occupy two whole books of this treatise. The third is of the same character. Moses lays down the wise practical rule that a night-burglar may be killed without incurring blood-guiltiness ; but if he be killed in daylight the slayer is guilty, since he ought rather to require restitution than revenge.[1] In Philo's hands this passage gives this

---

of etymologies. This method had also been learnt from the Stoics. In Latin they derived Mavors from "qui magna vertit, Saturnus quia se saturat annis, Minerva quia minuit," &c. (Cic. *De Nat. Deor.* ii. 18).

[1] Ex. xxii. 2.

strange result :—if any man cuts down the reason, and is found standing over the reason thus wounded and destroyed, he is a thief, who takes away what belongs to God and receives a severe blow, namely, arrogance. " But," says Philo, " Moses says nothing as to the name of the smiter, for the smiter and the smitten are the same " ! [1]

The death of Er is explained as follows:—Er means "leather," in other words "that leathern mass which covers us," namely, the body ! Elohim, and not Jehovah, is said to slay Er ; and the meaning is that goodness condemns the dead body to death. The touching incident of the blessing of the two sons of Joseph is made to signify that Jacob, the supplanter of the passions and practiser of virtue, gives his right hand to Ephraim, who stands for prolific memory, and his left to Manasseh, who stands for recollection aroused from forgetfulness. The Messianic promise, which Philo renders " He shall watch thy head and thou shalt watch his heel," is explained to mean that God says to pleasure " the mind shall watch your predominant and principal doctrine, and you shall watch the traces of the mind itself, and the foundation of the things which are pleasing to it, to which the heel has very naturally been likened." In the passage about Sihon and Heshbon (Numb. xxi. 28-30), Sihon is interpreted to mean the man who destroys the sound rule of truth ; Heshbon " sophistical riddles ; " and Debon " adjudication." Philo's comment on the budding of Aaron's rod is a tedious attempt to prove that " the nut signifies consummate virtue." [2] In the perfectly simple passage about the land of promise, Philo explains " cities " to mean " general virtues ; " houses " special virtues ; " wells " noble dispositions towards wisdom ; " vineyards and olive-trees imply cheerfulness and light, the fruits of a contem-

---

[1] The way in which Philo creates difficulties about the literal sense when there are none except in his own confusions of thought is shown by his comment upon the Mosaic rule for punishing an immodest woman, and also by his absurd remark about the punishment of cutting off the hand of a son who has struck father or mother (*De parent. col.* published by Angelo Mai). The naïve confession of St. Jerome, " Allegorice interpretatus sum Obadiam *cujus historiam nesciebam*," might have been made by other Allegorists.

[2] *Vit. Mos.* iii. § 22.

L

plative life.[1] The five Cities of the Plain are the five senses.
And thus every person, every living figure who passes across
the stage of Scripture history ceases for all practical purposes
to be himself, and becomes a dim personification. Moses is
intelligence; Aaron is speech; Enoch is repentance; Noah
righteousness. Abraham is virtue acquired by learning;
Isaac is innate virtue; Jacob is virtue obtained by struggle;
Lot is sensuality; Ishmael is sophistry; Esau is rude disobedience; Leah is patient virtue; Rachel innocence.[2] And
unhappily these counters, of which the significance is often
made to depend on a wild etymology, are interchangeable—
so that they may sometimes stand for one thing and sometimes for another thing which is entirely different. Japhet for
instance is in one sense permissible enjoyment; in another he
is insatiable desire.[3] The sun is sometimes the understanding
(which is the reason why Joseph marries the daughter of the
priest of Heliopolis, Gen. xli. 45); sometimes the bodily sense,
(so that the sun begins to rise when Jacob no longer sees
God, Gen. xxxii. 32); sometimes the Word of God; sometimes
God Himself. And thus the whole Bible becomes an insipid
philosophical romance of which the interpretation floats in
the air, and which can only be understood by the uncertain
aid of a dictionary of metaphors.

This kind of exegesis is not improved but rendered
still more valueless by the futile methods adopted to
sublimate these pale generalities out of narratives which
thrill with life, and are rich with the lessons of experience.
For instance, the parallel passages which are introduced
have nothing but the most distant verbal connection
with the passage explained. When we are told that
"God planted a garden in Eden," it is worse than superfluous to explain to us that the reason why Moses said

---

[1] *De Profugis*, § 31 ; *Quod Deus immut.* § 21.
[2] οὐ περὶ γυναικῶν λόγος ἀλλὰ διανοιῶν, *De Congr. erud.* 1–6, and *passim.*
Philo says (6) that Zilpah means "a mouth going forth," and Bilhah "a
swallowing."
[3] For Joseph see *Leg. allegg.* i. § 63 ; iii. §§ 85, 86. For Japhet see *De
Sobriet.* § 12 ; and *Quaest. in Gen.* ii. 80 ; and generally Siegfried, *Philo,*
190–196.

"Thou shalt not plant a grove for thyself," is that we are only to plant fruit-bearing trees, not wild trees, in our minds.[1] It is neither exegesis nor anything resembling it, to say that "she" is used in "*she* shall be called woman" because "there is another kind of outward sensation not derived from the mind." It is exegetical frivolity to say that by a change of accent the words ποῦ εἶ; "*Where art thou?*" in the Greek version may mean "*Thou art somewhere;*" and then to build an argument on both phrases.[2] Philo's method was equally alien from the natural interpretation of unsophisticated piety, and from the accepted results of scientific criticism. It was a hybrid born on both sides of illegitimate parentage. It was the strange offspring of Rabbinic dogma and Greek philosophy.

Philo held the most rigid views of inspiration, though when he deals with them practically he becomes vague and self-contradictory. To him Scripture is "the holy word," "the divine word," "the right word;" and its utterances are "sacred oracles."[3] Borrowing a theory from Plato, he imagines that the sacred books were written in a condition of ecstasy, which wholly obliterated the human powers. The vocal organs of the prophets, without any co-operation on their part, were but used by a divine ventriloquism. These views are the issue of nothing better than the pseudo-philosophic postulate, that "the mortal cannot dwell together with the immortal." He regards the books of Scripture as divine, and as having been written by "scholars of Moses," and as forming part of an indivisible whole, which was supernaturally significant down to its minutest parts. Aqiba himself used no stronger language on

---

[1] Deut. xvi. 21. The verse means "Thou shalt not set up an Asherah (or phallic emblem of the nature-goddess) of any wood."

[2] Philo, even if he had more than a smattering of Hebrew, yet speaks of the Greek as "our dialect," and of "us Greeks" as distinguished from the Hebrews. *De Conf. Ling.* 26; *De Congr. crud.* 8; and of "*our* Alexandria" (*Leg. ad Gaium,* 22).

[3] χρησμοί, λόγια, ἱερὰ βίβλος, ἱερώτατον γράμμα, ὁ ἱερὸς or θεῖος λόγος, or ὁ ὀρθὸς λόγος. *De Mut. Nom.* 8; *Quis. res. div.* 53; *Vit. Mos.* iii. 23; *De Monarch.* i. 9; *De Spec. Legg.* iv. 8. He even supposes that Moses wrote the account of his own death and burial! (*Vit. Mos.* iii. 39).

this subject than was used by Philo. Yet his theory of inspiration was a mere *nasus cereus.* His Bible practically consisted of the Pentateuch alone, and parts even of that he explains as mystical.[1] There are whole books of the Bible which he never mentions, and others of which he makes no use. He thinks so little of the historical books, that he blurs their vivid details into a phantasmagoria of dull and indistinct colours, and indignantly repudiates the notion of mere narrative as such being worthy of the dignity of Scripture.[2] He considers that the Scriptures were verbally dictated, yet quotes them with careless variations and in the freest possible paraphrases; mingles them with traditional details; combines them with views borrowed from Greek poets and philosophers whom he also reverences as inspired; and treats them in a manner purely arbitrary, derived from his own individual genius.[3] He would have been saved from many errors of detail if not of principle if he had been able or willing to study the original in which the Scriptures were written. But he did not think it necessary to do this, because he most mistakenly believed the Seventy to be not only "interpreters" but also "hierophants and prophets," in whom spoke the "divine" "the sacred" and unerring word.[4] Thus alone can we account for the singular phenomena of an acceptance of the most mechanical theory of inspiration,[5] combined with the acquiescence in a translation which constantly diverges from the inspired original.[6]

---

[1] He classed the contents of the Pentateuch under the heads of (1) oracles, (2) responses given to Moses, and (3) revelations given to him in a state of ecstasy.

[2] *De Somn.* i. § 10, οὐχ ἵνα ὡς παρὰ συγγραφέως ἱστορικοῦ μάθωμεν. *De Congr.* § 8, οὐχ ἱστορικὴ γενεαλογία ταῦτ᾽ ἔστιν.

[3] See Ewald, vi. 276–378 ; Siegfried in Hilgenfeld's *Zeitschr.* 1873.

[4] *Vit. Mos.* ii. 6, 7. On Philo's ignorance of Hebrew see Jost, *Judenth.* i. 352.

[5] *Vit. Mos.* iii. § 3 ; *Quis. Rer. Div. haer.* § 52 ; *De Praem.* § 9.

[6] *Vit. Mos.* iii. § 23. He uses the words ἐπιθείασαι, ἐνθουσιῶν, καταπνευσθείς. But it must be remembered that he by no means confines his theory of supernatural inspiration to the sacred writers ; for he takes the conception from Plato and the Greek philosophers (*Ion* 34 B &c.), and extends it to heathens and to himself (see Gfrörer, i. 51 ff.). Heathen Philosophy, not Scripture, was the source of such dogmas. The views of Josephus were less

VIII. When once the Jews had embraced the allegorical
method it was easy to support it by Scripture arguments. Philo
proves as follows that Scripture must have a mystic sense. In
Num. xxiii. 19, we find *God is not a man*; in Deut. i. 31,
we find, *The Lord thy God bare thee as a man doth bear his son.*
Philo sees in these two passages indications of the two
methods of divine legislation, the literal and the allegorical.[1]
The former is the body of Scripture, the latter the soul, which
like a fine fluid pervades the whole law.[2] The former is only
for the vulgar, the latter for the enlightened, the few, the men
of vision and faculty, the initiated who can perceive and see.[3]
These illuminated persons cover the living rock with accretions
which they refuse to share with any but their own followers,
and become so proud of the incrustation that they cease to be
conscious that there is a rock at all, and that it was meant for
the use of all mankind.

All this " madness " is reduced to " method " by a set of
rules, half Haggadistic, half Stoic, but entirely inapplicable.
By some of them the literal sense is positively excluded; by
others, the allegoric sense is indicated as existing with the
literal side by side.

1. The rules by which the literal sense is excluded are
chiefly Stoic.[4]

It is excluded when the statement is unworthy of God;[5]
when there is any contradiction; when the allegory is

extravagant, but he too extends inspiration to himself and to others besides
the Biblical writers (*B. J.* i. 2, § 8 ; iii. 8, § 3 ; iv.10, § 7). Ewald (vii. 203)
well points out that θεόπνευστος (2 Tim. iii. 16) is a far vaguer adjective
than "*a Deo inspiratus*" (Vulg.) or "*Von Gott eingegeben*" (Luther).

[1] Philo, *Quod Deus immut.* § 11 ; *De Somn.* i. § 40. See Gfrörer, *Philo,* i.
68–113 ; Dähne, i. 49 ; Hirschfeld, *Hagad. Exegese,* 156 ; Siegfried, 162-197.

[2] *De Migr. Abrah.* § 16.

[3] *De Abr.* §§ 29, 36 : *De Plant.* § 9 ; *De Cherub.* §§ 7, 8, and *passim ; De
Somn.* i. 33.

[4] See *De Somn.* ii. 2, 20 ; i. §§ 13–17 ; *De Abr.* § 15 ; *Leg. Allegg.* i. § 18 ;
De Cherub. §§ 7–9 ; *Quis Rer. Div.* § 57.

[5] The extraordinary notion that Scripture, of which they regarded every
word as being supernaturally inspired, is full of passages which in their obvious
sense are indecent, unbecoming, or derogatory to God is repeated after Philo
by centuries of Patristic and Christian expositors. Thus an extravagant and
unscriptural theory not only leads to allegory in one direction, but pleads
as a reason for the necessity of allegory, assertions which, if true, at once
disprove the theory itself.

obvious. If Scripture says that Adam "hid himself from God," the expression dishonours God who sees all things,—and therefore it must be allegory. If we are told that Jacob sends Joseph to look after his brethren when he had so many servants,—or that Cain had a wife or built a city,—or that Potiphar had a wife,—or that Israel is an "inheritance of God;"[1]—or if Abraham be called "the father" instead of grand-father of Jacob—those are "contradictions," and, therefore, the passages in which they occur must be allegorised.

2. The rules which prove the *simultaneous* existence of the allegorical with the literal sense are mainly Rabbinic.[2]

Thus if an expression be repeated as in "Abraham Abraham," the double name expresses first affection, then warning. Again, if a word be superfluous,[3] as in "eating thou shalt eat," it implies eating in a proper spirit and conscious knowledge. "He led him forth without" means that God loosed Abraham from all the fetters of his body.[4] If there be an apparent tautology, as when we are superfluously reminded that "Esau was Jacob's brother," the meaning is that Esau was still Jacob's brother though he was a sinner.[5] If there is a change in the expression, as from νὴ to οὐ, in the oath "by the health of Pharaoh," it not only indicates the wavering character of Joseph, but implies the difference between the discipline of Egypt and the discipline of home.

3. Again, words may be explained apart from their punctua-

---

[1] Ex. xv. 17.

[2] The exegetic principles of Philo differ, however, from the Talmudic in five respects : (1) He does not quote authorities or opinions ; (2) he comments on paragraphs more than on isolated verses ; (3) he is fond of a rhetorical style ; (4) he refers to the LXX. alone ; (5) he is more continuously arbitrary and allegorical (see Löw, p. 133). He interprets some passages in an anti-Rabbinic sense. Thus the Jews took pleasure in insulting and blaspheming the gods of the heathen, but Philo applied Ex. xxii. 28 to them also. The first Jewish writer who called attention to the forty-two works of Philo was Azariah de Rossi († 1578), who calls him "Jedidiah the Alexandrian," and doubts his orthodoxy, which Rappoport defends.

[3] Ex. xxi. 15. The rule is like that of Aqiba, Περιττὸν ὄνομα οὐδὲν τίθησιν ὁ νόμος (*De Profug.* 10). (Gen. ii. 17, LXX. βρώσει φάγῃ ; Gen. xv. 5, LXX. ἐξήγαγεν αὐτὸν ἔξω.)

[4] *Leg. Allegg.* i. 31.

[5] *Leg. Allegg.* 13. So in ἐκεῖ οὗ ἐστι ᾖ᾽ τὸ χρυσίον (Gen. ii. 11) the οὗ is made to mean that "prudence" (gold) *belongs to God.* For many instances of this baseless kind of interpretation see Siegfried, 168, fg.

tion.[1] Thus Jacob is saved by the Midrashim from telling a lie by being made to say " I am [Jacob : but Esau is] thy first-born ; "[2] and Philo says that Zoar both is and is not little ;[3] and that Jacob's words at Bethel mean " This is *not* the case, that the Lord is in this place "—since God is nowhere.[4]

4. Again, if synonyms are used, something allegorical is intended.[5] Thus if, in Gen. i. 27, God *"made"* man (ἐποίησεν), and in Gen. ii. 8 He *" moulded "* man (ἔπλασεν), the first word implies the earthly, and the second the heavenly, man. If in Gen. xvi. 2 we have ὑπήκουσε, and in Gen. xxviii. 7 εἰσήκουσε, the first word implies the obedient hearing of Abraham, and the second the careless hearing of Jacob.

5. Plays on words are admissible to educe a deeper sense.[6] Thus, if the Law bids redeem the firstling of an ass with a lamb,[7] then since ὄνος resembles πόνος and πρόβατον is derived from προβαίνειν, you get the idea of progress resulting from work ; and when it is added, *" and if thou wilt not redeem it thou shalt give its value,"*[8] the meaning is " leave off thy work, if thou makest no advance "![9]

6. Particles, adverbs, prepositions may be forced into the service of allegory. Parts of words may be made significant. Each word may have all its possible meanings apart from the context ; so that if ἐξ αὐτῆς means " from her," in Gen. xvii. 16, and also means " immediately," and also " out of her," to each of these meanings may be attached a mystic inference. Words may even be altered as in the Talmudic rule, *" read not so, but so."* Thus when Cain

---

[1] *De Migr. Abr.* § 29.
[2] Bereshith Rabba, c. 65.
[3] *De Abr.* § 31.
[4] *De Somn.* i. § 32.
[5] For many instances see Siegfried, 172, 173.
[6] *De Congr. erud. grat.* § 13.
[7] Ex. xiii. 13.
[8] A.V. "thou shalt break his neck." LXX. ἐὰν δὲ μὴ ἀλλάξῃς λυτρώσῃ αὐτό.
[9] So the use of ἐγκρυφίας ("cakes concealed in ashes to be baked ") implies that we must not reveal mysteries. *De Sacr. Ab. et Cain,* § 15.

killed Abel, ἀπέκτεινεν αὐτὸν is meant also to imply that ἀπέκτεινεν αὐτὸν,—*i.e.* by the same blow he spiritually killed himself. An unusual expression implies something mystical. Thus when, in Ex. vii. 15, Moses is bidden to stand by the Nile's "lip," the meaning is that he is to resist the seductive speeches of Pharaoh.[1] Lastly—but it is more than needless to furnish any further specimens—all numbers, animals, birds, plants, streams, materials, colours, circumstances, limbs, names of men and of countries may by etymological or other methods be made to stand, and are all meant to stand, as symbols for moral and spiritual things.[2]

Such was the system, such the presuppositions which could never be established, which Philo had traditionally received from a former generation of allegorists, but of which he was an eloquent and fertile expositor. He was determined to get circuitously what he could not get directly. And thus did he practically create a Bible of his own—a Bible infinitely less venerable and more obscure— endowed with claims and interpreted by methods which were not derived from its own pages but were a feeble exotic transplanted from the theories of Greek philosophers into a completely alien soil.

Let me however say in conclusion that the students of Philo's works receive a far more favourable impression of his powers than can be derived from mere references or extracts. If they cannot help perceiving the verbosity of the great Alexandrian, his want of logic, of lucidity, and of firm grasp over the thoughts which he is handling, they at least do justice to his high morality, his dignity and loftiness of soul, his wide learning, his burning enthusiasm, his obvious sincerity, his innocent gladness, his deep piety.[3] Undoubtedly,

---

[1] *De Somn.* ii. § 41. Comp. *De Migr. Abr.* 14.

[2] Unfortunately the etymologies on which Philo relied, and led the Fathers to rely, are often of the most absolutely uncritical character. A collection of his etymologies was once current. Euseb. *H. E.* ii. 18, § 7. See Ewald, vi. 267.

[3] See *Quod det. pot.* §§ 32-37 ; *De Mut. Nom.* § 23. Laughter is ὁ ἐνδιά- θετος υἱός. We get a very favourable view of Philo from the fine autobiographical passage in *De Spec. Legg. ad init.*

like the great philosophers in whose inspiration he believed, he
too had "knocked at the door of truth," and ardently longed
for the furtherance of virtue. But we are not here dealing with
the whole work of one who was a witness to the universal
circulation and abiding force of great human ideas, and who
"scattered seed in Judaism of which the noblest grains bore
fruit in Christianity." We are dealing only with his exegetic
system, and of that it must be said quite plainly and without
the least circumlocution that it is absolutely baseless. Its
futility becomes still more obvious when we find the same
text used for quite different purposes, and the same symbol
applied to entirely dissimilar things. Had the age of Philo
possessed in any measure the critical, literary, or historic sense,
—had it at all realised the exquisite human force, beauty, and
simplicity of the sacred narratives—the Alexandrians could
never have gone astray after such meteor-lights as these.
Whatever may be said of Philo's other merits as the Cicero
of Alexandrianism, his exegesis is radically false. It darkens
what is simple and fails to explain what is obscure. It
neglects the important and lays stress upon the insignificant.
It sometimes does injustice to what is loftiest and deteriorates
what is best. While it looks microscopically at words it
neglects entire passages, and gives us no conception of the
significance of whole books. Philo's system is one of vault-
ing ambition, which overleaps itself and falls on the other
side. It fails in consequence of its vain contempt of
grammar, of logic, of history, of archaeology, and of the most
ordinary canons of literary expression, and by the substitution
for them of arbitrary rules in the supposed interest of a
recklessly-invented theory of mechanical inspiration. That
theory led, as it always does, to two results equally
deplorable. It produced the slavish literalism of the Rabbis,
and the idealising rationalism of Alexandrian allegory.
It made an esoteric pride the common handmaid of both
systems; and being attached almost exclusively to the
Pentateuch, it extinguished, alike among the Rabbis and
the Alexandrians, the living inspiring hope of a personal

Messiah.[1] They clung to institutions which the earthquake
was rocking to its foundations; they lost entirely the things
which could not be shaken, and which remain.[2]

"Philo's whole system," it has been said, "may be
described as rhetoric turned into logic. Ignorant of the true
nature of language, presuming on its accuracy, allowing
nothing for its uncertainty and irregularity,"—misled, we may
add, by an eminently faulty translation, and drawing inferences
from its Greek mistakes as though they were supernaturally
inspired—borrowing from alien sources a system originally
mistaken and doubly inapplicable to the records of Scripture
—misled further by a totally different system of exegesis
which was indigenous among his countrymen, and was itself
based on an idolatrous and unspiritual letter-worship—" he
infers endless consequences from trivial expressions.　.　.　.
The worst extravagances of mystical interpretation among the
fathers, combined with the most tedious platitudes of a
modern sermon, convey a very faint idea of the manner in
which Philo improves Scripture." [3]　In snatching at shadows
the Alexandrians, no less than the Rabbis, lost the substance.
The Rabbis gained a crushingly elaborate ritual, the Alexandrians a pseudo-philosophical religion. Both schools alike
lost those beliefs which had been the heart and soul of
religion to the greatest of their fathers. The clouds were
already beginning to shine before the Sun of Righteous-

---

[1] On Philo's Messianic hopes, which were in no sense soteriological, but
only of a national and temporal character, see *De Execrat.* § 4 ; (Mangey
ii. 435). (Mangey, ii. 421-425. Ewald, vii. 231-235 E. T.) They had no
connection with Salvation. The Logos is not one of Philo's three Para-
cletes of reconciliation, which are (1) God's goodness ; (2) the holiness
of the forefathers of the Jews ; (3) amendment. As for the Rabbis some of
them took Herod for a Messiah, and others Barkokhba. Some say that
the Jews have forfeited him ; others curse all who try to calculate his
return. The school of Hillel seems to have thought that Hezekiah was the
Messiah. Others thought that there were two Messiahs—Messiah ben Joseph
the Sufferer, and ben David the Victor. For the views of Josephus, who
regarded Vespasian as a sort of Messiah, see *B. J.* vi. 5. § 4 ; *Antt.* iv. 6,
§ 5 ; Gerlach, *Weissag. d. A. T.* 86-89.

[2] Philo no less than the Rabbis thought that the Levitic institutions would
be eternal. *Vit. Mos.* ii. § 3 ; *De Monarch.* ii. § 3.

[3] Jowett, *St. Paul and Philo, Ep. to the Thessalonians,* i. 363. See the
wise remarks of Ewald, vii. 202 (E. T.).

ness, but the cold stone of the philosophic Memnon had no music to greet the dawn.

Such a work as Philo's—the result of a mere juxtaposition of alien elements, was, as a whole, foredoomed to failure. Mankind could make no use of a contradictory theology in which a God and a world at once flee from and seek each other ; of a God and a chaos both without attributes and coevally existent ;[1] of a system which placed true wisdom in asceticism and ecstasy ; of a reformation which knew nothing of the real evils of the world, and identified divine blessedness with egoistic self-sufficiency ;[2] of a religion which continued to insist on external ordinances, while it admitted that they generally led to gross superstition ; of a Judaism which undermined alike the past history and the future hopes of the chosen race ; of a Biblical exegesis which took scarcely any account of the noblest portions of the Hebrew Scriptures : of an illumination which " calling everything in question, making everything unnecessary, renounced the very foundation on which it stood and made no progress because it soared in the air."[3]

And yet we can hardly blame Philo if, under stress of circumstances, and the painful antagonism of Hellenic and Jewish culture—amid the taunting criticisms of philosophers and the grovelling letter-worship of Rabbis—he eagerly embraced a method which rested indeed on unverified presuppositions, but seemed to offer the possibility of reconciliation. Allegory in Philo's days was not an intentional falsification nor a hypocritical subterfuge. It was a phase of thought which seemed to be inevitable in the education

---

[1] The same epithet ἄποιος is given both to God and to Chaos.

[2] Philo, *De Cherub.* ταῦτα, ὢ μύσται, κεκαθαρμένοι τὰ ὦτα ὡς ἱερὰ ὄντως μυστήρια . . . παραδέχεσθε, κ.τ.λ.

[3] Keim, *l.c.* " It was equally partial in its application and its scope. It addressed only one part of man's nature, and one class of men. It suppressed the instincts of civil and domestic society which Christianity ennobled ; it perpetuated the barriers which Christianity removed ; it abandoned the conflict which Christianity carries out to victory." " Its tendency was to exalt knowledge in place of action ; its home was in the cells of the recluse and not in the field or the market ; its truest disciples were visionary Therapeutae, and not apostles charged with a Gospel for the world." Westcott, Introd. 77.

of the world. It is more astonishing, — and would be more culpable, if we could ever call men culpable for not rising superior to the religious opinions of their age—that Philo's methods, teeming as they do with impossibilities, and based as they are on the shifting sand, should yet have been adopted and practised by Christian commentators for thousands of years after the high-minded Alexandrian had passed away.[1] They rose superior indeed to his continuity of extravagance. They shook themselves free from the spell of Plato, though many of them only replaced it by the harder yoke of Aristotle. They discarded much of Philo's Pythagorean Kabbalism, and his vanishing combinations of abstract symbols. They learnt to value the historic books and the Prophets even more than the Pentateuch. Their logic was, on the whole, less feeble and fantastic. They do not show themselves wholly incapable of studying entire passages as well as fragmentary expressions, and entire books as well as separate paragraphs. They do not adopt the exclusively microscopic method of magnifying each phrase and clause as though it had no connexion with anything which lay out of the immediate field of vision. To them Abraham and the Patriarchs are something more than counters to be arbitrarily shuffled about as symbols of other things. Yet into many of these faults to a great extent they fell.[2] Centuries had to elapse before men ceased to explain Scripture in non-natural senses ; before they ceased to isolate and distort its separate expressions ; before they ceased to rely on purely verbal and accidental parallels; before they saw that Semitic literature was not to be interpreted by the

---

[1] The fables that Philo had met St. Peter at Rome (Euseb. *H. E.* ii. 17 ; Jer. *Catal.* 11), and that he had even embraced Christianity (Photius, *Cod.* cv. Suidas *s.v.* Φίλων) may be dismissed without further notice ; as well as the notions that in describing the Therapeutae (Ewald, v. 375-89) he was thinking of Christians. Such fancies are on a par with the notion that Seneca borrowed from St. Paul, and Plato from Moses. They arose from errors about the spurious *De Vit. contemplativa.*

[2] Allusions to Philo by the Fathers may be seen in Justin *Cohort.* pp. 10, 11, 14. Clem. Alex. *Strom.* i. p. 333, 360, 413. Orig. *C. Cels.* iv. p. 369, vi. p. 289. Euseb. *H. E.* ii. 4, 5, 16-18. *Praep. Ev.* vii. 12, viii. 5, &c. Ambros., *De Parad.* 4, Jer. *Catal. Praef. in Job,* &c. Aug. *C. Faustum,* xii. &c. See Mangey, i. pp. xxi-xxix.

rigid syllogisms of Western logic; before they ceased to bring to Scripture what they could never have fairly deduced from it; before they dreamed of applying to Holy Writ the verifying faculties of a reason and conscience informed by the Gospel and illuminated by the Spirit of God Himself; before they suspected the absurdity of rationalising here and spiritualising there in accordance with rules which had no foundation; before they thought it in the least necessary to master the original languages in which the Scriptures were written; before they ceased to quote it in defence of their own worst passions and their own least venial ignorance; before they attained any conception of it, as being composed of books of very unequal value, the far from homogeneous literature of two millenniums—as being a progressive revelation, fragmentary and multifarious, though from the first dimly prophesying of a final perfection.

IX. Yet let us not fail to notice, again and again, that there is a *Divine Progress*, an Evangelical Preparation. Humanity advances through the midst of errors, but it advances still. Truth wins its way though it have to struggle on " from scaffold to scaffold, and from stake to stake." God speaks in many voices. He has means of communicating with the soul other than through the letters of a Book. Even those who had no sacred Book were not left without witness that we are all His offspring. That which may be known of God was still manifested unto them. Neither Halakha, nor Haggada, not Qabbala, nor rules borrowed from Chrysippus in support of theories derived from Plato, can wholly rob mankind of the plain truths of God. They who have the priceless blessing of a sacred Canon may indeed misinterpret it by false methods, and mingle it with alien elements; but no faithful soul can wholly miss its most essential truths. All who search it with an honest and good heart will find therein all things necessary to salvation. The Alexandrians, widely as they erred in exegesis, had still high truths to teach. In reading their best aspirations we are, as it were, " fanned by the air of the New Testament."

The dim Logos of Philo appears clothed with the true and eternal glory of Divine Humanity in the Gospel of St. John ; and some of Philo's phrases and conceptions are used with yet nobler purpose in the Epistle to the Hebrews. If the question has occurred to us " How were the souls of men kept pure and holy amid the externalism of the Rabbis, and the vague allegoric philosophy of the Alexandrians ? " the answer is not far to seek. It shall be given in the voice of an Alexandrian : " Thou, oh God, canst show thy strength at all times when thou wilt. Thou hast mercy upon all, for thou canst do all things, and winkest at the sins of men because they shall amend. For thou lovest all the things that are, and abhorrest nothing which thou hast made. But thou *sparest all ; for they are thine, oh Lord, Thou lover of souls.*" [1]

It shall be given in the yet sweeter and loftier language of the Psalmist : " The statutes of the Lord are right, and rejoice the heart ; the commandment of the Lord is pure, and giveth light unto the eyes. . . Moreover by them is thy servant warned, and in keeping of them there is great reward."

[1] Wisdom, xi. 23-26.

" Reliqui Scripturas quidem confitentur, interpretatione vero conver
tunt."—Iren. *Adv. Haer.* iii. 12.

" Tantum veritati obstrepit adulter sensus quantum et corruptor
stylus."—Tert. *Apol.* 17.

" Sunt enim multa verba in Scripturis divinis quæ possunt trahi ad
eum sensum quem sibi unusquisque præsumit."—*Recogn. Clem.* x. 42.

" Sed ad sensum suum incongrua aptant testimonia, quasi grande sit
et non vitiosissimum docendi genus depravare sententias, et ad voluntatem suam Scripturam trahere repugnantem."—Jer. *Ad Paulin.* ep.
53, 7.

" Concerning the mystical sense it may be observed that we may err
in two ways, either by seeing it where it is not, or by taking it otherwise than it ought to be taken."—Dante, *De Monarchia*, iii.

LECTURE IV.

PATRISTIC EXEGESIS.

"That your faith should not stand in the wisdom of men."—1 COR. ii. 5.

IN supporting some special dogma, or private interpretation—in asserting the infallible accuracy of some party
opinion which would fain claim to be that of the universal
Church [1]—ecclesiastical controversialists have often appealed
to Christ's promise of the Spirit which should lead the
Apostles into all truth,[2] and they have usually identified this
promise with a power of rightly interpreting the language of
Scripture. It is strange that facts the most obvious, and
drawn from every branch of human investigation, have not
been sufficient to expose the folly of claiming that promise
without its obvious limitations. "Into all truth" which is in
any way necessary to salvation—"into all truth" which is
essential to the eternal welfare of the human soul—the Holy
Spirit of God has in all ages guided all who have not resisted
His gracious influence; but He has never taught men the
truths which are independently attainable by the exercise of
human intellect, or those which are left to be revealed by
the broadening light of universal experience. Nor can we
except from this statement a multitude of truths, which
many would represent as of primary importance. The stern

---

[1] "Granting that Christianity is the pure truth, who will answer for it,
that the orthodoxy which prevails at any one time is equivalent with pure
Christianity?" Chalybäus, *History of Special Philosophie*, p. 419, etc.
[2] John xvi. 13.

M

logic of circumstance, the clear verdict of history, is decisive against *a priori* theories and subjective fancies. The Scriptures contain the Word of God; and in the Scriptures every honest and earnest soul may find the few and simple things which the Lord requires of him. Yet the Scriptures never claim for themselves as a whole the supernatural dictation or miraculous infallibility which from the days of the Rabbis have been claimed for them. They do not even furnish any test of their own canonicity; nor do they protect themselves from grievous mistranslation; nor do they give any definition of the nature of their own inspiration; nor do they lay down any of its limits or degrees; nor has their text been kept free from numberless variations; nor do they furnish any rules whatever as to the manner in which their difficulties should rightly be explained. All such questions are left to the candour, the honesty, the wisdom, the experience of those who seek for truth by the appointed means; and who even then will have no claim to infallibility, nor have it in their power to impose " the senses of men upon the words of God, the special senses of men upon the general words of God," or to lay them upon men's consciences together under the equal penalty of death and damnation.[1]

The history of exegesis thus far has been in great measure a history of aberrations. If we turn to the Fathers with the hope that now at last we shall enter the region of unimpeachable methods and certain applications, we shall be disappointed. I would earnestly ask not to be misunderstood. I gladly admit that there are in the writings of the Fathers not only many noble truths but also many felicitous expositions. I also frankly allow that much of the staple of all recent commentaries, so far as they are simply moral and spiritual, is to be found in their pages. But this does not shake the fact that their exegesis in the proper sense of the word needs complete revision both in its principles and in its details. There are but few of them whose pages are not rife with errors—errors of method, errors

[1] Chillingworth, c. iv. § 16.

of fact, errors of history, of grammar, and even of doctrine.
This is the language of simple truth, not of slighting disparagement. I should be most unwilling to speak with
disrespect of the Fathers of the Church. They, like ourselves, were the children of their age. They were hampered
by the conditions, influenced by the culture, swayed by the
prejudices of the times in which they lived. Some of them
were men pre-eminent in holiness; a few of them were wise,
eloquent, deeply read in the human heart, fired with the
kindling enthusiasm of spiritual life; several of them were
men of wide learning; one or two of them were also men of
high genius. Their original thoughts, their pious exhortations, their homiletic skill, their spiritual insight, their practical
application of the lessons of Scripture will always be valuable.
The diligence of some of them has preserved for us traditional
information by which light is thrown on various passages. I
would not echo the scornful language either of Milton, of
Grotius,[1] of Chillingworth, or of Middleton.[2] " Whatsoever,"
says Milton, " time or the heedless hand of blind chance hath
drawn from of old to this present in her huge Dragnet, whether
Fish or Sea-weed, Shells or Shrubbs, unpicked, unchosen, those
are the Fathers;" and "it came into my thoughts . . . that I
could do Religion and my Country no better service for the
time than doing my utmost endeavour to re-call the People
of God from this vain foraging after Straw, and to reduce
them to their firm Stations under the Standard of the Gospel;
by making appear to them, first the insufficiency, next the
inconveniency, and lastly the impiety of these gay Testimonies

---

[1] Compare Grotius, *De Studiis instit.* (1635), p. 238. " Patres et Patrum
eruditionem . . . maximi facio, sed tamen tibi autor non sim ut illos hâc
quidem aetate legas sed differas . . . Nam multa habent non solum fluxa,
ambigua, futilia, et superstitiosa, sed etiam quaedam non usquequaque proba et
sana." He goes on to add that they are often unorthodox. I need only allude
to Daillé, *Traité de l'Emploi des Saints Pères*, 1632 (answered by W. Reeves,
The Apologie of the Fathers (1709), and the Rev. Prof. Blunt, *On the Right Use
of the Fathers* (1857), and Barbeyrac, *Traité de la Morale des Pères.*

[2] Middleton, *Free Enquiry*, 1729. Among others who have spoken very
slightingly of the Fathers might be mentioned Simon Episcopius. See him
quoted by Dr. Pusey, *Tract* No. 57, p. 10. Coleridge said of Luther,
Melanchthon, Calvin, that "the least of them was not inferior to St. Augustine
and worth a brigade of Cyprians, Firmilians, and the like" (*Remains*, iii. 276).

that their great Doctors would bring them to dote on."[1] We
can hardly wonder at the accent of indignation which rings
through the words of the mighty Puritan poet,[2] when we
remember that the Fathers had been thrust into a position of
autocracy which they repeatedly and emphatically disclaim,
and which had they ever claimed it would have been completely nullified by their own writings. Their glory is for the
most part the glory, not of intellect, but of righteousness and
faith.

The Church writers of the earlier ages were surrounded
with difficulties. It was not till the fourth century that the
Canon of the New Testament was finally established; it was
not till the sixteenth that the Canon of even the Old Testament was clearly defined. The views entertained about the
Old Testament and the methods of its interpretation were to
a great extent those of the Jewish schools. It was regarded
not as the history of a partial revelation, of which the main
provisions had been altered by the New Covenant, but as a
supernatural and homogeneous document of equal authority
with the writings of the Apostles and Evangelists. And the
entire library of thirty-nine books, which hardly any of the
Fathers could read in the original, was appealed to as the
final authority alike by Ebionites, who taking them literally
maintained the eternal validity of Mosaism, and by Gnostics,
who interpreting them allegorically deduced from their pages
the wildest extravagances of heresy. Without deep learning,
without linguistic knowledge, without literary culture, without any final principles either as to the nature of the sacred

---

[1] Of *Prelatical Episcopacy.*
[2] He speaks also of "the labyrinth of Councils and Fathers, an entangled
wood which the Papist loves to fight in."—Milton, *Of True Religion, ad
init.* "Many Fathers discover more heresies than they will refute, and that
often for heresy which is the truer opinion." "I dare to be known to think
our sage and serious poet Spenser to be a better teacher than Scotus or
Aquinas."—*Areopagitica.* It is wrong, he says, "to dote upon immeasurable,
innumerable, and therefore unnecessary and unmerciful volumes, choosing
rather to err with the specious name of the Fathers, than to take a sound
truth at the hands of a plain upright man, &c."—*Of Reformation in England.*
"Redis ad Patrum commentationes, de quibus hoc summatim, accipe. Quicquid illi dixerint, neque ex libris sacris aut ratione aliqua satis idonea confirm-
averint, perinde mihi erit ac si quis alius e vulgo dixisset."—*Defens. c. 4.*

writings or the method by which they should be interpreted
—surrounded by Paganism, Judaism, and heresy of every
description, and wholly dependent on a faulty translation,—
the earliest Fathers and Apologists add little or nothing to our
understanding of Scripture. They are not to be blamed for
deficiencies which were inevitable. They could not transcend
the resources of the days in which they lived. It is their
eternal glory that they won the battle of Christianity by their
innocence, their courage, their faithfulness even unto death
to the Gospel message with which they had been intrusted ;
but we turn to them in vain for the justification of any claim
to the possession of an infallible tradition. Their acquaintance with the Old Testament is incorrect, popular, and full
of mistakes ; their Scriptural arguments are often baseless;
their exegesis—novel in application only—is a chaos of
elements unconsciously borrowed on the one hand from
Philo, and on the other from Rabbis and Kabbalists. They
claim " a grace " of exposition, which is not justified by the
results they offer, and they suppose themselves to be in
possession of a Christian Gnosis [1] of which the specimens
offered are for the most part entirely untenable.[2]

1. The only Bible used by the APOSTOLIC FATHERS was the
Septuagint, and they rely on its supposed inspiration even
when it differs widely from the original Hebrew. But while
they proclaim the words of the Bible to be the very words of
the Holy Spirit, they treat them with the strangest freedom.
They alter ; they misquote ; they combine widely different
passages of different authors ; they introduce incidents
borrowed from Jewish ritual and Jewish legend ; they
make more use of the Old Testament than of the New ; [3]

---

[1] *Ep. Barnab.* c. ix. and *passim.* Bede on 1 Sam. i. 1, 2.

[2] For some remarks on the Fathers see Hare, *Vindication of Luther*, p. 81.

[3] The dissemination of the New Testament writings was not of course in-
stantaneous. It took some time for them all to become known, and also to
be recognised as being of coordinate authority with the Jewish Scriptures.
The epistle of Clement is to a great extent a cento of phrases. He makes
large use both of some of St. Paul's Epistles and of the Epistle to the Hebrews,
but says nothing about their inspiration. According to Funk (*Patres
Apostolici*, i. 566–578) Clement quotes 157 times from the Old Testament, the
Apocrypha, and the Assumption of Moses ; 158 times from the New Testament
but with only 3 *direct* quotations.

they not only appeal to apocryphal writings as of inspired authority, but build arguments upon them. In matters of interpretation they show so little title to authority that their views have been abandoned by the whole Christian world.

Passing over the author of the *Teaching of the Twelve Apostles,* who makes but little use of either Testament,[1] we come to CLEMENT OF ROME. This ancient bishop quotes not only from the book of Judith, but apparently even from such books as the Pseudo-Ezekiel and the Assumption of Moses.[2] He is the first who refers to the Phoenix as a sign of the Resurrection;[3] the first also who endows Rahab with the gift of prophecy, because by the scarlet cord hung out of her window she made it manifest that redemption should flow by the blood of the Lord to all them that believe and hope in God.[4] As the pictorial fancy of a preacher, such an illustration would be harmless; but when it is offered as the explanation of an actual prophecy it is the earliest instance of the overstrained Allegory, which was afterwards to affect the whole life of Christian exegesis. We see the reason for this. Allegory was already a familiar method among the

---

[1] He quotes the Old Testament thrice, and the Apocrypha four times; of the New Testament writers he seems only to have been familiar with St. Matthew.

[2] c. viii. The quotation in this chapter may be a confused reminiscence of several passages (Ps. ciii. 10, 11 ; Jer. iii. 4, 19 ; Is. i. 18 ; Ez. xviii. 30, &c.), but Clemens of Alexandria (*Paedag.* i. 10, § 91) quotes it from "Ezekiel." It may be either from the Alexandrian poet of that name or from apocryphal additions to Ezekiel. Photius says that Clement quoted from several apocryphal books "as from Scripture" (*Bibl. Cod.* 126). Nac. 17, ἐγὼ δέ εἰμι ἀτμὶς ἀπὸ κύθρας is ascribed to Moses and may be from the Assumption of Moses, though not for the reason assigned by Hilgenfeld. Bishop Lightfoot thinks that the quotation in c. 23 comes from Eldad and Medad. There are other apocryphal quotations in c. 29 and c. 46.

[3] c. 25. Clemens is not more credulous than Tacitus (*Ann.* vi. 28) or Pliny (*H.N.* x. 2) ; but I am only showing how far he stands below the level of St. John and St. Paul. And it should be observed that Pliny and Tacitus (1) express some doubts on the matter ; and (2) are not elevated into half-inspired authorities ; and (3) do not appeal to the fable in support of a religious truth. Perhaps he was misled by the Seventy in Ps. xc. 12 ; Job xxix. 18, or by the Assumption of Moses (see Hilgenfeld *Nov. Test. extr. can.* i. 99, and Bishop Lightfoot's note).

[4] *Ep. ad Cor.* 12, ὁρᾶτε, ἀγαπητοί, οὐ μόνον πίστις ἀλλὰ προφητεία ἐν τῇ γυναικὶ γέγονε. The same specimen of exegetic gnosis is adopted by Justin Martyr *Dial.* 111 ; Iren. *Haer.* iv. 20 ; Origen *in Matt.* xxvii. 28 ; Ambrose *De Fide,* 4 ; Paulinus, *Carm.* 23 ; Aug. *in Ps.* lxxxvi. 4 ; and many others. See the note of Cotelerius *in loc.* (i. p. 155).

Jews, and just as the Alexandrians had adopted it in order to find in Moses an anticipation of Greek philosophy, so the Apostolic Fathers, before the full formation of the New Testament Canon, were driven to it in order to make the Old Testament an immediate witness for Christian truth.[1] The Epistle of Clement to the Corinthians breathes the spirit of a sincere and beautiful piety, but its inferiority to even the humblest of the canonical writings shows us that with the close of the sacred Canon the whisper of divine inspiration breathed far more faintly over the intellectual powers of men. "The Bible," it has been said, "is not like a city of modern Europe which subsides through suburban gardens, and groves, and mansions into the open country, but like an Eastern City in the Desert from which the traveller passes by a single step" if not quite "into a barren waste" yet into poor and infertile fields.

2. The Epistle of BARNABAS has a more direct bearing on the History of Interpretation. It presents to us a singular spectacle. Intensely anti-Judaic in tone, yet directly Judaic in method, it is marked by no coherent and intelligible theory. The writer, though full of satisfaction respecting his own gift of insight, was no thinker, and he leaves side by side things quite irreconcilable. He appears to suppose that part of the Old Testament was meant for the Jews and part for the Christians, [2] but suggests no principle by which one part is to be discriminated from the other. He can hardly have been ignorant that Christ was circumcised and yet he quotes various passages to show that circumcision was not meant to be of the flesh and that the Jews were led into it by the delusion of an evil angel.[3] He believes that Judaism

---

[1] Arnobius (*Adv. Gentes*, iv. 33, v. 32—45) energetically repudiates the principle of allegory as applied by the Gentile philosophers to the fables about their gods. He asks a very pertinent question, "Quod cum ita se habeat, quî potestis res certas rebus a dubiis sumere, atque unam adjungere significationem dicto, quod per modos videtis innumeros expositionum varietate deduci?" (v. 34).

[2] *Ep. Barnab.* 4. 14. I should have thought it hardly worth saying that the writer of this Epistle could not have been *the Apostle* Barnabas, if Prof. Milligan had not thought it probable (*Dict. of Christ. Biog.* p. 261).

[3] *Ep. Barnab.* 9. So Ignatius (*Ad Magnes.* 10) calls Judaism ἡ κακὴ ζύμη.

was only an expression of God's will when it is explained by Christian gnosis ; and that God's intended covenant with the Jews had been dissolved and transferred to the Christians at the moment when Moses broke the tables of stone. The only glimmer of an exegetic principle which he discloses is to find throughout the Old Testament something which can be referred to Christ or to Christianity.[1] Thus, by loosely mixing up two separate events, he says, that Abraham circumcised his 318 servants, and then he explains this in a kabbalistic manner. The number, he says, may be expressed by the letters TIH of which T stands for the cross and IH for IHσοῦς, and this was the mystery which Abraham meant to imply.[2] " No one," he adds, " has been admitted by me to a more excellent piece of knowledge than this. But I know that ye are worthy." And this mixture of two kabbalistic methods,[3] purely Jewish and wholly arbitrary, is eagerly adopted not only by Clement of Alexandria, but by Tertullian, Ambrose, Augustine, Paulinus, Gregory, Isidore, and Bede.[4] It never even occurred to Barnabas or to any who adopted this singular specimen of exposition that there was any absurdity in attributing to a Chaldean Emir an application of mystic processes and numerical values to the letters of an alphabet which had no existence till hundreds of years after he had returned to dust.

Comp. *Ep. ad Diognet.* See Baur, *Church Hist.* i. 138 (E.T.) ; Hilgenfeld, *Die apost. Väter,* 37 *fg.* ; Reuss, *Théol. Chrét.* ii.

[1] He quotes Is. xlv. 1, as follows, " The Lord said to my Christ the Lord " apparently confusing Κύρῳ with Κυρίῳ, *Ep. Barnab.* 12. The only *direct* New Testament quotations in Barnabas (cc. iv. v.) are from Matt. xxii. 14 ; ix. 13. He quotes once from 4 Esdras ; four times from Book of Enoch ; and frequently from the Old Testament. The writer, had he been the Apostle Barnabas, could never have spoken of the Twelve as ὑπὲρ πᾶσαν ἁμαρτίαν ἀνομωτέρους. c. v. (See however *Dict. of Christian Biog. l.c.*)

[2] *Ep. Barnab.* 9. In this he is followed by Clemens Alex. (*Strom.* vi. 11 ; § 84); Ambrose, *De Fide,* i. ; Aug. *Quaest. in Jud.* 37 ; Hilary, *De Synod.* 86, &c., and apparently by Dr. Pusey (*Tract* 89). We have already seen the inference drawn by the Rabbis from the fact that the name Eliezer also yields the number 318. Bereshith Rabba, c. 27. Yet the Fathers complain of Valentinian for inferring that the letters IH indicated 18 aeons. (Epiphan. *Haer.* ii. 14.) So familiar were the early Christians with this form of the Qabbala that Prudentius says we must fight our vices with 318 servants, *i.e. figurâ mysticâ ; Praef. in Psychomachiam.*

[3] *Gematria,* see *ante,* p. 98 ; *Temoorah,* see p. 102.

[4] See Cotelerius *ad loc.*

It is in Barnabas also that we find the earliest of the many Christian attempts to follow Aristobulus in giving a mystic reason for the laws about clean and unclean meats. The hyaena, he says, is not to be eaten, to show that men must not be corrupters, since that animal annually changes its sex; nor the weasel, because it conceives with the mouth![1] In explaining the sacrifice of the Red Heifer as a type of Christ he adds, among other particulars borrowed from the Oral Law, that three boys had to sprinkle the people with scarlet wool and hyssop bound round a stick; and that the calf was to be offered by men of perfect wickedness. The men are explained to be symbols of those who led Christ to death and then (apparently) of the Apostles.[2] The boys that sprinkle are " those that have proclaimed to us the remission of sins," and are three in number in witness of Abraham, Isaac and Jacob. The stick is, of course, made a type of the cross and in some unexplained way the scarlet wool also; and the hyssop is to show that the days of Christ's kingdom will be evil. All these things he says, "we explain *as the Lord intended.*"[3] The comment on the first Psalm is equally fantastic. "*Blessed is the man who hath not walked in the counsel of the ungodly,*" even as the fishes—the lamprey, polypus, and cuttle-fish, which may not be eaten—go in darkness to the depths of the sea; "*and hath not stood in the way of sinners,*" even as those who profess to fear the Lord, but go astray like the swine; "*and hath not sat in the seat of the scorners,*" even as those birds that lie in wait for prey. This, he says, "is spiritual knowledge." "*He shall be as a tree planted by the waters,*" indicates both baptism and the cross. "*His leaf also shall not wither,*" means that "every word proceeding out of your mouth in faith and love shall tend to

---

[1] Allegorical explanations of these wise and practical prohibitions are found in many of the Fathers. Tertullian goes so far as to say " Quid tam *contemtibile* quam ciborum exceptio ?" and explains it as "sapientia in occulto," *C. Marc.* v. 5 ; Origen, *Hom. in Levit.* makes a similar remark, and *De Princ.* iv. 1 ; *C. Cels.* iv. 93.

[2] *Ep. Barnab. c.* 10. The passage is extremely obscure and confused ; but this seems to be the meaning.

[3] *Id.* c. 10 *ad fin.*

bring conversion and hope to many." Among the prophecies of the cross, Barnabas is the first of the Fathers to quote the apocryphal verse, " And the Lord saith, When a tree shall be bent down, and shall again arise, and when blood shall flow out of wood."[1] He blesses God for making him understand what is meant by "the land flowing with milk and honey," and explains it, "in accordance with true gnosis," to mean, "Trust in Jesus." For the "land" stands for "man," and "honey" for "faith;" and "milk" for "the word."[2] Barnabas is the earliest Christian writer who based the notion that the world was to last six thousand years upon the six days of creation, and the Psalmist's expression, " One day is with the Lord as a thousand years." In this fantastic inference he is followed by Irenaeus, Hippolytus, Lactantius, Hilary, Jerome, and many others.[3]

But while no sane man can now fail to see that such explanations are "in the highest degree foolish and unnatural," we must not set them down to the special incompetence of the writer. "The Christian Church," says Professor Milligan, "has afforded too many examples of the adoption of the most perverted principles of interpretation by gifted minds, and by large sections of her members, to make folly in that particular direction a proof of general mental weakness."[4] So far from being despised, the Epistle of Barnabas was regarded as pre-eminently edifying, and it was a matter of doubt for a time whether it should not be admitted into the sacred canon. Like the Pastor of Hermas, and the Epistles of Clement and Polycarp, it was even read in many churches in public worship.[5]

---

[1] *Id.* 12 (2 Esdr. v. 5).　　[2] *Ep. Barn.* 6.

[3] *Ep. Barn.* 15 (Gen. ii. 2 ; Ps. xc. 4) ; Iren. *Haer.* v. 28, 29 ; Hippolytus, *ap.* Phot. *cod.* cii. ; Lactant. *Instt.* vii. 25 ; ·Jer. *Ep.* 139, &c. See Cotelerius, i. 44.

[4] *Dict. of Christian Antiquities, s.v.* Barnabas.

[5] Into the theology of the early Fathers I do not enter. Jerome admits that before Arius arose like a demon of the noonday, "innocenter quaedam et minus caute locuti sunt, et quae non possint perversorum hominum calumniam declinare." *Apol. adv. Rufin.* ii. No one would blame them for this, but it shows that they cannot be regarded as authorities. See Petavius, *De Trin.* i. v. 7 ; Newman, *Ess. on Development,* 12—15.

3. HERMAS furnishes little or nothing to our purpose, and
indeed has not one direct quotation from either the Old or New
Testament, unless, "Many be called but few chosen" be taken
from St. Matthew.[1] Nor do POLYCARP and IGNATIUS indulge
in direct exegesis.[2] TATIAN wrote a book on Scripture
difficulties,[3] consisting of comments on St. Paul, which are no
longer extant. In his oration, he like Barnabas uses the Old
Testament as the source of all knowledge.[4] ATHENAGORAS
also held the mechanical theory of inspiration and uses the
allegoric method.[5] He says, "that the Spirit uses the writers
as a flute-player might blow into his flute."[6] THEOPHILUS
of ANTIOCH looked to the Bible even for physical and
scientific teaching. Thus he quotes the cry of Abel's blood
from the ground as the cause why blood coagulates when
it is spilled upon the earth.[7] Like many of the Fathers,
wherever he finds λόγος in the Old Testament he at once
applies the passage to Christ,[8] and interprets the first
words of Genesis to mean that the Son was in the Father.
His exegesis of the New Testament is equally arbitrary. In
John i. 3, "*without Him was nothing made which was made*,"
he says, that "nothing" means an idol, because the Apostle
says, "we know that an idol is nothing in the world." We
learn from St. Jerome, that in dealing with the parable of
the Unjust Steward he explained him to be St. Paul.[9]

---

[1] Matt. xxii. 14, in *Vision*, ii. 2. The same quotation occurs in Barnabas,
c. 4, and something like it in 4 Esdras. The scriptural parallels to passages
of Hermas are given by Funk, i. 575. Origen regarded "the shepherd" as
divinely inspired (*Comm. on Rom.* x. 31), but Tertullian despises it (*De
Pudic.* 20).

[2] No specially distinctive *exegetic* data are to be derived from Papias, or the
Ep. to Diognetus (which ignores the Old Testament).

[3] Euseb. *H. E.* v. 13, προβλημάτων βιβλίον.

[4] The translator of the Armenian version of the commentary on Tatian's
Diatessaron, by Ephraem Syrus, published by the Mechitarist Fathers at Venice,
happily proves that Tatian, a pupil of Justin, used the Gospel of St. John as
well as the Synoptists.   [5] *Apol.* 9.

[6] *Quaest. ad Autolyc.* ii. 9. He also quotes the Sibylline oracles as inspired
(*id.* ii. 9). The word Τριὰς first occurs in this book, and *Trinitas* in Tert.
C. Prax. 4. Jerome speaks slightingly of his commentaries, but does not
seem to feel sure of their genuineness. That on the Gospels would be the
earliest extant commentary if genuine. R. Simon, *Hist. Crit. der Comment.*
p. 5.   [7] *Id.* ii. 29.

[8] Thus in Ps. xlv. 1, "Eructavit cor meum *Verbum bonum i.e.* Christum."

[9] Jer. *Ep. ad Algas.* 151, qu. 6. Had the Key (κλείς) of Melito of Sardis

4. For the New Testament JUSTIN MARTYR not only offers
no exegesis,[1] but seems uneasy unless he can base its simplest
statements upon prophecies in the Old Testament. Indeed
he seems to regard even Christ less as a teacher than as an
interpreter of the Old Testament, which He had inspired.[2]
Like Philo, he supposes that the Greek philosophers borrowed
their wisdom from Moses.[3] He believes in verbal dictation,
yet quotes the Sibyl and Hystaspes as genuine prophetic
books.[4] He relies exclusively upon the skill which he
supposed himself to possess as an interpreter;[5] yet he was
ignorant of Hebrew,[6] and accepted the fables of Pseudo-
Aristeas about the Septuagint.[7] He was entirely uncritical.
He appeals to the so-called Acts of Pilate.[8] He speaks of the

and his commentary on the Apocalypse survived, they would have had great
exegetic importance. To him we owe the first Christian canon of the Old
Testament.

[1] The only book of the New Testament which he mentions by name is the
Revelation of St. John (*Dial.* 81). He never mentions St. Paul, and has no
certain traces of the Acts, the Catholic Epistles, or the Hebrews. He refers
to the Gospels as "Memorials" of the Apostles (*Dial.* 103), but only five of
his references agree *verbally* with St. Matthew and St. Luke. On the other
hand, though he does not quote the New Testament as "Holy Scripture," he
seems to imply the inspiration of its writers (*Apol.* i. 39, 50 ; *Dial.* 119).
For his quotations see Otto, *Corp. Apolog.* ii. 579–592 ; Bishop Kaye, p. 146.

[2] *Apol.* i. 32. After quoting the words, "Unless ye be born again ye shall
not enter into the kingdom of God" (John iii. 5), he refers also to Is. i. 17
(*Apol.* i. 61). It is true that this may partially be explained by the exigencies
of his controversy ; but it is in curious contrast to the Epistle of Polycarp,
which alludes but slightly to the Old Testament. In the Epistle of Ignatius
the practice of relying exclusively on the Old Testament is blamed (*Ep. ad
Philad.* 8).

[3] Justin is however most unfavourable to the Jewish Law. *Dial.* 19, 23,
27, &c.

[4] *Apol.* i. 20, 44 ; *Cohort. ad Graecos,* § 37 (if this work be genuine). Comp.
Tert. *ad Natt.* ii. 12, &c.

[5] *Dial.* 56, 58. Like Clement and Barnabas he regards the typical and
allegoric explanations as *Gnosis* derived from spiritual grace (χάρις), *Dial.* 112.

[6] He may have known by hearsay the strange derivations (?) of "Satan"
(from *Sata,* "apostate," and *Nas,* " serpent "), and of "Israel" ("the man
conquering power"). *Dial.* 125. See Siegfried, *Philo,* 269. Justin sometimes refers quotations to wrong authors (*Apol.* i. 35, 49, 51, 53), and sometimes quotes the same passage in different ways. *Apol.* i. 45 ; *Dial.* 32, 33.
Thirlby talks of his " *incredibilis in recitandis scripturis inconstantia,*" and
" *incredibilis in scribendo festinatio.*"

[7] *Cohort.* 13. *Dial.* 71. He appears to have taken an inscription to the
Sabine god Semo Sancus for one to Simon Magus, *Apol.* i. 26, 56. In *Apol.* i.
31, he says that Ptolemy sent messengers to *Herod.*

[8] *Apol.* i. 35, 48. The name "Acts of Pilate" was sometimes given to
the Gospel of Nicodemus. and the passages referred to by Justin are to be
found in that apocryphal book.

Law and circumcision as proofs of peculiar evil in the Jews, and regards God's approval of them as nothing but an "accommodation" to their sins.[1] He relies mainly on prophecy, and charges the Jews with having struck four passages out of the Septuagint, of which three do not occur in any manuscript, and one occurs in all.[2] Following in the footsteps of the Rabbis he denies the plainest historical facts. He explains the apparent justification of polygamy in the Old Testament by some great mystery, and allegorises the stories about Judah's immorality, and David's adultery, and Jacob's wives.[3] Thus, like Barnabas, he thinks that the Old Testament was meant mainly for Christians,[4] and, as Middleton sarcastically, but hardly with exaggeration, observes, "he applied all the sticks and pieces of wood in the Old Testament to the cross."[5] In every Old Testament Theophany he sees a certain Christophany. He sometimes presses into his allegory facts for which he has no scriptural authority, as when he says that there were *twelve* bells on the High Priest's robe, and that they symbolised the Apostles; that Jesus was born in a cave;[6] that the ass at Bethphage was found tied to a vine;[7] that Christ, as a carpenter, made yokes and ploughs; that a fire was kindled in Jordan at His baptism; that His feet as well as His hands were nailed to the cross.[8] He even adopts such mere fables as that not only did the clothes of the Israelites not grow old in the desert, but those of the younger Israelites grew as they grew.[9] Justin's whole system of interpretation depends on

---

[1] *Dial.* 27.

[2] *Dial.* 71–73. One of these is attributed by Irenaeus (iii. 20 ; iv. 22) first to Isaiah, then to Jeremiah. He unjustly charges with bad faith the render-ing of עַלְמָה by νεᾶνις instead of παρθένος in Is. vii. 14 (*Dial.* 43), and says that the Jewish corruption of the Scriptures was a worse crime than even Moloch-worship. *Dial.* 73.

[3] *Dial.* 86, 134, 141.   [4] *Dial.* 57, 137, 140.

[5] See *Dial.* 86–96. The rod of Moses, the pilled wands of Jacob, his staff, his ladder, Judah's wand, David's rod, the wood which Elisha threw into the Jordan, &c., &c.

[6] Is. xxxiii. 16 ; *Dial.* 78.

[7] Gen. xlix. 10 ; *Apol.* i. 32.

[8] See *Dial.* 88, 103 ; *Apol.* i. 35.

[9] *Dial.* 131. ἀλλὰ καὶ τὰ τῶν νεωτέρων συνηύξανε.

the assumption that the Old Testament writers always spoke in mysteries, types, and symbols.[1] When we read the passage in which Jacob and Noah are treated as types of Christ, we sympathise with the complaints of Trypho, that while God's words were sacred, Justin's exegesis of them was purely artificial.[3] We may concede to Celsus, that the proof of Christianity must rest on clearer images and less dubious indications than these.[4] The extent to which Justin was influenced by Jewish methods may be seen by his application of the verse, " *The Lord rained upon Sodom brimstone and fire from the Lord*" (Gen. xix. 24), to prove the divinity of Christ.[5] Philo uses analogous modes of argument, and Philo as we know was an object of Justin's admiration.[6] From him Justin borrowed the theory of passive ecstasy as the condition of prophetic utterance, and so far from feeling any misgiving about his exegetic system, he attributes it to the possession of a special grace.[7]

5. We might have hoped that some fragments of genuine Apostolic, wisdom would have reached IRENAEUS through Polycarp or his aged predecessor Pothinus.[8] But whatever may be his other gifts he shows no special wisdom in the

---

[1] παρακεκαλυμμένως ἐν μυστηρίῳ.

[2] *Dial.* 134, 140.

[3] *Dial.* 79. τὰ μὲν τοῦ Θεοῦ ἅγιά ἐστιν, αἱ δὲ ὑμέτεραι ἐξηγήσεις τετεχνασμέναι. For instance "Jacob served Laban for speckled and many-spotted sheep, and Christ served . . . . for the various and many-formed races of mankind. Leah was weak-eyed, *for* the eyes of your souls are weak. Rachel stole the gods of Laban and we have lost our paternal and maternal gods" (*Dial.* 134).

[4] Orig. *C. Cels.* ii. 30. παρέρριψε δὲ ὁ Κέλσος τοῦτο· Θεὸν δὲ καὶ τοῦ Θεοῦ υἱὸν οὐδεὶς ἐκ τοιούτων παρακουσμάτων οὐδ' ἐξ οὕτως ἀγεννῶν τεκμηρίων συνίστησιν.

[5] *Dial.* 56. A similar use was made of the text in Iren. *Haer.* iii. 6 ; Tert. *Adv. Praxean.* 13 ; Euseb. *Dem. Evang.* v. 23 ; Ambros. *De Fide*, i. 2 (see Feuardent *in loc. Iren.*) and see *infra.* The Council of Sirmium anathematised any one who understood the verse differently. Hilar. *De Synod.* p. 373. A similar interpretation was given to 2 Tim. i. 18.

[6] *Cohort. ad Graec.* 9. He calls him and Josephus οἱ σοφώτατοι. Renan says of him, "Justin n'était un grand esprit ; il manquait à la fois de philosophie et de la critique ; son exégèse surtout passerait aujourd'hui pour très défectueuse . . . il avait cette espèce de crédulité médiocre qui permet de raisonner sensément sur des prémisses puériles et de s'arrêter à temps de façon à n'être qu'à moitié absurde."—*L'Eglise Chrétienne,* 356.

[7] *Cohort. ad Graec.* 8.

[8] "Constat Polycarpi . . hunc fuisse discipulum." Jer. *Catal. s.v.*

application of hermeneutic methods.[1] He, too, relied simply on
the Septuagint and regarded all who preferred other readings
as *vere impudicos et audaces*.[2] He quotes the Book of Baruch
and Bel and the Dragon as genuine Scripture. He constantly
appeals to " tradition; " [3] and he says that the true exposition
of Scripture must be learnt by Presbyters from Bishops who
could claim apostolic succession, and had received therewith
a sure charism of truth. Nevertheless, his own exposition
is based on the same erroneous principles as that of his predecessors. He was quite able to expose futile and fantastic
exegesis when it was used by heretics, and he compares it to
twisting ropes of sand.[4] Nothing can be more admirable than
his remarks on the arbitrary juxtaposition of irrelevant and perverted texts which in all ages has passed for scriptural proof.
He compares it to the centos made of Homeric verses,[5] and
to the breaking up of the mosaic of a king in order to work
the separate fragments into the mosaic of a dog or fox.[6] He
insists on the excellent rule that enigmatic passages are not
to be explained by those which are still more enigmatic, but
only by what is clear and plain.[7] Unhappily, however, his
own exegesis often falls far short of his theories. Since the
Gnostics used apocryphal gospels he tries to prove that there
could only be four Gospels because there are four quarters of

---

[1] *Haer.* iii. 21, § 2. He is the earliest Father who quotes as largely from
the New Testament as from the Old, and in his fourth book he proves against
Marcion the unity of the two covenants. The edition of Irenaeus to which I
refer is Massuet's, 1710.

[2] For his quotations see Stieren, i. 996–1005.

[3] ἡ δύναμις τῆς παραδόσεως μία καὶ ἡ αὐτή. *Haer.* i. 10, § 2. ἡ ἀπὸ τῆς
ἐκκλησίας κηρυσσομένη ἀλήθεια, i. 9, § 5. Comp. v. 20, § 2 ; iii. 3, § 1-4. By
tradition he sometimes appears to mean the shorter form of the old Roman
creed ; but he also appeals to tradition for special facts (see Routh, *Rel. Sacrae*,
42—65, ed. 1814).

[4] *Haer.* i. 8, § 1, τοιαύτης δὲ τῆς ὑποθέσεως αὐτῶν οὔσης ἣν οὔτε Προφῆται
ἐκήρυξαν, οὔτε ὁ Κύριος ἐδίδαξεν οὔτε Ἀπόστολοι παρέδωκαν τὴν περὶ τῶν ὅλων
αὐχοῦσι πλεῖον τῶν ἄλλων ἐγνωκέναι, ἐξ ἀγράφων ἀναγιγνώσκοντες, καὶ τὸ δὴ
λεγόμενον ἐξ ἄμμου σχοινία πλέκειν ἐπιτηδεύοντες (comp. *id.* ii. 10, § 1).

[5] *Haer.* i. 9, § 4, λέξεις καὶ ὀνόματα σποράδην κείμενα συλλέγοντες
μεταφέρουσι. Comp. Jer. *Ep.* liii. § 7 " Quasi non legerimus Homerocentonas
et Virgiliocentonas ! "

[6] *Haer.* i. 8, § 1, ὅνπερ τρόπον εἴ τις . . . πείθοι ὅτι αὕτη ἡ σαποὰ τῆς
ἀλώπεκος ἰδέα ἐκείνη ἐστιν ἡ καλὴ τοῦ βασιλέως εἰκών. He gives us some
specimens of Valentinian allegory, and preserves a comment of Ptolemaeus
on the Prologue of St. John (§ 5).

[7] *Haer.* ii. 10, § 2.

the world, four winds, and four cherubic forms.[1] He blames the Gnostics for drawing arguments from numbers, letters, and syllables,[2] yet even in a matter so important as an explanation of the name Jesus he adopts the Rabbinic method of *Notarikon.*[3] He says that in Hebrew the word consists of two and a half letters and implies that Jesus is Lord of Heaven and earth.[4] He appeals to tradition against the Gnostics, but he frequently uses the same methods, of which, in their case, he repudiates the application.[5]

In theology Irenaeus is the first who, if he be rightly interpreted, suggests the disastrous view that Christ's ransom of our race was paid to Satan [6]—a notion which recurs in the writings of theologians almost unquestioned till the days of Anselm. Even as regards events which were then recent Irenaeus is a most unsafe authority. He quotes the evidence of " elders who received it from the Apostles " for the assertion that our Lord at His death was more than forty years of age [7] —an opinion rejected by the whole Christian world. He makes the highly questionable statement that the Apocalypse was not written till the reign of Domitian.[8] He repeats after

---

[1] *Haer.* iii. 11, § 8.

[2] *Haer.* i. 3, § 3 ; ii. 24, §§ 1-6, where many instances are given.

[3] See *supra*, p. 101.

[4] *Haer.* ii. 24, § 2. The initials of the word ‏ישו‎ may be made by Notarikon to stand for *Y*ehovah, *Sh*amaîm, *V*e-ha-arets. Nothing can be made of the present reading, "Terra autem iterum *sura user* dicitur."

[5] Judg. vi. 37 (*Haer.* iii. 17, § 3) ; Jon. ii. 1 (*Haer.* iii. 20, § 1) ; Dan. ii. 34 (*Haer.* iii. 21, § 7), referred to by Lipsius *Dict. of Christian Biogr.* ii. 270. In each instance the allegories are adopted by Augustine, Jerome, &c. See Diestel, pp. 56-60.

[6] *Haer.* v. 1, § 1. Athanasius furnishes a brilliant exception to this error. Archdeacon Norris understands Irenaeus differently (*Rudiments of Theology,* p. 274), but Origen and many others certainly held this view. It must not be forgotten that even in Theology the Fathers are not always safe guides. Cardinal Newman remarks that out of some thirty authors cited by Bishop Bull, he has to *explain* nearly twenty (*Ess on Development,* p. 158).

[7] *Haer.* ii. 22, § 5. The passage is quoted by Eusebius *H. E.* iii. 25, πάντες οἱ πρεσβύτεροι μαρτυροῦσι, οἱ κατὰ τὴν Ἀσίαν, Ἰωάννῃ . . . συμβεβληκότες παραδεδωκέναι [ταῦτα] τὸν Ἰωάννην, and for other mistakes see ii. 21, §§ 1-10. The mistake about the age of Jesus is the more strange because a little before he had pointed out the Passovers in the Gospels to disprove the "one-year" theory.

[8] In *Haer.* iii. 7, § 1, Irenaeus makes the true remark that St. Paul sometimes uses *hyperbata* " *propter velocitatem sermonum suorum ;* " but his application of the figure to 2 Cor. iv. 2 is unfortunate. He refers to a book of his own " On the peculiarities of the style of St. Paul."

Polycarp a most improbable story about St. John and Cerinthus, which is so unworthy of the Apostle that we can only hope that it is without foundation.[1] These examples sufficiently prove that if we are to judge the value of tradition even from such early writings as those of Irenæus we shall find that neither in theology, nor in exegesis, nor in the simplest matters of fact, does it establish any claim to our reverent acceptance.[2]

II. The Fathers of the third and later centuries may be divided into three exegetical schools. Those schools are the LITERAL and REALISTIC as represented predominantly by Tertullian ; the ALLEGORICAL, of which Origen is the foremost exponent ; and the HISTORIC and GRAMMATICAL, which flourished chiefly in Antioch, and of which Theodore of Mopsuestia was the acknowledged chief.

1. TERTULLIAN, like other Fathers, always speaks of Scripture as uttered by God, and dictated by the Holy Ghost.[3] He will not allow to Valentinian that there are any varying degrees of inspiration, nor to Marcion that Paul's insight was any deeper than that of other Apostles. Like the Rabbis, he placed all the Scriptures exactly on the same level.[4] He held that they contained all truth ; that they had no contradictory elements ; and that their cosmogony, chronology, anthropology, and history, were infallibly inspired.[5] If his views on this question are to be regarded as authoritative they must

---

[1] The story of Cerinthus and the Bath (see Epiphan. *Haer.* lxxviii. 14 ; Lampe, *Proleg.* p. 69). I have pointed out elsewhere the grounds on which I doubt the truth of the story (*Early Days of Christianity,* i. 163).

[2] See, for instance, the wild passage about the Millennial grapes, which he tells on the authority of the weak and credulous Papias, who professes to have heard it from Polycarp (*Haer.* v. 33, § 3 ; Euseb. *H. E.* iii. *ad fin. ;* Routh, *Rel. Sacr.* p. 9). When such authority is cited for such a Rabbinic absurdity, we cannot estimate very highly the boasted "tradition" on which Irenaeus relies. For other instances see Routh, *Rel. Sacrae,* i. pp. 46-68, 95-101 (Rahab's cord, $\dot{\epsilon}\nu \, \dot{\alpha}\rho\chi\hat{\eta} = \dot{\epsilon}\nu \, \Lambda\dot{o}\gamma\wp$, &c.).

[3] *Apol.* 18.

[4] *De Pudic.* 17, "Hanc *aequalitatem* Spiritus Sancti qui observaverit, ab Ipso deducetur in sensus ejus." He makes Ps. i. 1 a *prophecy* of Joseph of Arimathaea (*De spectac.* 3).

[5] *De Anim.* 1, 2 ; *C. Hermog.* 39, 40. He quotes from all the New Testament except 2 Pet., James, and 3 John, and held that the Old Testament belongs specially to Christians (*Apol.* 21). He knew no Hebrew, and relies on the "inspiration" of the Seventy (*Apol.* 18).

N

be equally claimed for the Book of Enoch, and "the Sibyl who lies not."[1] He mixes up different quotations, refers to them inaccurately, and relies for proof on verses which do not occur in Scripture at all.[2] He thinks that Noah may have received the Book of Enoch from his grandfather, or that, if the Book was lost in the Deluge, he might have restored it by immediate revelation, as Ezra reproduced the whole Scriptures.[3] How can such opinions be appealed to as having any weight? Before a scientific exegesis many of Tertullian's statements, so far from being a part of the Christian verity, vanish like mist before the sun.[4] He protests against literalism, except when time, manner, and circumstance are taken into consideration, yet he believes in a corporeal God, and accepts literally such metaphors as "the hand of God," and the "drop of water" in the Parable of Dives, and thinks that everything is forbidden which is not in Scripture expressly permitted.[5] He rightly blames the Gnostics for their abuse of allegory.[6] Yet he does not hesitate to allegorise whenever it suits him. Orthodoxy was accepted as a sufficient warrant for exegetic extravagance. He finds a symbol of the Twelve Apostles in the twelve wells of Elim, in the twelve gems on the High Priest's breast, in the twelve stones taken from Jordan;[7] and he thinks that *literal* prohibitions about clean and unclean kinds of food would be quite contemptible. The eloquent, fiery, uncompromising African practically makes Scripture say

---

[1] *De Idol.* 15 ; *De Cult. Fem.* i. 3 ; *ad Natt.* ii. 12, " Illa scilicet Sibylla veri vera vates."

[2] *De Cult. Fem.* i. 2, 3. See Bishop Kaye, *Writings of Tertullian*, p. 320 ; Porson, *Letters to Travis*, p. 273. Tertullian is too reckless a controversialist to be accepted as authoritative in his appeals to the actual autographs of the Apostles (*Haer.* v. 30, 31), or the census of Augustus (*C. Marc.* v. 7), or the supposed letter of Tiberius to the Senate about the divinity of Christ (*Apol.* 5), or the official report of the Crucifixion by Pilate (*Apol.* 21).

[3] He borrows this Jewish fable from 2 Esdras, xiv. 21-44.

[4] See Böhringer, iii. 787–790.

[5] *De Cor. Mil.* 2 ; *De Monogam.* 4, " Negat scriptura quod non notat."

[6] *De Resurr. Carnis*, 19, " Non omnia sunt imagines sed et veritates ; nec omnia umbrae sed et corpora." Comp. too *id. ib.* 20-33, *De Praescr.* 39 ; *C. Hermog.* 34, &c.

[7] *C. Marc.* iv. 13. See too *De Orat.* 4, *C. Prax.* 7, *De Baptismo*, iii. ix. and *passim.*

exactly what he himself chooses. When, like Athenagoras,[1] he condemns second marriage as "specious adultery," he has no manner of doubt that he is expressing the opinion of St. Paul, though St. Paul says the exact opposite.[2] If in spite of St. Paul's express disclaimer he insists on the resurrection of the identical flesh, he asserts that St. Paul does so likewise.[3] At one time Scripture has no meaning for him unless it coincides with what he recognises as tradition,[4] and at another time tradition is valueless if it does not correspond with his individual convictions. Thus he sometimes speaks the language of Luther, and sometimes that of the Council of Trent. If heretics appeal to the text, "Prove all things, hold fast that which is good," he loftily replies that "*we*" have no need of curiosity, and that "when we believe, we do not desire to believe anything further."[5] While he is in this mood he is so far carried away by his own sophistry as to speak with something like contempt of Biblical studies, as springing from curiosity, and tending to vainglory;[6] and by way of criticising our Lord's promise, "Seek and ye shall find," he implies that it was only applicable to the beginning of His teaching, while it was still doubted whether He was the Christ.[7] He contemptuously says that in arguing with heretics it is useless to appeal to Scriptural arguments, in which there is either an uncertain victory, or none at all, but that the appeal must be to Apostolic tradition.[8] And yet

---

[1] Athenag. *Legat.* 33, ὁ δεύτερος γάμος εὐπρεπής ἐστι μοιχεία, comp. Orig. *Hom. in Luc.* xvii. ; Theophil. *ad Autolyc.* iii. 15 ; Iren. *Haer.* iii. 17; § 2.

[2] 1 Tim. v. 14 ; *De Monogam.* 8.

[3] *De Resurr. Carnis*, 35, 47. 1 Cor. xv. 37. He calls those who disagree with him "lucifugae isti scripturarum." Comp. Iren. *Haer.* v. xii. § 3.

[4] *De Praescr.* 4.

[5] *De Praescr.* 7, "Nobis curiositate opus non est post Christum Jesum, nec inquisitione post evangelium."

[6] *De Praescr.* 14, "Fides in regula posita est . . . cedat curiositas fidei." 17, "Quid promovebis, exercitatissime Scripturarum, cum si quid defenderis negetur ex adverso, si quid negaveris defendatur?" The sentiment was finally crystallised in the "Tenendum quod semper, quod ubique, quod ab omnibus creditum est" of Vincentius Lerinensis, *Commonitor.* i. 3.

[7] *De Praescr.* 8. "Whatever answer Tertullian had ready for other objectors, these he could silence with a dashing peremptory interpretation of our Lord's words. . . . I find it hard to stifle my indignation at such trifling with the Divine precept."—Maurice, *Eccl. Hist.* p. 279.

[8] "Ego sum haeres apostolorum" (*De Praescr.* 37). This is the argument

when tradition no longer answers him according to his own
idols, he insists as forcibly as the Reformers, that Christ
calls Himself Truth, not Custom,[1] and, claiming what he has
so fiercely denied to others, he maintains that private judgment
is a natural and inalienable right.[2] The most inexorable of
traditionalists when he is arguing against heretics, he became
in his arguments against heathens the first clear asserter of
the Protestant principle of freedom of faith and conscience
as an inherent attribute of the conception of religion.[3]

Insisting on the verse, " God hath chosen the weak things
of the world to confound the strong," he adopted the paradox,
Credo quia absurdum est, and the wild conclusion that the
more repugnant to sound reason a statement was, it ought
so much the more to be deemed worthy of God.[4] And alas!
the vehement "father of Latin orthodoxy" erred from the
Catholic dogma. The maintainer of tradition became the
champion of a schism. The *malleus haereticorum* died a heretic.[5]

2. CYPRIAN is the only other prominent writer of the school
of Tertullian. He is said to have been so great an admirer
of his writings, that when he asked for them he used to
say *Da magistrum.*[6] But he was a man of less impetuous

---

of the whole *De Praescr. Haereticorum,* and Tertullian states it more formally than Irenaeus. *Praescriptio* means legally, an argument that the other
side ought not be heard. Tertullian charges heretics with having a different
canon, and with corrupting and mutilating Scripture. Heretics might certainly object to proofs from the Book of Enoch and from non-existent texts;
but to a very large extent they adopted the very same canon as Tertullian
himself.

[1] "Christus veritas est, non consuetudo" (*De Virg. vel.* 1).

[2] "Humani juris et naturalis potestatis est unicuique quod putaverit
colligere ; sed nec religionis est cogere religionem quae sponte suscipi debeat
non vi" (*Ad Scap.* 2). 　　　　　　　　　　[3] Baur, *K. G.* i. 428.

[4] On the deeply interesting personality of Tertullian, see Niebuhr, *Anct.
Hist.* ii. 54 ; Neander, *Ch. Hist.* i. 683 ; Newman, *Tracts,* p. 119 ; Renan,
Marc. Aurel. 456, "un mélange inouï de talent, de fausseté d'esprit, d'élo-
quence, et de mauvais goût." "Miserrimus ego," he says, "semper aeger
caloribus impatientiae" (*De Patient.* 1).

[5] "Every page almost of Tertullian would furnish terrible instances of
the irreverent torturing of Scripture to his own purposes—of a resolute
determination that it shall never contradict or weaken any purpose of
his—all the while that he professes to take it as his guide and judge."
Maurice, *Eccl. Hist.* p. 334.

[6] Jer. *Catal. s.v.* Tert. A certain Paulus, who had known Cyprian, told
Jerome "Nunquam Cyprianum absque Tertulliani lectione unam diem
praeteriisse."

genius, and all that is distinctive in his exegesis is
vitiated by the fatal fault of unreality.[1] He reads an
ecclesiastical tradition into Scripture as it pleases him.
If he wishes to prove the unity of the Church he does
so—in a manner almost ludicrous in its want of cogency
—from the Passover commandment "In one house shall
it be eaten;"[2] from the sentence, "My dove, my un-
defiled is one;"[3] and from the command of the spies to
Rahab to collect all her family into her house.[4] If he wants
to prove against the Aquarians that wine ought to be used
in the Eucharist,[5] he does so from the verse, " I am the true
vine;" from Noah's drunkenness, which he treats as a sign
of the Passion; from the hospitality of Melchizedek; from
the blessing on Judah; from the voice of wisdom in Proverbs;
from the red garments of the avenger;[6] and from the expression "my cup runneth over."[7] While insisting that
everything is to be done exactly as Christ did it, he yet
demands that the Holy Communion should be celebrated
in the morning. It is obvious that such exegesis is wholly
unscientific. It originates only in the necessity for con-
fronting Gnosticism in defence of beliefs or practices for which
there was no direct Scriptural warrant. It was forced to
maintain the view of the Jewish Rabbis, revived in modern
days by Dr. Newman, that Scripture is inconclusive without
the comment of tradition.[8] Every verse is interpreted *à*

---

[1] The Fathers have often rendered themselves liable to the very same complaints which they make against the heretics. Tert. *Praescr.* 38. "Alius
(Marcion) manuscripturas, alius (Valentinus) sensus expositione intervertit.
. . . Valentinus . . . materiam ad Scripturas excogitavit . . . adjiciens
dispositiones non comparentium rerum." Epiphan *Opp.* i. 396, κέχρηνται
παλαιᾷ καὶ νεᾷ διαθήκῃ κατὰ τὸν νοῦν τὸν ἴδιον μεταποιούμενοι. Euseb. *H. E.*
iv. 29, χρῶνται εὐαγγελίοις ἰδίως (Reuss, § 504).

[2] Ex. xii. 46.   [3] Cant. vi. 9.   [4] Josh. ii. 18.
[5] *Ep.* 63, *ad Caecil.*   [6] Is. lxiii. 2.   [7] Ps. xxiii. 5.

[8] It practically said "However you may interpret Scripture, Truth is with
us." "Quod apud multos unum invenitur," says Tertullian, "non est erratum
sed traditum." *De Praescr.* 28. See this subject excellently treated by Baur,
Church History, E. T. ii. 8-14. This side of Tertullian's and Cyprian's
opinions is most fully developed by Cardinal Newman's *Tracts for the Times*,
No. 85. He makes the remark, which would indeed be disastrous if it should
be proved, that "all persons, with very few exceptions, *who try to go by Scripture
only fall away from the Church and her doctrines,*" p. 2.

priori. If we are warned against eating and drinking the sacramental elements "*unworthily,*"[1] that is supposed to prove the necessity of formal penance and absolution.[2] If our Lord says, "He that is not with me is against me," that is explained to mean that all who are not Catholic Episcopalians are Antichrists. Cyprian has no glimpse of the relations of the Law to the Gospel. Whatever is said in the Old Testament about sacrificial priests is applied without hesitation to Christian presbyters. The remark of Optatus to Parmenian might be applied to Cyprian, "You batter the Law to such purpose that wherever you find the word water, there you conjure out of it some sense to our disadvantage." "He has," says Archbishop Benson, "a free ideal scheme before him, but in details falls from it, and so makes riddles of texts."[3] His exegesis yields any result that is required, and, therefore, yields no result of any intrinsic worth.[4] Yet, like Tertullian, he sets tradition aside where it interferes with his own opinions, and makes remarks which Calvin himself might have adopted—"Tradition without truth is only antiquated error," and "We must convince by reason, not prescribe by tradition."[5]

III. It was in the great catechetical school of Alexandria, founded, as tradition says, by St. Mark,[6] that there sprang up the chief school of Christian exegesis. Its object, like that of Philo, was to unite philosophy with revelation,[7] and

---

[1] 1 Cor. xi. 27.   [2] *Ep.* 16, § 2.

[3] Article "Cyprian" in Smith and Wace. Archbishop Benson refers to Cyprian's *Comments on Acts,* ii. 38 ; Phil. i. 18 (*Epp.* 73, 74, 75). It was a common complaint of the Fathers that the heretics quoted Scripture in their own sense. See Tertullian : "Valentinus non ad materiam Scripturas, sed materiam ad Scripturas excogitavit." *De Praescr. Haer.* 8, *De Anima,* 18. But do not the Fathers do the same ?

[4] Böhringer, ii. 1037.

[5] "Consuetudo sine veritate vetustas erroris est." The chief exponent of traditionalism in interpretation is St. Vincent of Lerins, who makes every decision turn on *ecclesiasticae intelligentiae auctoritas.* See Vincent. Ler. *C. Haer.* ii. iv. xli. and *passim.*

[6] Euseb. *H. E.* v. 10 ; vi. 3 ; Jer. *Catal.* 38 ; Sozomen, iii. 15. On the school of Alexandria see the treatises of Guericke, Matter, Vacherot, and others mentioned in the Bibliography.

[7] Clemens (*Strom.* i. § 9 ; vii. § 32) and Origen (*Hom. in Gen.* xiv. § 3) believed in the divine origin of Greek philosophy. For their views of Gnosis see *Strom.* vii. 10, § 55 ; Orig. *De Princip.* Praef. i. § 3.

thus to use the borrowed jewels of Egypt to adorn the sanctuary of God.[1] Hence, Clemens of Alexandria and Origen furnish the direct antithesis to Tertullian and Irenaeus. Clement appeals to a *secret* tradition, Tertullian denies its existence.[2] The Alexandrians aimed at the establishment of Christian Gnosticism, and many of their philosophic sympathies have such an affinity with those of the leading Gnostics that Gnosticism could not have been completely defeated by their methods.[3] Tertullian and Irenaeus, on the other hand, though with less learning, less depth, and less power repudiate all attempts to philosophise in matters of simple faith, and refuse to evaporate into speculative ideas the positive truths of historical Christianity. Nothing can be more unlike the spirit of the Alexandrians than the blunt question of Tertullian, "What has the Church to do with the Academy?"[4] Clement gives to philosophy a divine origin, Tertullian thinks it incompatible with Christian faith.[5]

1. The first teacher of the school who rose to fame was the venerable Pantaenus, a converted Stoic, of whose writings only a few fragments remain.[6] He was succeeded by CLEMENT OF ALEXANDRIA who, believing in the divine origin of Greek philosophy,[7] openly propounded the principle that all Scripture must be allegorically understood. The motto of the

---

[1] Origen, *Fragm. Ep. ad Greg. Thaumat.*

[2] See Kaye's *Clement*, 362 ; *Tertullian*, 31-234.

[3] Mosheim thinks that Christian Platonism defeated the Gnostics ; "verum ipso morbo nocentius longe remedium erat." (*De turbatâ per recentiores Eccles.* 1767, pp. 118 *sq.*)

[4] *De Praescr.* 7, "*Quid ergo Athenis et Hierosolymis? Quid Academiae et Ecclesiae? Nostra institutio est de porticu Salomonis qui et ipse tradiderat Dominum in simplicitate cordis esse quaerendum. Viderint qui Stoicum et Platonicum et dialecticum Christianismum protulerunt.*"

[5] For Clement's views on the relation of philosophy to Judaism and to Christianity see *Strom.* i. *passim* ; on its divine origin, see *id.* §§ 91-100 ; on its educational function, §§ 1-58. He holds that Greek philosophy was borrowed from what he calls "the philosophy of Moses," *id.* §§ 66-90, 167-179. Comp. vi. 42, 44; 47, 159. Tertullian on the other hand called the philosophers "the patriarchs of heretics."

[6] Routh, *Reliquiae Sacrae*, i. 375-383 ; Jer. *Catal.* 36. He must have favoured the allegoric method, for he applied to the Church what is written of Paradise. See Redepenning, *Origenes*, i. 63. Jerome says, "Magis viva voce ecclesiis profuit."

[7] *Strom.* i. § 28 ; vii. § 6 ; Origen, *Hom. in Gen.* xiv.

school was—"Unless ye believe ye will not understand."[1]
By way of proving this proposition he fell into the
prevalent error of giving an universal application to isolated
phrases.[2] He interpreted of a whole literature what was
originally intended of a single psalm or a single circumstance.[3]
The reasons which he assigns for the cryptic character
of Holy Writ are the antiquity of parabolic teaching, the
desire to stimulate research, and the assertion that the
hidden senses of Scripture are not fitted for all, but only
for those perfect Christians who are marked out by election
for the true Gnosis.[4] He does not deny the literal sense,
but thinks that it only furnishes an elementary faith. The
literal sense is the milk of the word, but the esoteric vision
furnishes strong meat.[5] "To the Gnostics," he says (*i.e.* to
philosophic Christians), "the Scriptures have conceived."[6]
Too often, alas, to such "Gnostics" they had only, in the
words of Isaiah, "brought forth wind."

His attitude towards the inspired writings is that of his
age. He makes room for legends even in the New Testament story.[7] His quotations are loose and paraphrastic, and
are sometimes attributed to a wrong author.[8] He quotes
verses which have no existence.[9] He refers to Apocryphal

---

[1] Is. vii. 9 ; LXX. ἐὰν μὴ πιστεύσητε οὐδὲ μὴ συνῆτε. The verse is mis-
translated and misapplied. On the Alexandrian contrast between "faith"
and "knowledge," see *Strom.* v. §§ 1–13 ; and for the exegetic principles of
Clement, specially *Strom.* i. § 32 ; v. § 20 ; vi. §§ 80–83, 127–132.

[2] *Strom.* i. § 32.

[3] For these scriptural proofs—which have not a shadow of validity—from
Ps. lxxviii. 2 ; Matt. x. 27 ; Mark iv. 34 ; 1 Cor. ii. 6, see *Strom.* v. §§ 25, 26 ;
vi. §§ 115-118. So as Neander says (*Ch. Hist.* ii. 265) "many texts from
Luther's translation of the Bible became current proof-passages for propositions
relating to Christian faith or practice, although this application of them *was
wholly inconsistent with the sense which they had in the original.*"

[4] *Strom.* i. § 7 ; v. §§ 16, 21 ; vi. §§ 1, 30 ; vii. § 35. See the passages
quoted in Gieseler, i. 233.

[5] In order to get rid of the objection that "knowledge puffeth up" (1 Cor.
viii. 1), Clement gives to φυσιοῖ the sense of "causes men to think great and
true thoughts" ! *Strom.* vii. § 104.

[6] *Strom.* vii. § 94. The distinction between the philosophic Christian (the
"true Gnostic") and the ordinary Christian runs all through the *Stromateis,*
see vi. §§ 26–109 ; vii. §§ 55, 57–95.

[7] The story about Salome is from "the Gospel to the Egyptians." *Strom.*
iii. § 63.

[8] See Kaye, p. 407.

[9] *Strom.* ii. § 45 ; vii. § 94.

writings as though they were inspired.[1] He attributes the
book of Wisdom to Solomon, and the Book of Baruch to
Jeremiah. He quotes even the "Revelation" and "Preaching" of Peter,[2] as well as the Epistle of Barnabas[3] and the
"Teaching of the Twelve Apostles," as having Scriptural
authority. He believes in the miraculous inspiration of
the Septuagint,[4] the Sibyl, and Hystaspes,[5] and he calls
Plato "all but an evangelical prophet."[6]

The characteristic features of his system are as follows:—

a. He believes that *esoteric teaching* was communicated by
Christ, not in writing, but orally after the Resurrection to
James, Peter, and John, who transmitted it to the seventy
disciples.[7] Pearls, he says, are not to be thrown before swine.
Some things were, therefore, only said and done, not because
they were right or true in the abstract, but only κατ'
οἰκονομίαν.[8]

b. He claims for his "ecclesiastical gnosis" the authority
of a *tradition*, to which he repeatedly appeals against the
perverted interpretations of heretics,[9] and which he calls
"the Apostolic orthodoxy," "the evangelical canon," "the
glorious and venerable rule of tradition."[10] This, he says, is
"the key" of the true Gnostics, while the heretics have only
an "anti-key."[11] But this tradition seems, on examination,
to be nothing more than the method of Pantaenus and other

---

[1] See Lardner, *Credibility*, ii. c. 22, § 13.

[2] *Strom.* i. § 182 ; vi. §§ 39, 48, 128.

[3] *Strom.* ii. § 31. He also quotes the Gospel according to the Hebrews.
Strom. ii. § 45.

[4] *Strom.* i. §§ 124, 148.

[5] *Paed.* ii. § 27 ; iii. § 15 ; *Strom.* i. § 108 ; v. § 13 ; vi. § 43. In *Strom.*
vi. § 42, St. Paul is made to quote the Sibyl and Hystaspes, Kaye, p. 406.

[6] *Strom.* i. § 10, Ὁ Πλάτων μονόνουχι προφητεύων τὴν σωτηρίου οἰκονομίαν.
ὁ ἐξ Ἑβραίων φιλόσοφος Πλάτων. *Strom.* i. § 150, τί γάρ ἐστι Πλάτων ἢ
Μωϋσῆς ἀττικίζων. *Paed.* iii. § 54, ὁ πάντα ἄριστος Πλάτων . . οἷον θεοφορούμενος.
Comp. *Strom.* i. §§ 28–32, where Heathen Philosophy is treated as a source
of sacred truth.

[7] Clem. *Hypotyp. ap.* Euseb. *H.E.* ii. 1, § 2 ; *Strom.* i. §§ 11, 96 ; vi.
§§ 61, 68, 125 ; vii. §§ 94, 107 ; Orig. *C. Cels.* vi. § 279.

[8] He instances not very appositely St. Paul's circumcision of Timothy. See
Kaye's *Writings of Tert.* p. 399. His Scriptural references are sometimes
inaccurate.

[9] *Strom.* vii. § 97. For reference to the "canon of tradition," see *Strom.*
i. §§ 11, 88, 179 ; vii. § 94. *Hypot.* vii. (*ap.* Euseb. *H. E.* ii. 1, § 2).

[10] See Kaye, p. 366. [11] *Strom.* vii. § 106.

Alexandrians. At any rate, the results to which it leads are, to quote Canon Westcott's phrase, often so "visionary and puerile" that we can attach to them but little importance. Different interpretations are sometimes furnished of the same passage. His explanations of the story of Abraham and Sarah are in principle identical with Philo's, as are his views concerning the symbolism of the Tabernacle.[1] Abraham's lifting up his eyes on the third day and seeing the place which God had appointed,[2] is explained to mean that on the first day he attained to the sight of what is fair, on the second to the best desires of the soul, and on the third to an insight into spiritual things; or else the three days are interpreted of the mystery of the seal of baptism, whereby man believes on God, who, as Plato says, is "the place of ideas." Joseph's coat is made a symbol of various knowledge which his brethren envied. In Ex. xvi. 36 we are told that "an omer is the tenth part of an ephah," or, as it is in the LXX., "of the three measures" ($\tau\hat{\omega}\nu$ $\tau\rho\iota\hat{\omega}\nu$ $\mu\acute{\epsilon}\tau\rho\omega\nu$), and these three measures are said to be the three criteria of sensation, speech, and understanding. The "clean beasts" imply the orthodox who are steadfast and meditative, since rumination stands for thought, and a divided hoof implies stability. The forbidden animals, which ruminate but do not divide the hoof, stand for the Jews; those which divide the hoof but do not ruminate are heretics; those who do neither are the impure.[3] Clement even allegorises the Decalogue, and in the New Testament treats the miracles exactly as if they were parables. Thus, in the feeding of the five thousand, he says that "the barley loaves" indicate the preparation of the Jews for divine knowledge, because barley ripens earlier than wheat; and "the fishes" the preparation of the Gentiles by Greek philosophy, because philosophy was born amid the waves of heathendom, and given to those who

---

[1] See Rosenmüller, *Hist. Interp.* i. 219. Kaye, pp. 374-403.
[2] Gen. xxii. 8.
[3] *Strom.* v. § 52 ; vii. § 109. Comp. Iren. *Haer.* v. 8. See Kaye, pp. 220, 380. In Is. xi. 7, Clement makes "the ox" stand for the Jews, and "the bear" for the Gentiles. For other untenable interpretations see *Strom.* v. vi. *passim.*

lie on the ground. Or one of the fishes may stand, he says, for encyclical instruction, and the others for philosophy, which is taught later on, the two being subsequently collected together by the word of the Lord! But, as Bishop Kaye says, " to follow Clement through all his allegorical interpretations would be a wearisome and unprofitable labour." [1] The worst evil of the system was that it led the Alexandrian teachers into very unsound views about " accommodation" and " esoteric teaching," of which the first became fatally akin to tampering with the truth, and the other was apt to deaden brotherly love, and to inflate a spiritual pride.[2]

IV. Of ORIGEN, the greatest master of this school, it would be impossible to speak in any terms but those of the highest admiration and respect.[3] While living he was the victim of episcopal jealousy and party intrigue and his very memory has been for many ages the butt for ignorant malice and brutal calumny. Envy never pardons.[4] History itself has been falsified, and the decrees of Councils misrepresented, to vilify one who was equally great in the value of his labours and in the sanctity of his life. There is no man to whom the Church of Christ owes a more awful debt of reparation than to this incomparable saint, who, though his memory has been branded and his salvation denied, rendered

---

[1] On Clement see, besides the books here quoted, Bishop Reinken's *De Clemente Presbytero Alexandrino,* 1851 ; and Abbé Freppel, *Clement d'Alexandrie,* 1860.

[2] This is the least pleasing aspect of the teaching of the school of Alexandria. Clemens is the first Father who uses οἰκονομία in the sense of "accommodation." "Condescension" (συγκατάβασις) occurs in Chrys. *Hom. in Tit.* iii. The Fathers attribute it not only to St. Paul, but even to our Lord, of which the worst instance is in Basil's remark on Matt. xxiv. 37, τοῦτο διὰ προσποιητῆς ἀγνοίας οἰκονομεῖ (*Ep.* 84). The doctrine was first borrowed from Plato (*De Rep.* iii.) by Philo (*Quod Deus sit immut.*). Clement approves of circuitous modes of stating truth (συμπεριφερόμενοι, κατὰ συμπεριφοράν). Origen says that a man "who is *obliged to speak falsely* (!) should be very careful" (Orig. *Strom.* vi.; *ap.* Jer. *Apol. I. in Rufin.* 18). For a practical instance see *C. Cels.* iii. 159. On the esoteric doctrines of these Fathers see *C. Cels.* i. 7 ; *De Princ.* 1, vi. § 1 ; *Hom. in Lev.* ix. Synesius adopted these views to the full (*Ep.* 105). See Schröckh, *K.G.* x. 380-395 ; Daillé, *De Usu Patrum,* vi.

[3] Jerome, who so often spoke bitterly of him, called him an Arian, and argued that he approved of telling lies, talks of his "immortale ingenium." *Catal. s. v.* Origen.

[4] Jeremie, *Hist. of Second and Third Cent.* p. 95.

to her greater services than all her other teachers—from whom
in fact those teachers for many centuries derived an immense
part of their knowledge and their thoughts—but whom
her hierarchal representatives cruelly persecuted while he was
living, and virulently anathematised after he was dead. By
his Tetrapla and Hexapla he became the founder of all
textual criticism ; by his Homilies he fixed the type of a
popular exposition; his *Scholia* were the earliest specimens
of marginal explanations ; his Commentaries furnished the
Church with her first continuous exegesis ; his book on "First
Principles" was "the earliest attempt at a systematic view of
the Christian Faith ; " [1] his knowledge of the Bible, and his
contributions to its interpretation were absolutely unrivalled.
His labours mark an epoch. Like the influence of Socrates
in Greek Philosophy, so the influence of Origen in Church
History is the watershed of multitudes of different streams
of thought. "Certainly," says Mosheim, "if any man deserves
to stand first in the catalogue of saints and martyrs, and to
be annually held up as an example to Christians, this is the
man ; for except the Apostles of Jesus Christ and their
companions, I know of no one among all those ennobled and
honoured as saints who excelled Origen in virtue and holiness." "In spite of his very patent faults," says Bishop
Lightfoot, "which it costs nothing to denounce, a very considerable part of what is valuable in subsequent commentaries,
whether ancient or modern, is due to him. A deep thinker,
an accurate grammarian, a most laborious worker, and a most
earnest Christian, he not only laid the foundation, but, to a very
great extent, built up the fabric of Biblical interpretation." [2]

---

[1] See Huet, *Origeniana*, iii. 2, p. 238 ; Westcott in *Contemp. Rev.* vol.
xxxv. p. 337. His Scholia (or Σημειώσεις) are mostly lost ; his Homilies are,
for the most part, preserved in the Latin translations of Jerome and Rufinus,
which, unhappily, cannot be relied on, since the translators thought fit to
modify and tamper with them. They fill three folios, though much is lost.
His Commentaries (τόμοι) extended over the whole Old Testament, except
Ruth, Esther, and Ecclesiastes ; and the whole New Testament except Mark,
1 and 2 Cor., 1 and 2 Pet., 1, 2 and 3 John, James, Jude, and the Apocalypse.
See Rufin. *Invect. in Hieron.* ii.

[2] *On Galatians*, p. 217. For the use made of Origen by Hilary and Victorinus, see Jer. *Ep.* 41, *ad Pammach.* Some of his commentaries (*e.g.* that
on 1 Cor.) are much freer from allegory than others.

It is a circumstance due to I know not what Nemesis, but certainly strange and sad, that Origen's name as a thinker is popularly associated with a complete misunderstanding of his most dubious speculations, and that his name as an exegete is chiefly remembered in connection with the least solid and the most erroneous of his methods.[1] His errors were canonised, his name was condemned. In the paragraph from which I have just quoted, the Bishop of Durham expresses his regret that he has chiefly to allude to Origen by way of correction, " because his opinion has rarely been recorded by later writers except where his authority was needed to sanction some false or questionable interpretation." But the impression thus produced, he adds, is most unjust to his reputation, since " there can be no doubt that all subsequent writers are, directly or indirectly, indebted to him to a very large extent." His Commentaries were in fact the common mine in which all his successors dug ; and it must not be forgotten that he was the father of grammatical as well as of allegoric exegesis. Compilers seized on his fanciful perversions; they neglected his noblest thoughts.[2] Hilary, Ambrose, Jerome, Augustine, the Latin fathers who had the profoundest influence on the Church· of the West, perpetuated the least tenable parts of his method. The School of Antioch, no less than that of Alexandria, owed its origin to the mighty impulse which the Christian world received from his labours, but unhappily for the cause of sound learning the School of Antioch was crushed by charges of heresy, and the allegorical tendencies of the School of Alexandria prevailed.

Origen shared many of the views about Scripture which we have already noticed in writers like Philo, Barnabas, Justin, and Clement of Alexandria. He believed in the inspiration of the Septuagint, and saw hidden mysteries in its solecisms and errors.[3] He appeals to Apocryphal books

---

[1] See for full information Huet, *Origeniana, passim.*

[2] See Westcott, Gospel of St. John (*Speaker's Commentary*, p. xcv.).

[3] *Philokal.* p. 33 ; *Comm. in Oseam* (Huet, i. p. 201). Like Plato he often contrasts τὸ ῥητόν, τὸ σωματικόν κ.τ.λ. with τὸ ἀπόρρητόν, ἡ ἀλληγορία, ἡ ἀναγωγή, πνευματικὴ διήγησις, θεωρία κ.τ.λ.

as authoritative and inspired. He is too much given
to hortatory and dogmatic divergences. He shows clear
traces of methods traditionally received both from the
Palestinian Rabbis and the Alexandrian theosophists.[1] He
admits that the New Testament is not written in the best
Greek, but says that this is unimportant, because the revelation consists not in the words but in the things revealed.
Yet, he held in its strongest form the theory of verbal
inspiration. Not one iota, he said, of Scripture is empty:
and it must not be forgotten that his Scripture included the
Apocrypha. His proof of this statement is the purely verbal
application of isolated sentences which bear no relation to the
matter on hand. "God," he says, "gave the command *Thou
shalt not appear before me empty*, and therefore He cannot
speak anything which is empty"![2] The infinite confusions
involved in such a proof show the chaotic condition of
thought which was prevalent on the question of Scripture
Inspiration.

The errors of the exegesis which Origen tended to
establish for more than a thousand years had their root in
the assumption that the Bible is throughout homogeneous
and in every particular supernaturally perfect.

He did indeed attempt a proof of this thesis.[3] He
appealed, as has been done in all ages, to the subjective
impression effected by the Bible. But he fails to observe
that this impression is produced by its fundamental truths
and its essential message, not by all its books or narratives,
still less by its every word or detail. Many indeed of these
he considered to be, in their obvious meaning, derogatory to
God's greatness. He said that the Scriptures must be divine
because they speak of Christ Who is divine, a proof which
does not rise above the dignity of a mere play on words.
He referred to the prophecies which they contain as a proof

---

[1] He professes himself indebted to a Jew for explaining to him what was
meant by the words "by your tradition." *Hom. in Matt.* 245.

[2] *Philokal. fragm.*

[3] *De Princ.* iv. περὶ τοῦ θεοπνεύστου τῆς θείας γραφῆς. His hermeneutics
are here theoretically stated.

of supernatural inspiration, failing to observe that this argument has no bearing upon whole books from which the element of prophecy is altogether absent. But in point of fact
Origen's proofs are but the after-thoughts devised in support
of an unexamined tradition. They could not have had a
particle of validity for any logical or independent mind.

How small is their demonstrative force may be seen in
the fact that to Origen, and to many of the Fathers, they
were as valid for Bel and the Dragon and the Story of
Susanna, if not even for the Sibyl, Hystaspes, and the Book
of Enoch, as for the Prophecy of Isaiah and the Gospel of
St. John.

The false theory at once necessitated a false system for its
support. Origen saw, as plainly as Philo and Barnabas and
Justin and Clement had done before him, that the dogma of
verbal dictation is at once confronted by the most decisive
proofs of its impossibility if Scripture be taken as it stands.
He could not help seeing that it would be simple blasphemy
to predicate of every clause of the Old Testament that it is,
taken literally, the direct utterance of God.

a. He saw, for instance, and insisted on the fact, that the
Bible is full of the frankest anthropomorphism,[1] such as led
Tertullian and the Egyptian Monks to believe exclusively in
a corporeal God.

b. He saw much in the Old Testament narratives which
seemed to him immoral and unbecoming. His system rose in
reality not from reverence for the Scriptures, but from a
dislike to their plain sense which had at all costs to be set
aside. Origen had no key to understand what Pascal calls the
"*sots contes*" of Scripture. How, he asked, could it possibly
profit any one to read about the drunkenness of Noah, or
about Jacob, his wives and his concubines, or about the

---

[1] He borrows from Philo the notion that it is unworthy to speak of God
planting trees, or walking in the garden. *Philokal.* 12. No one has ever
stated more frankly and fully than Dr. Newman the fact that the whole
phenomena of the Bible as it stands are *primâ facie* entirely opposed to the
doctrine of plenary and verbal inspiration. See *Tracts for the Times*, No.
85, pp. 30, *sq.;* and that the reader may see all that can be said and best
said for schemes of mystic interpretation see *id. ib.* No. 87, pp. 21, *sq.*

horrid incest of Lot, or about the foul story of Judah and Tamar? All these, he said, could be nothing but "mystic œconomies." [1]

c. He argued that there were many things in the letter of Scripture—such as the prohibition to eat vultures—which are inherently absurd. [2]

d. Some of the precepts of Scripture, understood in their obvious sense, seemed to him unworthy and unjust;—such for instance as the menace that the uncircumcised man-child should be cut off, whereas the punishment of excision ought rather to fall upon his parents. [3]

e. Other commands again, such as that which bids every man to abide in his place all the Sabbath day [4]—and other prohibitions such as that to eat of the unicorn (τραγέλαφος), a creature which has no existence—showed, he said, by their very impossibility that they could not have been literally intended. [5] He applied the same remark to large parts of the prophecies about Nebuchadnezzar, Tyre and Egypt, and even to passages in the New Testament such as "salute no man by the way," and "if any man smite thee on thy right cheek," and the details of the Second Temptation, where Christ was made to see all the kingdoms of the world. [6]

---

[1] Bede argues in much the same way. See *infra*, Lecture V. How, asks Origen, could hearers possibly be edified by the trivialities of Leviticus, or Numbers? and how could God have given minute regulations about fat and leaven? or how could He have narrated small unimportant facts about Abraham? or have justified bloody wars and fierce imprecations? Literalism, he said, would destroy the possibility of the Christian faith. See *In Lev. Hom.* v. 5. *In Gen. Hom.* iv. 3 ; vii. 1—3. *In Num. Hom.* xvi. 8, &c.

[2] Deut. xiv. 5. So Jerome, *In Matt.* xxi. "Ubi materia vel turpitudinem habeat vel impossibilitatem ad altiora transmittimur." In supporting his view Origen quoted Ezek. xx. 25, δικαιώματα οὐ καλὰ, but said that mystically understood (πρὸς διάνοιαν) the commandments were good. *C. Cels.* vii. 20. He speaks of the σκάνδαλα καὶ προσκόμματα καὶ ἀδύνατα in the literal sense of Scripture. "Unde *vilitas literae* ad preciositatem nos spiritualis remittit intelligentiae." *In Num. Hom.* xii. 1.

[3] Gen. xvii. 14 ; *De Princ.* iv. 17. One of the Chapters of the *Philokalia* is περὶ τοῦ δεῖν τοῦ θεοῦ ἄξιον νοῦν ἐν τοιούτοις ζητεῖν.

[4] Ex. xvi. 29.

[5] *De Princ.* iv. 18 ; πολλοὶ τὸ ἄλογον ἐμφαίνουσι, ἕτεροι δὲ τὸ ἀδύνατόν. Συνύφηνεν ἡ γραφὴ τῇ ἱστορίᾳ τὸ μὴ γενόμενον. πῇ μὲν μὴ δυνατὸν γενέσθαι πῇ δὲ δυνατὸν μὲν γενέσθαι οὐ μὴν γεγενημένον (*id.* 15). See *C. Cels.* iv. 44 ; *Philokal.* 12 ; *In Levit. Hom.* vii. 5.

[6] *De Princ.* iv. 16 (Matt. v. 39 ; Luke x. 2, &c.). After touching on these passages he adds, πλησίως δὲ τούτοις καὶ ἄλλα μυρία ἔνεστι τὸν ἀκριβοῦντα

f. He said that in the Evangelists there were many things which, taken literally, involved not only discrepancies but direct contradictions ; and that many doctrines were not announced by the Apostles with perfect distinctness who therefore left the more precise proof and determination of dogmas to "the disciples of science."[1] Even a Peter and a Paul saw but a fragment of the truth.[2] Thus Origen was perhaps the first propounder of a definite "doctrine of development."

In reading most of Origen's difficulties about the Bible in its literal meaning, we stand amazed. We might have supposed that it would not have needed the additional insight of so many centuries to show any man that by the slightest application of literary criticism they vanish at a touch. They are simply the birth of that openly avowed presupposition ($\pi\rho\delta\lambda\eta\psi\iota\varsigma$) which the Alexandrians brought with them to the study of Holy Writ. Had Origen been taught to take Scripture as the literature of a chosen race, and to claim for it no more than it professes, no more than it claims in each part for itself ; had he abstained from applying to the whole of Scripture mere fragments of clauses often divorced from their meaning and dissevered from their context, which, in any case, can have had no further extent of application than that to which they were originally applied, he would have contemplated such difficulties with a smile. It was only because he saw Scripture in a false light that he was unable to account for its most salient phenomena except by explaining them away. Allegory by no means sprang from spontaneous piety, but was the child of Rationalism which owed its birth to the heathen theories of Plato.[3] It deserved its name, for

τηρῆσαι ὑπὲρ τοῦ συγκαταθέσθαι ταῖς κατὰ τὸ ῥητὸν γεγενημέναις ἱστορίαις ἕτερα μὴ συμβεβηκότα.

[1] He also speaks of the solecisms in John, and says that in one passage the literal sense involves an irreconcilable contradiction ; and he speaks of the heavy and intricate style of the Epistle to the Romans.

[2] *Hom. in Jerem.* viii. Origen's chief exegetic views are scattered through the 3rd and 4th books of the *De Principiis.*

[3] See the very pertinent remark of Mosheim *De turbata,* &c. p. 211. It will of course be clear that I am not here deprecating the value of teaching professedly allegoric (see Trench *on the Parables,* pp. 12, 13), but only the distortion of plain narratives into allegories which have no connexion with the

O

it made Scripture say something else (ἄλλο ἀγορεύειν) than
it really meant.[1]

Such being the assumptions of Origen it was easy for him to
persuade himself further of very contradictory views about
the literal sense. He thought that it would serve well enough
for the faith of the masses, nay, even that the physical sounds
of Scripture might have a value for the multitude akin
to that of magic formulae ;[2] and yet he says that the literal
sense, if uncorrected, has a tendency to lead both to moral
and intellectual aberrations—to carnal views of God like
those of the Marcionites ; or to Gnostic distinctions between
God and the Demiurge of the Old Testament ; or to idolatrous
practices ; to unbelief ; to heresy ; and even to immoral
deeds.[3] Judaism was, in his opinion, but a veiled Christianity,
and the New Testament itself but an introduction to an
unwritten and spiritual reality.

It was as easy for Origen as for Philo to find Scripture arguments in favour of his own theories. Just as it was said of the
Holy Sufferer in Isaiah, "He hath no form nor comeliness,"
and yet on the Mountain of Transfiguration the body of the

---

literal sense. See, however, Burton, *Eccl. Hist.* ii. 283. The *positive* arguments of the Fathers in favour of allegory are founded on misapplications
which have long been rejected as untenable ; and they confused allegory
with typology (as in 1 Cor. v. 7, 8), and with arguments *a fortiori* such as
2 Cor. iii. 7–13, 14.

[1] Baur points out clearly the origin of the allegoric interpretation. The
minds of men were full of new ideas, and yet their ancestral faith asserted its
indefeasible authority. Since the Scriptures were accepted as the source of
all truth it became necessary to force the new ideas out of them. "All that
was necessary was to find the right key for the explanation of the books of the
Old. Testament, and then exegesis could bring forth out of those books the
ideas which the commentator had unconsciously put into them. They fancied
that they were keeping a firm hold of the old faith, but in reality they had
substituted entirely new ideas in its place." *Ch. Hist.* i. 19.

[2] *C. Cels.* i. 18, ὅρα ὁποῖα μᾶλλον δύναται ἐπιστρέψαι καὶ αὐτόθεν τοὺς
ἀκούοντας κ.τ.λ.

[3] He thought that neither Jews nor heretics could be convinced by the
literal sense, *Philokal.* 6. He says (*id.* 7) that from the Scriptures, taken
literally, many τοιαῦτα ὑπολαμβάνουσι περὶ τοῦ Θεοῦ ὁποῖα οὐδὲ περὶ τοῦ ὠμοτ-
άτου καὶ ἀδικωτάτου ἀνθρώπου· αἰτία δὲ πᾶσι τοῖς προειρημένοις ψευδοδοξιῶν καὶ
ἀσεβειῶν ἢ ἰδιωτικῶν περὶ Θεοῦ λόγων οὐκ ἄλλη τις εἶναι δοκεῖ ἢ ἡ γραφὴ κατὰ τὰ
πνευματικὰ μὴ νενοημένη ἀλλ' ὡς πρὸς τὸ ψιλὸν γράμμα ἐξειλημμένη. The most
remarkable expression of his opinion that the literal sense leads to immorality
is to be found in his *Stromata* (*ap.* Jer. in Gal. v.). It ends with "Multorum
ergo malorum occasio est si quis in Scripturae carne permaneat." See Orig.
Hom. in Gen. vi., *Hom. in Levit.* vii.

Lord shone with dazzling lustre, so, he says, the nature of the divine word shines forth to those who ascend the mountain to gaze on it. The ascension of the mount is to him the application of the allegoric method. Origen seems to have been unconscious that any particular sentence of Scripture is not to be made applicable to the whole of Scripture. If St. Paul incidentally uses the passage of the Israelites through the Red Sea as furnishing an analogy of baptism,[1] or in one single instance gives an allegoric turn to the story of Sarah and Hagar,[2] Origen argues that therefore a mystical meaning must have been intended throughout the whole narrative of Scripture. St. Paul said "*the letter killeth, but the Spirit giveth life.*"[3] If by this he had meant that all Scripture was to be allegorically interpreted it is clear that his phrase "the letter killeth" would in the strongest way have condemned the literal sense altogether. His meaning was quite different, and the Fathers who did *not* wholly exclude the literal sense only took so much of the phrase as suited their controversial purpose.[4] If St. Paul spoke of marriage as "*a great mystery*,"[5] what had this to do with the interpretation of the whole Old Testament? Or what was the bearing upon this question of the remark in the Epistle to the Hebrews that Christians have come not to Sinai but to Mount Sion?[6] It is obvious that such proofs are either absolutely irrelevant or are wholly

---

[1] 1 Cor. x. 1. He also refers to 1 Cor. ii. 6, 7 ; ix. 9, 10 (which is simply a merciful analogy, not an explanation) ; and to 1 Tim. 1, 8 ; Eph. v. 32, which are *nihil ad rem* (*C. Cels.* iv. p. 197 *ed.* Spencer).

[2] Gal. iv. 21.

[3] 2 Cor. iii. 6 ; this passage is appealed to by Greg. Nyss. *Prooem. in Cant. ;* Greg. Naz. *Orat.* 1 ; Didymus, *ap.* Jer. and many other Fathers.

[4] St. Paul probably means, as Theodoret and Chrysostom interpret him, that the written Law of Moses was a law which threatens death, and that the grace of the Spirit was life.

[5] Eph. v. 31.

[6] We constantly find in the Fathers this radically vicious method of giving universal application to isolated passages. Commenting on the words, "I will open my mouth in a parable," Jerome says, "Ex qua intelligimus *universa quae scripta sunt* (!) parabolice sentienda, nec manifestam tantum sonare literam, sed abscondita sacramenta." One very intelligible limitation of Allegory and Typology has been adopted by some English divines, viz. that we should only admit them when actually sanctioned in Scripture. This is the view of Bishops Marsh and Van Mildert, *Bampt. Lect.* p. 239, and Macknight, *St. Paul's Epistles,* iv. 439.

inadequate to sustain the mountain-loads of inference which were made to rest upon them.

St. Paul borrows an incidental illustration from the methods of the Rabbis, without for a moment disturbing the literal sense; Origen borrows from heathen Platonists and from Jewish philosophers a method which converts the whole of Scripture, alike the New and the Old Testament, into a series of clumsy, varying, and incredible enigmas. Allegory helped him to get rid of Chiliasm and superstitious literalism and the "antitheses" of the Gnostics, but it opened the door for deadlier evils.[1]

For the allegoric system might be claimed by a Valentinus no less than by an Origen, and the "proofs" of the one were— if, such a method be supposed to furnish *any* proofs—just as valid as those of the other.[2] In fact if Origen's principles and example were valid it was idle for him to complain of those who interpreted even our Lord's miracles of spiritual diseases only.[3]

But Origen went still further. Having started with the assumption that every clause of the Bible was infallible, supernatural, and divinely dictated, and having proved to his own satisfaction that it could not be intended in its literal sense, he proceeded to systematise his own false conclusions. The Bible, he argued, is meant for the salvation of man; but man, as Plato tells us, consists of three parts—body, soul, and spirit. Scripture therefore must have a threefold sense corresponding to this trichotomy.[4] It has a literal, a moral, and

---

[1] See Iren. i. 3, 8 ; ii. 24.

[2] Dr. Maitland (*Dark Ages,* p. 174) speaks much more strongly than I have done. "If Origen's plaything were not the word of God we might often be amused by his childish fooleries ; but when we consider what mischief has been done to truth by the way of allegorising (or as it is now called spiritualising) the Bible, it cannot be looked on without disgust." See too Bishop Wordsworth's *Miscellanies,* ii. 17 (on the Interpretation of Scripture).

[3] See *Hom. in Joann.* viii.

[4] See Orig. *De Princip.* iv. 8, 11, 12, 14, 19 ; *Hom. in Levit.* v. ; Redepenning, *Origenes,* i. 232 ; Gieseler, i. 232, 243.

Origen's threefold sense is practically the fourfold sense of the Fathers, for his "spiritual" sense involves both allegory and anagoge, though he does not practically make this division (Redepenning, i. 226). He uses the word ἀναγωγή of explanations which are simply allegories. Thus he gives an allegoric sense to Matt. xiv. 13. and says μετὰ τὸ ῥητὸν καὶ κατὰ ἀναγωγὴν τὸν τόπον ἐξεταστέον.

a mystic meaning analogous to the body, to the soul, to the spirit. This conclusion also he supported by quoting what seems to be a mere mistake of the Septuagint.[1] In Prov. xxii. 20 " Have I not written unto thee excellent things (שָׁלִישִׁים) in wisdom and in knowledge," the LXX. has καὶ σὺ δὲ ἀπόγραψαι αὐτὰ τρισσῶς, and the Vulgate, *Ecce descripsi tibi tripliciter.*[2] If the Hebrew marginal reading be right, and if the idea of three things lies in the Hebrew word at all, it refers at most to three subsequent verses. But Origen relying on the translation applied to the entire Bible an isolated reference to a single passage. He thus gave to his own fancy, what he took to be an inspired sanction, and contributed a pure mistake to the blind acceptance of the exegetes of a thousand years.

But of two of these three supposed senses Origen makes very little use. To the moral sense he refers but seldom ;[3] to the literal sense scarcely at all.[4] Indeed in many passages he speaks disparagingly of the literal truth of the Scripture narratives.[5] This constitutes his retrogressive and disastrous originality.[6] He constantly uses allegory where his own principles give him no excuse for doing so. He had so completely deadened in his own mind the feeling of historic truth that he allegorises not only such narratives as that of the Creation, but even the Law, the Histories, and the Prophets. The acceptance of the

---

[1] The Chaldee and Syriac agree with the Vulgate in adopting this reading ; some have supposed allusions to Proverbs, Ecclesiastes and Canticles ; or to the Law, the Prophets, and the Hagiographa. Both interpretations are as untenable as that of Origen. If the idea of "three things" lies in the word at all it may refer to verses 22, 24, 26. The Fathers following Origen apply it to the literal, tropologic, and anagogic sense.

[2] Orig. *Philokal.* 8 ; *De Princ.* iv. 11.

[3] He disparagingly compares it to the earth, the body ; and yet with curious literalism he argues that the stars are living beings from Job xxv. 5 (*De Princ.* i. 7). For passages which depreciate the literal sense see *C. Cels.* vi. 70 ; vii. 20 ; *Hom. in Gen.* vi. § 3 ; x. § 4 ; *De Princ.* iv. 8–28.

[4] Chiefly in the Homilies, and not always happily. Thus he comments on "Joseph died, and the children of Israel multiplied," by saying that if Joseph died in us, *i.e.* if we carry in our bodies the death of Christ, our spiritual graces will grow and multiply. *Hom. in Exod.* i.

[5] Thus on John i. 20, he says ὥσπερ ἐπιβάθρᾳ χρησάμενοι τῇ ἱστορίᾳ τὰ ἴχνη τῆς ἀληθείας ζητοῦντες ἐν γράμματι.

[6] See this amply proved by Origen's remarks, *Hom. in Gen.* iii. 4-6 ; vii. 5 ; x. 1 ; *Hom. in Levit.* vi. 3 ; *Hom. in Num.* xxiii. 5. See these and other passages quoted in Denis, p. 41.

simple narrative becomes too commonplace for him ; he compares it to the transgression of eating raw the Paschal Lamb.[1]
Thus, like Philo, he loses much of the historic grandeur, the
poetic beauty, the human tenderness of the Scriptures. They
become to him a book of Alexandrian mysticism, into which
he everywhere reads the views which alone he considers to be
" eternal truths."[2] Arbitrary in its purport, immeasurable in
its extent, a great part of this allegoric comment becomes a mere
shuffling of subjective commonplaces.[3] It is the servile handmaid of a fancied Gnosis, and almost deserves the scornful
remark of Porphyry, that it attributes all kinds of strange
meanings to what had been said by Moses with perfect clearness.[4] " *Hoc divinare magis est quam explanare* " was the just
criticism passed upon him (as he frankly tells us) even by his
contemporaries.[5]

In details Origen is constantly misled by defective literary
canons and imperfect linguistic knowledge. He was not
sufficiently acquainted with the laws of Hebrew parallelism
to prevent him from drawing mystic inferences from synonyms
and repetitions. Thus he thinks that there is a mystery in
the repetition of the word " God " in " I am the God of
Abraham, the God of Isaac, and the God of Jacob ; "[6] and
that the expression " Rebecca was a virgin, neither had any

---

[1] Ex. xii. 8, οὐκ ὤμην οὖν βρωτέον τὴν σάρκα τοῦ ἀμνοῦ ὥσπερ ποιοῦσιν οἱ
τῆς λέξεως δοῦλοι τρόπον ἀλόγων ζώων κ.τ.λ.
[2] *Hom. in Num.* xxv. 3, " Non tam reges quam *vitiorum nomina*
quae regnant in hominibus." *Hom. in Jos.* i. 7, " Intra nos enim sunt
omnes gentes istae vitiorum." *Hom. in Gen.* x. 4, " In his *non historiae
narrantur, sed mysteria contexuntur.*"
[3] See Böhringer, iii. 366-373. " Allegorical interpretation amounted, in
practice, only to a species of aphoristical philosophy on the occasion of Bible
passages," Ueberweg, i. 319.
[4] Porphyry κατὰ Χριστιανῶν iii. (*ap.* Euseb. *H. E.* vi. 19). Αἰνίγματα τὰ
παρὰ Μωϋσεῖ φανερῶς λεγόμενα εἶναι κομπάσαντες καὶ ἐπιθειάσαντες ὡς θεσπίσματα
πλήρη κρυφίων μυστηρίων. He goes on to charge him with Hellenising, and
clothing Hellenic thoughts in Jewish myths. He says that Origen borrowed
the principles of Plato, Numenius, the Stoics, Chaeremon and Cornutus,
—παρ' ὧν τὸν μεταληπτικὸν τῶν παρ' Ἕλλησι μυστηρίων γνοὺς τρόπον ταῖς
Ἰουδαϊκαῖς προσῆψε γραφαῖς. Even Jerome, who is himself an offender, complains that Origen's treatise on Hosea is chiefly occupied by explaining the
meaning of " Ephraim " ; that in his three volumes on Malachi " Historiam
omnino non tetigit, et more suo in allegoriae interpretatione versatus est."
[5] *Hom. in Exod.* xiii. 2.
[6] Ex. iii. 16 ; *Hom. in Joann.* ii. § 16.

man known her " (Gen. xxiv. 16), must mean that Christ is the husband of the soul when it is converted, and that Satan becomes the husband of the soul when it falls away.[1]

One or two brief specimens of his method must suffice. When we are told that Rebecca comes to draw water at the well and so meets the servant of Abraham, the meaning is, according to Origen, that we must daily come to the wells of Scripture in order to meet with Christ. He thinks that there is a contradiction because in Ex. i. 5 the midwives are not said to have killed the female children as well as to have saved the male children. A glance at the text shows that there is no difficulty whatever in an expression of the plainest kind. But failing to see that the Scriptures are written according to the ordinary rules of language, he explains the female children to mean carnal affections, and the male children the reasonable sense and intellectual spirit. So that when men live their life in pleasure Pharaoh is killing the males in them and preserving the females. In the twenty-first verse of the same chapter Origen follows the mistranslation of the LXX. " because the midwives feared God *they made for themselves houses,*" [2] and declaring it to be inconsequent, takes it to mean that if we act like the midwives in keeping alive the spiritual sense we shall gain eternal life. In Gen. xviii. 2, the Septuagint says that the three men stood *above* Abraham,[3] and this is interpreted to mean that Abraham submitted himself to the will of God. Of what use, he asks, is it to me, who have come to hear what the Holy Spirit teaches the human race, to be told that Abraham stood under the oak of Mamre? Mamre means " Vision," and the sense of the passage is that God was pleased with the insight of Abraham. What meaning can there possibly be, he asks, in our being told that " the Lord opened the eyes of Agar " ? Where do we read that she had closed

---

[1] *Hom. in Rom.* vii. § 8 (De la Rue, iv. 604). It need hardly be said that the tautology is only due to the descriptive fulness of Hebrew style, just as " I am a widow woman, and my husband is dead," 2 Sam. xiv. 5.

[2] Ex. i. 21, ἐποίησαν ἑαυταῖς οἰκίας, LXX.

[3] Gen xviii. 2, εἰστήκεισαν ἐπάνω αὐτοῦ, LXX.

eyes? Is it not clear as daylight that the mystic sense
implies the blindness of the Jewish synagogue!

But the allegoric method is still more inexcusable when it
invades the simplest and most precious passages of the New
Testament. St. Mark tells us (x. 50) that Bartimaeus when
he hastened to Jesus flung off his coat. Origen cannot conceive that the dignity of the Evangelist would have allowed
him to record such a trivial circumstance (as he regards this
to be) without a mystic meaning.[1] We feel it to be singularly
out of place when the mention of divorce in Matt. xix. leads
Origen into a long digression about the marriage of the soul
with its guardian angel. We cannot value the method which
explains " the water-pots of stone containing two or three
firkins apiece," to be the Scriptures which were intended to
purify the Jews, and which sometimes contain two firkins,
namely, the moral and literal sense, and sometimes three,
namely also the spiritual; nor are we able to see the
smallest relevance in the remark about the six water-pots
that the world was made in six days. There are many
beautiful and touching lessons in the humble triumph of
Palm Sunday, but it loses every particle of its natural instruc-
tiveness when we are told that the ass represents the letter
of the Old Testament, the ass's foal, which was gentle and
submissive, the New Testament, and that the two Apostles
who go to loose them are the moral and mystic sense.[2] Nor
are we in any better position to understand " whose shoe's
latchet I am not worthy to bear," or " to unloose," when it
is made to refer to Christ's Incarnation and descent into
Hades, " whatever Hades may be." [3] All such comments
are a μετάβασις εἰς ἄλλο γένος. They do but weary
and offend us with a sense of incongruous unreality. They

---

[1] Orig. *Comm. in Matt.* (xx. 33).

[2] For abundant specimens of Origen's allegorising methods see Huet,
Origeniana, II. 2 Ger. 13 ; (De la Rue iv. App. 240–244).

[3] *Hom. in Joann.* vi. § 18 (De la Rue, iv. p. 136). The passage is long
and difficult. Εἰ δὲ μυστικὸς ὁ περὶ τῶν ὑποδημάτων τόπος οὐδὲ τοῦτον παρελ-
θεῖν ἄξιον. οἶμαι τοίνυν τὴν μὲν ἐνανθρώπησιν ὅτε σάρκα καὶ αἷμα ἀναλαμβάνει ὁ
τοῦ Θεοῦ υἱὸς τὸ ἕτερον εἶναι τῶν ὑποδημάτων, τὴν δὲ εἰς ᾅδου κατάβασιν, ὅστις
ποτέ ἐστιν ὁ ᾅδης, κ.τ.λ.

change tender human narratives into dreary and ill-constructed riddles. With the highest admiration, and even the deepest reverence for Origen, whose spiritual teaching is often full of beauty and depth, and whose isolated comments are often valuable, we can only come to the conclusion that the foundations of his exegetic system are built upon the sand.

V. The influence of Origen was wide and deep,[1] and all the more so because he did but expand and systematise in the Christian Church, as Philo had done in the Jewish, the principles which we have already seen at work in the writings of the Fathers. Even those who, like Methodius and Cyril, opposed some of the best parts of Origen's teaching, yet interpreted Scripture in a similar way. Methodius, an ardent Platonist,[2] commenting on Gen. xv. 9, explains "the calf, the goat, and the ram of three years"[3] in Abraham's sacrifices to mean his soul, his sentient faculty, and his mind.[4] The same arbitrary mixture of allegory and dogma is found in the works of Cyril. It is needless and impossible to speak separately of him, and many others of the Fathers, and in point of fact there is no new or original principle observable in their comments.[5] Gregory

---

[1] Gieseler says that "his exegetical writings were the model and sources for all succeeding Greek commentators" (i. 232) ; he might have added, and for most Latin ones also.

[2] See his only extant work, the *Symposium*, or περὶ ἀγνείας. It is printed in Migne, vol. xviii.

[3] That Hippolytus explained Scripture by the same methods we see from his comment on Gen. xlix. 12 in his book *De Christo et Antichristo*. His interpretation resembles that of Justin. Thus "His teeth are whiter than milk" is made to refer to the commands which come from the mouth of Christ, which are white like milk. He still more clearly shows the basis of his system in his book on Daniel. Explaining the Story of Susanna as forming part of the Book of Daniel, he says that Susanna represents the Church ; her husband Joacim is Christ ; the garden is the calling of the Saints ; Babylon is the world ; the bath is baptism; the two Elders are the Jews and the Gentiles ; and the two handmaids are Love to God and Faith in Christ.

[4] In Cant. vi. 7 Methodius says that the 60 queens are royal souls like those of Enoch, Seth ; and the concubines, the souls of the Prophets after the Deluge. In Judg. ix. he explains the trees who went to choose a king to be sinful souls before the Incarnation which now implore the mercy of God (see Photius, *Cod.* 234–237 ; Schröck, *K. G.* iv. 427, *sq.* ; Rosenmüller, *Hist. Interpr.* iii. 187, *sq.*).

[5] Euseb. *H. E.* vi. 46 ; Steph. Gobar. *ap.* Phot. *Cod.* 232 ; Guerike, *De Schol. Alex.* 67.

Thaumaturgus,[1] the martyr Pamphilus,[2] Athanasius,[3] Didymus the Blind,[4] Pierius,[5] Theognostus,[6] Hierax of Leontopolis,[7] Eusebius of Vercellae,[8] Eusebius of Cæsarea,[9] Firmilian,[10] Victorinus of Pettau,[11] all made some contributions to exegesis in their day, but there is nothing distinctive in their special methods. Like many others they openly expressed their admiration of Origen, and largely borrowed from him in their writings. It was the express object of the Presbyter Rufinus to make him known in the West. The great Cappadocian Fathers adopted many of his views.[12] Gregory of Nyssa, the brother of Basil, was the most Origenising of all the Fathers of the Nicene age, and he adopted not only his exegetic system, but also many of his dogmatic opinions.[13] Even Tillemont [14] admits that, from the days of Origen to those of Chrysostom, there was not a single eminent commentator who did not borrow largely from the works of that great man. They found in them as Doucin says *Une source inépuisable de lumières.* In spite of the unjust and sweeping condemnation

---

[1] See his Apology for Origen in De La Rue's edition, vol. iv.

[2] Euseb. *H. E.* vi. 53 ; vii. 32 ; Jer. *Catal.* 75 ; Routh, *Rel. Sacr.* iii. 491–512 ; Böhringer, iii. 578 ; Schröck, *K. G.* xii. 93, *sq.*

[3] See Rosenmüller, *Hist. Int.* iii. 206, *sq.* He follows Origen in the remark that the literal sense is often unworthy of God. The genuineness of Athanasius's commentary on the Psalms is doubtful, but his letter to Marcellinus on the Psalms is excellent, and it is needless to point out the high value of his contributions to exegetic *theology.*

[4] Jer. *Ep.* 84 ; *Apol. adv. Ruf.* ; Socrates, *H. E.* iv. 25 ; Baronius, *Ann.* A.D. 347.

[5] He was called "the young Origen" (Phot. *Cod.* 119 ; Jer. *Catal.* 76 ; Euseb. *H. E.* vii. 32).

[6] He was a pupil of Origen, and was called " the Exegete."

[7] Epiphan. *Haer.* 67.

[8] Jerome calls him an admirer and imitator of Origen.

[9] Euseb. *H. E.* vi. 53 ; Photius, *Cod.* 118. He was greater as a scholar and historian than as an exegete. Fragments of his commentaries have been published by Mai, *Nov. Patr. Bibl.* iv. and Migne, vi. His Εὐαγγελίων διαφωνία is unfortunately lost.

[10] Euseb. *H. E.* vi. 27.   [11] Jer. *Ep.* lxv. 2

[12] Niceph. *H. E.* xi. 17 ; Schröck, *K. G.* xiv. ; R. Simon, *Hist. Crit.* (*N. T.*), p. 111, *sq.* ; Buddeus, *Isag.* 1385, *sq.*

[13] See Rupp, *Greg. v. Nyssa*, pp. 243–262 ; Schaff, *Ch. Hist.* ii. 907. For Gregory's exegetical preference of allegory see *Prooem. in Cant.* Basil, however, though not free from it, has some strong and wise protests against it (*Hexaem.* ii. 2 ; iii. 9 ; ix. 1 ; *Hom.* I. in § 9, c. 2).

[14] Tillemont, iii. 266.

of his theology, he yet was the chief teacher of even the
most orthodox of the Western Fathers.[1] They delighted in
a system which still left them some semblance of originality
and freedom. We need only instance the names of Hilary
of Poictiers and of Ambrose.

VI. HILARY, "the Athanasius of Gaul," admirable as a
theologian, and powerful as a writer,[2] but commonplace as an
exegete, was almost entirely dependent on Origen.[3] Jerome
says that in his Commentary on the Psalms, he imitated
Origen and added some things of his own, and that his commentary on St. Matthew and his book on Job were free translations of Origen.[4] Like many other Latin Fathers he knew
no Hebrew. A specimen of his remarks on passages of the Old
and New Testament will show the general character of his exegesis.[5] Writing about the inscription of the Psalms," To the
chief musician a Psalm of David," [6] he adopts the mistaken
rendering, " *In finem intellectus David,*" and infers that Psalms
headed " *in finem* " [7] had no relation to contemporary history,
but must all be explained of Christ. The 50th Psalm (A.V. li.)
refers to forgiveness, because its number is that of the year of

---

[1] See the remarkable testimony of Suidas *s.v.* Ὠριγένης. πλεῖστα καὶ
ἀναρίθμητα ἐκλέλοιπεν ὡς ἐξ ἐκείνου πάντας τοὺς μετέπειτα ἐκκλησίας
διδασκάλους καὶ ἀφορμὰς εἰληφέναι, ὡς ὁ θεολόγος φάσκει Γρηγόριος, Ὠριγένης
ἡ πάντων ἡμῶν ἀκονή.

[2] Jerome calls him "a Rhone of eloquence." Dorner's estimate of his
theology is very high.

[3] On Hilary see Schröck, xii. 252, *sq.* ; Rosenmüller, *Hist. Interp.*
301, *sq.* ; Buddeus, *Isagoge,* 1388, *sq.* Both Ambrose and Hilary speak of
the contradictions of Scripture from which we can only escape by allegory
(Diestel, pp. 80 ff.).

[4] Jer. *Catal.* 100, "Quos de Graeco Origenis in sensum transtulit." Hilary,
not quite honourably, avoided acknowledging his obligations to Origen—" *ut
Origeniani nominis invidiam vitaret* " (Erasm.).

[5] Jerome, perhaps unjustly, implies that he also knew but little Greek
(Graecorum literarum *quamdam aurulam* ceperat), and was assisted in under-
standing Origen by the Presbyter Heliodorus (*Ep. ad Marcell.* and *ad Paullin.
De Inst. Monach.*).

[6] לַמְנַצֵּחַ מַשְׂכִּיל לְדָוִד.

[7] LXX. εἰς τὸ τέλος. The remark is borrowed from Eusebius, who also
refers the superscription עַל־הַגִּתִּית περὶ ληνῶν, LXX. (*Pro torcularibus,* Vulg.)
of Ps. 8 to Christian altars and the wine of the Eucharist (Diestel, p. 119).
Hilary says that *Pro torcularibus* shows the Psalm to be about the new fruits
prepared out of men by God's Spirit. The inscription probably means "in
the manner of Gath."

jubilee. In Ps. li. (A.V. lii.) the Latin version has the inscription
" When Doeg the Edomite came and told Saul, David came to
the house of Ahimelech." Hilary says that Ahimelech means
" my brother's empire," and that St. Peter explains this when
he writes " Ye, as living stones, are built into spiritual
houses, to a holy priesthood." We, therefore, are to be built
into this spiritual house if by spiritual edification we become
like to God ; and Doeg's revelation to Saul that David had
gone into the house of Ahimelech refers to the betrayal of
Christ to Pilate. The same methods are applied to the
New Testament still more disastrously. Of all the comments
quoted from the Fathers in the *Catena Aurea*, those of Hilary
are usually the least satisfactory. They show as little insight
as those of Remigius or Rabanus Maurus. Peter's mother-
in-law becomes a type of infidelity. The birds of heaven
which sow not, neither do they gather into barns, are evil
spirits;[1] the lilies of the field are angels;[2] the " grass "
signifies the Gentiles; two sparrows which are sold for one
farthing are sinners made up of mind and body, who, though
born to fly with spiritual wings, sell themselves for the
smallest faults and become one, since the subtlety of the
soul grows heavy into the nature of bodies.[3] Yet Hilary
seems to have been so entirely convinced of the truth of this
dreary irrelevance, that after explaining the clouds in Psalm
cxlvi. to mean the writings of the Prophets, and the rain the
Gospel doctrine, and the mountains Prophets and Apostles,
and the beasts men, and the young ravens Gentiles, he adds

---

[1] Matt. vi. 26, 27, " Under the name of birds He exhorts us, by the
example of the *unclean spirits* to whom, without any trouble of their own,
provision of life is given by the power of the Eternal Wisdom." Remigius,
with just as much right, says, " By the birds of the air are meant *the saints.*"
[2] Matt. vi. 31, " By the lilies are to be understood the eminences of the
heavenly angels."
[3] Here are other specimens : Matt. iv. 18–22, " Leaving the ships, that is,
carnal desires, and their nets, that is, the love of the world, they followed
Christ ; by James is understood the Jewish nation . . . ; by John the Gentile
world. Zebedee, whom they leave (the name is interpreted ' falling ' and
' flying '), signifies the world which passes away and the Devil who fell from
Heaven," &c. Matt. viii. 28, " The demon held the two men among the tombs
without the town, *i.e.* without the synagogue of the Law and the Prophets,
that is, they infested the original seats of the two nations (Jews and Gentiles),
the abodes of the dead," &c.

that to understand these things otherwise would be a matter
not only of error but even of irreligion.[1] He seems to have
thought that it would have been better to leave many Scripture mysteries unexplained, but, he says, " We are compelled
by the vices of heretics and blasphemers to do things
unlawful, to climb heights, to utter things unspeakable, to
seize things unpermitted." [2]

VII. Nor is St. Ambrose a whit behind him in the adoption of Origenistic allegory, and Philonian methods,[3]
though he does not deny the literal sense. There is much
that is ingenious, pious, and forcible in the writings of
this great practical Bishop, but we can judge of the
wild license of his method when, in his comment on
Cant. viii. 1, he says that there the Emperor Gratian
declared to his brother of august memory, that he is
furnished with the fruits of divers virtues.[4] The allegoric interpretation of the locusts which John the Baptist ate; of the
second-first Sabbath; of the Moth and the Rust; of the days
of Creation; and many more details are all in the current style;
and his defence or extenuation of Peter's denial of Christ
deserves the sarcasm of Jerome that it defends Peter at the
expense of Christ who said, "Thou shalt deny me thrice."
Jerome says of his two commentaries on St. Matthew and
St. Luke, that the latter trifles in the words and drowses
in the meanings, and the other is dull in both.[5] Jerome,
however, was strongly prejudiced against him.[6] In his Cata-

---

[1] "Haec ita intelligere *non dicam erroris sed irreligiositatis est*" (Hil.
in Ps. 146).
[2] Hil. *De Trin.* ii. There is a monograph by Reinken, *Hilarius von
Poictiers*, 1864.
[3] See Siegfried, *Philo*, pp. 371-391.
[4] *Tract. de Obit. Valent.* ii. 12.
[5] Jerome says, "Nuper Ambrosius sic illius (Origenis) *Hexaemeron* com-
pilavit ut magis Hippolyti sententiam Basiliique sequeretur" (*Ep.* 84, 7);
"Ante paucos dies quorumdam in Matthaeum et Lucam commentarios vos
legisse dixistis e quibus alter et sensibus hebes esset, et alter in verbis luderet,
in sententiis dormitaret" (Rufinus, *Inv. in Hieron.* ii. 22-29). Augustine,
on the other hand, always speaks of him with high respect (see Aug. *Conf.*
vi. 4).
[6] On Ambrose see Schröck, xiv. 148, *sq.* ; Rosenm. iii. 313, *sq.* ; Buddeus,
Isag. 1306. Böhringer (iv. 66) says that in his numerous exegetic writings,
" Von Beachtung des Wortstandes, von grammatisch-historischen Auslegung

logue he only says that he will make no remark about him, because he is still living, and that he may not be blamed either for flattery or plain-speaking.[1] He compares the superficial and meagre commentary of Ambrose to the croaking of a raven which makes sport of the colours of all other birds, and yet is itself dark all over.[2] But Ambrose was perfectly modest about his own writings. "Snatched," he says, "from the tribunals to the priesthood, I have to learn while I teach, since I had no leisure to learn before."[3] Hence "the sacred books were to him what pastoral and didactic theology has always tended to make them, verbal materials for edification which was to be extracted from them by any and every kind of interpretation to which their letter could be subjected." [4]

VIII. Before passing to the school which endeavoured, not wholly in vain, to make a stand against the allegorising method of the Alexandrians, we must notice the two writers who furnish the finest pieces of Biblical criticism in this epoch. One of these is the great DIONYSIUS OF ALEXANDRIA († 265),[5] whose remarks on the Apocalypse are so precise and subtle that they might have been written in modern times. He came indeed to the erroneous conclusion that the Apocalypse could not have been written by St. John, and in his dislike

---

ist *fast nirgends eine Spur ;* das Meiste ist allegorisirend 'doch fehlt er nicht an sinnigen Bemerkungen." Ambrose says (*De Fide*) "*Historia simplex* sed alta mysteria . . . *quia litteralis sensus indignus est.*"
  [1] " Meum judicium subtraham ne in alterutram partem aut adulatio in me reprehendatur aut veritas " (*Cat. Virr. Illustr.* 124). Some have conjectured that Jerome had some personal dislike to Ambrose in connexion with his sudden departure from Aquileia, *Ep.* 3, 3. Zöckler, p. 40.
  [2] *Praef. in* xxxix. *Hom. Origenis in Lucam ap.* Rufinum ; *Invect.* ii. *adv. Hieron.* § 21. " Oscinem corvum audiam crocitantem et mirum in modum de cunctarum avium ridere coloribus, cum totus ipse tenebrosus sit." In § 23 Rufinus defends Ambrose, and calls him "omnium Ecclesiarum columna quaedam."
  [3] *De Offic.* I. i. 4. Heinz, in his severe criticism on this book (Walch, *Patrologia*, p. 668), complains especially of "Schlechte Auslegungen der Schriftsteller A. und N. T. die gewaltsam angezogen werden und nichts beweisen."
  [4] Rev. J. Ll. Davies in Smith and Wace. The Commentary of Ambrosiaster, which used to be printed with the works of Ambrose, is of uncertain authorship, but has high merits. Sixt. Senensis calls it "brief in words but weighty in matter."
  [5] He earned the title of "the Great" (Euseb. *H. E.* vi. 46, vii. 1 ; Basil, *Ep. ad Amphiloch.* Steph. Gobar, *ap.* Phot. *Cod.* 232 ; Guerike, *De Schol. Alex.*, p. 67, and Schröck, *K.G.* iv. 169).

to the crude literalism of the Chiliasts he endeavoured to attribute the book to another John (who probably had no separate existence). Yet the style and the keenness of his criticism shows how much greater advance might have been made in the study of Scripture if there had been less of arbitrary fancy and more of independent thought.[1] Nor are the contributions of JULIUS AFRICANUS († *c.* 240) less valuable. In a brief but vigorous letter to Origen he expresses his surprise that, in a discussion with Bassus, the great Alexandrian should have referred to the Story of Susanna. He says that at the time, as was only fitting, he did not like to make any remark; but in his letter he points out that the Story of Susanna is lacking in propriety; that it is full of improbabilities; that it attributes to Daniel a kind of prophetic insight unlike that displayed in his book; that it formed no part of the Jewish canon; and that it has two plays on words which would have been impossible in Hebrew.[2] Origen's answer to this letter shows signs of timidity, and appeals to a supposed infallibility of tradition. Though full of ingenuity, it is quite inferior to the criticism of Africanus in grasp and insight. Not less remarkable is Julius's solution of the problem presented by the two differing genealogies of Christ. In his letter to Aristides he rejects with wholesome scorn the notion which seems to have been then current even in the Church, that they are merely a "pious fraud," representing the desire to set forth Christ as descended from the kingly line of Solomon and the prophetic line of Nathan.[3] Relying on a

---

[1] His arguments are given by Euseb. *H. E.* vii. 25. He argued (1) from style and phraseology; (2) from the omission by John of his name in the Gospel and Epistle; (3) because he does not call himself anything but "a fellow-disciple;" (4) the name John was common; (5) the character of the Apocalypse is strange. But the fragment must be read at length by any who would do it justice. Canon Westcott (*s.v.* in Smith and Wace) says that this criticism "is perhaps unique among early writers for clearness and scholastic precision." For a full account of it see Lücke, *Einl. in die Offenbarung* (Bonn, 1852), pp. 605–621.

[2] See Euseb. *H. E.* vi. 31; Jer. *Catal.* 63; Photius, *Cod.* 34; Suidas, *s.v.* 'Αφρίκανος; Nicephorus, *H. E.* v. 21; Routh, *Rel. Sacr.* ii. 225. The letter was edited by Wetstein, with notes, in 1674; and in De la Rue's *Origen.*

[3] Μὴ δὴ κρατοίη οὗτος ὁ λόγος ἐν 'Εκκλησίᾳ Χριστοῦ ὅτι ψεῦδος σύγκειται εἰς αἶνον καὶ δοξολογίαν Χριστοῦ (Routh, *Rel. Sacr.* ii.).

tradition preserved among the Desposyni, or earthly kinsmen of the Lord's family who lived near Nazareth and Kokhaba, he says that Matthew gives the natural, and Luke the legal descent, and that the discrepancy is accounted for by the Jewish law of the levirate marriage. This account of the matter was accepted by Augustine, and has found wide currency in the Christian world.[1] One more service Julius rendered by his Chronology, though it was based on data necessarily imperfect.[2] He amply deserves his reputation as one of the most learned of the Ante-Nicene Fathers,[3] and by no means the least acute.

IX. We have seen that, even in Origen's lifetime, there were protests against his method of exegesis.[4] Clemens gives the name of "ignorant brawlers"[5] to those who repudiated the vaunted Gnosis of a philosophised religion. There were many who had no taste for the speculations which professed to be a "translation from the gospel of sense into the gospel of spirit;" nor would they surrender the historic fact in favour of the subjective caprice. They saw that the method could be used with equal effect by heretics.[6] They saw, too, that

---

[1] Euseb. *H. E.* i. 7 ; Routh, *Rel. Sacr.* ii. 228 ; Euseb. *ad Steph. Qu.* 4 (Mai, *Script. Nov. Coll.* i.) ; Aug. *Retr.* ii. 7 ; Mill, *Mythical Interpr.* p. 201 ; F. Spitta, *Der Brief des Jul. Afric. an Aristid. kritisch untersucht und hergestellt* (Halle, 1877).

[2] Euseb. *H. E.* vi. 11.

[3] Jer. *Ep. ad Magnum*, 83 ; Socr. *H. E.* ii. 35. If the Κέστοι were really by Julius they were not worthy of him ; but even if they be genuine, they have suffered from additions and mutilations.

[4] See *Hom. in Lucam*, xxv. ; *Hom. in Joann.* x. § 13, τρόπον ἀλόγων ζώων καὶ ἀποτεθηριωμένων πρὸς τοὺς ἀληθῶς λογικοὺς διὰ τοῦ συνιέναι βούλεσθαι τὰ πνευματικά ; in *Hom. in Gen.* xiii. § 3 he compares himself to Isaac, who dug wells which the Philistines came and disputed.

[5] 'Αμαθῶς ψοφωδεῖς. In the pseudo-Clementine *Recognitions* (x. 42) there is a protest against the arbitrary distortion of Scripture. Peter is made to say "There are many passages in Scripture which can be dragged into any sense which each reader chooses, which ought not to be done." Other protests are to be found in Theophilus, *Pasch.* i. ; Epiphan. *Ep. ad Joan. Jerosol.* 2 ; *Haer.* 64, § 4 ; Jer. *Ep.* 61 ; Basil, *Hexaem.* 9 ; Aug. *De Civ. Dei*, xiii. 21, &c. (Huet, *Origeniana*, qu. 13). The language of the Clementine Homilies (iii. 9, 10, 13, 14, 21, 22, 23, 47) opposes the mechanical theory of inspiration, and criticises the origin of the Pentateuch, &c., in a manner which reminds us of Kuenen and Wellhausen.

[6] Thus the Manichaeans argued that Christ had finally laid aside His human nature from the text "Posuit tabernaculum suum in sole" (Ps. xix. 4), which they interpreted to mean that He had left in the sun His mortal dwelling (σκήνωμα), *i.e.* His body.

the end of such idealism would be a subversion of the plain
truths of the Gospel,[1] and that a dangerous use might be
made of the determination to know Christ after the flesh no
more.[2] The danger was illustrated by the way in which
Origen explained the words spoken by Christ in His agony,[3]
" Let this cup pass from me." His gloss upon them was that
Christ desired a cup yet more bitter.

The Egyptian Bishop NEPOS wrote a Refutation of the
Allegorists,[4] and a different school of Scriptural study arose
in Syria. Even this school—it should not be forgotten—
owed its impulse to the many-sided genius of Origen.[5] If he
exercised an unfortunate influence by his exaggerated allegories,
he yet gave its main stimulus to the critical and philological
labours of the best school of ancient exegetes. One of the
forerunners of this school was the martyr LUCIAN, whose
revision of the Septuagint was known as the Κοινή, and was
used in Constantinople, Asia Minor, and Antioch.[6] The
presbyter DOROTHEUS was not only a student of classic
literature, but acquired the rare accomplishment of being
able to read the Old Testament in the Hebrew original.
Eusebius heard him expound the Hebrew text with moderation
at Antioch.[7]

The best representative of the Syrian school of Edessa was
EPHRAEM SYRUS, a man of singular personal sweetness, and a
laborious commentator, who died A.D. 381. Adopting to a
great extent the views of Origen, he abounds in allegories of
which a single specimen may stand for multitudes. Com-

---

[1] See the admirable remarks of Neander, *Ch. Hist.* ii. 295-302.

[2] Orig. *Hom. in Matt.* xv. § 3, ed. Huet.

[3] In his treatise on Martyrdom, 29. (ἀλλὰ δὲ τάχα βαρύτερον αἰτεῖν
λεληθότως.)

[4] Ἔλεγχος τῶν Ἀλληγοριστῶν. It was written in the interest of the
Chiliasts (Euseb. *H. E.* vii. 24), and was answered by Dionysius the Great in
his two books περὶ ἐπαγγελιῶν.

[5] The martyr Pamphilus, the ardent admirer and champion of Origen,
founded a great library and a theological school at Caesarea. Euseb. *H. E.*
vii. 32.

[6] His MSS. were called Λουκιανεῖα, Jer. *Catal.* 77. See Routh, *Rel. Sacr.*
iv. 3 ; Westcott on the Canon, p. 392 ; Westc. and Hort, *Greek Test.* ii. 138 ;
De Broglie, *L'Église et l'Empire*, i. 375 ; Newman, *Arians*, p. 414.

[7] Euseb. *H. E.* vii. 32 ; Neander, ii. 528 ; Gieseler, i. 247.

P

menting on the wisdom through which Rahab let down the
spies (Josh. ii. 15), he says that it represents the mystery
of the freedom of the mind uncorrupted by the darkness
of sin, which receives the teachers of spiritual mysteries,
and then cautiously sends them away to the God of the
Universe, while it hopes that they will return in due
time![1] But Ephraem's worst error is the mingling and confusion of the historic and mystic sense, which serve to show
that for centuries together exegesis was drifting hither and
thither on the open sea of fancy, with no compass of true
principle to guide its course. In one and the same passage,
even in one and the same verse, he takes one phrase literally,
and the next mystically, after the aimless fashion afterwards
systematised by Tichonius. Thus on Is. ix. 7 he remarks
that part of it refers to Hezekiah, and another part cannot
possibly apply to him. The first verses of that chapter refer,
he says, to Christ, the third and fourth verses to Hezekiah
or to Christ, the fifth and sixth verses to Christ only, except
that the epithets " Prince " and " Father " may also refer to
Hezekiah, whereas the first clause of the next verse can refer
to Christ alone![2]

X. The third great school, the SCHOOL OF ANTIOCH,
possessed a deeper insight into the true method of exegesis
than any which preceded or succeeded it during a thousand
years. We are not here speaking of theological questions,
nor am I concerned to enter into the bitter disputes of the
fourth century, or to inquire how far the Antiochene interpreters have been ignorantly misrepresented. All that
I here affirm is that their system of Biblical interpretation
approached more nearly than any other to that which is
now adopted by the Reformed Churches throughout the
world, and that if they had not been too uncharitably
anathematised by the angry tongue, and crushed by the

[1] For Ephraem's acquaintance with the Jewish *Midrash*, see Delitzsch,
Genesis, p. 62.
[2] On the merits and defects of Ephraem Syrus, see the admirable monograph of Caesar v. Lengerke, *De Ephr. Syri arte hermeneutica*, especially
pp. 160 *sq.* and pp. 168 *sq.* (Königsb. 1831.) See too Cave, i. 231, Fabricius,
viii. 217.

iron hand of a dominant orthodoxy, the study of their commentaries, and the adoption of their exegetic system, might
have saved Church commentaries from centuries of futility and
error. Cardinal Newman has talked about "the connexion
of heterodoxy with Biblical criticism," and has said that by
their contemporary appearance in some of the teachers of
Antioch "it may be almost laid down as an historic fact
that the mystical interpretation and orthodoxy will stand
or fall together." A more fatal admission could hardly be
made. If it were true, it could only mean that ecclesiastical orthodoxy shrinks from the light of knowledge, and
that its exegesis is an arbitrary fiction. The mystical
interpretation has had every opportunity of establishing
itself during a thousand years. It has been weighed in the
balance and found wanting. It consists of application,
not of explication. It ignores the human element which
Scripture shows on every page. While professing to reverence the Bible it detracts from its authority, and
substitutes in its place a hollow, gilded idol, which totters
upon its flimsy pedestal. It foists into the Bible its own
fancies which are not there. It approaches the Bible in the
interests of a system pre-conceived and pre-established.[1] It
was repudiated by the ablest interpreters of Scripture in its
own day and since. It was by rejecting it that Theodore of
Mopsuestia attained an exegetic skill which had been previously unknown. Chrysostom, the ablest of Christian
homilists, and one of the best of Christian men, uses language entirely inconsistent with the theory of inspiration on

---

[1] Here is a comment on Cant. iii. 9–11, by Cyril of Alexandria († 444).
The "palanquin" is the Cross; its "silver legs" the thirty pieces of silver
paid to Judas; its purple cushion the scarlet robe with which Christ was
mocked; the "nuptial crown" is the crown of thorns! See Ginsburg, *Song
of Songs*, p. 67. It is astonishing that any one should support such theories of
the meaning of the poem in the face of such passages as vii. 2, 3, 7, 8.
Neander wisely and truly says that "those who would not admit any human
element in Scripture and arbitrarily got rid of it by pretended mysteries
under the idea of showing special respect to the Bible, undesignedly de-
tracted from its authority . . . because they explained the whole as a
single production in a way foreign indeed to the sacred word, but pre-
conceived and pre-established as a divine one by themselves, thus foisting
into the Bible what was not really there," iv. 11.

which it is based; and even Irenaeus, Tertullian, Jerome, and Augustine, in the midst of their undefined and wavering views, are betrayed into phrases which show that the theory of homogeneous supernaturalism broke down under the force of facts.[1] Happily, in his assertion of a necessary connexion between orthodoxy and exegetic wilfulness, Cardinal Newman stands alone. Even Roman Catholic historians like Cardinal Hergenröther have done justice to the School of Antioch. If it were indeed true that sound faith cannot co-exist with Biblical criticism, this could only mean that the Bible is not consistent with ecclesiastical tradition. The attempt to enforce private interpretations by Church anathemas has led to the melancholy spectacle of Councils—as for instance that of Sirmium—denouncing as heretical the refusal to accept certain specimens of exegesis which are no longer deemed tenable by any ordinary Christian man.[2]

1. DIODORUS OF TARSUS († 393) must be regarded as the true founder of the School of Antioch.[3] He was a man of eminent learning and of undisputed piety. He was the teacher of Chrysostom and of Theodore of Mopsuestia. In the days of Valens he saved the Church of his province from being submerged by the waves of misbelief.[4] He commented

---

[1] Thus Irenaeus attributes St. Paul's *hyperbata* to the vehemence of his spirit (*Haer.* iii. 7). Tertullian supposes a growth of restraint and knowledge in the mind of St. Paul (*Paulus adhuc in gratia rudis, ferventer ut adhuc neophytus*, adversus Judaismum. *C. Marc.* i. 20, and *De Pudic.* 5). See Chrysostom, *Hom. in Matt.* Field, i. ed. Field, i. pp. 4, 5, 7 (where he admits in the Gospels discrepancies in minor matters); Jerome on Gal. v. 12, where he speaks of St. Paul being carried away by the vehemence of his feelings ("Ut homo, et *adhuc vasculo clausus infirmo*"). Even Augustine speaks of the Evangelists writing "*Ut quisque meminerat vel ut cuique cordi fuerat.*" Neander, iv. 10–13.

[2] "Si quis *Faciamus hominem* non Patrem ad Filium dixisse dicat . . . anathema sit . . . Si quis cum Jacobo non Filium quasi hominem colluctatum . . . dicat, anathema sit. . . . Si quis *Pluit Dominus a Domino* (Gen. xix. 24) non de Filio et Patre intelligat . . . anathema sit." *Conc. Sirm.* (A.D. 357; Canons xiv.–xvii.; Harduin, i. 702. See Rosenmüller, *Hist. Interp.* iv. 291).

[3] The "school" of Antioch was not like that of Alexandria, a succession of connected teachers. It was rather a theological tendency which continued at Nisibis and Edessa after the condemnation of Nestorius. See Schaff, *Ch. Hist.* ii. 816. To this school belong Ephraem Syrus, Eusebius of Emesa (on whom there are monographs by Augusti and Thilo), Chrysostom, Severianus, Theodore of Mopsuestia, and Theodoret.

[4] Theodoret, *H.E.* v. 4.

upon a large part of both Testaments with special reference
to the literal sense. His works were unhappily destroyed
by the Arians whom he had so successfully refuted, and he
was also anathematised by the Eutychians, though not, as
was commonly but erroneously asserted, by the Fifth
Oecumenical Council.[1] His books were devoted to an exposition of Scripture in its literal sense,[2] and he wrote a
treatise, now unhappily lost, " on the difference between
allegory and spiritual insight."[3]

2. But the ablest, the most decided, and the most logical
representative of the School of Antioch was THEODORE OF
MOPSUESTIA († 428). That clear-minded and original thinker
stands out like "a rock in the morass of ancient exegesis."
He was not, indeed, a Hebrew scholar.[4] This is shown
somewhat disastrously in his criticism on Job. He regarded
it as a very imperfect tragedy on a Jewish theme, and
inferred that the writer was a heathen because one of Job's
daughters was called "Amalthaea's horn"![5] He even
neglected the Peshito version which might have stood
him in such good stead, and he relies, like most other
Fathers, on the "inspired" LXX.[6] In his theory of types

---

[1] The anathemas are not in the genuine Acts of the Council. He is
defended by Facundus Hermianensis. "Should not the merits of St. Chrysostom seem rather to justify Diodorus than the errors of Theodore to condemn him ?" See Neander, iv. 209.

[2] Socrates, *H. E.* vi. 3. Διόδωρος δὲ . . . πολλὰ βιβλία συνέγραψε ψιλῷ
τῷ γράμματι τῶν θείων κατέχων γραφῶν, τῆς θεωρίας αὐτῶν ἐκτρεπόμενος.
Sozomen, *H. E.* viii. 2. Διόδωρος ὃν ἐπυθόμην ἰδίων συγγραμμάτων πολλὰς
καταλιπεῖν βίβλους, περὶ δὲ τὸ ῥητὸν τῶν ἱερῶν λόγων τὰς ἐξηγήσεις ποιήσασ-
θαι τῆς θεωρίας ἀποφυγόντα. Jer. *Catal.* 119.

[3] τίς διαφορὰ θεωρίας καὶ ἀλληγορίας. Suidas, *s.v.* Διόδ. By Theoria is
meant spiritual insight which is not content with the letter only.

[4] This appears from his remark on the word Remphan (Acts vii. 43, comp.
Amos v. 26) φασὶ δὲ τὸν Ἑωσφόρον οὕτω κατὰ τῶν Ἑβραίων καλεῖσθαι
γλῶτταν. Any Jew could have told him that the word is not Hebrew at all
but Egyptian.

[5] The name Qeren Happuk is rendered *Cornustibium* in the Vulg., and
Gregory the Great derives it from *cornu* and *tibia!* See Merx, *Joel*, p. 101.
Theodori Ep. Mops. *in Epp. B. Pauli Commentarii*, ed. H. B. Swete, Cambr.
1880. Some of Theodore's commentaries were long attributed by mistake to
Ambrose, and to Hilary of Poictiers, writers to whom he has not the least
resemblance. Dr. Hort's discovery of the true authorship, given in *Journ.
of Class. and Sacr. Philol.* iv. 302, is mentioned in Bishop Lightfoot's *Galatians*, p. 219.

[6] In Habak. ii. 11, where the LXX. has the curious word κάνθαρος, which
misled so many commentators, Theodore contents himself with saying that

there is a want of living connexion between rows of facts and no definite principle on which to decide why some facts were to be regarded as typical and others not. Like all the ancient interpreters he lacked the conception of Development, of a living growth and progress in the order of revelation. Again—not to enter on the defects and errors of his theology—he does not rise superior to the influence of "bias," which sometimes leads him to get rid of passages which tell against his special views.[1] It is, further, true that he is not eminent as a textual critic, and sometimes chooses his readings on arbitrary principles.[2] Once more, his interests are intellectual and dogmatic rather than devotional and spiritual, so that in these respects he is far inferior to his friend St. Chrysostom. Photius blamed his style for its diffuseness, obscurity, and tautology,[3] and we cannot but regret that he often attacks other commentators with scarcely merited derision. Some of his faults may be due to the self-reliance of an ardent and ingenious temperament; others to the rhetorical training which he had received in the School of Libanius; others again to restless productiveness; others perhaps to some uncertainty as to the scope and issue of views in which he was far before his time. "His literary faults," it has been said, "were but the reflexion of mental imperfections which to some extent vitiate his work as well as his style, his theology no less than the form in which it is cast."[4] But while his faults are thus freely admitted, it remains true that he was worthy of his title as "The

---

"*according to some*" the Syrian version renders the word by "peg"! Because the Apostles used the LXX. he seems always to assume that the LXX. is right, the Peshito wrong.

[1] Thus on Eph. iv. 10 (ὁ καταβὰς αὐτός ἐστιν καὶ ὁ ἀναβὰς) he denies that this is true literally; and on Col. i. 13 persuades himself that Christ's "adoption" of manhood is involved in τῆς ἀγαπῆς, that ἐν αὐτῷ points to the second or spiritual creation, and that the Pleroma which dwelt in Christ was the Church, His Body. See Swete's edition of Theodore of Mopsuestia, i. p. lxxi.

[2] In Eph. iii. 15 he reads φρατρία for πατριά. In Eph. ii. 22 he comments on ἀφὴ not οἰκοδομή.

[3] Photius, *Cod.* 4, but he calls him ταῖς διανοίαις καὶ τοῖς ἐπιχειρήμασι λίαν πυκνός, καὶ ταῖς γραφικαῖς ἄριστα πλουτῶν μαρτυρίαις.

[4] Swete, p. lxv.

Exegete " of the early Church, as Theodoret is the Annotator
and Chrysostom the Homilist. His merits are so conspicuous
that Theodoret does not shrink from calling him " The Master
of the whole Church."

For Theodore was a man " of bold independence and
masculine sagacity ;" a leader of thought ; a writer of rare
acumen, of fearless honesty, of prodigious industry, of ardent
sincerity, of unquestionable power. He was a Voice not an
Echo ; a Voice amid thousands of echoes which repeated only
the emptiest sounds. He rejected the theories of Origen, but he
had learnt from him the indispensable importance of attention
to linguistic details [1] especially in commenting on the New
Testament.[2] He pays close attention to particles, moods,
prepositions, and to terminology in general. He points out
the idiosyncrasies ($\iota\delta\iota\omega\mu\alpha\tau\alpha$) of St. Paul's style. He is
almost the earliest writer who gives much attention to
Hermeneutic matter, as for instance in his Introductions to
the Epistles to Ephesus and Colossae.[3] He enters into such
collateral questions as Church organisation, early ecclesiastical history, the condition of slaves and women in the
heathen world, and adds to the interest of his treatment
by references to contemporary matters such as sacerdotal
arrogance, false liberalism, and the spirit of persecution.
His highest merit is his constant endeavour to study each
passage as a whole and not as " an isolated congeries of separate
texts." He first considers the sequence of thought, then
examines the phraseology and the separate clauses, and
finally furnishes us with an exegesis which is often brilliantly
characteristic and profoundly suggestive.

But his crowning merit was the original yet unhappily
fruitless stand which he made against the subtle fascination

---

[1] Linguistic, but unfortunately not historical or geographical. Questions
about Tarshish, Bothrus (LXX. for קיר Am. ix. 7), &c., he flings aside as
$\pi\epsilon\rho\iota\tau\tau\grave{\eta}$ $\dot{\alpha}\kappa\rho\iota\beta\omicron\lambda\omicron\gamma\acute{\iota}\alpha$.

[2] Ambrose says that Origen was *" longe minor* in Novo Testamento," but in
spite of prolixity he is in fact better as a New Testament than as an Old Testament exegete, and his notes on the use of words (John i. 3 ; iv. 35, 44, &c.)
are often excellent. See Dr. Sanday in *Expositor*, xi. 371.

[3] Questions as to

"Quis, quid, ubi, quibus auspiciis, cur, quomodo, quando."

of Origenising allegory.[1] Part of the bitterness with which his memory was persecuted was due to the anger of the Origenists against him for the treatise which he had written to refute their principles.[2] The Syrian school held that the Scriptures are the basis of knowledge, and not either the esoteric Gnosis to which the Alexandrians had attached so much importance, nor the ecclesiastical tradition to which Irenaeus, Tertullian, and Cyprian had appealed. They were the Reformers, the Protestants, the Puritans, of the Ancient Church. Origen had held that the Old and New Testaments were equally important ; the Antiochenes had realised the vast difference which separates them. They recognised that the "grace of superintendency" (εὐδοκία), which they attributed to the Old Testament writers, admitted of degrees. They denied, and rightly denied, that the Jews had anything approaching to a real knowledge of such truths as the Trinity and the Incarnation. Theodore understood the Psalms in their historic sense, and, while he by no means denied their typical applicability, he was attacked by Leontius of Byzantium, and called a Judaiser, just as Calvin was in later times, because he referred them primarily to Hezekiah and Zerubbabel, and only allowed that three Psalms were directly Messianic.[3] He pointed out that the Song of Solomon does not once mention the name of God, and, like many eminent moderns, he rejected its mystic application. In the ninth chapter of Zechariah (8-10) he thought it an instance of frigid and foolish interpretation (ἀνοίας τῆς ἐσχάτης) to

[1] See the excellent remarks of Sieffert, *Theod. Mops. V. T. sobrie interpretandi vindex*, 1827, and Munter, *De Schola Antiochena*, 1811. The monograph of Fritzsche, *De Theod. Mops. Vita et Scriptis* (1836), is printed in Migne's *Patrologia*, vol. lxvi.

[2] Facundus of Hermiane (*Def. Triun. Capit.* iii. 6) cites a treatise of his, *De Allegoria et Historia*, in five books, and mentions the odium which it excited. Ebedjesu (Assemanni, iii. 34) also alludes to this.

[3] Leont. Byzant. *adv. Eutych.* iii. c. 11. "Omnes psalmos judaice ad Zorobabalem et Ezechiam retulit, tribus tantum [viii. xlv. cx.] ad Dominum rejectis." Facundus defends him very properly by saying that he did not dispute the applicability of all Messianic prophecy, and that there was no crime in the moral interpretation of the Psalms. And Theodore at least assigned reasons for his views. He could not allow Ps. xxii. to be exclusively Messianic, because in verse 1 the Septuagint has "*my transgressions.*" He is said to have written this commentary on the Psalms at the age of eighteen.

apply one clause historically and another allegorically, to refer one to Zerubbabel, the next to Christ, and then to go back again to Zerubbabel. He rightly refuses to read the latest revelations into the earliest utterances,—to see the doctrine of the Trinity in the first verse of Genesis, and the three spies of Exodus; of Redemption in Rahab's red cord; of the Resurrection in the law of levirate marriage; or of the evangelisation of the heathen in the Ethiopian wife of Moses. He stood his ground on the doctrine of Unity of Sense, and he deduced the sense on secure principles from the context, from the general laws of language, and from the usages of the particular writer.

Another of his conspicuous merits is this, that he had grasped the difference which separates the Jewish from the Alexandrian theory of inspiration, a difference which fundamentally affected the methods of the two schools. To some of the ablest thinkers among the Jews inspiration was *ethical* in its character; it consisted in the dilatation and ennoblement of the individual consciousness. To the Alexandrians, misled by Plato, inspiration was pathological; it consisted in a trance, and depression of the individual consciousness. The difference is that which also separates the ecstasy of Montanists from the inspired Christian preaching, to which the Apostles give the name of "prophecy." The different theories led to different methods of interpretation. The Alexandrian theory furnished the pretext for allegory—that is, for making the writers say something other than what they did say. The better Jewish theory, purified in Christianity, takes the teachings of the Old Dispensation literally, but sees in them, as did St. Paul, the shadow and germ of future developments. Allegory, though once used by St. Paul by way of passing illustration, is unknown to the other Apostles, and is never sanctioned by Christ.[1] But Christ Himself, as in the case of Jonah, and of the Brazen Serpent, sanctioned the use of types. The

---

[1] It is surely needless to point out the absolute difference between *parabolic teaching* and *allegorical interpretation*.

allegoric method triumphed from the days of Origen onwards. The true grasp of typology ceased from the fifth to the seventeenth century—from the days of Theodore to those of Cocceius.

It must not be supposed that Theodore rejected the whole argument from Prophecy. He neither accused the Apostles of error in their Old Testament references ; nor did he deny the progressive and providential governance of God in the History of the World. He held that the essence of Old Testament prophecy lay rather in an inspired hope than in conscious vaticination ; that Israel was under the special care (κηδεμονία) of God, and that God prophesies by deeds rather than by words. Hence he believed that the relation of the Old to the New Testament lay mainly in the homology of facts due to a sort of pre-established harmony; that by God's divine administration (οἰκονομία) the facts were themselves a dim revelation of the future, and that the Prophets were led by divine inspiration to express what they saw in larger terms (ὑπερβολικώτερον) than would have been warranted by contemporary circumstances.[1] It is on this principle that he explains the applications of the New Testament writers. He sees as clearly as we do that they are not proofs in the modern sense of the word, but rather illustrative applications which would have been specially valuable to those who had been trained in the methods on which they depended.[2] There can be no better indication of the fine original genius of Theodore than the fact that in these conclusions, without any aid from the immense apparatus of subsequently-accumulated

---

[1] See Theod. Mops. *Praef. in Jon.* ; Merx, *Joel*, p. 127, fg. Delitzsch on Ps. xxii. He held that the Prophets did not see distinctly, but had φαντασίαν τινα τῶν μελλόντων.

[2] The phrases he uses closely resemble those of Calvin. If Calvin says that the sacred writers " apply " this or that passage to Christ, "*piâ deflectione,*" so Theodore says of Heb. x. 5, that the passage quoted was originally applicable to the Jewish exiles, but that the writer altered the reading from ὠτία to σῶμα (μεταλλάξας οὖν αὐτὴν ὡς ἐκ προσώπου τοῦ Χριστοῦ ταύτῃ φησὶν ἀντὶ τοῦ ὠτία, σῶμα). He uses the words συγχρῆσθαι, καταχρῆσθαι, of the use made of Amos ix. 11, Is. xlv. 23, in Rom. xiv. 11 ; and defends such quotations on the ground that what was said of the Divine nature generally might be applied to the Son or the Holy Spirit.

thought, he anticipated by fourteen hundred years many of the accepted conclusions of modern days.

3. It is a matter of profound regret that, in the Western Church especially, the influence of Theodore was totally destroyed by the charge of Nestorianism.[1] In the Syrian Church, indeed, he produced a profound impression. His views were, to a certain extent, perpetuated by THEODORET, who depended almost entirely on Theodore and Chrysostom, whom he calls luminaries of the world. But Theodoret († 457), though safer and more terse, drew back from the advanced position of Theodore, and was wholly inferior to him in genius, courage, and literary power.[2] Theodore paid a terrible penalty for having been born in an age too soon. His aberrations from traditional dogma brought him into suspicion, and "a century later a pigmy generation anathematised exegetes, who were already half forgotten."[3] But his merits have been recognised in later days, and the stream of truth, having flowed for centuries in its subterranean course, once more emerged at the Reformation into regions of light and day.

4. The great Cappadocian triumvirate, BASIL THE GREAT, GREGORY OF NYSSA, "the Theologian," and GREGORY OF

---

[1] Among Theodore's predecessors might have been mentioned Aphraates, Eusebius of Emesa, and possibly Adrianus : among his successors his younger brother Polychronius Bishop of Apamea († 430) and Severianus Bishop of Gabala (see Schröck, x. 458, Cave, i. 375).

[2] On Theodoret see Schröck, xviii. 398 *sq.* ; Rosenmüller, iv. 93 ; Merx, *Joel*, p. 147, *fg.* Lightfoot, *Galatians*, p. 226. There is a monograph by Richter, *De Theodoreto Ep. Paulin. interprete*, 1822 ; and another by Specht, *Der exegetische Standpunkt Theodor's und Theodoret's.*

On Theodore's writings, of which we now possess some complete works in the original, see Fritzsche, *De Theod. Mops. Vita et scriptis*, Halae, 1836. Ernesti, *Opusc. Theol.* 502 ; Sieffert, *Theod. Mops. V. Test. sobrie interpretandi vindex*, 1827 ; Diestel, pp. 129-133 ; Merx, *Joel*, pp. 110-141 ; and the excellent introduction of the Rev. H. B. Swete to the edition of his *Commentaries on the Epistles of St. Paul.* The savage attack on him by Leontius may be read in Gallandi, *Bibl. Patr.* xii. 686 (*Libidinose pro sua et mente et lingua meretricia interpretatus*, sua supra modum incredibili audacia ex libris sacris abscidit," &c.). The style of the theological criticism of partisans was as violent and vulgar then as it has always been. It is to be feared, however, that Theodore in part provoked it by his own stinging expressions. For notices of the writers of the Antiochene School in general, see Rosenmüller, iii. 250. The merits of Theodore have been fully admitted by Merx (*Joel*, pp. 110–141), Bishop Lightfoot (*Galatians*, p. 220), and Dr. Sanday (*Expositor*, vol. xi.).

[3] Reuss, *Gesch.* § 521.

NAZIANZUS, followed in exegesis a *via media*. Their profound admiration of Origen is proved by the publication of the *Philokalia*, but they avoided as a rule the extravagances of allegory.[1] They sought a middle term between a slavish literalism and an *unlimited* play of fancy; but the three friends are more famous as orators and as theologians than for anything distinctive in their exegetical labours. In the last epoch of patristic exegesis three names tower above all others, the names of Chrysostom, Jerome, and Augustine; —Chrysostom the Homilist, Jerome the Commentator, and Augustine the Theologian.

5. In CHRYSOSTOM we see the "bright consummate flower" of the school of Antioch, to which he belongs as a faithful and admiring pupil of Diodorus of Tarsus.[2] If he showed less originality and intellectual many-sidedness than his younger fellow-pupil Theodore, he has more definiteness, a clearer insight, a more rigorous logic, a more practical wisdom. He was not so learned as Jerome, nor had he Origen's deep sympathy with the more mysterious aspects of the Gospel,[3] nor was he so profound a theologian as Augustine, nor was he in any sense a textual critic like Julius Africanus;[4] but as a Bishop inspired with genuine love for the souls of his flock; as a preacher of surpassing eloquence, whose popular exposition is based on fine scholarship and controlled by masterly good sense; as one who had a thorough familiarity with the whole of Scripture, and who felt its warm tingling human life throbbing in all his veins; as one who took the Bible as

---

[1] Basil stoutly says, "When I hear of grass, I understand it to mean grass, and so of plants, and fishes, and beasts, and cattle; all of them as they are spoken of, so I receive." He adds that "many interpreters *pervert all this according to meanings of their own, much like those who profess to interpret dreams;*" and that "some have tried by I know not what allurements and figures of speech *to get the Scriptures credit for a kind of dignity which is in fact of their own devising,*" and "under the show of interpretation to introduce matters of their own."—*Hexaem.* ix. 1.

[2] See Förster, *Chrysostomus in seinen Verhältniss zur Antiochenischer Schule,* 1869.

[3] Contrast for instance the treatment of St. John's Gospel in Chrysostom's homilies and Origen's comments; see Westcott, *St. John,* p. xcv.

[4] See Dr. Sanday, *Expositor,* vol. xii.; Lightfoot, *Galatians,* p. 218. Canon Westcott says (*St. John* in *Speaker's Comment.* p. xcv.) "The reader will probably miss the signs of a spontaneous sympathy with the more mysterious aspects of the Gospel."

he found it, and used it in its literal sense as a guide of
conduct rather than as an armoury of controversial weapons
or a field for metaphysical speculations—Chrysostom stands
unsurpassed among the ancient exegetes. St. Paul was his
ideal, but, while he had less of the Pauline nature than
Augustine, he may be rightly called "·another John" for his
glowing zeal and love, and he resembled St. James in his
practical tendency. Too actively employed to become a close
student, he was unacquainted with Hebrew,[1] and without even
a nice critical knowledge of the Greek which he wielded with
so much force.[2] Hampered by the traditional misconceptions
which had already been introduced into many passages, he
yet keeps himself, to a great extent, free from vain dogmatism
and baseless allegory.[3] There are fewer errors and vagaries
in his writings than in those of any one of the Fathers. His
manly moral nature, trained in a life of activity and struggle,
his noble and commanding individuality, his oratorical power,
his habit of studying every passage as a whole, his general
principle of *eliciting* instead of *introducing* a meaning,[4] his
exquisitely genial sympathy,[5] his frank recognition of the
human element in Scripture, and of the effect produced by
the personality of its writers,[6] justly earn for him the place
which Dante assigns to him in the Paradise, between Nathan
the Seer and St. Anselm, as one who "spoke before kings
and was not ashamed."[7]

> " Natan profeta l'metropolitano
> Crisostomo ed Anselmo."

---

[1] He was dependent mainly on the Seventy, but sometimes refers (without
name) to Theodotion, Symmachus, and Aquila.

[2] He makes however excellent grammatical remarks on John xii. 39 ; 2 Cor.
iii. 17 ; Gal. i. 18, iv. 5, v. 15 ; Eph. i. 10. See Dr. Sanday in *The Expositor*,
xii. 134 ff.

[3] He recognises allegory in theory (*Hom. in* 1 *Cor.* xxxix.) but for the most
part avoids it in practice (see Förster, *Chrysost. in seinen Verhältniss*, &c.
p. 21 ; Diestel, p. 135.)

[4] In Isai. v. 3 and vi.

[5] "His charm lies in his habit and his power of throwing himself into the
minds of others." Newman, *Ancient Saints*, chap. v. He furnishes beautiful illustrations from the notes of the *Catena Aurea*, on the narrative of the
Transfiguration.

[6] See his notes on Ps. lxiv. and *Hom. in* 1 *Cor.* xxix.

[7] *Parad.* xii. 136.

Yet he was no ecclesiastical statesman like St. Ambrose. He desired far more to see Christianity dominate in the individual heart than to see priests lording it over the heritage of God. No one of the Fathers insists so constantly on the importance of studying Scripture for personal instruction. He adopts, but generally with sobriety, the mystic sense.[1] He held, but did not abuse, the doctrine of "accommodation," and he combined his view of inspiration with a free admission of obvious limitations.[2] His discussion of discrepancies entitles him to be regarded as the founder of "Harmonistic," but his highest merit is the skill with which he develops the literal sense by a study of the context,[3] and a regard for the usage of special words.[4] He held that the larger part of Scripture was perfectly "perspicuous," and that the only aids required for its comprehension were a willing heart, the guidance of the wise, and the help of the Holy Spirit of God. The superiority of the Antiochene over the Alexandrian method may be readily seen by comparing the sober, moral, practical manner in which Chrysostom treats the subject of the Fall,[5] and the way in which the same topic is handled by a genuine Origenist like Gregory of Nyssa.

XI. But great as were the services of Chrysostom, his influence on the Biblical studies of succeeding ages was less powerful than that of JEROME. Jerome was the Origen of the Western Church. The great hermit of Bethlehem had less genius than Augustine, less purity and loftiness of character than Ambrose, less sovereign good sense and steadfastness than Chrysostom, less keenness of insight and consistency of courage than Theodore of Mopsuestia;[6] but in learning

---

[1] He gives his *via media* theory on Ps. xlvi. τά τε αἰσθητὰ νοοῦντες καὶ τὰ νοητὰ ἐκδεχόμενοι, and on Ps. cix. τὰ μὲν προοίμια εἰς ἕτερον, τὰ δὲ λειπόμενα εἰς ἄλλον λεγόμενά ἐστιν. This indefiniteness is at any rate better than baseless fancies.

[2] See *Hom. in Matt.* 26 ; Böhringer, *Chrysost.* p. 158.

[3] τὴν ἀκολουθίαν τῶν εἰρημένων.

[4] "Er hat's," said Luther, who admired him more than any of the Fathers, "*sensus literalis,* der thut's, da ist Leben, Kraft, und Wahreit drinnen."

[5] *Hom. in Gen.* xvii.

[6] *Apol. c. Rufin.* iii. 6. "Ego philosophus, rhetor, grammaticus, dialecticus, Hebraeus, Graecus, Latinus, trilinguis."

and versatile talent he was superior to them all. Deeply as
he was indebted to Origen, he surpassed him in the accuracy
of his conception as to what the true function of an exegete
should be. He was not a deep theologian; he was not a
great moralist; he was an excessively faulty saint; but his
wide learning, his intense and eloquent style, his literary
skill, his philological attainments, the use which he made of
Jewish authorities, the combination of a fiery and passionate
nature with immense and many-sided ability, the indomitable industry with which he continued to produce volume
after volume during years full of sickness, controversy, endless
correspondence, ascetic exercises, and barbarian invasion,[1]
enabled him to render services to the study of Scripture such
as are approached by Origen alone. As regards the Old Testament especially no comments were so useful to generations
of subsequent commentators as those which they borrowed
wholesale from the voluminous writings of Jerome. Those
writings have the additional advantage of being so illuminated
by flashes of epigram and passion that not one page of them
is dull.[2]

i. Foremost among his services must be placed the Vulgate
translation.[3] No doubt it is an easy task to point out the
defects and errors of that version, and critics like Simon and
Clericus have ventured to speak with contempt about Jerome's
knowledge of Hebrew.[4] It would of course be unjust to
compare it with that critical knowledge which can be obtained
by modern scholars with the help of grammars and lexicons.

---

[1] He wrote daily letters to Paula and Eustochium, *Catal.* 135. "Cui jugis
adversus malos pugna, perpetuumque certamen," says Sulp. Severus, who
stayed six months with him at Bethlehem (*Dial.* i. 4). He adds "Totus
semper in lectione, totus in libris est; non die, non nocte requiescit; aut
legit aliquid semper, aut scribit."

[2] In Jerome and in Tertullian may be found a fire which is wanting even in
Cicero. See Erasmus, *Epp.* v. 19 ; Ozanam (*Hist. de la Civilisat. chrét.* ii. 100)
calls him " Le maître de la prose chrétienne pour tous les siècles suivans." See
Zöckler, *Hieron.* pp. 323-340.

[3] On the Vulgate translation and its high importance see Hody, *De Text.
Bibl.* ; Routh (quoted in *Expositor,* xii. 217). The articles on the Vulgate by
Westcott in Smith's *Dictionary,* and Fritzsche in Herzog, xvii. 422, are of
great value.

[4] It was impossible for him with the scanty appliances within his reach to
attain to a thoroughly *critical* knowledge of Hebrew.

Jerome, though he could speak and understand Hebrew, was not a Hebrew scholar in the same sense as Gesenius, or Ewald, or Delitzsch.[1] But we must remember that he could only learn it *viva voce*, without any other assistance than that of a Hebrew Bible without vowel points or diacritical marks, and under the tuition of Jews, whose visits to him were an object of such deep suspicion alike to Christians and to their own countrymen that they often had to be made in secret.[2] Judged by the standard of his own age, Jerome's knowledge of Hebrew was probably more thorough than that of all the other Fathers. It is to the credit both of his diligence and his courage that he should have devoted twenty-three years (A.D. 382 to 405) to a task so formidable, and one which exposed him to such rude animadversions as his Latin translation of the Bible.[3] It is still more to his credit that he should have seen the impossibility of resting content with the endlessly variant and corrupted copies of the many old and incorrect Latin versions,[4] and should have dared to

---

[1] See "Hebrew Learning" in Smith and Wace, *Dict. of Christian Biography.*

[2] One of his teachers was Hillel, brother of R. Judah II., and grandson of R. Judah the Holy. His chief teacher was the learned Bar-Anina. *Ep.* lxxxiv. § 4. "Quo labore, quo pretio Baraninam *nocturnum* habui *doctorem* ; timebat enim Judaeos et mihi alterum exhibebat Nicodemum." Rufinus, *Apol.* ii. 12. "*Barabbam*, ejus de Synagoga magistrum." He also alludes to a Rabbi at Lydda, whose teaching was very expensive, and another from Tiberias. *Praef. in Osee ; Praef. in Chron.; in Esaiam*, xiii. 10 ; xxii. 1, &c. It is from the Haggada that he gets the rendering, "in *igne* Chaldaeorum," for "in *Ur* of the Chaldees," Gen. xi. 28.

[3] His "*pius labor sed periculosa praesumptio*" was undertaken at the request of Damasus († 384). See Clericus, *Quaest. Hieron.* (1700).

[4] Reuss, *Gesch. d. N. T.* §§ 449, 453. Engelstoft, *Hieronymus* (1797) ; Schröck, *K. G.* xi. 61 *sqq.* He complains bitterly of the abuse to which he was subjected. *Praef. in Evang. ad Damasum.* He defended his abandonment of the Seventy on the grounds that (1) the Church had done so in preferring Theodotion's version of Daniel ; (2) the Apostles often referred to the Hebrew ; (3) the Seventy had altered Messianic passages. *Praef. in Gen.* "Nescio quis primus auctor 70 cellulas Alexandriae mendacio suo extruxerit." *Comm. in Mich.* ii. 9. "Interpretatio LXX. (si tamen LXX. est, Josephus enim scribit quinque tantum libros ab eis translatos)." *Praef. in Paralip.* "70 cellulas quae vulgo sine auctore jactantur." See too *Praef. in Dan.* lib. ii. ; *in Rufin.* 33 ; Zöckler, 355. He had to suffer from incessant attacks of Obscurantists, and was annoyed by the timid warnings of Augustine, and the curious story about the African bishop who read "hedera" for "cucurbita," in Jonah. Augustine seems to have thought that venerable error was better than new truth in matters of translation, and the strange reception given to the Revised Version shows that many still share his views. See Aug. *Ep.* 82.

translate directly from the Hebrew and not from the half-deified Septuagint.[1] He mercilessly exposed the fables which invented for the work of the Seventy an inspired authority. He sets aside the pseudo-Aristeas, and thinks that only the Pentateuch was translated under Ptolemy I. He was in advance of his age, alike in knowledge and foresight, and centuries after his death inspiration was claimed for his own work which had been originally received, like all new versions, with suspicion and abuse.[2]

ii. Another of his services was the extent to which he helped to clear the views of the Church respecting the Canon. In spite of the wavering phrases which characterise every branch of his labours, he drew a marked line between the apocryphal and canonical books of the Old Testament,[3] while he absolutely, and even contemptuously, rejected the extra-canonical Christian writings which had sometimes been placed on a level with the genuine works of Apostles and Evangelists.

iii. It must further be put down to his credit that he almost equalled the School of Antioch in the care with which he endeavoured to develop the literal and historic sense. It is owing to his diligence in carrying out this endeavour, and the information on many topics which he was able to obtain, that his commentaries are to this day more necessary to the Expositor than those of any other of the Fathers. He was also one of the earliest to collect hermeneutic materials as a guide to the significance of each separate book.

But against these high merits must be set the four serious drawbacks of overhaste, second-handness, vehement prejudice, and incessant vacillation.

a. Of his own haste he has given us repeated proofs, which take the form of excuses.[4] In his various prefaces he tells us

---

§ 35 ; Klausen, *Augustinus,* 84. Augustine says, "Latinorum interpretum infinita varietas." *De Doctr. Christ.* ii. 2.

[1] In point of fact, however, he made large use of the Septuagint, as well as of the version of Symmachus and others. [2] Morinus, *Exerc. Bibl.* vi. 12.

[3] See his remarks on 4 Esdras in his letter to Vigilantius.

[4] These excuses occur very frequently in his letters. He would have done better to follow the rule of Marcus Aurelius, who tells us that he had learnt

Q

that he wrote, or rather dictated, his commentary[1] on the Galatians at the rate of 1000 lines a day, so fast that he could not keep in his memory either the order of the words or of the meaning. He says that his comment on St. Matthew was written during the fortnight of recovery from a severe illness, and that in reading it he hardly seemed to be reading his own work.[2] He tells his correspondents that he took three days to translate the three reputed books of Solomon, Proverbs, Ecclesiastes, and the Song of Songs,[3] though he was at the time *aegrotatione fractus.* Similar excuses occur in other prefaces. In his comment on Isaiah he speaks of the swiftness of his dictation, and in that on Obadiah he says that he dictated whatever came first to his lips. In one passage he gives an amusing description of the way in which, if he did but stop to think, his secretary rebuked him by his supercilious silence, relaxed the grasp of his fingers on the pen, wrinkled his forehead, and by every gesture of his body proclaimed that he had come for no purpose. This careless haste, to use his own recurrent phrase *dictare quodcunque in buccam venerit,*[4] is the more remarkable because in other respects he took the utmost pains. He visited Constantinople to hear Gregory of Nazianzus, and Alexandria to profit by the insight of Didymus the Blind. Nor did he ever spare himself expense. He disbursed large sums to secure Hebrew teaching, and he emptied his purse to buy the works of Origen.[5]

---

from the Platonist Alexander "never to say in a letter that I have no leisure," i. 12. In his letter to Paulinus he makes a series of futile excuses which practically mean that he did not mean to hold himself responsible for what he said in his hasty letters—"Non mihi debes imputare sed tibi, et *imperitae notariorum librariorumque incuriae.*"

[1] He calls it "commaticum interpretandi genus." The 244 verses of Tobit, the 339 of Judith, occupied him but a single day. "Hieronymus laborantissimus et desudatissimus." Notker, *Virr. ill.*

[2] *Ep.* 73, *ad Evangelum, c.* 10 ; *Praef. in Matthaeum.*

[3] *Praef. in libb. Salom.* At the close of his letter to Fabiola (lxiv. *De Veste sacerdotali*) he says (§ 23), "Satis intelligens magis me loquendi impetu, quam judicio scribentis fluere, et more torrentis turbidum proferre sermonem."

[4] See Zöckler, 377.

[5] *Ep.* 84, *ad Pammach. et Occan.* § 3. "Nostrum marsupium chartae Alexandrinae evacuarunt."

b. It was partly due to this want of reflexion and this hurried voluminousness of production that Jerome's method is too much that of a compiler. He tells us [1] that in many of his commentaries his way was to read the previous comments of Origen (whom he generally mentions first), Apollinaris, Hippolytus, Irenaeus, Eusebius of Emesa, Eusebius of Caesarea, Theophilus of Antioch, Theodore of Heraclea, Hilary, Victorinus, Fortunatianus, Eustathius of Antioch, Acacius, Diodore of Tarsus, and Didymus (whom, in allusion to his blindness, he calls *Videntem meum*), and then to dictate as fast as he could what might be accepted, either as his own or not his own, as the reader chose.[2] He makes his humility the excuse; but he had a sufficiently high and clear conception of the duty of an interpreter to feel that he thus laid himself open to the just criticism of his antagonist Rufinus.

c. Of the bitterness of his prejudices we need say but little. It appears in every line of his controversial writings, in which, with the vain excuse that there was a difference between saying a thing doctrinally (δογματικῶς) and saying it controversially (γυμναστικῶς), he too often " throws truth and decency to the winds."[3] He was avowedly guilty of the base modern view that controversial works have no other object than to win an immediate victory. To this end he often indulges in a style of interpretation which he theoretically repudiates.[4] Nothing, for instance, can be more grossly sophistical than his way of distorting Scripture to support his favourite monachal theory of virginity in his furious arguments against Jovinian.

---

[1] *Prooem. in Eph.* Jerome's views as to the duty of an expositor may be seen in his *Ep.* 57, *ad Pammachium* ("Libellus de optimo genere interpretandi scripturas") and in his answer to Rufinus. They are not so good as those of Augustine, though he surpassed Augustine as a commentator.

[2] *Ep.* 73, *ad Evangelum,* § 2 ; *Ep.* 119, *ad Minerv. et Alex. ; Ep.* 70, *ad Magnum,* §§ 4, 5, where he quotes thirty-three Greek and eight Latin Fathers. Zöckler, 154. An immense mass of ancient exegetical matter has perished. See Diestel, 110. In his *Prooem. in Matt.* Jerome says that he had no time to read the older writers.

[3] Donaldson, *Apostol. Fathers,* ii. 19.

[4] Thus he constantly violates the admirable rule which he lays down in his letter to Paulinus "not to distort expressions and wrest reluctant Scripture into agreement with one's own fancies." *Ep.* 53, § 7. Comp. *Ep.* 48, § 15. (I refer throughout to Vallarsi's edition.)

When Jovinian appeals to the primal command " Increase
and multiply," Jerome answers that " Marriages fill earth, but
virginity fills Paradise ; " that the second day of creation was
the only one of which it is not said that " God saw that it
was good ; " and that all the animals which entered two and
two into the ark were unclean.[1] When Jovinian urges that
the Song of Songs is full of the idea of marriage, Jerome
answers by an allegorical interpretation in which the
mountain of myrrh means those who mortify their bodies,
and the hill of Libanus means flocks of virgins. Again,
when he is arguing against Vigilantius, the Protestant of
the fifth century, whom in his usual style of abuse he calls
Dormitantius, he rages against his objection to the adoration
of relics by quoting the reference to the angels in the tomb
of Gethsemane, and the verse " Precious in the sight of the
Lord is the death of His saints." If he has to get over the
fact that St. Peter was married, he does so in one place by
the remark that Peter had " washed off the filth of marriage
in the blood of martyrdom "[2] (a remark which, disgracefully
anti-scriptural as it is, was the delight of the mediæval
monks),[3] and sometimes by the impudent fable that Peter
left his wife with his nets and his fishing-boat.[4] If he wishes
to explain away the Gospel passages about " the brethren of
the Lord," he does so by inventing a theory that they were
His cousins, which he himself drops when it has served his
immediate purpose. Jerome knew better than this ; but he
boldly defends his own perversions by misrepresenting the
method of St. Paul, who (he says) quoted the Old Testament
in an astute and dissimulating way.[5]

d. But Jerome's most serious fault, which no doubt is in
great measure the outcome of these other faults, is his total
lack of exegetic decision. He shows again and again, both

---

[1] *C. Jovin.* i. 16.
[2] *C. Jovin.* i. 26.
[3] Pet. Damian. *De perfect. Monach.* (Zöckler, p. 201).
[4] *Ep.* 118, § 4, *ad Julian. Cum reti cam et navicula dereliquit.*
[5] No other epithet than *deplorable* can be applied to Jerome's controversial
language, and his whole degrading style of abuse and Scripture misrepresenta-
tion in his wrangles with Jovinian, Vigilantius, Rufinus, and Helvidius.

in details and in principles, the vacillations of a hasty
and timid eclecticism. In the Vulgate he is content to
leave uncorrected renderings which he declared to be
erroneous, such as "*Apprehendite disciplinam*" for "*Adorate
Filium*" in Psalm ii. 12,[1] and in Psalm cxxvii. 4 "*filii
excussorum*" for "*filii juventutis*," the meaning accepted by
Aquila, Symmachus, and Theodotion.[2] We can never be
certain what Jerome is likely to say, because he constantly
contradicts himself. He sometimes extols Aquila, sometimes
abuses him. At one time he praises Origen with fervour, at
another he seems anxious to repudiate him altogether.[3] He
sometimes quotes the Septuagint translators as inspired
prophets, and sometimes all but treats them with contempt.
He speaks of the Jews sometimes with reasonable tolerance,
sometimes with blind hatred. In one Epistle he says that
at the Resurrection many of the spirits of them that slept
"were seen in the heavenly Jerusalem;"[4] in another he says
that "we are not in this place to think of the heavenly
Jerusalem as many persons ridiculously suppose."[5] He was
himself so conscious of these inconsistencies that he quotes
the verse "When they persecute you in one city, that is in
one book of Scripture, let us fly to other cities, *i.e.* to other
volumes."[6]

[1] *Adv. Rufinum*, lib. i. 19; "Quid igitur peccavi, qui in commentariolis,
ubi libertas est disserendi, dixeram 'adorate filium,' in ipso corpore ne violentus
viderer interpres et Judaicae calumniae locum darem 'adorate pure, sive electe,'
quod Aquila quoque et Symmachus transtulerunt?" See Zöckler, p. 363, *n.*

[2] A.V. "children of the youth," *i.e.* sons of early married life, LXX.
οἱ υἱοὶ τῶν ἐκτετιναγμένων. *Ep.* 34, *ad Marcellum,* § 3, "Ubi nos habemus
sicut filii excussorum," &c. Aquila "*filii pubertatum.*" Symm. Theodot.
filii juventutis. On this subject see R. Simon, *Hist. Crit. des Versions du
N.T.* cap. vii. ; Erasmi *Schol. in lib. Hier. adv. Helvid.*, and Zöckler, p. 123.

[3] Rufinus says that Jerome had translated more than seventy homiletic
books of Origen. See his *Epp.* 62, *ad Tranquill.*, and 33, *ad Paulam.* Jerome
says "In Origene miramur scientiam Scripturarum, et tamen dogmatum non
recipimus falsitatem," *c. Ruf.* iii. 27.

[4] *Ep. ad Heliodor.* 60, § 3, "Et visa sunt in coelesti Jerusalem." Origen,
Eusebius, and Hilary were of this opinion.

[5] *Ep.* 46, § 7. "Nec statim Hierosolyma coelestis, *sicut plerique ridicule
arbitrantur*, in hoc loco intelligitur."

[6] *Comm. in Matt.* x. 23 ; for some of his mistakes and self-contradictions
see Daillé, bk. ii. c. 4, and Gilly's *Vigilantius,* pp. 250-270. To take an
instance with which we are familiar in modern days :—when a Bishop dis-
agrees with you "Nihil interest inter Presbyterum et Episcopum ; " but when
he agrees with you "Apostolorum locum Episcopi tenent."

iv. Unfortunately, this wavering spirit of the hasty and prejudiced compiler vitiates much of his work. He abounds in isolated remarks of the utmost courage and value.[1] Had he kept his own principles steadily in view he might have saved the study of Scripture from a thousand years of retardation; but unhappily his principles had no stability, and were constantly set at nought by a more contagious practice.

v. It is, for instance, impossible to say what he really thought, if he thought anything distinctly, about the inspiration of the sacred writers. At one time he criticises them with all the freedom of an Ewald, and even of a Semler:[2] at another he speaks as if every word they had ever uttered were so mysterious and supernatural that even their contradictory statements were equally true.[3] He throws up the chronology of the Bible as hopeless, and offers no explanation, except the possibility of a corrupted text, for the difficulties and contradictions which he saw in it.[4] He freely points out errors in quotation and reference.[5] He criticises the style of St. Paul with perfect freedom, and ventures to talk about his barbarisms, cilicisms, and solecisms, trivialities, inefficient proofs, and want of taste.[6] He points out that in Greek and

---

[1] See, for instance, his remark on the original identity of Presbyters and Bishops (in Matt. xvi. 19), and on the Power of the Keys, by misunderstanding which he says that Bishops assume the pride of Pharisees, and think that they can condemn the innocent and absolve the guilty "*quum apud Deum non sententia sacerdotum sed reorum vita quaeratur.*"

[2] *Comm. in Ezech.* xi. ; *in Jer.* xxi. 2 ; *Ep.* 21, § 13. "Haec si secundum literam intelligimus, nonne ridicula sunt ?"

[3] This discrepancy between nominal theories and actual practice is seen in many of the greatest fathers. From Justin Martyr, Irenaeus, Tertullian, Origen, Jerome, Chrysostom and Augustine, not to mention other writers, may be collected not a few passages which not only freely admit the human element in Scripture, but even attribute immorality and impropriety to many passages taken literally ; and in such instances they usually apply, in a very aimless manner, a wrong meaning of the phrase "the letter killeth." Allegory therefore is practically due to rationalism, *i.e.* the attributing to Scripture senses other than those which its words convey. See Tholuck translated in *Journ. sacr. Lit.* July 1863. Neander, *Hist. of Doctrines*, i. 280.

[4] See *Ep.* 72, § 5. "Quid enim prodest haerere in litera et *vel scriptoris errorem* vel annorum seriem calumniari quum manifestissime scribatur *Litera occidit ?*"

[5] On Mark i. 2 ; ii. 25 ; Matt xxvii. 9 ; *Ep.* 57, *ad Pammach.* §§ 7–9.

[6] *Ep.* 121, *ad Algas.* 7–11 ; *Comm. in Acts* xxvi. 6 ; *Gal.* iii. 1 ; iv. 24 ;

Hebrew the plural of " seed " has a totally different sense from the singular,[1] and that *beríth* never means " will." [2] He comes to the extraordinary conclusion that, the Galatians being foolish, St. Paul makes himself foolish by way of accommodation to their infirmities, and wrote what would have offended the wise if he had not premised the phrase, " I speak as a man." [3] Elsewhere he speaks of St. Paul as carried away by his emotions, and as being unable to express profound thoughts in an alien tongue.[4] Yet in other passages he uses the current commonplaces of the theology of his day, and though he talks of some narratives as improper and impossible, says that there are mysteries in every word of Holy Writ, and that it was written throughout by the Holy Ghost.[5] He does not make the smallest attempt to co-ordinate his lax expressions with his orthodox assertions. The latter indicate his traditional profession, the former his real belief.[6]

vi. Once more, he is at complete variance with himself on the subject of allegory. He complains of Origen that " he mistook his own subjectivity for ecclesiastical mysteries," yet says himself, " *Singula scripturae verba singula sacramenta sunt.*" [7] In many places he entirely disparages allegory as mere

vi. 2 ; *Eph.* iii. 3, 8 ; Zöckler, 429–431. He says that St. Paul sometimes wrote *sermone trivii.* See *Ep.* 120, *ad Hedib. qu.* 11 ; *Ep. ad Algas. qu.* 10.

[1] *Comm. in Gal.* iv. 24. [2] *Comm. in Gal.* iii. 15.

[3] Nothing is so grossly offensive among Jerome's many faults as his belief in the permissibility of a *falsitas dispensativa* which he betrayed in the shocking theory that the scene between St. Paul and St. Peter at Antioch was collusive "ut hypocrisis conceptionis hypocrisi emendaretur." He says of St. Paul, "quam artifex, quam prudens, quam dissimulator sit ejus quod agit." See his letter to Pammachius in defence of his treatise against Jovinian ; and the fine criticism of Augustine *Ep. ad Hieron. de reprehenso Petro.* On the harm done by this doctrine of "accommodation" see Ribof, *De Economia Patrum,* and Coleridge, *The Friend,* Ess. v.

[4] *In Gal.* v. 12. " Nec mirum esse si apostolus, ut homo, et adhuc vasculo clausus infirmo, vidensque aliam legem in corpore suo . . . semel fuerit hoc locutus, &c." And again, " In vernaculo sermone doctissimus, profundos sensus aliena lingua exprimere non valebat." *Comm. in Tit.*

[5] *In Matt.* xxi. 4. " Ubi materia *vel turpitudinem habeat vel impossibilitatem* ad altiora transmittimur." Comp. *Comm. in Gal.* v. 12.

[6] *Comm. in Eph.* iii. 9 ; *in Mich.* vii. 7 ; *Ep.* 27, 1 ; *in Esaiam,* 29 ; *ad Marcell. Ep.* 46, 4 ; *ad Marcell. in Matt.* xiii.

[7] *Prol. in Es.* v. 10 ; *ad Ps.* xci.; Reuss, *Gesch.* § 517.

cloud and shadow.[1] He tells us that he ought to be pardoned
if in his youth he had written an allegorical commentary on
Obadiah, the reason being that he could not then understand
him historically.[2] He complains of Origen, Hippolytus, and
Didymus, because their exegesis is exclusively allegorical.
He boasts of his simple desire to let Scripture speak for
itself.[3] He complains that the faultiest style of teaching is
to corrupt the meaning of Scripture, and to drag its reluctant
utterance to our own will, making Scriptural mysteries out of
our own imaginations.[4] He blames Eusebius for lapsing into
extravagant allegories in the fashion of Origen.[5] And yet,
after repeated remarks of this kind, he talks of the *turpitudo
litterae,* and fills his books with specimens of allegoric interpretation no less arbitrary than those of Origen himself. He
calls the literal interpretation " Jewish," implies that it may
easily become heretical, and repeatedly says that it is inferior
to the "spiritual." He adopts the threefold sense almost as
if he had invented it,[6] and is always ready to "build the
superstructure," or " spread the sails," or " mingle the flowers,"
of mysticism, and to break up the hard clods of the letter.[7]
He treats every detail, almost every syllable, of the Levitic
law as full of mystic meanings. The passing allusion of
St. Paul to the passage of the Red Sea as an analogy to
baptism, furnishes him with the excuse of making a mystery
out of every one of the forty-four " stations " in the wilderness,
and so getting rid of geographical and other difficulties.[8] The
Book of Joshua becomes mainly an allegory about the Church

---

[1] *Comm. in Gal.* iii. 3 ; i. 6 ; *Comm. in Jer.* 27. "Delirat allegoricus interpres." . . "Nos qui ista contemnimus quasi pro brutis habent animalibus
et vocant πηλουσιῶτας."   Comp. *Ep. ad Pammach.* 84, § 9.

[2] *Comm. in Ezech.* c. 16, *init.*

[3] *Praef. in lib.* v. *Comm. in Esaiam.*

[4] *Ep.* 53, *ad Paulinum,* § 7. "Quicquid dixerint, hoc legem Dei putant."

[5] *Comm. in Amos,* 2 ; In *Ep. ad Pammach.* he says, "Hilarius non
assedit *literae dormitanti.*"

[6] *Ep.* 120, § 12, *ad Hedibiam ;* 1 *Ep.* 64, § 9 ; *adv. Lucif.* 27, &c.; *Ep.* 121,
ad Algas. § 2. He quotes Prov. xxii. 20, " descripśi ea *tripliciter,*" and refers
it to History, Tropology and the spiritual sense.

[7] *Praef. lib.* vi. *in Esai. ; Ep.* 64, *ad Fabiolam ; Comm. in Osee,* c. 10, &c.
See Zöckler, 370.

[8] *De* 42 *Mansionibus, ad Fabiolam.*

and the heavenly Jerusalem. In the Book of Judges there
are as many figures as there are leaders of the people. The
Book of Ruth is connected with Is. xvi. 1. The history of
the Kings becomes an enigma which indicates the struggle of
heretics against the Church.[1] The Ethiopian wife of Moses,
and the bride in the Canticles who is "black but comely," are
the Church. The adulteress in Hoshea becomes a Mary
Magdalene or a Rahab. The last chapter of the Book of
Joel is explained as referring to Pentecost and the Fall of
Jerusalem, but as to the locusts, Jerome gives a liberal
choice, for he says they may be Assyrians and Babylonians,
Medes and Persians, or Greeks, or Romans. Scripture
narratives, full of warning and instruction, are regarded
as too shocking to be matters of sacred history. It would
be an endless task to furnish specimens of his many frivolous
and tasteless fancies.[2] He cannot even abstain from allegorising such plain New Testament narratives as the stater in the
fish's mouth and Christ's entry into Jerusalem, or so simple
a text as, "Let not the sun go down upon your wrath."[3]
He flatters himself that he succeeded in steering safely
between the Scylla of allegory and the Charybdis of literalism,
whereas in reality his "multiple senses" and "whole forests
of spiritual meanings" are not worth one verse of the original.[4]
He was constantly swayed by a spirit of compromise, by
tradition, by boundless credulity, by the preference of the
facile talent of the compiler to the severe and sincere labour
of the original thinker. He found it easier to give a literary

---

[1] Abishag is divine wisdom. Taken literally, the story is 'no better than
the figment out of a mime, or even one of the Atellanae.' *Ep.* 52, *ad Nepotian.*
§ 2 ; yet he takes it literally, *c. Jovin.* i. 24. He calls Deut. xxi. 12, 13
"ridiculous" if taken literally. Tamar, Rahab, Delilah, Bathsheba, are all
allegorised.
[2] On Ecc. iv. 1, "If two sleep together they will be warm," he thinks it
necessary to refer to Elisha raising the son of the Shunamite ! In his *Ep.* 21
ad Damas. § 6, "He divided unto them his living" becomes "He gave
them free will."
[3] Eph. iv. 26.
[4] What Du Pin says of Paulinus is even more true of Jerome. "He
interlaced his discourses with endless texts and often gave them a forced
meaning." *Ann. Eccl.* iii. 449. See too Dr. Maitland, *Dark Ages*, p. 174, *n. ;
Church of the Catacombs*, p. 229, *n. ;* Gilly's *Vigilantius*, p. 93 &c., and for
the more favourable views Möhler, *Patrologie*, p. 21.

grace and a dogmatic colouring to the thoughts of others, than to work out his own genuine opinions with consistency and courage.[1]

XII. St. Augustine—"the oracle of thirteen centuries" —is greater as an Apologist and as a Theologian than as an interpreter of Scripture. Nothing, indeed, can be theoretically better than some of the rules which he lays down. He dwells on the desirability of multifarious knowledge.[2] He insists that allegory should be based on the historic sense.[3] He recognises the "more excellent way" of spiritual intuition derived from love. He perceived that there is in revelation a progressive element,[4] and that there is an inferiority in the degree of revelation furnished by the Old Testament.[5] But when we read his actual comments these principles are forgotten. He was badly equipped for the work of exposition. He knew no Hebrew, and had but a meagre knowledge of Greek.[6] He is misled by the LXX. and by the old Latin versions. He attempted to find "all," or "almost all," the truth of the Gospel in the Old Testament.[7]

[1] *C. Rufin.* 1. "Commentarii quid operis habent? *Alterius dicta edisserunt, multorum sententias replicant,*" *Prooem. in Gal.* "Legi haec omnia, et *in mente mea plurima coacervans* accito notario *vel mea vel aliena* dictavi." *Prooem. in Matt.* "Omnes legere qui in Evangelia scripserunt, deinde, adhibito judicio, quae optima sunt excerpere," and *Prooem. in Eph.* see *Praef. lib.* i. *Comm. in Jerem.*, where he answers the objections of Grynaeus (as he rudely calls Rufinus) and "indoctus calumniator" (Pelagius). R. Simon, *Comment. du N. T.* 230 ; Clericus, *Quaest. Hieron.* p. 493. On St. Jerome's life and works see Engelstoft, *Hieronymus* ; Amédée Thierry, *St. Jerome*, 1867 ; Zöckler, *Hieronymus*, 1865.

[2] *De Doctr. Christ.* ii. 16, § 24-28, § 42 ; *Ep.* 137, 1. He was the first to suggest something in the shape of a Biblical Dictionary, *id. ib.* c. 19, Trench, p. 15.

[3] *De Civ. Dei*, xiii. 21.

[4] *De Ver. Rel.* 17, § 34 ; *Enarr. in* Ps. lxxiii. 1. See Trench, *The Sermon on the Mount*, p. 42. His system of "periods" was seized by the later Reformed Theology. See *De Civ. Dei*, xv.–xvii., where he speaks of seven periods, of which the creative week was a type. This is the first attempt to treat Old Testament theology. Oehler, *Theol. of Old Testament*, i. 26–30 (E. T.).

[5] His *De Doctr. Christ.* is practically an exegetical treatise (*praecepta tractandarum Scripturarum*).

[6] *Confess.* i. 13, § 20 ; 14, § 23 ; xi. 3, § 5 ; *De Doctr. Christ.* ii. § 23 ; *De Trin.* iii. 1, § 23. This is admitted even by his Benedictine editors, and is the subject of severe remarks by Walch, *Bibl. Patr.* 352 ; Rosenm. *Hist. Interpr.* iii. 404 ; Winer, *in Gal.* p. 22 ; but see a more favourable view in Trench, l.c. p. 20. His etymologies are terribly weak.

[7] *C. Adim.* iii. 4. He corrects the "*nulla* quae illis veteribus libris desint" into "*paene nulla*" in the *Retract.* i. 22, § 2 ; comp. Tert. *C. Marc.* iv. Such

He actually ventures to maintain that David wrote the
whole Psalter but sometimes prefixed to a Psalm some
other name which he considered appropriate! If he
puts forth his best strength in resisting the unworthy view of
Jerome, that the dispute between St. Peter and St. Paul at
Antioch was a "pious collusion," he exhibits his greatest
weakness in the opposition which he offered to Jerome's new
translation.[1] In the former controversy he showed the power
of insight, in the latter the feebleness of traditionalism, and a
total absence of the critical faculty. By his dialectic skill
and speculative curiosity he became the father of scholasticism,
and at the same time he gave an impulse to the mediæval
mystics by his spiritual ardour.[2] His ecclesiastical tendencies
helped to strengthen the hierarchy of catholicism, and yet the
Jansenists relied on his writings to establish their doctrine of
grace, and more than any Father he became the favourite
doctor of the Reformation by virtue of his insistence on the
sufficiency and perspicuity of Holy Writ.[3] In all respects he
exercised a creative influence over future ages, but it would be
false to say that the influence was in all respects wholesome.
To him are due in no small degree the excesses of the subtle
and systematising spirit of the schoolmen; the over-weening
pretensions of sacerdotalism; the extravagant exaltation of
"the Church," as represented by an imperious hierarchy;
the exaggerated doctrine of total human depravity; and
above all the bitter spirit of theological hatred and persecution. His writings became the Bible of the Inquisition.
His name was adduced—and could there be a more terrible
Nemesis on his errors?—to justify the murder of Servetus,
to sanction the massacre of St. Bartholomew, to countenance
the revocation of the Edict of Nantes.[4] As the teacher of

views, as contrasted with the *Ep. of Barnabas*, show the strong reaction
against the *Antitheses* of Marcion.

[1] He believed in the inspiration of the Seventy, *De Doctr. Christ.* ii. § 22.

[2] Thus, as Liebner points out, Hugo of St. Victor who first united and
reconciled the principles of scholasticism and mysticism, was called *Lingua
Augustini*, and *Alter Augustinus* (see Trench, p. xii.).

[3] "Scriptura sacra . . . omnibus accessibilis quamvis paucissimis pene-
trabilis." *Ep.* 137, § 18. "Ut exciperet omnes populari sinu." *Conf.* vi. 5, § 8.

[4] See proofs of these facts in Owen, *Evenings with the Sceptics*, ii. 211, who

intolerance he has flung a dark shadow across the Church of Christ, and his intolerance was mainly the result of his views of Scriptural interpretation.

The exegesis of St. Augustine is marked by the most glaring defects. Almost as many specimens of prolix puerility and arbitrary perversion can be adduced from his pages as from those of his least gifted predecessors.[1] He was warped by dogmatic prepossessions. He laid down the rule that the Bible must be interpreted with reference to Church Orthodoxy,[2] and that no Scriptural expression can be out of accordance with any other. He therefore, in support of this view, demanded that all interpretation should be panharmonic, and he helped to stereotype the current misapplication of the phrase "*the analogy of faith.*"[3] He warns us against the fraud of those who distort the meaning of isolated texts, yet he is constantly guilty of the same fraud.[4] He could not fail to observe the human element in Scripture,[5] and he accounts for the

---

quotes Nourisson, *Philos. de St. Aug.* ii. 181 ; Flottes, *Études sur St. Aug.* p. 542. The Spanish Jesuits, in their indictment of St. Augustine in the seventeenth century, said that "his sentiments are too hard, and unworthy of the goodness and mercy of God."

[1] He began a commentary on the Romans, but after devoting a *whole book* to the salutation alone, found that it would be too laborious, and gave it up.

[2] *De Doctr. Christ.* iii. 10 : "Scriptura non asserit nisi fidem catholicam." Perhaps the most startling instance of the crude ecclesiasticism, which increased as Augustine grew older, is his remark, "Ego vero *Evangelio non crederem* nisi me Catholicae Ecclesiae commoverit auctoritas." *Ep. c. Manich.* 5, § 6. On this false and degrading opinion see Ritter, *Gesch. de Philos.* vi. 432. "*Setting forth the Church as the way to Christ,*" says Bishop Ewing, "*instead of setting forth Christ as the way to the Church,* has been a fountain of unnumbered evils." St. Augustine's reversal of the true order of things was exposed before Luther's days among others by Marsilio of Padua in his *Defensor Pacis,* and by John Wessel ("Evangelio credimus et propter Evangelium Ecclesiae, non Evangelio propter Ecclesiam"). See Owen, *Evenings with the Sceptics,* ii. 181.

[3] St. Chrysostom had explained the phrase rightly, *Hom. in Rom.* xii. "Faith, though it is a grace, is not poured forth at random but . . . letteth as much flow as it may find the vessel that is brought to be capable of."

[4] *C. Adimant.* xiv. § 2 : "Istorum fraus qui particulas quasdam e Scripturis eligunt quibus decipiant imperitos, non connectentes quae supra et infra scripta sunt, ex quibus voluntas et intentio scriptoris possit intelligi." Had the warning received the slightest attention, the majority of the texts quoted in party controversy would be seen to be wholly inapplicable. But Augustine was inevitably false to his own rule because he had to reconcile the teaching of Christ with all that the Church taught in the fourth century. See Neander, iii. 510.

[5] *De Cons. Evang.* ii. 12, 24, 28, 66, &c.

variations in the narrative of the Evangelists on purely human principles ;[1] and yet he uses the irreverent, misleading, and wholly unscriptural phrase, that the sacred writers were " pens of the Holy Ghost."[2] He held that whatever was revealed mysteriously and enigmatically in one part of Scripture was revealed clearly in another part,[3] yet fails to see that there could be nothing of real or independent value in the incessantly wavering interpretations of dim enigmas. After all his judicious theories he makes his exegesis the facile slave of his personal theology.

In the writings of St. Augustine we see the constant flashes of genius, and the rich results of insight and experience, which have given them their power over the minds of many generations. But these merits cannot save his exegetic writings from the charge of being radically unsound. Snatching up the old Philonian and Rabbinic rule which had been repeated for so many generations, that everything in Scripture which appeared to be unorthodox or immoral must be interpreted mystically, he introduced confusion into his dogma of supernatural inspiration by admitting that there are many passages " written by the Holy Ghost," which are objectionable when taken in their obvious sense.[4] He also opened the door to arbitrary fancy.[5] From the intolerable prolixity of his commentary on Genesis, down to his voluminous remarks on many books of the New Testament, we find incessant instances of that futile method which evacuated the Bible of a significance infinitely precious, in order to substitute for its real lessons the thinnest commonplaces of homiletic and dogmatic edification. By his acceptance of the rules of Tichonius he adopted a system of tropology in which " leaven " might everywhere

---

[1] "Inspiratus a Deo sed tamen homo," *in Joann. tract.* 1, § 1.

[2] *Conf.* vii. 21, *De Gen. ad Litt.* v. 8 ; see Trench, p. 50.

[3] *De Doctr. Christ.* iii. § 37, whence it passed into the *Summa* of St. Thomas i. *Qu.* 1, *Art.* 10.

[4] *De Doctr. Christ.* iii. § 14 : " Quidquid in sermone divino *neque ad morum honestatem neque ad fidei veritatem proprie referri potest* figuratum esse cognoscas."

[5] He adopts the unfortunate notion that all sorts of explanations must be admissible, because the Holy Spirit must have foreseen them (*id. ib.* 32). The heretics might have urged the same plea.

stand either for "truth" or for "wickedness," and "a lion" either for "the Devil" or for "Christ." In the narrative of the Fall the fig-leaves become hypocrisy, and the coats of skins mortality, and the four rivers of Eden the four cardinal virtues. In the story of the Deluge the Ark is pitched within and without with pitch to show the safety of the Church from inward and outward heresies. The drunkenness of Noah is, shocking to relate, "a figure of the death and passion of Christ."[1] The Books of Kings are distorted into a prophecy as much as a history. Nor is it only the Old Testament history which is throughout treated as an allegory.[2] Poetry and prophecy are similarly handled, till even Augustine's contemporaries were driven to complain.[3]

Thus the exquisite beauty and lyric tenderness of Psalm civ. is evaporated at a touch. " *The sun which knoweth his going down* " becomes Christ, who was aware of His own death; "*the beasts that get them away together* " become persecutors who dare not show themselves in the days of Christ's prosperity. If the Psalmist says, " *I laid me down, and slept, and rose up again*," Augustine asks whether any one can be so senseless (*ita desipit*) as to suppose that "the prophet" would have made so trivial a statement, unless the sleep intended had been the Death, and the awakening the Resurrection of Christ![4] Even the Gospels are not safe from this faithless invasion of predetermined dogmatism.[5] "No sober person," says one writer, "can believe that our Lord really had his feet anointed by a woman with precious ointment, as luxurious and wicked men are wont to do at feasts and the like, which we detest." [6] When once the principle of allegory is admitted, when once we start with the rule that whole passages and books of Scripture say one thing when they mean another, the

---

[1] *Hom. in Gen.* 13 § 3.　　　　　[2] *In Ps.* cxxxvi. 3.
[3] *De Civ. Dei*, xv. 20 ; xvi. 1.
[4] *Enarr. in Ps.* ciii. Even Sixtus Senensis says that since Augustine knew neither Hebrew nor Greek, "Necesse fuit illum a vero ac proprio literae sensu ad extortas allegorias deflectere " (*Bibl. Sanct.* p. 257).
[5] For a bad instance of exegesis warped by dogmatics see Augustine's remarks on Christ's blessing little children in *De Peccat. Remiss.* i. 19.
[6] "Aliud dicitur *ut* (!) aliud intelligatur." See *De Doctr. Christ.* iii. §§ 32-40. St. Augustine laughs at the allegorical arguments of the Donatists

reader is delivered bound hand and foot to the caprice of the interpreter. He can be sure of absolutely nothing except what is dictated to him by the Church, and in all ages the authority of "the Church" has been falsely claimed for the presumptuous tyranny of false prevalent opinions. In the days of Justin Martyr and of Origen Christians had been driven to allegory by an imperious necessity. It was the only means known to them by which to meet the shock which wrenched the Gospel free from the fetters of Judaism. They used it to defeat the crude literalism of fanatical heresies; or to reconcile the teachings of philosophy with the truths of the Gospel. But in the days of Augustine the method had degenerated into an artistic method of displaying ingenuity and supporting ecclesiasticism. It had become the resource of a faithlessness which declined to admit, of an ignorance which failed to appreciate, and of an indolence which refused to solve the real difficulties in which the sacred book abounds. It enabled would-be teachers to fill whole volumes with the semblance of teaching. With others it became the ready means for establishing Church dogmas and priestly traditions, and so of making Scripture an oracle which answered them according to their idols, and an echo which returned to them the disguised utterance of their own imaginations.[1]

Unhappily for the Church, unhappily for any real apprehension of Scripture, the allegorists, in spite of protest,[2] were completely victorious. The School of Antioch was

who from the words "in *meridie*" ("at noon") in Cant. i. 7, argued that the Church was only in the south, and defended the rebaptising of heretics from the strange mistranslation of the Vulg. in Ps. cxli. 5. But his own allegories are quite as baseless.

[1] On Augustine's work as a commentator see Klausen, *Aurel. Augustinus, S. S. interpres.* Abp. Trench, Aug. as an interpreter of Scripture (*Sermon on the Mount*) ; Breithaupt, *Institutio hermen. ex Aug. libris conquisita ;* Kilon, 1605. His theoretical rules were excellent, if he had but been faithful to them. Thus he says : 1. *Scripturae scopus est dilectio Dei.* 2. *Codices emendandi sunt.* 3. We must decide whether the sense is literal or mystic. 4. We must consider the context. 5. *Obscura per apertiora explicanda.* 6. Geography, &c., must be studied. 7. The original is important (but the LXX. is to be preferred even to the Hebrew !). 8. *Distingue tempora et concordabis Scripturas, &c.*

[2] See Rosenmüller, iii. 147.

discredited by anathemas. Origen was indeed attainted with equal violence, but his exegetical principles had already taken deep root alike in the East and in the West. Theodore and Theodoret were to a certain extent quoted in Glosses and Catenae, but their chief influence was confined to the churches of the Nestorians, and though glimmerings of their method appear here and there,[1] it received no development, and we soon descend to allegorical dictionaries of the three-fold sense, like that of Eucherius,[2] to the secondhandness of Cassiodorus († 562), and the interminable tedium of Gregory the Great († 604). The thirty-five books of Moralia on the Book of Job, by Gregory, awoke the intense admiration of the Middle Ages, but to any real knowledge of the sacred poem itself they contribute nothing. Such value as they possess is to be found solely in the masses of allegorical and homiletic commonplace which furnished ready materials for the sermons of a thousand years.[3] We trust that hundreds of those sermons may have been found rich in spiritual blessing by those who listened to them, but their instruc-tiveness was derived exclusively from the simple facts of the Gospel which they taught, or the moral truths in which there could be no ambiguity: they derive no particle of additional value from the so-called exegesis which, being based on an invented hypothesis, a supposed tradition, and an unwarrantable system, was no better than a house built upon the sand.

But let us once more thank God that, even in the study of Scripture, correct exegesis is of less importance than the saving apprehension of a few great truths. In understanding

[1] As in the anonymous comment on Joel printed among the works of Ru-finus. Pelagius (whose commentary on the Epistles is in the eleventh volume of Vallarsi's edition of the works of St. Jerome) may be compared to Diodore of Tarsus, and Julian of Eclane to Theodore of Mopsuestia, but as their opinions were condemned as heretical their exegesis had little influence. Lücke, *Grundriss*, p. 45 ; Walch, *Ketzereyen*, iv. 519.

[2] Eucherius, *Liber formularum spiritualis intelligentiae.*

[3] See some severe remarks on the *Moralia* in Hampden, *Bampt. Lect.* p. 275. Gregory knew neither Greek nor Hebrew, and in his allegorical expositions Job represents Christ, his sons the clergy, his three daughters the three classes of the laity who are to worship the Trinity, his friends the heretics, the oxen and she-asses the heathen (because of Is. i. 3) &c. &c.

its most essential messages we have little need of the labours of the commentator. Those messages are less intelligible to learning than to faith. If in exegesis the Fathers were often led astray by deficient knowledge and mistaken principles, on the other hand the minds of the best of them were " animated, informed, and kindled by the substance, the purpose, and the spirit of the sacred books." " There is," says Dean Church, " in these writers a kind of living contact of their whole being with the inspired words. Their whole soul is stirred and penetrated with words which to them are manifestly full of the things and the spirit of God. Their reading leaves them aflame with the enthusiasm of admiration, delight, awe, hope, analogous in a higher degree to the feeling which a glorious prospect, or a magnificent passage of poetry or oratory, leaves on the mind which takes it in, and is alive to its complete meaning and effect. This is the secret of their excellence and value," if not " as commentators," yet as that which is even higher and more important, as moral and spiritual teachers of mankind.

And when we think of them personally, when we recall the heroic fortitude of Justin, the ardent zeal of Cyprian, the dauntless courage with which Athanasius faced the world ; —when we think of Origen, banished, excommunicated, racked by torture, and dragging from prison his aged frame and dislocated limbs, " till the weary wheels of life stood still ; "—when we think of the tears and conversion of Augustine, of Jerome's struggle for self-conquest in his cell at Bethlehem, of Ambrose repelling his Emperor from the gates of his Cathedral because his hands were red with the blood of massacre ;—when we recall the picture of Chrysostom dying in his cruel exile with his favourite words δόξα τῷ θεῷ πάντων ἔνεκα upon his lips ;—when we recall the profound thoughts and eloquent exhortations of many of the Fathers—the many high examples which they set of holiness in life, and of courage even unto death—we give to them the hearty offering of our honour and esteem. We say of them, with St. Chrysostom, " Oh blessed and happy

R

men whose names are in the Book of Life." [1] We cannot elevate them into idols, or accept their utterances as oracles; but we look up to them with love and reverence, as to our elder brothers in the great family of God.

[1] See the fine passage quoted by Bishop Jeremy Taylor, "*Via Intelligentiae,*" *ad fin.*

ὁ γὰρ ἄλλα μὲν ἀγορεύων τρόπος, ἕτερα δὲ ὧν λέγει σημαίνων, ἐπωνύμως
Ἀλληγορία καλεῖται.—HERACLIDES PONTICUS, *Allegg. Homer.*

Ἦν ὅτε ἤκμαζε τὰ ἡμέτερα καὶ καλῶς εἶχεν, ἡνίκα τὸ μὲν περιττὸν τοῦτο καὶ
κατεγλωττισμένον τῆς θεολογίας καὶ ἔντεχνον οὐδὲ παρόδον εἶχεν εἰς τὰς
θείας αὐλάς.—GREG. NAZ. *Orat.* xxi.

"Melius est dubitare de occultis, quam litigare de incertis."—AUG.
De Gen. ad lit. c. v.

"Philosophia tua te vexat."—LUTHER *to* MELANCHTHON.

"That which by right exposition buildeth up Christian faith, being
misconstrued, breedeth error ; between true and false construction the
difference reason must show."—HOOKER, *Eccl. Pol.* iii. § 8.

"Theologia haec Scholastica, quanta quanta est, magis Ethnica quam
Christiana est, non ex S. Literis hausta, sed ex Aristotelis Metaphysica
consuta et conflata ; quae multo plus habet rixarum philosophicarum
quam Christianae pietatis."—GROTIUS, *De studiis instituendis* (1645),
p. 240.

"Deliver me . . . from unhealthy enquiries and interminable disputes."—PRAYER OF BISHOP ANDREWES.

"The plague of the Church for above a thousand years has been the
enlarging our creed, and making more fundamentals than God ever
made."—BAXTER.

"L'ignorance vaut beaucoup mieux que cette fausse science qui fait
que l'on s'imagine savoir ce qu'on ne sait pas."—ARNAULD, *Logique de
Port Royal.*

"Eine Spekulation auf dürrer Heide, eine Dialektik ohne das erforder-
liche Materiale der Kenntniss, ein Formalismus ohne Fülle des Inhaltes
und ohne Freiheit der Bewegungen."—KLAUSEN, *Hermen.* p. 190.

LECTURE V.

SCHOLASTIC EXEGESIS.

"Guard that which is committed unto thee, turning away from . . . the antitheses of the knowledge which is falsely so called; which some professing have missed the mark concerning the faith."—1 TIM. vi. 20.

GREGORY THE GREAT died in the year 604. With him the age of theological originality ceased for five centuries; and for four centuries more the study of the Bible was fettered by narrow restrictions, and misdirected in unprofitable efforts. We approach the subject of mediaeval exegesis with every desire to judge it in the kindliest spirit; but we are compelled to say that during the Dark Ages, from the seventh to the twelfth century, and during the scholastic epoch, from the twelfth to the sixteenth, there are but a few of the many who toiled in this field who added a single essential principle, or furnished a single original contribution to the explanation of the Word of God.[1] During these nine centuries we find very little except the "glimmerings and decays" of patristic exposition. Much of the learning which still continued to exist was devoted to something which was meant for exegesis, yet not one writer in hundreds showed any true conception of

---

[1] The word σχολαστικὸς is first found in a letter of Theophrastus, *ap.* Diog. Laert. v. 20; *Scholasticus* in Petronius. In the 'Αστεῖα of the Pseudo-Hierocles it is surrounded with grotesque associations. But it is perhaps simplest to derive the word "scholasticism" from the schools of Charlemagne. See Hauréau, *Philos. Scholastique,* i. 7; Brucker, *Hist. Phil.* iii. 710. In Art. 13 the Schoolmen are called "the School Authors." On the connection between Patristic and Scholastic systems, see Ueberweg, *Hist. of Philos.* i. 262.

what exegesis really implies. Sometimes, indeed, they repeat correct principles borrowed from Jerome and Augustine, but in practice they abandon these principles as soon as they are enunciated, and give us folio volumes of dogma, morality, and system, which profess to be based on Scripture, but have for the most part no real connection with the passages to which they are attached.[1]

The Papal system had established a secure despotism over the minds of men. The sources of all Christian truth were supposed to be furnished by Scripture and tradition; and the Church—by which was mainly meant the Pope—was held to be the infallible interpreter of both. In the seventh century the whole fabric of society still reeled with the terrible and continuous shocks which it had received from the storms of barbarian invasion, when Goths, Vandals, Sarmatians, Gepidae, Alani, Heruli, Huns, Suevi, Saxons, and Burgundians, had poured themselves upon the West. Learning naturally perished in the storm. "Woe to our days," exclaimed Gregory of Tours, "for the study of letters has perished from us."[2] When Didier, Archbishop of Vienne, tried to reintroduce the teaching of grammar, Gregory the Great, the most fertile and eloquent moralist of his dreary age, in words which irresistibly remind us of what Jack Cade says to Lord Saye and Sele in Shakespeare's *Henry VI.*, wrote to him, "I can scarcely mention without shame that your Fraternity explains grammar to certain persons. What a deadly and heinous fault!"[3] Fortunatus († 609), though a leading poet

---

[1] Homiletics have been to an incredible extent the *Phylloxera Vastatrix* of exegesis, and preachers with their habit of thrusting into texts an endless variety of commonplaces which have no connexion with them, have become privileged misinterpreters. They have ploughed with the unequally-yoked ox and ass of science and sermon-making, and made texts an excuse for saying this or that as it pleased them, with no thought of the real meaning of words.

[2] Greg. Tur. *Hist. Franc. Prooem.* Compare Lupus, *Ep.* 36 (Migne, vol. cxix.). King Alfred did not know one monk south of the Thames who could translate the Breviary.

[3] "Sine verecundia memorare non possumus fraternitatem tuam *Grammaticam* quibusdam exponere ! . . . Quam grave nefandumque !" Greg. M. *Epp.* xi. 54. So Jack Cade in *Henry VI.* pt. ii. act iv. sc. 7 : "Thou hast most traitorously corrupted the youth of the realm in erecting a grammar-school," &c. We must, however, bear in mind that Gregory regarded the end of the

of the age, confesses not only that he had never read Plato
or Aristotle, but not even Hilary, Ambrose, or Augustine.
"Many," wrote Ambrose Antpert in his comment on the
Apocalypse, "say that this is no time to discuss Scripture."
The eighth century was the most ignorant, the darkest, the
most barbarous, that France had ever seen.[1] There was
everywhere confusion and chaos, national, social, and political.
The energies of men were absorbed in the attempt to found
a new order upon the crumbling ruins of ancient civilisation.

Charlemagne, having seen that schools and learning still
existed in Italy, wished to revive them in his own kingdom,
and about 787 wrote to the Bishops the circular letter which
Ampère calls "*la charte constituante de la pensée moderne.*"
Then it was that the teaching of the *Trivium* and the
Quadrivium began.[2] As there was no diffusion of knowledge,
all education became ecclesiastical, all piety monastic in type.
There was a monotonous and absolute ascendency of sacerdotal
authority. And how could there be anything but an ever-
deepening misinterpretation of Scripture when so few Christian
interpreters possessed even a smattering of Hebrew; when
Greek was but little known; when men went to Scripture,
not to seek truth, but to find their own dogmas; when,
in spite of a nominal idolatry for the sacred writings, men
turned them into plastic enigmas; when the interpreter

---

world as being "in actual progress," and thought that the light of eternity
was already piercing the gloom of time. *Dialog.* iv. 41. Gregory, in his
thirty-five books of *Moralia* ("ein schweres, ein unausdehnliches Buch ")
thinks it "unworthy to bind the heavenly utterances by the rules of
Donatus." He says, "Primum quidem fundamenta Historiae ponimus ;
deinde per significatorem *typicam* in arcem fidei fabricam mentis erigimus ;
ad extremum quoque per *moralitatis* gratiam quasi superducto aedificium
colore vestimus." *Ep. ad Leandrum.*

[1] *Hist. Lit. de France,* ii. For the facts mentioned in the foregoing paragraphs see Hauréau, *Hist. de la Philos. Scholastique,* i. 1–16. Hallam,
Middle Ages, iii. 418. Bouquet, *Rer. Gallic. Script.* vol. v. Even Alcuin
grew up to disparage as "polluting" the study of Virgil. *Vita* (Migne) ;
Maitland, *Dark Ages,* p. 179.

[2] The three arts of grammar, dialectics, and rhetoric, and the four sciences
of arithmetic, geometry, music, and astronomy. See J. Bass Mullinger, *The
Schools of Charles the Great* (1877). Brucker, iii. 957. Hauréau (i. 21)
attributes the classification to Martianus Capella, but it is as old as Augustine
(*De Ordine,* 13). See J. Gow, *Short Hist. of Greek Mathematics,* p. 72 (1884).
Léon Maitre, *Les Écoles de l'occident ;* Monnier, *Alcuin et son influence.*
Manset, *Art. Logic. Rudimenta,* p. 28.

set himself practically above the text by making it answer him in accordance with his own idols, or not at all ?

The seventh and four following centuries were the age of sheer compilation, in the form, first of excerpts, and then of glosses.[1] John of Damascus was labouring at commentaries in the Eastern Church at the same time that Bede was devoting fifty-eight continuous years to them in the Western ; but both are compilers.[2] The Venerable BEDE († 735) was "a man whom it is easier to admire than to extol as he deserved;"[3] yet though quite capable by his genius and learning of exercising an independent criticism,[4] he only professes to collect passages from the Fathers, with the occasional addition of a few words of his own. In his preface to his comment on St. Luke, he says that it consists of extracts woven together from Ambrose, Augustine, Jerome,[5] and other Fathers, the authorship of each clause being marked by the initial of the writer's name which he entreats copyists not to omit.[6] Being thus dependent he is hopelessly led astray. He accepts as important the baseless rules of Tichonius. Jerome had said that Luke being a physician provides medicine for the soul also, and this remark furnished Bede with a sufficient reason for a constant introduction of allegory into the explanation of

[1] Excerpts or Catenae (σεῖραι, συλλογαί, ἑρμηνειῶν ἐπιτομαί), like those of Cassiodorus, Primasius, Sedulius, Florus Magister, Remigius, and in the Greek Church those of John of Damascus, were extremely numerous. Second-hand commentaries, like those of Procopius of Gaza, Isidore of Seville, Bede, Claudius Turinensis, Angelomus, and Pseudo-Haymo abounded and multiplied. The commentary of Chr. Druthmar on St. Matthew is an improvement on most of these ; yet in commenting on "*Liber generationis Jesu Christi*" he tells us "liber" also means "free," and "the bark of the tree ; " and he derives *panis* from πᾶν. "Scripturi maxime quae in Patrum exemplis invenimus hinc inde collecta ponere curabimus, sed et *nonnulla propria* ubi opportunum videbitur *interponemus*" (*Prol. in Marc.*).

[2] Bede, *Hist. Eccl. Introd.* On John Damascene's commentaries see Lupton, pp. 156 *sq.*

[3] William of Malmesbury.

[4] As he shows, especially in his *Retractationes*.

[5] "The teaching of the Latin Church rested on the authority of three Fathers—Ambrose, Jerome, Augustine. From the first she derived her conception of sacerdotal authority ; from the second her attachment to monasticism ; from the third her dogmatic theology ; and to these three conceptions the most remarkable phenomena in European History may undoubtedly be referred."—J. B. Mullinger, *The University of Cambridge*, i. p. 3. Milman, *Latin Christianity*, Bk. ii. c. 4.

[6] They have, however, done so.

a book exquisitely simple and transparently historical. In Old Testament comments he revels in the Philonian and Origenistic method. Laban means "whitened," and he is therefore a symbol of the devil transformed into an Angel of Light; he also represents the world pursuing the elect. Jacob took away his daughters—the daughters, that is, of the world and the devil—when Christ won Himself a Church from the Gentiles. Mandrakes, he says, are a kind of tree in the shape of a man, except that they have no head. They, therefore, represent humanity without Christ. In the beginning of Samuel the Vulgate has *Fuit vir unus, et nomen ejus Elcana.* Bede makes a mystery of the *unus*, and says that it points in the first place to Christ; next it implies the unity of the elect; and thirdly it points to a man who was not double-minded. What is it to us monks, he asks, to be told that Elkanah had two wives?[1] If we only draw such "old things" as the literal sense out of Scripture, we get no spiritual doctrine; but when we understand it allegorically, Elkanah is our Lord, and his two wives are the Synagogue and the Church. Any one, he says, who knows how to interpret the Book of Tobit allegorically, sees the inner sense to be as superior to the literal as fruit is to leaves.[2] Thus in the works of Bede we find ourselves for the most part among the sediments of patristic exposition. All the writers of this school speak like Bede of their *pusillitas* and their *temeritas*, and their *ingeniolum*, and profess to write only for the *rudis lector*. Of the Fathers, from which they so indiscriminately borrowed, they can only speak "with bated breath and whispering humbleness."[3]

Similarly in reading ALCUIN († 804), we find that the *Interrogationes* with which he is occupied are often as idle as

[1] Such remarks show that allegory was the daughter of rationalism. So Sixtus Senensis asks "Quid juvat scire antiquorum Judaeorum bella et seditiones?" and makes this a potent argument for allegorising. *Bibl. Sanct.* (*De duplici sensu*).

[2] "Si quis eundem allegorice novit interpretari quantum poma foliis tantum interiorem ejus sensum videt simplicitati literae praestare."

[3] Bede was himself reckoned afterwards among the Fathers. William of Conches says, "Non est fas Bedae *vel alicui alii sanctorum Patrum* contradicere" (*ap.* Cousin, *Œuvres Inéd. d'Abel.* p. 673).

the *Responsiones* are valueless, and he, too, most humbly prostrates his intellect at the feet of the Fathers—*Cautissimo stylo providens ne quid contrarium Patrum sensibus ponerem.*

The works of Haymo of Halberstadt, and Rabanus Maurus († 856) are equally servile, and the latter unconsciously exposed the futility of the allegoric method by the alphabetic register (*Liber Allegoriarum*), in which he tried to reduce it to system.[1] He tells us that he compiled his commentary on the Epistles from eleven Latin and three Greek Fathers (*Prol. in Matth.*). Paschasius Radbertus († 865) boasts that he "adhered to the footsteps" of Gregory, &c., and never deviated from them. How significant is the remark of Notker of St. Gall († 912), "*In Matthaeo Hieronymus sufficiat tibi, in Marco pedissequo Matthaei Baeda pedissequus Hieronymi.*"

Doubtless such compilations had a certain use when nothing better was to be had, and when books were few and not easily obtained; but they tended even in their own day to stereotype false positions and check original study.[2] They were made without criticism or choice on the most haphazard principles. They gyrate round a narrow circle of recognised interpreters. Being dependent on the chance of translations for the few Greek Fathers whom the writers consulted, they wholly ignore the masterly labours of the Antiochene expositors. They quote mutilated fragments of works often spurious, and these fragments are frequently misunderstood. The result is a mosaic of dubious and irreconcilable opinions. For modern times they might have preserved passages which would have been otherwise lost; but the quotations are so erroneous, and so often derived second, third, and fourth hand from bad translations and supposititious works, that even for this purpose they are of scarcely any use.[3]

---

[1] Rabanus Maurus is chiefly great as the "*primus Germaniae praeceptor,*" not as an Exegete.

[2] A distinction must be made between glosses (*glossae, Postillae, ἐπιτομαὶ, συλλογαὶ, συναγωγαὶ ἑρμηνειῶν, ἐξηγήσεις συλλεγεῖσαι,* &c.) and the later Catenae proper, which chiefly occur from the ninth to the sixteenth century. See Fritzsche in Herzog, *s.v.* Exeget. Collections. Cramer, *Praef. in Catcn.* New Testament.

[3] The *Quaestiones* of Photius († 890), and the compilations of Procopius of Gaza (sixth century), of Oecumenius (tenth century, chiefly from Chrysostom),

The Glosses whether marginal like that of Walafrid Strabo
(† 849), or interlinear like that of Anselm of Laon († 1117),
are of a still lower order of merit than the exegetic antho-
logies. Besides being compilations they were heaped together
without choice, order, or criticism, and they furnish a promiscuous mass of literal, moral, and mystic fragments,
intermingled with grammatical remarks of the most
elementary character.[1] With an *"aliter"* or *"potest etiam*
intelligi"* the reader is often left to choose between heterogeneous interpretations logically exclusive of each other.
Hermeneutic principle there is none. When Gisla and
Rectruda, daughters of Charlemagne, wrote to ask Alcuin for
a commentary on St. John, they never dreamed of asking for
anything original but said *" Collige multorum margaritas."*
Yet the *Glossa ordinaria* of Walafrid Strabo († 849) acquired
such extraordinary popularity that it was called *Lingua
Scripturae,* and even Peter Lombard quotes it under the title
of "the Authority."[2] A single specimen may serve to show

of Theophylact (eleventh century), and Euthymius Zigaebenus (twelfth century), in the Greek Church have a higher value. See Fabricius, *Bibl. Graec.*
vii. 727 ; Buddeus, *Isag.* p. 1422 ; Walch, *Bibl. Med.* iv. 192 fg. ; Elster,
De Med. Aevi Theolog. Exeget. p. 17 ; Bacon, *Advancement of Learning,* ii.
"This course of sums and commentaries is that which doth infallibly make
the body of sciences more immense in quantity and more base in substance."
Erasm. in 2 Cor. xi. 23 ; 1 Tim. ii. 15 ; *" Tumultuario Studio, hinc atque
hinc consarcinatis glossematis."* But no judgment can be severer than that of
the acute John of Salisbury. "Compilant omnium opiniones, et *illa quae
etiam a vilissimis dicta vel scripta sunt* ab inopia judicii scribunt et referunt ;
proponunt enim omnia *quia nesciunt praeferre meliora,"* &c. *Metalog.* ii. 7.
For a more favourable view see Newman's Pref. to the *Catena Aurea,* and
Ancient Saints, chap. v.

[1] See *Glossen* and *Exeget. Sammlungen* in Herzog's *Encyklop.* The success
of the *Glossa* was due in part to its (baseless) ingenuity. Thus on Gen. ix.
13, since the rainbow is blue and red, it is made to be a prophecy of the
Deluge and the final conflagration! See too Hieron. Magius, *De mundi
exustione* (1562), p. 9. Milton, even in his day, complains of the use made
by the clergy of "interlinearies . . . and other *loitering gear."* There were
nine editions of the *Glossa* between 1472 and 1634.

[2] Contemporary with Walafrid was his teacher, Rabanus Maurus († 856),
the author of the *Liber Allegoriarum.* He speaks of himself as *" Col-
lectarius quidam,"* and in his Prologue to St. Matthew tells us that his commentary is composed of extracts from eleven Latin and three Greek Fathers.
Great part even of his introduction is verbally identical with Bede's. Fabricius says that there were *hundreds* of Catenae in the Royal Library at Paris.
The manufacture was easy. See too *Hist. Lit. de France,* v. 62. The Douay
edition of the *Glossa Ordinaria* says that all succeeding writers used to consult
it "tamquam *officinam ecclesiasticorum sensuum."*

its character. It might have been thought that the first
verse of the Prophet Joel, " *The word of the Lord that came to
Joel the son of Pethuel*," needed little elucidation. In the
Glossa "the word" is as a matter of course absurdly and
irreverently referred to Christ, and "*quod factum est*" is
explained to mean that Christ was "made" not as regards
Himself but as regards him to whom He was made. "*Factum
est*," says Remigius, "is put for 'spoke'"! "This word," says
Rupert of Deutz, "is Christ the Son of God, whom Joel son
of Phaluck signifies both by his own and by his father's
name."[1] "The word," says Hugo of St. Victor, "involves the
sound, the form, the meaning. The sound is here addressed
to the enemy; the form of the word to the afflicted people;
the meaning of the word to the mind of the Prophet, and the
choir of the elect." It would be hardly possible more effectu-
ally to darken counsel by the multitude of words without
knowledge; yet with such comments the mediaeval writings
are filled in every page. The *Eruditio Didascaliae* by Hugo
of St. Victor shows that even the theory of exegesis was
hopelessly perverted.[2] Its practice consists for the most part
of moral platitudes; dogmatic iterations extorted from
passages with which they have not the remotest connexion;
mystic plays on numbers; erroneous etymologies; a use of
parallel phrases and passages which is often absurd in its
triviality, and which a glance at the original languages or the
context would have rendered impossible; and amidst these

---

[1] Rupert illustrates the possibility of subtle theological acumen co-existing
with very weak exegesis. John Wessel († 1489) when tired of the iteration of
the *Summistae* used to cross the Rhine and read the MSS. of Rupert in the
Abbey of Deutz.

[2] *Erudit. Didasc.* vi. In some respects there was more freedom of thought
in the ninth century than in the twelfth. Claudius of Turin († 839) and
Archbishop Agobard of Lyons († 840) were both of them independent thinkers.
The latter argues against verbal dictation (*ipsa corporalia verba*) of Scripture as
absurd, and rightly insists that its form is human, even when the sense is
divine (*Lib. c. Object. Fredegisii*, xii. 277). The passage is quoted by Mr.
Poole (*Med. Thought*, p. 46), who says that Gibbon's remark "that the
disciples of the Messiah were indulged in a freer latitude, both of faith and
practice, than has ever been allowed in succeeding ages," applies no less to the
ninth century. Agobard distinguished himself by protesting against the duel
and ordeal, and Reuter (*Rel. Auferklärung im Mittelalter*, i. 24) calls him
"the clearest head of the ninth century." On this period see R. Simon,
Hist. des Comment. pp. 422-468 ; Buddeus, *Isagoge*, lib. ii. cap. 8.

masses of exegetic nullity a total failure to grasp the simple
and often obvious meaning either of books, passages, texts, or
even words. Most of these Compilers and Glossators were
preachers; some of them were saints of God; many of them
were the most learned men of their day; but in spite of all
this, their exegesis is null and naught.[1]

Between this earlier epoch and the zenith of Papal supremacy stands the great name of JOHANNES SCOTUS ERIGENA.
Scholasticism practically sprang out of the brief collision
between Church authority and independent thought. It was
in part the outcome of controversies like that between Ratram
and Paschasius on the Eucharist (A.D. 844); between Lanfranc
and Berengarius on the Eucharist (1047); between Anselm
and Roscelin on Universals (1092); between Bernard and
Abelard on rationalism.[2] Erigena, who towers above his age,
was employed to answer Gotteschalc who was a Predestinarian,
but he was himself condemned by two Councils for "very
many heresies inferred by very many syllogisms," and his
books were burnt by Pope Honorius III.[3] Alone among his
predecessors, contemporaries, and successors, he shows independence and originality. "Let no authority terrify you,"
he says, "from conclusions which the reasonable persuasion

---

[1] Even Cardinal Newman says, "About the sixth or seventh century
this originality disappears; the oral or traditionary teaching which allowed
scope to the individual teacher *became hardened into a written tradition,* and
henceforth there is a uniform invariable character as well as substance of
Scripture interpretation." Pref. to *Catena Aurea,* p. ii. The lexicographers
Hesychius, Suidas, Phavorinus, Zonaras, &c., are not exegetes but furnish
good materials.

[2] Scholasticism may be divided into three epochs. 1. From Anselm († 1109)
to Peter Lombard († 1164). 2. From Peter Lombard to the death of Albertus
Magnus († 1280). 3. From the beginning of the thirteenth century to Gabriel
Biel († 1495). Hauréau divides it, 1. From Alcuin to the end of the twelfth
century. 2. From Alexander of Hales († 1245) to John Gerson († 1429).
Ueberweg's epochs are nearly the same, and so are those adopted by Tribbechovius and by Diestel. Philosophically, Mr. Lewes distinguishes three
epochs. 1. The debate on Universals. 2. The influence of Aristotle. 3.
The proclamation of the independence of reason (*Biogr. Hist. of Philos.* p.
290). Cousin distinguishes between the periods of (1) absolute subordination
and (2) commencing emancipation of philosophy (*Cours de l'hist. de la philos.*
Leçon ix.).

[3] Feb. 23, 1225. The writings of Erigena fell into the more suspicion
from the use made of them by Berengarius of Tours in the Eucharistic controversy (1050), and by Amalric of Bène. John Scotus was the first who
adopted a systematically syllogistic form of argument.

of right contemplation teaches. Reason and authority come alike from the one source of divine wisdom, and cannot contradict each other. Reason is not to be overruled by authority but the reverse, and therefore the opinions of the Fathers must only be introduced in case of necessity,[1] for the Fathers often contradict each other." [2] That voice was of a higher mood, but no one listened to it. Erigena unhappily was not a commentator. He held indeed that "the sense of divine utterance is manifold, and like a peacock's feather glows with many colours,"[3] but he also held that all creatures are manifestations of the divine. The chief influence he exercised was due to his translation and adoption of the views of the Syrian Neoplatonist whose works were attributed to Dionysius the Areopagite.[4] Those spurious writings, which probably originated at Edessa or under the influence of the Edessene School, about the beginning of the sixth century, wrought like a spell upon the mediaeval Church

---

[1] *De Div. Nat.* i. 66, 68, 71, iv. 9; Diestel, p. 159. He asserts the *identity* of Philosophy and Religion, not the vassalage of the former to the latter. Ueberweg, i. 357. So too Berengar. *adv. Lanfranc., Lib. posterior,* p. 105.

[2] *De Div. Nat.* iv. 16.

[3] *De Div. Nat.* iv. 5. This truly great work was condemned by the Synod of Valence (855) as a *commentum diaboli ;* and by Pope Honorius III. (1225) as "teeming with the venom of heretical depravity ;" and placed on the Index by Gregory XIII. See Schaff, *Mediaeval Christianity,* ii. 543.

[4] The writings of Pseudo-Dionysius are first heard of about 532, soon after the closing of the Neoplatonic schools of Athens by Justinian, and their authenticity was early disputed (Phot. *Cod.* 2). Cave (*Script. Ecc.* i. 177) attributes them to Apollinaris the elder, and others to Synesius. Neither suggestion is probable. See Gieseler, ii. 113 ; Meier, *De Dionysii et Mysticorum Doctrina,* 1845 ; Montet, *Des Livres du Pseudo-Dionysius ;* Dean Colet on the *Celestial Hierarchies of Dionysius* (ed. Lupton); Westcott *on Dionys. the Areop., Contemp. Rev.* May, 1867. "The effect of this work on the whole ecclesiastical system and on the popular faith it is almost impossible justly to estimate." Milman, *Lat. Christ.* iv. 334. "Proclus and Dionysius ploughed with one and the same Neoplatonic heifer" (Fabric. *Marini Procli Vita,* p. xii.). The books of Dionysius were translated by J. Scotus Erigena, and in the twelfth century by Saracenus ; but even in 757 his writings had been given by Paul I. to Pippin. They were favourites with the mystics, as also with Ficino and Pico of Mirandola. Some of Abelard's many troubles were caused by certain historic doubts as to Dionysius and St. Denys. Pope says with somewhat ignorant severity,

> " Go soar with Plato to th' empyreal sphere
> To the first good, first perfect, and first fair ;
> Or tread the mazy round his followers trod,
> And quitting sense call imitating God."
>
> *Essay on Man,* ii. 23-26.

and especially upon the mystics of the twelfth and the
Platonists of the fifteenth century. The φυγὴ μόνου πρὸς
μόνον of Plotinus [1] expresses the inmost idea of Mysticism,
and its influence is traceable not only in the mystics of the
Middle Ages but in Dean Colet,[2] in the Quietists, in the
Molinists, and even in the memorable remark of Cardinal
Newman about God and the soul as being the two supremely
and luminously self-evident existences.

It was not till the twelfth century that the slightest breath
of fresh life blew over the faded fields. The era of passivity
ends with Erigena. Thenceforth dogma assumes the aid of
dialectics, and is developed into a system. Just as Alexandrian Christianity was the result of a conflict with heretical
gnosis, so scholasticism was elicited by the efforts of free
inquiry. The era begins with the attempt of Anselm (1033-
1109) to raise the truths of faith to scientific certainty, and
so to fuse faith and reason as to save the one from being
blind, and the other from being autocratic.[3] The close of
this century is marked by the great names of Bernard (1091-
1153), of Abelard (1079-1142), of Rupert of Deutz († 1135),[4]
of Hugo († 1141), and of Richard de Sto Victore († 1173).

St. Bernard, the *Doctor Mellifluus*, and "Last of the
Fathers," is the able and eloquent representative of the ecclesiastical rule, but also the father of the mediaeval mystics.[5]
Mysticism is the natural resource of souls that cannot find sufficient to satisfy their religious needs in the tyranny of artificial
systems. The calm question of the author of the *Imitatio*,

---

[1] Plotin. *Ennead.* vi. 9. Creuzer says of the Ps. Dionysius, "His walls are
inlaid with Plotinian mosaic." Dante expresses the high estimate of him in
the Mediaeval Church (*Par.* x. 112 ; xxviii. 121).

[2] "Nisi poterit homo dicere secum Ego solus et Deus in mundo sum non
habebit requiem " (Colet).

[3] "Credo ut intelligam " (Anselm, *Prol.*).

[4] The remarks of Rupert (*Prol. in Joann.*) in favour of the view that commentators were still possible though Augustine had written, were thought
unusually bold. On the transcendent authority of Augustine, which even
Berengarius said it was "ne fas quidem contradicere," see Werner, *Schol. d.
Mittelalt.* i. 1-3.

[5] See Stöckl, *Gesch. d. Philos. d. Mittelalters*, i. 293. It is remarkable that
while Peter Lombard quotes Hugo of St. Victor, he never notices Bernard.
Thomasius thinks that this was out of kindness to the memory of his teacher
Abelard.

" *Quid nobis cum generibus et speciebus?* " expressed the rejection by the truest mystics of the discussions which occupied so many centuries. Mysticism was not an enemy to
scholasticism, but had a different aim. Scholasticism dealt
with *aetiology,* and aimed at the discovery of truth ; mysticism
dealt with *teleology,* and aimed at the realisation of holiness.[1]
All mysticism is included in the remark of St. Bernard,
" Causa diligendi Dei Deus est, modus est sine modo diligere "
(*De dilig. Deo,* opp. i. 974). It was fostered in the intellect
by the fancies of the Pseudo-Areopagite, and in the heart
by the unnatural asceticism of the monastic system. Deprived
of the refining influence of family life, shut up in an endless
round of services and self-denials which alike tended to
become mechanical, the monks were still unable to defy the
emotions and impulses of nature, and while they desired to
live in closest communion with the divine, constructed for
themselves in the next world an idealised form of the joys
which they gave up in this. There was one book of the
Bible which left scope to their imagination to revel in
thoughts which seemed to be innocent because they were
supposed to be Scriptural, and which gratified those yearnings
of the human heart which are too strong and too sacred to
be permanently crushed. It was the Song of Solomon.
Many of the Jewish Rabbis had felt doubts about the book,
until Aqiba with his usual dictatorial confidence had declared
that it was the very Holy of Holies of Scripture.[2] Whether
mystically interpreted of the soul or not, it was felt to be
a warm and glowing song of love, and Jewish youths were
not permitted to read it.[3] Such feelings were not transitory.
Abelard feared the effects which it would produce on the minds

---

[1] Hergenröther, *K. G.* i. 953. St. Bernard speaks (*Sermons,* ed. Marténe,
p. 21) " of Aristotelicae subtilitatis facunda quidem sed *infecunda loquacitas.*"

[2] " On the day when R. Eliezer ben Azariah was made President it was
decided that the books of Canticles and Ecclesiastes defile the hands (*i.e.*
are canonical). R. Aqiba said . . . No day in the history of the world is so
valued as the day when the Book of Canticles was given to Israel ; for all the
Scriptures are holy, but the Book of Canticles is the Holy of Holies "
(Yaddaim, c. iii.).

[3] Sanhedrin, f. 101, i. . . . " Whoever recites a verse of the Song of Solomon
as a secular song . . . causes evil to come upon the world."

of the virgins of the Paraclete.[1] When we read Jerome's letter
to Eustochium on Virginity we can see that there might be
both moral danger and gross bad taste in the manner in
which the images of Canticles were applied.[2] Something of
the same kind may be seen at the close of Hugo's treatise,
De Nuptiis. Jerome had mentioned the Canticles as the
goal for Paulla's theological studies.[3] Aquinas expounded it
almost with his dying breath. The monkish commentaries
upon it were unwholesomely numberless. In the eighty-
six Homilies of St. Bernard there are thoughts and passages
full of beauty, but the mystic interpretation of the book,
even if it be justifiable, degenerated in meaner hands into a
style of language of which it would be charitable to say
nothing worse than that it is too poetically sensuous for any
commentary on Holy Writ.

The monastery of St. Victor was the chief home of
mediaeval mysticism.[4] Over its gate was the inscription—

> " *Claustrum nolenti mors est, sed vita volenti ;*
> *Per claustri sedem coeli mercaberis Eden.*"

In that distich lay the whole theory of monasticism. Its
aim was to fly from the world, not to save it. It strove to
obtain personal salvation as the payment of present asceticism.
HUGO was driven into mysticism by disgusted conviction of
the danger and uselessness of the dialectics which had been
introduced into the service of religion. "The incorrupted
truth of things," he says, "cannot be discovered by ratio-

---

[1] *Ep. ad Virg. Paracl.* "Ne sub *carnalibus verbis* nuptiarum spiritualium,
epithalamium non intelligens vulneretur" (*Opp.* ed. Cousin, i. 227).

[2] Here are a few of St. Bernard's explanations : *Meliora sunt ubera tua
vino.* Though addressed to the Bride he refers them to Christ, and says that
they mean His *patience* and His *clemency* (which he proves at great length by
"parallel passages"). *Propterea adolescentulae te dilexerunt nimis.* The
adolescentulae are the Angels, and this gives Bernard an opportunity to
expatiate at length on the nine orders of Angels, &c.

[3] *Ep. ad Lactam.*

[4] Hugo, *Erudit. Didascal.* iii. 13. John of Salisbury had said, " *Claustrales
rectissime et tutissime philosophantur* " (*Polycrat.* viii. 13, 21). Bacon says,
" Quemadmodum corpora eorum in cellis coenobiorum, sic animus in uno
Aristotele conclusus fuit" (*De Augm. Scient.* i. 16) ; see Hauréau, i. 507.
Even Bede complains of the " innumera *monasticae servitutis* retinacula "

cination." [1] It was, however, of no importance that ratiocination should fail to discover truth, for according to Hugo truth had already attained its full and final objective existence in the system of the Church. *Disce prius quid tenendum sit* was his plain advice; first learn what you are to believe, and then go to Scripture to find it there! [2] Dogmatics were made the key to interpretation. He places the end of life in contemplation which he says follows after reading, meditation, prayer, and good works, and is a foretaste of heaven.[3] In his treatise on Contemplation, he tells his novices to read the Scriptures for instruction in morals, not for training in subtlety.[4] It was, however, the object of the Victorines not so much to reject the scholastic methods as to unite them with mysticism. RICHARD OF ST. VICTOR († 1173), in his *Benjamin Major*, defines and describes contemplation in a manner altogether scholastic.[5] In the fourteenth century mysticism became more simple. Tauler anticipates the Protestant demand for Scripture and Scripture only, and if he relies on the mystic interpretation it is because to him inspiration was the living inner word which corresponds with Scripture, and Scripture was only regarded as a witness to the revelation of God in Christ.[6]

In one sense mysticism was a protest against the bold and speculative inquiries of Abelard, who is justly regarded as

---

[1] *Erudit. Didascal.* i. 12. See Hauréau, *Hugues de St. Victor.* He said, "Tantum de veritate quisque potest videre, *quantum ipse est.*"

[2] *Erudit. Didasc.* vi. 4. An old Pope is reported to have said, "The Scripture is a book which, if a man will keep close to, he will quite ruin the Catholic faith."

[3] *Erud. Didasc.* i. 9. R. de Sto Victore said, "In tantum Deus cognoscitur in quantum amatur."

[4] *De Contemplatione et ejus Speciebus* (published in Hauréau's *H. de St. Victor*) ; "ubi caritas ibi claritas" (*De Sacr.* ii. 13, § 11). His own method is allegoric, monastic, and popular. On 1 K. iv. 10 he says that the ten fat oxen represent the Decalogue, the twenty pasture oxen the preaching in the New Testament, the 100 rams *perfectam ecclesiasticam praelationem.*

[5] See Vaughan, *St. Thomas Aquin.* i. 252. Hergenröther rightly says that in the hands of these writers Scholasticism and Mysticism were "nur verschiedene Auffassungs- und Darstellungsweisen der Dogmen" (*K. G.* p. 952).

[6] Tauler complains that "Man nimmt *fremde Glossen* aus der H. Schrift dass es zu erbarmen ist." See Böhringer, xvii. German mystics Tauler († 1361), Suso († 1365), Rusbroek († 1381), and the author of a "German Theology" (see Pfeiffer's *Deutsche Mystiker*, and Ullmann, *Reformatoren vor der Reformation*).

the chief founder of scholasticism proper. For mysticism
was introduced into the monastery of St. Victor by William
of Champeaux when he had been dialectically defeated by
the audacious arrogance of his dangerous pupil.[1] It rendered
one great service by the persistence with which the mystics
pointed out that the object of studying Scripture was not
speculative but practical and moral.[2] Their object was to
make men better; to give them, not *mirabilia*, but *salutifera*[3]
—the grace of eternal peace, or admiration, or the highest
love of God.[4]

It may seem strange that a man who is regarded as the
founder of scholasticism should have been a rationalist in his
tendencies.[5] Like Gregory of Nyssa ABELARD was orthodox,
but he wrote with a freedom which tended to separate the
dogmas of Theology and Philosophy, and Peter Lombard, like
Augustine, helped to restore Theology to its old supremacy.
Scholasticism, as represented by St. Thomas of Aquino, combined the authority of Scripture, tradition, and the Church,
—an authority not demonstrated but accepted as an incontrovertible axiom.[6] Abelard, by his *Sic et Non*, and his
own standpoint of indifference, helped to break down the
authority of tradition,[7] and even used language, which

---

[1] See Ueberweg, *Hist. of Philosophy*, i. 376, E. T.

[2] Hugo of St. Victor, *Erud. Didasc.* v. 10. Comp. Johann. Sarisb. *Polycrat.*
vii. 10. Augustine and Abelard had said the same.

[3] Richard of St. Victor.

[4] Bonaventura, *Breviloq., ad init.* In Richard of St. Victor's system there
are three powers of the soul—Imagination, Reason, Intelligence—to which
correspond three methods of knowledge—Thought, Meditation, Contemplation. The object of Contemplation is God, the means to it are virtue and
self-knowledge. It has six steps to it (which are very scholastically described),
and three grades—Dilatatio, Sublevatio, Alienatio (ecstasy). Rachel (the
reason) dies that Benjamin (ecstasy) may be born. It is here that Holy
Scripture comes in (like Moses and Elias at the Transfiguration) to prevent
self-deception or Satanic delusion.

[5] "Ce qui est certain c'est que la scholastique . . . ne cite point de plus
grand nom, et *consent à dater de lui*" (Rémusat, *Abélard*, i. 272).

[6] The universally accepted phrase "*Philosophia ancilla Theologiae*" seems
to come from Didymus (who makes Sara a symbol of theology, Hagar of
Dialectics) through John Damascene (*Dial.* i. 1)—see Rémusat, *Abélard*,
ii. 144.

[7] He does not scruple to head his sections "Quod non sit Deus singularis et
contra;" "Quod sit Deus tripartitus et contra;" "Quod sit finis sine prin-
cipio et contra;" "Quod omnia sciat Deus et non," &c. Yet Abelard was
rather an inquirer than a sceptic, and his *Sic et Non* was only meant (like

s 2

expressed somewhat less than the current adoration of
Scripture.[1] For, after showing the errors and inconsistencies
of the Fathers (to whom he yet attributes a special inspiration)
he adds, " What wonder, when it is acknowledged that even
Prophets and Apostles were not wholly free from error,[2] if
in such a multitude of writings of the Holy Fathers, some
things seem to be erroneously propounded and written ? " The
Prophets were not, he says, always filled with the grace of
God. He proceeds, however, to limit the errors of Prophets
to their lives; to erroneous citations due to the Scribes; and
to the fact that they necessarily spoke in popular language.[3]
Hence, if anything in Scripture seems to be absurd we are
not to set it down to the writer but to the fault of the manuscript or the mistake of the translation.[4] He rightly and
wisely distinguished between important and unimportant
elements in Scripture, and, like Luther, drew a distinction

the Stoic paradoxes and Kant's Antinomies) to stimulate inquiry (see
Maurice, *Mediaeval Philosophy*, p. 39). Comp. Tribbechovius, p. 325.

[1] Abelard always writes like a man of genius, but his answers to the strange
scholastic questions sent him by Héloise, and his own commentaries, prove,
as Tholuck says, that he was not a good historic interpreter. He is too full
of curiosities, *placita majorum, ecclesiae praecepta, quaestiones scholasticae,*
&c. (Tholuck, *De Thom. Aquin. et Abaelardo*). He often makes remarks which
would be stigmatised as "rationalistic." For instance, he preferred the version
of the Lord's Prayer in St. Matthew to that in St. Luke, because the latter
could only have heard it secondhand from St. Paul. Hence William of St.
Thierry complained that " he treated Scripture as he treated Logic . . . he is
the censor not the disciple of the faith, the corrector not the imitator of
our masters " (*ap.* Bern. *Opp. Ep.* 326). For specimens of " discrepancies "
in the Gospels and Fathers see the *Sic et Non*, p. 7 (ed. Cousin).

[2] " *Constat et prophetas ipsos quandoque prophetiae gratiâ caruisse*" (*Sic et
Non,* Prol.).

[3] *Sic et Non,* Prol. On the *Sic et Non* see S. Bernard, *Ep.* 326 ; *Tract. de
Erroribus Abaelardi,* i. ; *Opp.* i. 532, 1055 (Migne), Vaughan, *Life of St.
Thomas Aquinas,* i. 168, *sq.* ; Maurice, *Med. Philos.* pp. 138–141. In
Abelard's book *On the Trinity* there is said to have been the remark, " *Nec
quia Deus id dixerat creditur,* sed quia hoc sic esse convincitur, recipitur.*"
This bold assertion of the claims of reason was hateful to the traditionalists
(Poole, p. 153).

[4] This view created no difficulty, because something like it was found in
Augustine and Jerome. The *Correctoria Biblica* of Lanfranc, Stephen Harding,
R. Grostête († 1253), Cardinal Hugo of St. Cher († 1260) show that the need
of a better text was felt. Roger Bacon speaks of the impossibility of a translation conveying the exact sense of the original, and quotes Grostête as desiring
a new translation (*Opus Majus,* iii. 1). Hugo of St. Cher deserves special
mention as "the Father of Concordances" and the *first Postillator* of the
whole Bible. For specimens of his extravagance see the notes of Erasmus
on Matt. v. 16, xix. 22, John v. 2, 1 Pet. ii. 24, &c.

between "Scripture" and the "word of God." To Abelard, however, is mainly due the scholastic method of dialectics, and the restless spirit of unchecked speculation. As to the first he himself said "*Odiosum me mundo reddidit logica,*"[1] and took as his motto "By doubting we arrive at truth." As to the second we read the indignant complaint of Bernard, "He thrusts his face into heaven and peers into the secrets of God, and while he is ready to render a reason about all things, he assumes even those which are above reason and against reason and against faith. For what is more against reason than by reason to endeavour to transcend reason?"[2] Hence Abelard produced the two-fold reaction of the dogmatists and the mystics, who hated alike what they regarded as "profane verbal novelties," and to whom the very words *Sic et Non* sounded monstrous.[3] The dogmatists demanded oracles of certainty; the mystics required intuitions of rapturous communion.

PETER LOMBARD (✝ 1164), the famous "Master of the *Sentences,*" though he had been a pupil of Abelard, recoiled altogether from his position. His *Sentences* are a protest against the *Sic et Non,* as the *Sic et Non* had been perhaps itself a protest against the "*crede ut intelligas*" of Anselm.[4] They became with Aristotle and the Bible the "bases of the active intellect" of the thirteenth century. Peter was accused of heresy at first by Walter of

---

[1] *Apol. ad Helois.*, *Opp.* p. 308. Almost the only other voices which venture (more timidly) to dissent from the Fathers were those of Richard of St. Victor (*Opp.* ii. 1) and Rupert of Deutz. There was an old rule—

"Si Augustinus adest sufficit ipse tibi,"

and Rupert shows courage in the manly and beautiful passage of the preface to his commentary on St. John, in which he claims that though the eagle-wings of Augustine overshadow the Gospel, he did not exhaust the right of all Christians to handle the Gospel.

[2] Bernardi, *Ep.* xi. *ad Innocent.* "Nihil videt per speculum et in aenigmate, sed facie ad faciem omnia intuetur" is the mystic's characteristic complaint of the logician (*Ep.* 192). Abelard's Comments on the Hexaemeron (Marténe and Durand, *Thes. Nov. Anecd.*) is chiefly remarkable for its curious scientific (?) speculations.

[3] "Sicut monstruosi sunt nominis sic etiam monstruosi dogmatis." W. de St. Thierry.

[4] Hauréau, p. 384.

St. Victor, but his commentaries are little more than a compilation from Hilary, Ambrose and Augustine.[1] The Fathers lent themselves to his dogmatic method far more easily than the Scripture which he is too ready to explain away. He only refers to Aristotle incidentally,[2] and is always cautiously on his guard against the suspicion of independence. His ideal writer is John Damascene, whom he called the greatest of the Greek teachers, and whose book " on the orthodox faith," in which he expressly says ἐγὼ τοιγαροῦν ἐμὸν οὐδέν, had been translated by order of Pope Eugenius.[3] It is only in the *form* of his *Liber sententiarum*, and its speculative spirit that the Lombard shows whose pupil he had been.[4] He followed the Church and "used the weightiest words of the weightiest Fathers in the weightiest manner," but the method of questions and " distinctions " enabled him to combine disputation with deference, and "to comment and discuss without limit within the range of constituted authority." The publication of the *Sentences* formed an epoch. It showed that though the world of First Principles was "surrounded by Stygian waters " the spirit of inquiry might, with at least a semblance of freedom, launch into the open sea of inference and deduction. The *Sentences* of Peter became the text-book of scholasticism. They marked out its mission, which was not to discover but to formulate.[5] They were a

[1] *Sent.* i. ; *Dist.* 19.
[2] *Sent.* ii. ; *Dist.* i. § 5 ; and Maurice refers specially to his comments on John i. 9, 1 Tim. ii. 4.
[3] In one sense John of Damascus may be regarded as the Father of Scholasticism, for in his Πηγὴ γνώσεως he was "the first to apply Aristotelian dialectics to traditional theology."
[4] Dante, in the lines

" L'altro che appresso adorna il nostro coro
Quel Pietro fu, che con la poverella
Offerse a santa Chiesa il suo Tesoro,"

alludes to the Prologue to the *Sentences* where he says that he desires, with the poor widow, to cast something out of his poverty into the treasure of the Church ; "Cupientes aliquid de tenuitate nostra cum pauperculâ in gazophylacium Domini mittere."
[5] It was "the first of a long series of attempts to obtain for the doctrines of the Church a scientific system." Schwegler, *Hist. of Philos.* E. T. p. 144 ; *Hist. Litt. de la France*, xii. 589. "Round . . . . . the *Sentences* . . . . . the theology of the Schoolman was trained and trammelled over a rigid network of dialectics, where the flower often lost its perfume and the fruit perished." Mullinger, i. 63.

convenient handbook, which, with the *Summa* of Thomas
Aquinas, showed all inquiring spirits how they could unite
the restless impatience of the human mind with the arbitrary
determinations of the spiritual authority. During the following centuries the *Summa* and the *Sentences* were studied and
expounded far more than the Scriptures.[1] And without
professedly revolting from the hard and arid system which
was thus established, mysticism could take refuge in allegorising the Song of Songs, and in dreaming over "the Celestial
Hierarchy" of the supposed Areopagite. In both schools
Divinity was "reduced into an art, as into a cistern, and
the stream of doctrine derived from thence."[2]

The fortunes of Aristotle in the mediaeval Church were
strange. Through the Alexandrian schools, both Jewish and
Christian, Plato had exerted no small influence over the
discussions of theology, but during the early centuries the
works of Aristotle were in obscurity. His dialectical methods
had first been used by heretics, and especially by Artemon
and Theodotus in arguing against the doctrine of the Trinity.
No less than twenty of the Fathers from Justin to Cyril speak
disparagingly of him. "They place the whole virulence of
their poisons in dialectical disputation," says Ambrose of
the Arians.[3] "Wretched Aristotle," exclaims Tertullian,
"who trained the Valentinians in dialectics!"[4] But the
works of the great Stagirite crept into the Church imper-
ceptibly, and in spite of her opposition. At first only his
Organon and *Categories* were known to the Western world.
The school-discussions of the Middle Ages were originated by
a single passage from the introduction of Porphyry trans-

[1] As even Roger Bacon complains, *Opus Minus* (ed. Brewer), p. 329.
[2] Bacon, *Advancement of Learning.*
[3] *De Fide*, 21, 5 ; comp. Serm. xxii. in Ps. 118.
[4] Gregory of Nazianzus says that "the Christians knew nothing of the
craftiness of Aristotle's craft." *Orat.* xxvi. St. Vincent Ferrer was glad to
quote the assertion of Jerome : "Quod Aristoteles et Plato in inferno sunt."
Mullinger, i. 122. Roger Bacon said : "Had I the power, I would have all
the works of Aristotle burnt, as it is but waste time . . . . . to study them,"
Opus Minus (ed. Brewer), pp. 322–330. Grotius observes that many Platonists
(Clemens, Origen, &c.) became Christians, but none—or very few—of the
Aristotelians. *De Stud. Instit.* (1645), p. 221.

lated by Boethius.[1] He said that to understand Aristotle
it was necessary to know the meaning of the five words
genus, differentia, species, proprium and *accidens*, but he would
abstain from the more difficult question about *genera* and
species, whether they existed or only had a place in the
naked intellect, whether they were corporeal or incorporeal,
and whether separated from sensible things or placed in
them, or consisting around them. The questions whether
universals are real or are only mental conceptions, and
whether they do or do not exist apart from individuals
wasted more money, as John of Salisbury said, than the
treasures of Croesus, and occupied more time than it took the
Caesars to rule the world.[2]

At the beginning of the thirteenth century (from 1210
to 1225) *all* the works of Aristotle became known together
with those of Arab philosophy through the medium of
Spanish Jews.[3] They were received with profound distrust.
The errors of Amalric of Bène and David of Dinant were
attributed to the study of them, and the use of them was
thrice forbidden by Papal infallibility.[4] In spite of this
they crept from the threshold to the shrine, and added
new and predominant influences to the scholastic method.
The Popes soon saw their mistake in opposing a science which
was placed absolutely at the disposal of their most extravagant
claims. It is said that Aristotle's *Ethics* were sometimes

---

[1] "Un rayon dérobé à l'antiquité la produisit ; l'antiquité tout entière
[*i.e.* the Revival of Letters] l'étouffa." V. Cousin, *Fragments Philos.* p. 82.
See, too, J. B. Mullinger, *Hist. of Cambr.* pp. 50–54 ; Bain's *Mental and Moral
Science*, App. A.

[2] Johann. Sarisb. *Polycrat.* vii. 12.

[3] Through Avicenna in the East, and Averroes in the West they passed
from Mohammedans to Jews. Maimonides translated them into Hebrew. See
Renan, *Averroes*, p. 52 ; Jourdain, *Recherches critiques ;* Prantl, *Gesch. d. Logik*,
iii. 3. Up till 1100 the Logic of Aristotle was known, and that only
partially. Mullinger, *Hist. of Cambr.* i. 29.

[4] In 1209, 1215, and 1231, by Gregory IX. (See Landerer *s.v. Scholasticism*
in Herzog.) A Provincial council ordered that Masters of Arts should not
philosophise but "*satagant fieri Theododacti*" and should only discuss questions
"quae per libros theologicos et Sanctorum Patrum tractatus valeant terminari."
Lanfranc had expressed his strong preference for "sacred authorities" over
"dialectics." "Nec libri Aristotelis nec commenta legantur." Conc. Paris.
A.D. 1209. The prohibition was withdrawn by Urban V. in 1366.

read in Churches.[1] It is certain that they were more often referred to than the Decalogue,[2] and that more pains were taken to connect Aristotle with Christianity than to explain the relation between Moses and Christ. Before the close of the thirteenth century the world saw the full development of that scholastic theology which may be most shortly defined as " the reproduction of ancient philosophy under the control of ecclesiastical doctrine." It reminded Luther of a centaur, because it was a mixture of divine utterances and philosophic reasons. Erasmus says that theologians in his day " thought that all was up with the Christian religion if any one rejected the decrees of Aristotle." [3] Aristotle was called the "*praecursor Christi in naturalibus.*" On the other hand, the literal sense of Scripture appeared so worthless to the dominant dogmatism that Hugo compares it to mud used to anoint the eyes of the blind. " *Biblicus theologus*" became a term of contempt.[4]

How rapidly the influence of Aristotle spread may be seen in the works of Alexander of Hales († 1245),[5] Albertus Magnus († 1280), and Thomas Aquinas († 1274) who became acquainted with his *Metaphysics* through the medium of Averroes and Arabic translations. They did not in any way advance or alter dogma : they only systematised it, furnished it with an apparatus of scientific nomenclature, and transferred it from the Church to the School.[6] They all

[1] So Melanchthon complains *Apolog.* A. C. 62 ; Mathesius, *Vit. Luth.* i. 712 ; Brucker, iii. 886 ; Gabriel Biel is said to have offended in this way.
[2] "Quidam Doctor Theologus rogatus de Decalogo, negabat se *ejusmodi librum* in Bibliotheca umquam habuisse." Ridderus, *De Eruditione* (1680), p. 40.
[3] Erasm. *Schol.* p. 258.
[4] See Liebner, *Hugo von S. Victore,* p. 128 ; *Praenott. Elucid.* 5.
[5] He is the first who definitely quotes Averroes, and the first commentator on the *Sentences.* See Renan, *Averroes,* p. 176 ; Hauréau, i. 402 ; Ueberweg, i. 407, and on the Arabs generally, Munk, *Mélanges,* p. 313, *sq.* Owing to Arabian influences Aristotle " passed from the consulship to the Dictatorship of Philosophy." *Aristoteles* was made into the anagram, *iste sol erat.* In 1629 the Sorbonne decreed that to contradict Aristotle was to contradict the Church.
[6] Card. Hergenröther defines scholasticism as " dialektisch geordnete, systematische Theologie, die an die Philosophie sich anlehnte und die Dogmen theils als vernunftgemäss, theils als über jede vernünftige Einsprache erhaben zu begründen suchte." *Kirchengeschichte,* i. 952 ; compare Ueberweg, i. 355.

practised the dialectic method, and thought that they were establishing religious truth, while they were only framing a technical language. Following the example of Abelard [1] they fatally misapplied the maxim of Aristotle that "to frame doubts well" (τὸ διαπορῆσαι καλῶς) is a service to the discovery of truth.[2] They delighted their fettered ingenuity with the semblance of emancipation by furnishing vain answers to insoluble questions. Their theology is a science of definition in which analyses of language are taken for discoveries of fact, and in which a congeries of doubts is met by a concatenation of baseless assumptions. The result is a dull mythology in which abstractions are deified, not in the gracious atmosphere of Poetry, but in the sterile desert of logical discussion. They were thus enabled to unite obedience with rationalism, and the Hierarchy successfully disguised intense intolerance under an apparent permission to philosophise at will.[3]

In exegesis we see the Schoolmen at their worst. Scholasticism treats the letter of Scripture, even in its plainest

---

[1] Abelard's motto had been, Ecclus. xix. 4, "Qui cito credit levis est corde." "*Dubitando ad inquisitionem venimus, inquirendo veritatem percipimus.*" *Sic et Non*, p. 16, ed. Cousin. This resembles the remark of Diderot : "Le Scepticisme est donc le premier pas vers la vérité." Thomas Aquinas says that Theology has no need of Philosophy except by way of illustration, because it receives its principles immediately from God. *Summa*, I. *qu.* 1, 4, 5.

[2] Arist. *Metaph.* iii. 1. See Launoy, *De varia Aristotelis fortuna in Acad. Paris.* Hampden, *Bampt. Lect.* p. 63. In 1516, Luther wrote to J. Lange, "Nihil ita ardet animus quam *histrionem illum qui tam vere graecâ larvâ Ecclesiam lusit,* multis revelare *ignominiamque ejus* cunctis ostendere" (*Briefe*, i. 15), and in 1517 "Aristoteles descendit paulatim . . . ad ruinam prope futuram sempiternam." In his letter to the German nobility he complains that, *Aristotle, that blind heathen, has replaced Christ.* See further extracts from his *Responsio ad Prieratium* in Gieseler, v. 233. Roger Bacon stood almost alone in the 13th century in protesting alike against servile devotion to the Fathers, and against the authority of Aristotle, all of whose books he said that he would burn if he had the power. "Haec aetas" he says "*languet et asininat* circum male intellecta."

[3] See Hampden, *Bampt. Lectures.* A lively conception of the barren discussion of that age may be derived from the writings of John of Salisbury, particularly the *Metalogicus* and *Polycraticus,*

> "Quaevis
> Litera sordescit, logica sola placet."—*id. Entheticus.*

I have not touched on Anselm, who was rather a theologian than an exegete. See Rémusat, *St. Anselm*, p. 478.

histories, as an enigma which veils the latest after-thoughts of theology. It destroys the real meaning of the Old Testament in the attempt to make it speak the language of Church tradition. No one can doubt the greatness and goodness of ALBERTUS,[1] yet what can be more essentially irreverent in substance or more empty in method than his discussion of the reasons why it was necessary for an Angel to announce to Mary the immaculate conception, and not for God to be His own messenger?[2] The greatness of the Schoolmen was so paralysed by vicious methods, traditional errors, and foregone conclusions, that many of their comments on Scripture become not only inconsequent but childish. "*Let not the foot of pride come against me.*"[3] Why "foot" and not "feet"? asked Albertus. Because, he says, "he who walks on one foot falls more easily than he who walks on two![4] Could anything be less elucidatory than this distortion of the simplest passages?[5] His commentary on the Minor Prophets is nothing but a dry compilation, paraphrastic, verbose, and overladen with the formalism of useless distinctions. The comment on the opening clause of Joel is as follows. "*The word of the Lord that came to Joel.*" *Verbum* is used in the singular because the Word, so far as it is in God, is one and uncreate, yet is the reason and source and form of many words. This Word was made (*factum est*) to Joel, not so far as it is in the word, but in the mind of the Prophet. Joel calls himself "son of Pethuel, that spiritually

---

[1] "Questi che m'è a destra più vicino
  Frate e maestro fummi ; ed esso Alberto
  È di Cologna ; ed io Thomas d'Aquino.
        —DANTE, *Parad.* x. 97.

The works of Albertus filled twenty-one folios, of which five are commentaries. But the *Doctor Universalis* does not seem to have known either Greek, Arabic, or Hebrew, and was very feeble in history and philology. See Stöckl, ii. 358. Prantl calls him a mere compiler and "ein unklarer Kopf, und nicht befähigt irgend eine grundsätzliche Auffassung hinauszudenken" (*Gesch. d. Logik*, iii. 189). He says, "Alles durchweg Alles was er schreibt ist nur fremdes Gut." His real greatness was in science, in which he was very eminent.

[2] See Rosenmüller, *Hist. Int.* v. 250.

[3] Ps. xxxvi. ii.

[4] This takes us back to the region of pure Rabbinism.

[5] See by way of specimen his comment on Ps. xxxi. 9-12. His notes are chiefly glosses, burdened with unsifted parallel passages.

as well as carnally he may be known to have descended from
so great a father." Here, omitting some useless and irrelevant
parallels, we have first a mere play on words; then a passage
borrowed from the *Glossa ;* and lastly the idle Jewish fancy
that when a Prophet names his father, the father was also a
prophet.[1] " *That which the palmerworm hath left hath the
locust eaten.*"[2] This verse is first explained by a mosaic of
parallel places, which, being only taken from the Vulgate, is
entirely meaningless. Then we are told that Jerome takes
these species of locusts literally of Assyrians, Chaldaeans,
Babylonians, &c.; and morally to mean sadness, joy, fear,
and hope ; and that Gregory takes them morally to mean
either lust, vain-glory, gluttony, and anger, or (rather)
incipient passion, instability, habit, and despair. As to any
attempt to find the real or principal sense there is none.
" *For in Mount Sion and in Jerusalem shall be deliverance,*"[3]
that is, says Albertus, in the eminence of a speculative and
the peace of an active life. " *The mountains shall drop down
new wine, and the hills shall flow with milk.*"[4] The mountains,
he says, mean the heights of the three Persons in the Holy
Trinity, or even the heights of the Apostles ; and the hills,
that is the heights of the angels and saints, shall flow with
the truth of the white sweet doctrine of the Humanity of
Christ. " *Egypt shall be a desolation and Edom a desolate
wilderness*"—that is, spiritual and carnal sins shall be driven
where God and the Saints shall not be, because they have
shed the blood of martyrs ! This is not exegesis but homily-
work of the poorest description, allegorising passages which of
themselves are perfectly clear. " *Let the bridegroom go forth
of his chamber and the bride out of her closet.*"[5] That is, says
the Pseudo-Haymo of Halberstadt, "let Christ go out of the
bosom of the Father, and the flesh of Christ from the Virgin's

---

[1] See Merx, *Joel*, p. 369.   [2] Joel i. 4.
[3] Joel ii. 32.   [4] Joel iii. 18.
[5] Joel ii. 16. We find the same explanations with only slight differences
of detail in Hugo of St. Victor, Remigius, Rupert of Deutz, the *Glossa Ordinaria*, &c. The exegesis of Albertus Magnus like that of Peter Lombard is
chiefly derived third or fourth hand from the *Catenae* and glosses. See R.
Simon, *Hist. des Comment.* pp. 468, *sq.*

womb." The explanation, which is as old as the *Clavis* of Pseudo-Melito, reduces the passage as a whole to sheer nonsense.[1] It illustrates not only the helpless secondhandness of the mediaeval commentators, but also the absurdity to which their systematic allegorising often led them. It shows still more their fatal habit of looking at words without their connexion, and at texts without their context. "Or,"— continues Pseudo-Haymo—for the expositions of his day are always liberal of their futilities—"the bridegroom" may mean the divine word, and "the bride" (in the usual language of mysticism) the faithful soul. Mediaeval exposition very rarely explained the real meaning of the sacred writers.[2] It was a specious transition to a totally different order of thought.

Even Thomas of Aquino, with all his nobleness and greatness, profound as a thinker, incomparable as a theologian, is least successful in the interpretation of Scripture.[3] Imbued with the fatal dream of the fourfold sense of Scripture, he is meagre in the explanation of the literal sense, but diffuse in

---

[1] Pitra, *Spicil. Solesm.* iii. 75, *ap.* Merx, *Joel*, p. 377.

[2] Even Abelard looked on the necessity for allegory as a proof of "inspiration," and on this ground extended it to Plato. *Introd. ad Theol.* i. p. 46.

[3] Tholuck in his monograph *De Thoma Aquinate et Abaelardo interpretibus N. T.* says " *Quantum ad interpretandi dogmaticum genus attinet* hic ei campus laudum, hic *meriti corona*. Est argumenti dogmatici interpres diligens, indefessus qui ne voculam quidem praeterit quin excutiat." Erasmus said of him (on Rom. i. 2), "Meo quidem animo nullus est recentiorum theologorum cui par sit diligentia, cui sanius ingenium, cui solidior eruditio." On his work as an exegete see Vaughan, *Life of St. Thomas*, ii. 567, *sqq.* The present Pope (Leo XIII.) is the fourteenth who has loaded St. Thomas with eulogies. In his Encyclical *Aeterni Patris* (Aug. 4, 1879), while not vouching for oversubtlety or over rashness, or what is improbable, or not in accordance with the demonstrated doctrines of a later age, he recommends the study of his writings with a glowing eulogium to the whole Christian world. "Far above all other scholastic doctors," says the Encyclical, "towers Thomas Aquinas, their Master and Prince. Greatly enriched as he was with the science of God and the science of man, he is likened to the sun, for he warmed the whole earth with the fire of his holiness, and filled the whole earth with the splendour of his teaching." According to Natalis he found Philosophy wandering like Agar in the wilderness, and sent her back to be a bondslave in the tent of Abraham. Bucer said, "Tolle Thomam et Eccl. Romanam subvertam." Ventura says, "Il n'y a aucune erreur qu'il n'ait prévue, réfutée, pulverisée d'avance" (*La Raison philosophique*, ii. 129). *Catena Aurea* is a later name. He himself in his Dedication calls it *continua expositio*, and in older editions it is called *glossa continua*.

speculative discussions and dialectic developments. At the beginning of his comment on Job, he goes off into a long discussion about good and bad angels. When the patience of Job is mentioned he gives an essay on the views of the ancient philosophers respecting that virtue. He is so devoted to Augustine, as to have originated the saying that the soul of Augustine had passed into him by metempsychosis.[1] In his *Catena* on the Gospels he compiles mainly from twenty-two Greek and twenty Latin writers, and accepts without hesitation their most tasteless and empty allegories.[2] "Masterly and architectonic" as is the skill shown in that work which is "nearly perfect as a conspectus of patristic interpretations,"[3] yet being a *catena* only it did not contribute to exegetic progress. Thomas was acquainted with the writings of Maimonides and of Averroes, and has gained something from them as he shows in his remarks on prophecy. He does not, however, venture to mention the Jewish writer, whose works he was quoting side by side with those of Jerome and Gregory, at the very time that the brethren of his own Dominican order were condemning those works to the flames at Paris.[4] But neither Greek, nor Arab, nor Jewish learning produced any adequate effect on the exegesis of the Schoolmen. Even in the hands of St. Thomas it is dependent, traditional, unprogressive. He repeats the worst excesses of Hilary and even of Remigius. Thus John ate locusts and wild honey, because his preaching was to the crowds sweet like honey, but short of flight like locusts (Rem.). By John (*i.e.* "the Grace of God") is signified Christ who brought grace to the world; and by his camel's-hair robe is indicated the Church

---

[1] Sixt. Senens. *Bibl.* iv. 308.

[2] Frigerio (*Vita di S. Thomas*, ii. 115) speaks of his inexplicable reverence for the Fathers.

[3] Cardl. Newman, Pref. to vol. i. of *Catena Aurea*, Oxford, 1841 ; and Vaughan's *Life of St. Thomas*, ii. 547-574. The exquisite superiority of St. Chrysostom to other patristic commentators is constantly evinced in this *Catena*. A considerable drawback, however, to its usefulness arises from the fact that so many of the extracts are from spurious books.

[4] See Merx, *Joel*, p. 354. Jaraczewsky in *Zeitschr. für Philos.* xlvi. points out his influence on Scholasticism, and especially on Albertus. For the influence of Averroes see Renan, *Averroes*, pp. 231-236.

of the Gentiles (Hil.). Even throughout the simplest narratives of the Gospels he allegorises incessantly. Besides this he is full of contradictions.[1] A large part of his method consists in the ingenious juxtaposition of passages of which the verbal similarity depends only upon the Vulgate. From these imaginary identities of expression, by a method which seems to have survived from the days of Hillel, he deduces systems extremely ingenious but utterly without foundation. I need but mention one salient instance [2] in the arrangement which lies at the base of his commentary of 700 pages on the Pauline Epistles. The whole scheme is made to turn on the phrase "*a chosen vessel.*" St. Thomas arrives at the conclusion that all the fourteen Epistles (for he follows the popular view in attributing the Epistle to the Hebrews to St. Paul) treat of grace, and that the Epistle to the Galatians is a sort of appendix to the treatment of grace as it is in the sacraments![3] It would be difficult to conceive anything more ingeniously misleading, more historically groundless, more essentially partial, inadequate, and mistaken, than this celebrated scheme of the Epistles in which every critical and historical consideration, as well as every human element in the origin of the Epistles is fatally ignored in order that they may be symmetrically arranged into an artificial diagram of abstract doctrines.[4] The mere index to the word "Grace" in the chief edition of the works of St. Thomas fills many folio columns. How much has any reader really added to his understanding of the Scriptures, when he has read the multitudinous pages to which the index refers? In Divinity, as Bacon says, there cannot be this perfection and

[1] See the fifth Index to the *Summa* (Migne, i. *De Antilogiis*).
[2] His doctorial lecture on Ps. cv. 13 (see Vaughan's *Life*, ii. 113) gives a good specimen of his manner. For his views about allegory, tropology, and anagogy, see *Summ.* I. i. art. x.
[3] See *Opp.* vi. 3 (Venet. 1745).
[4] "Il ne peut être question de progrès dans un tel ordre d'exposition. . . . Partout ce sont les mêmes textes découpés et séparés de ce qui les explique, les même syllogismes triomphants, mais posant sur le vide, les mêmes défauts de critique historique, provenant de la confusion des dates et des milieux." Renan, *Souvenirs*, p. 281.

completeness. We cannot have the form of a total when there is but matter for a part.

We can hardly wonder that after his rapturous trance at Naples, Thomas of Aquino dropped the labour of his *Summa* and refused to write anything more.[1] He had seen such visions, he said, in the ecstasy of his long illness as to reduce to insignificance all that he had hitherto published. He so far yielded to the importunity of friends as to begin dictating a commentary on the Canticles, but he died in the midst of the task. There was in him a vein of pure mysticism,[2] which we should hardly have suspected when we read the pages of the *Summa*, so entirely free from rhetoric or emotion—" clear as water, passionless as marble, regular as mechanism, cold as ice."

Mysticism and scholasticism were even more commingled in the writings of St. Thomas's great contemporary, the Seraphic Doctor. In BONAVENTURA († 1274) indeed the mystic and Neoplatonist predominated; but the scholasticism of his day affected his writings no less than those of the two great monks of St. Victor.[3] Accepting the supernatural infallibility of every word of Scripture, his mode of commenting upon it is profoundly unscriptural. Some notion of his wearisome prolixity may be derived from his comment on " God saw the light that it was good." This verse is made the excuse for all sorts of diffuse and irrelevant remarks about vision, philosophy, and light, of which this is but one part of one sentence. " If truth is not, it is true that truth is not; something therefore is true ; and if something is true, it is true that there is truth; therefore, if truth is not there is truth. For truth prevails above all things." But perhaps nothing more is wanted to show the absolute lack of all exegetic insight than Bona-

---

[1] He said to his friend, Brother Reginald, "Omnia quae scripsi videntur mihi *paleae* respectu eorum quae vidi." *Prooem. De Vit. S. Thom. Aquin.*

[2] Corderius says that he derives almost all his theology from Dionysius (Migne, i. 96).

[3] He gives his views of exegesis in *Principium S. Scripturae.* See *Isagoge in Script. Sacr.* in which he says the New Testament is only the Old spiritually expounded.

ventura's application of the Psalter to the Virgin Mary.[1]
Bonaventura expatiates on the length, breadth, height, and
width, of Scripture; he says, that its altitude is unattainable
because of its inviolable authority, its plenitude inexhaustible
because of its inscrutable profundity, its certitude infallible
because of its irrefutable progress, its value inappreciable
because of its inestimable fruit, its pulchritude incontamin-
able because of its impermixtible purity, and so forth with all
the inexhaustible verbosity of scholastic eloquence, and with
an artificiality which lacks the ring of genuine feeling. This
supremacy, he says, belongs to God's Word, "in order that to
secular sciences which inflate the heart and overshadow the
intellect, there may be no room for glorying against Holy
Scripture."[2] But his many-syllabled eulogy only serves as
an introduction to an account of the river of Paradise which
divides itself into four heads, the rivers namely of histories,
of anagogies, of allegories, and of tropologies.[3] This fourfold
river of exegesis had its fountain not, as Bonaventura imagined,
in Paradise, but partly in the Greek Stoa and partly in
the Jewish Synagogue. It had broadened and deepened in
the works of interpreters who found in the mystic sense a
facile way of gratifying ingenuity, of concealing ignorance and
of furnishing homiletics. During the whole of this period
Christian exegesis resembled that of the Rabbinic school of
Tiberias in its age of decadence. Both had their oral
tradition with which they made the Word of God of none
effect. The Fathers took the same position as the Mishna,
and allegory as the Qabbala. From Rabbis and Alexandrians

---

[1] Bonaventura has been highly praised for his method of "explaining
Scripture by Scripture." But in the first place the method is not in the least
degree peculiar to him, and in the next the indiscriminate use of "parallel"
passages, which have nothing "parallel" in them, leads in all the Schoolmen
to mere confusion.

[2] *Procem. in Breviloquium.* Comp. Hugo, *Erudit. Didasc.* iv. 1 ; Johann.
Sarisb. *Polycrat.* vii. 12. The sciences which reveal the laws of God were
thus treated as menials "in the service of a mistress who had grown sluggish
and immovable."

[3] Bonaventura himself prefers to regard the Bible as a book with *seven*
seals, and not content even with the fourfold sense, he adds to it three more
senses—the symbolic, the synekdochic, and the hyperbolic !

T

the Christian teachers had taken without examination an
unscriptural view of inspiration, and they supported it by a
method which had been borrowed directly from Pagan
philosophers.[1]

But we meet at last with one green island among the
tideless waves of exegetic commonplace. NICOLAS OF LYRA [2]
(† 1340) — the *Doctor planus et utilis*—was the Jerome
of the fourteenth century. From him came the revival
which reached its full force more than two centuries after he
had gone to rest. The fresh life came from the reviving
studies of the French and Spanish Jews. The old method
of Biblical study, the fantastic child of Rabbinism and the
Stoa, had long fallen, it has been said, into a magic sleep,
and the trees rustled in vain over the enchanted castle. It
had drunk at the hands of Bede the opiate of Jerome's
vague wavering elegant compilations ; and had fed to
repletion upon the sermon-material so abundantly supplied
by Gregory. But meanwhile, on the banks of the Tigris
and in Andalusia, Jews trained in Arabic schools of wisdom
had found the charm to open its closed eyes. That charm
was Hebrew grammar. A thoughtful monk, sitting in
his lonely cell, first found its efficacy in his own enlightenment, and forcing his way through the brushwood and under-
growth of centuries awoke the sleeper. That monk was
Nicolas of Lyra.[3]

Since the days of Ibn Ezra († 1167), a change had come
over the spirit of the Jewish commentators. He had distinguished between five methods of Biblical commentary :—

---

[1] A word of at least passing recognition should be given to the textual and
practical (though hardly to the exegetical) labours of Hugo of St. Cher (†1260),
who in his *Correctoria* attempted some improvement of the text of the
Vulgate. His book first made the division of the Bible into chapters general.
His efforts were due to the hints of the greatest genius of the thirteenth
century, Roger Bacon.

[2] So called from his birthplace, Lyra, in Normandy. Sixtus Senensis
says : "Natione *Anglus* vel . . . . . ex Lyra *Brabantiae* oppido." *Bibl.
Sanct.* p. 276. There seems to be little or no proof of the common notion
that he was, on his mother's side, of Jewish birth. At an early age he
became a Franciscan.

[3] Merx, *Eine Rede vom Auslegen.*

The Verbal, which dwells on every separate word.

The purely Subjective, which pays no attention at all to tradition.

The Allegoric, which reads mysteries into the sacred text.

The Kabbalistic, which develops secrets out of letters, numbers, and syllables.

The Literal, which confines itself to developing the actual meaning of the writers.[1]

Of these five methods he had himself chosen the last. In the same century the labours of the Qimchis had greatly facilitated the study of Hebrew grammar. Rashi († 1170), while following traditional views, had done much to elucidate the literal sense, and Maimonides "the Light of the West," "the Eagle of the Rabbis" († 1204), whom the stricter Jews of his day regarded as a rationalist, had practically rejected much of Talmudism, and reverting to the written Law had endeavoured to show by Aristotelian and Alexandrian methods that the written Law was founded on immutable reason.[2] Nicolas had studied Rashi and had often followed him so closely as to be called *Simia Salomonis*.[3] He seems intuitively to have seized on some of the best principles hitherto enunciated. Here and there he had met with hints as to the corruption of manuscripts; the necessity for a better text; the importance of understanding the original languages; the folly of splitting up texts into endless fragments; the difference between true exposition and a confused chaos of possible suggestions; the primary duty of

---

[1] See Sale's *Koran*, p. 87.

[2] On the Jewish mediaeval interpreters see Schröck, *K. G.* xxv. 391 ; Rosenmüller, *Hist. Interp.* v. 211, *sq.* ; Meyer, i. 85-93 ; Merx, *Joel*, 207-296 ; Siegfried " Ueber Rashi's Einfluss " (Merx, *Archiv*, i. 431). In the latter paper is shown the extent of Rashi's influence over Luther as well as over Nicolas of Lyra.

[3] Rashi is the abbreviated name of Rabbi Solomon Jizchaki. It was probably from Rashi that Lyra learnt the admirable old rule which he renders " *Scriptura loquitur secundum modum nostrum loquendi* " (note on Gen. viii. 1, " Recordatus est "). Nicolas says, " Intendo non solum doctorum catholicorum sed etiam Hebraiorum explanationes, maxime R. Salomon, qui inter doctores Hebraeos locutus est rationabilius ad declarationem sensus literalis (פשט)."

building all developments upon a secure basis of the literal
sense. Nicolas combines these views. He does not ostensibly
abandon the current opinions. His definitions, divisions,
and terminology show that he is still a Schoolman.[1] He
repeats the phrase that God is the *auctor principalis* of
Scripture, and follows Thomas Aquinas in the remark that
the literal sense develops the meaning of the words, and the
mystic sense the meaning of the things which the words
signify.[2] He even adopts the seven rules of Tichonius, and
repeats the common definitions of the fourfold sense,[3] and
gives the stock illustration which was supposed to be
furnished by the word " Jerusalem." On the other hand he
evinces rare clearness and sobriety ; he insists on the Protestant
principle of referring to the original ; he complains that the
mystic sense had been almost allowed to choke (*suffocare*) the
literal ; he says that when the mystic exposition is discrepant
from the literal it is *indecens et inepta ;* [4] he demands that the
literal sense alone should be used in proving doctrines.[5]
Practically, therefore, he only admits two possible senses—

---

[1] He characteristically meets the objection that "either man must now
have a rib too few and be imperfect, or must have had one too many, and be a
monster," by the remark that a thing may be superfluous, *ratione individui*,
but not *ratione speciei.*

[2] Thom. Aquin. *Summa*, 1, Qu. 1, art. 10. Nicolas says, "Habet ille
liber hoc speciale, quod una litera continet plures sensus."

[3] To him are attributed the lines—

" *Littera* gesta docet, quae credas *Allegoria*,
Moralis quid agas, quo tendas *Anagogia ;* "

but he only quotes them in his first preface, where he explains the four senses.
In his second preface he compares Scripture to the book written *within* (the
mystic sense) and *without* (the literal sense).

[4] "Vel saltem minus decens ceteris paribus et apta," he cautiously adds.
Lyra firmly states his object in the words, " *Cum Dei adjutorio intendo circa
literalem sensum insistere, et paucas valde et breves expositiones mysticas ali-
quando interponere ; licet raro.*" Prol. 2.

[5] "Cum ex solo sensu literali et non ex mystico posset argumentum fieri
ad probandum." He wrote eighty-five books of Postills, of which fifty were
literal and thirty-five *moralitates.* The name *Postilla* is as old as the eighth
century, and is derived from *post illa* (*s.c.* verba textus). If we read Nicolas
of Lyra on Gen. i. after Hugo of St. Cher we see an immense advance. In
the "allegoric" division of the fourfold sense in Hugo, "*Creavit coelum*"
becomes "He made the New Testament ;" both Testaments are *coelum*,
regarded on the side of Christ's Divinity, *terra* on the side of His humanity.
The Old and New Testaments are symbolised by the coverings of the tabernacle (Ex. xxvi.) made *opere plumario.* "Pluma est acus, acus vero Christus,
perforatus in passione, pungit in secundo sicut acus," &c., &c.

the literal and the mystic, and he founds the latter exclusively upon the former. No mere eclectic, he everywhere exhibits a vigorous independence and originality with the clear feeling that he is opening fresh paths. He does not hesitate sometimes to prefer the explanations of Rashi and the Jews to those of the idolised Latin Fathers, even in passages which had been accepted Messianically; and sometimes he sets aside both Jewish and Christian interpretations in favour of some view of his own.[1] While, therefore, he wrote in a tone of extreme modesty, and submitted all his works to the decision of the Church,[2] he did more than any other writer to break down the tyranny of ecclesiastical tradition, and to overthrow the blind belief in the bad method of many centuries. The old proverb *Si Lyra non lyrasset, Lutherus non saltasset* may only express a popular view of history; but Luther, while blaming his dependence on Rashi, both made great use of Lyra and expressed for him the utmost admiration.[3] He can have no juster eulogy than the distich of his epitaph—

> " Littera nempe nimis quae quondam obscura jacebat,
> Omnes per partes clara labore meo est." [4]

Although the folios of Lyra almost immediately drove other commentaries, except the *Glossa ordinaria,* into

---

[1] See his note on Gen. xlix. 11, where he says, " Exponunt de Christi passione sed ista expositio videtur mihi magis mystica quam literalis." He refuses to see any allusion to the Trinity in Gen. xviii. 1.

[2] He modestly says that he has only written *Scholastice et in modum exercitii,* and subjects his views to the correction *sanctae matris ecclesiae et cujuslibet sapientis.* The vigour of his independence is well shown in his comment on Ezek. xl.–xlviii. (on which see Hengstenberg, *Christologie,* ii. 595 ; Merx, *Joel,* 331–335). He examines the views of Rashi, Jerome, Gregory, Richard, and Hugo of St. Victor, and differs from them all for the better.

[3] Luther said, " Ego Lyranum ideo amo et inter optimos pono quod ubique diligenter retinet et persequitur historiam, quamquam auctoritate Patrum se vinci patitur et nonnunquam eorum exemplo deflectit . . . ad ineptas allegorias." Flacius (*Catal.* xviii. 809) speaks of him no less highly. In Luther's comment on Genesis (as Siegfried has proved) Lyra is traceable in almost every verse. Luther adds little to him except polemical and dogmatic biblicism. R. Simon, iii. 432.

[4] On Nicolas of Lyra see Fabric. *Bibl. Lat.* v. 114 *sq.*; Le Long, *Bibl. Sacr.* iii. 357, *sq.* ; Rosenmüller, *Hist. Int.* v. 280 ; Flacius, *Catal. test. Verit.* xviii.; Buddeus, *Isagoge,* 1420, *sq.* ; Meyer, *Gesch. d. Schrifterkl.* i. 109–121 ; Diestel, pp. 198-201 ; Merx, *Joel,* 305–335 ; Klausen, *Hermeneutik,* p. 210 ; Grätz, *Gesch. d. Jud.* vii. 513 &c.

oblivion, he had no adequate followers.[1] The converted Jew, Solomon Levita, known as Paulus of Burgos († 1435), published *Additiones* to Nicolas of Lyra, which were purely reactionary,[2] and deserved the *Correctorium corruptoris Burgensis* of Matthias Doring.[3] Paulus repeats the old secular misquotation of "the letter killeth," and makes the slavish and sophistic remark that, "Since God is the author of Scripture, and must have intended the literal sense, the Church decision always *must* be the literal sense, even when it seems least to resemble it."[4] This argument, which has been repeated by a leading theologian in the last decade, makes God responsible for the follies and ignorances of men. It recklessly confuses predestination with foreknowledge, and it amounts to saying that if a passage has been universally misunderstood, the misconception or perversion of it must have been a part of the intended meaning![5] Thus does theological error try to hide itself under the shield of omnipotence, and to fulminate its ignorances with the voice of infallibility.

After the death of Nicolas of Lyra there was no important addition to the study of Scripture till the dawn of the Reformation. Wiclif, indeed, made the important remark that "the whole error in the knowledge of Scripture, and the source of its debasement and falsification by incompetent

---

[1] See Paul. Burgens. *Prol. Addit.* In some lines by Angelo Rocca (*Bibl. Theol. Epitome,* 1594) he says, in a patronising way,

"*At brevis et facilis, non est spernenda tironi,*
Lyrensis expositio.*"

Pope in the *Dunciad* (i. 153) says of the bookshelves of Colley Cibber,—

"De Lyra there a dreadful front extends;"

and adds in his note that De Lyra's works were printed in five vast folio volumes in 1472. Pope may possibly have confused him with Harpsfield; if so he gives a wrong date.

[2] He repeatedly returns to the unnatural glosses which Lyra's honesty and good sense had rejected.

[3] Doring called his book *Replicae defensivae.* See Buddeus, *Isag.* p. 1433.

[4] "Sensus literalis non debet dici ille qui repugnat ecclesiae auctoritati." *Prol. in Additiones.* So too Gerson, "Sensus literalis judicandus est prout ecclesia . . . determinavit." *Propp. de sens. lit.* 3.

[5] This dangerous notion is first found in Augustine, and is repeated by Cocceius, "Impossibile est aliquid fieri in mundo de quo verba Spiritus Sancti usurpari possunt, *ut id non intuitus sit Spiritus S. . . . et non voluerit legentem ea verba ei rei accommodare.*"

persons, was the ignorance of grammar and logic ; " [1] and Hus by the sobriety of his writings earned the praise of Luther, that he was "skilful and weighty in the treatment of Scripture." The value of Savonarola's comments is exclusively practical.[2] The *Propositiones de sensu literali* of Gerson († 1429) lay down some excellent principles, but he entirely nullifies their value by making the interpretation of Scripture depend exclusively on the authority of the Church.[3]

His comments on the Canticles and the Penitential Psalms, apart from their devotional remarks, are of the poorest description. Picus of Mirandola († 1494) was chiefly occupied with Platonism and Kabbalism.[4] Tostatus († 1454), the *"Stupor mundi qui scibile discutit omne,"* turned to but poor account his knowledge of Hebrew, used Nicolas of Lyra often without acknowledgment, and filled his interminable pages with irrelevant disquisitions, prolix speculations, and valueless questions.[5] Turrecremata († 1468) blindly followed the old traditional lines. The Jewish convert, Jacob Perez of Valentia († 1492), mixed them up with the poorest lees of Rabbinism.[6] John Wessel—*Lux Mundi*—who

---

[1] *Trialog.* i. 8. On his views see Vaughan, ii. 315. Wiclif is allegorical and dialectical in his own methods, but he said that "all things necessary in Scripture are contained in its proper literal and historic sense."

[2] Savonarola's sermons are full of the fourfold sense (see Villari, i. 114, E. T.).

[3] See *Propp.* iii. vi. vii. *Opp.* 1, 3, ed. Du Pin.

[4] See Pic. Mirand. *Opp.* p. 71, and Cudworth, *Intellect. Syst.* 301, *sq.* ; Archangelus, *Artis Kabbal. Scriptores,* 1587.

[5] Such as, Was Adam wiser than Solomon ? Did he name the fish which could not be brought to him ? If God ceased to create after the six days, how come creatures to be formed out of putrefaction ? &c. In the New Testament, Was it fit that the Virgin should be married ? Why did not Joseph ask her, *quomodo conceperit ?* Quid faciebant parentes videntes eam praegnantem ? &c. On Matt. iii. 25, *Quomodo movebatur ista columba ?* . . . Si fuit vera columba potuit moveri multipliciter. Uno modo a vento, &c., &c.! Seven folios were devoted to St. Matthew and one to the fifth chapter alone ! His works occupied twenty-seven massive folios. The value of his verbal disquisitions on the New Testament may be estimated by the fact that he argues from the Vulgate. Hence his glaring errors about the word παραδειγματίσαι and ῥῆμα (Matt. i. 19 ; iv. 4).

[6] Not content with the seven rules of Tichonius he adds three more of the same kind. In Ps. xxii. 12 he makes the "garments" the letter and the mystic sense of the Old Testament. He makes the four-cornered Psaltery a type of the four Evangelists ; the ten strings are the ten mysteries. The triangular harp indicates the three virtues, and the three marks of holiness (*visio, tentatio, fruitio*). The timbrel, which is beaten, is a type of Christ's sufferings.

died in 1489, was, indeed, an excellent expounder, and was
warmly appreciated by Luther ; but in this respect he stands
almost alone.[1] In the Mammothrectus, a book which Erasmus
says made him nearly die with laughing, we reach the lowest
depths of imbecility ; but it must simply be regarded as an
illustration of the profound ignorance of the clergy in the
age in which he lived.[2] During the whole of this epoch the
Greek Church produced *Catenae*, but little else.

It does not fall under my subject to trace the history of
Scholasticism itself. Its ruin was due partly to its own excesses and divisions, partly to the general awakenment of the
human mind.[3] With Duns Scotus († 1308) begins the decay
which ended in dissolution. His constant phrase " it cannot
be *proved* that" led to scepticism. His purely negative
criticism, and his method of *quodlibets*—the statement of arguments *pro* and *contra* without any mediation—gradually dissolved the union between faith and science which Anselm had
endeavoured to establish. Hence Hauréau calls his system
"Spinozism before Spinoza." He also, as well as Raymond
Lulli († 1315), helped to open men's eyes to the fact that
the whole school system dealt far more with words than with
things. What Wetstein calls " the tyrannous and exclusive
dominance of that methodic, dry, dead, wooden, strawy, artificial theology which was a mixture of philosophy, technicality,
and dialectics," was rendered *ipso facto* impossible, when, as
Erasmus tells us, a " theologian" could boast "that it would
take more than nine years to understand what Duns Scotus
wrote as a mere preface to the *Sentences ;* and that unless a
man had all the metaphysical system of Scotus in his head,

The first Psalm refutes the Stoics, Peripatetics, Avicenna, Algazel, &c. In
the third we see Christ's sufferings ; in the fourth His miracles ; in the fifth
the Pharisees ; in the sixth the Eucharist, &c. See Fabr. *Bibl. Lat.* iv. 102 ;
Meyer, i. 322 *sq.* (who quotes some deplorable specimens). The "sensus *mere*
literalis " is to him always " *inutilis.*"

[1] See Ullmann, *Reformers before the Reformation.* For the views of Anton
de Nebrissa I can simply refer to Meyer, i. 332-339.

[2] " *Nuper cum in hunc codicem incidissem, minimum abfuit quin risu
dissilirem.*" Erasm. *Colloq.* 561. The author of the book was Joannes
Marchesinus. For a kindly remark about him see Hallam, *Lit. of Europe,*
i. 286*n.* See too Sixtus Senensis, p. 273.

[3] See Hergenröther, i. 953.

he could not understand one sentence of his writings." Men began to perceive that years of study of these subtle technicalities only made them masters of a cumbrous and useless terminology, and took them no nearer to the comprehension of the *incircumscriptibilitates,* as Scotus barbarously called them, which they were supposed to elucidate.[1]

The system of the Schools received a yet deadlier blow when WILLIAM OF OCCAM († 1347) became the subtle and clear-minded champion of nominalism. The Platonic doctrine of ideas—the belief in *Universalia ante rem*—had been the band of union between theology and philosophy. The Church had adopted the rule *Invisibilia non decipiunt,* and she had maintained that apart from Realism there could be no belief in the Trinity or in Transubstantiation. Thus Realism was favourable to dogma, for it could reason deductively from truths assumed to be certainly known. The earlier Nominalists had been crushed by accusations of heresy. Roscelin had been charged with Tritheism; Abelard with Sabellianism. Occam by arguing that universals were names, words, *flatus vocis,* which had their exclusive birth in the human reason,[2] snapped the link between theology and philosophy. His two axioms, *Entia non sunt multiplicanda praeter necessitatem* and *Frustra fit per plura quod fieri potest per pauciora,* cut away the ground under many traditional assumptions.[3] Unintentionally perhaps, but surely, Occam weakened the hold of the entire traditional system of Christianity by resting it on the authority of the Church alone, and by the absurdities, contradictions, and frivolities with which he unwisely and irreverently connected the Christian dogmas when regarded by themselves.[4] No less surely did he weaken the pride of sacerdotal tyranny, when he addressed to the Emperor Lewis of Bavaria the famous

---

[1] See Hauréau, 351–353.

[2] *Universalia post rem.* See Hampden, *Bampt. Lect.* p. 71.

[3] "Le caractère propre du nominalisme c'est la simplicité."—Hauréau. The name *Doctor Invincibilis* was given him by Pope John xxii.

[4] See Landerer, *s.v.* Scholasticism, in Herzog's *Encykl.* and *Occam und Luther* (*Theolog. Stud. u. Krit.* 1839). These extravagances chiefly occur in Occam's *Quodlibeta* and *Centilogium.*

words " *Tu me defende gladio, ego te defendam calamo ;* "[1] and when in his *Epistola Defensoria* he became the earliest defender of the Liberty of the Press.[2] The nominalist Gabriel Biel († 1495) was the last of the Schoolmen.

Nominalism rejects the ideas of Plato, yet the reintroduction of Platonic studies in the fifteenth century had their share also in the downfall of Scholasticism.[3] It led the way to a freer and more spiritual Christianity. The study of Plato was not monopolised by the semi-pagan humanists. St. Thomas Aquinas had spoken of Augustine as "*doctrinis Platonicorum imbutus.*"[4] Lorenzo de Medici went so far as to say, that " without Plato a man could not well be a good citizen or skilled in Christian doctrine."[5] The Fathers had been Platonists.[6] "*Academia Platonis Ecclesiae velut vestibulum,*" says Baronius. Ficino, the translator of Plato, also lectured on St. Paul. Colet, whose name stands so deservedly high among English theologians, studied Plato as well as Plotinus and Dionysius. The Church had long been under the sway of Aristotle, and had much to learn from Plato's analytic method of searching for truth instead of starting from synthetic maxims. " The most zealous defenders of Christianity," says Van Heusden,[7] " have esteemed the doctrine of Plato a prelude to the truest Christianity." Christian students thought that they found Platonic idealism in the Epistle to the Hebrews.[8] The works of Plato had become known to Europe in the Revival of Letters, and it has been said that the Christian Mirandola was as eager in the cause of reconciling Plato with Aristotle, as the anti-Christian Porphyry

---

[1] In 1328.

[2] Hauréau, ii. 420. Marsilio of Padua is said to have learnt from Occam the fine conceptions of liberty which appear in his *Defensor Pacis.*

[3] All that was known of Plato by mediaeval scholars was derived from a translation by Chalcidius of part of the *Timaeus*, references in St. Augustine, and the *De dogmate Platonis* of Apuleius. Ueberweg, i. 367.

[4] *Summ.* i. qu. 84, art. 5.

[5] Valorius, *Laurentii Medici Vita,* p. 18.

[6] See Aug. *De Civ. Dei*, viii. 12 ; *c. Academ.* iii. 19, " In multis quae ad philosophiam pertinent Augustinus utitur opinionibus Platonis." Thom. Aq. *Summ.* i. qu. 77, art. 5.

[7] *Characterismi*, p. 189.

[8] Even in its most Aristotelian epoch the Church was Realist. Thomas Aquin. *Summa Ima. qu.* xv. 1 ; xliv. 3.

had been twelve centuries before. This was one object of the nine hundred theses with which, at the age of twenty-four, he challenged the Christian world in Rome. Platonism and Nominalism were opposite influences, but each of them acted as a solvent on the hard shell of the Scholastic system.[1] Their work was powerfully aided by the development of Commerce, the growth of the Universities,[2] the spread of inductive philosophy, the Revival of Letters, the acquaintance with the great mediaeval Jewish commentators, the increasing study of Hebrew and other languages, and the immorality and ignorance of the monks and clergy which tended to bring their extravagant pretensions into absolute contempt.

The defects of scholastic exegesis were due to many causes. 1. One of these, and the source of all the rest, was a vague, superstitious, unproved, and purely traditional conception of inspiration. It was confused with verbal dictation, and the Bible was turned into an amulet or fetish with which the hierarchy, which arrogantly usurped the name of "the Church," could do as they liked. The result was "to nullify the use of Scripture as a record of the divine dealings with the successive generations of mankind. The voice of God was no longer heard as it spoke at sundry times and in divers manners to holy men of old, but simply as uttering the hallowed symbols of an oracular wisdom. The whole of Scripture was treated as one contemporaneous production of which the several parts might be expounded without reference to the circumstances in which each was delivered." And thus the Bible was degraded to the level of the Koran, and "the piety of the Schoolmen became a superstition, transubstantiating the Word of God into the verbal elements by which it was signified."[3] A false and extravagant system of

---

[1] See Mosheim, *De turbatâ per recentiores Platonicos Eccl.* 1677 ; Brucker, *Miscell. Hist. Philos.* 1748 ; Delacluze, *Florence et Ses Vicissitudes*, 1837.

[2] On the growth of the universities see Cardinal Hergenröther, *K. G.* 946–952. He attributes the fall of Scholasticism to an "hochgetriebene Sucht nach Spitzfindigkeiten, innere Zerwürfnisse, und das Ueberwiegen der humanistischen Studien." See too Ueberweg, *Hist. of Philos.* ii. 34, 461.

[3] Hampden, *Bampt. Lect.* pp. 88-92. The Fathers, the Church canons, and the forged decretals of Isidore were also treated as more or less "inspired."

interpretation has always been the Nemesis of a false and extravagant theory of supernatural infallibility. Nothing but
perversion could come from this system of treating the Bible
as a series of propositions all on the same level, each absolute
in itself, and warranting every inference which could be
logically deduced from the phraseology.

2. The whole system of Scholasticism necessarily fell with
the Renaissance and the Reformation, because it had been
essentially fettered, papal, sacerdotal, and monkish.[1] When
Constantinople had been taken by the Turks in 1453, and
the intellect of Europe once more came into close contact
with the glorious literature of antiquity; when the invention
of printing led to a tenfold diffusion of knowledge; when the
vernacular languages were used in every branch of general
education; when the laity discovered that the Church had
no longer the pretension to any monopoly of knowledge—
Scholasticism was doomed. It was not only *Philosophia
ancilla Theologiae*, but *Philosophia in servitutem theologiae
papeae redacta*.[2] It was the vassalage of philosophy which
was forbidden to stir beyond impassable limits fixed by the
dogmas of the Church.[3] If alike the humanists and the
Reformers—on the one hand men like Faber Stapulensis,
Sadoletus, Hermolaus Barbarus, Laurentius Valla, Bacon,
Descartes, and the Encyclopaedists, on the other Erasmus
and Luther—have spoken of the whole system with the
bitterest disdain, it must be remembered that for more
than four centuries it exercised a colossal tyranny, and
often used that tyranny on behalf of the Papal usurpations,
the monastic system, and the obscurantist theories which
became objects of deadly antipathy to many minds.

3. A third cause of the failure of Scholasticism was the lack
of due equipment in the writers.

[1] Peter Damian said that human intellect was not to claim mastership "sed
velut ancilla dominae quodam famulatus obsequio subservire." The Council of
Constance forbade laymen to teach in public, "sed aurem iis qui docendi
gratiam acceperint aperire" (*Can.* 64).
[2] Heumann, Prol. to Tribbechovius, *De doctr. Schol. et Corrupta per eos div.
hum. rerum Scientia*, 1665.
[3] Ueberweg, *Hist. Phil.* i. 66.

For instance the historic feeling and the critical faculty are entirely in abeyance in their writings. The narratives of the Old Testament are rich with human experiences, and full of interest, warning, and instruction. Those of the New Testament are not only infinitely pathetic, but contain the very heart of God's revelation of Himself in the life of men. Yet for all that is real and deep in these narratives, literally understood, the claustral narrowness of mediaeval exegesis had no feeling whatever.[1] Ignorant for the most part of classical literature, and therefore destitute of a training which was invaluable to the greatest of the Fathers, the Schoolmen were also cut off from a true knowledge of life by the narrowing walls and soul-dwarfing externalism of their monastic routine. For us the history of David thrills with life, beauty, and divine attractiveness; for the Schoolmen David became for the most part a dull and misty abstraction, and his Psalms cumbrous and obscure enigmas. "Here," says Albertus, writing on the forty-first Psalm, "the whole Church is called David, which groaning desires to reach its end." In the narrative of the Transfiguration, "Jesus," he says, "signifies the preaching of the gospel;" "Peter, one who learns;" "John, one in whom is the grace of God;" "James, a supplanter." Jesus took them up the mountain "after six days" because the world was made in six days, or, as St. Luke says, "after eight days," because the Resurrection was on the eighth day.[2] "They therefore who have ascended above the world can be led by the words of the Gospel into the mountains of sublime intelligence" and so forth. If we turn to the *Catena Aurea* of St. Thomas Aquinas, we find him quoting Rabanus Maurus, who explains the six days as a reference to the six ages before the Resurrection; and

---

[1] Even "the Universal Doctor," Albertus Magnus, numbers the Pythagoreans among the Stoics, calls Socrates a Macedonian, and says that Empedocles and Anaxagoras were Italians. See Elster, *De Med. Aevi Theol. exeget.* p. 39.

[2] The helplessness with which the reader is left to choose between "six days" (Matt. xvii. 1) and "eight days" (Luke ix. 28), without a glimpse of direction as to which period was meant, is very characteristic. There is not an attempt to give the very obvious solution of the apparent discrepancy.

Origen, who refers them to the six days of creation; and he thinks that the Three Apostles remind us of Shem, Ham, and Japheth, *or* (as Hilary says) of the Holy Trinity! With the historic sense thus atrophied it does not surprise us to find that the critical faculty is also dead; that though the Scriptures are declared to be written "by the Triune God," the Apocrypha and the Fathers are put very nearly on a level with them; that the Celestial Hierarchy could be confidently attributed to St. Paul's Athenian convert; and that even Roger Bacon supposes that the Church did not admit the Book of Enoch and the Testament of the Twelve Patriarchs into the Canon only " because of their too great antiquity."[1]

4. The neglect of Philology by the Schoolmen was equally fatal. Only one or two of them possessed even a smattering of Hebrew, and the vast majority of them were no less ignorant of Greek.[2] They philosophised and theologised over what they assumed to be the supernatural accuracy of largely vitiated manuscripts of a very imperfect translation; and often with no better aid than heterogeneous glosses from the Fathers, and those not unfrequently from poor versions and spurious writings. And as they "rack the text and so to speak drag it along by the hair," they constantly rely on the most grotesque etymologies.[3] If, as Luther said,

---

[1] *Opus Majus*, ii. 8. He said that they contained the articles of faith " *longe expressius quam in canone.*" Roger Bacon had hinted at the relative freedom of non-biblical branches of knowledge, but his view was not accepted. Hugo said that the Bible contains " *totius universi continentiam* " and it was used to settle all questions alike.

[2] Even Thomas Aquinas, if he knew some Greek, "has in several instances quite missed the sense of the Greek."—Newman.

[3] See the *Calendarium Etymologicum* (Hilarius = altus ares. Ignatius = ignem patius, &c.) Brucker, iii. 854. Roger Bacon derives παρασκευὴ from *parari coenam.* Hervaeus Dolensis derives *epistola* from *epi* and *stola*, and says that they were so called because they were sent over and above the Gospels. Hugo of St. Victor derives ἅγιος from ἀ and γῆ. Thomas Aquinas, terra—quia *teritur* pedibus ; tenebras—quasi *tenens umbram ;* abyssus from *a* and *byssus*, or *a* and *basis.* Albertus derives Endymion from *en* and *dymion*, " intellect ; " Durandus Alleluia from Alle *salvum*, leu, *me*, and ja, *fac ;* Hervaeus Dolensis says that Timotheus means " beneficial " and that the Epistle to the Hebrews was written to *those who had crossed over* from worldliness. See Tribbechovius *De Doctoribus Scholasticis* (1719), pp. 212 *sqq.*, or a curious later specimen, see Colet's *Letters to Radulphus* (ed. Lupton), p. 81. A very wonderful list might be made of the inferences drawn from absurd etymologies and sheer mistakes. In the *Glossa Ordinaria* Amram (= *pater excelsus*) is Christ ; Jochebed (= *Dei Gratia*) is the Church : from their union

"the science of theology is nothing else than grammar applied to the words of the Holy Spirit," the Schoolmen were indeed ill-prepared. In Heb. ii. 9 Thomas Aquinas, following Primasius, mistakes *gratiâ Dei* ($\chi \acute{a} \rho \iota \tau \iota$ $\Theta \epsilon o \hat{v}$) for a nominative and a title of Christ. He says that the name Paul cannot be of Hebrew origin because the Hebrew does not possess the letter P, but it may be from a word beginning with a letter like P, in which case it means "wonderful" or "elect;" if it be a Greek word it means "quiet;" if Latin, it means "small;" and he proceeds at great length to show from Scripture how each of these three meanings suits St. Paul! Gregory the Great said that it was of no consequence to know who wrote any particular book of Scripture, because we do not enquire with what pen a great writer wrote, and the sacred writers are only pens of the Triune God.

5. It naturally resulted from these defects that much of the exegesis of even the greatest Schoolmen consisted in an arbitrary juxtaposition of texts, a mere abuse of imaginary verbal resemblances. The method of Thomas Aquinas seems to have been to explain a passage by adducing all the other places where *in the Latin version* the same prominent word occurs. Thus, on Isaiah lx. 1, he chooses the texts in which "light" occurs; on Isaiah xliv. 3, he draws out a scheme of three ways in which "*the Spirit*" is given severally to beginners, to proficients, and to the perfect. When "washing" is spoken of, he collects the texts, and says that we are washed by water of baptism (Acts xxii. 16); by tears of contrition (Luke vii. 38); by the wine of Divine love (Gen. xlix. 11); by the milk of the Divine Word (Cant. v. 12); with the blood of the Passion (1 Cor. vi. 11); and with a view to our correction (John xiii. 5). This may be harmless when it is simply artificial, but it is sometimes purely misleading, as in the note of Albertus Magnus on Psalm lxix. 3, where he tries to show that the meaning of the word "substance" is fourfold—a matter which has nothing to do with his text—

comes Moses (!) who is the spiritual law; and Aaron the clergy. For other etymologies see Binder, *Scholastica Theologia*, p. 34.

from the uses of the word *substantia* in the Vulgate.[1] Here, again, is the comment of St. Thomas Aquinas on Isaiah xi. 1, " There shall come forth a rod out of the stem of Jesse." The Blessed Virgin, he says, is " a rod." (1) As *consoling* in tribulation, which he illustrates by the *rod* of Moses dividing the Red Sea. (2) As *fructifying*, because Aaron's *rod* budded. (3) As *satiating*, because the *rod* of Moses drew water from the rock. (4) As *scourging*, because a *rod* was to smite the corners of Moab. (5) As *watching*, because in Jer. 1. 11, we read in the Vulgate *Virgam vigilantem ego video.* Unhappily, however, for this curious piece of perverted exegesis, the word for "rod," in Isaiah xi. 1, is *choter* (חֹטֶר) ; in Numbers xvii. 8, xx. 11, is *matteh* (מַטֶּה) ; and in Jer. i. 11, is *maqqeel* (מַקֵּל) and means " an early or wakeful tree " (A.V. " rod of an almond tree," LXX. βακτηρίαν καρυΐνήν). The parallel passages are therefore no parallels at all, and the only light thrown on the passage, apart from its arbitrary application to the Virgin, is a false and fantastic light. This concordance-like juxtaposition of the purely semblable identities of expression furnished by a translator has misled exegetes since the days of Hillel, who invented it. If it were justifiable, the Manichees had a perfect right to explain " In sole posuit tabernaculum suum " (Psalm xix. 4) to mean that Christ had ascended incorporeally to the Father, leaving His *tabernacle, i.e.* His body, in the sun. The method it appears was perfectly orthodox, though the inference was altogether heretical.

6. Another radical defect of scholastic commentaries is the abuse of the dialectic method, which led too readily to sophistry and logomachy, and even to the *mendacium officiosum* of pledged controversialists.[2]

The object of the Schoolmen is often far less to explain the meaning of a passage than to work it up dialectically,

---

[1] 1. Earthly goods (Gen. xiii. 6). 2. Stability of life. 3. Virtue (Prov. xiii. 11, sua est *substantia* cui non est peccatum in conscientia). 4. All nature.

[2] Thom. Aquin. *Summ.* II. 2 ; cx. 2 and 4. Petavius admits σοφιστικὴ and ἐριστικὴ to defeat heresy (*Dogmata, Prol.* 4, p. 14).

under the categories of Aristotle, and to arrange in the systematic form of endless subdivisions every possible lesson, which they think can be extorted from it.[1] They thought with Berengar that " God is a logician." [2] They treated theology geometrically, after the fashion of a proposition of Euclid. Spinning out of their own subjectivity by the aid of objections, solutions, definitions, conclusions, corollaries, propositions, proofs, replies, reasons, refutations, exceptions, and distinctions,[3] they weave, as Bacon said, interminable webs, " marvellous for the tenacity of the thread and workmanship, but for any useful purpose trivial and inane." [4] " In divine things," says Ludovicus Vives, " they divide, singularise, particularise, completely, incompletely, as though they were dealing with an apple." [5] Hence follows that *coacervatio*, as Sixtus Senensis calls it, which is so inexpressibly wearisome. A perfectly empty schematism led to a boundless prolixity. Langenstein in four large folios had only got to the fourth chapter of Genesis, and more real elucidation of the meaning could probably be given in four lines. Hasselbach wrote twenty-four books on the first chapter of Isaiah,[6] and an indefinitely truer conception of its meaning could be furnished in two pages. It took mankind several centuries to arrive at the conviction that " it had not pleased God to

---

[1] As early even as Lanfranc, the dogmatics of the day are set forth in the scholastic manner, with syllogisms and dialectic examination of proofs and counterproofs. "They did not *define* doctrine," says Baur, "they refined upon it." *Versöhnungslehre*, p. 147.

[2] Ampère, *Hist. Lit. de France*, iii. 333.

[3] Erasm. *Encom. Mor.* p. 193 (ed. 1696).

[4] Bacon, *De Augm. Scient.* i. 16. "This degenerate kind of learning was chiefly prevalent among the Schoolmen, who, having sharp wits, abundant leisure, small variety of reading, and knowing little history, whether of nature or time, spun laborious webs of learning which are extant in their books."

[5] Lud. Vives, *De Corrupt. Art.* I.; *ap.* Tribbechovius, *De Doctor. Schol.* p. 24 Some accuse Abelard (Trithemius, *Cat. S. E.* p. 97), others Peter Lombard (Aventinus *Annal.* vi. Baur, *Dogmengesch.* p. 159), some Duns Scotus (*Sent.* iii. *dist.* 24, *qu.* 1. See Brucker, ii. 875), and some Albertus (see Vaughan, *Life of St. Thomas*, i. 248) of thus "introducing Aristotle into Christianity."

[6] The phantom of a "multiple sense" led them yet deeper into these quagmires of prolixity. Bede boasts that a single line of Scripture is so fecund that it " will fill many pages with the sweetness of its spiritual meaning."

U

reveal His salvation in dialectics," and that " dialectics are inefficacious if unsupported by other knowledge." [1] Duns Scotus had said that the certitude of the Scriptures is a certitude not of reason but of authority; that they give no demonstrations and do not argue *definitive et devise.*[2] Scholasticism made the vain attempt to remedy the supposed deficiency, and by trying to combine word-splitting and stringent dogmatism became at once servile and tyrannical.[3]

7. A fatal defect was the barbarous nature of their language. "Person" is defined in a mass of verbiage which could not possibly convey a definite meaning to the mind of a single learner. Erasmus said that if Jerome or Augustine could have come to life again they would have been derided for their ignorance, because they could not have understood such portentous words as "instances, relations, ampliations, restrictions, formalities, haecceities, and quiddities." Everything was considered alien from theologic erudition which was not intertwisted with thorny syllogisms, and if St. Paul was quoted to the later Schoolmen they imagined themselves removed to another world.[4] That special theological mystery the *circuminsessio,* and *communicatio idiomatum,* in other words, the relation to each other of the two Natures in the Person of Christ, is defined as "*Subsistentis in subsistente realiter distincto mutua praesentialitis assistentia in eadem essentia.*" The Hypostatic union is "*Relatio disquiparentiae realis quidem in uno extremo cui in altero nulla realis relatio respondet.*"[5] These are but slight specimens of a terminology which rapidly degenerated into a nonsensical jargon. Even Nicolas of Lyra gives an account of the word *act,* of which so learned a scholar as Dr. Siegfried is compelled to ask, " whether in any age whatever any human being whatever

---

[1] Johann. Sarisbur. *Metalog.* ii. 9.

[2] Duns Scot. *Opp.* ii. 175.

[3] See Maurice, *Med. Philosophy,* p. 154.

[4] Erasm, *De Rat. Ver. Theol.* p. 87.

[5] " Hujusmodi tricarum" says Erasmus (on 1 Tim. i. 6) " apud istos plena sunt omnia." " Ea explicant verbis non modo sordidis sed adeo obscuris et involutis ut tanti non sit sic discere." On this use of mere words see the admirable remarks of Locke, *Ess. on the Hum. Understanding,* ii. cx. § 4.

could have possibly gained from it a single distinct conception?"[1]

8. Yet their barbarous phraseology was not half so pernicious as their micrological subtlety: what Bacon calls their unwholesome and vermiculate questions, their vain imaginations, vain altercations and vain affectations. Such wordy wars about mere nomenclature were foredoomed to sterility. When they had ploughed aside philology and history with the share of empty speculation, over the whole field of their exegesis

"Infelix lolium et steriles dominantur avenae."[2]

The *"quodlibetarii"* were worse offenders in this matter than the *"Sententiarii"* or *"Summistae."* They abounded in what Calvin calls the "wandering speculations that ravish unto them light spirits."[3]

St. Paul's one word, ματαιολογία, sums up folios of the scholastic *quodlibets.* The question how many angels could dance upon the point of a pin is only an *instantia elucescens* of futility, nor is it more intrinsically absurd than St. Thomas's serious discussion of such *quaestiunculae*, as whether angels could be in two places at once; or whether many angels could be in the same place at once; or whether Adam in a state of innocence could discern the essence of angels; or whether local distance has any effect on the speech of angels; or whether there is a definite number of angels, and whether

---

[1] Siegfried, *Rashis Einfluss über Nic. v. Lyra und Luther* (Merx, *Archiv.*, i. 431). The one man to whom, besides St. John, the Church has allowed the title of "the Divine," Gregory of Nazianzus, bewails the growth of theological technicalities. Διάπτυέ μοι ἐνστάσεις καὶ τὰς ἀντιθέσεις τῆς νέας εὐσέβειας καὶ τὴν μικρολόγον σοφίαν . . . ἐν δίδασκε φοβεῖσθαι μόνον, τὸ λύειν τὴν πίστιν ἐν τοῖς σοφίσμασιν. *Orat.* xxiii.

[2] Sixtus Senensis who, like Luther, was educated in Scholasticism, speaks of it with equal disfavour (*Bibl. Sanct.* p. 218). He says that the five methods of the Schoolmen were, 1. *Divisio,* applied to the shortest clauses. 2. *Distinctio,* applied to nearly every word. 3. *Allegatio,* the reference to endless authorities, &c. See his sketch of a scholastic sermon, with its references to material, formal, efficient, and final causes ; its Prooems, Tractatio, Mysteries, Narratio, questions from Albert, Alexander, &c., and illustrations from the *Manipulus Florum* and *Polyanthea.*

[3] "La première fois que Casaubon vint en Sorbonne . . . on lui dit 'Voilà une salle où il y a quatre cents ans qu'on dispute :' il dit 'Qu' a-t-on décidé ?'" *Menagiana,* ii. 387 (Pattison's *Casaubon,* p. 479).

they all belong to the same genus, and whether they are
composed of matter and form.[1] Nor is it one whit more
empty than Bonaventura's speculations as to the difference
between the morning and evening vision of celestial in-
telligences.[2] These questions are almost as meaningless as
that of Rabelais about the "chimaera buzzing in a vacuum."[3]
And this *vaniloquium*, this λεπτολεσχία, became at times
little short of blasphemous. If even St. Thomas can discuss
whether a disembodied soul can move things from one place
to another, or "can God sin if He wishes to do so?" or
"if the sacrament had been administered between the
Crucifixion and the Resurrection would Christ have died in
it?"—we cannot wonder if meaner intellects discussed such
nonsense as "whether we can say that the Son is the Father
and is not the Father," or "whether the Father produces
the Son by intellect or by will."[4] The Schoolmen fell into
the fundamental error of supposing that an elaboration of
phraseology is a science of theology, and that we can add to
our knowledge of God by dialectic formulae about Him.
Can any other name but nonsense be given to discussions

[1] St. Thomas frequently says "ut docet Dionysius;" and in the Celestial
Hierarchies there are fifteen long chapters about the distinctions, &c. of
Angels, arranged in a sort of feudal system. See Dante, *Parad.* xxviii. 97.
St. Thomas's argument for the number of angels is derived from the fact
that incorruptible bodies are incomparably larger than corruptible, so that it
is reasonable to suppose that immaterial substances incomparably exceed
material in number (*Summ.* i. qu. 50, *art.* 3). Duns held that any *a priori*
proof of the matter was impossible, but that it might be proved *a posteriori*
"quia tot (intelligentiae) sint necessariae ad motus orbium" (ii. *dist.* 9, qu. 4,
art. 1).

[2] See *Die Angelologie der nachscottischen Scholastik*, in Werner, ii.
181-201.

[3] Scholasticism cared all the less for genuine exegesis because it was occupied with questions to which Scripture deigned to give no answer. Hence its
exegesis was mainly an attempt to read asceticism, mysticism, and papal
supremacy into Old Testament books, especially into the Canticles. "Too
many scholars," says Jeremy Taylor, "have lived upon air and empty
nothings, falling out about nothings and being very wise about things that
are not and work not." *Via Intelligentiae.* (*Works*, viii. 384.)

[4] Lud. Vives, *De Corrupt. Art.* iii. Many such questions are given by
Binder, *De Theol. Schol.* p. 24 (1624). I select a few. "*Utrum plus conveniat
Deo non posse facere impossibile, quam impossibilia non posse fieri a Deo?
Utrum unio sit entitas aut relatio? Utrum corpus V. Mariae fuerit expositum
influentiis stellarum? Utrum Christus est tantus in una parva hostia sicut in
una magna?*" and so on. No one could condemn the "worship of inutility"
in the schools more strongly than John of Salisbury. *Polycrat.* vii. 12.

as to whether the Father begets the Divine Essence, or whether the Divine Essence begets the Son? Whether the Essence begets the Essence, or whether the Essence itself neither begets nor is begotten? Such questions, as Erasmus says, it is more learned to ignore than to know.[1] For all these years, he says, we have been frivolously cavilling in the schools whether we should say that Christ is *composed* or that He *consists* of two natures; and whether the right word to use respecting their union is "conflate," or "commixed," or "conglutinate," or "coagmentate," or "copulated," or "ferruminate." What, again, are we to say of the immense and long-continued discussions as to whether the host still continued to be the body of Christ if it was eaten by a mouse, or the wine to be His blood when tasted by an insect which had fallen into the chalice?[2] Still more degrading and shocking was the dispute with those who were called *Stercorianists*.[3] Such questions show the dangers which arise from a mixture of intellectual subtlety and dogmatic servitude, of crude materialism and unfathomable superstition. They are, as Luther says (omitting his epithet *diabolica*), "an art of litigating about idle and useless speculations." They are, as Bacon says, "*portentosae et latrantes quaestiones.*" In the long run they can lead to nothing but hypocrisy and scepticism. Might not the Schoolmen have recalled with advantage the wise caution of St. Augustine, "*Melius est dubitare de rebus occultis quam litigare de incertis*"?[4]

---

[1] *Encom. Mor.* p. 114. Gregory of Nazianzus compares such language to jugglery. ταὐτὸν ἦν ψηφοῖς τε παίζειν τὴν ὄψιν κλεπτούσαις τῷ τάχει τῆς μεταθέσεως ἢ κατορχεῖσθαι τῶν θεατῶν παντοίοις καὶ ἀνδρογύνοις λυγίσμασιν καὶ περὶ θεοῦ λέγειν καὶ ἀκούειν καινότερόν τι καὶ περίεργον. *Orat.* xxi. It is to such discussions that Pope alludes in the lines about *Paradise Lost:*

"In *quibbles* angels and archangels join,
And God the Father turns a *School Divine.*"

[2] Brulifer († 1483), who, among many others (Bonaventura, Alexander of Hales, Thomas Aquinas, Marsilius, Paulus of Burgos, Durandus, &c.), discusses the question, draws distinctions between *alvus, uterus,* and *venter ;* between *trajicere* and *projicere in ventrem ;* between *edere* and *vorare ;* between the mouse as made of earth, and as made of water, &c. *In Sent.* iv. *dist.* 13, *qu.* 5.

[3] As to this miserable controversy, the natural outcome of unspiritual superstition, see Schaff, *Med. Christianity*, ii. 552.

[4] On this subject nothing can be added to the wise remarks of Bacon, *Advancement of Learning*, and the valuable note of Erasmus on *Con-*

9. But while the Scriptural exegesis of the Schoolmen was injured by all these causes, the worst plague-spot of it was the assumption that every part of Scripture admitted of a *multiplex intelligentia.* Some teachers, as John of Salisbury said, declared in true Rabbinic style, " *singuli apices divinis pleni sunt sacramentis,*" and " *litera inutilis est nec curandum quid loquatur.*" [1] Both notions were borrowed from the school of R. Aqiba, who had been the inveterate enemy of Christian truth. They owe their parentage not to Scripture but to Talmudism and Kabbalism.[2] They filtered down to the Schoolmen through the Alexandrians and the Fathers, and were unfortunately perpetuated by the authority of Jerome and Augustine.[3] Origen was, as we have seen, the earliest to develop the conception that Scripture was written with a triple meaning ; the Latin fathers had separated his " spiritual sense" into allegoric and anagogic.[4] A favourite illustration of this

vertuntur in vaniloquium ; 1 Tim. i. 6. He speaks of them as " *de frivolis nugis sine fine digladiantes,*" and says that for ages they had in huge volumes discussed (" *usque ad clamorem, usque ad convicia*) quaestiunculae of which some were useless, others insoluble, others ridiculous, others profane. " Un des côtés les plus faux de cette scolastique *c'était de chercher et de trouver partout des erreurs.* Nous avons de ces énumérations d'erreurs qui remplissent des volumes, et souvent parmi ces prétendues erreurs condamnées, il y a de très bonnes choses." Renan.

[1] Joh. Sarisb. *Polycrat.* vii. 12. This lively thinker knew well how to warn, in similar cases, against the follies to which such a view must lead. " *Fiunt in puerilibus Academici senes ; omnem dictorum excutiunt syllabam immo et literam, dubitantes ad omnia, quaerentes semper sed nunquam ad scientiam pervenientes,*" *Metalog.* ii. 7. (He is speaking primarily of logicians.) The Faculties of Louvain and Douai called it " an intolerable and great blasphemy " to say that there was an otiose word in Scripture. " Every phrase, syllable, tittle and point, is full of a Divine sense." See Cardinal Manning *On the Insp. of Script.*

[2] The Rabbinic phrase for the *multiplex sensus* was טעמים כמה (Löw, p. 65). " The Kabbalists, who are the anatomists of words, and have a theological alchemy to draw sovereign tinctures and spirits from plain and gross literal matter, observe in every variety some great mystic signification ; but so it is almost in every Hebrew name and word." Donne, *Essays in Divinity,* p. 122.

[3] No doubt the Schoolmen could have quoted loose popular passages of the Fathers which seemed to point to " verbal dictation." But few if any of the Fathers had any clear and fixed conception of the subject. Certainly the Apostolic Fathers had not (see J. Delitzsch, *De inspir. S. Script.* Leipzig, 1872); and no less an author than Tholuck (*Die Inspirationslehre,* 1850) says that the ancient Church unmistakably held the *language* of Scripture to be human and imperfect, and ascribed to the Bible contradictions both in words and facts (see Ladd, *Dict. of S. Script.* ii. 29).

[4] They all continue to say after St. Augustine that the literal sense must

supposed fourfold sense was the word "Jerusalem," which might stand for a city, for a faithful soul, for the Church militant, or for the Church triumphant. Another was the word "water," which literally means an element; tropologically may stand for sorrow, or wisdom, or heresies, or prosperity; allegorically may refer to baptism, nations, or grace; anagogically to eternal happiness.[1] "Light" was another illustrative word. Thomas Aquinas tells us that "*Let there be light*" may mean historically an act of creation; allegorically, "Let Christ be love;" anagogically, "May we be led by Christ to glory;" and, tropologically, "May we be mentally illumined by Christ." Even these instances, though chosen as special proofs of the fourfold sense, show the emptiness of the method. Hugo of St. Cher and others compare those four meanings to the four coverings of the tabernacle; the four colours of the veil of the tabernacle; to the four winds; to the fourfold cherubim; the four rivers of Paradise; the four legs of the table of the Lord.[2] Bishop Longland preaching before the University of Oxford in 1525, on "*She hath also furnished her Table*,"[3] explained it to mean

come first (cf. Greg. *Praef. in Job*), but they despised it, as may be seen (among hundreds of other proofs) in Hugo's line—

"*Parvis* imbutus tentabis grandia tutus,"

where he explains the *parva* to be all that elucidates the literal sense. *Erudit. Didasc.* v. 2. Bonaventura says that even in a single letter the Scripture begets a multiform wisdom, but that "sub *cortice* literae occultatur mystica et profunda intelligentia." An anonymous monk of St. Victor falls back, however, on the old remark of the Rabbis, Origen, Augustine, and Jerome, that the *letter* of Scripture, without allegory, has many things "*falsa, inepta, inutilia, impeditiva ad aeternam vitam.*" Diestel, p. 188.

[1] Eucherius, *Spirituales Formulae*, referring to Gen. i. 9 (literal); Ps. lxv. 12; Prov. xviii. 4; John iv. 14 (tropological); Ezek. xxxvi. 25; Rev. xvii. 15; John vii. 38 (allegoric); Jer. ii. 13; Ps. cxlviii. 4 (anagogic). Basil, with infinitely more good sense, says that when the Bible says *water* it usually means *water.*

[2] *Prol. in Gen.* Durandus († 1296), the *Doctor resolutissimus*, author of the *Rationale div. officiorum*, says that the beam from which church bells hang represents the Cross, and the rope the Scriptures; and "as the rope consists of three strands, so does Scripture consist of a threefold strain, namely history, allegory, and morality, and the descent of the rope from the wood in the hands of the priest is the descent of Scripture from its mystery in the mouth of the preacher"!

[3] Prov. ix. 1, 2. Bishop Longland also defended the fourfold sense in a sermon in Westminster Abbey, November 27, 1527. "Si sola grammatica

that Wisdom had set forth in her Scriptural banquet the four courses of History, Tropology, Anagogy, and Allegory. Not content even with the fourfold sense, Bonaventura and others contend for sevenfold or even eightfold senses,[1] and there is just as much reason for the one number as for the other. In point of fact any book may by these methods be made to bear any number of meanings, and the student in the *Epistolae Obscurorum Virorum* may scarcely have been exaggerating when he says that he had attended *unam lectionem in poetria* where he had heard Ovid expounded *naturaliter, literaliter, historialiter, et spiritualiter.*[2] To apply such a system to the Bible after all that God has revealed to us respecting it can only be regarded as an immense anachronism.[3] It is subversive of all exactitude, even if it be not fatal to all truth.

10. But the system, besides saving the trouble of much study, was advantageous to hierarchic usurpations. It made of Scripture an Apocalyptic book with seven seals, which only priests and monks were able to unlock.[4] It made a standing dogma of the "obscurity" of Scripture, which was thus kept safely out of the hands of the multitude.[5] It made the Pope the doorkeeper of Scripture, not the Holy Spirit. It placed at the disposal of the hierarchy an indefinite number of flaccid symbols which might be oracularly applied to prove whatever

---

sufficeret," he says, "esset grammaticae peritus factus illico consummatus theologus."

[1] Angelomus, because of the seven-sealed book in the Apocalypse (!) explained the Book of Kings in seven senses, historic, allegoric, parabolic, dogmatic, &c. See Rosenmüller, *Hist. Int.* v. 153.

[2] Some read Virgil only to allegorise him. Lupton's edition of Colet on *The Corinthians*, introd. p. xxiv. Bernard Sylvester of Chartres († 1167) allegorised the whole history of Æneas, whom he made the symbol of the soul (see Johann. Sarisb. *Metalog.* iii. 4), and his *Glossules* may be taken "as a good *argumentum ad absurdum* for the entire method of allegorising." Poole, *Med. Thoughts*, p. 119.

[3] Dr. J. M. Neale says, "If Scripture *has not an undercurrent of meaning, double, treble, quadruple, or even yet more manifold*, all primitive and mediaeval commentators from the first century to the Reformation . . . . have been substituting their fancies for God's immutable verities—have adopted a system which is alike the offspring and the parent of error." *Dissertation*, p. 377.

[4] Bellarmine (*De Verbo Dei*, iii. 3) says that exegesis needs the aid of the Spirit, who is only found in a council approved by the Pope.

[5] Albertus Magnus uses this argument.

they desired. Tropology was at the service alike of ecclesiastical dogma and priestly usurpation. Jesus raising the dead before a few witnesses was used to prove the duty of private confession to a priest. While Scripture narratives were, in the literal sense, treated as "bare dead histories which concern men no more,"[1] the Levitical system was adduced in absolute defiance of the whole idea of the New Testament to shew that Christian presbyters were sacrificial priests.[2] "*Domini sunt cardines terrae*," the Vulgate rendering of "the pillars of the earth are the Lord's" (1 Sam. ii. 8), was applied to the cardinals. The eighth Psalm was used by Antonius, Bishop of Florence, to mean that God put all things under the feet of the Pope,—sheep, *i.e.*, Christians; oxen, *i.e.*, Jews and heretics; beasts of the field, *i.e.*, pagans; and fishes of the sea, *i.e.*, souls in purgatory. "Thou hast broken the heads of the dragon in the waters" (Ps. lxxiv. 13) proved the expulsion of demons by baptism.[3] The celibacy of priests was supported by the comparison, in Canticles, of the cheeks of the beloved to doves.[4] The root of the tree in Daniel's vision (Dan. iv. 12) furnished a proof of the Immaculate Conception of the Virgin. The two rods of Zechariah (xi. 7) are types of the Dominicans and Franciscans. The papal canonisation of saints was maintained by a reference to the putting of a lamp on a lampstand (Matt. v. 15). So far back as the ninth century Rabanus Maurus († 856) in his *De Clericorum Institutione* had found *chorepiscopi* in the seventy elders, "Readers" in Ezek. xxxiii. 7, and the Roman Catholic system of service generally in Mosaism and the Psalms. Baronius pretended to discover that our Lord put on a pontifical vestment for the celebration of the Lord's supper.[5] Nor must it be supposed that these were treated as passing

---

[1] Luther.

[2] Hervaeus Dolensis on Matt. ix. 18–26.

[3] Compare similar interpretations of Job i. 14, in Neale's *Mediaeval Preachers,* p. xxx., where this style of exegesis is defended.

[4] Cardinal Cusanus admits that Rome made the sense of Scripture vary with her own practice. *Opp.* p. 833.

[5] *Annales*, i. 154. The rebuke of Casaubon is "Hoccine est Divina oracula cum timore tractare, humana figmenta sacris narrationibus ex suo semper immiscere?" (*Exercitationes*, p. 439, *ap.* Thirlwall, *Charges*, i. 150).

applications. On the contrary, as we have already seen, they were endowed with a demonstrative force by Innocent III. and Boniface VIII. in crises of intense seriousness.[1] Because kings were not excepted in the command "*Feed my lambs,*" Boniface maintained that a Papal Legate might trample on the decrees of Emperors. Even the plural "keys" was a sufficient proof that the Pope was to exercise kingly as well as pontifical power, and that the (forged) "donation" of Constantine was only a restitution. He explained "*Launch into the deep*" to mean "Go to Rome; betake thyself to the city which has dominion over all nations, and there lay down thy net."[2] The hideous and unutterable infamies of the Inquisition were defended by the words, "*they gather them in bundles and burn them.*" "*O temerariam impudentiam,*" exclaims Luther of this and similar allegories, "*et scelestam ambitionem !*"[3]

We may perhaps wonder that there had been no stronger and earlier revolt against this vast usurpation. But there is no need to wonder. There was no Prophet more. The priests loved to have it so, for it offered boundless facility for sermons, and gave a fine semblance of freedom. The people loved to have it so, for they did not want to be troubled with independent thought. They were glad to resign the responsibility for their beliefs and their future salvation into the hands of those who claimed to have the infallibility of knowledge and the keys of heaven and hell. Like the Israelites of old, the mass of men did not wish to hear the voice of God. They had said to the Pope

---

[1] "The greater light" is the Papacy, Innocent III. *Decret.* Gregor. ix. lib. i. tit. xxxiii. The two swords, Boniface VIII. *Extrav.* lib. i. tit. viii. It was convenient to forget the wise rule, "Theologia parabolica non est demonstrativa."

[2]
  " l'Evangelio e i Dottor magni
  Son derelitti, e solo ai Decretali
  Si studia sì che parea a' lor vigagni.
 A questo intende il Papa e i Cardinali :
  Non vanno i lor pensieri a Nazzarette
  Là dove Gabbriello aperse l'ali."—DANTE, *Parad.* ix.
133-138. Comp. *id. De Monarchia,* iii. p. 137.

[3] See Milman, *Lat. Christianity,* vi. 405.

"Speak thou to us. Let not God speak with us." "And the people stood afar off." [1]

But since the Papal Church could thus prove to her own satisfaction the infallibility of every doctrine of mediaeval sacerdotalism; since she could openly maintain that if the Bible seemed to collide with any crystallised dogma of her scholasticism, the Bible must give way ; since she could extract from Scripture the defence of her own unlimited pretensions in hundreds of ways inconceivably remote from the intentions of the sacred writers; since she held the Bible thus bound with the double chains of dogma and allegory, it is clear that nothing short of the Reformation was required to shake down the prison-walls of system, and to rescue the Scriptures from these centuries of misuse. To maintain the fourfold sense was for mediaeval Romanism a matter of life and death. It was necessary for her power that dogmatic prepossession and traditional authority should reign supreme. The more ingeniously texts were manipulated in her interests, the more loudly she proclaimed that such interpretations alone were "spiritual" and were due to "illuminating grace." The motto of the Bernardines, like that of the Alexandrians, *Nisi credideritis non intelligetis* was practically made to mean "Protestants despise our arguments from allegories because they are devoid of the Spirit." [2] The vitality of such notions is astonishing. In 1777 a book was published called *Samson's Hair, an Eminent Representation of the Church of God.* "Some," says the writer, "may object against this that the hair of a man's head is a mean thing to represent so great and glorious a thing as the Church of Christ. To which I answer, 'Glory over me, thou infidelity, thou first-born of the devil, if thou canst.'" [3]

But the fourfold sense which might have survived Erasmus, and even Luther, received its death-blow from the masculine good sense of the English Reformers. "We may borrow

[1] Ex. xx. 19-21. See Lange, *Grundriss*, p. 4.
[2] Salmeron on 2 Cor. iii.
[3] E. Jones Trevecka (quoted by the Rev. Prof. Conybeare in his Bampton Lectures, 1824).

similitudes or allegories from the Scriptures," says the great translator Tyndale, "and apply them to our purposes, which allegories are no sense of the Scriptures, but free things besides the Scriptures altogether in the liberty of the Spirit. Such allegory proveth nothing, it is a mere simile. God is a Spirit, and all his words are spiritual, and *His literal sense is spiritual.*" [1] "As to those three spiritual senses," says Whitaker, the opponent of Bellarmine,[2] "it is surely foolish to say there are as many senses in Scripture as the words themselves may be transferred and accommodated to bear. For although the words may be applied and accommodated tropologically, anagogically, allegorically, *or any other way, yet there are not therefore various senses, various interpretations, and explications of Scripture, but there is but one sense and that the literal,* which may be variously accommodated, and from which various things may be collected." [3]

It is always an evil to create any discontinuity between ourselves and the past. It has not been my object to hunt out the details of ancient error; still less to glory in the superiority of modern insight. If we are compelled to study

[1] See his chapter on "The Four Senses of Scripture" in *Obedience of a Christian Man.*

[2] *Dispute on Holy Scripture*, p. 409 (Parker Society).

[3] Even Dean Colet, though he admitted the fourfold sense, yet says that the New Testament "has for the most part the sense that appears on the surface ; nor is one thing said and another meant, but the very thing is meant which is said, and the sense is wholly literal." See further, Colet, *On the Hierarchies of Dionysius*, p. 107 (ed. Lupton), and on Gal. iv. 24. Colet compares the anagogic sense to the Kabbala (*l. c.* p. 112), and had been deeply influenced by Mirandola and Plotinus. Mr. Lupton also kindly refers me to Mr. Alexander Gill (High Master of St. Paul's), who, in his *Sacred Philosophie of the Holy Scriptures* (1635, p. 165), compares David's cutting off the lap of Saul's robe to Ps. xxii. 18—"*They parted my garments among them*" —"For," he says, "Saul was a figure of Christ." He adds, "But, you say, *the Scripture is not to be strained, for by that means everie thing can be made of any thing.*" His answer to this very natural objection is supremely invalid. "At the Reformation," says Bishop Marsh, "it became a maxim among Protestants, that the words of Scripture had only one sense, and that they who ascribed to them *various* senses made the meaning of Scripture altogether uncertain." *Criticism and Interpretation*, Lect. xii., p. 506. "No such universal rule " (for allegorical interpretation), says Bishop van Mildert, "is to be found in Scripture. It is nowhere laid down as a maxim, that there is in every part of the sacred writings, nor even in the greater part, a hidden spiritual sense." *Bampton Lect.*, p. 250.

and to point out the errors of the past, it should be in a
spirit of humility, and not of malice ; it should be that we
may faithfully learn, not vainly triumph. Nothing can be
more beautiful than the character and example of many of
the Schoolmen, nothing keener than their intellectual subtlety,
nothing more admirable than their unwearied diligence.
When we think of the blameless life of the Venerable Bede,
devoted from the age of seven years upwards to the study of
Scripture in the calm retirement of Jarrow, and ended while
he was dictating to his young scholar the last words of his
comment on St. John ; [1]—of the young Bernard of Clairvaux,
standing neck-deep in the ice-cold stream to subdue the passions of the flesh, and devoting his life to saintly self-denial ;—
of his unhappy rival, the brilliant Abelard, hiding his shame
and agony in the monastery of St. Gildas de Rhuys, and
dying in humble peace under the gentle care of Peter of
Clugny ;—of Bonaventura, of whom his master, Alexander
of Hales, used to say that "in Bonaventura Adam did not
sin ;" who, when appointed Cardinal, was found humbly
washing the vessels of his monastery, and when his great
contemporary asked him the source of his vast learning,
pointed in silence to his crucifix ;—of the chancellor Gerson
gathering the little children round his sick bed, and bidding
them uplift their little white hands with the prayer, " Lord,
have mercy on thy poor servant Jean Gerson ;"—of Albert
the Great preferring his position of a humble monk to the
Bishopric of Ratisbon which he resigned ;—of Thomas of
Aquino in his profound humility, his rapturous visions, his
glorious daily prayer, *Da mihi Domine cor nobile quod nulla
ad terram detrahat terrena affectio,* his holy answer to the
Vision " Bene scripsisti de me, Thoma ; quam mercedem a me
accipies ? " *Non aliam nisi te, Domine ;*—of the incredible
diligence, sanctity, and learning of Duns Scotus, who had
influenced the entire theology and philosophy of his day
before his early death at the age of thirty-four ; [2]—of the iron

---

[1] Sigebert, *De Script. Eccles.* 88. Bede's version of St. John is the first
extant specimen of English prose.
[2] Milman, *Latin Christianity,* bk. xiv. 3.

logic and dauntless courage with which Occam, the *Doctor Invincibilis,* "the demagogue of scholasticism," braved in defence of civil liberty the excommunication of the Pope, and in defence of absolute poverty the excommunication of his own order—when we think of the mingled holiness and intellectual power of these great men, we revolt at the thought of speaking about them with flippancy or disrespect. If they had left nothing else to the Church, they have left the best of all legacies—the legacy of holy lives and an immortal example; the legacy of men who during years of unselfish sincerity spurned delights and lived laborious days. The writings of some of them will be always valuable for the spirit of deep devotion which they breathe, for high moral teaching, for profound philosophical and theological investigation. But their lives were better than their learning. They had found Christ, even though they read His name by wrong methods. I have not been speaking of their writings in general, or of the many high services which they rendered to their generation and to mankind. I have been speaking only of their exegesis, and respecting that branch of their labours it is impossible to avoid pronouncing the judgment that it was radically defective—defective in fundamental principles, and rife on every page of it with all sorts of erroneous details. It demonstrates the amazing vitality of error; the fatally stupefying effects which result from the attempt to crush free inquiry under the leaden weight of authority and tradition; the hopeless insecurity of superstructures, even when they have been elaborated with the utmost care and skill, which have been based on shallow, imaginary, or untested foundations. But the sadness of these facts is irradiated by one truth of which they furnish the strongest evidence. It is that the Bible may be obscured for centuries by bad translations, and buried under mountain-loads of valueless and erroneous exposition; that it may be withheld from the ignorant, and grossly mis-interpreted by the learned; that it may even be abused as a bulwark of immense follies, and a pretext for enormous crimes; and yet that there is in the truths which constitute its essence so divine a preciousness, so innate a force, that never in any age has it ceased to teach men the way of salvation, never has it lost the power to brighten happiness and to console affliction, to inspire men with courage for the amelioration of social wrongs, for the overthrow of popular idols, for the assault on ancient errors, for the restatement of forgotten and neglected truths. Men may still continue to misunderstand and to misrepresent it ; to turn it into a grim idol or a mechanical fetish ; to betray it with the kiss of false devotion, and to thrust it between the soul and the God Whom it was designed to reveal ; but to the end of all time—and herein consists its divine authority—it shall guide the souls of the humble to the strait gate and the narrow way which leadeth to eternal life—to the end of all time "an highway shall be there, and a way, and it shall be called The way of holiness; the unclean shall not pass over it; but whosoever walketh in the way, yea, and even fools, shall not err therein." [1]

[1] Is. xxxv. 7, 8.

"Proinde volo liber esse."—LUTHER.

"So wird diese Geschichte nicht allein Geschichte der Finsterniss und der Verringungen ; sie wird auch eine Geschichte der Dämmerung, der Morgenröthe, und des endlich angebrochenen hellen Tages werden."
—G. W. MEYER, *Gesch. d. Schrifterklärung*, i. 6.

> " Unless—what whispers me of times to come ?
> What if it be the mission of that age
> My death will usher into life, to shake
> This torpor of assurance from our creed,
> As we broke up that old faith of the world
> Have we, next age, to break up thus the new—
> Faith in the thing grown faith in the report—
> Whence need to bravely disbelieve report
> Through increased faith in thing reports belie ? "
> —The Pope in *The Ring and the Book* (BROWNING).

LECTURE VI.

THE REFORMERS.

"He that hath my word, let him speak my word faithfully. What hath the straw to do with the wheat? saith the Lord."—Jer. xxiii. 28.

THE Reformation is very inadequately and negatively represented by the word "Protestantism."[1] If in its narrower aspect it was a revolt against Romanism, it was in reality but one scene in the vast drama of human progress in which Rome herself was compelled to take her part. Her awakenment, her purification, her better line of Popes, her Council of Trent, her Society of Jesus, resulted in no small degree from the work which owed its personal impulse to the mighty passion and genius of Luther. Those who reconcile it with their sense of justice to call him the father of infidelity, might with just as much truth have called him the restorer of the Papacy. For the work of Luther, like that of Origen, was the watershed of many divergent influences. If in the one direction he is to be held responsible for the teaching of Denck and Müntzer, and in another of Lessing and Strauss; assuredly he was also the cause of a marked improvement in the Romish Church, of the energy of her counter-Reformation, and of the improvement in morality and discipline within her pale.

---

[1] It should however be observed that the Protest of Spiers, if negative against particular doctrines, was positive in its assertion of the liberty of conscience.

But in point of fact, as history has proved again and again, it is absurd and misleading to charge men with all the results which may spring indirectly from their teaching or character. Their work must be judged with reference to the times and circumstances in which it was accomplished. We might as well make St. Paul responsible for Marcion or St. John for Valentinus, or charge Christianity with the follies and extravagances of Gnosticism, or lay at the door of Las Casas the guilt of negro slavery, or brand the memory of Lafayette with the blood spilt in the Reign of Terror, as lay at Luther's door the errors which have arisen among the sects and churches which were first called into existence by his heroic personality. He was but one among many influences mightier than himself, and his work was but a single current in a tide of which the forces are to this day unspent. The Reformation was "the life of the Renaissance infused into religion under the influence of men of the grave and earnest Teutonic race; a return to nature which was not a rebellion against God, an appeal to reason which left room for loyal allegiance to the Bible and to Christ."[1]

He must indeed be incapable of fairness who can ignore the services once rendered by the Papacy to the cause of civilisation and humanity. These services have been recognised as generously by Comte[2] and Mazzini[3] as by De Lamennais[4] and Le Maistre.[5] But

"The old order changeth, giving place to new,
And God fulfils Himself in many ways
Lest one good custom should corrupt the world."

In the sixteenth century the whole Papal system had, even on the confession of its own historians, sunk into a formalism and corruption which made it a curse to mankind.

---

[1] Beard, *Hibbert Lectures*, p. 2. Perhaps rather "Religion infused into the Renaissance." What the Renaissance was without the Reformation may be seen in such men as Leo X., Bembo, Bibbiena, Panormita, Filelfo, Politian, Pomponatius, &c. (see Gieseler, v. 181–184).

[2] *Cours de Politique Positive.*

[3] See the very powerful and eloquent testimony of Mazzini in the *Fortnightly Review*, 1870, p. 731.

[4] *Essai sur l' Indifférence*, 1817.

[5] *Du Pape*, 1819.

An even more tremendous indictment against the decadent morality of Rome and her priesthood might be drawn from the writings of Petrarch, Gerson, Machiavelli, Picus of Mirandola, or Savonarola, than from those of Boccaccio and the Italian novelists.[1] Even in the *Paradiso* of Dante you may hear the cry of holy indignation wrung from the assembled saints while St. Pietro Damiano denounces the gross luxuries of the priesthood ; and in the same mighty song the unworthiness of the successors of St. Peter had made the living topazes of heaven bicker into ruby hues of fiery wrath while the great Apostle fulminates his more than papal anathema against the blood-stained and avaricious pontiffs who have usurped on earth "My place, my place, MY PLACE!" And things grew worse and worse. How could Rome be respected when the world saw such pontiffs as Sixtus IV., Innocent VIII., Alexander VI., Julius II., and Clement VII., not to mention such a once-dissolute sophist as Pius II. (Aeneas Sylvius), or such an elegant epicurean as Leo X.? How could the world tolerate on the lips of simonists, nepotists, adulterers, and worse, the claim to absolute dominion over religion, the claim to be sole interpreters of Scripture, and the immediate recipients of the power and authority of Christ?[2] How could men endure that such persons should be addressed by a trembling sycophancy as "our Lord and God"? How could they suffer a man so vile as Sixtus IV. to found, unquestioned, that Spanish Inquisition which is perhaps the most abhorrent phenomenon ever presented to the loathing of the world? Was his successor, Innocent VIII., amid his life of criminal luxury to let loose, unquestioned, a man like Sprenger, whose *Malleus Maleficarum* has well been called "a monstrous

---

[1] See proofs only too overwhelming in Gieseler, v. § 139.

[2] See Dorner, *Hist. of Prot. Theol.* i. 35, E. I. The most extravagant statement of Papal claims may be found in Augustin Trionfo, *De Potestate Ecclesiae*, who says that "worship, equal to that due to the saints, greater than that to the angels, belongs to the Pope" (Trionfo, ix. 72). Papal claims were supported by such exegesis as this : Quod Papa sit *Deus Imperatoris* juxta illud "Ecce constitui te *Deum Pharaonis*." Gerson (*De Potest. Eccl.* 1 ; *Considerat.* 10), protests against these extravagances.

bastard of priestcraft and scholasticism?" Were popes, of
whom some were equal to Nero and Domitian in crime, but
from their positions and their professions far viler in infamy, to
be suffered for ever to wield in the name of Jesus, a power
with which that even of the Caesars was not to be compared?
The ecclesiastical casuistry which could not quite suffocate
the moral sense or suppress the burning blush of the Emperor
Sigismund at the Council of Constance, was still less able to
crush a rebellion which was headed, on all sides, by the noble
indignation and the revolted conscience of mankind.

The institutions of piety were thoroughly corrupted. Theology had sunk into a dull, dead, and cumbrous scholasticism,[1]
which so far from reconciling faith with knowledge had but
deepened the chasm between the two. If John of Salisbury
in the twelfth century had complained of its slavish dependence, and miserable pettiness—if Roger Bacon in the
thirteenth had said that it *languet et asininat circum male
intellecta*—in the course of three more centuries its questions
had become more "vermiculate," its terminology more barbarous, and its whole foundationless superstructure, reared
only on the sand, was tottering under the waterfloods, which
began to burst upon it. A sacerdotalism at once arrogant,
intolerant, immoral, and idle, headed by a Pope who might be
at once a "priest, an atheist, and a god," had radically corrupted the lifeblood of the Church by dividing it into two
classes, the ruling and the ruled. It had poisoned the veins
of all Christian life by substituting a visionary satisfaction
for a true reconciliation, and a mechanical conformity for a
holy life. Piety was practically identified with the observance of ecclesiastical rules. Impunity was sold to the living
and deliverance to the dead.[2] Monasticism, itself polluted

---

[1] "Theologiae tum materia non sacrae literae et Scripturae divinae erant,
sed quaedam obscurae et spinosae intricataeque quaestiones, quarum nugatoria
subtilitate exercebantur et defatigabantur ingenia" (Camerarius, *Vit. Melanchth.* c. iii.).

[2] See a very fine passage of Erasmus (*Annott.* in 1 Tim. i. 6), which is too
long to quote, but is full of indignant eloquence against the slothful and
corrupt priesthood—"Metuebant tyrannidi suae, si mundus resipisceret"
(*Opp.* ix. 490). But perhaps some may be more open to conviction if I

by confessed and countless abominations, seized upon selfishness as the basis of religion, and expanded it to infinity. Asceticism, darkening at once the teaching of Scripture, the meaning of life, and the character of God, taught that celibacy was holier than marriage, and that self-inflicted tortures could expiate for spiritual sins. The very conception of morality was vitiated. A priesthood calling itself the Church—a priesthood whose vices were the complaint of the theologian and the motive of the novelist, the despair of the good and the execration of the multitude—claimed absolute authority over men's bodies and souls, shut the Bible from the many, turned Christ into a wrathful Avenger, made it easier for the rich than for the poor to escape damnation, and gave even to the grace of God the aspect of capricious concession to the purchased intercessions of the Virgin Mary. The Christian Rome of Borgia had come to deserve every one of the denunciations which had been hurled at the Pagan Rome of Nero by the Apocalyptic seer. The name of faith was prostituted by being bestowed on the abject acceptance of unproved postulates ; the name of morals was conferred upon a blind obedience to human traditions ; the name of grace was confined to the mechanical operation of perverted sacraments ; the name of truth to a mass of infallible falsehoods ; the name of orthodoxy to the passive repetition of traditional ignorance. The results were frightful. There was mental coercion and moral disorder.[1] Even Bellarmine acknowledges that some years before the Reformation "there was no strictness in spiritual courts, no chastity in manners, no reverence in presence of what was sacred, no scholarship, in short almost no religion." [2]

The necessary deliverance came through the study of the Holy Scriptures. Long before the days of Luther some, at

---

summon a Pope as witness. Pope Adrian VI., at the Diet of Nürnberg, which was convened to suppress Lutheranism, declared through the Bishop of Fabriane that "these disorders had sprung . . . *more especially from the sins of priests and prelates ;* even in the Holy Chair many horrible crimes have been committed."

[1] See Hampden, *Bampton Lectures*, p. 38.
[2] See Dorner, i. 23-49.

least of the few who studied the Bible with open eyes, had
seen how different was primitive Christianity from mediaeval
Romanism, how deep and impassable was the gulf between
the Church of the Apostles and the Church of Alexander VI.
and Leo X. There had been Reformers long before the
Reformation. Already at the beginning of the fourteenth
century Dante had said,

> " Ah, Constantine, of how much ill was cause,
> Not thy conversion, but those rich domains
> That the first wealthy Pope received of thee ! "

but it was not till the sixteenth that men's eyes were fully
opened to the falsehood of the pretended Donation of
Constantine and the forgery of the Decretals of Isidore. The
Mystics,—Greek, Latin, and German—had tried to walk in the
light of Eternity. The Waldenses had desired to make the
Bible their sole authority. Wiclif had translated it, and
put it into the hands of the poor. Hus had inaugurated
the Bohemian reformation. The Brethren of the Common
Life, and other retired bodies, had peacefully studied the
Scriptures.[1] John Wessel († 1489), in his *Farrago Rerum
Theologicarum*, had so far anticipated the views of Luther that
Luther expresses his surprise at the identity of thought
between them.[2] Similarly in 1520 he wrote, " I have hitherto
unknowingly held and taught all John Hus's doctrines; in a
like unknowingness has John Staupitz taught them ; briefly
we are all unconscious Hussites. Paul and Augustine are
Hussites to the letter." [3]

But there were others, who on different grounds from
these had in various directions contributed powerfully to the
Reformation, and had helped to form the views of Scripture
exegesis on which it so largely depended.

1. First among these we may mention LORENZO VALLA
(† 1465). Valla, a Canon of St. John Lateran, was not a

---

[1] See Ullmann, *Reformers before the Reformation.* Gieseler, v. 172–177.

[2] " If I had read Wessel first, mine adversaries might have imagined that I
had taken everything from Wessel—*adeo spiritus utriusque concordat.*"—
Werke, xiv. 220, ed. Walch (Pref. to Wessel). Wessel, in his *Mare Magnum*,
borrowed largely from Rupert of Deutz.

[3] *Briefe*, ed. De Wette, p. 425 ; Beard, *Hibbert Lectures*, p. 30.

man of deep religious feelings, but he is one chief link between the Renaissance and the Reformation. He had at least learnt from the revival of letters that Scripture must be interpreted by the laws of grammar and the laws of language. He showed his courage and independence in many ways.[1] In days when scholasticism was still dominant he wonders that schoolmen who were ignorant of Greek, should ever have ventured to comment on St. Paul.[2] In defiance of the whole Dominican order he contemptuously rejects the monkish legend that St. Paul had appeared to St. Thomas Aquinas and said that no one had so well understood his Epistles ; for "why," he asks, "did not St. Paul in that case warn him of his mistakes ?"[3] Undaunted by the Papal power he showed the spuriousness of the Donation of Constantine, in a pamphlet republished in 1517 by Ulric von Hutten.[4] He expressed his doubts as to the genuineness of the works attributed to Dionysius the Areopagite.[5] He denied the fictions about the composition of the Apostles' Creed. He did not scruple to criticise St. Augustine[6] and the Vulgate.[7] Above all he drew up Annotations on the New

---

[1] No one who has looked at Valla's works, especially at his disgraceful *De Voluptate et Vero Bono*, can have the least sympathy with him as a man ; but this must not blind us to his real services. On Valla see Oudin, *Script. Eccl.* p. 2439 ; Fabric, *Bibl. Lat.* vi. 282 ; Meyer, *Gesch. der Schrifterklär.* i. 155.

[2] "Quem (Remigium) et item Thomam Aquinatem . . . ignaros omnino linguae Graecae, miror ausos commentari Paulum Graece loquentem " (*Annott.* in 1 Cor. ix. 26).

[3] "*Peream nisi id commenticium, nam cur eum Paulus non admonuit erratorum suorum*, cum ob alia tum de ignorantiâ linguae graecae " (*Annott.* in 1 Cor. ix. 13 ; comp. in Acts xiii. 9.)

[4] Dante (*Infern.* xix. 115. *Parad.* xx. 55, *De Monarch.* ii. *ad fin.*) ; Wiclif, (*Trialog.*, Tracts and Treatises, ed. Vaughan, p. 174), and Ariosto (*Orl. Furioso*, xxviv. st. 80) alike protested against the effects of the Donation of Constantine. Aeneas Sylvius (Pius II.) had even in 1443 expressed doubts of its authenticity (Pez, *Thes. Anecd.* iv. 316), as also did Bishop Pecock and Cardinal de Cusa (Brown, *Fascic.* i. 57). But Valla went further. See Döllinger, *Fables of the Popes*, pp. 107-176. After Baronius gave up the "Donation" no one had a word more to say.

[5] *Annott.* in Acts xvii. 34. Grocyn after beginning to lecture on the *Celestial Hierarchies* about 1500, and severely censuring Valla, confessed after a few weeks that he had come round to Valla's opinion, that the works were spurious. See Erasm. *Annot.* in *Acts* xvii. 34 (*ed.* 1519).

[6] *Annott.* in John xviii. 28.

[7] *Annott.* in Mark x. 49, Luke ii. 14, John x. 29, &c. The low state of critical knowledge led him into frequent errors, *e.g.* in his notes on Matt. vi. 1 and John xviii. 1. But his remarks helped to show the extreme importance of philology and criticism.

Testament, in which, though they have little religious or spiritual interest, he recognised the supreme importance of abandoning erroneous renderings and of ascertaining what the Apostles and Evangelists really wrote and really meant.[1] Though Bellarmine calls him "a precursor of the Lutherans," Valla remained to the last a Humanist. He escaped the Inquisition by a cynical conformity, and became the secretary of Nicholas V., who thought more of Ciceronian style than of theologic accuracy. But he may claim the honour of being one of the founders of textual criticism,[2] and Erasmus was so much struck with his Annotations, of which he found a MS. in a monastic library at Brussels, that he republished them with a warm eulogy in 1505, forty years after the death of their author.[3]

2. With Valla must be mentioned JACQUES LE FEVRE D'Étaples, usually known as *Faber Stapulensis*, who also helped to break the heavy yoke of ecclesiastical and scholastic tradition. Encouraged by the example of Valla he made a new Latin translation of St. Paul's Epistles, and has the high honour of having published in 1523 the first French version of the entire Scriptures.[4]

3. Still greater were the services of REUCHLIN.[5] Regarded in his own lifetime as being, with Erasmus, one of the two eyes of Europe, he may fairly claim to have effected for the study of the Old Testament even more than Erasmus achieved for the New. With his *eruditio trilinguis* he was regarded as a new St. Jerome. He was born in 1455, the year that Gutenberg sent forth from Mainz the first printed book, the Mazarin Bible; and although he was a layman, a lawyer, an ambassador, a Humanist, he had learnt the rudiments of Hebrew from John Wessel in his youth, and

---

[1] Hallam's remark that these are "the earliest specimens of explanations founded on the original language" (*Lit. of Europe*, i. 147) requires qualification.

[2] "*Collatis aliquot vetustis atque emendatis Graecorum exemplaribus*" (Erasm. *Ep.* ciii.).

[3] When Cornelius Aurotinus called Valla "*corvus crocitans*," Erasmus said that he ought rather to have called him *suadae medulla*.

[4] It is anonymous, but there is little doubt that it is by him.

[5] Luther wrote, "*Fuisti tu sane organum consilii Dei.*"

devoted himself to the study of languages with the express object of elucidating the Scriptures.[1] In one characteristic sentence he gives us the secret of his great services : "*Novum Testamentum graece lego, Vetus hebraice, in cujus expositione malo confidere meo quam alterius ingenio.*" At great cost, ever spending upon learning what he had gained by teaching, he acquired a knowledge of Hebrew from Jacob Jehiel Loans, and is said to have once paid ten gold pieces to a Jew for the explanation of a single phrase.[2] Although his *Rudimenta Linguae Hebraicae* was preceded by the imperfect book of Pellican, he had a right to conclude it with the verse, " *Exegi monumentum aere perennius.*" So great in that age was the ignorance of Hebrew, that he had to begin by a full and emphatic notice that Hebrew is read from right to left.[3] His grammar was mostly derived from David Qimchi, but in the commentary on the seven penitential psalms he also consulted the works of Rashi, Ibn Ezra, Saadia, Maimonides, Levi Ben Gerson, and the Targums of Jonathan and Onkelos.[4] He frequently corrects the Vulgate in favour of the *Hebraica Veritas.* It is to be regretted that he should have wasted so much time over the delusions of Kabbalism,[5] and this had the further ill effect of exposing him to the fury of the priests, theologians, Dominicans, and Inquisitors. They were already suspicious of one who studied the language of the Old Testament, which they stupidly denounced as an accursed tongue. When Reuchlin lectured on it at Heidelberg he had to do so secretly. The collision with Pfefferkorn[6] and Hoog-

---

[1] Beard, p. 43 ; see Geiger, *Johann Reuchlin,* 1871. Chairs for Oriental languages, with a view to missionary work, had been formed in 1311, but till Reuchlin's time they had not produced much fruit.

[2] " Universalem stipem quam discendo impendi, docendo acquisivi" *Praef. (ad fratrem).* His desire to find the literal sense is emphasised in his *De Accentibus.*

[3] The first edition was published at Pforzheim in 1506.

[4] When reproved for doing so he replied, " Quamquam Hieronynum veneror ut angelum et Lyram colo ut magistrum, tamen . . . veritatem adoro ut Deum" (*Praef. Rudim. Hebr. lib.* iii.).

[5] *De Verbo Mirifico,* 1495 ; *De Arte Kabbalistica,* 1515. Erasmus wrote to the Archbishop of Mainz, "Cabbala et Thalmud, *quidquid hoc est,* meo animo nunquam arrisit" (*Ep.* 477). Luther spoke of his Jewish *Alfanzerei.*

[6] Pfefferkorn, an apostate Jew, wanted to have the copies of the Talmud searched out and burnt. The Talmud has been almost as much persecuted as

straten embittered Reuchlin's declining years, which he might
have spent so happily among his white peacocks in the peaceful retirement of Stuttgart. But this quarrel opened men's
eyes to the presumptuous ignorance of a clergy who still
claimed for their opinions an infallible authority. Even
the coarse satire of the *Epistolae Obscurorum Virorum* emphasised the general conviction that the coming struggle
between the Reformers and the Papacy was a struggle of
knowledge against ignorance, of light against darkness, of
freedom against a servility which was at once degrading and
intolerable to the awakening conscience of mankind.[1]

4. But more than any man except Luther it was DESIDERIUS
ERASMUS of Rotterdam, who in widening the knowledge of
Scripture advanced the cause of the Reformation. In the
person of this brilliant humanist and admirable theologian
"Greece rose from the dead with the New Testament in her
hand." There is no one whose writings show a more distinct
and decided emancipation from untenable traditions. His
editio princeps of the New Testament (1516) "formed a
great epoch in the history of Western Christendom, and
was a gift of incalculable value to the Church."[2] It was
to it that the English martyr Bilney owed his conversion.
Tyndale and Coverdale used it as well as Luther. It was
from Erasmus that Tyndale borrowed his immortal answer
to the theologian who had said, "We had better be without
God's laws than the Pope's;" that "If God spare my life,
ere many years I will cause the boy that driveth the
plough to know more of Scripture than thou dost." For

the Jews. Justinian condemned it in 533 ; it was burnt in 1244 and 1288 ;
Julius III. in 1555 ; Paul IV. in 1559 ; Pius V. in 1566 ; Clement VIII. in
1599. In 1307 Clement V. had shown greater wisdom by founding professor-
ships of Oriental languages in Paris, Salamanca, Bologna, and Oxford, in order
to learn what the Talmud really was (*Constt. Clementis V. in Conc. Viennensi*,
p. 277). Reuchlin said that to burn the book was a mere *Bacchanten-argu-
ment.* "On brûlait le Talmud et quelquefois le Juif avec le Talmud" (Vict.
le Clerc, *Disc. sur l'Hist. Lit. de France*).

[1] There was a story current, and by no means impossible, of a priest who
thought that Greek and the New Testament were two recent heresies.

[2] See Westcott, *Hist. of Eng. Bible*, pp. 26, 140, 203–205. By an order
in Council in 1547, every English parish church was bound to have a copy
of his *Paraphrases* (Hallam, *Lit. of Eur.* i. 373 ; Milman, *Lat. Christianity*,
vi. 439).

in direct opposition to the prevailing hierarchical sentiment, in an age when even Luther could grow up to the age of twenty-six without having read a complete Bible, Erasmus had proclaimed the privilege of even the unlearned to read for themselves the messages of a Gospel which was proclaimed to Scythians, and slaves, and peasants, and women, no less than to Greeks and kings.[1] He had assailed immemorial custom in deploring the fact that ".men and women chattered like parrots the Psalms and prayers which they did not understand." He had expressed the wish to see Christ honoured in all languages, to hear the Psalms sung by the labourer at the plough, and the Gospel read to poor women as they sat spinning at the wheel. " I should prefer," he said, " to hear young maidens talking about Christ than some who in the opinion of the vulgar are consummate Rabbis "; and he could claim it as the glorious result of his labours that " the veil of the Temple has now been rent in twain, and it is no longer a single High Priest who can enter into the Holy of Holies."[2]

Erasmus had some right, then, to reject the taunt of Stunica, *Erasmus lutherissat,* and to answer that in truth *Lutherus erasmissat.* The fame of his ability, the brilliancy of his wit, the force of his learning, the vivacity and manliness of his Latin style, the mordant humour of his attacks upon a purblind yet autocratic theology, rendered the subsequent work of Luther more easy, and paved the way for the wide and immediate acceptance of his German Bible. Though Erasmus edited many of the Fathers[3] he helped to break down the extravagant belief in their authority. He freely and forcibly exposes the mistakes and ignorance of the

---

[1] *Praef. in Paraphr. Matth.* How rapidly and thoroughly his hopes were fulfilled may be seen by the complaint of Cochlaeus (*De Act. et Script. M. Lutheri, ad ann.* 1522), that even cobblers and women, *quilibet idiotae,* knew the New Testament by heart, and carried it in their pockets.

[2] The Complutensian Polyglot was printed in 1514, but not published till 1520. The second edition of Erasmus's New Testament was published in 1518. In later editions (1522, 1527, 1535) he consulted the Complutensian.

[3] Irenaeus, Cyprian, Hilary, Ambrose, Jerome, Augustine, Basil, Chrysostom and others.

Schoolmen.[1] The Dominicans would allow no dissent from the decisions of Thomas Aquinas or Hugo of St. Cher; the Franciscans gave implicit allegiance to Nicolas of Lyra; the Augustinians were indignant if any man departed a hairsbreadth from the interpretation of St. Augustine. Erasmus does not hesitate to point out that Peter Lombard [2] and Aquinas [3] made serious mistakes; that Hugo of St. Cher was full of grotesque misinterpretations; [4] that even Augustine had left much to be done, and that no great teacher had ever claimed the authority which was then accorded to writings which were but human and full of glaring imperfections. [5] Nor is this all. He expressly repudiates the exegetic infallibility not only of the Pope but even of Churches.[6] He never hesitates to reject a so-called "Scripture proof" when it seemed to him to be misapplied or untenable, [7] nor to retain a Scripture phrase even though it might seem liable to abuse. [8] His philological merits were of a high order, and his notes on many of the rarer words and phrases in the Greek Testament, may still be read with advantage. He sets aside theological quibbles and scholastic subtleties with the brief remark *quae supra nos nihil ad nos*, and his comments on "the commandments of men," on sacerdotal Pharisaism, on marriage dispensations, on the spirituality of true religion,

---

[1] Pope expresses the popular view about Erasmus in the lines,

"At length Erasmus, that great injured name,
(The glory of the Priesthood and the shame,)
Stemmed the wild torrent of a barbarous age
And drove the holy Vandals off the stage."

[2] See his note on the *pudendus lapsus* of the Master of the Sentences (παραδειγματίσαι = *rem habere cum sponsa*) in Matt. i. 19 (see his notes on Rom. i. 4 ; 1 Cor. i. 10 ; 1 Cor. vii. 42 ; 1 Tim. ii. 21, v. 18, &c.).

[3] He blames the confidence with which Aquinas "spoke of things which he did not understand" (see notes on 1 Cor. xiv. 11 ; Heb. xi. 37). Colet's disapproval joined to study of the *Summa* weakened *Erasmus's* original estimate of Aquinas. See Seebohm, *Oxf. Reformers*, p. 110.

[4] See his notes on Matt. v. 16, xix. 12 ; John v. 2 ; Acts xxvii. 12 ; 1 Tim. i. 18 ; 2 Tim. iii. 2 ; Tit. i. 7 ; 1 Pet. ii. 24.

[5] *Annott.* in Luke ii. 35, 1 Tim. i. 7. On John v. 2, he says, "Eatenus debetur sanctis viris reverentia, ut siquid errarint, *nam errant et sancti*, citra personae contumeliam veritati patrocinemur."

[6] *Annott* in 1 Cor. vii. 39 ; 2 Cor. x. 8 ; 1 Tim. i. 7.

[7] See on Matt. ii. 5 ; Rom. v. 12 ; Phil. ii. 6 ; 1 Tim. i. 17 ; 1 John v. 7, 20.

[8] See his note on Matt. xxiv. 36.

on monkish divisions, on religious mendicancy, and on the non-existence of any earthly infallibility, were all contributions to the emancipation of the Church from the tyrannous burdens and false traditions of the days in which his lot was cast.

In all this Erasmus showed a courage which, though it cost something in his as in every age, is often the *best* service which any man can render to his own generation. It has been the fashion to sneer at his supposed timidity in not throwing himself heart and soul into the work of Luther.[1] But the natures of Luther and Erasmus were antipathetic. Erasmus felt a constitutional dislike of Luther's methods, as well as a theological repulsion from many of his opinions.[2] Personally he was shocked by Luther's roughness; intellectually he could attach no meaning to his chief watchword. Doubtless he was not wholly free from the feeling of self-interest and the desire to avoid conflict. Luther charged him with wishing to walk upon eggs without crushing them, and among glasses without breaking them. But he never allowed these weaknesses to show themselves in the region of his most sincere convictions. It must not be forgotten that he willingly braved the intense hatred of a powerful and unscrupulous majority. Many a sermon was directed against him in his lifetime by enraged obscurantists, who, as is common with that class, had not even read the books which they so vehemently denounced.[3] On one occasion, in his presence, a Carmelite preacher, in the violet hood and cap of a doctor, charged him with two out of the three sins against the Holy Ghost; namely, presumption, for having ventured to correct the Magnificat and the Lord's Prayer;—and the impugning of recognised truth, because, after hearing two preachers

---

[1] He bravely took Luther's part for some time (*Ep.* 513), as even Luther admitted (De Wette, i. 241, 396.) Erasmus urged his schoolfellow Pope Adrian VI. to mildness and concessions, and he says, "Romae me faciunt Lutheranum," *Ep.* 667.

[2] "Videor mihi fere omnia docuisse quae docet Lutherus, nisi quod non tam atrociter, quodque abstinui et quibusdam aenigmatibus et parodoxis." Erasmus to Zwingli (Milman, *Essays*, p. 127).

[3] See *Ep.* 417 (ad Campegium), A D. 1519.

on the same day, he had remarked that neither of them understood his subject.[1] His *Colloquies* were burnt in Spain and put on the Index at Rome. He was censured by the Theological Faculty of Paris, and among the many who attacked him was Caranza, who published a book called, *The Blasphemies and Impieties of Erasmus.*[2]

Erasmus may be regarded as the chief founder of modern textual and Biblical criticism. He must always hold an honoured place among the interpreters of Scripture. In his *Paraphrases*, which Luther bitterly called *Paraphroneses*, he endeavoured, he says, " to supply gaps, to soften the abrupt, to arrange the confused, to simplify the involved, to untie the knotty, to throw light on the obscure, to give the Roman franchise to Hebraisms . . . to say the same things though in another way." It was his aim, above all, to brighten the meaning of words which had been partly deadened by familiarity, partly perverted by mistaken applications.[3] In his edition of the Greek Testament, he was one of the first to apply critical principles, and to convince the Church of the now admitted spuriousness of the verse about the three heavenly witnesses.[4] He pointed out the strange textual phenomena of the passage about the woman taken in adultery. In his *Annotations* he described the general characteristics of Hellenistic Greek, and many of the peculiarities which mark the style of St. Paul. He did not deny the possibility of trivial errors and discrepancies in the sacred writers.[5] He usefully illustrates the form into which our Lord sometimes threw His teaching. He did not confuse inspiration with

---

[1] *Ep.* vi. p. 344, and xxii. *Ep.* 31 ; Rosenmüller, v. 432.

[2] The letter of Dorpius to Erasmus, in which he argues that the Vulgate must be free from error because the Church had accepted it, is a specimen of common *a priori* reasoning. Erasmus in his reply said, " You follow in the steps of those *vulgar divines who attribute ecclesiastical authority to whatever creeps into general use.*" Lee, afterwards Archbishop of York, was chastised by Sir T. More as a "monachulus et obscurus et indoctus " for his attack on Erasmus.

[3] *Dedicat. Paraphr.* in *Ep. ad Rom.* Herder said that his *Paraphrases* were worth their weight in gold. Tischendorf, Lachmann, and Tregelles do justice to his merits.

[4] 1 John v. 7.

[5] *Annott.* in Luke xxii. 36 ; John ii. 19, 20, &c.

supernatural infallibility in expressions and details.[1] "Christ alone," he said, "is called the Truth. He alone was free from all error." He allowed for the human element in Scripture. His views on the authorship of the Epistle to the Hebrews, on St. James, and on the Apocalypse, have found wide acceptance among recent scholars. In the matter of allegory he vacillates. It is not indeed often that he countenances it by his example,[2] but he made the two unfortunate observations, that without a mystic sense the Book of Kings' would be no more profitable than Livy,[3] and, "give chief attention to those expositors who depart as widely as possible from the letter." But we can best estimate the advance he made when we recall that in his day there were thousands of theologians who did not know whether the Apostles wrote in Hebrew, in Greek, or in Latin; and when, as Bellarmine says, "The better grammarian a man was, the worse theologian was he considered to be."[4] Robert Stephens, in his *Apologia*, quotes the remark of a Professor of the Sorbonne, who, in a declamation against Scripture during the course of a public lecture, exclaimed, "By heavens! I was more than fifty years old before I knew what the New Testament was." The custom of these theologians was, he adds, "to draw their theology not from the sacred codex of the oracles of God, but from their Master

---

[1] Passus est errare suos Christus etiam post acceptum Paracletum sed non usque ad fidei periculum. See Drummond, *Erasmus*, i. 307. Compare the remark in his *Ratio Verae Theologiae*, and on Colet's views, in *Opp.* iii. 459.

[2] Yet he allegorises the raising of Jairus' daughter. *Eccles.* ed. 1730, pp. 70, *sqq.* We may be proud of the influence of Colet over Erasmus.

[3] *Enchirid. Mil. Christ.* ed. 1523, leaf *g.* 2. In this passage the "mysterium in literis omnibus" is insisted on. See too *De Copia rerum* (ed. 1545, p. 165); *De tedio et pavore Christi* (ed. 1515, p. 128); *Praef. in Annott.* (ed. 1535); *Ennarratio in* Ps. lxxxvi. (ed. 1652, p. 19). Yet he ridicules the *abuse* of allegory in *Encom. Moriae* and *Instit. Principis Christiani* (ed. 1628, p. 121). For these references I am indebted to the kindness of the Rev. J. H. Lupton.

[4] Bellarmine, *De Rom. Pontif.* iv. 12. Melanchthon says, "*Itali dicunt 'Bonus est grammaticus; ergo est haereticus'*" (*Postill.* iii. 660). Erasmus has excellent philological notes on Acts i. 4; Rom. v. 12, ix. 5; Phil. ii. 6; Col. ii. 18, &c., and his linguistic attainments were of a high order, though Lee made the somewhat cheap remark, that he could point out 300 errors in his New Testament. Luther, who exceedingly disliked Erasmus as a theologian, and even used unbecoming language about him, stigmatising him as "a foe to all religion and a thorough sham," yet estimated him highly as a grammarian (*Ep. ad Spalat.* 1518; *Briefe*, iv. 507; *Tischreden*, ii. 402, 419).

Y

of the Sentences, the sophist Aristotle, and the Mahometan Averroes." [1]

The work then which Erasmus achieved, and achieved with brilliant ability and no mean courage, was the work of a pioneer. He had no desire to break wholly with the past. He was a man of cosmopolitan sympathies ; a theologian, yet the prince of Humanists; a pitiless exposer of religious abuses, yet an ally of Popes and Cardinals ; an editor of the Fathers, yet a friend of those who overthrew their dictatorship ; a Biblical critic, yet the author of the *Colloquies,* and the *Encomium Moriae.* "*Erasmus est homo pro se*" is the definition given of him in the *Epistolae obscurorum virorum.* "Words without deeds," "*Verba non res,*" was Luther's severe judgment of him. But "words" are often the most powerful of deeds, and Erasmus was fully entitled to the praise that he had made the path easy for all who followed him. "We by our diligence," he says, "have smoothed a road which previously was rugged and troublesome, but in which henceforth great theologians may ride more easily with steeds and chariots. We have levelled the soil of the arena, in which, with fewer obstacles, they may now display those splendid processions of their wisdom. We have cleansed with harrows the fallow land which heretofore was impeded with briars and burs. We have swept away the impediments, and opened a field wherein they who may hereafter wish to explain the secrets of Scripture may either play together with greater freedom, or join battle with more convenience."

5. God endows His chosen instruments with such gifts as they specially need. It required a personality far different from that of Erasmus to bring about that emancipation of Christendom from sacerdotal tyranny and false exegesis which was the essence of the Reformation.[2] Revolutions have

---

[1] See similar remarks quoted in Seebohm, *Oxford Reformers,* ch. ii.

[2] Erasmus said, "*Ego peperi ovum gallinaceum, Lutherus exclusit pullum longe dissimillimum*" (*Epp.* iii. p. 840) ; "*Videor mihi fere omnia docuisse quae docet Lutherus*" (Letter to Zwingli) ; "*Quid mihi cum causa Capnionis et Lutheri?*" (*Ep.* 477) ; see Beard, *Hibbert Lectures,* p. 69. In 1520 Erasmus writes to Leo X., "Lutherum non novi, nec libros illius umquam legi, *nisi forte decem aut duodecim pagellas, easque captim.*" Could this be true ?

usually been wrought by men whose sympathies were all the more intense and concentrated from their very narrowness, not by men of delicate refinement and many-sided powers of appreciation. The genius of Erasmus, and the learning of Melanchthon would have produced but small results without the Titanic force of Luther, the sovereign good sense of Zwingli, the remorseless logic of Calvin;—and of these three the greatest was MARTIN LUTHER.

Luther was the "intensified self" of the German nation.[1] This man it is a recent fashion in the Church of England to revile—and would to God that they who revile him would render to mankind but one of the very least of his many services! He gave to the Germans their Bible; he gave them the perfection of their language; he gave them the sense of their unity; he gave them the conviction of their freedom before God; he gave them the prayers which rise night and morning from thousands of hearts; he gave them the burning hymns, rich in essential truth, and set to mighty music, which are still daily poured forth by millions of voices; he gave them the example of a family life, pure, simple, and humbly dependent upon God. "To have lifted the load of sin from many consciences—to have reconciled nature and duty, purity and passion—to have made woman once more the faithful helpmeet of God's servants as of other men—to have been the founder of countless sweet and peaceful homes—is no small part of Luther's true glory." But his highest glory—the glory he valued most—was to have fulfilled the vow of the Doctorate—*Juro me veritatem evangelicam pro virili defensurum*—and to have given to the people whom he loved an open Bible which could be closed no more.

And he not only gave them the open Bible, but taught them and all the world how best it might be interpreted. His Commentary on the Galatians was his only complete and continuous contribution to the exegesis of the New Testament,[2] yet that single work would have proved to be a

---

[1] See Döllinger, *Kirche und Kirchenthum*, 386 ; Dorner, *Prot. Theol.* i. 81-125.
[2] 1519. Re-edited in 1524, and 1535. Luther says " Es ist Dolmetschen nicht einer jeglichen Kunst; es gehört dazu ein recht from, treu, fleisig,

blessing to millions, had it produced no other effect than to
lead (as it did) to the enlightenment of John Bunyan and John
Wesley. But Luther's German Bible is more than a translation. It forms also an admirable commentary,[1] and in
his *Prefaces* and in all his other works he enunciated rules to
which the complete revolution of exegetic methods in modern
times has been principally due.

There are four well-marked stages of his religious
advance—

1. Till the age of twenty-six (A.D. 1508) he studied
scholasticism, and the *Sententiarii.* He could almost repeat
Gabriel Biel and Peter of Alliacum by heart and was an
eager student of Occam;[2] but he knew no Greek and no
Hebrew, and had read no more of the Bible than the
Church lessons.[3] His incessant study of the Vulgate, which
he found in the library of his monastery at Erfurt, caused him
even then to be suspected of heterodoxy; but he was still
imprisoned in the bonds of ecclesiastical tradition, was
content with the secondhand fancies of the *Glossa Ordinaria,*
and had only begun to grasp the importance of the verse
which influenced his life, " *The just shall live by faith.*"

2. For ten years more (1509-1517), though he lectured on
furchtsam, christlich, gelehrt, erfahren, geübt Herz" (*Sensdchr. vom
Dolmetschen*).

[1] The cases in which he shewed dogmatic bias (2 Sam. xxiii. 1 ; Ps. lxviii.
12, 19 ; Rom. v. 28 (*allein* durch den Glauben), Eph. iv. 16 (*und das alles*) are
honourably few (see Reuss, *Gesch. d. N.T.* p. 449). Luther, born 1483 ;
Theses, 1517 ; Leipzig discussion, 1519 ; excommunicated, 1520 ; Diet of
Worms, 1521 ; returns to Wittenberg from Wartburg, 1522 ; Peasants' War,
1525 ; marriage, 1525 ; Augsburg confession, 1530 ; Articles of Smalcald,
1537 ; death, 1546.

[2] "Diu multumque legit scripta Occam." Melanchthon, *Vit. Luth.* p. 7.
Even at this period, however, Martin of Mellerstadt prophesied that Luther
would alter the then common studies, *id.* p. 11 ; Gieseler, v. 220.

[3] See Jurgens, *Luther's Leben,* i. 487. "Von dreissig Jahren war die Bibel
unbekannt. . . *Da ich zwanzig Jahr alt war hatte ich noch keine gesehen.*
Ich meinete es wären keine Evangelia noch Episteln *mehr denn die in den Pos-
tillen sind.* Endlich fand ich in der Liberei in Erfurt eine Bibel, die las ich
oft *mit grosser Verwunderung Dr. Staupitzen.*" *Tischreden,* iii. 229. See too
Mathesius, *Leben d. M. Luther Erste Pred.* p. 6. In spite of what Dr. Maitland
says (*Dark Ages,* pp. 468-508), it is clear from the decree of Charles V. in the
Netherlands that the common reading of the Bible *was regarded as a crime
which deserved death by burning.* And Carlstadt tells us that he had been a
Doctor of Divinity for eight years before he read the whole New Testament.
See the anecdotes of Archbishop Albert in Sixt. of Amama (*Antibarb. Bibl.*
ii. 7) and of Linacre in Balaeus, *Cent.* 8.

the Bible at Wittenberg in a practical way, and had abandoned scholasticism, he was still partly content with the
Vulgate, the Fathers, and the fourfold sense.[1]

3. The next four years (1518-1521) were marked by a
great advance.[2] He began to study Hebrew and Greek, to
draw from his own rich spiritual experiences, and to depend
less and less on the Fathers. The discovery that *poenitentia*
was the equivalent of μετάνοια, and meant something much
more than, and very different from *penance*, brought home to
him with a tumult of joy and conviction the indispensable
necessity of reverting to the original languages of Scripture.[3]
He began to understand the extent to which words often
repeated tend to ossify the organs of intelligence. His
comments during this period were popular and practical,
with the one aim of bringing Scripture home to the hearts
and consciences of men.[4]

4. It was only in his fourth stage that he gained a clear
grasp of the principles which through all the Reformed
and Lutheran Churches have thenceforth been steadily
recognised in the interpretation of Scripture.[5]

What are those principles ?

i. First among them was the supreme and final authority
of Scripture itself, apart from all ecclesiastical authority
or interference. This was with Luther a *Hauptfunda-*

---

[1] See *Werke*, xxxv. 24 (Erlang.). The Erfurt monks told him that Scripture was an obscure confused mass, and that he should go to Fathers and
Schoolmen (*Tischreden*, lxxii. 108, Erlang.). He became a Doctor in 1512.
In 1516, he wrote to J. Lange, " Pars crucis meae vel maxima est quod videre
cogor fratrum ingenia ' *in istis coenis* ' (Aristotle, &c.) vitam agere et operam
perdere." In his theses in defence of Augustinianism (1517) the 41st was
" *Tota fere Aristotelis ethica pessima gratiae inimica.*"

[2] Luther's conference with Cardinal Cajetan took place in 1518. The liberality of Cajetan as a commentator, his preference of the literal sense, his free
admission of the defects of the Vulgate, &c., may have been due in part to the
influence of Reformation principles. See Weiszäcker in Herzog.

[3] *Briefe*, i. 116 (ed. De Wette). Up to that time he says that he had disliked Nicolas of Lyra, because of his attention to the literal sense ; "sed nunc
hanc ipsam ob commendationem omnibus fere Scripturae interpretibus eum
antepono." *Opp. Exeget. Lat.* ii. 320.

[4] To this period belong his *Operationes in Psalmos*, "the first scientifically
exegetic book of the Reformation."

[5] He began to translate the N.T. in 1521, using Erasmus's edition and the
Vulgate (*Briefe*, ii. 123-176). His invaluable Prefaces may be read in the lxiii.
vol. of his works (ed. Erlangen).

ment which he refused even to discuss, because it was theoretically admitted even by his opponents. It was in his controversy with Eck, in 1519, that he was first led to reject as fallible the authority of councils, and to declare that "a layman who has Scripture is more than Pope or council without it." He learnt to feel the utmost scorn for current glosses. "When Papists quote the Scriptures," he says, "it is in this style. ' *Ye are the salt of the earth,*' *i.e.* ' Ye are Priests.' ' *Praise God in His saints,*' *i.e.* ' The Pope has the power of canonisation.' " Vincentius of Lerins had laid down the rule that interpretation was to follow the lines of Church tradition.[1] Luther, on the other hand, maintained that "the Church is the creature of the Gospel, incomparably inferior to the Gospel." "The Church cannot create articles of faith; she can only recognise and confess them as a slave does the seal of his lord." "The censure of the Church will not separate me from the Church, if truth joins me to the Church." "The Pythagorean *ipse dixit* is not to be tolerated in the Church." "Let us not heap to ourselves Fathers, Councils, Doctors, Decretals, and the slough of human traditions and opinions." Thus Luther refused to allow the Pope—as in his rough way he expressed it—" to sit upon the eggs, and be our idol." [2] He recognised the truth that "to set forth the Church as the way to Christ, instead of setting forth Christ as the way to the Church, is the fountain of unnumbered errors." " *Ecclesia non facit Verbum sed fit Verbo.*"

[1] Vinc. Ler. *Commonitor, Ep.* 2 ; " *Interpretationis linea secundum ecclesiastici et catholici sensus normam dirigatur.*" The rule was formally reaffirmed by the Council of Trent (*Sess.* iv.), and had been again and again repeated from the days of Irenaeus, Tertullian and Cyprian downwards. Comp. Bellarmine, *De Verb. Dei,* iii. 3. " Hic in genere dicimus judicem veri sensus Scripturae et omnium controversiarum ecclesiam esse, *id est Pontificem.*" The rule, however great its vitality, however high the authorities which may be quoted in its favour, resembles the assertion that no sidereal phenomena must ever henceforth be allowed to interfere with the laws of Kepler and Newton. If there be one truth which History has demonstrated more decisively than another it is that no Church, and no combination of Churches, has ever possessed the attribute of exegetic infallibility.

[2] See Fabricius, *Loci Commun. M. Lutheri,* i. 120. Köstlin, *Luther's Theologie,* i. 272–278. Bellarmine said, " Summum judicium esse summi Pontificis." *De Verb. Dei,* iv. 1.

ii. Secondly he asserted not only the supreme authority but the *sufficiency* of Scripture. The Christian man, he said, needed Scripture and nothing else, not even a commentary. "I ask for Scripture," he said, "and Eck offers me the Fathers. I ask for the sun, and he shows me his lanterns. I ask, 'Where is your Scripture proof?' and he adduces Ambrose and Cyril." He saw that the Fathers have repeatedly erred, and that, except in the very simplest doctrines, there is no such thing as an "unanimous consent" among them. "With all due respect to the Fathers," he said, at Leipzig, "I prefer the authority of Scripture."[1]

iii. Like all the other reformers he set aside the dreary fiction of the fourfold sense. In this respect he was in advance of Erasmus, who thought that the Holy Spirit had meant words to be taken in various senses, and that this was not the "uncertainty," but the "fecundity" of Scripture. "The literal sense of Scripture alone," said Luther, "is the whole essence of faith and of Christian theology."[2] "I have observed this, that all heresies and errors have originated, not from the simple words of Scripture, as is so universally asserted, but from *neglecting* the simple words of Scripture, and from the affectation of purely subjective (*ex proprio cerebro*) tropes and inferences." "In the schools of theologians it is a well-known rule that Scripture is to be understood in four ways, literal, allegoric, moral, anagogic. But if we wish to handle Scripture aright, our one effort will be to obtain *unum, simplicem, germanum, et certum sensum literalem*." "Each passage has one clear, definite, and true sense of its own. All others are but doubtful and uncertain opinions." He saw as clearly as Melanchthon[3] that the

---

[1] "Salvis reverentiis Patrum ego praefero auctoritatem Scripturae." For Luther's opinion on the Fathers see *infra*. Bishop Jewel is one of the many English theologians who deny the existence of any "unanimous consent of the Fathers;" and even Cardinal Newman admits of the "quod semper, quod ubique," &c., that "it is hardly available now."

[2] Unfortunately however, Luther opened the postern door for the re-intrusion of artificial dogmas by saying too unguardedly, "Grammatica non debet regere res sed servire rebus." "Grammaticam decet Theologiae cedere." *Praef. in Cant.*; and on Gen. xvi.

[3] *De Rhetorica*, ii. "Fit enim incerta oratio in tot sententias discerpta. Nos meminerimus unam quandam ac certam et simplicem sententiam ubique

pretence of a *multiplex intelligentia* destroyed the whole meaning of Scripture and deprived it of any *certain* sense at all,
while it left room for the most extravagant perversions, and
became a subtle method for transferring to human fallibility
what belonged exclusively to the domain of revelation.

iv. It need hardly be said, therefore, that Luther, like most
of the Reformers, rejected the validity of allegory.[1] He
totally denied its claim to be regarded as a *spiritual*
interpretation. " An interpreter," he said, " must as much
as possible avoid allegory, that he may not wander in
idle dreams." " Origen's allegories are not worth so
much dirt." " Allegories are empty speculations, and as
it were the scum of Holy Scripture." " Allegory is a sort
of beautiful harlot, who proves herself specially seductive
to idle men." " To allegorise is to juggle with Scripture."
" Allegorising may degenerate into a mere monkey-game
(*Affenspiel*)." " Allegories are awkward, absurd, invented,
obsolete, loose rags." [2] Since Paul, *after furnishing a proof*,
had borrowed an illustration from allegory, we may use them
as mere spangles and pretty ornaments (*Schmuck und schöne
Spangen*), but nothing more.[3]

v. Luther also maintained the *perspicuity* of Scripture, that
is, its *perspicuitas finalis* in the chief matters which pertain to
the Law and Gospel. He sometimes came near to the modern
remark that, " the Bible is to be interpreted like any other

quaerendam esse. *Nam oratio quae non habet unam ac simplicem sententiam
nihil docet."* Elsewhere he says that it produces a *prodigiosa metamor-
phosis* in the meaning of Scripture. For other quotations see Flacius, *Clavis
Sacr. Scripturae* (ii. 65), and for Calvin's views, see his remarks on Gen. ii.
8 ; vi. 14. The fourfold sense of Flacius (words, context, purpose, doctrine)
is much more real than that of the schoolmen.

[1] The *single* sense of Scripture was maintained in the sixteenth century by
Luther Erasmus, Melanchthon, Camerarius, Osiander, Chemnitz, Calixt,
Zwingli, Bucer, Calvin, Beza, Casaubon, Drusius, Scaliger ; in the seventeenth
by J. and L. Cappellus, L. de Dieu, Lightfoot, Arminius, Grotius, Episcopius,
Clericus, and many others. Even Cajetan († 1534) avoids allegory and
expounds *juxta sensum literalem. Dedic. ad Carol. v.*

[2] He speaks more temperately in his *Table Talk* (see Hazlitt's *Transl.* pp.
326-328. See too Beza on Gal. iv. 22-31).

[3] These remarks are chiefly found in Luther's *Comm. in Gen.* iii., xv., xxx.
See Fabricius, *Loc. Comm.*, i. 73, *sq.* and *Opp. Lat.* vii. 37. He is least true to
his own principle in the comments on Job, Psalms, and Canticles, and is by no
means always consistent.

book." "The Holy Ghost," he said, "is the all-simplest writer that is in heaven or earth ; therefore his words can have no more than one simplest sense, which we call the scriptural or literal meaning." [1] He did not of course deny that there are difficulties in Scripture, and is fond of quoting Gregory's remark, that it is "a river in which the lamb may ford and the elephant must swim." When confronted with the fact that there is scarcely a verse in Scripture which has not been interpreted in different ways, he can only attribute it to malice and pravity, or with Melanchthon to "mere petulance and diabolical sophistry." The explanation is inadequate. The strife of perfectly honest interpreters cries aloud to heaven. Even such passages as Christ's promise to St. Peter, and the authority given to the Apostles, and the institution of the Eucharist have met with interpretations equally honest yet fundamentally diverse. The Scripture is perfectly perspicuous in those few and simple truths which suffice for salvation, but as to many other subjects, and even as to subjects which have been deemed to be of consummate importance, it may almost be said *Quot viri, tot sententiae.* We can only say with Chrysostom, πάντα τὰ ἀναγκαῖα δῆλα.[2] Scripture reveals distinctly all necessary truth, but whole passages and even books of Scripture are of uncertain significance to the Christian Church.

vi. Luther maintained with all his force, and almost for the first time in history, the absolute indefeasible *right of private judgment*, which, with the doctrine of the spiritual priesthood of all Christians, lies at the base of all Protestantism, I might even say at the base of all manly, sure, and thoughtful religion. He felt that the Christian especially is not permitted to resign—that it is a mere effeminate pusillanimity to resign—into the hands of any one the exercise of that spiritual faculty—the gift which comes from the unction of the Holy One—which is promised to all Christian

---

[1] Answer to Emser. See Köstlin, *Luther's Theol.* ii. 58, 284.

[2] Chrys. in 2 Thess. The "*perspicuity*" of Scripture must certainly be limited. Luther *insisted* on the literal sense ; Erasmus says that those commentators were to be preferred who were farthest removed from the literal sense. Jeremy Taylor (*Liberty of Prophesying, Works,* vi. 403–419) exaggerates the difficulties of Scripture.

men alike. He indignantly swept aside the fiction of a usurping hierarchy, that priests were in any sense the sole authorised interpreters of Scripture. The first wall which he threw down in his attack on the Papacy was the Romish distinction between the spiritual capacity of the laity and the clergy. There was no truth to which Luther clung more firmly, none which he felt to be nobler, more inspiring, or more eternally necessary, than the fact that Christ has not *two* bodies but *one* body, wherein every member has his office, which is to be a priest therein. Among Christians, he maintained, there is a difference of *office*, but no difference in spiritual rights, and that it is baptism, not ordination, unction, or tonsure, which makes any one "a religious" or a spiritual man. He held that henceforth there is no such thing as a priest in the sacrificial sense except Christ alone, nor is any minister a priest in *that* sense except by metaphor, and by exactly the same metaphor whereby every other Christian is every whit as much a priest as he.[1] The use of the word "priest" except in the sense of presbyter, to describe the functions of the clerical order, and the confusion of the ἱερεὺς with the Christian minister, was, in Luther's opinion a defiance alike of the whole letter and spirit of the New Testament. The word of God was a word not to the clerisy, and not for the sole interpretation of the clerisy, but a word to all.[2] He held that the Holy Spirit was given to all Christians, and therefore that the laity had a higher function than merely to register the decrees and interpretations of a ministerial class.

There was nothing which Luther found it more difficult to maintain with unflinching faithfulness than this indefeasible right to private judgment. He was sorely tried by the excesses of individual opinion. The doctrine of tolerance was

---

[1] It is needless to repeat that ἱερεὺς is *never* used in the New Testament of Christian ministers, but only of heathen and Jewish priests, or of Christ, or *of the whole body of Christian men* (1 Pet. ii. 5, 9 ; Rev. i. 6 ; v. 10 ; xx. 6).

[2] This is the direct antithesis to the views of Gerson, who not only protested with all his might against the right of individual judgment, but said that the exegetic views of the Church were inspired, and that any who disputed them should not be argued with, but legally punished.

as yet unhappily unknown. Luther was perplexed and pained by the fact that in the sacramentarian controversy Zwingli, in the political controversies the Anabaptists, in the controversy about free-will Erasmus, in other controversies Campanus and Emser and Carlstadt and the Zwickau prophets, all appealed to Scripture as constantly and, to all appearance, as sincerely as himself, and claimed the right to interpret it in their own way. Melanchthon dreamed of getting over the difficulty by " a consensus of pious men," [1] which was only another way of re-enthroning the fallibility of councils, and of restoring that external dictation of the sense of Scripture which Luther in his letter to the Pope had expressly repudiated.[2] Calvin, too naturally dictatorial to admit the right of individual judgment, talked with futility about a " synod of true Bishops." [3] But Luther, like a true man, held fast to the claim of Christian liberty. He preferred the hurricane of controversies to the stagnation of enforced uniformity, and the pestilence of authoritative error. He saw the worthlessness of merely nominal unity, which only meant the torpor of an unreasoning acquiescence, and in spite of all trials he continued to assert to the last, that it was at once the duty and the privilege of every Christian to test his faith by the Scriptures. " To ascertain and judge about doctrine pertains," he says, " to all and to every Christian; and in such a way that let him be anathema who injures their right by a single hair." [4]

In accordance with these principles, Luther, in his preface to Isaiah (1528) and in other parts of his writings, lays down what he conceives to be the true rules of Scripture

---

[1] " Interpretatio est donum piorum " Melanchthon's *Loci Communes*, p. 369. Unless " *interpretatio* " be confined to the *apprehension of spiritual truths*, which is a totally different thing from the exegesis of a very large part of the Old, and even of the New Testament, the remark is absolutely untrue.

[2] 1520. " *Leges* interpretandi verbum Dei non patior." See Köstlin, *Luther's Theologie*, ii. 63. Bunsen, *God in History*, iii. 199-201.

[3] Calvin, *Inst.* iv. 9, § 13. The only test of a " true " Bishop would have been one who accepted the views of Calvin.

[4] *Werke*, xxviii. 339 (Erl. ed.). He founded the right on Matt. vii. 15 ; John x. 4, 5 ; 1 John iv. 1 ; 1 Thess. v. 21 ; 1 Cor. ii. 15 ; iii. 22. So too Flacius, *Clavis*, i. 472. " De interpretatione lis est, penes quem ea potestas sit ? Responsio est *unumquemque piorum* . . habere jus interpretandi."

interpretation. He insists (1) on the necessity for grammatical knowledge; (2) on the importance of taking into consideration times, circumstances, and conditions; (3) on the observance of the context; (4) on the need of faith and spiritual illumination; (5) on keeping what he called "the proportion of faith"; and (6) on the reference of all Scripture to Christ. Of the former requirements nothing need be said, but the three latter contained the germs of many subsequent errors.

(1) It is true and right to say that faith and spiritual enlightenment are necessary for the saving knowledge of Scripture, and for the saving apprehension of Gospel truths. It is further true that the Scripture deals with the will of God and the heart of man, and that, therefore, the insight of a saint may often be of more value for its explanation than the skill of a grammarian. But except in power to understand the few and simple truths which are essential to salvation, it is not true that piety and orthodoxy can claim any inward light or infallible authority for the interpretation of the Bible, and in the face of the age-long mistakes of even the holiest men it is nothing short of spiritual arrogance to put forth such a claim. It requires faith, it requires the aid of the Holy Spirit, so to read the Holy Scriptures as to attain that best end which the reading of them serves—namely, to become thereby wise unto salvation. But when we speak of the whole Bible we speak of the national literature of many hundreds of years, and throughout by far the largest part of the sacred writings the decision of what the authors say and mean, apart from its personal application, pertains far less to piety than to grammar, intelligence, unbiassed candour, historical knowledge, and literary tact.

(2) *Analogia fidei*—the proportion of faith—is a watchword which occurs hundreds of times in the writings of the Reformers.[1] As is the case with nine out of every ten

---

[1] It is practically confused with the obscure rule that Scripture interprets itself, a rule which exegetically considered has no meaning. "Non aliunde quam ex ipsa sacra Scriptura certa et infallibilis potest haberi interpretatio. Scriptura enim, vel potius Spiritus Sanctus in scriptura loquens, est sui ipsius

dogmatic Shibboleths it involved the misapplication of a
Scriptural phrase. St. Paul has said that if we have the gift
of prophecy—that is of religious teaching—we ought severally
to exercise it κατὰ τὴν ἀναλογίαν τῆς πίστεως, *i.e.* as St.
Chrysostom rightly explains it, "*according to the proportion
of our faith,*" according to the greater or less measure of
the faith which we have acquired.[1] This phrase was first
inaccurately used to mean *Analogia Scripturae*—the rule
that we ought to explain Scripture in accordance with
Scripture.[2] So far as it forbade men to isolate and distort
any one passage into authoritative contradiction to the
whole tenor of Scripture teaching, the misapplied phrase is
susceptible of a wise use. It was soon, however, made to
mean the same as the old Romish rule that no explanation is
to be admitted which runs counter to the current ecclesiastical
dogmas.[3] It thus paved the way for the distortions and
sophistries of the later Protestant scholasticism, and turned
the Old Testament especially into "a sort of obscure forest in
which dogma and allegory hunt in couples to catch what
they can."

(3) Nor is Luther's rule "to find Christ everywhere in
Scripture" free from liability to grave abuse.[4] Homiletically
indeed the rule is true. The end of the law is Christ. He
is the hid treasure and the pearl of great price.[5] But while

legitimus interpres." Quenstedt, i. 137. Such a view is true only of the
simplest essentials of the faith. There is no *mechanical* unity in the Bible.

[1] The "proportion of faith" was greatly decided by parallel passages
which, as Luther felt, might be egregiously abused. He said that "to cull
diverse passages from diverse places without any reference to the sequence of
thought, is the most current cause of going wrong."

[2] S. Thom. Aquin., *Summ. Ima. qu.* i. *art.* 10. "Cum veritas unius
Scripturae ostenditur veritati alterius non repugnare." In old writers "the
analogy of faith" was used as a practical synonym for the "*regula* fidei."
Iren. *Haer.* ii. 47 ; Aug. *De Cons. Ev.* i. 1 ; *De Civ. Dei*, ii. 13 ; *c. Faustin.*
ii. 6 ; Tert. *Enchirid.* 56.

[3] The first trace of this rule is found in Origen, *De Princip.* iv. 26. Its
most distinct assertor was Vincent of Lerins. *Commonitor. Ep.* 2. See *Conc.
Trident. Sess.* iv.

[4] Auch ist das der rechte Prüfestein alle Bücher zu tadeln, wenn man siehet
ob sie Christum treiben oder nicht," *Werke*, lxiii. 157. On this rule see
Flacius, *Clavis S. Script.* p. 7, and Schleiermacher, *Hermeneutik*, § 13.

[5] "Wir erleuchten die alte Heilige Schrift durch das Evangelium," *Werke*,
iv. 1728. "Here (in the O.T.) shalt thou find the swaddling-clothes and the

homiletically we may with St. Augustine tolerate any comment *modo pia sit*, it is an exegetical fraud to read developed Christian dogmas between the lines of Jewish narratives. It may be morally edifying but it is historically false to give to Genesis the meaning of the Apocalypse, and to the Song of Solomon that of the First Epistle of St. John.[1] When Luther reads the doctrines of the Trinity, and the Incarnation, and Justification by Faith, and Reformation dogmatics and polemics, into passages written more than a thousand years before the Christian era—when, in a spirit worthy of R. Aqiba himself, he infers the Divinity of the Messiah and the "Communication of Idioms" from the particle את in Gen. v. 22,[2] he is adopting an unreal method which had been rejected a millennium earlier by the clearer insight and more unbiassed wisdom of the School of Antioch.[3] As a consequence of this method, in his commentary on Genesis he adds nothing to Lyra except a misplaced dogmatic treatment of patriarchal history.

It was, however, a result of this last rule of interpretation that Luther assumed the attitude of manly independence

manger in which Christ lies. *Poor and of little value are the swaddling-clothes*, but dear is Christ the treasure that lies in them." *Pref. to O.T. of* 1523. "*Externa variant, interna manent.*" *In* Ps. xx. "Quodsi adversarii Scripturam urserint contra Christum, nos urgemus Christum contra Scripturam."

[1] "There is nothing more miserable as specimens of perverted ingenuity than the attempts of certain commentators and preachers to find remote and recondite and intended allusions to Christ everywhere (in the Bible) . . . This perverted mode of comment is not merely harmless, idle, useless, it is positively dangerous. This is to make the Holy Spirit speak riddles and conundrums, and the interpretation of Scripture but clever riddle-guessing" (F. W. Robertson).

[2] He renders the words יִתְהַלֵּךְ אֶת־הָאֱלֹהִים, "*ambulavit Deum*," and finds in it the *communicatio idiomatum*, but not by the Understanding, which is only *Rauchloch und Schlaffenlande*. See his explanation of the last words of David, 1543.

[3] See Hazlitt's edition of the *Table Talk*, p. 74, where Luther talks much as Colet does about triads (*On the Hierarchies*, ed. Lupton, p. 192).

[4] Lyra and Rashi are traceable throughout, and in his polemical remarks on iv. 11 ; v. 22 ; xv. 7, &c., Simon says, "il n'a le plus souvent consulté que les préjugés dont il était rempli." See Luther's notes on Gen. i. 26 ; ii. 7, 14 ; iii. 21 ; iv. 1 ; xi. 7-9 ; Num. vi. 22 ; 2 Sam. xxiii. 2, &c. Siegfried, *Rashi's Einfluss*, &c. (Merx, *Archiv*, i. 432). Yet Luther praised Hilary's rule "*Optimus* interpres hic est qui sensum e Scripturâ potius retulerit quam attulerit nec cogat hoc in dictu contentum videri quod ante intelligentiam docere praesumserit." Fabricius, i. 72.

towards the Bible which made him "the most radical critic
of the Church of the Reformation."[1] We cannot find the
New Testament in the ordinary historic narratives of the Old
without large recourse to some form or other of the figurative
interpretation which Luther had so decisively rejected. He
drew a deep distinction between *this* method of making
Scripture self-interpreting, and that "uncertain understanding of the Scriptures by which the devil gets us on
his fork and tosses us hither and thither like a withered
leaf." But there were books of Scripture which failed to
come up to his test of canonicity, and when this was the case,
he unhesitatingly placed them in a lower position. Had he
accepted an infallible canon it could only have been on a
human tradition which he fundamentally refused to recognise
as authoritative. "That which does not teach Christ is not
apostolic," he said, "even if a Peter or a Paul taught it."
Hence he put some books far above others in value. He
declared that St. Paul's Epistles were more a gospel than
Matthew, Mark, and Luke, and that St. John's Gospel, the
Epistle to the Romans, and the First Epistle of Peter were
"the right kernel and marrow of all books."[2] He has little
to say of the Book of Esther.[3] He saw the complete historic
inferiority of the Books of Chronicles as compared with the
Books of Kings.[4] He saw that some of the Old Testament books had passed through revising hands. He refused
to believe that Solomon could have written Canticles.[5] He
points out the unchronological order of the present arrangement of the Book of Jeremiah. Believing that all the
prophets had built on the one foundation, he thought that
there was hay and stubble as well as gold and precious stones
in the superstructure. He was evidently startled and per-

---

[1] Keim, *Jesu von Nazara*, i. 142 (E. T.). On this subject see Köstlin,
Luther's Theologie, ii. 258-285.

[2] "Die rechten gewissen Hauptbücher des N.T."

[3] "Ich bin dem Buche (2 Macc.) und Esther so feind dass ich wollte sie
wären gar nicht vorhanden, denn sie judenzen zu sehr und haben viel heidn-
ischer Unart." See *Werke*, lxiii. 93-104.

[4] He only regarded the Books of Kings as "a Jewish Calendar." *Tischreden*, iv. 405.

[5] *Werke*, lxiii. 35-41.

plexed by the story of Jonah. He regarded the Book of
Job as a drama in glorification of resignation.[1] He believed
that the Book of Ecclesiastes belonged to the time of the
Maccabees. He considered one of St. Paul's proofs in the
Galatians too weak to hold. Of the Epistle to the Hebrews,
he said, "Who wrote it is unknown, but also it does not
matter."[2] He believed the Epistle of St. Jude to be unnecessary, second-hand, and non-apostolic.[3] He called the
Epistle of St. James a right strawy epistle and one which
flatly (*stracks*) contradicted St. Paul, and he did not believe
it to be written by an Apostle at all.[4] Of the Apocalypse he
said that "his spirit could not accommodate itself to the book,
and that it was sufficient reason for the small esteem in which
he held it, that Christ was neither taught in it nor recognised."[5]
He classed it with Esdras, and did not believe it to be
inspired. He thought it a matter of no consequence whether
Moses had written the Pentateuch or not. Thus without the
least hesitation he sought for the canon within the canon. It
need hardly be said that he rejected the Apocrypha without
any ceremony. Esdras, he says, "*mirum in modum esther-
issat et mardochissat.*" He wished that the second book of
Maccabees had never been written, because it contains too
much heathen folly. He had a profound contempt for those
who had a way of "quoting some single text and then setting
up their horns against all Scripture." "We will neither see
nor hear Moses," he exclaims, "for Moses was only given to
the Jewish people and does not concern us Gentiles and

---

[1] *Werke,* lxiii. 25 *ff.* "Like the comedies of Terence," *Tischreden,* iii. 130.

[2] He was the first to make the brilliant and now commonly-accepted con-
jecture that it was written by Apollos. He thought it a hard knot that this
Epistle "stracks verneinet und versagt die Busse den Sündern," and that
Heb. xii. 17, "wie es lauter scheinet, wider alle Evangelia und Episteln S.
Pauli zu seyn." See Köstlin, *Luther's Theol.* ii. 272.

[3] "Eine unnöthige Epistel unter die Hauptbücher zu rechnen."

[4] "Denn sie doch keine evangelische Art an ihr hat" (Köstlin, ii. 257.)

[5] In some of these views he was preceded by Carlstadt, and followed by
Melanchthon, Flacius (*Clavis,* ii. 46), Calvin, the Magdeburg Centuriators, and
even Cajetan. But criticism of the canon is as old as the Rabbis. Some of
them had doubts about Job, Esther, Ezekiel (Shabbath, f. 13, 2), and the Song
of Solomon (Yadaim, iii. 5).

Christians." [1] "When a contradiction occurs in Holy Scripture," he says, "so let it go." [2] It is very hard to reconcile
such remarks with his formal declaration that "one letter,
yea, a single tittle, of the Scripture is of more and greater consequence than heaven or earth." [3] In point of fact his theory
and his current language about inspiration are as completely
at variance with his methods of criticism as were those of
Origen, Jerome, and Augustine.

Some of these views were doubtless rash; they were
caused by an almost inevitable deficiency in the nascent
science of Biblical criticism; nor did he desire to press
them upon others. And yet it would have been well for the
peace of Christendom, it would have robbed many controversies, even in our own lifetime, of their miserable bitterness, if Christians had acquired the strong spiritual confidence
which enabled Luther to seize essentials without being
troubled by minor details. "The eagle that soars near the
sun does not worry itself how to cross the rivers." Luther at
least saw with truth that the Bible is a forest which contains
many very different trees. It is little short of childish to
call Luther a rationalist, in a bad sense, because of views like
these. [4] They arose not from rationalism but from its very
opposite—the sovereign supremacy of a faith which read the
Bible with fresh unbiassed eyes, and felt the closeness of the
immediate communion with God and Christ. In point of fact,
Allegory and Mysticism are as regards the Bible far more
rationalistic. They avowedly refuse to accept it as it is.
They avowedly make it say something else than it actually
does say. They start with the repeated assertion that the
letter of the Bible is in many passages too crude, or too
trivial for their acceptance. Luther had little need for such
expedients. With him faith and the Scriptures were not

---

[1] See Köstlin, ii. 78, *sq.*, 258, *sq.*; Diestel, pp. 250, 251.
[2] He expresses his indifference to small points of variation in the Gospels
(*Werke*, xliv. 174).
[3] We may refer generally to his remarks on Heb. ii. 13; Gal. iv.
22, &c.
[4] The charge is first found in Krause, *Opusc.* p. 199.

disparate things which hindered or excluded each other; they were things which had a like origin in the Holy Spirit which proceeds from the Father and the Son, and there could therefore be no enmity or discordance between them.[1] No one has used stronger language than this so-called rationalist against the unwarranted and exclusive reliance on the human understanding.[2] His free criticisms were due not to the insolence of reason but to the assurance of belief. " I have on my side," he said, " the Master and the Lord of Scripture, and let them go on in their hostile cry that the Scriptures contradict themselves. Hear thou well, thou art almost a bully with the Scriptures, which are nevertheless under Christ as a servant, and for this end *thou bringest out of them what is not altogether the best portion.* For this I do not care in the slightest; boast away of the servant, I, however, glory in Christ who is the true Lord and Sovereign of the Scriptures. Him have I, and by Him I abide." At the same time he believed that the Scriptures could not contradict themselves, and that therefore a criticism of the canon by faith was a criticism of the Scriptures by themselves. He strove " to equalise the Scriptures and the Christian conscience." He believed in the Holy Ghost.

These deep and far-reaching opinions of Luther's, which differentiate him from the mass of his predecessors, are not indeed elaborated into a system, or thoroughly coordinated with each other. He never makes it perfectly clear to us now he could place in Scripture a confidence so absolute, and yet subject it to a criticism so fearless. But he set forth one or two principles on the right apprehension of which the future of the Christian Faith, amid the advancing noon of knowledge, must certainly depend.

---

[1] Dorner, i. 250.

[2] He calls Reason "a poisonous beast with many dragon's heads ; " " old Madam Weather-witch " (*die alte Frau Wettermacherin*) ; " a devil's bride ; " " a beautiful strumpet ; " " a mangy, leprous harlot," &c., *Werke*, viii. 294 ; xii. 1530, 1533, 1537 (Beard, p. 156). It did not strike him that such language is absurd. Even at Worms he saw that he must be refuted out of Scripture or "*evidentissimis rationibus.*" But by "reason" he sometimes meant the purely psychical " understanding."

I. One of these is that *the Word of God is not to be regarded
as identical and coextensive with the Holy Scriptures.*[1] He indubitably admitted "a difference between the Word of God
and the Holy Scriptures, not merely in reference to the form,
but also in reference to the subject-matter."[2] He made a
distinction between author and author. He set one book far
above another in value. Christ, and Christ alone, was to him
without all error—was alone the essential Word of God.[3]

II. *His view of Inspiration was not verbal.*[4] The Bible was
not to him a stereotyped collection of supernatural syllables.
He took a living and historical view of the origin of the
sacred books. He held that they were not dictated by the
Holy Spirit, but that His illumination produced in the
minds of their writers the knowledge of salvation, so that
divine truth had been expressed in human form, and the
knowledge of God had become a personal possession of man.
The actual writing was a human not a supernatural act.[5] It
had been accomplished in full human consciousness, and not
as the Alexandrians taught, in a spasm of self-annihilating
ecstasy. The sacred authors received the historical matter
not by inspiration, but (as St. Luke and others so clearly tell
us) by purely historical research; and it was only under a

---

[1] Diestel (p. 283) says that the *identification* of the Bible with the Word of
God (of course he means after the Reformation) is first found in G. Major, *De
Origine Verbi Dei*, 1550. See Heppe, *Alt. Prot. Dogmatik*, i. 257.

[2] Dorner, i. 244. He did not regard all the Bible as one equally divine
Book, but as a living organism. See his remarks on John v. 39, and Romberg,
Die Lehre Luther's von den heil. Schrift (Wittenb. 1868), p. 5.

[3] *Werke.* xxii. 654, Erlang. "Gesetz und Evangelium sind zwei ganz
widerwärtige Dinge die sich mit oder neben einander nicht leiden oder ver-
tragen können." He spoke of some parts of the ceremonial law as "gleich
närrisch und vergeblich anzusehen." He recognises in the living whole of
scripture "edlere und minder edle Glieder, fundamentale und nicht fundamentale Glaubenslehren," Romberg, p. 15.

[4] Hence he even speaks of Ecclesiasticus as "Holy Scripture" written by
some poet or prophet "*aus dem Heiligen Geist*" (*Vorreden zu den Bibl. Büchern*).
"Luther die göttliche offenbarung nicht als *mechanische Mittheilung* übernatur-
licher Erkenntniss sondern als dynamische Lebensentwicklung auffasst," Romberg, 27.

[5] From this strong recognition of the human element, he speaks of Joel as
"ein gütiger und sanfter Mann ;" and says of Amos, "Er ist aber auch heftig
und schilt das Volk Israel fast durch das ganze Buch aus . . dass er wohl
mag heissen *Amos*, d. i. eine Last, oder der schwer und verdriesslich ist"

z 2

grace of general superintendence that they sifted and arranged it in proportion to the power and illumination they had received. Luther was never guilty of the inexcusable misuse of language and confusion of thought which makes inspiration involve infallibility. He saw clearly that just as the Spirit of the Lord may come upon a Samson, a David, and a Peter, and yet leave them liable to moral aberrations, so the same Spirit may dilate and illumine the faculties of a writer while it left him in all respects a human writer still.[1]

III. Once more, he held that *the Word of God is not in the Scriptures alone.* Inspiration still continues. It was no mere exhausted spasm of the past. It is not to Christians that the eternal oracles are dumb. The essential Word is still a living and a speaking Word. It does not consist in any collection of dead sounds. " God," he said, " does not speak grammatical vocables, but true essential things. Thus, sun and moon, Peter and Paul, thou and I, are nothing but words of God." [2] What may once have been a word of God in times past unto the Fathers, is not necessarily the word of God to us. The multitude of Christians in believing that God spoke to holy men of old have altogether forgotten that He speaks to them still, though neither then nor now does He raise the finite to the capacities of the infinite, so that neither they nor we were made either perfect or all-wise, or on all subjects infallible, although moved by the Holy Ghost. There was a time when patriarchs and prophets had no Old Testament, when saints and martyrs had no New Testament. As Zwingli said, " He who is born of the Spirit is no longer solely dependent on a book." [3]

---

[1] Hence he admits the existence of (unimportant) chronological and historic errors. Romberg, p. 16 ; Dorner, i. 255. *" Jacobus delirae."* See Köstlin, ii. 257.

[2] " In the deepest meaning of the essential and only truth . . all things in the world are only variously-embodied *words* of the Creator, inasmuch as by this mighty word alone they are upheld in being. Hence דָּבָר and ῥῆμα in Scripture signify both word and thing."—Stier, *Words of the Lord Jesus,* i. 38. Raymond of Sabieude (1430) was one of the first to recognise (in his *Theologia Naturalis*) that Nature is a Book of God. See the thought developed in Bacon, *De Augm. Scient.* (ed. Spedding, i. 149).

[3] Zwingli, *Opp.* ii. p. 250 (*ed.* Schuler and Schulthess) *ap.* Dorner, i. 290. " Piety is a fact and an experience, not a doctrine or a science." *Opp.* iii. 202.

Such were the views of Luther and it is impossible to exaggerate their importance. They shew a clearer vision and a more vital faith in the Holy Spirit than had ever been fully manifested since the Apostolic age, or than has since been attained by any but a brave and faithful few. They were the ripe fruit of the long results of Christian time, and they furnished to the principles of manly Christian exegesis a more valuable contribution than interminable folios of traditional commentary.

6. It will be needless to dwell at length on a multitude of other names. If Luther was the prophet of the Reformation MELANCHTHON was the teacher. If "the miner's son drew forth the metal of faith out of the deep pit, the armourer's son fashioned the metal for defiance and defence." [1] Carlstadt,[2] Seb. Franck,[3] Denck,[4] even the unhappy Müntzer [5] helped forward the cause of a truer interpretation. ZWINGLI, with absolute independence, had arrived at opinions on this subject which in all essential particulars coincided with those of Luther; only that his sunny and practical turn of mind had led him to choose the Gospel of St. Matthew, the Acts of the Apostles, and the two Epistles to Timothy, rather than the Epistles to the Romans and Galatians, as his basis for scrip-

---

[1] See Thilo, *Melanchthon im Dienste an heiliger Schrift*, Berlin, 1860. G. T. Strobel, *Hist. Litt. Nachricht von Phil. Melanchthon's Verdiensten um die heilige Schrift*, Altdorf, 1773. Galle, *Versuch. einer Charakteristik Melanchthons*, Halle, 1840. Melanchthon's most important services as an exegete were philological and theological. He says, "Ignavus in grammatica est ignavus in theologia." *Postill.* iv. 428.

[2] See his *Libellus de Canonicis Scripturis*, Augsb. 1520 ; Dorner, i. 126–132.

[3] "To the devout," he said, "all is an open book, wherein he learns more from the creatures and work of God than a godless man out of all Bibles." "Antichrist, who is now tired of the Pope . . will put on another disguise, and . . be more learned in Scripture than we. . . Many are making an idol of Scripture." "The *Scriptures* are only the shell, cradle, sheath, lantern, court, letter, veil, and surrounding of the *Word of God*, which is the kernel, infantry sword, light, sanctuary, spirit and life, fulness and reality." *Id.* i. 193. He regarded all history as a Bible, and distinguished between the written and the unwritten word.

[4] "He regarded the world as the great word of God, and individuals as letters of the word." *Id.* i. 191. "I esteem the Holy Scriptures," he said, "above all human treasures ; but not so highly as the Word of God, which is living, powerful, eternal, free and independent of all elements of this world ; spirit, and not letter, written without pen and paper." See Hase, *Seb. Franck*.

[5] Dorner, i. 135–139.

tural instruction [1] A host of Reformation expositors endeavoured to spread the truths to which they had been led by the German and Swiss Reformers. It will be sufficient here merely to mention the names of Oecolampadius (†1581), Bucer (†1551), Brenz (†1570), Bugenhagen (†1558), Musculus (†1563), Camerarius (†1574), Bullinger (†1575), Chemnitz (†1586), and Beza (†1605). Among all of these there was a general agreement in principles, a rejection of scholastic methods, a refusal to acknowledge the exclusive dominance of patristic authority and church tradition; a repudiation of the hitherto dominant fourfold meaning; an avoidance of allegory; a study of the original languages; a close attention to the literal sense; a belief in the perspicuity and sufficiency of Scripture; the study of Scripture as a whole, and the reference of its total contents to Christ. These principles were followed in many writings and commentaries, and found their clearest statement and most systematic development in the *Clavis Scripturae Sacrae* of Flacius Illyricus.[2]

7. But the greatest exegete and theologian of the Reformation was undoubtedly CALVIN.

i. He is not an attractive figure in the history of that great movement. The mass of mankind revolt against the ruthless logical rigidity of his "horrible decree." They fling it from their belief with the eternal "God forbid!" of an inspired natural horror. They dislike the tyranny of theocratic sacerdotalism which he established at Geneva. Nevertheless his Commentaries, almost alone among those of his epoch,[3] are still

[1] Dorner, i. 287 290 "The Scriptures are in his view chiefly the *revelation* or *memorial* of the will of God."

[2] Flacius, *Clavis, Praef.* Matthias Flacius Illyricus († 1575) was—one of the most learned theologians among the early Lutherans, and his *Clavis Scripturae Sacrae* is full of learning and vigour. In the dedication there is a brief but clear sketch of the previous epochs of exegesis. Klausen (*Hermen.* 237–241) gives an outline of its general principles. Diestel (p. 953), who says that they are little more than a mixture of Jerome, Augustine, and Luther, hardly does him justice.

[3] The Reformation period produced hosts of commentators—Luther, Melanchthon, Zwingli, Musculus, Pellicanus, Chytraeus, Brenz, Bugenhagen, Bullinger, Beza, Bucer, Mercer, Camerarius, and many more. Calvin was more indebted to Bucer than any one else. In his Dedication to the *Gospel Harmony* he says, "Bucerum praesertim . . eximium Ecclesiae doctorem sum imitatus." The opinions of Beza had great weight with our English reformers,

a living force.[1] They are far more profound than those of
Zwingli, more thorough and scientific, if less original and
less spiritual, than those of Luther. In spite of his many
defects—the inequality of his works, his masterful arrogance
of tone, his inconsequent and in part retrogressive view
of inspiration, the manner in which he explains away
every passage which runs counter to his dogmatic prepossessions [2]—in spite, too, of his "hard expressions and
injurious declamations—"[3] he is one of the greatest interpreters of Scripture who ever lived. He owes that position
to a combination of merits. He had a vigorous intellect, a
dauntless spirit, a logical mind, a quick insight, a thorough
knowledge of the human heart, quickened by rich and strange
experience; above all, a manly and glowing sense of the grandeur of the Divine.[4] The neatness, precision, and lucidity of his
style, his classic training and wide knowledge, his methodical
accuracy of procedure, his manly independence, his avoidance
of needless and commonplace homiletics, his deep religious
feeling, his careful attention to the entire scope and context of
every passage, and the fact that he has commented on almost

who regarded him as the greatest theologian of his day. Out of 252 passages Dr. Scrivener has shown that our translators of 1611 have preferred his
readings to those of Stephen, Erasmus, the Vulgate, and the Complutensian.
From his Latin version they adopted some of their worst marginal renderings
(Mark i. 34; Luke iv. 41; Acts i. 8; Rom. xi. 17), though their good sense
delivered them from following him still more disastrously in Matt. i. 23; John
xviii 20; Acts ii. 41; Rom. ii. 7; v. 16; xi. 32; 1 Cor. xiii. 2; James, ii.
14, &c.

[1] This is illustrated by their translation into English and republication very
recently. Poole, in the preface to his *Synopsis*, excuses himself for not referring
more frequently to Calvin on the ground that others have borrowed from him
so largely that to quote them is to quote him! See Bayle's notice of him,
and further, Klausen, *Hermeneutik*, pp. 227 *fg.*; Meyer, *Gesch. d. Schrifterkl.*
ii. 448–475; Diestel, pp. 241 *sq.*; Reuss, *Gesch. d. Heilig. Schrift.* § 569;
Beard, *Hibbert Lectures*, 258 *fg.*; Tholuck, *Die Verdienste Calvin's als Ausleger der Heiligen Schrift* (*Verm. Schriften.* ii. 330–360); Merx, *Joel*, pp 428–
444; Haag, *La France Protestante*, Art. Calvin.

[2] G. W. Meyer, *Gesch. d. Schrifterklärung*, ii. 450. See Simon's *Hist. Crit.
des Comment. du N. T.* p. 747. Simon is unjust in his depreciation of
Calvin's learning. He had received a classic training, his first book was an
edition of Seneca, *De Clementia*, and in his Commentaries he quotes Plato,
Plutarch, Polybius, Cicero, Ovid, Quintilian, Aulus Gellius, &c.

[3] In a commentary on St. John we are shocked to stumble very soon on
such a sentence as "*Servetus, superbissimus ex gente Hispanica nebulo.*"

[4] He speaks of tradition and of the Fathers more respectfully than Luther
does. See *Praef. in Rom.* and *Praef. in Inst.*

the whole of the Bible, make him tower above the great majority of those who have written on Holy Scripture.[1] Nothing can furnish a greater contrast to many helpless commentaries, with their congeries of vacillating *variorum* annotations heaped together in aimless multiplicity, than the terse and decisive notes of the great Genevan theologian. He was a foe to all vagueness, prolixity, and digression. " I hold," he wrote to his friend Grynaeus, " that the chief excellence of an Expositor consists in clearness and brevity." [2] He fulfilled his own ideal in an exposition " brief, facile, luminous, full of rare sagacity, and entire good faith." Hundreds of pages have been written about " a woman having power on her head." Calvin says all that is essential in the three lines that the word " power " means by metonymy " a symbol of her husband's power over her," and is here used for some sort of veil. He never drags his weary reader through a bewildering mass of opinions, of which some are absurd, the majority impossible, and of which all but one must be wrong. " *Dimoveri non possum,*" he says, " *ab amore compendii.*"

ii. Nor is it a less supreme merit that he has a contempt for all exegetic falsities and frivolities, such as still show a fatal vitality in the commentaries of to-day.[3] We have already seen the comments of Rabbis, Fathers, and schoolmen on the first verse of Joel, the son of Pethuel. Since Pethuel is mentioned, said the Rabbis, he too must have been a

---

[1] He is at his best in his Commentaries on the Acts, on St. Paul's Epistles, and on the Psalms. The notes on the minor Prophets were much less elaborate. Hooker, in a MS. note quoted by Keble, says that "the sense of Scripture which Calvin alloweth," was held to be of more force than if "ten thousand Augustines, Jeromes, Chrysostoms, Cyprians were brought forth." He compares his influence to that of Peter Lombard among the Schoolmen. *Eccl. Pol.*, *Pref.* ii. 8.

[2] See *Praef. in Rom.* In this preface, and in his letter to Viret (May 19, 1540), he gives us his conception of the duty of an expositor. Schleiermacher says, " Die glückliche Ausübung der Kunst (des Auslegens) beruht auf dem Sprachtalent und dem Talent der einzelnen Menschenkenntniss " (*Hermeneutik*, § 10). Calvin had both, and the latter enabled him to enter into the feelings of the sacred writers.

[3] See his notes on John i. 3 ; Heb. xi. 13 ; Gen. iii. 21 (" *Non sic accipi haec verba convenit quasi Deus fuerit pellifex. Credibile est . . necessitate coactos mactasse aliqua (animalia) quorum se corio tegerent* ").

Prophet. "We see how impudent they were," says Calvin, "in such fictitious comments; when they have no reason to offer, they invent a fable, and obtrude it as an oracle." Nor is he less disdainful of Christian figments. It had (as we have seen) been irresistible to Jerome and other patristic and mediaeval commentators to drag the phrase " *Verbum* Dei quod *factum est* ad Joel," into a sign of the Incarnation, as though it implied the same as "the Word was made flesh!" The strong good sense of Calvin regarded such comments as a discreditable paltering with words, and he swept the fiction aside with the one contemptuous word, *Nugae!* Hence he carries out the principles of Luther and Melanchthon with more consistent thoroughness. He will not tamper with allegory as they do, even for ornamental and homiletic purposes.[1] He saw more clearly than Luther that the method has no foundation, and is liable to gross error.[2] He will not give a mystic significance even to the Levitic law, because, he says, "It is better to confess ignorance than to play with frivolous guesses."

iii. A characteristic feature of Calvin's exegesis is its abhorrence of hollow orthodoxy. He regarded it as a disgraceful offering to a God of truth. He did not hold the theory of verbal dictation. He will never defend or harmonise what he regards as an oversight or mistake in the sacred writers.[3] He scorns to support a good cause by bad reasoning. In Gen. iii. 15, he says that "seed" is a collective term for "posterity" and was only interpreted of Christ by subsequent experience. He will not admit the force of arguments in favour of the Trinity drawn from the plural

---

[1] See his note on Gal. iv. 22. He quotes Chrysostom to show that "allegory" is here used in an improper sense (καταχρηστικῶς), and that Moses meant the history only in a literal sense. He calls it a " *commentum Satanae*, to annihilate the dignity of Scripture." He says that allegories are "puerile" and "farfetched," and that "he gladly abstains from them because there is in them nothing firm and solid." " *Affinis sacrilegio audacia est Scripturas temere huc illuc versare et quasi in re lusoria lascivire.*" *Praef. in Rom.*

[2] Peter Martyr in his *Loci Communes Theol.* dwells on the imprudence of using a method which Anabaptists used, " *ad paradoxa sua imperitis comprobanda.*"

[3] Matt. xxvii. 9 ; Acts vii. 16 ("hic locus corrigendus est").

"let us make," nor from the three angels who appeared to Abraham, nor from the Trisagion.[1] He will not with Luther see a sign of the Incarnation in the Burning Bush.[2] He sets aside many of the untenable arguments drawn from passages in Isaiah in favour of the Divinity of Christ,[3] which, he says, would only appear ludicrous to Jews. In saying that it is absurd to interpret the "stone cut without hands" of the virgin birth of Christ he rejects an interpretation common to the Fathers.[4] He says that he would not dare to press a Sabellian with such a phrase as "the breath of his mouth." Nor was he less independent in his views on the New Testament.[5] His robust honesty in these particulars drew on him the most savage hatred. Montacute charged him with wresting their weapons out of the hands of Christian athletes.[6] Walch said "he expounded oracles about the Trinity and the Messiah in accordance with Jewish and Socinian views."[7] The Roman Catholics called him a Mohammedan,[8] and the Protestant Hunnius, in his *Calvinus Judaisans,* said that he had corrupted Scripture in a detestable manner, and that he ought to have been burnt.[9]

iv. But the most characteristic and original feature of his Commentaries is his anticipation of modern criticism in his views about the Messianic prophecies. He saw that the words of psalmists and prophets, while they not only admit of

---

[1] See his notes on Gen. xviii. 2; Is. vi. 3.

[2] Note on Ex. iii. 2.

[3] See notes on Is. iv. 9 ; xlviii. 16.

[4] Justin, Tertullian, Origen, Basil, Jerome, Augustine, all apply it to Christ. See Rosenmüller, ii. 917. Feuardentius called Calvin's view "*Judaicam plane impietatem.*"

[5] See his notes cn Matt. xi. 11 ; xvi. 18 (where, in opposition to Luther, he makes the Rock to be *Peter* as the representative of all believers) ; John x. 30 (which he applies to the *will* of Christ, not to the *Homoousian*) ; John i. 51 ; v. 31, 32 : 2 Cor. xii. 7 ; 1 Pet. iii. 19, &c.

[6] *Orig. Eccl.* i. 310.

[7] Walch, *Bibl. Theol.* iv. 413.

[8] Limborch, *Theol. Christ.* p. 34.

[9] A.D. 1593. Hunnius was answered by Pareus in his *Orthodoxus Calvinus,* who, with equal amenity, assigned the work of Hunnius to the authorship of the devil. See Buddeus, *Isagoge,* pp. 1062 *sq.* ; Limborch, *Theol.* p. 34. Calvin might reply as Facundus did for Theodore of Mopsuestia.—"Conse-quens non est ut evacuet omnes in Christum factas prophetias qui aliqua mystice in eum dicta moraliter quoque tractaverit."

but demand "germinant and springing developments," were yet primarily applicable to the events and circumstances of their own days. The use made of them by Evangelists and Apostles he regarded as ἐπεξεργάσιαι; as illustrative references; as skilful adaptations; as admissible transferences; as metaphoric allusions; as fair accommodations; as pious deflections.[1] It must not be supposed for a moment that he denied the reality of Messianic prophecy, or failed to see in it the very heart of spiritual Judaism. But he would not confuse the generality of a Divine Promise, or the yearning of faithful hearts for a promised Deliverer, with minute vaticinations, which, torn from their context, would have had no significance for those to whom the prophets addressed their words. It will be clear to all who have an adequate knowledge of the subject, that whether Calvin's phrases in reference to the New Testament quotations were happy or not, they can only be judged with reference to the entire view of prophecy of which they form a part. That view, which is now all but universally accepted, so far from degrading prophecy gives to it a diviner grandeur and elevation. It lifts it from the level of a heathen oracle to the inspired utterance of an indefeasible conviction. It hears in the ancient prophets of Israel the voice of a living God, and in His promises the assurance of an eternal and unfading hope in the advent of a Deliverer, who for themselves and for the nation would make "life's broken purpose whole."

In his Preface to the Romans Calvin laid down the golden rule, that "it is the first business of an interpreter to let his author say what he does say, instead of attributing to him what we think he ought to say." Multitudes of previous writers—even Hilary—had said something of the same kind, yet scarcely one among them all had been able to withstand the sway of dogmatic prepossessions. Nor was Calvin any exception.[2] He had been taught much by the experience of life. It is this which makes his Commentary on the Psalms a

---

[1] See note *infra*, p. 472.

[2] See his notes on John i. 12, where he makes ἐξουσίαν mean "dignity," and the shocking note on "Lead us not into temptation" in Luke xi. 4.

masterpiece of psychological analysis. He called the Psalter
" an anatomy of all the parts of the soul; " and just as Luther
said that the stricken heart and the troubled conscience
had enabled him to understand St. Paul, so Calvin
described the advantages which he had gained from the
combats in which " God had so led and whirled him about as
to bring him into light and action by leaving him no repose
in any place whatever." [1] On the other hand the determination not to be disturbed in the convictions which he thus
had gained has undoubtedly led him at times to be untrue to
his own exegetic principles, by dragging his special dogma
into passages where it is not to be found, and by putting an
unfair gloss on others which tell in the opposite direction.
One flagrant instance may suffice. In Joel ii. 13, he is
naturally perplexed by the phrase, " It repenteth Him of the
evil," which conflicts with his favourite idol of " irreversible
decrees." How does he meet it? "This," he says, " has
reference to human capacities. Whatever has come out of
the mouth of God ought to be looked at in the light of an
irreversible decree. *But meanwhile God often threatens us conditionally*, and the condition must be understood though it
is not expressed. But when God is appeased, and relaxes for
us the punishment *which had been already in some respects
(quodammodo) decreed to us as far as outward words are concerned
(secundum externun verbum)*, then He is said to be influenced
by repentance." This is nothing more or less than the argument of Archbishop Tillotson, who hoped for the ultimate
salvation of the wicked on the ground that God's decrees are
sometimes reversible and conditional. But while we can
understand such an argument in the mild system of Tillotson,
we cannot harmonise it with the inexorable severity of
Calvinism. On the very next page Calvin writes, " *Scimus
iram Dei grassari usque ad ipsos infantes.*" But if God's
decrees sometimes depend on unexpressed conditions without
any hint to us that they do so—if the outward utterance is to

---

[1] Luther said that he had learnt from Ps. 118 that three things taught
theology—*oratio, meditatio, temptatio.*

be regarded as an irreversible decree while that which corresponds to it is variable according to unknown conditions—it is strange that one who had been trained as a jurist, and had been the pupil of Alciati, should have failed to see that he cut away the ground under the clay feet of his own system, and that the " *decretum horribile* " might, on his own confession, be but an ostensible threat, an accommodation to human needs. Nor is this the only instance in which the dogmatist gets the better of the exegete, because the exegete had failed to grasp the progressiveness of revelation and the external circumstances of age and relative knowledge by which it is conditioned.[1]

Such comments prepare us for the fact that in spite of his logical intellect, Calvin is in some respects more loose and inconsequent in his views of inspiration than even Luther was. Like all the Reformers he speaks incessantly of the supreme and final authority of Scripture. Yet he leaves his statements as though they were incontrovertible axioms, and, not considering the case of heathens, for instance, or of unbelievers, has furnished no argument but that of a supposed self-evidence by which the supremacy of Scripture can be proved.[2] The Reformed Churches admitted no such questions about canonicity as those which Luther had discussed, for in their forms of confession they enumerate the books which form the Canon.[3] Calvin neither insists as Luther did on the relative independence of Christian truth; nor does he follow Zwingli in drawing a distinction between the outer and the inner word, the written Bible and "the Bible in the heart." Yet if he held that Scripture flowed from the very mouth of God,[4] he gives us no explanation of his own admission of inaccuracies in Scripture,[5] of his free tone of criticism,[6] of his almost contemptuous

---

[1] See Merx, *Joel*, 433–435.   [2] *Instit.* i. 7, §§ 1–4.
[3] Conf. Belg. 9, ii.–iv. ; Gallic. ii. 5 ; Helvet. i. 2 ; Westmr. Conf. i. § 2, art. vi. ; Dorner, i. 391.
[4] *Instit.* i. 7, § 5.
[5] See his notes on Matt. xxvii. 9 ; Acts vii. 16, &c.
[6] See his remarks on the Epistle to the Hebrews, 2 Peter, and John viii. 1 ; 1 John ii. 14 ; v. 7.

rejection of the whole sacrificial and ceremonial law. How, for instance, can a theory of supernatural dictation agree with the remark that the notion of God making a throne of the Mercy Seat was "a crass figment," from which even a David and a Hezekiah were not free? So far as any philosophical view is concerned of the relations between the Old and the New Testament Calvin must be regarded as distinctly retrogressive, and his defective views led him into strange and miserable quagmires. The intolerance which stains his name is directly traceable to this strange mixture of letter-worship with independence. Free in historical criticism, he is as rigorous as Melanchthon in the dogmatic treatment of the Old Testament. It would have been a less harmful error if Calvin had allegorised the whole Mosaic law than that he should have accepted the imperfect morality of the days of ignorance as a rule for Christian men. But he stood far below Luther in making no distinction between different parts of the Bible. When Réné, Duchess of Ferrara, daughter of Louis XII., had in a letter made the wise remark that David's example in hating his enemies is not applicable to us, Calvin curtly and sternly answered that "such a gloss would upset all Scripture," that even in his hatred David is an example to us and a type of Christ, and "should we presume to set up ourselves as superior to Christ in sweetness and humanity?" It is strange that he should never have thought of the Sermon on the Mount—"It was said to them of old time, Thou shalt love thy neighbour and hate thine enemy; but I say unto you, Love your enemies." Doubtless indeed he would have found some subtle means of reconciling Christ's plain words with the idolatry of his dogmatic theory. Theologians in all ages have been skilful in letting in through the narrow wicket of a text the evil notions

---

[1] Calvin said that the only difference between the Old and the New Testament was *ad modum administrationis*, not *ad substantiam*. *Instit.* ii. 11. This became the ordinary post-Reformation view. Bellarmine called the doctrine of the Old Testament *inchoate*, not perfect; but Gerhard replied, "Doctrina Vet. Test. nequaquam est imperfecta siquidem *eosdem* fundamentales fidei articulos tradit *quos Christus et Apostoli repetunt !*" See Oehler, *Old Testament Theology*, i. 41 (E. T.).

which were meant to be kept out by every wall, tower, and fortress of the whole Christian system. Calvin, honest as he meant to be, found the same fatal facility of reading into Scripture what he wished to find there. If he did not altogether look at the world through the lurid mist which the Anabaptists had raised out of the pages of the Apocalypse, yet from his failure to apprehend the full force of the new commandment he ruthlessly burnt Servetus,[1] recommended persecution to the Protector Somerset,[2] and raised no voice to aid the miserable and exiled congregation of John à Lasco. Dogma reacts on character, and Grotius rightly said that Calvinists for the most part were as severe as they imagined God to be to the greater part of the human race. Not in the Inquisition only, but no less in the acerbities of Puritanism, in the ruthlessness of the Pilgrim Fathers, in the perennial ferocity of sects, in the constant recrudescence of intolerance and persecution, in the unscrupulous malice, factions, and intrigues of living partisans, and in the injuries thus inflicted on the cause of religion, we see the fatal consequences of the mental confusion which made no distinction between the authority of the two Testaments. It is the opposite extreme to that of Marcion's *Antitheses*, but an extreme hardly less perilous.[3] Neither Melanchthon, nor even Luther, though he was averse to employing force in the cause of religion, had learnt the chasm which separates the Elijah-spirit and the Christ-spirit. The worst stain upon their names—the concession to the bigamous marriage of Philip of Hesse—arose, not from want of courage, but from

---

[1] It is usual to defend this disgraceful and grossly illegal act by the sanction of Melanchthon, but Beza tells us (*Vita Calvini*, A.D. 1550) that even in his own day it was widely and severely condemned. Martinus Bellius in his *Farrago* showed that not only the best Reformers, but even the Fathers had opposed the capital punishment of heretics. The sentence about Servetus in Calvin's letter to Farel (Feb. 1546), "*Si venerit, modo valeat mea auctoritas vivum exire non patiar*," shows him at his very worst.

[2] In a letter dated Oct. 22, 1548.

[3] The utterances of Reformation theology on this important subject are quite unsatisfactory, and merely swim in the air. Quenstedt talks of the Old Testament as a "*perpetua norma fidei ac vitae in universâ Ecclesia*," and Hollaz, and the *Formula Concordiae* vaguely extol the Old Testament, and irrelevantly quote Ps. cxix. 105; Gal. i. 8. See Hase, p. 570.

confused notions about the Old Testament. Calvin would hardly have fallen into this error, for he had no esteem for the Levitic law; but unfortunately he could not see that the actions of Gideon, and Jael, and even David, furnish no fit ideals for the Christian moralist. Intolerance has been the curse and the ruin of Calvinism, and has drowned its dogmas in the general abhorrence of mankind. It is at once a blunder and a crime :—a blunder, for as Luther said, "Heresy is a spiritual thing which cannot be hewn with any axe, or burned with any fire, or drowned with any water " :—a crime, because as the Emperor Maximilian says, it attempts to storm the conscience of man, which is the very citadel of heaven. The humble minister in *Old Mortality* spoke deeper wisdom than the world-famous Reformer. "By what law," says Henry Morton to Balfour of Burley, "would you justify the atrocity you would commit ? " "If *thou* art ignorant of it," replied Burley, "thy companion is well aware of the law which gave the men of Jericho to the sword of Joshua the son of Nun." "Yes, but we," answered the divine, "live under a better dispensation, which instructeth us to return good for evil, and to pray for those who despitefully use us and persecute us." Even Augustine—in his later years the fatal patron of religious persecution, and thereby the cause of unnumbered miseries to the Church of God—even Augustine said—though neither he nor any other interpreter for a thousand years rightly applied the force of the remark —"*Distingue tempora et concordabis Scripturas.*" [1]

8. But whatever may have been the faults and limitations of the expositors of the Reformation, their very enemies could not deny that they had made a greater advance in the interpretation of Scripture than had been made during many previous centuries. "Merciful God ! " exclaimed Flacius, " I say it with grief and groaning, almost from the very times of Christ down to this age of ours how has nothing less been

---

[1] The indifference to hermeneutics is one chief source of Calvin's weakness. He says "that it does not much matter when Jonah or Obadiah lived," which may be true enough for the homilist, but is singularly false for the exegete. See Merx, *Joel*, 428–444.

the aim of theologians than the clear explanation of the very word, sense, and text of the sacred writings!"[1] "We may most truly declare," says Calvin, "that we have brought more light to bear on the understanding of Scripture than all the authors who have sprung up amongst Christians since the rise of the Papacy; nor do they themselves venture to rob us of this praise."[2]

Yes! to the Reformers was fulfilled once more the old promise, "Ye shall know the truth, and the truth shall make you free." Fragments of the Bible had been used to shut men in the prison-house of human dogmas, and to bind their souls in the chains of religious despotism. In the true knowledge of the Bible as a whole, lay the force which delivered them. It was the Voice of the Living Spirit of God speaking to them in Scripture, and in the heart, which enabled men to burst the gates of brass, and smite the bars of iron in sunder. So it has been; so it will ever be. Christianity has been perpetuated, far less through the letter of its records than through "the Apostolic succession of inspired personalities;"[3] of Prophets who have stood, if need be,

[1] Calvin, *Antid. in Conc. Trident.* sess. iv. Bacon says of English theologians that "if the choice and best observations which have been made dispersedly in our English sermons . . had been set down in a continuance, it would be the best work in divinity that hath been written since the Apostles' times." The licence of allegorising seems to be somewhat alien from the practical good sense of the English character, for it has never been found among our great divines. They are content to admit its theoretical validity (as even Locke does on Rom. iii. 25; v. 14). Such books as *Bibliotheca Biblica* of Parker (1720), Vertue's *Parallels*, Keach's *Sacred Typology*, &c., have never been accepted as having any authority. Even Jeremy Taylor says, "Of these things there is no beginning and no end, no certain principles, and no good conclusion." *Sermon on Ministerial Duties.* "This (the work of drawing out mystic meanings), to speak freely my opinion," says Waterland, "appears to be a work of such a kind as scarce one in a thousand will be fit to be trusted with" (Pref. to *Scripture Vindicated*).

[2] *Comm. in Joel*, iii. 1. See some remarks on the subject in Hooker, *Eccl. Pol. III.* viii. §§ 16–18. How strikingly this was the case with Dean Colet, may be seen in Mr. Lupton's editions of his *Commentaries*, and in Seebohm's *Oxford Reformers*, ch. ii.

[3] "The form in which the Divine Spirit accomplishes every important change in the world is that of gifted men, by whom He diffuses His own ideas and works them out. And thus the gifted man becomes the mediator of the Divine Spirit, in behalf of those who are not served at first-hand by these ideas. He knows himself to be this by two signs; the one his consciousness of self-sacrificing enthusiasm; the other his consciousness of originative power."—J. H. Fichte, *Spek. Theol.*, p. 655.

A A

alone against priests, and against the world ; of men who have flashed into dead generations the electric spark of truth. Churches need many Pentecosts, and many Resurrections. And God grants them. Sooner or later He shakes down from their flimsy pedestals the gilded idols which men set up for themselves to worship, and delivers His children from the burning fiery furnaces kindled for them by those who would slay them in His name. Sooner or later He bids His lightnings stab through the dim but irreligious light of voluntary illusion, with which men swathe their own imaginations. He did so in the sixteenth century. He did so in the eighteenth century. He will do so again in the nineteenth, or in the twentieth, and if need be again and yet again. He will raise new Prophets when the old have been slain or silenced ; and those new Prophets shall, like the Reformers, lead us back once more to simplicity from artificiality, to truth from tradition, to the Word of God from the inventions of men.

"Man nimmt fremde Glossen aus der Heiligen Schrift dass es zu erbarmen ist."—TAULER.

"Majestas theologica quam multi pluris faciunt quam Christum."—ERASMUS to LUTHER (*Epp.* i. 427).

"We should not interpret the Scriptures by the Creeds, but the Creeds by the Scriptures."—SPENER, *Bedenken,* iii. 478.

"Tous les scholasticismes me rendent douteux de ce qu'ils démontrent, parce qu'au lieu de chercher ils affirment dès le début. Leur objet est de construire les retranchements autour d'un préjugé, et non de découvrir la vérité."—AMIEL, *Journal Intime,* ii. 136.

LECTURE VII.

POST-REFORMATION EPOCH.

." Questionings and disputes of words, whereof cometh envy, strife, railings, evil surmisings, wranglings."—1 TIM. vi. 4.

IF the slow but general and permanent adoption of principles by the Christian world be any proof of their correctness, it must be admitted that the Reformers gave a mighty impulse to the science of Scriptural interpretation. They made the Bible accessible to all; they tore away and scattered to the winds the dense cobwebs of arbitrary tradition which had been spun for so many centuries over every book, and every text of it; they put the Apocrypha on an altogether lower level than the sacred books; they carefully studied the original languages; they developed the plain, literal sense; they used it for the strengthening and refreshing of the spiritual life.

> " Thus truth was multiplied on truth ; the world
>   Like one great garden showed,
> And through the wreaths of floating dark upcurled
>   Rare sunrise flowed.
> And Freedom reared in that august sunrise
>   Her beautiful bold brow,
> When rites and forms before her burning eyes
>   Melted like snow."

We might have hoped that the splendid progress would have been continuous, but, alas, the experience of mankind has made us only too familiar with the spectacle of arrest and of retrogression in the history of thought. Imperfection and failure are stamped on all human efforts, on all human institutions. Toilsome and incomplete is all that men accomplish. The Epigoni of the Reformation were far feebler and less large-hearted than their mighty predecessors. During the space of one hundred and fifty years the torch burned dim, and it was only rekindled into brightness by those who were at first denounced as renegades and heretics, but who, in the increasing purpose of the ages, were the true heirs of Erasmus and of Luther.

I. In spite of much theological labour and activity,[1] the period at which we are about to glance in the history of exegesis is very cheerless. It was a period in which liberty was exchanged for bondage; universal principles for beggarly elements; truth for dogmatism; independence for tradition; religion for system. A living reverence for Scripture was superseded by a dead theory of inspiration. Genial orthodoxy gave place to iron uniformity, and living thought to controversial dialectics.[2] The Reformation had broken the leaden sceptre of the old Scholasticism, but the Protestant Churches introduced a new Scholasticism whose rod was of iron. The *Sentences* of Peter Lombard and the *Summa* of Thomas Aquinas were built on the Bible, Tradition, and the Fathers. The Bible only was the professed basis of the *Loci Communes* of Chemnitz, the *Loci Theologici* of Gerhard, the *Theologia Didactico-polemica* of Quenstedt, and the *Systema locorum* of Calovius. The *Reformed* dogmatists vainly fancied that their building would be eternal, but it was built on party Creeds, not on Christ, and therefore it has crumbled into the dust. The Protestant Churches bit and devoured one another, and suffered terribly in consequence. "The Reformation soon parted company with free learning, turned its back upon culture, held out no hand to awaking science,[3] and lost itself in a maze of theological controversies."

---

[1] For an account of the German universities and their celebrated scholars at this epoch, see Tholuck's *Das Akadem. Leben,* ii. 15–202, and a useful summary in Dorner, *Hist. of Prot. Theol.* ii. 103–108.

[2] Romberg, *Die Lehre Luther,* p. 18, "Man war aus der Region der Lebenswarmen und seines Heil-bringenden Glaubens, in die Eisregion des Verstandes getreten . . . des schematisirenden und reflectirenden Verstandes."

[3] Witness the attacks on Kepler and Descartes, and Calovius's declaration that the revolution of the earth round the sun was "contrary to Scripture"—

The whole of this epoch was retarded, and its labour vitiated, by a threefold curse: the curse of tyrannous confessionalism; the curse of exorbitant systems; the curse of contentious bitterness.

1. It was the age of Creeds, Symbols, Confessions, theological systems, rigid formulae. At one time almost every important city or principality had its own favourite creed. There was the *Corpus Pomeranicum,* the *Corpus Prutenicum, Brandeburgicum,* and so forth. Even Lüneburg had its *Corpus Wilhelminum,* and Brunswick-Wolfenbüttel its *Corpus Julium.* Besides these minor statements of belief, there were, among many others, in 1529, the Articles of Marburg; in 1530, the *Confessio Tetrapolitana* and the Confession of Augsburg; in 1536, the Wittenberg Concord; in 1537, the Articles of Schmalkald; in 1566, the *Confessio Helvetica Posterior;* in 1580, the triumph of rigid Lutheranism in the *Formula Concordiae;* in 1562, the Thirty-nine Articles; in 1643, the Westminster Confession.[1] Men fell into the error of supposing that unity could be secured by a nominal uniformity, or controversies precluded—instead of created and multiplied—by the minuteness of doctrinal formulae.[2] These symbols differ *toto coelo* from the early professions of faith—the Apostles' Creed and the Nicene Creed—which, in spite of all controversies, amply sufficed for the first eight centuries of Christians. They fill many dreary and often highly disputable pages. The *Consensus repetitus* formally repudiated the "heresy" of supposing that the Apostles' Creed contained everything necessary for salvation, or that the Trinity was not clearly revealed in the Old Testament. Now the Vine of the Church cannot

a phrase which has been applied to almost every scientific discovery in turn. See Brewster's *Martyrs of Science,* pp. 2, 52, 76, 193.

[1] There were also the *Confessio Belgica, Gallicana, Hafnica, Marchica, Saxonica,* and *Scotica.*

[2] The protest of Milton is characteristic in its energy and manliness. He speaks in the *Areopagitica* (1644) of "planting one faith now in the Convocation House, and another while in the Chapel at Westminster; where all the faith and religion which shall there be canonised is not sufficient without plain convincement and the charity of patient instruction, to supple the least bruise of conscience, to edify the meanest Christian who desires to walk in the spirit and not in the letter of human trust, for all the number of voices that can be there made."

grow in the dusty and blighting soil of acrimonious theology. God has left many truths in the penumbra which alone suits our finite capacities. The Post-Reformation Churches refused to recognise how large a part of theological definition belongs solely to the uncertain and unessential. Their dogmas were based not upon secure evidence, but on dominant authority, and it was therefore necessary to enforce them by anathema and banishment, yes, even by axe and stake.[1] This terrorism of Formulae prevailed throughout all the Churches. The *Formula Concordiae* swayed the Lutherans; the Synod of Dort was supposed to have uttered the last word for the Reformed Churches; the Council of Trent for Romanists; even for Socinians the Racovian Catechism. These were more or less imposed upon men's consciences with the syllogism of violence. The world forgot the memorable saying of Luther that "thoughts are toll-free." The consequence was a total loss of originality, a complete arrest of progress, the crushing of spontaneous thought under the dead weight of petrified dogmas. Sterile repetition, narrow scrupulosity, burning recriminations, religious factiousness everywhere prevailed. The very names which different writers have given to this period indicate the impression left upon the mind by its dreary history. It has been called by no less than seven different historians the age of "Symbololatry," of "creed-bondage," of "Lutheran patristics," of "Protestant scholasticism," of "Dogmatic traditionalism," of "dead orthodoxy," of "theorising system," of "ecclesiastico-confessional," or "polemico-dogmatic interpretation."[2] The Council of Trent practically reduces exegesis to a register of non-existent unanimity. It puts forth no authorised commentary, nor even any hermeneutic theory, and it relies upon a version which is full of errors. The Greek Church, laying down the rule that those only can interpret who can enter into "the

---

[1] There is a touch of quite unconscious humour in the Abbé Glaire's remark about Calvin, "Il fit brûler Michael Servet *parce qu'il enseignait d'autres erreurs que les siennes*" (*Dictionnaire*, i. 377).

[2] These names are applied to it by Klausen, Dorner, Hagenbach, Landerer, Fritzsche, Reuss, Kurz. The old rules, "Nihil contra Scripturas" and "Nihil contra Ecclesiam," became "Nihil contra Symbolos."

depths of the Spirit," refers to the faulty LXX., and specially forbids the reading of certain parts of the Old Testament.[1] Protestant Schoolmen practically bound themselves by the limits of their current confessions. Each Church of Christendom had its own Version, and its own Canon, and its own exegetic rules, and not one of them lays down any test of the differences between the value of the Old and of the New Testament, or furnishes any intelligible hint as to how we are to distinguish between relative and absolute truths. The Protestant theologians reasoned upon *à priori* assumptions, and proved once more that "Men only need to bring to the Bible sufficiently strong prepossessions, sufficiently fixed opinions, to have them reflected back in all the glamour of infallible authority."[2]

2. As a consequence of the bondage to Formulae this was also the age of huge books of theology, which were produced in astonishing numbers, and of which the majority now sleep in the dust of oblivion. These system-building folios, to which the *Summa* is light reading, seemed ever to grow in size. For some time they followed what is called the *local* or *porismatic* method, that is, they began by the statement of *loci* or theological commonplaces, which were inordinately expanded with precise definitions and harmonisations into symmetrical completeness.[3] Melanchthon's *Loci* were the development of Lectures on the Epistle to the Romans. Luther characteristically said that they were "worthy of a place in the Canon of Scripture," and Cochlaeus sarcastically called them "the Alkoran of Lutheranism." They kept growing from 1521 to 1543, till they more and more resembled a book of the Schoolmen.[4] Calvin's *Institutio* began in 1536 with

[1] *Dosithei Confessio*, *Qu.* 1 (Kimmel), *Monumenta Fidei Eccles. Orient.* i. 465.   [2] Beard, *Hibbert Lectures*, p. 192.

[3] The "*porismatic*" method consisted in the abstraction of dogmatic results. Thus in Baldwin's *Commentary on the Pauline Epistles*, "*Multiplices commonefactiones e textu eruuntur.*" This method was superseded by the *analytic* after the example set by Calixtus.

[4] R. Simon says, a little too severely, of Melanchthon's exegesis, "On n'y voit que des disputes. . . Il faut lire beaucoup pour trouver quelque chose qui regarde l'auteur qu'il fait profession d'interpréter" (*H. Critique . . . V. T.*).

six chapters, and ended in 1559 with eighty. The *Loci* of
John Gerhard (1610-1622), which are regarded as the palmary
work of Lutheran theology, originally occupied nine quarto
volumes, and were developed into twenty by later writers.
Quenstedt, "the book-keeper of Lutheran orthodoxy," Hütter,
the most slavish upholder of symbolical traditionalism,
Calovius (1655-1677), in the twelve quarto volumes of his
Systema, Dannhauer in his *Hodosophia,* Baier in his *Compendium Theologiae,* and hosts of other writers, all base their
labours on the assumption that the scheme of salvation can
be set forth in its minutest details with Aristotelian dialectics.
They started with a belief falsified by the whole history of
the Jewish and Christian Churches alike, that the Bible
contains a consistent and symmetrical system of doctrine,
which is complete and necessary and self-evident, and can
be extracted from it by ordinary reasoning.

3. As regards the third great curse of this period,
dogmatic inflexibility, unsoftened by Christian love, led
to contentiousness, which regarded trifling matters as important, and too often esteemed the weightiest as trifles.
The air was full of burning questions which have long
ago "burnt themselves out." [1] There was the Lutheran and
Reformed controversy, the Flacianist and Philippist controversy, the Antinomian controversy, the Osiandrian controversy, the Majorist controversy, the Ubiquitarian controversy,
the Synergistic controversy, the Adiaphoristic controversy, the
Crypto-Calvinistic controversy, the Arminian and Gomarist
controversy, the Calixtine or Syncretistic controversy, the
Kenotic controversy, the Rathmann controversy, the Pietist
controversy, the Amyraldian controversy, the Karg controversy,
the Huber controversy, and many more.[2] In the French
Church there were the discussions about Pajonism and

---

[1] Dorner, ii. 1.

[2] A brief sketch of these controversies which so unprofitably occupied the
last half of the sixteenth century is given by Kurz, *Hist. of the Christian
Church,* pp. 112-121 (E. T.). See too Schlüsselberg, *Haereticorum Catalogus*
(Frankfort, 1597-1599), which Frank calls "Das Arsenal zu diesen nachre-
formatorischen Streitigkeiten."

Jansenism and Quietism; in the English Church about Quakerism and Semi-Socinianism; in the Dutch and Swiss Churches about Calvinism and Arminianism; in the Lutheran Churches about Mysticism and Humanism.[1] Many of these controversies were waged with a fierceness in proportion to the entire doubtfulness of the question at stake.[2] An age of egoism, of party spirit—of what St. Paul calls ἐριθεία—must always produce false interpretation. There never was an epoch in which men were so much occupied in discovering each other's errors, or in which they called each other by so many opprobrious names. Deutschmann of Halle (1695) charged the gentle and holy Spener with 264 errors, and the Wittenberg Faculty charged him with 283.[3] Carpzov called him a "*procella ecclesiae,*" and Fecht all but denied his salvation.[4] Löscher in Dresden published an anti-pietistic journal in thirty-one volumes. The University of Wittenberg in 1655 endeavoured to carry a *Consensus repetitus fidei vere Lutheranae,* which enumerated eighty-eight errors of Calixtus and the Syncretists. Religion was cast by some evil spirit into a paroxysm of theological condemnations.[5] John Arndt, "the Fénélon of Lutheranism,"[6] was accused by his colleague Denecke, and other Lutheran zealots, of "Papistry, Monkery, Calvinism, Pelagianism, Osiandrianism, Flacianism, Schwenkfeldianism, Weigelianism, Paracelsism, Alchemy," and other enormities.[7] Men were separatists (διορίζοντες) and Pharisees, and therefore they could not keep the unity of the Spirit in the bond of peace. They read the Bible by the unnatural

---

[1] Rom. ii. 8 ; Lange, *Grundriss*, p. 3.

[2] Alles verzerrt sich in eine kleinliche Polemik ; die ganze theologische Literatur dient ihrem Interesse, überall ein lauernder Verdacht der auf jedes unbedachte Wort fahndet, &c. Frank, *Gesch. d. prot. Med.* i. 92. See too Witte, *Memoriae Theologorum* (1674).

[3] In the *Christlutherische Vorstellung.* Happily Spener was able to say that "the attacks of his enemies had never given him a sleepless night."

[4] Fecht, *De Beatitudine Mortuorum.*

[5] "Un des côtés les plus faux de cette scolastique, c'était de chercher et de trouver partout des erreurs. Nous avons de ces énumérations d'erreurs qui remplissent des volumes, et souvent parmi ces prétendues erreurs condamnées, il y a de très bonnes choses" (Renan, *Le Judaïsme*).

[6] Author of *Wahres Christenthum.*

[7] Kurz, ii. 107 ; see Wildenhahn, *J. Arndt, ein Zeitbild*, 1847.

glare of theological hatred.[1] They " imposed the senses of men upon the words of God, the special senses of men upon the general words of God, and forced them upon men's consciences together under the equal penalty of death and damnation." FLACIUS ILLYRICUS, a passionate and determined controversialist, became a very thorn in the side of Melanchthon, and, in spite of the merits of his *Clavis,* his *Catalogus testium,* and his share in the Magdeburg centuries, we can hardly except him from the blame of bitter uncharitableness.[2] Of another theologian of this epoch—Osiander—Tholuck says " that the Holy Spirit seems to have appeared to him in the form rather of a raven than of a dove ; " and of another—Myslenta— that he was "a volcano constantly vomiting fire and mud." Both remarks are applicable to ABRAHAM CALOV († 1686), in whose person the seventeenth century produced a man of stupendous diligence and wide learning, but the very type of a bitter dogmatist. He is said to have daily uttered the perverse prayer, *Imple me, Deus, odio haereticorum.* Alas ! the bale-fires of religious animosity need not to be fanned into fiercer flame by the pure breath of prayer. If the story be true, the spirit of hatred was granted him by way of punishment, and the hatred was often poured out upon men ten times less heretical than himself. He was a born heresy-hunter, one of those other people's bishops (ἀλλοτριοεπίσκοποι) who think it their special mission to take in charge the orthodoxy of all their fellow men. He flew to the attack of everybody who differed from his own confessional standard. Luther was his " Megalander" and the Lutheran symbols his standard of infallibility. He wrote no less than twenty-eight controversial pamphlets. The very titles of his books, *Mataeologia papistica, Socinianismus profligatus, Theses de Labadismo, Anti-Boehmius, Discussio controversiarum,* are

---

[1] See a disgraceful scene described at Schlüsselberg's examination for his M.A. degree, which ended in the sentence " *Nunc anathema pronuntiamus ac te tamquam diaboli vivum organum totis pectoribus exsecramur.*" Guttmann, *Annal. d. Universität zu Wittenberg,* i. 153-155.

[2] The judgment pronounced on him by Camerarius (*Vit. Melanchth.* clxxxii.) is very severe. See too Planck, *Prot. Lehrbegriff,* and Maitland's *Letters to King.*

menacing with antagonism. His *Systema,* in twelve quarto volumes, is "a ponderous engine of war against Calixtus." His *Biblia illustrata,* in four volumes (1672), turned the sacred book into a heap of controversial missiles against Grotius, and its very title was a challenge.[1] This fury for polemics is the invariable result of a dead and formal theology. It defends Christianity in the spirit of Antichrist, and turns the words of Eternal Life into an excuse for eternal litigation. During this prevalence of sectarian contentiousness, the Universities of North Germany showed few signs of vitality and none of progress.[2] The Gospel of Peace became in such hands a war of words. Dogmas were orthodox, but spirituality was extinguished. Theology was triumphant, but love was quenched.[3] Science was reduced to impotence. The " Analogy of Faith," and the " Analogy of Scripture," were made the pretext for regarding the Bible as a sort of quartz-bed, in which was to be found the occasional gold of a proof-text. Those passages were chiefly dwelt upon which could be most usefully applied or misapplied for controversial purposes. The Creeds were demonstrated, the Christ was forgotten.[4] Sometimes the theologic system is deduced from the whole Old Testament, sometimes by strange perversions it was read in its entirety between the

---

[1] " *Biblia Illustrata, in quibus Grotianae depravationes et ψευδερμηνεῖαι justo examine sistuntur et exploduntur.*" Calov's hatred for Grotius, whom he considers to be "*nullius religionis*" and "*deterior Judaeis,*" amounted to fanaticism. It sometimes makes him almost witty, as when he accuses Grotius of implying that the Cherubim were "*aliquod bituminis genus!*" His own commentary is a perfect hotbed of violent errors, on which he insists as the only orthodoxy. He often leaves important passages unexplained, but *never* omits an opportunity of attacking "heretics." But Grotius is still valued and Calov is forgotten. Exegesis which is mainly controversial stands self-condemned.

[2] Mullinger, ii. 106 ; Döllinger, *Die Universitäten sonst und jetst* (1871).

[3] " Was auch als Wahreit oder Fabel
In tausend Büchern dir erscheint,
Das Alles ist ein Thurm zu Babel
Wenn es die Liebe nicht vereint."—GOETHE, *Xenien.*

[4] "The Bible is not a collection of aphorisms designed to serve as proof-texts for Dogmatics. The anxiety of dogma to quote Biblical proofs may easily betray theologians into an atomistic mode of procedure which tears passages out of the context and makes them isolated groups for isolated theses" (J. Müller in Herzog, *s.v. Dogmatics*).

lines of some single book. The excesses of this view are
almost inconceivable. In Calov, Quenstedt, Hollaz, and even
in Gerhard, the testimony of the Holy Spirit becomes mainly
an inward assurance that their private opinions about Holy
Scripture are irrefragably true.[1] In Wernsdorf the work of the
Spirit is degraded into a recalling to memory of the texts
which prove our judgment about doctrines; and our judgment must itself be based on the fact that we hold true
doctrine! Scripture was declared to be not "an inanimate
instrument," but a sort of oracular teraph, a self-efficacious
organism, which had the inherent power of emanating true
theology.[2] This mechanical infallibility was so far attributed
to the symbolic books that Calovius and his followers speak
of them also as possessing a normative power and a mediate
inspiration. The bad rule, *Consequentiae aequipollent revelatis,*
was everywhere prevalent, and the endeavour to establish
unnatural *emphases* destroyed the bases of true interpretation.
Controversy tried (so to speak) to underline every word from
which an argument could be extracted.[3] Men were harassed
by dubious texts "blown backwards and forwards at the
opening of opposite windows." Thus did the dogmatists set
up their idols in their heart, and put the stumbling-block of
their opinionativeness before their face.

4. Two controversies which wasted the energies and evoked
the mutual anathemas of the Reformed and Lutheran
Churches will serve to illustrate how grave is the misuse of
Scripture when it is applied to the polemic elaboration of
minute and sectarian dogma.

i. One is the dispute, or rather the series of disputes,
which arose out of Calvinism. The Church has long since
shown a practical determination to cease prying into the

[1] Dorner, ii. 123–127, who quotes Gerhard, *Loci,* pt. ii. §§ 20, 36, 44 ;
Quenstedt, pt. i. p. 97, iii. 569 ; Hollatius, i. 136, &c.
[2] Dorner, ii. 132–141.
[3] For instance, Rambach says, "Merito vocibus tanta significationis am-
plitudo, tantumque pondus assignatur, quantum per rei substratae naturam
sustinere possunt ;" and Pfeiffer still more precisely, "*Tanta cuilibet voci
tribuenda est emphasis quanta potest*" (see Zöckler, *Handb. d. Theol. Wissenschaften,* p. 658).

councils of God, and has remained content with the double certainty on the one hand of God's love, on the other of man's freedom. She rightly refuses to follow the example of Milton's fallen angels who reasoned high

> " Of providence, foreknowledge, will and fate,
> Fixed fate, free will, foreknowledge absolute,
> And found no end, in wandering mazes lost."

In the seventeenth century it was otherwise. Men sincerely imagined that they could find certain warrant in Holy Scripture to decide not only that God had passed upon millions of miserable men a "horrible decree" of eternal and inevitable reprobation, but also whether He had passed that decree upon man after he had fallen or before. Such was the controversy of the Sublapsarians with the Supralapsarians. Could there be a stronger indication that nothing is too sacred for the dogmatic passion to touch, too difficult for it to attempt to resolve ? Could there be a more instructive proof of the folly of attempting to fly up into the secrets of the Deity on the waxen wings of the understanding ?

ii. Yet dogmatism intruded with bold step and unabashed forehead into matters yet more inscrutably mysterious. Every Christian must deplore the bitter and interminable disputes about the double nature of Christ—disputes into which the New Testament never enters, because it was only the mission of the Apostles and Evangelists to reveal what was necessary for man's deliverance, and within the reach of his finite comprehension. The Church for 300 years remained content with the plain teaching of the New Testament, that Christ was both Divine and Human, at once God and Man. When the Arian, Apollinarian, Nestorian, and Eutychian heresies arose, she was content, after fierce disputings and many evil surmises, with the four words of definition which she had accepted at four great oecumenical Councils— ἀληθῶς, τελέως, ἀδιαιρέτως, ἀσυγχύτως—that Christ was truly God, perfectly Man, indivisibly God-Man, and distinctly God and Man. The refining and speculating genius of Greek theologians had ventured further to define the relation

of the two natures in Christ by the word περιχώρησις, which
was translated into Latin by *circuminsessio*, and was treated
of by the Schoolmen as the *communicatio idiomatum.*[1] Luther
in his early days was not fond of these scholastic terms. He
pointed out that not only *Homoousion* but even *Trinitas* are
post-scriptural expressions.[2] In his catechism he speaks of
the Trinity "oeconomically" as corresponding to creation,
redemption and sanctification. He said emphatically "the
simplicity of Scripture is to be observed, nor let men presume
to speak more clearly or more simply than God Himself has
spoken." So, in Melanchthon's early editions of the *Loci*,
there was no attempt at Theosophy. It is only in later
editions that he tries to achieve a speculative construction of
the doctrine of the Trinity, " as the eternal necessary process
of the divine self-consciousness, in which God, Whose thoughts
are realities, eternally sets Himself over against Himself, but
also again unites with Himself." Luther, too, was led to
speculate, in a manner closely bordering upon Gnosticism,
about the Divinity concealing or withholding itself in Christ's
Passion. But this is nothing to the developments of the
later Protestant scholastics. In Chemnitz and Calov not even
the *communicatio idiomatum* is enough. It becomes something threefold—the *genus idiomaticum, genus apotelesmaticum,*
and *genus αὐχηματικὸν* or *majestaticum.*[3] As though "a sort
of a something" by way of meaning could in any way be
attached to such aerial and wholly unscriptural speculations!
Yet even on this subject arose furious quarrels between
Mentzer and the theologians of Marburg and Giessen on the
one side, and Osiander and those of Tübingen on the other;—
the former maintaining that Christ's incarnation was a κένωσις
or emptying of omnipotence and omnipresence, and the latter
that it was only a κρύψις or concealment. Thus was it assumed
that not only the whole of Christianity, with all its aspirations,

---

[1] *Form. Concordiae* (1580). The favourite Post-Reformation illustration of
the περιχώρησις is the burning bush (see Calov, *ad loc.*).
[2] *Werke*, xi. 1547, xiii. 2631. Τριὰς is first found in Theophilus of Antioch,
Trinitas in Tertullian. Ὁμοούσιον was originally borrowed from Neo-Platonists.
[3] Calovius, *Systema*, 636 ; *Form. Conc.* sol. 2, decl. viii. 36 ; Dorner, ii.
148 ; Baur, *Dreieinigkeit*, iii. pt. i. c. 8.

and spiritual insight into things which surpass man's understanding and elude the feeble powers of man's expression, but
even the most secret things of God, and what took place, to
use the bad phrase of some theologians, " in the innermost
council-chambers of the Trinity," could be stated like a
geometrical proposition, labelled with theological technicalities,
and enforced in the belief of others with abuse and violence !

" Vain wisdom all and false philosophy ! "

It was an idle attempt to know Christ by subtle definitions,
whereas He is only to be known by sympathy, by spiritual
feeling, by spiritual responsiveness, by mystic union. Is it
possible to doubt that St. Paul, had he read or heard such
speculations, would have exclaimed, I marvel that ye are so
soon corrupted from the simplicity that is towards Christ
Jesus ?[1]

5. The πρῶτον ψεῦδος of the whole unprofitable development was—once again—Biblical Supernaturalism ; an irreverent identification of " inspiration " with " verbal dictation."
Whoever was the first dogmatist to make the terms "the
Bible " and " the Word of God " synonymous, rendered to the
cause of truth and of religion an immense disservice. The
phrase in that sense has no shadow of Scriptural authority.
It occurs from three to four hundred times in the Old
Testament, and about a hundred times in the New ; and in
not one of all those instances is it applied to the Scriptures.[2]
Archbishop Agobard of Lyons even in the ninth century had
argued against the absurdity of reducing the Prophets to a
level no higher than that of the dumb ass.[3] The formula
of the Reformation in its best days, like that of the Church
of England, was not "Scriptura *est* Verbum Dei," but
"Scriptura *complectitur* Verbum Dei."[4] Had inspiration been

---

[1] See 2 Cor. xi. 3 ; Gal. i. 6.
[2] See Bishop Thirlwall, *Charges*, i. 71.
[3] " Quodsi ita sentitis quanta absurditas sequatur quis dinumerare poterit ?
. . . Restat ergo ut sicut ministerio angelico vox articulata formata est in ore
asinae ita dicatis formari in ore prophetarum " (Agobard).
[4] See Art. vi., " Holy Scripture *containeth* all things necessary to salvation."
And in the services for the ordering of Priests and Bishops, " Are you persuaded that the Holy Scriptures *contain* sufficiently all doctrine required of

capable of definition as a supernatural verbal dictation which secured infallibility to the inspired writers, nothing would have been easier than so to define it. The Church has never laid down any such definition of it, or indeed any theory or definition of it whatever.

The meaning of Inspiration, as indicated by all the greatest writers of theology, and by the decisive usage of our own Church,[1] does not imply an exclusive *Theopneustia* for the sacred writers, and still less for every word which they uttered or recorded. It meant the influence of the Holy Spirit of God revealing Himself in every great thought and utterance of the soul of man; given in the bestowal of " every good and every perfect gift."

6. It is easy to see how the doctrine arose. Papal infallibility had been set aside. In the perplexity of opinions men yearned to substitute some objective authority in the place of it, and so to acquire, or to imagine that there could exist, respecting every conceivable detail of theological speculation, a certitude which, as regards such details, is nothing but an idle dream. The Reformed and Lutheran Churches having gained—often by heroic struggles and through seas of blood —the undisturbed possession, not only of certain Christian verities, but also each of its own special theories; and, being compelled to maintain this heritage of opinion against Anabaptists, against Socinians, against Romanists, wanted something to which they could appeal as a decisive oracle.[2]

necessity for eternal salvation ?" And again in the Homilies, "Unto a Christian man there can be nothing more necessary than the knowledge of Holy Scripture, forasmuch as *in it is contained* God's true Word."

[1] The word "Inspiration" occurs five or six times in the Prayer-book and Homilies of the *ordinary* gifts of the Holy Spirit which are wholly apart from infallibility.

[2] They rejected the three principles insisted on (later) by the Council of Trent, namely (1) the authority of Ecclesiastical tradition ; (2) the canon and authority of the Vulgate ; (3) the necessity of conforming interpretation to Church authority and the unanimous consent of the Fathers. They said that tradition was invalid ; that the Vulgate is full of errors and its canon untenable ; and that there is no such thing as a consent of the Fathers nor would it be decisive if there were (see Robertson Smith, *The Old Test. in the Jewish Church*). On the other hand, they extravagantly and unscripturally exaggerate the *affectiones Scripturae*, on which see Quenstedt, *Theol.* i. 59. They are (1) *divina auctoritas;* (2) *perfectio;* (3) *perspicuitas;* (4) *semet interpretandi facultas.*

They made the Holy Scriptures such an oracle, but they made the oracle answer them according to their own idols. They substituted for its interpretation their own ready-made theology. They assumed that the Bible formed a homogeneous, self-interpreting, and verbally dictated whole, and that the inferences drawn from it by dialectics and compacted into a technical system were as certain and as sacred as itself.[1] In this way a difference of exegetical opinion became, not only an intellectual error, but a civil crime. Step by step we mark the full imposition of this dogma. It was not itself discussed. There was no attempt to place it on a scientific basis. It was an *à priori* assumption which was pushed into the utmost extreme of unreasonable fanaticism,[2] and which directly contradicted the principle of the Apostle that "he that is spiritual judgeth all things and he himself is judged of no man."[3] It was based, not on exact principles, but on vague assertions which floated in the air. The great Reformers, as we have seen, never attempted to bind themselves by the only possible consequences of such a doctrine. They used current phrases, but practically they left themselves a wide liberty to criticise not only the separate utter-

---

[1] Rambach's *Institutiones Hermen. Sacrae*, 1723, is a learned book, and characteristic of the epoch in its attacks on Grotius and Arminian exegesis; its irrelevances and digressions; its scholastic formalism; and the superstition with which it claims an inward enlightenment apart from other gifts in mere matters of interpretation (see Klausen, pp. 272–276). All these theologians set up their personal impressions as the common measure of truth, and so made them an instrument of aggression on the rights of conscience. See Bishop Thirlwall's *Charges*, i. 274.

[2] Gerhard makes no difference between Revelation and the record of it, and Hollaz, arguing throughout on the rule that "Whatever Scripture teaches is infallibly certain," transfers the same infallible certainty to all his own conclusions. The dogma was more and more strongly asserted but never proved. Quenstedt borrows the bad phrase, "*Scripturae auctoritas est tanta, quanta Dei,*" and says, "*Invicte concludimus omnem et totam Scripturam Sacram nullâ ejus vel minimâ parte exceptâ, esse θεοπνευστόν*" (*System Theol.* i. 69). So too Hollaz, Lange, Calov, Carpzov, Baier, Buxtorf, &c. And yet they practically abrogated not a few "God saids," beginning with the decree of the First Council at Jerusalem (Acts xv. 9), to say nothing of the whole Levitic Law. It is Christian practice merely which has drawn a distinction between the Universal and the Partial, the Temporary and the Permanent.

[3] 1 Cor. ii. 15. Corn. à Lapide draws from this verse the conclusion that "the spiritual man" will have recourse to the better judgment of "the Church."

ances of individual writers, but even the very composition of the canon. They preferred to be inconsequent rather than to be fettered, and gave to Faith an authority co-ordinate with that of Scripture. But their successors regarded Faith as the *exclusive* product of Scripture, and dependent for its authority on Scripture only.[1] They turned the inspiration-dogma into "an iron formula, a painful juridical fetter of conscience to be imposed on Christians to the detriment of fresh religious life and the destruction of a just appreciation of the Bible." [2] And thus they directly impaired the authority of Scripture. For "as incredible praises given to men," says Hooker,[3] "do often abate and impair the credit of the deserved commendation, so we must likewise take great heed lest by attributing to Scripture more than it can have, the incredibility of that do cause even those things which it hath abundantly to be less reverently esteemed!" "It is," says Richard Baxter, "the Devil's last method to undo by over-doing, and so to destroy the authority of the Apostles by over-magnifying."

Rathmann of Lübeck (1612—1628) tried to make a stand against these errors. He argued that to restrict all real communication with God to a study of the Scriptures, to *confine* to them the agency of the Holy Spirit, and to endow them with the living powers of the Deity was to dishonour Christ and the Holy Spirit, and to put fellowship with an impersonal thing in the place of fellowship with a living Saviour. He called the Scriptures "*a passive instrument, the light of an object, instrumental, historical.*" But his truer views were indignantly rejected. The theological faculties of six universities,[4] ascribing to Scripture an inherent efficacy for salvation, condemned him as a Calvinist, as a despiser of

---

[1] The commentators of the Reformed Churches (Calvin, Beza, Zwingli, Bucer, Mercer, &c.), were more independently exegetical than the Lutheran commentators (Musculus, Chytraeus, Brentius, Bugenhagen, Bullinger, &c.), who proved Lutheran dogmatics by digressions (see Göbel, *Die Rel. Eigenthümlichkeit d. Ref. und Luth. Kirche*, Bonn, 1837 ; Tholuck, *Verm. Schriften*, ii. 330).

[2] Hagenbach, *Hist. of Ref.* i. 161.

[3] *Eccl. Pol.* bk. ii. c. 8, § 1.

[4] Wittenberg, Königsberg, Helmstädt, Dantzig, Jena, Leipzig.

the external word, as a sympathiser with Schwenckfeld and
with mystic fanaticism. In their system the sole work of the
Holy Ghost is to give us assurance that the doctrines of
Scripture are true. Chemnitz seems to deny the possibility
of faith in Christ unless it be preceded by faith in the whole
of Scripture as undoubted truth. We soon arrive at such
superstitious phrases as that the writers of Scripture are
"*amanuenses of God, hands of Christ, Scribes and notaries of
the Holy Spirit ;*"[1] not even instrumental authors, but only
"*living and writing pens.*"[2] Holy Scripture is described, not
as the *record* of revelation but as revelation itself. Christianity,
which existed so many years before a single Gospel or
Epistle had been written, was robbed of its power. In
defiance of every historic fact the inspiration of the Apostles
was regarded as the annihilation of their proper individuality.
This sort of dogmatism became more and more pernicious.
God's presence and providence in the history of the world
were practically ignored. The Bible was spoken of as "a
divine effluence," "a part of God." Nitzsche even seriously
discussed whether Holy Scripture could be called a creature,
and decided that it could not. The Old and New Testaments were treated as one book, of which all the words and
every word were immediately dictated.[3] The view fell far
below that of the wiser Rabbis, who at least distinguished
between different grades of inspiration. It was a revival
of the worst form of that Talmudic φλυαρία καὶ ματαιότης,[4]
which said that Jehovah had dictated every letter of the Torah
from " I am the Lord thy God," down to " Timnath was the
concubine of Eliphaz." Men like Maimonides, Abarbanel,
Qimchi, had long seen that such inventions can only be
maintained by degrading casuistry.

[1] So Gerhard. Quenstedt says, "Scriptura est infallibilis veritatis fons,
omnisque erroris expers, omnia et singula sunt verissima . . . sive dogmatica,
sive moralia, sive historica, &c."
[2] "*Calami Spiritus sacri dictantis.*" Gregory the Great seems to have been
the first to give currency to this bad phrase. So Calovius, *Systema*, i. cap. 4,
ii. cap. 1, and *passim.* Compare Hollaz, *Exam. Theol.* p. 73 ; Calov. *System.*
i. 594 ; Quenstedt, *Theol. Didact.* i. 55. Differences of style, &c., were
"accommodations" of the Spirit (*id.* i. 76).
[3] Hollaz.   [4] Gregory of Nyssa.

And thus the old ecclesiastical authority, which Luther had so decidedly rejected, was brought back. Even the *impius orthodoxus* was supposed to be illuminated *ex opere operato* by the reading of the Scriptures.[1] Questions about genuineness and integrity were held to be irrelevant because, according to Calov, the Church had decided, or, according to Quenstedt, because each book sufficiently proves its own canonicity.[2] "To correct even acknowledged errors in Luther's translation was regarded as 'dangerous;' nay, the very typographical errors of his editions were to be left intact—a sure sign of what kind of faith was being set up."[3] Although Jerome had so freely pointed out the *cilicisms* of St. Paul, Quenstedt, Hollaz, Calov, and the Wittenberg faculty in 1638 decreed that to speak of barbarisms and soloecisms in the Greek of the New Testament would be *a blasphemy* against the writers of Holy Scripture, and against the Holy Ghost.[4] Orthodox purists thought that the very doctrine of inspiration was imperilled unless the inspiration was conveyed in perfect Greek. Hebraisms were only the desire of the Holy Spirit to assimilate the style of the Old Testament to that of the New. Hellenistic Greek, according to Pfeiffer, is simply Holy Greek—a form of speech peculiar to God.[5] The *Formula Consensus Helvetica* (drawn up in 1675 by F. Heidegger and

---

[1] Dorner (ii. 134), to whom I am here chiefly indebted, refers to Tholuck, *Das Kirchl. Leben*, i. 65.

[2] Protests against this confusion came specially from the mystics. "The external word is the human voice, in which there is included no divine virtue" (Schwenkenfeld, *Ep.* 79). "If thou sayest among the inexperienced that the letter is God's word, thou art . . . a deceiver" (Weigel, *Postills*, i.). But as far back as the eighth century the eminently orthodox Father,-St. John of Damascus, had said, "We apply not to the written word of Scripture the title due to the incarnate Word of God." He says that when the Scriptures are called λογία Θεοῦ, the phrase is only figurative. *Disput. Christiani et Saraceni* (see Lupton, *St. John of Damasc.* p. 95).

[3] Thus Luther—under his current title of Megalander—was erected into a sort of Pope, while the Lutherans were diverging most widely from the spirit of his writings.

[4] Quenstedt censures Beza for not having held this view (*System.* i. 84).

[5] Pfeiffer, *Hermeneutica Sacra*, c. 8; *Dubia Vexata*, pp. 457, *sq.* The same views were maintained by Walther (*Harmon. Biblica*), Buxtorf (*Anticritica*), Wasmuth (*Vindiciae*), Calov, &c. (see Meyer, *Gesch. d. Schrifterkl.* iii. 295), and by Samuel Clark in his *Divine Authority of the Holy Scriptures*, 1699; and John Owen. They were rejected by Ussher, Voss, Hody, Casaubon, Grotius, Bellarmine, Clericus, &c.

Turretin [1]) laid it down as the doctrine of the Church that the very vowel points and accents of the Hebrew Bible were divinely inspired.[2] The Holy Spirit, it was seriously maintained, had altogether abdicated His agency to the written word.[3] Such were the prevalent views of the current opinion which called itself "orthodox" in France, in Holland, and in Germany, both among the Lutheran and the Reformed Churches. We can now scarcely repeat such statements without an apology for irreverence. And yet for the correctness of these serious mis-applications appeal was made to the inner testimony of the Holy Spirit—an appeal which often sounds "like a horrible irony."[4] Even among the Romanists—as was proved by the able and learned works of Richard Simon, of Calmet, even of Bellarmine—freer views had begun to prevail—views less burdensome to the consciences of men, less dishonouring to the majesty of God.[5] Thus did the Post-Reformation Theologians repeat the old error of the Scribes and Pharisees. They were not faithful enough to believe that the Divine Revelation could stand without the dense hedge of human dogmas which they erected in its defence. They idolised the record to such an extent as wholly to miss its essential meaning. They strangled all spiritual life, or at any rate impeded all spiritual growth, by the tight-wound swaddling-bands of polemic orthodoxy. They turned Christianity into a theology and forgot that it was a life. They wrote folios full of theological hatred about problems as to which Christ

[1] Kurz, ii. 264.

[2] Bleek, *Einleit.* 126. Calovius, who has the melancholy honour of having made most dogmatic statements of this epoch in their most absurd and objectionable form, said "It is impious and profane audacity to change a single point in the Word of God, and to substitute a smooth breathing for a rough for a smooth."

[3] As, for instance, in Seb. Schmidt's *Collegium Biblicum Prius* (V. T.) *et Posterius* (N. T.), 1670.

[4] Reuss, *Gesch. d. Heil. Schriften*, ii. 295.

[5] We may be thankful for the gulf of difference between the truthful moderation of our VIth Article, "Holy Scripture *containeth all things neces-sary* to salvation," and the wild extravagance of the *Form. Consensus Hel-vetica*, "Hebraeus codex tum quoad consonas, tum quoad vocalia, sive puncta ipsa, sive punctorum saltem potestatem, Θεοπνευστός." The older reformed confessions (*e.g. Conf. Gall.* art. 5, "*complectens* quicquid . . . requiratur ; *Conf. Belg.* art. 7, "Credimus . . . Scripturam . . . omnem Dei voluntatem *complecti*), contrast favourably in this respect with the later.

was silent; they persecuted as heretics those whom He would most have loved.

Of course under such a system true exegesis became impossible.[1] The tone of it became petty, jealous, unspiritual, and it was perpetually hunting after " *emphases* " which were purely imaginary. Some fragments of former truth were indeed preserved in Hermeneutic treatises; but they were repeated without being utilised.[2] In historic, archaeological, and linguistic researches, amid much that was absurd and irrelevant, there was some accumulation of *materials* for the understanding of Scripture. But a fettered and suspicious exegesis is always sterile, and the living power of Scripture, together with all progress in its comprehension, ceases when it is turned into an idol. The only works, and the only commentaries of this epoch which still retain any vitality are, with all their faults, the works of men like the Arminians, Grotius, Le Clerc, and Spencer; the Cocceians, Lampe, Vitringa, and Van Til; the Pietist Bengel, and the freer critics like J. J. Wetstein and G. A. Turretin, by whom orthodox theology felt itself injured, and against some of whom it directed its most indignant anathemas.

English Christians were happily insulated from the incessant bickerings of the Lutheran and Reformed Churches. The active intercourse with the Continent in the days of Luther and Calvin—the days when Beza, Bucer, and Peter Martyr had exercised so large an influence in England— were followed by a period of isolation, in which the English Church was almost exclusively occupied with her own concerns. Jewel had died in 1571, and Hooker in 1600; but she produced during the seventeenth century and the first half

---

[1] "Die eingeschüchterte Wissenschaft . . . tractirte geringfügige Dinge mit dem lächerlichen Apparat einer pedantischen Gelehrsamkeit" (Reuss, *Gesch. d. Heil. Schrift.* ii. 296)." "If the enquiry is to be free, it is impossible consistently to prescribe its results." Thirlwall, *Charges*, i. 61.

[2] Such treatises were very numerous. Among them were Gerhard, *De Interpr. S. Script.* 1610; Glassius, *Philolog. Sacr.* 1623; Rivetus, *Isagoge*, 1627; Pfeiffer, *Herm. Sacr.* 1684; Dannhauer, *Idea Boni Interpretis*, 1642; L. Meyer, *Philosophia Scripturae Interpres.* 1666 (by a friend of Spinoza); Francke, *Praelectiones Hermeneuticae*, 1717; Rambach, *Inst. Hermen.* 1720.

of the eighteenth many eminent theologians and scholars, such as Bull († 1710), Pearson († 1686), Ussher († 1656), Selden († 1654), Beveridge († 1708), Cave († 1713), and Bingham († 1733). Among those who rendered the highest services to criticism and history may be mentioned Bryan Walton, whose Polyglott appeared in 1657; the Arabic scholar Pococke († 1691), Castell, Hyde, Spencer, Shuckford, Prideaux, and especially Lightfoot († 1675) whose Talmudic annotations still retain their value. Bishop Lowth in his *De Sacra Poesi Hebraeorum* (1753) and his Isaiah (1779) rendered to the English Church some of the services for which Europe was afterwards indebted to the works of Herder. The *Novum Testamentum* of Mill laid the foundations of New Testament criticism. Whittaker, Hammond and Whitby wrote commentaries which contain much that is of permanent interest. Men like Fowler, Leighton, Tillotson, and Burnet, adorned the pulpit. Among the nonconformist communities Baxter, Bunyan, Owen, Howe, and Isaac Watts helped to keep alive the flame of spiritual life, while Hales and Chillingworth, Locke and Cudworth, Smith and Whichcote the Cambridge Platonists and other "moderate divines abusively called Latitudinarians," showed how large a share must always be contributed to the development of truth by wide sympathies and unfettered thought. The work of Tindal called forth Butler's *Analogy;* that of Morgan was answered in Warburton's *Divine Legation.* Wesley and Whitfield did for England what Pietism effected for Germany. By such men—each in his own way and measure, each according to the proportion of his faith—it may be fairly said that all which was anti-Christian and perilous in the writings of the English deists was defeated all along the line.

II. And step by step, in every Protestant country of the Continent, the unbending system of creed-bondage, with its idolatrous letter-worship, was gradually broken down. Freer movements of all kinds began. These, even when they were purely spiritual, were opposed by the dominant orthodoxy with every weapon in their power;—but they were opposed in vain. The true exposition of the Bible which had freed men from the tyrannies of a decadent Romanism was powerful enough to free them once more from the renewed tyrannies of orthodox scholasticism.

And the deliverance came, as it always comes, not from majorities, but from the few; not from multitudes, but from individuals; not from the favourites of erring Churches, but from rebels against their formalism and their tyranny; not from the smooth adherents of conventional religionism, but from its inspired martyrs and heroic revolutionists. In other words the deliverance comes always from the prophets and the children of the prophets: spiritually, from an Antony, a Benedict, a Francis; socially and morally from a Howard, a Clarkson, a Wilberforce; doctrinally, from an Athanasius, a Wiclif, a Hus, a Luther, a Wesley. And so it came to the "ghastly smooth life, dead at heart" of this age of disputatious dogma and loveless religionism. And so it always will come. It will come, not always from men whom Churches bless, but from those whom they anathematise: not only from those whom churchmen praise, but from those whom they call Beelzebub; not always from those whom Bishops have ordained, but from men who have heard voices which others cannot hear, and have felt upon their heads the hands of an unrecognised and invisible consecration. In such conditions it has been said men become electric. They flash in upon the hearts and consciences of others something of their own enthusiasm. Even in the deadest ages there are always more persons than we suppose who revolt against the prevailing fashions, who take courage from one another, and support one another, until communities are led into higher moral principles and purer intellectual beliefs. As their numbers multiply they catch fire with a common idea and a common indignation, and ultimately burst out into open war with the falsities that surround them. So it was in the days of Elijah and in the days of Jeremiah. So it was also in the days of the Son of Man. So it was in the last century. Seven influences helped one by one to redeem the age from its false development ; and those seven movements were mainly due to seven men—Arminius, Spener, Calixtus, Descartes, Böhme, Cappell, and Cocceius. All the movements were not equally pure and spiritual, but all were wholesome in their effects, and through them, to quote the words of St. Augustine, " Christ appeared to the men of a decrepit age, that they might receive a new and youthful life."

1. About the year 1600 Holland succeeded Geneva in the Hegemony of Calvinism. But although the views of Zwingli had been silenced they were not wholly repressed. The hedge of flourishing Dutch universities,[1] reared by the new Pharisaism, could not exclude the milder theology of ARMINIUS († 1609). Refusing to explain the Bible by creeds, he found rigid Calvinism to be Scripturally untenable. Even the fulminations of the Synod of Dort (1618-1619) were ineffectual against so splendid a succession of Arminian theologians as Episcopius († 1643),[2] Grotius († 1645), Limborch († 1711),[3] Clericus († 1736),[4] († 1645) Wetstein († 1754),. Many of these theologians were not afraid to agree with Romanists and Socinians who alike rejected the idol of verbal infallibility. Although the works of Grotius were

---

[1] Dutch universities and their theologians :—

FRANECKER : Lydius, Drusius, Maccovius, Amesius, Amama, Cocceius, Vitringa, Witsius, Gürtler.

UTRECHT : Voetius, Hoornbeck, Leydecker, Lampe.

GRONINGEN : Gomarus, Maresius, J. H. and Jac. Alting.

LEYDEN : Junius, de Dieu, Rivet, the Spanheims, G. J. Voss, Erpenius, Burmann, Witlich.

For details see Dorner, ii. 9–12.

[2] In 1610 Episcopius drew up the Remonstrance in five articles against the Gomarists, who charged the Arminian school with Pelagianism. Hence the name " Remonstrants."

[3] Limborch was author of the *Theologia Christiana.* He opposed an extravagant allegorising and typology, and is consequently censured by Rambach, *Hermeneutica Sacra*, 155, *sq.*

[4] Le Clerc (*Ars Critica*, 3 vols. 1696 ; *Dissertatio de Opt. Gen. Interpretum*, 1693) carried too far his theory of accommodation, and is severely dealt with by Rambach. He represents the strong reaction against the extravagances of the Cocceian school, as also do Turretin, Werenfels, &c. Turretin († 1737) was a Professor at Geneva. He protests against the assumption that "an inner light," which was able to discover indefinite meanings in Scripture, was of value, and in his *Tractatus de S. Scr. interpretandae methodo* he lays down the rule that the interpreter requires " *animus vacuus . .* instar tabulae rasae ut genuinum sensum percipiat." He was a friend of Burnet, Tillotson, and Wake, and endeavoured to unite the Lutheran and Reformed Churches.

received with a storm of disapprobation, his classical learning, his masterly good sense, his brevity, independence, and incomparable lucidity make his annotations more valuable than those of any one of his immediate contemporaries.[1] In the writings of Le Clerc and Spencer there was a misplaced ingenuity and an extravagant utilitarianism, but even these faults have not robbed their learning of all its value, and their works exercised a permanent influence equally removed from disputatious dogma and intolerant self-satisfaction.[2]

2. Another breath of fresh life came from the Pietists. To the icy stiffness of orthodoxy not only the dreams of Böhme, but even the glowing holiness of Arndt had been offensive. But the influence of Arndt was revived by PHILIP JAMES SPENER, a man at once learned, profound, and tolerant. He was chosen minister at Frankfort in 1666, at the age of thirty-one. He became court preacher at Dresden in 1686, and provost at Berlin in 1691. He had read the works of Baxter, and translated into German two books of Molinos. A faithful Lutheran, he yet could not help seeing that living holiness was being buried under dead formalism and a sterile theology of words.[3] "The Lord mercifully keep us," he

---

[1] On Grotius, see Bayle; Simon, *Hist. Crit. du V. T.* p. 443; *Des Comment. du N. T.* p. 803; Buddeus, *Isag.* 1517 : Herder, *Briefe d. Stud. Theol.* p. 357; Meyer, *Gesch. der Schrifterklärung*, iii. 435. Grotius was largely followed by Hammond in his *Paraphrase and Annotations*, 1675 ; *Psalms and Proverbs*, 1684. There was a current saying "Grotium *nusquam* in sacris litteris invenire Christum, Cocceium ubique." It is not true. On Ps. xv. 10 Grotius says, "Latet sensus mysticus . . *ut in plerisque Psalmis.*" Some of his freer views may be seen in the notes on Gen. i. 26 ; iii. 15 ; Ps. ii. ; xvi. ; Is. vii 14 ; ix. 6 ; xi. 1 ; Mic. v. 1 ; Matt. i. 22 ; iii. 15 ; vi. 13, &c. Grotius was called a Papist because he would not call the whole Roman priesthood "ministers of Antichrist" ; a Socinian, though he refuted Socinus ; and (by Calov) an atheist, though he was the author of the *De Veritate.* In the learning and good sense of his notes he has in multitudes of instances anticipated the conclusions of modern exegesis. His view of inspiration was "A Spiritu Sancto dictari historias non fuit opus. Satis fuit Scriptorem memoria valere." *Vot. pro pac. Eccles.*

[2] Bähr says (*Symbolik.* i. 41) that in their system "God appears as a Jesuit using bad means for a good end."

[3] The Lutheran Churches had produced nothing of first-rate importance in exegesis since the death of Flacius in 1575. The most important Lutheran Theologians of the 17th century were Gerhard, S. Glass, Dannhauer, A. Pfeiffer, Camerarius, Chemnitz, Chyträus, Hunnius, Tarnov, and G. Calixt. The chief exegetes of the Reformed Churches were Arminius, Episcopius,

prayed, " from interpreting Scripture solely from our creeds, and so erecting the genuine popedom in the midst of our Church." He desired to add an inward life to the outward profession, and in his *Pia Desideria* (1675), and Spiritual Priesthood (1677) he pointed out with touching humility the necessity for reform. He recalled the forgotten doctrine of the priesthood of every Christian believer, and by his *Collegia pietatis* or, as we should call them, Bible classes and prayer meetings, he revived a sincere religion in many hearts. He was no separatist ; but Pietism was passionate for the holiness about which orthodoxy was indifferent, and indifferent about the formulae for which orthodoxy was passionate. Spener early despaired of doing more than to found *ecclesiolam in ecclesiâ,* and to lead back Christian doctrine from the head to the heart. Part of the great and good work which he effected was the revival of that gift of preaching which is known in the New Testament by the name of "prophecy." Even preaching had withered into inanition amid the combats of theology. It had become almost exclusively dogmatic, controversial, and scholastic in its spirit, and it therefore failed to elevate the life or to touch the heart. It followed various methods known by the barbarous and pedantic titles of Pancratian, Porismatic, Hoppnerian, Zetetic, and Ursinian,[1] and was in fact everything except edifying and spiritual. But Spener's example helped to sweep away this mass of artificial rules, and by reintroducing the genuine Homily he gave a fresh impulse to the careful study of Scriptural thoughts. The views of Spener were adopted by three young Masters of Arts, A. H. Francke, Anton, and Schade, who held Bible meetings at Leipzig.[2] They tried to do at Leipzig exactly what the Wesleys tried to do at Oxford. Even so pure and spiritual a movement as this [3] was violently denounced by all who mistook

Chamier, Sixt. Amama. Grotius, A. Rivet, Drusius, L. de Dieu, Gomarus, Cappellus, Cocceius, Lipsius, Bochart. Among the Socinians, F. Socinus († 1562) Crell, Schlichting. [1] See Herzog, *Art. Ev. Homiletik.*

[2] These *collegia philobiblica* resembled those of Wesley and the young Methodists at Oxford.

[3] Pietism was defined as follows :

"Was ist ein Pietist ? der Gottes Wort studirt
Und nach demselben auch ein heilig Leben führt."

for temples the whitened sepulchres of their own formalism. Spener was compelled to leave Dresden. Francke and his friends were driven from Leipzig by the theological faculty headed by J. B. Carpzov. But though many States prohibited these religious meetings, Pietism found a home at the new University of Halle, and became a powerful factor in German life.[2] A Church, as Calvin said, "has need of many resurrections," and the need is never greater than in the days when genuine piety is an object of suspicion, and Enthusiasm becomes the "red spectre" of orthodoxies which have only a name to live when they are dead.

3. A third powerful protest against the ossification of religion by theological Scholasticism came in the direction of tolerance and culture. GEORG CALIXTUS (†1656) for forty-two years professor at Helmstädt, had lived through the fury of the Thirty Years' War; he had received a Humanist training, and in his early travels had lived among Lutherans, among Roman Catholics, and in the Reformed Churches. In England he had shared the enlightened wisdom of Casaubon and Thuanus. In these travels he had learned to see "that faith and love are not the exclusive possession of any party," and to say with Jerome that "Christ is not so poor as to have a Church only in Sardinia."[3] His watchwords were concord and tolerance, and he thought that they might be found by returning to early Church history, and leaving the confused whirl of contemporary controversies. He was one of the last to cherish some hope of a reunion with Romanism on neutral

---

[1] Spener was attacked by Schelwig, Carpzov, Alberti, Deutschmann, and the faculty of Wittenberg. Francke by Mayer, and the University of Leipzig. If my remark seems severe, it is not more so than that of Dorner. Speaking of the opponents of Pietism, he says (ii. 205) "Trusting in 'correctness of doctrine' they surrendered themselves to a security which pleased itself with dreams of a *florentissimus status ecclesiae*, and ignored the fact that they had themselves adulterated the Gospel into a law of dogma and a doctrinal codex, confused nature and grace, and frittered away the ideas of faith and regeneration."

[2] See Kurz, ii. 207 ; J. H. and C. B. Michaelis and their pupil Rambach belong to Halle, and 6000 theological students had been educated at Halle, before Francke died.

[3] He wrote *De tolerantia Reformatorum* and *Desiderium Concordiae Eccl. sarciendae*, 1650.

grounds, a hope defeated as much by the sectarianism of the Jesuits as by the vehemence of the Lutherans. His Syncretism as it was derisively called,[1] was partly dependent on a return to a truer estimate of Scripture. Abandoning the extravagant aberrations of prevalent bibliolatry he recalled the old distinction between *revelatio* and *assistentia divina*.[2] He did not wholly extinguish the co-ordinate authority of Faith, and regarding inspiration as a grace of superintendency he mitigated "the more than Alexandrian asperities" of the prevailing view.[3]

4. Again, the dawning philosophy of modern days was not without its liberating influence. DESCARTES († 1650) was not thinking only of philosophers when in his discourse on Method he spoke of "speculations of which men are more vain the more remote they are from common sense, because they will then have been forced to employ more ingenious subtlety to render them plausible." His views were vehemently opposed by Voetius, a theological professor at Utrecht, who secured from the States a prohibition of his philosophy. Calixt died in the very year (1656) in which SPINOZA was excommunicated with the most awful curses by his enraged co-religionists. No one can read the works of that virtuous and keen-sighted thinker without feeling that he was at any rate "almost a Christian." His pantheism resulted from philosophic reaction against the crude anthropomorphic

[1] Because Calixtus, like the *Cretans*, entered into unscrupulous alliances! This derivation is given by Plutarch, *De Frat. Amore.* I do not know on what authority Littré and others derive it from σὺν κερᾷν. In modern times, the use of the word had been revived by Erasmus in a letter to Melanchthon. The anonymous *Historia Syncretistica* of Calov was answered by F. U. Calixt in his *Via ad Pacem*, 1700. Syncretism, says Gass, "means the overthrow of all ecclesiastical exclusiveness by a deeper conception of the doctrines in question."

[2] In this he was followed by Grotius, Clericus, &c. See the valuable article by Tholuck on Inspiration in Herzog. I have not specially noticed the exegesis of the Socinians because it was so utterly and inexcusably bad. See Reuss, § 556 ; Diestel, pp. 387–534, *fg.*

[3] Scripture is not called divine because everything which is contained in it ought to be imputed to a special divine revelation." *Respons. thes.* 72. Professor Ladd (*Doctrine of Sacred Script.* ii. 212–214) shows that the views of Calixt resembled those of Baxter, Doddridge, and Lowth. Monographs on Calixt and the Syncretism have been written by Schmid, Henke, and Gass.

views in which he had been trained. He is the intellectual
successor of Moses Maimonides, the intellectual precursor of
Moses Mendelssohn, and he anticipated many of the critical
and hermeneutic views which are now widely accepted.
Lessing reverenced him; Goethe named him with Shak-
speare and Linnaeus as one of the masters of his mind;
Fichte and Hegel were deeply influenced by his method
and his thoughts. It was not till a century later that his
influence was felt in exegesis, but when it was felt men
remembered his saying, that "though it was not wholly
necessary to know Christ after the flesh, yet it was necessary
to know that Eternal Son of God, that is the Eternal Wisdom
of God, which has manifested itself in all things, especially in
the mind of man, and far most of all in Christ Jesus. . .
And because the wisdom was chiefly manifested by Jesus
Christ, therefore his disciples preached it, so far as it had
been revealed by Him to them." It may at least be hoped
that he who wrote this, and who also lived a life of singular
moral nobleness and beauty,—whatever may have been his
errors,—was "not far from the kingdom of heaven." [1]

5. The liberation of the Church was further helped on,
fifthly, by mysticism. Though few now read the works of
J. Böhme, "the mighty cobbler of Görlitz" († 1624), his influence was widely felt. His *Aurora oder Morgenröthe im
Aufgang*, was a sort of commentary on the Book of Genesis,
rich in poetic feeling and profound speculation. In England
he was reverently studied by William Law. In Germany the
"*philosophus teutonicus*" as he was called, prepared the way
for a revival of spirituality, and of that "enthusiasm" which
to a formal religion was a favourite object of denunciation.
How touching is the story of his death! "Do you hear that

---

[1] Spinoza derived his views of interpretation in part from Ibn Ezra and
Maimonides. He held that Scripture was its own best interpreter. Novalis
calls him "a God-intoxicated man." Schleiermacher did not hesitate to write
of him, "Offer reverently with me a lock to the Manes of holy rejected
Spinoza. . . In holy innocence and deep humility he beheld His image in the
eternal world. . . He was full of religion and of the Holy Spirit." He
influenced Lessing, Goethe, Schelling, Hegel, and foreshadowed the views on
the one hand of Semler and Eichhorn, on the other of Strauss, Baur, and
Renan. (For his critical views see especially Capp. viii.-x. of his *Tractatus*.)

sweet harmonious music ? " he asked of his son. " No," replied the youth. " Open the door," said Böhme, " that you may the better hear it." It would have been well for the Church of Osiander and of Calov, had it opened the door a little more widely to hear the heavenly music which soothed the deathbed of Jacob Böhme.

6. Two other powerful movements yet remain to be characterised—the influence of Cocceius, and the growth of criticism.

JOHN KOCH, Professor at Leyden († 1669), profoundly affected the religious tendencies of his day.[1] Few theologians have succeeded in doing at once so much good and so much harm by their special opinions.[2] On the one hand his " Federal Theology," the conception of a double covenant,— one of nature and works with Adam in innocence, the other of grace and faith in Christ,—helped once more to lead men back to the Bible. His theology became in fact a soteriology, a history of Redemption. He gave predominance to the *guidance* rather than to the *election* of grace, and almost for the first time developed the correct and fruitful conception of the progressiveness of Revelation as the ruling principle of theological inquiry. Being independent, he was, after the fashion of his day, charged with Judaism, Chiliasm, Pelagianism, and all imaginable heresies ; but he helped to expel the Aristotelian dogmatics which passed for orthodoxy, revived the original investigation of Scripture, and in his beautiful little book, *Summa Doctrinae de Foedere*, taught his contemporaries to study the structure of the Bible, and to abandon the unfruitful method of splitting it into isolated texts.[3] Unhappily, however, the good which Cocceius did in

---

[1] Cocceius was born in 1602. He was a professor first at Bremen, then at Franecker (1636–1650), and then at Leyden. As a youth he had been influenced by the orthodoxy of Maccovius, the Puritanism of Ames, and the scholarship of Amama.

[2] See Pfaff, *Hist. Lit. Theol.* i. 14 ; Alb. v. d. Flier, *De J. Cocceio anti-scholastico*, 1859 ; Schröck, viii. 344, *sq.* ; Gesenius in Ersch und Grüber's *Encykl.* i. 18 ; and Ebrard in Herzog. J. H. Majus said of him, "Animum imprimis ad fontes intendit, et *nulli se mancipavit.*"

[3] The dispensation of Grace after the Fall was treated under three divisions : 1. Before the Law. 2. Under the Law. 3. Under the Gospel. He thought

one direction he undid in another. He emancipated exegesis
from a dull tyranny, but subjected it to an extravagant
typology.[1] He was the first to sanction a system of parallels
between the Old and New Testament of which many were
purely fanciful.[2] His flexible axiom that the words of
Scripture signify all that they can be made to signify[3]
introduced a false plurality of meanings, by a fatal confusion
between the actual sense and all possible applications. Under
this system passages in Isaiah became actual prophecies of the
dispute between the successors of Constantine,[4] the history
of Karl the Great,[5] and the death of Gustavus Adolphus.[6]
In reading Gürtler's *Systema Theologiae,* we can see why
Cocceianism became proverbial for artificiality and caprice.[7]
The movement begun by Cocceius, like almost every
other movement during this epoch, seems by some
fatality to have been cursed by the falsehood of extremes.
Fortunately, however, Cocceius had successors like F. Burmann, Witsius, Van Til, Vitringa, and Lampe, who toned down
the exuberance of his system, and made important contributions to Scriptural interpretation.[8]

7. The growth of criticism helped still more completely
to break down the hard superstition on which the whole
system of Protestant Scholasticism was based. First among
the names of the critics who rendered this service stands
that of Ludovicus Cappellus (†1722). His *Critica Sacra,* pub-

---

that the Old Testament provides a praeter-mission (πάρεσις) but not a *remission* (ἄφεσις) of sins. Rom. iii. 25.

[1] The current phrase of the day was "Grotium nusquam in sacris literis
invenire Christum, Cocceium ubique." See p. 380, *n.* i.

[2] See Vitringa, *Typus Doctrinae Propheticae* ; Venema, *Methodus Prophetica,
Praef.* 1775 ; Lampe, *De Scala Jacobi* ; Cremer, *Antiquitates Theol. Typicae* ;
Kurz, ii. ; Oehler, *Old Test. Theol.* i. 42 ; Klausen, *Hermen.* 282 ; Dorner,
ii. 35, *sq.* Gass, *Gesch. d. Prot. Dogmatik,* ii. 319.

[3] "Id significant verba quod significare possunt in integra oratione sic ut
omnino inter se conveniant" (*ap. Roman.* § 35). So too Turretin, *De Interpr.
Sacr.* p. 126.

[4] Is. xix. 2.   [5] Is. xxiii. 11.
[6] Is. xxxiiii. 7.

[7] I have already quoted his unwise principle that every prophetic application attached to a passage was foreseen, and therefore was intended.

[8] Vitringa († 1722) tried to unite the methods of Grotius and Cocceius.
Some of the Cocceians were much influenced by Cartesianism. Meyer in his
Philosophia S. Scripturae called Cartesianism the only key to Scripture.

lished in 1650, marked an epoch.[1] Among the extravagances of reformed theology had been an assertion as to the miraculously perfect integrity of the text. Gerhard had maintained that it had neither been corrupted by the malice of the Jews nor by the carelessness of copyists. Cappellus admitted that there had been no wilful corruption; but from parallel passages, from the differences in numbers, from New Testament quotations, from references in Philo, Josephus, and the Fathers, from the *Keri* and *Kethib*, from the readings of Ben Asher and Ben Naphthali, from the Jewish and Samaritan MSS., and from the variations of the LXX. and the Paraphrasts, he proved that the Masoretic text furnishes numberless examples of the infirmity, somnolence, and ignorance of Scribes.[2] After the publication of his book no reasonable man could doubt that the Jewish notion of a correspondence of the Holy Books with the supposed autographs of Moses or Ezra down to the very apices of the letters, was a preposterous fiction. Robert Stephens said that he had found 2,384 variations in the oldest MSS. of the New Testament. It was admitted on all sides that these variations did not affect a single matter of faith, and scholars like Sixtinus Amama, Grotius, Brian Walton, Bochart, Ussher, Voss, Hody, and others, at once accepted the conclusion of Cappellus. But since these facts tended to show how untenable was the theory of verbal dictation, they were met with strange absurdities. Pfeiffer, with unconscious irreverence, argued that the Holy Ghost used paronomasias for our delight and advantage; that He showed His freedom by altering proper names; that, for instance, by omitting some letters in

---

[1] The *Exercitationes Biblicae* of J. Morinus (1633) were much cruder. But it is remarkable that, whilst Protestants vehemently opposed the publication of the *Critica Sacra*, the Catholics Morinus and Petavius procured the royal *imprimatur* for it. In the controversy raised by the book the Buxtorffs, with all their learning, were absolutely defeated, because their views on biblical dictation led them to hold that the Masoretic punctuation originated with Moses, or at least with Ezra.

[2] "Nobis jam satis est utcumque probasse argumentis non omnino contemnendis, puncta illa hebraica a Masorethis esse excogitata, et textui sacro addita, circa Christi Ann. 500, et saltem post 400" (Cappellus, *Critica Sacra*, ii. 28, p. 790).

the acrostic Psalms He meant to indicate some pause in music, or to call attention to some hidden mystery.

" Sic placuit Domino dicere plura nefas." [1]

The two Buxtorffs tried to prove that even the vowel points were inspired, and that to hold this was necessitated by the doctrine of Scripture inspiration.[2] That Hebrew was a divine and primaeval language, and that the present square character was at least as old as Ezra, were equally maintained with unavailing casuistry.[3] As the labours of Jewish scholars like Joseph Albo and Elias Levita became known, and were adopted by all the most eminent scholars of Europe, these masses of obscurantism were scattered like mist before the sun. It soon became a matter of certainty that the text of the Bible had suffered from exactly the same causes as those which have affected the text of every other ancient writing in the world.[4]

III. These seven movements then, each in its own way, corrected the false dip of the balance, and contributed to the advancement of sound learning and true religion. We may thank God that, though many a separate wave seems to retreat, the great tide of truth slowly advances through the centuries ;—

> For while the tired waves, vainly breaking,
> Seem here no painful inch to gain,
> Far back through creeks and inlets making
> Comes silent, flooding in, the main.

We may thank God also that no age is ever entirely barren, that no honest human labour is ever wholly lost. Even when the sway of *à priori* dogma was least resisted, the

---

[1] On the bad principle of inventing mysteries to account for variations, it was said that the Yod in כארי, as read in Ps. xxii. 17, was a *vau diminutivum*, and stood for 1230, the years between the writing of the Psalm and the Crucifixion ! (Diestel, p. 328).

[2] Heidegger (*Loci*, ii. § 58) proved it by the command to Moses to write the words on stones *plainly !*

[3] *E.g.* by Hugh Broughton, Buxtorff, Fuller, Bayle, Dilherr, Kircher, Leusden, Morinus, Löscher, Carpzov, &c. (Diestel, p. 384).

[4] Kennicott came to the conclusion that we have no Hebrew MS. of the Old Testament older than A.D. 1100, and that the oldest are full of clerical errors. Bengel was perhaps the first to attempt the classification of MSS.

Church was gaining wisdom from the toils of the learned and the meditations of the good. Such well-known works on various branches of Scriptural chronology, archaeology, geography, natural history, history, and general illustration, as those of Schultens, the Buxtorffs, Castell, Hottinger, Heidegger, Celsius, Bochart, Reland, Vitringa, Glass, Schröder, Ussher, Spannheim, Selden, Buddeus, Pfeiffer, Prideaux, Deyling, Wähner, Scaliger, Petavius, Goodwin, Lightfoot, Schöttgen, and many others, were storehouses of valuable material which were not affected by current quarrels, or "the rage of theologians," from which Melanchthon had yearned to be delivered.[1] And when tendencies and movements proved themselves to be inefficient, because of a large inter-mixture of error, or because they spent their force and had to be carried on by weaker agencies, they left their legacy to men who availed themselves of all their elements of truth and goodness. Mysticism in the followers of Böhme degenerated into a self-deceiving claim of illumination. Pietism, so pure and hopeful in its origin, withered into an inquisitorial hypocrisy. Cocceianism deteriorated into arbitrary super-stition. The Syncretistic movement split into sections by which Romanism and Indifferentism alike profited. Free criticism, looked on by orthodoxy with a jealous eye, was too apt to ally itself with an unspiritual philosophy. But though every one of these influences which had endeavoured to strike life into the decay of religion had gradually dwindled, they produced men of vast erudition, of conspicuous wisdom, and of exemplary holiness. Their combined value was seen in some whose names will stand recorded for ever among those whom the Church honours and loves. Among these I will here select three: Count ZINZENDORF, JOHN JAMES WETSTEIN, and JOHN ALBERT BENGEL.

i. In ZINZENDORF, and his Moravian brotherhoods, we see the undying force of Practical Christianity. He was born in

---

[1] See Reuss, § 566 ; Diestel, §§ 458 ff. The *Critica Sacra* were published in London, 1660, and Poole's *Synopsis* in 1669. Both books were highly creditable to English industry and scholarship.

1700, and as a child had received the blessing and happy prophecy of his aged godfather Philip Spener. Even as a schoolboy under Francke, at the High School of Halle, he had founded among his schoolfellows "the order of the grain of mustard seed," of which the token was a gold ring inscribed with the words "No man liveth to himself." Impressed by an *Ecce Homo* at Düsseldorf under which was the inscription :—

> "I did all this for thee,
> What hast thou done for me?"[1]

—impressed also during his travels with "the splendid misery of a world dying of envy amid its own pitiable littlenesses," he determined to devote his life to the cause of Christ.[2] "I have but one passion," he said, "and it is He, only He." Like every good man he was abused and misrepresented by sectarian bigotry. So busy was calumny with his pure name that Frederick William of Prussia said of him that "all the devils in hell could not lie worse than he had been lied to about Zinzendorf." But his pious journeys did much to bring back to the Church the love of Unity, and the colonies which he planted from Greenland to Ethiopia, from Persia to New Guinea, from Russia to the huts of the Hottentots, not only renewed the lost ideal of missionary activity, but showed to the world the power of spiritual holiness.[3] If we would estimate the extent and blessedness of his work, let us not forget that the deep practical piety of John Wesley was matured in a Moravian brotherhood ; and that Schleiermacher wrote from a Moravian colony in 1802, "Here it was that for the first time I woke to the consciousness of the relations of man to a higher world. . . After all that I have passed through I have become a Moravian again, only of a higher order."[4]

---

[1] "Hoc feci pro te,
Quid facis pro me?"

[2] In founding the community of Herrnhut he was deeply influenced by the *Ratio disciplinae* of the Bohemian Bishop, Amos Comenius.

[3] Perhaps his most characteristic thoughts are to be found in his *Gedanken über Evangelische Wahrheiten*, Gnadau, 1840. His best-known hymns are "Jesu, geh' voran," and "Christi Blut und Gerechtigkeit," (Jesu, Thy blood and righteousness).

[4] On Zinzendorf, see Bishop E. de Schweinitz, in Herzog's *Encykl.*; Tholuck, *Verm. Schriften*, i. 6 ; V. von Ense, *Leben Zinzendorfs*, 1846 ; Bonet, *Le Comte*

ii. In JOHN JAMES WETSTEIN, Professor at Basle († 1754), we see all that is best in this epoch on the side of learning and criticism. In his *Libelli ad Crisin atque Interpretationem Nov. Testamenti*, he dwelt on the necessity for considering the New Testament on its human side as an historical and literary product, and of devoting to it a free and unprejudiced study.[1] The same rules hold, he says, for the interpretation of Scripture as for that of other books. The sense of its words and phrases must be learnt by studying the usage of the writers and of their contemporaries. Its language is influenced by the times in which it was written and the needs, peculiarities, and habits of thought of the persons to whom it is addressed. Wetstein's invaluable labours on the text and meaning illustrate the remark of Goethe, that "the Bible becomes more beautiful the more we study it,—that is the more clearly we see that every word has received a certain distinct character according to the separate conditions of time and place when it was given." He was one of the ablest pioneers in the renewed and more sober Scriptural labours of the eighteenth century. His New Testament was only published in 1751, four years before his death. But he had devoted to its preparation a life of study.[2] He was, as a matter of course, like all the best workers in this field, accused of heresy, and was compelled to give up his Professorship at Basle for one in the Remonstrants' College at Amsterdam.[3] There he carried on and improved the best labours of Grotius. His commentary is one of the richest repositories of classical and Rabbinic illustration, and has, to an extent almost incredible, been rifled again and again by his successors. It is one of the very few produced in the

---

de Zinzendorf, 1860 ; Hagenbach, *Germ. Rationalism*, 128–153 (E. T.) ; Kurz, ii. 941, *sq.* ; Dorner, ii. 245–248 ; Kahnis, pp. 100-105.

[1] Some characteristic quotations from his *Libelli ad Crisin* are given in Klausen, *Hermen.* 298.

[2] Among other things he was condemned for Arianism and Socinianism in 1730, because he followed the now all but universally accepted reading, ὅς for θεὸς in 1 Tim. iii. 16. See Herzog, *Bible Texts*.

[3] He succeeded Clericus.

seventeenth and eighteenth centuries, which are still indispensable to the student of Scripture. [1]

iii. Still greater and more blessed, as well as somewhat earlier, was the work of the illustrious BENGEL († 1752). [2] He was the heir and continuator of all that was best in Pietism and Mysticism, without either the gloom of the one or the sentimentality of the other. Orthodox with none of the narrow blindness, obstinate creed-worship, and uninquiring dulness of passive traditionalism ; exquisitely open-minded ; a friend to science ; a friend to freedom ; the first great German critic of the text of the New Testament ; [3] profoundly humble yet thoroughly original, he towers above all the scholars and theologians of the Lutheran Church. [4] He entirely abandoned the notion of mechanical Inspiration, which then erected a barrier against all spiritual progress, and recognised the distinct individualities and manifold differences of the sacred writers. He regarded Piety not as the loveless personal pride into which Pietism had degenerated, but as an apprehension of the sweetness, gentleness, and grace of the Divine mysteries. He regarded Orthodoxy, not as a bristling antagonism to every slight deviation from current confessions, but as a faithful adherence to all primary truths.

---

[1] See Glöckner, *Interpretandi ratio a J. J. Wetsteino adhibita*, 1754, and the Prolegomena to his New Testament, published anonymously in 1730. He was the first to distinguish uncial MSS. by capitals, and cursives by Arabic figures.

[2] See Burk, *Bengel's Leben und Werke*, 1831 : Wächter, *J. A. Bengel, Lebensabriss*, &c. Bengel was born in 1687 at Winnenden, near Stuttgart. In 1731 he became tutor at Denkendorf. In 1741 he was made Bishop of Herbrechtingen. His *Gnomon* was first published in 1742 : his *Apparatus Criticus* and New Testament in 1734.

[3] He collected twenty-four Greek MSS. and some Latin ones, as enumerated in his *Apparatus Criticus*. He boldly pronounced the Doxology in Matt. vi. 13 to be spurious. His excellent rule was "Put nothing into the Scriptures, but draw out of them, and suffer nothing that is in them to remain hid." His remarks (*Praefatio*) on the uselessness of reading and refuting a multitude of baseless exegetical conjectures, or of refuting all the views from which we differ, would have helped, if attended to, to clear modern commentaries of much useless matter.

[4] The least fortunate part of his influence was the exaggerated devotion to the "futurist" speculations of Apocalyptic students. But, as Principal Edwards says, "His marvellous felicities must ever remain inimitable and he is mighty to quicken thought." *On* 1 *Cor.* p. xxxv.

"As to things indifferent," he said, "I am not fond of them, but the cord has been too tightly drawn." He opposed all too stringent subscriptions. "It is easy," he said, "for all who are content to live on like the rest of the world, to be orthodox. They believe what was believed before them, and never trouble themselves with testing it. But when a soul is anxious about truth, then things are not quite so easy. How wrong is it then to rush in upon just such sensitive souls, to cross-question, to gag, and stun them, when we ought on the contrary, to give them liberty of speech that they may gain confidence, and suffer themselves to be led aright." The fundamental virtue of Bengel was perfect conscientiousness,[1] and his fundamental merit as an exegete was that while he was diligent about minute points of textual criticism and Greek philology, he could also, like Chrysostom and like Luther, enter into the very soul of the sacred writers, and reproduce for others the melodies which once rang in their hearts.[2] Bengel regarded Scripture not as a dead Oracle, but as a living organism—"as an incomparable narrative of the divine government of the human race throughout all ages of the world, from the beginning to the end of all things." Independent though perfectly faithful, it was his not uncommon lot to be frowned upon by professional theologians and the clerical order in general; but, as he himself ventured to predict, the Church has at last learnt to estimate aright the value of his labours. His *Gnomon* is a mine of priceless gems.[3] It contains sentence

---

[1] See Kahnis, E. T. p. 105. Fresenius in his funeral sermon called Bengel "An angel of peace who was as pious as he was laborious, as child-like as he was learned, as rich in spirit as he was acute in mind, as humble as he was great."

[2] The necessity for a psychological element in the highest exegesis was pointed out by Schleiermacher. It was recognised also in the Greek Church. *Dosithei Confessio,* Qu. i. Kimmel, *Monumenta Fidei,* i. 465.

[3] *Gnomon N. T. in quo ex nativa verborum vi simplicitas, profunditas, concinnitas, salubritas sensuum coelestium indicatur.* Tüb. 1742. Its merits are gratefully acknowledged by John Wesley in his *Notes to the New Testament,* 1755. Even the Apocalyptic studies to which Bengel was led by mystic and Pietist influences give proofs of his power and insight. See Hartmann, *Art.* "Bengel" in Herzog. In *his* case at any rate "the path to the New Jerusalem did *not* lie near the madhouse."

after sentence exquisitely terse and finished, and throbbing with spiritual light. Few writers have so admirably succeeded in expressing in a few words the inmost purpose of each of the Epistles. A generation crowded with writers whose theology abounded in mutual anathemas is yet redeemed from the charge of sterility which has produced such a theologian as Bengel. His work must continue to have its value so long as men can recognise the richest fruits of a noble intellect, a pure spirit, and a blameless life.[1] "Lord Jesus, unto Thee I live, unto Thee I suffer, unto Thee I die ; Thine J am, living or dying." These words were repeated to him in his last moments, and on hearing them he pointed with his right hand to his heart, and fell asleep in peace.[2]

---

[1] In the Preface to the third edition of the *Gnomon*, his son gives us some biographical particulars of him. Oetinger beautifully describes his death which he had always wished to be "as if one is incidentally called out of doors from amidst the dust of his daily labours."

[2] I have not touched in this Lecture either on the Puritan or the Roman Catholic expositors, not only because I had no space at command, but because, apart from their theology, they added no new impulse and contributed no specially original element to Scripture interpretation. The greatest Puritan expositor is perhaps Owen (especially in his *Exposition of the Hebrews*). The best Roman Catholic expositors are Estius († 1613) and Corn. à Lapide († 1637)

" Deus scientiarum Dominus est, et ipsi praeparantur cogitationes.'
—1 SAM. ii. 3.

" Res Dei, Ratio."—TERT. *De Poenitent.* I.

" Christianity is all for practice, and so much time as is spent in quarrels about it is a diminution to its interest. Men inquire so much what it is, that they have but little time left to be Christians. I remember a saying of Erasmus, 'that when he first read the New Testament, with fear and a good mind, with a purpose to understand it and obey it, he found it very useful and very pleasant ; but when, afterwards, he fell on reading the vast differences of commentaries, then he understood it less than he did before, then he began not to understand it :' for, indeed, the truths of God are best dressed in the plain culture and simplicity of the Spirit ; but the truths that men commonly teach are like the reflections of a multiplying-glass. For one piece of good money you shall have forty that are fantastical."—JEREMY TAYLOR, *Via Intelligentiae.*

" Let none so superstitiously go back to former ages as to be angry with new opinions and displayings of light, either in reason or religion. Who dare oppose the wisdom and goodness of God if He shall enamour the world with the beauty of some pearls and jewels which in former days have been hid or trampled on ; if He shall discover some more light upon earth, as He hath let some new stars be found in the heavens ? "—CULVERWELL, *Light of Nature*, p. 136.

" I am persuaded that the Lord hath more truths yet to come for us out of His Holy word. Neither Luther nor Calvin have penetrated into the whole Council of God."—JOHN ROBINSON, *Farewell Address to the Pilgrim Fathers.*

" The Gospel itself rests on an immovable rock, while human systems of theology are everywhere undergoing a purifying process. We live in the time of a great crisis."—NEANDER.

LECTURE VIII.

MODERN EXEGESIS.

"It shall come to pass in that day that the light shall not be clear, nor
dark . . . but it shall come to pass at evening time it shall be light."—
ZECH. xiv. 6, 7.

THERE are three reasons which give peculiar difficulty to
the treatment of the final phases of Scripture interpretation.
One is their complexity, and the multiplication of their
literary memorials; a second is the rapidity with which
they vary from decade to decade in consequence of that susceptibility to surrounding influences which marks a literary
age ; a third is the impossibility of forming a final impression
of movements which have not yet attained their full
development.

The disruption of Protestant Scholasticism was hastened
and completed by philosophic inquiries. The malady of
scepticism had been rendered more acute by the un-
skilful violence of a self-styled orthodoxy. Such books as
Voltaire's *La Bible enfin Expliquée* were the natural Nemesis of
such books as Calov's *Biblia Illustrata*. The furious squabbles
of Lutheran and Reformed Churches about the *arcana* of
Theology had paved the way for English deists, French
infidels, and German neologians.[1] The gravity and gentleness
of Spinoza's manner, no less than his keen sagacity, had

---

[1] "So long as I see that one of the chief of Christ's commandments, to
love our enemies, is not better observed than it is, so long shall I doubt
whether those who give themselves out as Christians are really such"
(Lessing).

given weight to the criticisms of his *Tractatus Theologico-
Politicus,* and, crude as some of them were, he rendered a real
service by enforcing attention to that human element of
Scripture, which he had probably been taught to recognise by
the writings of Maimonides. His "Pantheism" was opposed
by Leibnitz († 1716), who substituted for it the theory of
self-subsisting monads held in union by a pre-established
harmony. Leibnitz was a hearty friend to Christianity, and
he so strongly desired to bring theology into the circle of the
exact sciences, that in his *Theodicaea* he pledged himself to
prove, if not the objective certainty, yet at least the possibility
of the deepest Christian mysteries—even of the Trinity, the
Incarnation, the Eucharist.[1] WOLFF († 1754), systematising the methods of Leibnitz in a mathematical form,[2]
aimed at deducing the truths of revelation from the abstract
ideas of the mind. In spite of his pedantic formalism, he
roused enthusiasm among the students of Halle. He was
angrily opposed by the Pietists, who saw in his doctrines
a fatalistic tendency which would destroy all interest in
revealed religion. They were right in their instinctive
conviction that Christianity has nothing to gain from
precarious arguments in favour of its abstract possibility.
An address in which Wolff had extravagantly eulogised
the moral teachings of Confucius was made the pretext
for his banishment on pain of the gibbet from Halle and
from the whole kingdom of Prussia. Thus failed the earliest

---

[1] Leibnitz added "the principle of the sufficient reason" as a criterion of
truth to Aristotle's "principle of contradiction." "The great foundation of
mathematics," he says in his correspondence with Dr. Clarke, "is the principle of *contradiction or identity ; i.e.* that a proposition cannot be true and
false at the same time. But in order to proceed from Mathematics to treat
Philosophy another principle is requisite (as I have observed in my *Theodicaea*),
I mean the principle of the sufficient reason, or in other words, that nothing
happens without a *reason* why it should be so rather than otherwise. Now
by this single principle can be demonstrated the Being of a God," &c.

[2] Wolff's chief works were *Vernünftige Gedanken von Gott, der Welt,
und der Seele* (1719), and *V. G. von der Menschen Thun und Lassen* (1721).
He studied mathematics, *methodi gratia,* in order to give diligence to reduce
theology to incontrovertible certainty. Even his opponent, Lange, had a
similar notion, and just at this period there arose an unprofitable fashion of
"hairsplitting analysis and dreary tabulation." Wolff's banishment was
hastened by stupid jests as to "prae-established harmony," at Frederic
William's "tobacco-Parliament."

attempt to reconcile a nascent philosophy with an old religion. But the expulsion of Wolff, and his subsequent triumphant recall, practically became the death-blow of Pietism which had outlived its functions, and had sunk into a system of morbid fanaticism maintained by inquisitorial forms.

Meanwhile many movements arose, which, in the dearth of a free and spiritual holiness, developed destructive tendencies. Mankind can never long be satisfied with vague eudaemonism and half-hearted compromise. LESSING († 1781) was as little hostile to Christianity as Leibnitz and Wolff had been, but in the then condition of Scriptural studies he seems to have held the opinion of St. Jerome, that almost anything may be said if it be only said tentatively. He gave an *impulse* to thought rather than a *direction*. He was "the versatile Proteus" of his age. His *Nathan der Weise*, exquisite in its spirit of tolerance, was weak in its indifferentism, and hardly accords with his own fruitful view of God as the educator of the human race. He was opposed to Spinoza's inert eternity of substance. He wanted something better than the demonstrations of Wolff and his followers, that Christianity contained nothing against the *principium contradictionis*, and the *principium rationis sufficientis*. There were germs of truth in his belief in a primitive oral Gospel; in his separation of Christianity from the weak evidences by which it is often supported; in the distinction which he drew between the Christianity of the heart and the Christianity of theologians, and even between the Christian religion and the religion of Christ. His quick susceptibility enabled him to grasp truths akin to those held alike by Mendelssohn and Kant and Herder; and if, no less than they, he lacked the vivifying power of personal and intellectual union with the divine humanity of Christ, the theology of his day must share the blame. Protestant divines could not expect the world to sympathise with them in their attempts to hunt up heresies in each other's sermons. Lessing was himself conscious of an unsatisfied want. He despised the popular incredulity as " a botchwork of ignoramuses." " It is not since yesterday only," he wrote to Mendelssohn, " that I have felt anxious, lest in casting off many prejudices I may not also have cast away much which I may have again to fetch back. If I have not done so already it is because I fear to drag back as well all the trash into the house again."

Lessing did not himself agree with the Wolfenbüttel fragments of Reimarus,[1] but his publication of them in 1774 produced a profound sensation. It was from the absence of adequate answers to the crude negations of the Fragmentist that they disseminated far and wide a spirit of disbelief. This disbelief found its expression in the so-called " enlightenment-period," which resulted from the influences of French and English deism. In one respect Reimarus sank even lower than the French deists. Not only Rousseau, but even Voltaire, still preserved an overwhelming sense of awe before the personality of Christ. Reimarus does not scruple to lay profane hands upon His holiness, and to accuse His Apostles of sheer deceit. Such views could never long prevail. The worst harm done by Reimarus was the way in which he pointed out the variations in the Gospel narrative of the Resurrection, of which the post-Reformation system had neither prepared men to see the reconciliation, nor to estimate the non-importance. Unhappily, since Scholasticism and Pietism were alike dead, and no force had risen to replace them, the epoch of a dreary illuminism was only met on the other side by timid concessions. But this phase of opinion was short-lived. It was specially discredited by the miserable failure and degradation of F. A. Bahrdt. Though " smitten," as he himself confesses, " with the disease of levity," he proclaimed himself an instrument of Providence for the welfare of men,

---

[1] " The Bible is not the Spirit, and the Bible is not religion. Consequently objections against the latter, as well as against the Bible, are not precisely objections against the Spirit and religion. For the Bible evidently contains more than belongs to religion, and it is a mere supposition that in the additional matter it must be equally infallible. Moreover, religion existed before there was a Bible, and Christianity before Evangelists and Apostles had written." Lessing, *Werke*, x. 10, ed. Lachmann. " What others, even good Lutherans, have asserted of whole books of the Bible, we may surely assert of single facts " (*id.* p. 137).

together with Moses, Confucius, Socrates, and One whose Divine Name I will not degrade by mentioning it in connection with such claims. This would-be regenerator of the human race lived a life of pollution, and died in an ale-house after having been imprisoned as a writer of scurrilous lampoons.

The tendency to crude infidelity, which was now fostered for the first time by periodical literature,[1] was only influential through the feebleness of the opposition which was offered to it. The work of Spener and Francke had spent its beneficent force.[2] Of the clergy, some shut themselves up in a sullen dogmatic obstinacy. Others in alarm were willing to reduce religion to a system of utilitarianism and sentimentality, and acted, says Tholuck, like a man who, crying that his house is on fire, throws his best mirrors out of the window in order to save them. The truest defence of the Church was to be found in the sincere holiness of men like Stelling, Oberlin, Claudius, and Lavater. Preachers were living, among whom the teaching of the early Pietists still " lingered like the fragrance of a flower." Lavater especially, the friend of men like Goethe and Fichte, maintained in the most advanced and polished circles a profound respect for the religion of which he was not ashamed. In the words of Goethe, he still raised the clear crystal to his lips, and, as he quaffed the divine draught, even let it pour profusely over the sides of the goblet. In that age, too, as in many others,

> " Piety hath found
> Friends in the friends of science, and true prayer
> Hath flowed from lips wet with Castalian dews."

If the clergy produced but little to stem the rising tide of infidelity, a poet, a physiologist, a mathematician, showed openly that they were not ashamed of Christ or of His Gospel. The hymns of GELLERT—the Watts of Germany— still kept alive the spirit of the older strains which had

---

[1] *E.g.* the *Allgemeine Deutsche Bibliothek* of Nicolai and Lessing. The work of Mendelssohn in the Jewish community was analogous to that of Lessing in the Church. His followers were called Biuristic (באור, "Illumination ").

[2] Even Zinzendorf spoke of the Halle Pietists as "those miserable Christians whom no one calls Pietists but themselves."

D D

glowed in the *Lyra Germanica.* HALLER, one of the founders of modern physiology († 1777), with the whole strength of his genius made a stand against the growth of materialism. EULER († 1763), one of the greatest mathematicians of his age, ventured even in Berlin, and surrounded by the sceptics who formed the court of Frederic the Great, to publish in 1747 his *Defence of Revelation against the Attacks of Free-thinkers.*

Turning to works which bore directly on exegesis we notice how cold was the orthodoxy which succeeded the best days of Pietism. Amid the shallowness of the current philosophic views, all men felt the necessity of recurring to the solid ground of history. But even these historic researches partook of the character of the age. They lacked enthusiasm, spontaneity, and faith. The critical learning and moderate rationalism of MICHAELIS († 1791) and ERNESTI († 1781) represent the chief efforts to elucidate the Old and New Testaments on principles of formal philology. Michaelis reduces Moses to a clever statesman who gave to utility a religious sanction.[1] He was followed by EICHHORN and PAULUS who, with all their learning, could find no better explanation for the supernatural element in both dispensations than a theory of mistake, hyperbole, and ignorance. The naturalism of Paulus received its death-blow from the mordant sarcasm of Strauss. Ernesti was, perhaps, the first to formulate with perfect clearness the principle which has been much discussed in our own day, " that the verbal sense of Scripture must be determined in the same way in which we ascertain that of other books." He found a pupil greater than himself in the earnest-minded and learned Semler.[2]

SEMLER († 1791) marks a distinct epoch. He was neither

---

[1] See Hengstenberg, *Pentateuch*, I. xiii. It is said that the term "rationalism" first occurs in the *Theologia Naturalis* of Amos Comenius, 1661. "Supernaturalism" was first used as the antithesis to "Rationalism" by Gabler (*Hengst. Theol. Journ.* 1801). Descartes in 1650 had formulated his proposition, *De omnibus dubitandum est.*

[2] Dr. A. S. Farrar in his learned Bampton Lectures (p. 311) points out that Leipzig was the chief home of the dogmatic school ; Göttingen of the critical ; Tübingen and Halle of the Pietist and Scholastic.

a prophet like Herder, nor an originator like Schleiermacher, but by his 171 books he gave an impulse to exegetic study, which is still far from exhausted. Trained among the Pietists who had taught him the difference between theology and religion, he united to marked liberality and independence a sincere and pious orthodoxy. His spiritual experiences, and the vast reading which revealed to him the divergences of theological opinions, had convinced him that men must often separate as it were for themselves a religion which meets their own needs. He lived in what has been called "the epoch of subjectivity"—the epoch in which men had convinced themselves that "every man must see with his own eyes, and examine with his own judgment, and comprehend with his own understanding, all things in the political, literary and religious world." [1] He regarded it as a part of his religious duty to discriminate between those elements of the Bible which are temporary and Judaic, and that part which is of eternal validity.[2] The teaching of Ernesti, the study of R. Simon, of Spinoza, and of Michaelis, had led him to view the Bible on its human, external, and historical side; to consider it in its diversity rather than in its unity; in its fragmentary divisions and various methods rather than as an organic whole. He examined the Canon as independently as Luther had done, and on much the same principles. He pointed out the distinction between Judaising and Pauline theology, which is the germ of the criticisms of the school of Tübingen. He gave to exegesis a new direction. In the early Church its method had been typical; among most of the Fathers allegorical; in the middle ages dogmatic; after the

[1] Something of this tendency is expressed by the doctrine of Frederic the Great that "every man must be left to get to heaven in his own way." "Semler did all he could to take off the halo which rested on the first centuries" (Kahnis), and "uttered the magic word which emancipated theology from the fetters of tradition" (Reuss). See Myers, *Catholic Thoughts*, p. 288.

[2] "It is inconceivable how thoughtful Christians confound the sacred Scripture of the Jews and the Word of God which is here and there contained and enveloped therein." Semler, *Abhandl. v. freier Untersuchen d. Kanons*, i. 48 (4 vols. 1771-1775). He also wrote a special book, *Der Unterschied d. Heil. Schrift und des Wortes Gottes.* See many passages from his writings quoted by Sonntag (*De Doctrina Inspirationis*, pp. 162, fg.), who points out the importance of his distinction between "inspiration" and "revelation."

Reformation confessional; in the Renaissance, and recently again under the influence of Ernesti, it had become predominantly grammatical. Semler added, or greatly developed, the *historic* method, which lays predominant stress on the circumstances and conditions by which the original writers had been surrounded.[1] But he was rather the child of his epoch than its leader, and, in his later years, having laid but a bewildered hand on the sacred harp, he

> " Back recoiled, he knew not why,
> E'en at the sound himself had made." [2]

The worst feature of his system was the extent to which he allowed the principle of " accommodation." That there is such a thing as the ' oeconomy' (οἰκονομία) or ' condescension' (συγκατάβασις) of which Origen and the Fathers had spoken is admitted. It is, in fact, a necessity.[3] Anthropomorphism is itself a concession to finite capacities. Only by some sort of condescension to our infirmities can the Infinite be revealed. Nor again can it be denied that something which may be called " accommodation" is implied by the progressiveness of revelation.[4] There were times of ignorance which " God winked at." Some things, as our Lord said, had been permitted by Moses, not because of their intrinsic desirability but because of the hardness of men's hearts.[5] But Semler gave to this principle an abnormal and even a repulsive development. He pushed it to an extent which *seemed*, at least, to make Him who is " the Truth" responsible for a suppression of truth which is hardly distinguishable from a suggestion of falsehood.[6] No such system is consistent

---

[1] " Le trait caractéristique du 19me siècle est d'avoir substitué la méthode historique à la méthode dogmatique, dans toutes les études relatives à l'esprit humain." Renan, *Averroes*, p. vi. It is needless to say that Semler was the subject of fierce attacks. The *Nova Bibl. Ecclesiastica* called him " *homo impius, et Judaeis pejor*."

[2] He died, Kurz says, " brokenhearted," at the height of the controversy raised by the Wolfenbüttel Fragments. See Semler's *Beantwortung der Fragmente eines Ungenannten*, 1779.

[3] See Colet's *Letters to Radulphus*, p. 28 (ed. Lupton).

[4] It is defined as " oeconomicum dicendi genus." See Carus, *Hist. antiquior Sent. Eccl. Graec. de Accommodatione*, 1793.

Ezek. xx. 25. Matt. xix. 8.

[6] Each system of interpretation has generally appealed to a favourite *dictum probans*. That of Semler was ἐλάλει αὐτοῖς τὸν λόγον καθὼς ἠδύναντο ἀκούειν,

with a living Christianity. If the words even of the Master
rested on illusion and compromise, then

> "The solid firmament is rottenness,
> And earth's base built on stubble." [1]

But there could be no permanent life in principles of
exegesis which were lacking in positive elements.[2] "Men
thought too much about the Jews and knew too little of
Christ."[3] Their interpretation was "*humilis et demissa*" to
an extent far greater than that of the School of Antioch.
From so dead an historical analysis the Church was saved by
the genial influence of HERDER (†1803). "In Herder all the
blossoms of Humanism ripened; in him the palms of the
East, the olives of Greece, the oaks of the North are all
thriving. In him we find the shady walks of philosophy,
the great perspective of history, the serene temple-path of a
religion of Humanism."[4] Herder no less than Semler was
able to see the human side and progressive revelation of
Scripture, but he infused into the lifeless learning of his day
the glowing heat of a poetic soul. He used the Scriptures
to elevate his conception of humanity, not to dwarf his sense
of the divine. "Poetry, philosophy, history, are," he
said, "in my opinion, the three lights which illuminate the
peoples, the sects, and the generations—a holy triangle." In
Scripture, "he saw alike vivid poetry, a practical history,
and an eternal philosophy." "Christianity," he said, and
this is the keynote of his system, "commands the purest
humanity in the purest way." And thus he met illuminism

Mark iv. 33. It was no less misapplied than the κατὰ τὴν ἀναλογίαν τῆς
πίστεως (Rom. xii. 6) of the Reformation epoch, and the τὸ γράμμα ἀποκτείνει
(2 Cor. iii. 6) of the Fathers and Schoolmen, or "the love of Christ" which
was used by the Pietists as a plea for holy ignorance.

[1] Perhaps the extreme outcome of Semler's tendencies may be seen in Teller's
Wörterbuch des N.T. 1772, which reduces Christianity to commonplace
morals.

[2] On the important influence of Semler, see his own autobiography (1781) ;
H. Schmid, *Die Theologie Semlers*, 1858 ; Tholuck, *Verm. Schriften*, ii. 39 ;
Nösselt, *De J. S. Semlero* (Rigae, 1792), and the notices of him in Dorner
Diestel, Meyer, Kahnis, Hagenbach, &c.

[3] Reuss, *Heil. Schrift*, ii. 323.

[4] Kahnis, *Germ. Protestantism*, E. T. p. 70. "More poet than theologian,
and for that reason only the more lovely." Reuss, § 578.

with its own weapons. Christ in his view was divinest in His divine humanity, and under His own chosen title as the Son of God who called Himself "the Son of Man."[1] At the very time when men like Nicolai and Bahrdt were sneering at the Bible as "an obsolete, incomprehensible book, an arsenal of old prejudices," Herder, whom the most illuminated among them could not venture to depreciate, was labouring, as Luther did, to place it as the candle in the centre of the sanctuary.[2] While they were attempting to put Homer and Plato on a level with Isaiah and St. John, Herder, who valued the great Greek writers as highly and knew them better, said that in comparison with the prophets and poets of the Old Testament the greatest of them were but as a drop to the ocean.[3] "The Bible," so he wrote in his letters on the study of theology, "must be read in a human manner, for it is a book written by men for men. The best reading of this divine book is human. The more humanly we read the Word of God, the nearer we come to the design of its Author, who created man in His image, and acts humanly in all the deeds and mercies, wherein He manifests Himself as our God." Thus he rescued the Bible from the hands which only tore and tangled the rich threads of its poetry and life. He dealt but little with "the theological metaphysics which neither teach how to live or die, but only how to quarrel scientifically." He always tried to find the Revelation of God centred in the person of Christ, and not in minute and unscriptural formulae concerning Him. Large tolerance, a loving spirit, gladness of heart, sympathy with the East, literary insight, noble and melodious language, the ideal colouring which he shed over all that he taught—these were Herder's special gifts. They helped him in counteracting the utilitarianism of pulpit teaching, the conceit of French infidelity, and the incapacity of the prevailing criticism. He left upon the Church the

---

[1] Herder, *Vom Erlöser d. Menschen*, 1796 ; *Von Gottes Sohn*, 1797.
[2] Hagenbach, *Germ. Rationalism*, p. 191.
[3] *Zur Schönen Literatur und Kunst*, p. 67 (1769).

impress which she then most needed.[1] Perhaps no small
part of his depth and spirituality were due to his loving
study of the Gospel of St. John. "It is," he said, "a still
deep sea in which the heavens with the sun and stars are
mirrored. If there are eternal truths for the human race,
(and such there are,) they are to be found in the Gospel of
St. John." [2]

But it seems [3] as if all human services must inevitably be
imperfect and liable to abuse. The magical garden of Herder
was but a labyrinth. His romanticism had fulfilled a necessary
function, but sterner elements were required for the regeneration of theology. The opinions of the age had been sent
drifting upon the open sea of doubt, and men were still
searching for some anchor of the soul, by which they
could moor in a safe harbour the faith which had long
been rolling like a dismantled hulk on stormy and turbid
waves.

For a time it seemed as if rest was to be found in the new
attempt of KANT (†1804) to form a union between philosophy
and religion.[4] But so far as religion is concerned, the
sole service of Kant was to establish against utilitarian
morals the awful supremacy of conscience. With incomparable distinctness, he, "like a philosophic Moses,
proclaimed once more the supernatural majesty of the moral
law." [5] Had this been all it would have been well; but Kant's
system, in vindicating against Lutheranism the grandeur of
human freedom, unhappily denied the necessity of divine

[1] The best exegetical works collected in Herder's twelve volumes of *Theolog.
Werke* were *Aelteste Urkunde des Menschengeschlechts,* 1774 ; *Lieder der Liebe,*
1778 ; *Maran Atha,* 1779 ; *Vom Geiste d. Hebr. Poesie,* 1782 ; *Briefe das
Studium d. Theologie betreffend,* 1780.
[2] In this sketch of Herder I have been much helped by Hagenbach,
who speaks of him with great enthusiasm and fulness. *Germ. Rationalism,*
pp. 166-212. See too the singularly glowing estimate of Lücke, *Grundriss,*
p. 75.
[3] Kahnis, p. 78.
[4] "To seek for theology in philosophy is to seek for the living among the
dead ; to seek for philosophy in theology is to seek for the dead among the
living." Bacon.
[5] Dorner, ii. 22. See Archer Butler, *Development of Christian Doctrine,*
p. 87. In Kant's system God is revealed by the law of duty, and the freedom
and immortality of the soul are postulates of the idea of duty.

grace. Religion became as it were but an adjunct to morals; and since it was branded as venality to do what is right for God's sake, God became little more than "a stream of tendency," and Christ not an historic Person, but that "divine idea of man which expiates our sinful mortality." It is true that, recognising the enslavement of the Practical Reason by an enigmatic selfishness, Kant postulates the necessity for an ideal Church, which presupposes an ideal Founder.[1] But the supernaturalism for which Kant, as it were by an afterthought, found room in his system, was obviously superfluous if it offered to the reason nothing more than its own contents. We cannot therefore be surprised that in the Idealism to which Kant paved the way from the older Rationalism, God became as distant from man as the Stoic "Providence." To exegesis he only contributed the rationalising suggestion that it, or its application, should be purely allegorical and moral;[2] and since he too, like Semler, had allowed the free use of "accommodation," Paulus applied his system in a truly ludicrous explanation of the New Testament miracles. In this system, as Dorner says, "the miraculous power is transferred to the exegete, who does not indeed make something out of nothing, but who manages to change something into nothing, and then gives out this nothing as something, throwing away the kernel of the history in order only to retain the shell." Under the impulse which Kant had given, Christianity was replaced by vague religionism, which gave way to bare morality, which in its turn was replaced once more by the very eudaemonism which Kant most disliked.[3]

---

[1] The language of Kant, as of many of even the most advanced sceptics, was profoundly reverential towards Christ. He rebuked Borowski for mentioning his name in any nearness to that of Christ. "Namen davon der eine geheiligt, der andere aber eines armen Ihn nach Vermögen auslegenden Stümper's ist." *Werke*, xi. 131.

[2] Here we have once more an illustration of the fact that Allegory is in reality the offspring of Rationalism.

[3] Dorner, ii. 328. Among theologians Wegscheider specially represents the views of Kant. "The Kantian rationalism pretended to commemorate the mysteries of Christianity from behind the veil of its terminology in a clearer and glorified light." Chalybäus, Lect. 17.

It is not here necessary to dwell on the successors of Kant. Kant had recognised the objective reality of the "thing in itself." FICHTE tried to get rid of this Kantian dualism, by treating the *Non-Ego* as a mere postulate of *Ego;* by making the *Ego* to be everything, even God; or by saying that the *Ego* has no existence at all, and that there is nothing but God [1]—a God, however, who, as far as Fichte's philosophy was concerned, was without personality and without self-consciousness. If Kant's categorical imperative could bear no living fruits, neither could this resolution of everything into self or into the absolute. Jacobi, among his constant oscillations, at least saw distinctly that we cannot pray to a God which we simply possess as the *Ego*, or even to a God who is "the moral order of the world," but to a God who can say to us, " I am that I am." The system of Fichte might serve for an unanswerable philosophy, it is useless for every purpose of personal religion. That could only be derived, as it was by Fichte himself, from far different sources.[2] Philosophy had served no other religious purpose than to help Protestantism to shake off the tyranny of narrow dogmas. It could offer nothing substantial in their place.

The more constructive movement of the new epoch began with SCHLEIERMACHER (†1834), the Origen of Germany, who exercised a profound influence alike on religion and on biblical interpretation. He is the founder of what may be called the psychological school of exegesis. Like Lessing, Semler, and Herder, he was a man of deep piety, but he had a clearer insight and a profounder faith than any of the

---

[1] The *Non-Ego*, according to Fichte, has no reality without us, but is produced by the activity and unconscious intuition of the *Ego ;* and this creative *Ego* is not the individual but the absolute *Ego*.

[2] "God is infinite, therefore beyond the reach of our *science*, but not beyond our faith." Fichte, *Sittenlehre.* Claudius compared an ideal religion without historical basis to a painted horse, which you can admire but not ride. Hagenbach, *Germ. Rat.* p. 296.

[3] Fichte, *Spekulative Theologie*, 1846. It is a characteristic fact that both Fichte and Schelling dwelt on the primary importance of the Gospel of St. John (see Westcott's *St. John*, p. xcvi.).

three.[1] He saw as distinctly as they the difference between religion and dogma, between the Church and the school of theology, between the Scriptures as a whole and the collections of "proof-texts" which had been drawn from them. But, because Piety had been, as he says, the womb in whose holy darkness his young life was nourished,[2] he also saw, as they had not done, the power and the function of Faith, and the need for the redemptive work of Christ. It was through this apprehension of Christ that he was able to understand the New Testament,[3] and while rising above sectarian bigotry to feel the necessity for something beyond the philosophical probabilities of Leibnitz, the historical inquiries of Semler, and the poetic sympathies of Herder. His *Monologues,* published in 1800, were the fitting commencement of an influence which was to affect so powerfully the new century.[4] His main work was to vindicate for Christianity its place in the emotions, and not to treat it either as a series of dogmas, a philosophical problem, or a system of morals. The Rationalists called him a mystic because he was a sincere believer; the orthodox called him a Rationalist because he claimed the right to the free criticism which since the days of Luther had scarcely dared to breathe or whisper. He belonged to neither party; he was greater than them both. Uniting the deepest principles of Syncretism and Pietism, he was the Luther, the Calixt, the Spener, and the Semler of a new and philosophic theology based on religious consciousness. " Speculation and

---

[1] "Not even Herder," says Strauss, "so distinctly and emphatically asserted the divinity of Christ as he did." *New Life of Jesus,* introd. § 5. He gave a greater impulse to exegesis than any one since Calvin.

[2] As a boy of fifteen he had been sent to the Moravian school of Niesky, and he afterwards entered the Moravian College at Barby. He went to Halle at the age of nineteen in 1787.

[3] He contributed little or nothing to the understanding of the Old Testament. He wished to unite the Lutheran and Reformed Churches, and said, "Christ is the quickening centre of the Church; from Him all comes, to Him all returns." In his last moments he celebrated the Holy Communion with his family, and solemnly expressed his faith in Christ his Saviour, and in the atoning merits of His death.

[4] They were the moral completion of the *Reden über die Religion,* published in 1799, which were addressed rather to the bigoted than to the indifferent.

faith," says W. von Humboldt, " are often regarded as being
hostile to each other; but it was peculiar to this man that he
united both most intimately, without doing injustice to the
freedom and depth of the one, or to the simplicity of the
other." The consequence was that if he did not become
the founder of a school, he yet inspired many who were
more or less his followers. Most of those followers worked
in the field of exegesis. Among them we may number
men of very different schools: men of strict orthodoxy like
Twesten, Nitzsch, and J. Müller; men with a leaning to
rationalism like De Wette,[1] Bleek, and Gieseler; men who
occupied an intermediate position like Olshausen, Tholuck,
Riehm, Weiss, Hagenbach, Uhllorn, Lücke, Neander, Umbreit,
Ullmann, Dorner, and other writers, at whose feet the
theologians of England, though they too have done a
great and lasting work, have been content for many years to
sit and learn. The first work of the ablest prelate of modern
days, the late Bishop Thirlwall of St. David's, was a translation of Schleiermacher's *Introduction to St. Luke.*

But in spite of Schleiermacher's powerful and, on the
whole, healthy influence the conflict was by no means over.
Its most acute crisis was yet to come. HEGEL was born in
1770, two years later than Schleiermacher. In his system
the world has probably seen the last attempt to make
religion a phase of philosophy. Schleiermacher had endeavoured to establish a conviction of the truth of Christianity by finding it psychologically in its adaptation to
human needs, and its satisfaction of human aspirations.
Schelling had ascribed the power to grasp the ideal of God
to " intellectual intuition ; " Jacobi to a mixture of feeling
and intuition. Hegel once more revived the tendency to
ideology, and treated religious dogma as the explanation of

---

[1] See Schwarz, *Gesch. d. neuest. Theol.* p. 27. Schleiermacher not only influenced De Wette, but even gave to the Tübingen school some impulse
by his letter to Gass on the Pastoral Epistles (1817), and his introduction to
St. Luke (1824). His chief book, *Der Christliche Glaube* (2 vols. 1821)
bore the same relation to modern German theology as Calvin's *Institutio* to
that of the Reformed Churches. Schleiermacher never entered into current
controversies.

a priori principles.[1] Thus Hegel's Trinity—which consists of an unconditioned subtraction, a conditioned reality, and the identity of the two—is indefinitely far removed from that of Athanasius, and still farther from that of Scripture. Hegel's Christ is neither the Christ of scholastic dogma, nor Kant's Ideal of Humanity, nor the historic Christ of Schleiermacher, nor the Redeeming Saviour of Spener and Francke, but only a speculative Christ, a sort of identity between the known and the knowing. The Holy Spirit of Hegel is not the Holy Ghost the Comforter, but "that which brings the Father and the Son in the essence of God to a unity of consciousness." [2] The knowledge of such a Trinity is not life, but a mere logical notion, a mere etherealised shadow of arbitrary thought.[3]

It is not for us to ask how far Hegel was in earnest with this strange orthodoxy, or how far his orthodoxy was mere self-delusion, and that of his followers the mistaking of words for realities.[4] But though some of them certainly, like Daub and Marheinecke († 1846), were perfectly sincere, the natural results of his system appeared very rapidly, on the one hand, in Strauss, Bruno Bauer, and Feuerbach, on the

---

[1] "Like the ancient Gnosticism, the Hegelian philosophy believed in dogmatic Christianity, because it descended from an *a priori* principle, in which it found the explanation of it" (Dr. A. S. Farrar, *Free Thought*, p. 373). "Der Grundgedanke seiner Philosophie ist daher ; das Absolute ist Process, ist die Selbstentwickelung der Substanz zum Subject" (Schwarz, p. 15). "The existence of a personal God is admitted neither within nor without the Universe, but is reduced simply to the knowledge of the human being. The hope of conscious immortality is scoffed at as a sensuously selfish illusion ; and the antagonism of good and evil is suppressed, evil being regarded as necessary, and good as only relative, while both may relapse into each other" (Chalybäus, Lect. 18).

[2] "The Universality can be regarded as the absolute essence (the Father) which by the world's reality (the Son, as the momentum of particularity) mediates itself into the identity (the Holy Ghost)," Chalybäus, Lect. 16.

[3] The influence of Hegel is clearly seen in Wilhelm Vatke, who applied Hegel's method to Old Testament criticism. See Dr. Geldardt, in *Mod. Review*, 1884.

[4] Hegel's *Religionsphilosophie* was only published after his death, in 1832. Of the *Christliche Glaubenslehre* of Strauss, it has been said that "it resembles a theology in the same way that a cemetery resembles a city." A letter in the life of Vatke (September, 1828) gives a curious picture of the theological currents in Berlin when Schleiermacher, Neander, and Marheinecke were Professors.

other, in Ferdinand Christian Baur, and the school of
Tübingen.[1]

Hegel had not been four years in his grave before the
appearance, in 1835, of a book by one who had been
his pupil, which produced in theology the sensation of an
earthquake. That book was Strauss's *Life of Jesus.* It
illustrated the danger which Claus Harms had prophesied
in his theses of 1817, that "Lutheranism would be progressively reformed back into heathenism." It did not
so much make an epoch as cause a crisis; it did not so
much constitute a beginning as a close.[2] It was the *reductio
ad horribile* of current scepticism. Kant had seen in the
existence of the Church a proof of the existence of its Founder.
Strauss inverted the relation, and saw in the idea of Christ
an invention of the already existing Church. The ability of
the book, its clearness, its mastery of the critical studies
which Hegel had despised, its union of Hegelian construc-
tiveness with ruthless criticism, its adoption of the historic
method which was peculiarly suited to the tendencies of
the century, all increased the shock which the *Leben Jesu*
caused in the minds of Christians.[3] The theory of the book
was as original as it was audacious. There was little or no
attempt at flimsy and fantastic ideology. With great acute-
ness Strauss marshalled and magnified the difficulties
and discrepancies which, though they are innocuous to
any reasonable view of truthful testimony, fell with fatal
force on the hollow idol of the dictation dogma which
had so long been enthroned on the pedestal of a false
orthodoxy. And when, on these grounds, he had denied the
genuineness and credibility of the Gospels, he proceeded
to account for their existence by the theory of myths; in

---

[1] See Hegel's *Philosophy of History* (E. T. J. Sibree, 1857); Véra, *Philosophie
Hégelienne,* and *Introd. à la Philosophie de Hegel.*

[2] Schwarz, *Gesch. d. neuest. Theol.* p. 3. Strauss, then a Repetent in
Theology, had gone from Tübingen to Berlin in 1831 on purpose to hear
Schleiermacher's lectures on the Life of Christ, and "Sie gaben ihm den
stärksten Anstoss zu seinem Zerstörungswerk," p. 29.

[3] It was translated into French by Littré, 1839; into English anonymously
by Miss Evans, 1846.

other words, he treated the facts narrated in the Gospels as stories evolved out of the idea. For Christ he substituted mankind in general as the only incarnation of God, and in his subsequent work, the *Glaubenslehre,* he declared the absolute irreconcilability of Christianity with modern culture.[1] Strauss was rapidly followed by men who showed whither his teaching led. Bruno Bauer spoke of the Gospels with ridicule, and declared them to be due to conscious fiction; Feuerbach argued that it is man only who exists and not God, and that every positive religion is due to nothing but the self-delusion of mankind.

At such an epoch the hearts of many began to fail them for fear, and still more when FERDINARD BAUR endeavoured (to use his own language) to take by regular siege the fortress which Strauss had thought to surprise by storm. Baur was a man deserving of all respect. His intellect was keen, his learning immense, his industry inexhaustible, his heart sincere. In his powerful answer to Möhler's *Symbolik* he had already proved himself to be a great theologian, and the cause of Christian Apologetics seemed to be seriously imperilled when he attacked the genuineness of the greater part of the New Testament. Supplementing Strauss's view of the Gospel history by a close criticism of the Gospels themselves, he endeavoured to undermine their authority by emphasising into contradictoriness the different points of view in the Synoptists and St. John.

But true Christianity has nothing to fear at any time. The strength and consummate equipment of these attacks has but rendered more evident the impregnability of the sacred citadel. NEANDER showed the calmness of his own courageous convictions when he withstood the proposal of the Prussian Government to prohibit the introduction into Prussia of Strauss's books. The *Leben Jesu,* which seemed likely to be so fatal, was but one more of the many waves which have dashed themselves in vain upon the rock, and

---

[1] Strauss wrote to Vatke: "Schleiermacher has stirred me deeply . . . but he does not say the last word. This word I will utter."

been scattered into mist upon the wind and scum upon the shore. It called forth a multitude of answers equal to it in ability and learning, infinitely superior to it in power and depth. It was Neander, more than any man, —Neander, that "saint of Protestantism," that last of the Fathers of the Church, as he has been affectionately called,—Neander, with his fanaticism of mildness and intolerance of intolerance, who stemmed the rising tide of infidelity. His motto was *pectus facit theologum,* and many sneered at his followers as *pectoralists,* but he relied on deep learning quite as much as on pious emotion. Those who have read such lives of Christ as were written in answer to Strauss by Neander, Ullmann, Tholuck, Lange, Ewald, Riggenbach, and many others—those who have since studied the profound and powerful works of Weiss and Keim—will see, even amid some concessions which they may regret, how jejune and transitory was the work of Strauss. The feelings with which it was read even by Christians of moderate erudition were well expressed by the earnest and eloquent Lacordaire. Studying the book paragraph by paragraph, and then opening the Gospels to read the texts which had been criticised, he says that, in spite of a sort of involuntary terror inspired by the writer's erudition, " it never needed more than ten minutes to dissipate the charm of a vain science, and to enable me to smile inwardly at the impotence to which God has condemned error." [1]

As Strauss had laughed out of the field the naturalism of Paulus, so it was Baur who showed the radical weakness of the mythical theory of Strauss. Neither he, nor the able writers who followed him, could fall into the extreme folly of denying the historical existence of Jesus, or the fact that the faith in Him sprang from His own transcendent personality. Even the ingenuity of Baur could not put the date of the Gospels low enough to allow for the evolution of myths, nor could his candour deny the certain genuineness of at least the

---

[1] *Conférences* (1846), p. 155.

Apocalypse and the four greatest Epistles of St. Paul.[1] Many of his arguments for the spuriousness of the New Testament were strangely futile, and his own school has had to admit the genuineness of books which he declared to be apocryphal. But meanwhile if the main results of his criticism had been successful, enough would have remained even in the Apocalypse and the four Epistles to prove the truth of the historic Gospel. Baur, in fact, rendered a threefold service. The germ of his tendency-theory, founded on an hostility between the Judaic and Pauline elements in the Church, was true and full of suggestiveness, though his developments of this view were utterly extravagant. His criticisms led to a yet closer and more thorough examination of the Canon, which has tended to establish every book of it, with very few exceptions, on an even more certain basis than before.[2] And meanwhile he had shown, not to the world only, but even to Strauss himself, that the book which was to have convulsed Christianity to its foundations was but an idle dream. In subsequent editions Strauss undid his own work by making an unavailing attempt to remodel his theory on the views of Baur and Feuerbach,[3] allotting more space to conscious and intentional fiction. The argument failed as egregiously as before. The inherent simplicity and truthfulness of the Gospels defeats every attempt to brand them with intentional imposture. Twenty-five years after the *Leben Jesu* had been published, its author, with ill-concealed chagrin, alluded to the fact that it was already beginning to be forgotten and overlooked.

And in many other ways God brought good out of evil, and mercifully vindicated His truth to man. These attempts to represent the Saviour of the World as one who could stoop

---

[1] Such discoveries as the lost "Teaching of the Twelve Apostles" and the inscription on the tomb of Abercius, Bishop of Hieropolis, found last year by Mr. Ramsay in Phrygia, are alone sufficient—apart from the certain date of some of the canonical writings—to shake to the dust the whole mythic theory which once seemed to loom so large.

[2] Baur has been followed by Schwegler, Hilgenfeld, Zeller, Volkmar, &c., and opposed by Thiersch, Dorner, Ewald, Bleek, &c.

[3] *Leben Jesu für das Deutsche Volk bearbeitet*, p. 158 (1864).

to deceit horrified the feelings of all Christendom. So far from convincing they repelled. The work of Strauss had an effect very different from that which he had intended. It was the dissolution not of Christianity, but of the pretentious philosophy which had posed at first as its protector.[1] It gave an impulse to the concentration, the revival, even the enlightenment of Christian life. It is true that the orthodox reaction evoked by his *Life of Jesus* contained some unworthy elements. In the hands of domineering partisans it sought to maintain itself by the terrorism of anonymous journalism, aided by majorities and denunciations, by protests and depositions. It invoked the anti-Christian bitterness of religious partisanship to secure the prosperity of the clericalism which it perniciously identified with Christianity. Had this been its only result the brief revival would have been doomed to swift and more overwhelming catastrophe.[2] But the deadly attack of Strauss upon the centre of Christian faith stimulated in a far healthier way than this the negligences of the Christian life. The pulpits rang once more with vital truth and manly eloquence. The clergy saw the necessity for something beyond official studies, and found that the rusty armour of scholastic orthodoxy was useless against the cannon of modern warfare. The laity began to remember that they too, no less than the clergy, were a spiritual priesthood called to the duty of good works. Missions became more active and more earnest; education

---

[1] See Kahnis, p. 249.

[2] The failure of Hengstenberg and his short-lived school of reaction into "confessional orthodoxy" was due to the fatal attempt to stake the whole of divine revelation on the weakness of any particular link, and also to the snarling party-newspaper style of controversy and the ecclesiastical terrorism on which it relied. Hengstenberg was the Calov of the nineteenth century, and the *Evangelische Kirchenzeitung*, during the period of its influence (1835–1848) occupied the same unhappy position as the *Record* did twenty years ago. But no heresy-hunting, no religious espionage, no hounding of theological hatred against unpopular names could give life to a school of retrogression animated by unscrupulous and bitter animosities. It was soon seen that the strange new orthodoxy of an Evangelical Loyola or Torquemada, using evil means that supposed good might come, was a complete anachronism (see Schwarz, pp. 58–92, Kurz, p. 299). So retrogressive was Hengstenberg's commentary on the Canticles, that Bunsen called it a disgrace to Germany.

more thorough and religious. Above all faith was deepened, and was restored to its due supremacy in the economy of the Christian life. The whole Christian world had learnt to see that in the Holy Scriptures there are many unsolved difficulties, many unreconciled antinomies. They saw that the soul could not be sustained in its convictions exclusively by the biblical supernaturalism which had not come unscathed out of the assaults of so many writers from Spinoza down to Baur. They saw that questions like the genuineness of this or that particular book, could never alone become so certain that upon them could be built the majestic superstructure of a Christian's faith. They realised that there was something both radically unscriptural and profoundly irreverent in questions as to whether a book was written by a man or by " the pen of the Triune God." They remembered that the spiritual life of many a hero and patriarch had been sustained and inspired by a Word of God which was not the written word, but of Whom the written word is to us a revelation ; and that the earliest Christians, who had been Christians indeed, were heirs of the new covenant, though not a line of the New Testament had yet been penned. They returned, says the ablest and deepest historian of this epoch to " the power and certainty of the material principle of the Faith—whence critical operations may be contemplated with serenity, nay, actively shared in without anxiety." [1]

On a Faith thus strengthened—on a Faith which had attained to a deeper certainty than historical criticism could either bestow or shake—all subsequent storms fell in vain. " We older men," says Meyer, in the Preface to his fourth edition of the Epistle to the Romans, " have seen the day when Dr. Paulus and his devices were in vogue ; he died without leaving a disciple behind him. We passed through the tempest raised by Strauss, and with what a sense of solitariness might its author now celebrate his jubilee ! We saw the constellation of Tübingen arise, and even before Baur departed its lustre had waned. A firmer basis and

[1] Dorner, ii. 397.

a more complete apprehension of the truth were the blessings which these waves left behind them." Christian students availed themselves of many important lessons which critics had brought into prominence while they rejected their more extravagant conclusions. Renan's *Vie de Jésus* failed to shake a general conviction. It was accepted as a picture—in its better aspect a pathetic picture— of the life of Christ in its purely external features while no one whose faith had not been previously shaken felt anything but regret and pity for its negation of the supernatural at the expense of the truthfulness of Christ. And meanwhile the literature of a strong and wise theology was being yearly enriched by the labours of men whose learning and diligence were unsurpassed. WINER for the first time produced a thorough grammar of the Hellenistic dialect. THOLUCK, outliving the times in which his house was attacked and his person insulted because he reverenced the Bible, outliving, too, the day when he could only find one of his theological students who read the Bible for devotional purposes, began a new epoch by his Commentary on the Epistle to the Hebrews, and once more taught men to regard the whole religion of the Old Testament as being in its essence one great and unassailable prophecy. From schools of orthodox reaction, more or less rigidly Lutheran or reformed, came such works as those of Keil, and Hävernick, of Stier, Olshausen, and Lange. From the so-called "Mediating Theology"—a school of freer spirit, but not untouched by the scepticism of the age, came the works of GESENIUS, HITZIG, DELITZSCH, HUTHER, DE WETTE.[1] NEANDER shed over Church history the glow of his ripe learning and large-hearted piety. MEYER published his critical and luminous edition of the New Testament. DORNER in his *Christology* produced a book which for its speculative depth and historic erudition was worthy to take

---

[1] Very touching were the words used by De Wette shortly before his death in 1848 : "I fell into a time of confusion ; the unity of faith was destroyed. I too mixed myself up with this struggle—in vain ! I have not settled it."

its place beside the very greatest works of Christian orthodoxy. EWALD, at once a prophet and a critic, combining in an unusual degree the gifts of learning, originality, and eloquence, stood haughtily alone on a peculiar eminence, and flung over every part of Scripture the meteoric gleam of his stormy genius.[1] In every Protestant Church of Europe was felt the stirring of a new life. In France there have been such labourers in various fields as VINET, MONOD, BERSIER, BUNGENER, NAVILLE, REUSS, GODET, DE PRESSENSÉ. In German Switzerland, HAGENBACH, AUBERLEN, STÄHELIN, RIGGENBACH, IMMER, and KEIM. In Holland, KUENEN, SCHOLTEN, VAN OOSTERZEE. In Sweden and Denmark such men as KLAUSEN and MARTENSEN. And there is scarcely one among all these theologians, and a multitude of the highest merit who are here left unnamed, who does not combine the deepest reverence for the divine authority of the Holy Scriptures with an entire rejection of that dogma of mechanical inspiration, which, in addition to many other evils has, age after age, introduced so much of weakness and of confusion into the whole system of interpretation of those by whom it has been maintained.

The English Church, since the days of Bede and Alcuin, has rarely, perhaps never, been in the forefront of Scriptural studies. She has produced many masters of theology, such as Hooker, Andrewes, Chillingworth, Whichcote, Leighton, Pearson, Barrow, Bull, Beveridge, Waterland, and Butler. She has had unequalled preachers, like Latimer, Donne, Henry More, Barrow, Jeremy Taylor, South, Burnet, and Tillotson. She has had true saints of God, like Bishop Ken, and Bishop Wilson, and Bishop Berkeley. She has had great scholars and critics, like Selden, Brian Walton, Pocock, Lightfoot, Bentley, Mill, and Archbishop Lawrence. She has had incomparable translators, like Wiclif, William Tyndale, Miles Coverdale, and those

---

[1] Kurz says of his *Jahrbücher* that "in them he held a yearly *auto-da-fè* over the collected theological and biblical literature of the departed year."

of 1611. She has had laborious students in various branches of biblical study, like Ussher, Prideaux, Matthew Poole, Lardner, and the editors of the *Critici Sacri;* but, with the exception of Colet and one or two others, she has had but few great exegetes till present times. She has had indeed Hammond, Whitby, Leighton, Patrick, Horsley; but is there a single English commentary before the last generation, except the Isaiah of Bishop Lowth, of which any one could say without extravagance that it struck out a new line or marked a new epoch? Can there be a better proof of the stagnation of fifty years ago than that the popular commentary was the "variorum" mediocrity of D'Oyly and Mant?

The views of our theologians down to very recent times have been conservative, with a caution which has not seldom proved itself to be retrogressive. The dogma, which had so long maintained the absolute, supernatural, homogeneous infallibility of every word and letter contained in the Bible, had been weighed for centuries in the balances, and never without being found wanting. Every argument and principle on which it had staked its existence had been exploded by deeper investigation. No conception more subversive of Scriptural authority has ever been devised than the assertion, that in the Bible we must accept everything or nothing. That notion, which so irremediably confounds the truth of God with the theological notions of men, has been responsible for crimes and errors innumerable. The canon which it maintained was indefensible; its science has been proved to be childish; its ethics are tainted with hatred and intolerance; its history and chronology are obsolete; its harmonistic methods are casuistical to dishonesty; its views about the inspiration of the vowel-points, and the perfect accuracy of the text have been covered with confusion; its whole method of interpretation has been discredited and abandoned. Wherever the systems built upon this dogma have been rejected, the Bible has become more dear and more widely understood. And yet for a considerable period the main body of the English Church, ignoring the philosophy and the history of the Continent, clung with tenacity to obsolete conceptions, and failed not only to further the progress of Scriptural study, but even to avail themselves of the sources of knowledge which other Churches so largely used.

Fifty years ago the Shibboleth of popular orthodoxy was the indiscriminate anathema of "German theology." If in later days the Church of England has made an immense advance, the progress is perhaps more due to Samuel Taylor Coleridge than to any ordained or professional theologian.[1] He helped to deliver English Churchmen from their ignorance of German literature, and their terror of German speculation. In his *Aids to Reflection* he sketched out a philosophy of religion in which he combined the highest teaching of the best English theologians—of men like Hooker, and Jeremy Taylor, and Archbishop Leighton—with influences derived from the Neoplatonic studies of his youth, and with truths which he had learnt from Kant and Schelling in his maturer years. In his *Confessions of an Inquiring Spirit* he was the first to show his fellow countrymen [2] with convincing illustrations and impassioned eloquence that the Rabbinic, mediaeval and post-Reformation dogma of inspiration could only lead to irreverence or casuistry. He taught them to acquire their estimate of Scripture from the contents and from the claims of Scripture itself, not from the theories and inventions of men respecting it. He proved how clearly a Christian thinker could see that the various books of the Bible greatly differ from each other in value, and could yet honour the Bible as deeply as the Apostles

[1] In his later years (1816–1834) Coleridge more or less entirely abandoned poetry for philosophy and theology. His *Confessions of an Inquiring Spirit* were not published till 1840, six years after his death.

[2] Archdeacon Hare, Professor Maurice, Sterling, and Cardinal Newman all testify to the influence of Coleridge, nor will their estimate be weakened by the characteristically splenetic sneers of Carlyle (see J. S. Mill's *Dissertations;* Dr. Hort in *Cambridge Essays* for 1856 ; Rémusat, *Rev. des Deux Mondes,* October, 1856 ; Dr. A. S. Farrar's *Bampton Lectures,* pp. 475-479 ; Rigg's *Mod. Anglican Theol.* 1857 ; Principal Tulloch on Coleridge as a Thinker in the *Nineteenth Century* for January, 1885).

themselves. He showed how possible it was to love the
Bible as a book which contains the word of God, and yet
to read it—as one of the most unimpeachably orthodox of
German theologians says that it should be read—"as a book
which, with all its Divinity, with its divine origin and divine
ends, is still written by human hands for human beings, for a
human eye, a human heart, a human understanding; as a
book which, though written for all times, even for eternity,
still refers to certain times and occasions, and must from
these given times and occasions be interpreted." [1]   It was for
every reason which made him prize and revere the Scriptures
—prize, revere, and love them beyond all other books—that
he rejected as no longer tenable a theory which falsified the
whole body of their harmonies and symmetrical gradations,
and "turned their breathing organism into a colossal
Memnon's head with a hollow passage for a voice."

It was this spirit which animated many great English
teachers in modern days. To it were due the sermons of
Arnold and of Robertson, of Whately and Thirlwall, of Hare
and Kingsley, which have been so rich in the noblest influences
alike upon the young and the old. It was in this spirit that
one whom the foremost of living statesmen has rightly called
"a spiritual splendour" — Frederic Denison Maurice —
laboured for years amid religious obloquy and opposition,
leaving to the English Church the legacy not only of writings
full of thought, beauty, and tenderness, but also of a stainless
example and a holy life. It was this spirit which has given
us in the Greek Testament of Alford, in the dictionaries of
the Bible and of Christian biography, and in some recent
commentaries, worthy monuments of English candour and
erudition. It was this spirit which shone forth in Milman's
History of the Jews and *History of Christianity*. It was
this spirit which enabled the vivid historic genius of
Arthur Penrhyn Stanley to recall before us the stately and
heroic figures, the stirring and memorable scenes, of Scripture
history, till the pages of Genesis, Exodus, Judges, and the

[1] Hagenbach, *Germ. Rationalism*, p. 192.

Kings, once more thrilled with the life and teemed with the instructiveness of which they had been deprived by an irrational conventionality. These men during all their days had the honour to endure the beatitude of malediction. They were pursued by the attacks of no small portion of the clergy, and of those who called themselves the religious world. But they handed on the torch of sincerity and truth. If their works were received at the time of their appearance with vehement dislike and strong denunciation, as regards the dead at any rate the opposition is silenced, the denunciation has rolled away into idle echoes. They have taken their place among the acknowledged worthies of their Church and nation, and in spite of derision and reproach, " how are they numbered among the children of God and their lot among the saints ! "

And so far from being disturbed or shaken by their free, glad, and earnest investigations, it is by means of those very investigations that the Bible has triumphed over keen ridicule, over charges of fiction, over naturalist explanations, over mythical theories, over destructive criticism. By the combined labours of many learned men, the spirit not of fear but of love, and a sound mind, has given us a Revised Version, which—after having been received as once the Septuagint, and the Vulgate, and Luther's version, and our own Authorised Version were received, with dislike and suspicion—is quietly but surely winning its way into honour and reverence. Our own day has given us comments on St. Paul's Epistles, and on the Gospel and Epistles of St. John, superior in some respects to any which have yet been produced in any age or any branch of the church of Christ. The history which we have been considering is not exclusively a history of darkness and of mistake; it is a history also of the triumph of light over darkness, of truth over error, of faith and freedom over tyranny and persecution. It is a history of the dawning light and of the broadening day. By the grace of God the majority have not been too obstinate to unlearn the errors, or to pluck up the deeply-rooted prejudices of the past, and hence in a

Church as courageous, as active, as rich in all good works as in any age of the past, we can still say with thankful hearts, *Manet immota Fides.*

In that Church a living piety was kindled once more by the Evangelical revival; the spirit of reverence, and the sense of historic continuity were renewed by the Oxford movement; and the connexion with all that was progressive in the learning, science, and culture of the age, was maintained in other schools of large tolerance and comprehensive charity. The mercy of God has given us many outpourings of the Pentecost. Unless it be through our own guilt, our blindness, our formalism, our religious factions, our retrogression along the steps of our Exodus from the land of intellectual darkness and spiritual thraldom we may trust that the golden candlestick of our Church in England will never be removed.

But that we may dare to encourage such a hope, something more is needful than that we learn to despise the wrangling pettiness of party spirit, the spurious and dishonest criticism of party journalism, and the idle reiteration of party shibboleths. We shall never rightly understand the Holy Scriptures unless we keep alive among us the Spirit of Freedom and the Spirit of Progress. It is necessary that we should read the handwriting of God written upon the palace-walls of all tyrannies, whether secular or sacerdotal. It is necessary that we should learn that "there is nothing so dangerous, because there is nothing so revolutionary and convulsive, as the strain to keep things fixed, when all the world is by the very law of its creation in eternal progress." It is necessary that we should read in God's Bible of History that "the cause of all the evil in the world may be traced to that deadly error of human indolence and corruption, that it is our duty to preserve, and not to improve." [1] It is above all essential that we should see the hand of God in current events, and understand the thoughts which He is expressing by the movements in the midst of which we live. Since the days of the Fathers

[1] Dr. Arnold.

and the Schoolmen every sphere of knowledge has been almost immeasurably dilated, and many conceptions regarded as irrefragable have been utterly revolutionised. Again and again have God's other revelations flashed upon the sacred page a light which has convicted its most positive interpreters of fundamental errors. Nine years before the Confession of Augsburg (1530) Magellan had sailed round the world ; three years before the death of Luther (1546) Copernicus had published his *De Revolutionibus Orbium Coelestium*. The Synod of Dort was sitting, and Gerhard was elaborating his *Loci* during the very years in which Galileo and Kepler were making their discoveries. Newton was discovering the law of gravitation while Calovius was writing his *Biblia Illustrata*. Since the phases of Venus were revealed to the telescope of Galileo we have learnt the existence of infinite space thronged with innumerable worlds. Since fossil bones were submitted to the prophetic eye of Cuvier we have learnt that infinite time has been peopled with innumerable existences. The search into caves and river-beds has shown us the immemorial relics and flint implements of primeval man. The discoveries of philology have laid open to us the earliest records of his language. A scientific observer, second perhaps to none since the days of Newton, after having been treated all his life long as an enemy to religion, was laid, but three years ago, in his honoured grave in Westminster Abbey. His theories, which have been scores of times denounced from this very pulpit, are now not only accepted by the great majority of scientific men throughout the world, but have been admitted by many leading theologians to be in no sense irreconcilable with sacred truths. Entirely apart from his central, and as yet unproven hypothesis, he has illustrated the necessity for scientific methods, and has furnished us with new and startling conceptions of the order, development, and maintenance of living organisms. It would be idle to suppose that discoveries so vast and hypotheses so splendid should have no effect on the deepest beliefs of men. The students of science have exercised a mighty influence over theology, were it only that by their linear progress and magnificent achievements they have stimulated that spirit of inquiry which for many centuries had only gyrated within limits prescribed too often by the ignorance of priests.

What should be the attitude of religion towards those who have enriched the life of man by these superb contributions of advancing knowledge ? We know what it *has* been. It has been an attitude first of fierce persecution, then of timid compromise, lastly, of thankless and inevitable acceptance. Although some great discoverers have belonged, like Roger Bacon and Copernicus, to the ranks of the clergy, there is scarcely a nascent science which the accredited defenders of religion have not in their ignorance striven to overwhelm ; scarcely a great discovery which, in the first instance, they did not denounce as heretical or blasphemous. Such an attitude deserved the defeats which it has received—defeats, not of religion, not of Christianity, not of the very smallest fraction of the truths of God, but defeats of the obstructiveness, the obscurantism, or at best the arrogant imperfection of those who misinterpreted the requirements of true religion, and mistook for its oracles the echoes of their own prejudice and pride.[1] Five hundred years of mistaken opposition, from the days of Roger Bacon down to those of Darwin, may, it is to be hoped, have convinced theologians that all their teachings are neither infallible nor divine. It is only the foundation of God that remaineth sure, and on that foundation have been built also the irrefragable conclusions of science. We are not, indeed, called upon to accept at once every unproven hypothesis, or to mistake for science mere assertions about that which is unknowable, or that which can only be spiritually discerned. It is quite true that the votaries of science have often had as little right to speak in the name of science as the theologians have had little right to speak in the name

---

[1] The lives of Virgilius, Roger Bacon, Copernicus, Campanella, Columbus, Vesalius, Galileo, Kepler, Descartes, and very many more are full of warnings against the rash abuse of Scripture texts.

of God.   Nevertheless it remains certain that true science
and true religion are twin sisters, each studying her own
sacred book of God, and nothing but disaster has arisen from
the petulant scorn of the one and the false fear and cruel
tyrannies of the other.   Let them study in mutual love and
honour side by side, and each pronounçe respecting those
things which alone she knows.

But the advance of the human intellect has not lain solely
in the realm of natural science.   Philosophy and psychology
—the labours of Descartes, Spinoza, Leibnitz, Wolff, Kant,
Fichte, Jacobi, Schelling, Hegel, and of their successors—
have turned men's thoughts inwards, and have shown the
necessary limitations of human knowledge, while they have
failed to shake the fundamentals of faith.

The study of comparative religion, a study of yesterday,
and mainly founded by students who still live and work
in the midst of us, has shown how many are the religious
books of Humanity, and how they too—though they stand so
immeasurably below the Scriptures in worth and sacredness—
have suffered from the analogous misinterpretations of an
ill-directed superstition.

Nor while physical science and metaphysical inquiry were
thus advancing by leaps and springs was it likely that criticism
should remain stationary.   The demonstration of the forgery
of the Donation of Constantine and the Decretals of Isidore
on which had been built the great fabric of papal supremacy
over the national Churches ; [1] the examination by Daillé of
the Ignatian Epistles (1666); the letters of Bentley on the
Epistles of Phalaris (1699); the theory of Wolf as to the
origin of the Homeric poems ; the rejection of the genuineness
of the so-called works of Dionysius the Areopagite ; [2] and
many similar discoveries, awoke the minds of men during the
course of two centuries to the fact that pseudepigraphy
was a common phenomenon alike of Jewish, heathen, and

[1] Valla's discourse, *De Potest. Imp. et Eccl.* was written in 1440.
[2] By Valla, who is followed by Erasmus, *Annott.* in Acts xviii. 34.   See
Ussher, *Dissert. de Scriptis Dionysio Suppositis*, 1690.

Christian literature, and showed them the decisive character of internal evidence. Niebuhr applied the solvent of criticism to the series of legends which passed for Roman history, and a multitude of successors in his school has proved the futility of much which had once received unquestioned credence.

Amid this outburst of new and varied knowledge which has enlarged in so many directions our comprehension of God's dealings with our race, it would be disheartening indeed, and it would be a contradiction to the whole course of history, if we had made no advance in our knowledge of Scripture. It would have been shameful if we had remained content with the exegesis of the Rabbis, who were children of an imperfect and abrogated dispensation, or the Fathers who "lived among the falling and fallen leaves of the old world," or the Schoolmen in the ages of an all but universal ignorance. It was inevitable, nay, it was most necessary, nay, more, the sacredness of truth—which "is as impossible to be soiled by any outward touch as the sunbeam"—made it imperative that new principles of inquiry and modern methods of criticism should be extended to those records of revelation in which it was certain that nothing could suffer which was intrinsically truthful or divine. Even in the dawn of the Reformation a Cajetan no less than a Luther, and in the next age a Simon no less than a Spinoza, had recognised the freedom of Scriptural criticism. The Reformers had struck the Apocrypha out of the Canon, and gone far to place some books of the Bible—as had been done centuries earlier by some of the Rabbis, and by some of the Fathers—in the ranks of deutero-canonicity. In the year 1753 the French physician, Astruc, discovered the double stratum of Elohistic and Jehovistic elements in the Book of Genesis. Since his day criticism, both historic and philological, has been applied to every narrative and every section of Scripture. Many of its results have taken their place among valued truths; many of its assertions have been triumphantly refuted. It has overthrown false human theories, it has not shaken so much as the fringe of a single truth. But the notion of verbal infallibility could not possibly survive the birth of historic inquiry, which showed in Scripture as elsewhere an organic growth, and therefore a necessary period of immature development. And meanwhile we have been taught of God a fearlessness which enables us to examine every critical question with tolerance and candour. We have learnt to see, not only that everything is not lost, but even that nothing is lost if criticism succeeds in proving that the Pentateuch is composed of different elements, and the Book of Chronicles a late and one-sided narrative, or that there were two Isaiahs, and two Zechariahs, or that the old Antilegomena must still be regarded as of dubious genuineness. Nay, more, all is not lost if we were even compelled to make the extravagant admission that the Pastoral Epistles were pseudonymous, and the Fourth Gospel was not written by St. John. Where the Spirit of God is there is liberty. All these questions have been under discussion for many years ; yet to multitudes of those who on these questions have come to decisions which are in opposition to the current opinions, the Bible is still the divinest of all books and the Lord Jesus Christ is still the Son of God, the Saviour of the World.

And if any man ask, " How are we to discriminate between that which in the Bible ought to be to us the immediate word of God, and that which, having been but relative and transient, is not His word to us ? "—I answer that not only is there not the slightest practical difficulty in doing so, but that the question shows, surely, a strange and unworthy timidity. In the first place, no theory which can be invented will give the certitude which is claimed for every petty detail of sectarian dissidence or theological terminology ; nor can any pretence of an infallible decision ever give infallibility to hosts of fallible and varying interpretations. But for all essential truths, have we nothing to guide us into certainty ? Have we no reason "lighted by God, and lighting to God, *res illuminata, illuminans* " ? Have we within us no voice of Conscience, " that aboriginal Vicar of Christ, a

Prophet in its informations, a Monarch in its peremptoriness, a Priest in its blessings and anathemas"? Have we no Spirit of God to guide us, or has He abdicated His office since the days of St. John, or, at any rate, since the days of St. Augustine? Is it not enough that, to us, the test of God's word is the teaching of Him who is the Word of God? Is it not an absolutely plain and simple rule that anything in the Bible which teaches or seems to teach anything which is not in accordance with the love, the gentleness, the truthfulness, the purity of Christ's gospel, is not God's word to us, however clearly it stands on the Bible page?[1] The Bible, as I have already said, has been quoted to sanction despotism, tyrannicide, priestly usurpation, polygamy, slavery, cunning, assassination. cruel superstitions, remorseless intolerance, exterminating war. It has been quoted to slander the Apostle, to crush the reformer, to discourage the student, to break the hearts of the saints of God. Such applications of Holy Writ, even though an Angel from heaven utter them, are not and cannot be to us the word of God. We shall find in Scripture all that is necessary for the salvation of our souls; we shall find in it the few great moral principles which suffice for the guidance of our life. Whenever we are quoting it to stimulate the energy, to alleviate the misery, to promote the happiness of mankind—whenever we are able to use its words as arrows of lightning to slay the Python of corruption, or to shatter the strongholds of oppression, robbery, and wrong,—then we are using it in accordance with Christ's spirit,—then we are indubitably and indisputably right. But when we use it to oppose science, to stimulate hatred, to check progress, to crush independence, to buttress tyranny, then we are using it for the injury of mankind, and therefore not to promote, but to hinder the will of Him Who spake in times past unto the fathers by the Prophets, but hath in these last days spoken unto us by His Son.

In the name of that Son of God is the secret of our progress,

[1] See the remarks of Luther quoted by Köstlin, ii. 260.

of our security, of our freedom, of our strength.[1] If we build upon Him, we build on the one Foundation. It is because they put themselves in place of Him, that hierarchies have fallen into corruption and ruin. It is because they failed to comprehend His nature that philosophies have passed away. It is because they thrust the dead letter in the place of His living Spirit, that religious movements have ended in hatred and obstructiveness. It is because they have mistaken the dawn for a conflagration that theologians have so often been the foes of light.[2] It is because they have appealed to self-deceiving intuitions as infallible proofs of their own human interpretations, that their cherished conclusions have so often been overthrown. But no Church, and no system, and no man who has been rooted and grounded in Him in love has ever failed to increase with the increase of God. Amid the tyrannies of priestcraft, amid the aberrations of theology, amid the doubts and difficulties of criticism, the Bible has continued to be the inalienable possession of the Christian Church. No attempt to keep the sacred writings as a seven-sealed book in the hands of the clergy, no insuperable difficulties created by dogmas about inspiration, no false systems of interpretation built upon those dogmas, have been able to snatch the Bible wholly from the hands of the vast unknown multitude whom God has known for His, and who have departed from iniquity. To them—the simple and the unselfish and the pure in heart—it has ever been as still it is a guide to the feet and a lamp to the path, and in the quaint language of our Translators' Preface " a granary of wholesome food against fenowed traditions." For them there has always been that pure exegesis of the heart which to the pride of an anathematising theology has often been unknown. Reading the Scriptures

---

[1] "All the seeming contradictions of Scripture are reconciled in Jesus Christ " (Pascal, *Pensées II.* ix. § 13).

[2] When John Owen (*Works*, xix. 310) said that Newton's discoveries were "built on fallible phenomena, and advanced by many arbitrary presumptions *against evident testimonies of Scripture*," his sentences may stand as but one specimen of hundreds and thousands of the obscurantist utterances of theologians who attribute infallibility to their own exegetical errors.

not with the eyes of partisanship, of suspicion, or of self-interest, but with the eyes of love, and "into the soul's vernacular," they have found it rich in blessing and consolation. The secret of the Lord has been with them that fear Him, and He has shown them His covenant. For more than 1700 years party theologians, who have sought mainly for proof-texts to confound the heresies of others and to build up despotism for themselves, have gone astray; but also for more than 1700 years, with no more need than the early Christians had for dialectic definitions or elaborate theories, the simple have learned wisdom. Unencumbered by ponderous learning, uncrushed by a vast apparatus of systems, unterrified by difficulties, indifferent to wranglings, unperverted by aberrations, they have not been seduced from the simplicity which is in Christ Jesus into pathless labyrinths of allegory and dogma. They have not seen but have yet believed, and have never been disappointed of their hope.[1] Bengel in his brief summary of the epochs of exegesis calls the first *Nativa*, and that—without its Judaic and Rabbinic weakness—all true Christians however humble have always enjoyed. The saving knowledge of Holy Scripture "is a science," as Pascal said, "not of the intellect, but of the heart." [2] And therefore in this respect also the history at which we have glanced is full of encouragement. The supremacy of the Scriptures is assured when they are seen to be human as well as divine, and are not regarded as the sole source of revelation, but rather as the record of its progressive development. They are indeed the witness to evangelic truth, but for that truth when once attained we have the yet surer witness of Faith. When the Church has forgotten this co-ordinate claim of Faith, when she has rested content in slothful bondage, when she has

---

[1] "The unlearned multitude have obtained more good from the Bible than the learned schools, because, following the hermeneutics of nature, they do not attempt to enjoy it all at once. For that is beyond human power. For every day its care, for every time its text ; there are texts for all times. The devout heart finds it out from amidst the mass, and with its meaning consoles itself for the rest." Reuss, p. 599, E. T.

[2] Pascal, *Pensées*, ii. 17, § 106.

F F

thrust a book, even the most sacred, between herself and the living continuous operations of the Holy Spirit of God,—when she has confounded theology with religion and the clergy with the Church—then, by salutary discipline, by needful epochs of defeats and apathy, God has led her back from her wanderings, and once more turned her gaze to the Sun of Righteousness, and set her feet on the one Rock against which the gates of hell shall not prevail.

And lastly, if we need for the understanding of Holy Scripture a Guide who cannot fail, if we would learn such principles of interpretation as shall secure us not indeed against literary errors of criticism and theory, which must always be incident to our fallible natures, but against every error which could be pernicious to mankind or perilous to our own souls, we need but to study the method of the Lord Christ Himself. He is the one Divine *Angelus Interpres et Divinae veritatis internuntius.* [1]   The errors of which we have been unwilling witnesses could never have arisen if men had followed, instead of reversing, the methods which He taught by His precepts and illustrated by His example. By no word that He uttered did He sanction that mechanical theory of inspiration which "is at variance with the whole form and fashion of the Bible, and is destructive of all that is holiest in man and highest in religion." [2]   When He lived on earth a system of interpretation had already attained to its full proportions, to which His own was so entirely opposed, that one of the first things which the multitudes observed respecting Him was that He condemned it by His example. That system was the Rabbinic, the Pharisaic, the method of the Scribes—a system servile, secondhand, traditional, superstitious, self-interested, denunciative, fantastic—and its main features have been continued by direct affiliation through the Christian centuries down to our own. What was His atti-

---

[1] Buddeus, *Praef. ad* Rambach, *Instt. Herm.*, *ad fin.* Comp. Merx, *Eine Rede vom Auslegen*, p. 43 ; "*Wann wird das Thema bearbeitet werden : Jesus Veteris Testamenti interpres primarius ?*"
[2] Westcott, *Introd. to the Gospels*, p. 5.

tude towards that system? There is not one of its erroneous principles which He did not tacitly discountenance or expressly condemn. The Scribes relied on precedent; He taught with authority. They overlaid the Law with inferences; He told them that they set the Word of God at naught by their traditions. They claimed the power to shut out all except their adherents from the Kingdom of Heaven; He flung open its gates to all the world. They clutched in their own hands the key of knowledge; He wrenched it from their grasp and gave it to fishermen and publicans. They with false reverence had counted the very letters of their Bible; He told them that they were ignorant of its most essential principles. They explained Scripture theologically, scientifically, with infinite and elaborate subtlety; He seized the one essential message of its spiritual teaching.[1] They insisted on dogmas and minutiae; He broadened the significance of Scripture into that of its central truths. They were ready to stone a man for blasphemy against Moses if, in spite of the progressing ages, he treated any utterance of the Pentateuch as being other than eternally valid and supernaturally divine; He taught that some of the Mosaic regulations, in themselves intrinsically imperfect, were only a concession to the hardness of men's hearts. They, lastly, were ever extracting from the Scriptures some pretext for condemning Him, for condemning His disciples, for condemning the great mass of mankind except themselves; His favourite and thrice-repeated quotation—condemning the spirit of hatred, condemning the spirit of letter-worship, condemning the bondage of formalism—was "Go ye and learn what that meaneth, I will have mercy and not sacrifice." It was thus that Christ supported the Divine authority of the Holy Scriptures. Schemes of interpretation, whether Rabbinic, Kabbalistic, Alexandrian, Patristic, Scholastic, Dogmatic, Philosophical, Psychological, or Practical, may follow false developments and abound in erroneous details;[2] and so far as

---

[1] See Matt. xxii. 29–32; Mark xii. 24–27; Luke xx. 34–38.
[2] βεβήλους κενοφωνίας, 1 Tim. vi. 20; 2 Tim. ii. 16.

those who apply them are dominated by the spirit of pride,
jealousy, hatred, or partisanship their oppressive narrowness
may inflict immeasurable wrongs on the heart and intellect
of man.[1] But no such schemes receive any sanction from
the approval or practice of our Lord. He has but one
principle, which is to go to the very heart of the central
idea, and to fill it with the large liberality of love. God is
righteous. If we be sons of God we must hate falsity and
injustice and all "lying for God" with a perfect hatred.
God is a Spirit. If we be in living communion with God
we must not only believe in the continuous inspiration of
His Spirit, but we must speak with tongues and must
interpret. God is Love. We shall never go far astray in the
interpretation of Scripture even though we be but wayfaring
men and fools, if we strive by our theology to regulate our
life, and to sway the whole movement of our intellect by the
spirit which Christ manifested and by the Divine example
which He set;[2]—by the golden rule which it may be that He
clothed in these very words, "Never be joyful save when
ye look upon the face of your brother in love."[3]

Porro unum necessarium. Let me, as my last word, leave
with you the hexameters of a poet of the fourth century :—

> " Discussi fateor sectas attentius omnes,
> 　Plurima quaesivi, per singula quaeque cucurri,
> 　Nec quicquam inveni melius quam credere Christo."[4]

---

[1] "Out upon you that will read Scripture only to copy those things which
are held out to us as warnings, not as examples."—Kenilworth. Take two
instances of age-long crimes—persecution and slavery. Of persecution supported by Scripture texts I have said enough. For slavery one quotation out
of thousands may suffice. "From its *inherent nature*," said Bishop Hopkins
of Vermont, "*slavery has been a curse and blight wherever it exists : yet it is
warranted by the Bible.* Therefore, as slavery is recognised by the Bible,
every man has a right to own slaves, provided they are not treated with
unnecessary cruelty."

[2] Quisquis . . talem inde sententiam duxerit ut . . aedificandae caritati
sit utilis . . non perniciose fallitur, nec omnino mentitur." Aug. *De Doctr.
Christ.* iii.

[3] "Et nunquam, inquit, laeti sitis, nisi quum fratrem vestrum videritis in
caritate." Quoted by Jerome from the "Gospel of the Hebrews." Jer. *in
Eph.* v. 3.

[4] Antonius.

I too have examined many sects; I have considered many phases of teaching; I have found nothing better than to believe in Christ. We may differ about many things, and the less Christian be our disposition the more bitter will be our religious differences; but though there may be many readers who will disagree with me in much that I have said, I trust that they will all agree with me, heart and soul, in believing that the one end of all Scriptural study, the one object of all Christian life, the one thing needful to be desired in all the world, is this: to find Christ, and to be found in Him, not having a righteousness of our own, even that which is of the Law, but that which is through faith in Christ, the righteousness which is of God by faith.

NOTES.

NOTES.

NOTES.

LECTURE II.

NOTE I.

SELF-GLORIFICATION OF THE RABBIS.

Rashi on Deut. xvii. 11, says, "The Rabbis are to be believed even when they say that right is left, and left is right."

"He that quarrels with his Rabbi quarrels as it were with the Shekinah." See Sanhedrin, f. 110, 1; Num. xxvi. 9.

"The curse of a Rabbi comes to pass even when it is without cause." Sanhedrin, f. 20, 2 (a flat contradiction of Prov. xxvi. 2).

"Even the conditional curse of a Rabbi is certain to come to pass." Makkoth, f. 111, 1.

"When the Rabbis look at a man in displeasure, he dies or becomes poor." Chagiga, f. 5, 6.

"A Rabbi is greater than a prophet."

"A man should respect his Rabbi more than his father."

"At the death of Rabbi, meekness and fear of sin were at an end. 'Say not meekness,' exclaimed Rav Joseph, 'for I am still here.' 'Say not fear of sin,' exclaimed Rav Nachman, 'for I am still here.'" Sota, f. 49, 2.

The Rabbis, like the Schoolmen, rejoiced in bestowing pompous titles upon each other, such as:

Hillel the Nasî.	"The Modest, the Patient, the Elder, the Great."
R. Johanan ben Zakkai.	"Upright Pillar," or "Mighty Hammer." [1]
R. Meir.	"The Brilliant" (Meir) [2] and "*Baal nes*, Lord of Wonders."

[1] Berakhoth, f. 28, 2.
[2] His real name was Nehoraii. 'Erubin, f. 13, 2.

R. Eleazar ben Hyrkanos.	" A closed cistern."
R. Judah.	" The Holy, the Prince, Our Rabbi."
R. Tarphon.	" A pile of nuts."
R. Ishmael.	" A handy store."
R. Aqiba.	" A well-stocked storehouse."
R. Eliezer ben Jacob.	" A *Kab*, but clean."
R. Jose.	" Always ready."
R. Johanan ben Nuri.	" A heap of Halakhoth."
Rabbah.	" Rooter up of mountains." [1]
R. Jose the Galilean.	"A beautiful compiler." [2]
R. Eleazar ben Arak.	" A welling spring."
R. Joseph.	" Sinai."
R. Joshua ben Chananiah.	" The light of the world." [3]

NOTE

THE TARGUMS AND MIDRASHIM.

The word Targum is of uncertain derivation, and is used for the Aramaic versions of the Old Testament. The first trace of such a vernacular (oral) rendering is in Heb. viii. 8, where the word *Mephorash* (A. V. " distinctly ") is in the Talmud (Megilla, 3, 1 ; Nedarim, 37, 2) explained to mean " with a Targum." In Sanhedrin, f. 212, we are told that Ezra introduced the Targum, and the square character of the Hebrew letters.

The chief Targums are those of Onqelos, Jonathan Ben Uzziel, Pseudo-Jonathan and the Targum Jerushalmi. Full accounts of them will be found in Deutsch's *Remains*, pp. 319-403. Wogue, *Hist. de la Bible*, pp. 145-157 ; and Weber, *Alt.-Synag. Theologie*, viii.-xix.

THE MIDRASH.

Jewish literature is, 1. *Halakhic and Haggadic :* the Mishna ; the Talmuds.

2. *Expository* in a wider sense : the Midrashim and (incidentally) the Targums.

3. *Massoretic*, the great and little Massora.

---

[1] Berakhoth, f. 64, 1 ; Horaioth, f. 14, 1.

[2] R. Tarphon also called him " the horned ram," and applied Dan. viii. 3-7 to him, from his skill in rebutting the arguments of R. Aqiba. These and other titles are given in Gittin, f. 67, 1, and the Aboth of R. Nathan, xviii. I am indebted for these references to Mr. P. J. Hershon.

[3] Aboth, ii. 10, " Happy is she that bare him." The title " Lux mundi " was given in the Middle Ages to John Wessel.

4. *Historical,* Chananiah, The Books of Maccabees, Josephus, Josippon, &c.

5. *Philosophic* (Alexandrian).

The Midrash of the schools was mainly Halakhic; that of the synagogues mostly Haggadic.

The word " Midrash " first occurs in 2 Chron. xiii. 22; "the *Midrash* of the prophet Iddo," xxiv. 24; "the *Midrash* of the Book of Kings."

The epochs of the Midrashim are three.

1. Its development from B.C. 30—A.D. 400. From Hillel to Gamaliel V.

2. Its collection from A.D. 400-750. From Gamaliel V. to R. Anan the Karaite.

3. Its decline from A.D. 750-900. From death of Anan to R. Aron ben Asher in Tiberias.

The Midrash is founded on extravagant application of the two principles that

i. Nothing in Scripture is indifferent or accidental.

ii. All Scripture is capable of indefinite interpretations (some said 49, and some 70).

The chief Midrashim are, in the first epoch during which the Halakha is predominant,

1. Mekhiltaï (" Tenor ") An Halakhic commentary on parts of Exodus, based on the methods of R. Aqiba.

2. Siphra (" The Book ") or *Torath Kohanim,* on Leviticus. It originated in the school of Rab in Sara (ספרא דבי רב).

3. Siphri (" Books ") on Numbers and Deuteronomy.

In the second epoch the Haggada was greatly developed, and the following works belong to it :—

4. Pesikhta. On sections or selections of the Law and the Prophets by Rab. Kahana.

5. Midrash Rabba : one of the *catenae* collected in the thirteenth century. It consists of

> Bereshith Rabba, on Genesis. [1]
> Shemoth Rabba, on Exodus.
> Vajikra Rabba, on Leviticus.
> Bamidbar Rabba, on Numbers.
> Debarim Rabba, on Deuteronomy.

---

[1] This is the best and oldest. It is Palestinian of the 6th century. It resembles, and quotes the Jerusalem Gemara.

and of the five Megilloth (" Rolls ").

> Schir Rabba on Canticles.
> Midrash Ruth.
> „ Esther.
> „ Koheleth.
> Echa Rabbathi on Lamentations.

6. Tanchuma; on the Pentateuch. It is sometimes called Yelamdenu from its formula, " Our Rabbis have taught us." [1]

During the third epoch the Halakha became absolutely lifeless, and R. Anan the Karaite demanded a return to the natural and rational method of interpreting Scripture : but Haggadic *catenae* continued to be produced.

7. Jalqut Shimeoni ; on the Old Testament. This was drawn up by R. Simeon in the thirteenth century, and resembles the Patristic *catenae*.

8. Jalqut Chadash. It was compiled out of the Book Zohar in the Middle Ages.

Halakhic traditions outside the Mishna are called " extraneous " (*Boraïtoth* [2]), and are collected in the Tosephta.[3] The additions to the Mishna are called Tosephtoth ; those to the Gemara are called Tosaphoth.

NOTE III.

RABBI JOHANAN BEN ZAKKAI.

It was the happy method of R. Johanan to propose a subject for discussion, to listen to the opinions given by all his associates, and finally to give his own judgment. Thus on one occasion he told his disciples to consider " *which was the good way in which men should walk.*" They defended their several views as follows :

> *R. Eliezer.* He should have a kindly eye.
> *R. Joshua.* He should gain a sure friend.
> *R. Jose.* He should strive to win a good neighbour.
> *R. Simon.* He should always consider the consequences.
> *R. Eleazar.* He should have a good heart.

[1] יְלַמְדֵנוּ רַבֵּן.
[2] *Baria,* " exterior."
[3] From *yasaph,* " to add." The Tosephta was drawn up by R. Chija bar Abba, a Tanaite, who also drew up a collection of Boraïtoth.

R. Johanan summed up the discussion by saying, "The best answer has been given by R. Eleazar, for the blessing which he has mentioned comprises all the others."

On another occasion he proposed for discussion Prov. xiv. 34, which was rendered, "Righteousness exalteth a nation, but the mercy (וחסר) of nations is sin."

> *R. Eliezer.* Righteousness exalteth Israel, but any good deeds done by the Gentiles are only sin.
>
> *R. Joshua.* (To the same effect with different proofs.)
>
> *Rabbon Gamaliel II.* (who was still a disciple). (To the same effect with other proofs, and an expression of uncertainty.)
>
> *R. Eliezer.* (Still the same, with fresh proofs.)
>
> *R. Nechunjah.* Righteousness and mercy exalt Israel, but sin degrades the nations.
>
> *R. Johanan.* Righteousness atones for the nations of the world, just as a sin-offering does for Israel.[1]

This view showed at least the kindness of his heart (comp. Acts x. 34, 35); but he afterwards accepted R. Nechunjah's in preference.[2]

Specimens of the admirable sayings and parables of R. Eliezer are given by Löw (*Praktische Einleitung*, 95, 103).

NOTE IV.

FURTHER INSTANCES OF EXEGETIC AND SYMBOLIC KABBALISM.

1. *Gematria.*

Is. xxx. 8. "Blessed are all those that wait upon Him" (לו). The value of לו is 36, so Abaii said that there are 36 in every generation who receive the presence of the Shekhinah. Sanhedrin, f. 97, 2.

Is. xx. 1. This is made a prophecy of Habakkuk (comp. Hab. ii. 1) because "lion" = 216 = Habakkuk (see Rashi, Kimchi, and Ibn Ezra, *ad loc.*).

Gen. xi. 1. All the inhabitants of the earth were of one language. Here אֶחָת = 409, and is equivalent to הַקֹּדֶשׁ = 409 whence it was assumed that Hebrew was the primeval tongue.

---

[1] The word חסר usually means "mercy" or "piety," and taking it in this sense Schultens and Grotius practically agree with R. Johanan, and make the verse mean "piety is an atonement for the people." But חסר is rendered ὄνειδος by the LXX. in Lev. xx. 17 (A.V. "ungodliness;" R.V. "a shameful thing"). Kalisch thinks that it gets this sense by *antiphrasis*.

[2] Baba Bathra, f. 10, 2.

Gen. xviii. 2. "And lo! these men" = by Gematria, "These are Michael, Gabriel, and Raphael."

Jacob's *ladder* (סלם) is identified with Sinai (סיני), because both words = 130.

Gen. xlii. 2. "*Go down*" (רדו) = 210, therefore the Egyptian bondage was to last 210 years.

Lev. xvi. 3. "*Thus* shall Aaron come into the Holy Place." , "thus," = 410 = 2 + 7 + 1 + 400, therefore the first temple was to last 410 years.

Deut. xxxiii. 27. God is often described as "the Place" (*maqom*), because maqom = 186, and Jehovah = $10^2 + 5^2 + 6^2 + 5^2$.

On the tomb of Emmanuel Deutsch in the Jewish cemetery at Alexandria, the Hebrew inscription, written by Dr. Hermann Adler, says that he "died in the year '*Arise, shine, for thy light is come.*'" It is a sort of chronogram. The text quoted gives the number 1873, the year in which the brilliant scholar died.

For other instances see Buxtorf, *Lex. Chald. s.v.* נמטריא ; Buddeus, *Philos. Ebr.* p. 323.

2. *Notarikon.*

Each letter of the words "a father of many nations have I made thee" is made significant. Shabbath, f. 105, 1.

From Gen. xxxvii. 3 it is inferred that the "coat of many colours" was the source of all Joseph's troubles, because the letters of פסם stand for the initials of the Hebrew words for "Potiphar, merchants, Ishmaelites, Midianites."

Deut. xxx. 12, "Who will go up for us?" In the Hebrew the initials of these words give מלה, "circumcision," and the final letters יהוה, "Jehovah." Hence it is inferred that circumcision is the way to Heaven. (See further Ginsburg, *The Kabbalah*, pp. 12, 50 ; *Eccles.* p. 30.)

3. *Inferences from changing the reading.*

("Read not so but so.") א. תקרי כן אלא כן

Gen. xxv. 23. "Two nations are in thy womb." Read not גוים, "nations," but גיים, "men" (as the Massora reads). The two men are Rabbi (Judah the Holy), the compiler of the Mishna, and his friend Antoninus the Emperor.

Deut. xxxiii. 4. "Moses commanded us a law, the inheritance of the congregation of Jacob." Read not מורשה, "inheritance," but מאורסה, "espoused," which shows that the Law is as a bride. Pesachim, f. 42, 2.

Gen. xlix. 22. "Joseph is . . . a fruitful bough by a well." Read not עלי עין, "by a well," but עולי עין, "above the eye" which shows that Joseph and his descendants are not affected by the evil eye. Berakhoth, f. 55, 2.

Eccl. xi. 1. "Cast thy bread upon the waters, and thou shalt find it after many days." Read not ברוב חמים, "upon the waters," but ברוב הימים, "in much water." (This was illustrated by stories of R. Aqiba's escape from shipwreck.) Aboth of R. Nathan, ch. iii.

Ex. xxxii. 16. "Graven upon the tables." Read not חרות, "graven," but חֵרוּת, "freedom ;" for only students of the law are free. Aboth, ch. vi.

Cant. iv. 3. "Thy temples are like a piece of pomegranate." Read not "thy temples," but "thy empty ones," to show that even transgressors of Israel are as full of good works as a pomegranate of pips. Chagiga, f. 27, 1.

Cant. i. In Yadaim iii. the first chapter of Canticles is explained by R. Chasdah, and in Shabbath, f. 88, 2, by other Rabbis. The explanation turns on incessant changes of words. (See Dr. Ginsburg, *Song of Songs*, p. 28.)

4. *Importance attached to letters.*

Ex. iii. 15. The name of Jehovah must not be altered because לעלם "for ever" is here written without ו, and therefore means "to hide." Qiddushin, f. 71.

Gen. i. 31. Why the superfluous article in "the sixth" day (הששי) ? Because ה = 5, and it means that if Israel does not receive the five books of the Law, the world shall return to chaos. Shabbath, f. 88, i. a.

"Job said, Perhaps a storm wind changed by name from Job (איוב) to 'enemy' (אויב)." Baba Bathra, f. 16, 1.

Gen. xlvii. 12. The word *eth* is dotted to show that they meant to feed not the flock but themselves. Aboth of R. Nathan, 34.

5. *Inferences from the repetition of words.*

A Sadducee once said to Rabbi Iddith, "It is written (Ex. xxiv. 1), 'And God said unto Moses, Come up unto the Lord.' Should it not be 'Come up unto Me'?" "No," said the Rabbi, "Metatron is here called by the name of the Lord." Sanhedrin, f. 38, 2.

The child of R. Simeon ben Lakish asked Rabbi why the verb was repeated in '*Tithing thou shalt tithe*' (Deut. xiv. 22). The Rabbi said, "Give tithes that thou mayest become rich " (עשת has both meanings). Taanith, f. 9, 1.

2 Sam. vi. 2. "The Ark upon which the name, the name of the Lord is called." "Name" is repeated to show that the broken tables also were deposited in the Ark. Baba Bathra, f. 14, 2.

Gen. xix. 24. "The Lord rained . . . fire from the Lord." A Sadducee remarked that it should be "from Himself." A washer-man who was present, obtaining leave to answer him, referred to Gen. iv. 23 ; Lamech said, "Hear my voice, ye wives of Lamech." Sanhedrin, f. 38, 2. The perfectly sensible remark that it was only a peculiarity of speech was given by R. Meir ; yet this text is used by Fathers and Schoolmen to prove the Divinity of Christ.

6. *Inferences from impersonal verbs.*

Esth. vi. 1. "And he commanded to bring the books of the chronicles, and *they were read.*" It means they were read of themselves (by no visible agent). "*And it was found written.*" It means that Shimsai (? Ezra iv. 8) kept erasing the words, and Gabriel wrote them afresh. Megilla, f. 15, 2.

7. *Inferences from Plurals.*

Ex. xxiv. 6. "Long-sufferings." Why in the plural ? Because it extends both to the righteous and to the wicked. 'Erubin, f. 22, 1.

Gen. xlv. 16. "Benjamin's *necks.*" Had Benjamin two necks ? No, he wept for the destruction of the two Temples. Megilla, f. 16, 2.

Gen. iv. 10. "Thy brother's *bloods.*" It means that his blood was scattered on trees and stones. Sanhedrin, f. 37, 1.

Dan. vii. 9. "The *thrones* were placed." R. Jose. "One throne for justice, one for mercy." R. Eleazar. "One for a throne, the other for a footstool." R. Aqiba. "One for Himself, one for the Messiah." Sanhedrin, f. 38, 2.

8. *Miscellaneous.*

Gen. xiv. 3. As a reward for refusing a thread and a shoe-latchet which were not his, Abraham's children received two profitable commandments, to have a sky-blue thread in the fringes, and a leathern strap to the phylacteries. Sota, f. 17, 1.

Gen. xix. 2. "The cry of Sodom is great." Since רבה in Talmudic Hebrew also means "a girl," they had a story of a girl in Sodom who for giving a piece of bread to a poor man was smeared with honey and stung to death by bees. Sanhedrin, f 109, 2.

Rabbi Jehudah says, "He that renders a verse literally says what is not true ; and he who adds to it is a blasphemer," Qiddushin, f. 49, 1. (Rashi adds that the additions in the Targums of Onqelos were derived from Moses.)

Cant. viii. 10. "I am a wall," *i.e.* the Law ; "and my breasts like towers," *i.e.* the Pupils of the Wise. Baba Bathra, f. 8, 1.

NOTE V.

THE KARAITES.

The Karaites—whom I have called the Protestants of Judaism—date their distinct position from the days of the Khalif Almanzor (753-774) in Bagdad. Just as the Mohammedan Schiites reject, and the Sunnites accept, "tradition" apart from the Koran, so the Karaites reject the tradition of the Rabbinists, and acknowledge only the authority of Scripture (*Beni Mikra*). A learned Karaite in the fifteenth century, Kaleb Afendopulo, says that the Karaites differed from Talmudists : 1. In rejecting the oral law. 2. In rejecting traditional exegesis, and maintaining (like the Reformers) the "perspicuity" of Scripture. 3. In denying all right to add to, or take from, the Law.

We read in a Jewish periodical that a Jewish boy once asked his father, "Who are the Karaites ?" The answer was, "They are Jews who eat chickens fried in butter." The boy immediately (according to the common Jewish form of execration) spat on the ground and said, "May their name and memorial be blotted out."[1] The meaning was that they violate the law, "Thou shalt not seethe a kid in its mother's milk," because they reject the preposterous extensions given by the Rabbis to that precept.

The founder of the Karaites was Anan ben David Abba,[2] who being excluded from the position of Gaon, went to Jerusalem with his son, friends, and followers, and developed his opinions undisturbed. He shook off the yoke of Rabbinism and tradition, and proclaimed the right of private judgment. He is still commemorated by the Karaites in their mention of the dead, as one who opened for them the gates of the Law.

The Karaites claim, however, a much higher antiquity though not as a separate sect. In a Karaite book published in 1834, and quoted in the *Jewish World* (Jan. 27, 1882), we read, "The Jews murdered the good Jesus, the son of Miriam, *because he was a Karaite*, and because he opposed the Mishna, as his Karaite ancestors had always done."[3]

The influence of the Karaites told strongly even on the Rabbinists, and led to the development of the Massora. Their determination to

---

[1] The initial letters of the words of this curse form the word יש״ו, "Jesus.'
[2] See Munk, *Mélanges*, p. 479 *sqq.*
See Matt. xv. 6 ; Mark vii. 13 ; John v. 39. The Prophets Isaiah and Jeremiah certainly express Karaite views (Is. iii. 12 ; viii. 20 ; ix. 16 ; lvi. 10-12, &c. Jer. ii. 13 ; viii. 12 ; xviii. 8-23, &c.). Karaites are mentioned in the Mishna, Megilla, f. 24, 2.

abide by the literal sense gave an impulse to Hebrew philology, which was peculiarly difficult when there was neither grammar nor lexicon in existence.

The Karaites claim the right to constant progress without regarding themselves as unfaithful to their earlier teachers.

They have eight exegetical rules drawn up by Abu Jakub el Bazir.

NOTE VI.

THE MASSORA.

The word Massora is derived from *Masar*, "to deliver," and in its original sense the word means the traditional writing of the Biblical text of the Sopherim which R. Aqiba regarded as "a hedge round the law."

The necessity for the collection and preservation of the old textual traditions began with the decay of Jewish learning after the sixth century. The most important part of this task was the system of punctuation and vocalisation. The origin of the *Keri* ("read") and *Kethib* ("written") is attributed to the Sopherim (see Wogue, *Hist. de la Bible*, pp. 110-127) and the Massoretic material must have early existed, for the germs of it are alluded to even in the Mishna.

After the eighth century the word is used in a narrower sense to describe the knowledge of the words, letters, verses, vowels and points of the text. The Massorets counted the number of verses in each book, how many began and ended in the same way, how many times a word occurred in the Bible or in a particular book. Many of these results are preserved in Elias Levita. The Hebrew Bible (if any one cares to know) contains 815,280 letters.

The Massora was grammatic, lexical, and exegetic. The exegetic remarks, constituting the great and the little Massora, are written in the margin. The Massora was completed in the ninth century by Aron ben Asher, and Moseh ben David ben Naphthali, who laboured specially on the text.

Before the invention of printing the Bibles were written by scribes, "punctators" (   ) who added the vowel points and accents, and correctors (מניהים) who revised the whole. One of the most celebrated of these scribes was Samson the Nakdan, who wrote a book on the subject in the thirteenth century.

The Bible was early divided into Lessons from the Law (פרשיות) and from the Prophets (הפטרות). Rabbi Isaak Nathan in the fifteenth century wrote a concordance, in which the Jews first availed themselves of Hugo de St. Caro's division of the Bible into verses.

See Dillmann, in Herzog, *s.v. Bible Text.* Löw, *Praktische Einleitung*, pp. 115-117, and especially Dr. Ginsburg's translation of the Massoreth Ha Massoreth by Elias Levita, 1548 (London, 1867).

NOTE VII.

TALMUDIC CRYPTOGRAPHS.

From want of space I must content myself with a reference to my paper on this subject in the *Expositor* vii. 40-58, where several very important instances are given.

Want of space also compels me to omit a number of estimates of the Talmudic writings both favourable and unfavourable drawn from many writers, mediaeval and modern.

LECTURE III.

NOTE I.

PHILO'S USE OF THE SEPTUAGINT.

Siegfried, in three papers contributed to Hilgenfeld's *Zeitschrift* for 1873 has carefully examined Philo's use of the Septuagint. He finds from classifying Philo's quotations,

1. That he often cites from memory and parenthetically.
2. That he often mixes up his quotations with remarks of his own.
3. That he sometimes varies the terms of the same quotation.
4. That some of his professed quotations are no longer extant in any MSS.
5. That they occasionally represent more accurately the meaning of the Hebrew.
6. That they sometimes show traces of a different Hebrew text.
7. That they sometimes do not occur at all in our text.
8. That two quotations are sometimes mingled.

See too Gfrörer, Philo, i. 51 ; Dähne, ii. 2 *sq.*

Similar phenomena appear both in the quotations made from the Old Testament in the New, and in the writings of the Fathers.

NOTE II.

THE EXEGETICAL PRINCIPLES OF JOSEPHUS.

Although Josephus is primarily a historian, it was impossible for him to write a history of his people without giving many indications of the methods of interpretation which he adopted, and those methods were chiefly Palestinian. Nearly all that he has in common with Philo is the strong desire to narrate the Bible histories in such a manner as to be most acceptable to his Gentile readers, and so as least to excite their sense of the ridiculous.

He professes the intention of being perfectly faithful to the written records. But

1. He adopts allegorical explanations—as in his account of the Tabernacle. He says that two parts of it represented the land and sea which are open to all men; the third part symbolised the Heaven which is reserved for God. The twelve loaves of shewbread represent the twelve months; the candlestick was composed of seventy pieces to indicate the constellations; the seven branches indicated sun, moon, and planets, &c.

See *Antt., Proem.* § 4 ; i. 7, § 1 ; iii. 11, § 11.

2. He indulges in Hagadoth. Thus in his account of Abraham he says that the Patriarch taught Astrology, Arithmetic, &c., to the Egyptians from whom the Greeks learnt those sciences ; and he has many remarkable legends about the youth of Moses, &c.

3. He imitates the Greeks in putting speeches into the mouth of Moses, &c. (as Philo also does).

4. He adopts as often as possible a natural explanation of supernatural narratives, as in his account of the Manna, the Passage over the Red Sea, the crossing of Jordan, the appearance of the angel to the wife of Manoah, &c.

5. Like the Rabbis, he is fond of introducing proverbs, such as "Remorse is the daughter of obstinacy and thoughtlessness," "The mob is always changeable," "Envy waits on Prosperity," &c.

6. He assimilates Jewish views to those of the Greek philosophers. See *Antt.* vi. 11, § 8 ; viii. 4, § 2 ; *c. Ap.* ii. 39.

On the whole we must regard Josephus as presenting a strange mixture of Rabbinic, Pharisaic, and Rationalistic notions. He was wholly wanting in the religious earnestness of Philo.

NOTE III.

THE SEPTUAGINT VERSION.

A translator may either offer a free paraphrase, or may adhere to the original with slavish accuracy ; or may steer a middle course between these extremes. Many of the LXX. translators adopted the first view of their duty ; Aquila the second ; Theodotion and Symmachus the third.

i. The Seventy sometimes omit. The omission in some MSS. of 1 Sam.
xvii. 12-31, and 55-58 is due to the desire to avoid a contradiction.
The omission of Ex. xxxii. 9 is due to the same national vanity
which led them to alter "set on mischief" into "impetuous" in
Ex. xxxii. 22.

ii. They make Halakhic additions, as in Gen. ix. 4 ; Ex. xii. 15, 18 ;
xiii. 16 (*ἀσάλευτα*) ; xxii. 9 ; Lev. xix. 19 ; xxiv. 7 ; Deut. xxvi. 12,
&c. See Franker, *Vorstudien*, pp. 86-92.

iii. They add Haggadistic particulars, as in Gen. ii. 2 ; iv. 4 ; Ex. xiii.
18 ; Num. xxxii. 12 ; Deut. xxxii. 8 ; Josh. xiii. 22 ; xxiv. 30 ;
1 Sam. v. 4, 5, 10 ; xvii. 39-43 ; xix. 13-16 ; xx. 30 ; xxi. 13 ;
Eccl. xi. 9 ; xii. 9, &c.

iv. They explain and modify so as to get rid of anything which savoured
of difficulty or unorthodoxy, as in Ex. ii. 1 ; iv. 6 ; vi. 12, 20 ; xii.
40 ; 1 Sam. xvi. 12 ; xx. 30 ; Eccl. ii. 15, 17 ; xi. 9, &c.

v. They soften down Anthropomorphic and Anthropopathic expressions,
as in Gen. xviii. 30 ; Ex. iii. 1 ; iv. 16, 20, 24 ; v. 3 ; xv. 3 ; xvii.
16 ; xix. 13 ; xxiv. 10, 11 ; xxv. 8.

vi. As for their positive mistakes, they arose :

a. From the use of an unpunctuated text, as in Hos. vi. 5, Ps.
cvi. 7.

β. From the non-existence of vowel-points, as in
1 Sam. xiv. 45 ; 1 Chron. xix. 6 ; Ps. lxxxvii. 4, &c., where
they confuse *im* "with" and *am* "people."
1 Sam. ii. 16 ; viii. 19 ; x. 19, &c., confusions of לֹא and לוֹ.

γ. From confusion of letters, *e.g.* ד with ר or *vice versa*, as in
1 Sam. ix. 25 ; Is. xxix. 3 ; comp. 1 Sam. xvii. 8 ; xxxi. 3.
Some of these changes may be due to intentional anagram
&c. See Eccl. i. 18 ; ii. 3 ; viii. 6.

δ. From ignorance of proper names, as in
Gen. xxii. 13 ; Is. vii. 3, &c.

ε. From not understanding difficult words, as in
1 Sam. xv. 32 ; xvi. 20 ; xvii. 20 ; xxvi. 5 ; Ruth iv. 1 ; 2
Kings vi. 8.[1]

Aquila's version (A.D. 150) is slavishly literal, and was spoken of as
κατὰ ἀκρίβειαν (Jer. in Ezek. iii. 15). The LXX. sometimes render את
by σὺν (*e.g.* twenty-nine times in Ecclesiastes alone, i. 14 ; ii. 17, &c.).
Aquila, in deference to Aqiba's views, always did so. See Jer. *Ed. ad
Pammach.* The Talmud praises Aquila's version (Shabbath, 8 ;

---

[1] I have remarked on some of these errors of the LXX. in the version of
1 Samuel in the first vol. of the *Expositor*, pp. 104-119.

Yoma, f. 41, 1).[1] Theodotion's version seems to have been necessitated by the obscurity of Aquila's. Symmachus's version was far more intelligible and perspicuous.

NOTE IV.

Philo calls the literal sense :

τὰ ῥητὰ. *De Abrah.* § 38.
τὸ ῥητὸν, αἱ ῥηταὶ διερμηνεύσεις. *Quod det. pot.* §§ 6, 46.
ἡ ῥητὴ ἐπίσκεψις. *De Agric.* § 30.
ἡ ῥητὴ καὶ πρόχειρος διάταξις. *Quod Deus sit immut.* § 28.
αἱ πρόχειροι ἀποδόσεις ἐκ τῆς φανερᾶς τῶν νόμων γραφῆς.
ἡ πρόχειρος ἐκδοχὴ τοῦ λόγου. *De Conf. Ling.* p. 34.
ἡ ῥητὴ διήγησις. *De Joseph.* § 6.
κυρίως. *De Opif. Mundi,* § 54.
ἡ ῥητὴ καὶ φανερὰ ἀπόδοσις. *De Abrah.* § 36.
αἱ ῥηταὶ γραφαί. *id.* § 41.

Sometimes his phrases betray his strong dislike to literalism ; thus he calls it

ἡ κατὰ τὴν φράσιν ὑψηγορία. *Quod det. pot.*
ἡ φανερὰ καὶ πρὸς τοὺς πολλοὺς ἀπόδοσις. *De Abrah.* § 29.
πρὸς τοὺς τῆς ῥητῆς πραγματείας σοφιστὰς καὶ λίαν τὰς ὀφρῦς ἀνεσπακότας. *De Somn.* i. 17.

Of the allegorical sense he speaks as

νόμων ἱερῶν ἀλληγορίαι, αἱ δι' ὑπονοιῶν ἀποδόσεις. *De Abrah.* § 18.
                                                         De Agric. § 6.
                                                          De Cherub. § 7.
                                                          De Joseph. § 6.

αἰνίττεσθαι δι' ὑπονοιῶν. *Quod det. pot.*
διὰ συμβόλων. *Quod Deus sit immut.* § 27.
συμβολικῶς. *De Mund. Opif.* § 54.
τροπικαὶ ἀποδόσεις. *De Conf. Ling.* § 37.
τὰ ἐμφαινόμενα νοήματα. *Quod det. pot.* § 169.
τὰ νοητά. *De Abrah.* § 38.
ἀσώματα καὶ γυμνὰ πράγματα. *id.* § 41.

---

[1] R. Joshua b. Chananiah applied Ps. xlv. 3 to Aquila. Wogue, p. 139.

τὰ ἐν ὑπονοίαις. *De Joseph.* § 6.
ἡ τροπικωτέρα ἀπόδοσις. *id.* § 22.
ἡ ἐν ἀλληγορίᾳ θεωρία. *De Abrah.* § 25.
ἡ πρὸς διανοίαν ἐπιστήμη φιλομαθής. *De Spec. Legg.* p. 191
ἡ ἐν ἀποκρύφῳ καὶ πρὸς ὀλίγους ἀπόδοσις. *De Abrah.* § 29.

How complete in Philo's opinion was the superiority of this allegoric sense is seen in the fact that he calls it ὁρατικοῖς φίλη ἀνδράσιν, *De Plantat.* § 9. He says that it is obscure to the many, but is the sense held by the initiated (μύσται) and ἣν οἱ τὰ νοητὰ πρὸ τῶν αἰσθητῶν ἀποδεχόμενοι καὶ ὁρᾶν δυνάμενοι γνωρίζουσιν, *De Abrah.* § 36. He calls Allegory "the wise architect," *De Somn.* ii. § 2. In his view allegory was ἡ πρὸς τὸ ἀληθὲς ἐπινεύουσα ὁδός, and literalism only ἡ πρὸς τὰς νωθεστέρων δόξας.

Arbitrary as was Philo's method, it still *was* a method. It had its own rules (κάνονες τῆς ἀλληγορίας, *De Somn.* i. § 13 ; *De Vict. Offer.* § 5 ; νόμοι τῆς ἀλληγορίας, *De Abrah.* § 15). He quite sincerely believed that he was developing the true sense of Scripture, and after laying down the distinctly Platonic doctrine of Ideas says Μωσέως ἔστι δόγμα οὐκ ἐμόν, *De Opif. Mund.* § 6.

The two *loci classici* for Philo's conceptions of allegory are in the tracts *Quod Deus immutabilis,* § 11, and *De Somn.* i. § 40. In the first he argues from the apparent contradiction between the statements " God is not a man" (Num. xxiii. 19), and " God is as a man" (Deut. i. 31) that God has two methods of instruction, one for "the companions of the soul," and the other for "those who enter into agreements and alliances with the body." In the latter passage he says that to "incorporeal souls" God converses as a friend, whereas he trains the sensuous by condescension and fear. On the expression " God came down " he says, ταῦτα... ἀνθρωπολογεῖται παρὰ τῷ νομοθέτῃ περὶ τοῦ μὴ ἀνθρωπομόρφου Θεοῦ διὰ τὰς τῶν παιδευομένων ἡμῶν ὠφελείας (*De Conf. Ling.* § 27), and that to take it literally would be ὑπερωκεάνιος καὶ μετακόσμιος ἀσέβεια.

His two strongest and plainest statements on the subject are *De Joseph.* § 6, Σχέδον γὰρ τὰ πάντα ἢ τὰ πλεῖστα τῆς νομοθεσίας ἀλληγορεῖται : and *De Spec. Legg.* § 39, τὰ πλεῖστα τῶν ἐν νόμοις σύμβολα φανερὰ ἀφανῶν καὶ ῥητὰ ἀρρήτων. He sometimes puts aside the literal sense entirely, *e.g.* writing on Ecc. vii. 15, he says οὐδὲ γὰρ περὶ ποταμῶν ἐστιν ἱστορίας ἡ παροῦσα σπουδὴ περὶ δὲ τῶν βίων κ.τ.λ. : and, speaking of Sarah and Hagar, he says οὐ γὰρ περὶ γυναικῶν ἐστον ὁ λόγος ἀλλὰ διανοιῶν.

See Dähne, *Alex. Religionsphilos.* i. 49-80.
Siegfried, *Philo,* 160-165.

NOTE V.

PHILO AND MESSIANIC HOPES.

In the lull of persecution and the growth of prosperity among the Alexandrian Jews, the Messianic hopes, which had once been the stay and inspiration of their fathers, seem to have become very conventional and faint.

The word Messiah does not occur in Philo's writings, nor does he even comment on the great Evangelical prophecies. When he alludes to those which occur in the Pentateuch, it is only to minimise their Messianic significance.

Thus in his *Legis Allegoriae* (iii. §§ 63-70), he gives a truly deplorable specimen of exegesis on Gen. iii. 15. The enmity between the woman and the serpent is the conflict between pleasure and sense, passion and mind. His extraordinary comment on "It ($\alpha\vec{v}\tau\dot{o}s$) shall bruise ($\tau\eta\rho\dot{\eta}\sigma\epsilon\iota$) thy head, and thou shalt bruise his heel," is that the expression is a barbarism, but that this is corrected by the significance. For he says that the "he" ($\alpha\vec{v}\tau\dot{o}s$) refers to the woman, and should therefore be $\alpha\vec{v}\tau\dot{\eta}$. But, he says, Moses has passed from the woman to the seed, and its principle which is "mind" ($vo\hat{v}s$) and therefore masculine. The "mind" shall bruise, or following the ordinary meaning of the word in the LXX. "shall observe," the head (*i.e.* the predominant doctrine) of pleasure, and thou shalt observe the steps of the mind, and the supporter of things which please it, to which the "heels" are naturally likened. Going on to comment on the curious phrase of the LXX. ($\tau\eta\rho\dot{\eta}\sigma\epsilon\iota$) [1] he says that it may mean either "shall guard" ($\delta\iota\alpha\sigma\dot{\omega}\sigma\epsilon\iota$, $\delta\iota\alpha\phi\upsilon\lambda\dot{\alpha}\xi\epsilon\iota$) or "shall watch with a view to destruction." The former applies to the worthless mind which treasures up pleasures, and the latter to the earnest mind, which looks out for the attacks of pleasure, and tries to destroy it : and then follows a digressive allegorical illustration about Jacob. It will be seen at once that there is no Messianism here, and that in the hands of Philo the passage loses its profound and far-reaching significance, and is evaporated into moral platitudes.

So again with the marvellous promise to Abraham, "And in thy seed shall all the nations of the earth be blessed." This is what Philo has to say upon it in *De Somniis* (i. § 29). " This prophecy," he says, " accords with what is true both to a man individually and in his relation to others. For if my own inward mind be purified by perfect

[1] On the possible origin and meaning of this rendering, I must content myself with a reference to Schleusner, *s.v.*

virtue, and the tribes of the earthly around me are also swept away, namely my natural senses, and if any one in a family, or city, or country, or nation has become a lover of prudences, then the family, and country, and nation necessarily enjoys a better life. For just as odorous substance diffuses its sweet aroma to all who come near it, so all who are neighbours of the wise are bettered in character as they breathe the outpoured fragrancy." This may be a poetic commonplace, but all the glowing Messianic element of the most glorious of the Jewish hopes has disappeared.

It is quite clear that Philo in no sense identifies the Messiah with the Logos. There is an allusion to national victories under some great coming leader in *De Proemiis* (§ 16), and to the share of heathen proselytes in Jewish blessings in *De Execrationibus,* § 6.

Did Philo ever see Jesus? It is just possible that he did, for he tells us in his book on "Providence" (Aucher, ii. 107) that he once visited Jerusalem and there offered a sacrifice. But if he saw Christ he knew nothing of Him, and he rejected the very possibility of an Incarnation as a mere hypothetical absurdity which could hardly be even thought of without impiety. For in condemning the insane attempt of the Emperor Gaius to place a colossal statue of himself in the Temple of Jerusalem, he calls it "the gravest impiety" to liken the uncreated and incorruptible God to the created and corruptible nature of men, and adds by way of scornful parenthesis or *reductio ad absurdum,* θᾶττον γὰρ εἰς ἄνθρωπον θεὸν ἢ εἰς θεὸν ἄνθρωπον μεταβαλεῖν.[1]

---

[1] On this and other questions connected with Philo's theology there is an interesting sermon by Professor (now Bishop) Wordsworth "On Jewish Interpretation of Messianic Prophecy," preached before the University of Oxford in March, 1880.

LECTURE IV.

1. The asserted unworthiness of the letter.

"Historia simplex sed alta mysteria ; aliud enim gerebatur, aliud figurabatur; *quia litteralis sensus indignus est.*" Ambr. *De Fide.*

"Ubi materia vel turpitudinem habeat vel impossibilitatem ad altiora transmittimur."—Jer. *in Matt.* xxi. 4.

"Quidquid in sermone divino *neque ad morum honestatem, neque ad fidei veritatem proprie referri potest,* figuratum esse cognoscas." Aug. *De Doctr. Christ.* iii. § 13.

2. The unwarranted extension of isolated expressions to the whole Scriptures.

Jerome, after quoting Ps. lxxviii. 2, says, "*Ex quo* intelligimus *universa quae scripta sunt* parabolice sentienda, nec manifestum tantum sonare litteram sed abscondita sacramenta." *In Matt.* xiii. 35.

3. Entire misapplication of the verse, "*The letter killeth,* but the Spirit giveth life" 2 Cor. iii. 6).

This verse is quoted times without number by the Fathers and Schoolmen. It is obvious that if by "the letter" were meant "the literal sense," St. Paul would have been condemning the literal sense altogether as being of a fatal tendency. The context shows the meaning to be that the Law has nothing to say, but to threaten death to transgressors : or else that the Law, taken alone, causes first sin and then death (Rom. vii. 10 *fg.*).

4. The notion that all senses (within the limits of the Christian faith) are applicable because they must have been foreseen by the Spirit ; this argument would cover and justify all the divergences of all the Christian sects.

"Ille quippe auctor in eisdem verbis quae intelligere volumus, et ipsam sententiam forsitan vidit, *et certe Dei Spiritus* . . etiam ipsam occursuram lectori praevidit, immo ut occurreret . . sine dubitatione *providit.*" Aug. *De Doctr. Christ.* iii. p. 32.

This astonishing assumption is repeated by Cocceius (see the passage quoted in Lecture VII., and recently by Dr. Pusey).

5. The supposed use of allegory by St. Paul.

6. Passages adduced as sanctioning allegoric interpretation. Every passage which can by any possibility be pressed into such a conclusion is given by Sixtus Senensis, in his *Bibliotheca Sancta,* and by Waterland, Preface to *Scripture Vindicated.* In various passages of these Lectures I have shown their want of validity. Sixtus Senensis clearly shows that allegory is the result, not of loyalty to Scripture, but of radical disloyalty to it as it is, in such remarks as the following. He says that to take Scripture literally is inevitably "contaminari et inquinari Judaicis institutis ;" that it involves the duty of keeping the Ceremonial Law, "caeterasque Hebraeorum umbras quae jam illucescente Evangelii luce evanuerunt." If we take the Old Testament literally we shall have no answer when men ask, "Cur Deus dederit tam absurdas leges—amputare praeputii pelliculam, occidere agnum, &c., sanguine beluino cuncta foedare, gerere paxillum in balteo et egesta humo felium more proprii corporis excrementa contigere," &c. He adds the remarkable words " *Videbuntur nobis omnia insipida, agrestia, insana, et prorsus divina majestate indigna esse, quae Deus* praecipit de agno, de ariete, de bove," &c. " Quid enim ad salutem juvat scire antiquorum Judaeorum bella et seditiones, si in eis nihil aliud quam strages et effusiones sanguinis intelligimus ? "

Thus in Aqiba ; in Philo ; in Jerome, Augustine, Hilary, and most of the Fathers ; in Bede ; in Albertus, and most of the Schoolmen ; and even in writers who, like Sixtus Senensis, wrote late in the seventeenth century (1666), we see a repetition of the same traditional devices for getting rid of "difficulties" which only originate in a totally false conception of God's progressive revelation. Allegory was used to force Scripture into accordance with men's *à priori* conceptions. The Bible is treated as a sovereign who, being declared by his courtiers to be of divine origin and supreme authority, is yet reduced to a *Roi fainéant,* and made at all costs to speak their language and obey their behests.

LECTURE V.

NOTE I.

MEDIAEVAL JEWISH COMMENTATORS.

The golden age of Jewish interpretation was between A.D. 900-1500. It began with R. Saadia Gaon, and continued till Isaak Abravanel. The chief writers on Scripture flourished in Africa, Spain, France, Germany, and Italy. The fresh impulse came from the Arabian scholars, as in former days it had come from the Greek philosophers.[1]

R. Saadia Gaon (A.D. 892-942) was called "the pioneer of the Exegetes," and his merits were so great that Maimonides said, "The sense of the Law would have been quite lost had not R. Saadiah come forth to reveal what was hidden, and to establish what was being weakened." He turned his attention to the Language, the Interpretation, and the Teaching of Scripture. He often refers to the Targum, the Mishna, and the analogy of Arabic words. Like Josephus and Philo, he endeavours to remove the more startling elements of Scripture, and explains the speaking both of the serpent to Eve, and of the ass to Balaam metaphorically. He points out that the rainbow could not have been first created after the Deluge, but merely *taken as a sign*. He rejected, however, the naturalistic explanation of miracles suggested by his contemporaries Chamiel and Ha Kalbi, and also the allegoric explanations of the Karaites. He said, "We have two sources of knowledge beside the Bible, namely, the Understanding, and Tradition." He found an acute opponent in the Karaite Salmon ben Jerocham, and in Joseph ben Jacob, whose book, *The Great Light*, written in A.D. 930, is still valued.

Saadia is the author of the oldest extant Philosophy of Religion, a system of Faith and Morals (אמונות ודעות) of which the third section treats "Of the Revelation of God's Word, and the Eternal Validity of the Law." In writing this work he set the excellent example of familiarising himself with the philosophical writings and translations

---

[1] I have referred to Wolf, *Bibl. Hebraica*, i. 337, *sq.*, iii. 599, *sq.* ; Buddeus, *Isagoge*, p. 1446, *sq.* ; Wogue, *Hist. de la Bible* (Paris, 1881) ; Löw, *Prakt. Einleitung*, &c.

of the Arabians. He was "a fruit of the Jewish soil, modified by grafts from the Arabian garden," [1] A.D. 980.

The grammatical and philosophic gains of the Jews in Africa and Eastern Asia were introduced into Spain by the happy accident of the shipwreck of Moses "clad in sackcloth." [2]

The first pre-eminent name of mediaeval Jewish exegesis is that of R. Solomon ben Jizchak of Troyes, born in 1040, and best known as RASHI. [3] He died in 1105. His Midrashic comment on the Law was long a standard book among the Jews. It was the first Hebrew book which was printed (at Reggio, Feb. 5, 1470), and has been translated into German by L. Dukes. It had a powerful influence over Nicolas of Lyra, and indirectly over Luther.

Saadia had written in Arabic, Rashi wrote in Hebrew. Saadia, influenced by the Karaites, built primarily upon the literal sense ; Rashi was untouched by Karaite opinions, and is not troubled by the divergence of the Midrash from the simple sense. Saadia strove to remove objections to the Bible narrative ; Rashi absolutely ignores them. Saadia has scientific digressions : Rashi abides by the text, sometimes furnishing the literal explanation, and sometimes adding passages of the Midrashim. He was not wholly uninfluenced by the reactions in favour of literal and grammatical exegesis, but on the whole he adheres to traditional views. [4]

The commentaries of RASHBAM (R. Samuel ben Meier, † 1167), the grandson of Rashi, show a great advance in the abandonment of Midrashic lore for a literal and grammatical interpretation. [5]

JUDA HA-LEVI, the author of the celebrated *Khozari*, flourished A.D. 1140. [6] He headed the reaction against extraneous philosophical influences.

Not less illustrious than Rashi was R. Abraham IBN EZRA (Rabe), born 1092, [7] and famous for his scientific discoveries no less than for his Scriptural commentaries on almost the whole of the Old Testament. It was his one object to develop, grammatically and historically, the literal sense. He disliked the allegoric method. Previous exegetes had

[1] Jost, *Judenth.* ii. 279 ; Weill, *Le Judaïsme,* passim ; Munk, *Mélanges,* 477 *sq.* ; Ewald und Dukes, *Beiträge zur Gesch. d. ältesten Auslegung in Spracherklärung d. Alten Testamentes.* Stuttgart, 1844.

[2] See Milman, *Hist. of the Jews,* iii. 147.

[3] Often incorrectly called Jarchi. A life of him has been published by Bloch, 1840. See too Jost, *Gesch. d. Judenthums.* His comment on Genesis has been translated into German by Haymann.

[4] As, for instance, in his commentary on Koheleth. See Ginsburg, p. 38.

[5] *Id.* p. 43. Dr. Ginsburg gives valuable specimens of these Jewish commentators.

[6] See Munk, *Mélanges,* 485 *sq.*

[7] See Grätz, *Gesch.* vi. 198 *fg.* ; 440, *fg.*

chosen, he said, five different paths.[1] 1. Some, like Saadia, mingled
alien scientific digressions with their comments. 2. Others, like Anan,
rejected Tradition. 3. Some were addicted to Allegories. 4. Some
followed the Midrash. 5. Some, to whom he himself belongs, sought
the simple grammatical sense.[2] We see in his commentaries that
difficulties required entirely new solutions, as allegory was abandoned.
Thus both in Ibn Ezra and in the Zohar an attempt is made to get rid
of the numerous apparent contradictions in the Book of Ecclesiastes by
the supposition that they represent the hypothetical or actual remarks of
others and not of Solomon.

MAIMONIDES. R. Mo3e ben Maimon, born in 1135, belonged to one
of the Jewish families which had been nominally compelled to embrace
Mohammedanism, and till the age of sixteen he was a professed Mussul-
man. He attained to a position of the highest honour, and left a deep
impress on the Jewish mind, although the teachings of himself and his
followers were for a century resisted with the utmost vehemence.
Fanatical Rabbis charged him with "selling Holy Scriptures to the
Greeks," and even tried to use the Inquisition to put him down.[3]

The great work which he accomplished in his *Moreh Nebuchim*
(*Doctor Perplexorum*) was to establish the right of free examination as
against the absolute principle of authority. He held that there were
branches of knowledge which were independent of faith, and that in
passages which touched on these the literal sense of Scripture was to be
allegorically explained. To counteract this view Abraham ben Dior,
in his book of the Qabbala, inserted a list of all the eminent teachers
who had received the "tradition" from the days of Adam down to his
own.[4] Maimonides assigned to Aristotle unconditional authority in all
matters not connected with religion, and "by giving prominence to the
spiritual and moral ideas of Judaism, he exerted on all Jewish theology
a salutary, and, in spite of violent reaction, a permanent influence."
He died in 1204.[5]

[1] So Algarrati divided "the sects of the faithful" into four classes :--
i. The Dogmatists. ii. The Allegorists (*Bastînîs*). iii. The Philosophers, or
Logicians. iv. The Soufis, or Mystics.
[2] He was one of the first Jewish writers to adopt Aristotelian methods.
Though unacquainted with the works of Philo, he attaches great mystic
importance to numbers. His style is far from easy, and his system has
recently been explained by Krochmal. His admirable commentary on Isaiah
has been translated by Friedländer. (Lond. 1873.)
[3] On Maimonides see Munk's edition of the "*Moreh Nebuchim*," and
Franck in *Dict. des Sciences philos.* iv. 31.
[4] See Schwab, *Berachoth, Introd.* p. xiv.
[5] "C'est par la lecture du *Guide* que les plus grands génies des Juifs
Modernes, les Spinoza, les Mendelssohn, les Salomon Maimon et beaucoup
d'autres ont été introduits dans le sanctuaire de la philosophie." Munk,
Mélanges, 487.

The Jews partake incontestably with the Arabs the glory of having preserved and propagated philosophy in ages of barbarism, and so of having exercised for a time a civilising influence over the European world.[1]

The family of THE QIMCHIS of Narbonne—R. Joseph Qimchi and his two sons, R. David and R. Moses—rendered the highest services to Hebrew philology, and to the natural interpretation of the Bible. So highly was the grammar of David Qimchi valued that the Jews applied to him a proverb from the Mishna, " Where there is no Qimchi, there is no knowledge of the Law."[2]

The revival of Kabbalism by R. Moses ben Nachman (Nachmanides) sometimes called Ramban (born 1194) was partly due to the inevitable reaction against a cold, historic, and rationalising exegesis.

To this epoch, according to some, belongs the Zohar, a Kabbalistic Midrash on the Pentateuch, founded on the Talmud, the Midrashim, and the works of Ibn Gebirol, Ibn Ezra, and others.

R. Joseph Albo (✝ 1444), the author of the *Sepher Ikkarim,* is chiefly known as a theologian. He followed the Midrash, but in a tasteful and philosophic manner.

Abravanel (Don Isaak ben Judah Abravanel), born in 1437 at Lisbon, was one of the Jews who were banished from Spain in 1492 by the brutal and suicidal decree of Ferdinand. He was eminent as a commentator, and made free use of Christian writings. His special characteristics were that : 1. He shook off the fetters of Aristotelianism. 2. He rejected Kabbalism. 3. He returned to the neglected grammatical methods of the Qimchis and R. Levi ben Gerson (Ralbag). 4. He brought his wide experience of life as a traveller and statesman to bear on the historical books. 5. Though he did not possess the works of R. Tanchum, who had been the first to write a general introduction to the sacred books, he paid special attention to Hermeneutics, pointing out the times and circumstances in which books were written.[3]

Elias Levita (✝ 1549), the teacher of bishops and cardinals, wrote grammatical treatises, which are so highly valued that R. Simon urged all who desired to know Hebrew to study them. He is highly praised by Gesenius, and his book on the Massora has been translated into English by Dr. Ginsburg.

---

[1] Munk, *Mélanges,* 511.

[2] The word קמֹחת means "meal," and the phrase originally meant that men cannot study the Law when they are starving. Dr. McCaul has translated David Qimchi's *Commentary on Zechariah* (Lond. 1837).

[3] See Grätz, *Gesch.* viii. 334 ; ix. 6.

NOTE II.

TITLES OF THE SCHOOLMEN.[1]

Baeda.	Venerabilis.
Anselm of Laon.	Doctor Scholasticus.
St. Thomas Aquinas.	Doctor Angelicus *and* Communis.
St. Bonaventura.	Doctor Seraphicus.
Alexander of Hales.	Doctor Irrefragabilis.
Albertus Magnus.	Doctor Universalis.
Franciscus de Mayronis.	Doctor Illuminatissimus.
Roger Bacon.	Doctor Mirabilis.
William Varro de Anglia.	Doctor Fundatus.
Aegidius of Colonna.	Doctor Fundatissimus *and* Princeps. Theologorum.
Hugo de Sto. Victore.	Didascalus.
Joannes Baconthorpius.	Doctor Resolutus.
Durandus.	Doctor Resolutissimus.
Peter Lombard.	Magister Sententiarum.
William of Champeaux.	Columna doctorum.
St. Bernard.	Doctor Mellifluus.
Nicolas of Lyra.	Doctor Planus et Perspicuus.
John Bradwardine.	Doctor Profundus.
Petrus Aureolis.	Doctor Facundus, *or* Abundans.
William of Occam.	Doctor Singularis et Invincibilis *and* Venerabilis Inceptor.
Duns Scotus.	Doctor Subtilis.
Henry of Ghent.	Doctor Solemnis.
Jean Gerson.	Doctor Christianissimus.
Wiclif.	Doctor Evangelicus.
Dionysius of Rickel.	Doctor Ecstaticus.
John Wessel.	Lux Mundi, *and* Magister Contradictionis.

[1] See Heumann, *Act. Philos.* iii. 921 ; Brucker, *Hist. Philos.* iii. 889, and *passim.*

H H

NOTE III.

ORIGIN OF SCHOLASTICISM.

The precursor, though not the founder, of Scholasticism, was St. John of Damascus. His book, *Fons Scientiae* (πηγὴ γνώσεως), consists of three parts :—1. *Capita Philosophica.* 2. *De Haeresibus.* 3. *Expositio accurata Fidei orthodoxae.* This third part is "one of the most important works that have come down to us from Christian antiquity." For it is the first complete "Body of Divinity" that we possess, and as such has had an influence that cannot easily be measured on the theology of the West. It was made known to the Latin Church by the version of Burgundio of Pisa in 1150. The statement that Peter Lombard had this version before him when preparing his Book of the Sentences "thus becomes quite probable. Without, therefore, taking account of Aquinas, whose indebtedness to the work of Damascenus is admittedly great, we have here a visible link of connection between the Eastern Church and the Western." [1]

"It is chiefly as a framer of systems that we are indebted to him. . . Making theology a part of philosophy, as Aristotle had done before him, he applied to it a philosophic method. Taking for his basis the existence of God . . he organises, step by step, the whole body of religion and Christian truth. He is thus the progenitor of Scholasticism. Though the proposition has been disputed as an exercise of scholastic skill, it is the all but unanimous verdict that the great treatise on the 'Orthodox Faith' was the starting-point of the Scholastic system which afterwards grew to such dimensions in the West." [2]

There is, however, no proof that the *earliest* Schoolmen were acquainted with the *Fides Orthodoxa* of the Damascene. It was first translated by the order of Pope Eugenius III. in 1143. From the time of Peter Lombard it became a favourite authority of the "school authors." [3] The Calvinists in later days reproached Melanchthon for having imitated it, and even Luther said of him, "*Nimium philosophatur.*" [4]

Some date the beginning of Scholasticism from John Scotus Erigena. [5]

[1] See Lupton, *St. John of Damascus*, pp. 65–88 ; Rémusat, *Abélard*, ii. 158.
[2] Lupton, p. 211, who refers to Dr. Gérando, *Hist. Comp.* iv. 159.
[3] Tribbechovius, *De Doct. Schol.* p. 280.
[4] Buddeus, *Isag.* p. 319 ; Lequien, *Opp. Joann. Damasc.* Praef. p. 5.
[5] See R. L. Poole, *Mediaev. Thought*, p. 76. He was "the father of Nominalism," and greatly influenced Gilbert de la Porrée.

Others date the beginning of Scholasticism from Lanfranc or Anselm.[1]

Others from Peter Lombard.[2]

Others from Alexander of Hales.[3]

Others from Albertus Magnus.[4]

The truest view seems to be that given in the text, that Scholasticism proper began with the conflicts between traditionalism and free inquiry. Scholastic philosophy began with Roscelin, and Scholastic theology with Abelard. Such is the view of Tribbechovius. Trithemius says of Abelard, " Ab hoc tempore philosophia secularis sacram theologiam sua curiositate inutili foedare coepit."[5]

One secret of Abelard's influence was his lucidity. John of Salisbury says, " Non enim occasio quaerenda est ingerendae difficultatis sed ubique facilitas generanda. *Quem morem secutum recolo Peripateticum Palatinum ;*[6] . . . rerum intellectui serviebat."[7]

Deriving the Scholastic philosophy from the sentence of Porphyry preserved in the Latin translation of Boethius, which stated the question as to the nature of genera (εἴδη), Cousin places its *infancy* from the eleventh to the thirteenth century, when the University of Paris was organised ; its *manhood* from the thirteenth to the fifteenth, when the great Universities and the religious orders were flourishing ; and its *decline* from the fifteenth to the end of the sixteenth.[8] As a *philosophy* it turned entirely on the difference between realism and nominalism. Its theology furnishes the singular spectacle of a realist and Platonising spirit expressing itself in a dialectic and Aristotelian form. There was more real independence and originality in Scholasticism during its infancy, before all the works of Aristotle were translated into Latin, than afterwards ; but in all its epochs there was nothing absolutely

---

[1] Danaeus, *Prolegom. in Lombardi Sent.* p. 18. *Sententiae* had, however, been written before his day by Gilbert de la Porrée, and others.

[2] Calixtus, *Apparat.* p. 143 ; Aventinus, *Annal.* vi. ; Baur, *Dogmengesch.* p. 156 ; Kling in Herzog's *Encykl. s.v.*

[3] Chemnitz, *c. Conc. Trident.* p. 371.

[4] "Albertus et similes, qui dediti fuerant doctrinae Aristotelis, transformare Ecclesiae doctrinam in Philosophiam coeperunt."—Melanchthon, *Vit. Lutheri,* c. xiii.

[5] Trithemius, *De Script. Eccles.* p. 161 (Coloniae, 1546) ; Thomasius, *Hist. Sap. et Stult.* iii. 23 ; Cent. Magdeburg, p. 148 ; Victor Cousin, *Ouvr. inéd. d'Abélard,* Introd. p. iii. " C'est l'invention d'un nouveau système philosophique et l'application de ce système et en général de la philosophie à la théologie . . . c'est Abélard qui l'érigea en principe ; c'est donc lui qui contribua le plus à fonder la scolastique." Cousin calls Descartes the destroyer of this system and the founder of modern philosophy.

[6] This is the name which John of Salisbury repeatedly gives to Abelard. It means " the dialectician of Palais,"—the place where Abelard was born.

[7] *Metalog.* iii. 1.

[8] V. Cousin, *Ouvr. inéd. d'Ab.* p. lxv.

original. " Advance is measured less by the power with which men used their intellects, than by the skill with which they used their materials."[1]

NOTE IV.

THE " SIC ET NON " OF ABELARD.

When William of St. Thierry wrote to complain to St. Bernard of Abelard's theology, he had only heard a rumour about the *Sic et Non.* " Sunt autem," he says, " *ut audio* adhuc alia ejus opuscula quorum nomina sunt *Sic et Non, Scito teipsum,* et alia quaedam de quibus timeo ne, sicut monstruosi sunt nominis, sic etiam sint monstruosi dogmatis ; *sed, sicut dicunt, oderunt lucem, nec etiam quaesita inveniuntur.*"[2]

Such was the terror which the book inspired that this is said to be the only mention of the *Sic et Non* in the middle ages.

Martène and Durand found a copy of it at St. Germain, but did no dare to publish it for fear of scandal. They say that, in it, Abelard " genio suo indulgens omnia Christianae religionis mysteria in utramque partem versat, negans quod asseruerat et asserens quod negaverat." Their colleague Dachery after careful study of it " *aeternis tenebris* potius quam luce dignum existimavit."[3]

Little or nothing was known of it until it was published by M. Victor Cousin in the *Ouvrages inédits d'Abélard,* 1836.

It deals with the subjects which formed the basis of Abelard's theology. He quotes from Augustine, Jerome, Ambrose, Hilary, Isidore, Gregory, and Bede ; but being very superficially acquainted with Greek, he refers but little to Greek Fathers and only to those whose works had been translated into Latin. He also quotes from Aristotle, Boethius, Seneca, Cicero, and once from Ovid and Prudentius.

Three things are specially observable in the *Sic et Non* besides the singular boldness of the general plan.

I. One is the audacious statement of the questions considered ; such as,

> Q. 6. Quod sit Deus tripartitus ? et contra.
> Q. 14. Quod sit Filius sine principio ? et contra.
> Q. 63. Quod Filius Dei mutatus sit suscipiendo carnem ? et contra.
> Q. 35. Quod nihil fiat Deo nolente ? et contra.

---

[1] Lane, *Illustrations of Med. Thought,* p. 2.   [2] *Ap.* S. Bern. *Opp.* i. 301.
[3] *Praef. ad Thes. Nov. Anecd.* t. iv.

The twenty-third question, *Quod philosophi quoque Trinitatem seu verbum Dei crediderint? et non*, indicates the favourable view of heathen philosophy which was so suspicious to St. Bernard [1] who still shared the spirit shown by Tertullian's remark, *Haereticorum patriarchae philosophi*.[2] This with his anti-realism was the base of Bernard's tremendous indictment of his theology, "Cum de Trinitate loquitur sapit Arium, cum de gratia sapit Pelagium, cum de persona Christi sapit Nestorium." [3] Yet John of Salisbury, a man of unreproached orthodoxy, calls him "*Abaelardus noster*," speaks of him constantly with praise and affection, and adopted his conceptualism ; and it was the *Sic et Non* which gave the original conception of the famous *Liber Sententiarum.*

II. The distinct formulation of Aristotle's view, that doubt leads to discussion, and discussion to truth, "*Dubitando enim ad inquisitionem venimus, inquirendo veritatem percipimus,*" which Abelard very precariously compares with "Seek and ye shall find."

III. The anticipation of modern criticism in the passages in which he deals with the difficulties of Scripture interpretation, *e.g.* the apparent contradictions, the corruption of the text, the number of spurious writings, the ignorance of copyists, the danger of confusing comments with the text, and the differences of sense which may be attached to the same word.

NOTE V.

THE ABUSE OF "PARALLEL PASSAGES."

The use of allegory was largely eked out by the juxtaposition of similar expressions from different books. Scholastic exegesis consisted mainly of "glossarial annotations, groaning beneath the burden of numberless unsifted examples and parallel passages." We have already seen that when this led to the habit of educing parallels derived only from translations it was a most unsatisfactory method.

The amazing extent to which the principle was used may be seen in such a comment as that of Prosper of Aquitaine on the Tabernacle. He says that the joining of the sides indicated that mercy and truth were met together ; the goat's hair curtains the penitence of the world ; and the fact that there were eleven curtains has reference to the eleventh Psalm (the twelfth in our version) which begins " Help, Lord " ! [4]

---

[1] *Ep. ad Papam Innocent.* Opp. i. 650.
[3] Opp. i. 185.
[2] Tert. *adv. Hermog.* 8.
[4] *De Promiss.* ii. 2.

The custom of crowding the margin of "reference Bibles" with passages supposed to be illustrative has been greatly overdone. In the Bible of 1611 there were about 9000 ; these by gradual accretion have mounted to nearly 63,000. Large numbers were added by Dr. Paris (1768), Dr. Blayney (1769), Canne (1747), Crutwell (1785), Clarke (1810), and Scott (1822). They need the stringent revision which they have received in the Cambridge Paragraph Bible. Some of them are hopelessly wrong ; some are founded on sheer mistakes ; others are misprints; others are only parallels in the English phrase, but not in the Greek or Hebrew original ; others again are frivolous, irrelevant, questionable, or even untrue, and in some of these instances they become positively misleading. How suggestive and truly illustrative they may often be when they are well chosen, may be seen in the *Commentary wholly Biblical.*

For some very interesting particulars about the marginal references of our version, see Dr. Scrivener's *Authorised Version of the English Bible,* (Cambr. 1884) pp. 116-127.

NOTE VI.

OPINIONS ON SCHOLASTICISM.

Favourable judgments of Scholasticism are not easily to be found. I may however refer (merely by way of example) to—

Hooker, *Answer to Travers,* 16 (who refers to Calvin's *Instit.* i. 16, § 9.
Pearson, *Opera Minora* (ed. Churton, i. 1).
Newman, *Lectures on Univ. subjects,* p. 282.
Rémusat, *Abélard,* i. 289.

Unfavourable views of Scholasticism are very numerous and very weighty. See by way of specimens—

Lud. Vives, *De Corrupt. Art.* iii.
Cornel. Agrippa, *De Vanitat. Scient.* 8.
Bacon, *Advancement of Learning.*
Melanchthon, *Vit. Lutheri,* c. xiii.
Luther, *passim.*
Tribbechovius, *De Doctoribus Scholasticis* (1665).
Brucker, *Hist. Philos.* iii. 709.
Wetstein, *Praef. in N. Test.,* ed. 3.
Hallam, *Middle Ages,* ii. 485-489.
G. H. Lewes, *Biogr. Hist. of Philosophy,* 291.
Renan, *Souvenirs,* xiv.

LECTURE VI.

NOTE I.

"Respectu Patrum vermis sum; attamen quo magis illorum scripta lego eo plus offendor. Nam res ipsa clamat eos homines fuisse et ipsorum auctoritas Apostolorum scripta oppressit. Attamen Papistae audent Scripturam sacram obscuram blasphemare, quasi Patres eam declarare debent; sed ita declarare est obscurare." Aurifaber, *Colloqu.* ii. 235 (ed. 1571).

"Observate quaeso quantae tenebrae fuerunt apud Patres de doctrinâ fidei. *Hieronymus* supra Matthaeum, Galatas et ad Titum frigidosissime scripsit. *Ambrosius* sex libros super Genesim. Quam exiguus hominum intellectus! Nullus fere commentarius in Epp. ad Romanos et Galatas aliquid sincere tradit."

On reading *Cyprian* he sighed, "Mirabatur tanti viri ineptias, dubitans utrum ille liber sit Cypriani; sed non est mirum, nam si Dei verbum relinquimus, tunc omnibus offendiculis nos involvimus."

He was very unjust to *Chrysostom*, of whom he says, "Multos splendidos composuit libros, sed tantum fuit chaos et saccus verborum." He calls him "seditiosus et garrulus," and adds, "Ideo Erasmo placet, qui negligit fidem et tantum moralia tradit." He quotes the remark of Schurff, who, after purchasing and reading the works of Chrysostom, said "Multa lego, nihil disco."

He had a strong prejudice against *Jerome*. "Scripsit xii. libros super Genesim, et tamen vix dimidium capitis primi pertractat." "Nihil de Christo tractat nisi quod nomine utitur. Tantum de virginitate, jejuniis, cibis scripsit."

He remarks generally, "Patres habuerunt magnam auctoritatem, et interim facta est injuria bibliorum. Ambrosius, Basilius sunt frigidi et Gregorius Nazianzanus accusatur quod . . . nihil sincere de Deo scripsit. Spiritus Sanctus non patitur ut verbis et larvis obligetur." *Colloqu.* ii. 159.

NOTE II.

Porphyry in the third century had asserted "that the Apostles in their references to the Old Testament had abused the simplicity and ignorance of their readers." Jerome replies that they had done nothing of the kind, but that they strengthened the facts of the present by the testimonies of the past, by spiritually applying to Christ's first coming the promises which the Jews applied carnally to His second coming. But we find in few ancient authors anything like a clear conception of the "argument from prophecy." Calvin has expressed himself more boldly on this subject than any other theologian, and has not sufficiently guarded himself by any adequate statement of the true conception of the Messianic prophecies.

The following are some of his notes.

Matt. ii. 15. "Perinde sit hoc nobis extra controversiam locum (Hos. xi. 1) non debere ad Christum restringi. Neque tamen a Matthaeo torquetur, sed *scite aptatur* ad praesentem causam."

Matt. ii. 23. "Tantum est allusio."

Matt. viii. 17. "Quod apud Jesaiam (Is. liii. 4) de animae vitiis dici certum est, Matthaeus ad corporales morbos *transfert*."

John xix. 37. Locum hunc (Zech. xii. 10), qui secundum literam de Christo exponere conantur, nimis violenter *torquent.* Nec vero in hunc finem ab evangelista citatur ; sed potius ut ostendat Christum esse deum illum, qui olim conquestus fuit per Zechariam, sibi pectus a Judaeis transfodi."

Heb. iv. 4. "Jam locum illum quem citaverat ex Davide exornare incipit ; hactenus eum tractavit secundum litteram, hunc autem expoliendo amplificat, *ideoque alludit magis ad verba Davidis quam interpretatur.* Ejusmodi ἐπεξεργασία est apud Paulum ad Rom. x. 6."

Heb. xi. 21. "Quod vulgo receptum erat Apostolus non dubitat suo instituto accommodare. Judaeis quidem scribebat sed qui . . . patriam linguam Graeca mutaverant. *Scimus autem hac in parte Apostolos non adeo fuisse scrupulosos.*"

LECTURE VIII.

SOME EXEGETIC RULES AND PRINCIPLES.[1]

1. *Everything essential in Scripture is clearly revealed.*

   πάντα τὰ ἀναγκαῖα δῆλα. Chrys. *Comm. in* 2 *Thess.*

   This rule is our chief source of consolation amid the endless perplexities of divergent interpretation. If a truth be essential to salvation, it must appear clearly on the pages which contain a Divine Revelation : otherwise the Revelation would not be a Revelation. The preceding clause of St. Chrysostom, πάντα σαφῆ καὶ εὐθέα τὰ παρὰ ταῖς θείαις γραφαῖς, is not true. It is belied by the whole history of exegesis, which in different ages has come to opposite conclusions about matters of much importance.

2. *The true sense can only be decided by the original.*

   Very numerous errors, often perpetuated for long periods, have arisen from reliance on current versions. They prove the necessity for not depending on translations, whether the LXX., the Vulgate, the German, the Rheims, and Douay, or the Anglican. Even when a rendering is literally correct, it may in some cases connote a very different order of thought from that originally intended.

   " *Impossibile est quod proprietas unius linguae servetur in alia.*" Roger Bacon (*Opus majus,* iii. 1 ; quoting Jerome, " si ad verbum interpretor, absurdum est ").

3. *Every doctrine and every inference drawn from any passage must be deduced from the literal sense.*

   "Omnes sensus fundantur super unum, scilicet literalem ; *ex quo solo potest trahi* argumentum, non autem ex his quae secundum allegoriam dicuntur. Nec tamen Scripturae idcirco aliquid deperit quia nihil sub spirituali sensu continetur fidei necessarium, quod

---

[1] The word "*Hermeneutic*" implies the Science and Theory, the word *Exegesis* the Art and Practice of Scriptural Interpretation. See Lücke, *Grundriss,* p. 6 ; Wollius, *Introd. in Hermeneuticam,* p. 36 ; Semler, *Hermen. Vorbereit.* 26. The distinction is merely one of usage, for the words ἑρμηνεία and ἐξήγησις imply no such difference.

Scripturae non alicubi per literalem sensum manifeste tradant."
Thomas Aquinas, *Summa* I. Qu. 2, art. 10.

"Si litera tollitur Scriptura quid est? Lege ergo Scripturam et
disce primum diligenter quae corporaliter narrat." Hugo de Sto
Victore.

This is incomparably more true than the sentiment quoted by
Johannes Sarisb., " Litera inutilis est, nec curandum quid loquatur "
(*Polycrat.* vii. 12) ; but it must be added that neither Hugo de
Sto Victore nor many others who enunciated this axiom made any
real use of it.

It is true that John of Salisbury places the sentence about the
uselessness of the letter among the "ineptiae nugatorum," but at
the close of the same chapter he half endorses their views.

4. *Ignorance of the certain meaning of many passages must be freely
admitted.*

לַמֵּד לִשׁוֹנְךָ לְאָמֹר אֵינֶנִּי יוֹדֵעַ. " *Teach thy tongue to say 'I do
not know.' "*

I do not remember to have seen this Talmudic rule ever propounded as a principle of exegesis, but it seems to me an extremely
important one. "Melius est," says Augustine, "dubitare de
rebus occultis quam litigare de incertis " (*De Gen. ad litt.* viii. 5).
Thus he frankly confesses that he does not know whom or what
St. Paul meant by the Man of Sin.

5. *Theological conclusions cannot be founded on the language of metaphor
and parable.*

" Theologica parabolica non est demonstrativa."

"Pium quidem posse esse sensum allegoriae sed nunquam para-
bolas et dubiam aenigmatum intelligentiam ad auctoritatem dogmatum posse proficere." Jer. *in Matt.* xiii.

This rule, if properly attended to, would have cut away by the
roots a large number of the spurious inferences of which the
commentaries of all ages furnish many specimens. St. Augustine
insisted on this rule when arguing against the Donatists, but he
often neglects it himself. "Quis autem nisi impudentissime nitatur
aliquid in allegoria positum pro se interpretari nisi habeat et mani-
festa testimonia quorum lumine illustrantur obscura?" Aug. *in
Ep.* 48, *ad Vincent.*

6. *Omnis Scriptura sacra eo spiritu debet legi quo scripta est.* Thomas
à Kempis.

This resembles the remark of St. Augustine, That the true sense
of Scripture is Scripture, and no other sense.

7. *Scripture must be interpreted in accordance with the ordinary rules of human language.*

"The law speaks in the tongue of the sons of men."

"Nullo locutionis genere utitur Scriptura quod in consuetudine hominum non inveniatur, quia utique hominibus loquitur." Aug.

"Quaecumque scripta sunt ad nostram doctrinam scripta sunt ; hinc divinae litterae sunt humana capacitate humanoque sermoni accommodata." *Id. de Trin.* i. 12.

This kind of condescension (συγκατάβασις) points to the necessity for Anthropomorphism, Anthropopathy, &c., "just as conversing with barbarians," says Chrysostom, "we make use of their own tongue." The recognition of the truth that the language of Scripture is ordinary language does away with multitudes of spurious inferences in the Talmud, in Philo, in the Fathers, in the Schoolmen, and in modern commentators.

8. "*Distingue tempora et concordabis Scripturas.*" Aug.

These words of St. Augustine are capable of an application far wider than he gave to them. They may be used to express the progressiveness of revelation, and the necessity for interpreting Scripture with reference to the views and morals of the age in which its various books were written. Commentators of all epochs have been compared to the painters who paint Italian cities and customs as the background to Scripture scenes, or surround sacred personages with groups of Dutch burgomasters.

9. *Bias and party spirit are frequent and fatal sources of exegetic error.*

"Vitiosissimum dicendi genus depravare sententias et ad voluntatem suam Scripturam trahere repugnantem." Jerome (*Ep. ad Paulinum*, liii. 7 ; compare *Praef. Comm. in Joann.*, and *Ep.* (lxiv. ad Fabiolam).

"Das ist der beste Lehrer, der seine Meinung nicht in die Schrift, sondern aus der Schrift bringt." Luther (*Werke*, xxxiv. 131, Erlang.).

"Absint praeconceptae opiniones et studia partium quibus veritas non potest non impediri." Kimedonc, *De Scripto Dei Verbo*, p. 622.

10. "*Adsit quidem pia curiositas et curiosa pietas.*" Erasmus.

We must welcome lights from all quarters. "Our faith, so far as it is in knowledge, is imperfect, and requires not only enlargement, but correction. Great movements of the human spirit are not hostile to theology, but introduce the conditions of a more perfect development of it." The Reformed religion will be false to all its own deepest principles, if it seeks relief from hostile perplexity by throwing itself into the arms of obscurantism.

11. "Interpret literally and grammatically."

"Illustrate where possible by reference to history, topography, and antiquities."

"Interpret with reference to the context."

"Elicit the full significance of details."

These four rules are given by Bishop Ellicott in *Aids to Faith*, pp. 426-440, where they will be found expanded and illustrated. He adds the rules

"Interpret according to the analogy of Scripture."

"Interpret according to the analogy of Faith."

These two last rules may be reasonably and wisely interpreted, but we have sufficiently seen in the previous pages that they have been seriously abused and perverted. The first has been misapplied to force upon passages of Scripture wholly alien from each other in meaning a deceptive semblance of identity of purport. The other has been used to fetter the freedom of inquiry by dictating beforehand, in each particular branch of the Church, the conclusion at which the expositor must arrive.

12. One rule is always valuable :— *Interpret in a spirit of piety and humility.*

"Scriptura sacra non temerarios et superbos accusatores sed diligentes et pios requirit lectores." Aug. *c. Adimant.* iii. 6.

BIBLIOGRAPHY.

BIBLIOGRAPHY OF GENERAL EXEGESIS.[1]

LECTURE I.

Cave, Scriptores Ecclesiastici. London. 1688.
Oudin, De Scriptoribus Ecclesiae. Leipzig. 1722.
R. Simon, Histoire Critique du Vieux Testament. Paris. 1680.
———— Hist. Crit. des Principaux Commentateurs du Nouveau Testament.
   Rotterdam. 1693.
S. Glass, Philologia Sacra. Amsterdam. 1694.
Pfaff, Hist. Lit. Theologiae. Tübingen. 1720.
J. F. Buddeus, Isagoge Hist. Theol. Leipzig. 1727.
J. G. Walch, Bibliotheca Theol. Jena. 1757-1765.
S. F. N. Morus, Acroases super Hermeneutica. Leipzig. 1797-1802.
J. G. Rosenmüller, Historia Interpretationis. 5 vols. Leipzig. 1795-1814.
J. A. Fabricius, Bibliographia Antiquaria. Hamburg. 1713.
Schröck, Christliche Kirchengeschichte. 45 vols. 1768-1812.
Ernesti, Institutio Interpretis Novi Test. Leipzig. 1761.
Böhringer, Die Kirche Christi und ihre Zeugen. 2te Ausg. Stuttgart.
   1873.
Sonntag, De Doctrina Inspirationis. Heidelberg. 1810.
Klausen, Hermeneutik. Germ. Transl. Leipzig. 1841.
Lücke, Grundriss d. Neut. Hermeneutik. Göttingen. 1817.
J. L. S. Lutz, Biblische Hermeneutik. Berne. 1849.
Lange, Grundriss d. Bibl. Hermeneutik. 1874.
Immer, Hermeneutik. Wittenb. 1873.
Diestel, Gesch. d. Alt. Testamentes in der Christlichen Kirche. Jena. 1869.
Bishop Wordsworth, On the Interpretation of the Bible. Miscellanies II.
   1-100.
S. Davidson, Introduction to the New Testament. London. 1868.
Reuss, Gesch. d. Heiligen Schriften Neuen Testaments. Braunschweig.
   1874.
———— Gesch. der Heiligen Schriften Alten Testaments. Braunschweig.
   1882.

---

[1] It is possible that some readers may be glad to be referred to the works
mentioned in the following list. I have not attempted to make the Bibliography complete ; that would require a volume. The dates are often those
of editions which I have used, and the titles are given in the briefest form.
Other works of a more special character are referred to in the notes. "Quibus
parum vel quibus nimium est mihi ignoscant."

Ewald und Dukes, Beiträge zur Gesch. d. Ausleg. A. T.   3 vols.   1844.
L. Wogue, Hist. de la Bible et de l'Exégèse jusqu' à nos Jours.   Paris.   1881.
Hamburger, Real-Encyklopädie für Bibel und Talmud, vol. i. *s. v.* Schrift,
    Schriften, Sprache.   Breslau.   1870 : vol. ii. *s. vv.* Bibel, Bibelübersetzung,
    Exegese, Halacha, Agada, Kabbala, Talmud, Text der Bibel, &c.   Strelitz.
    1883.
Herzog, Real-Encyklopädie für Prot. Theol. u. Kirche *s. v.* Hermeneutik, &c.
Encyclopaedia Britannica, *Art.* Hermeneutics.
Merx, Eine Rede vom Auslegen insbesondre d. Alten Testaments.   Halle.
    1879.
————Die Prophetie des Joel und ihre Ausleger von der aeltesten Zeiten bis
    zu den Reformatoren.   Halle.   1879.

Scattered notices are to be found in various Introductions, such as—
Sixtus Senensis, Bibliotheca Sancta.   Rome.   1586.
Hottinger, Thesaurus Philologicus.   Zürich.   1649.
Huet, Demonstratio Evangelica.   Rouen.   1681.
J. G. Carpzov, Introd. ad Libros Canonicos.   Leipzig.   1721.
Eichhorn, Einleitung.   Leipzig.   1780-1783.
Michaelis, Introduction to the New Testament.   ed. Marsh.   Cambridge.
    1801.
Jahn, Introd. in Libros Sacros.   Vienna.   1804.
Zöckler, Handbuch d. Theologischen Wissenschaften.   Nördlingen.   1883.
Ladd, The Doctrine of Sacred Scripture.   Edinburgh.   1883.

And in the works of Hilgenfeld, De Wette, Kurz, Oehler, Baur, Neander,
Gieseler, &c. ; and in the various Biblical and Theological Dictionaries and
Encyclopaedias.

LECTURE II.

Mischna.   Surenhusius.   6 vols. fol.   Amsterdam.   1698-1703.
Mishna Treatises, De Sola and Raphall.   London.   1843.
The Midrashim.   Bibliotheca Rabbinica, eine Sammlung alter Midrashim,
    übertragen von Dr. A. Wünsche.   Leipzig.   1882-1884.
Le Talmud de Jérusalem.   Traduit pour la première fois, par Moïse Schwab.
    Paris.   1871-1883.
Der Jerusalemische Talmud in Seinen Haggadischen Bestandtheilen, übertragen
    von Dr. A. Wünsche.   Zürich.   1880.
Etheridge, Translation of the Targums to the Pentateuch.   London.   1862-
    1884.
Fl. Josephi Opera.   ed. Haverkamp.   Amsterdam.   1726.   ed. Richter.
    Leipzig.   1826.
Maimonides, More Nevochim.   (Ductor Perplexorum.)   ed. Buxtorf.   Basle,
    1629.
Raymond Martin, Pugio Fidei.   Paris.   1651.
Eisenmenger, Entdecktes Judenthum.   Königsberg   Ed. 1711.
J. Buxtorf, Synagoga Judaica.   Basle.   1604.
———— De Abbreviaturis Hebraicis.   Basle.   1613.
Wagenseil, Tela Ignea Satanae.   Amsterdam.   1681.
Ewald, Abodah Zarah.   Nürnberg.   1856.
Lightfoot, Works.   Ed. Pitman.   London.   1822-1825.
Schöttgen, Horae Hebraicae.   Dresden.   1733.
Meuschen, Nov. Test. ex Talmude illustratum.   Leipzig.   1736.
J. J. Buxtorf, Lexicon Chaldaicum, Talmudicum et Rabbinicum.   Basle.
    1639.

Vitringa, De Synagoga Vetere. Franeker. 1696.
Waehner, Antiquitates Ebraeorum. Göttingen. 1743.
J. C. Wolf, Bibliotheca Hebraea. 1715-1735.
Beer, Gesch. d. religiosen Secten d. Juden. Berlin. 1822.
Fürst, Kultur- und Literatur-Geschichte der Juden in Asien. Leipzig.
  1849.
Fürst, Der Talmud in Seiner Nichtigkeit. Warsaw. 1848.
Hirschfeld, Halachische Exegese. Berlin. 1840.
————— Hagadische Exegese. Berlin. 1847.
Zunz, Gottesdienstliche Vorträge. Berlin. 1832.
——— Synagogal. Poesie d. Mittelalters. Berlin. 1855.
Hamburger, Real-Encykl. für Bibel und Talmud. Abth. i. Breslau. 1870.
  Abth. ii. Strelitz. 1883.
L. Wogue. Hist. de la Bible et l'Exégèse Biblique jusqu'à nos Jours. Paris.
  1881.
Löw המפתח . Praktische Einleitung und Gesch. d. Schriftauslegung.
  Gross-Kanischa. 1855.
Chiarini, Théorie du Judaïsme. Paris. 1830.
Weber. System der Altsynagogalen Theologie. Leipzig. 1880.
Talmudische Studien, R. Joshua ben H'anania. Berlin. No date.
Friedländer, Geschichtsbilder aus der Zeit der Tanaiten und Amoräer. Brünn.
  1879.
Weill, Le Judaïsme, ses Dogmes et sa Mission. Paris. 1866.
Revue des Études Juives. Paris. 1885.
Encycl. d. Sciences religieuses. *Art.* Talmud.
Derenbourg, Hist. de la Palestine d'après les Talmuds. Paris. 1867.
Neubauer, La Géographie du Talmud. Paris. 1868.
Wellhausen, Die Pharisäer und die Sadducäer. Greifwald. 1874.
————— Geschichte Israels. Berlin. 1878.
Ginsburg, The Massorah Ha Massoreth of Elias Levita. London. 1867.
Trenel, Vie de Hillel. 1867.
Delitzsch, Jesus und Hillel. Erlangen. 3rd edition. 1879.
Jost, Geschichte des Judenthums. Leipzig. 1859.
Grätz, Geschichte der Juden. Leipzig. 1871.
Herzfeld, Geschichte des Volkes Israel. Leipzig. 1863.
Geiger, Das Judenthum und seine Geschichte. Breslau. 2nd edition. 1865.
Jahn, Archaeologia Biblica. Ed. Upham. Oxford. 1836.
Munter, Der Judische Krieg unter d. Kaisern Trajan und Hadrian. 1821.
Ewald, Gesch. d. Volkes Israel, vol. v. 3rd ed. Göttingen. 1867.
Milman, Hist. of the Jews, vols. ii. and iii. London. 1863.
Eisenlohr, Das Volk Israel. Leipzig. 1856.
Schürer, Neutest Zeitgeschichte. Leipzig. 1874.
Kuenen, The Religion of Israel. E. Tr. Edinburgh. 1874.
Steinschneider, Jewish Literature. London. 1857. A translation of the
  Article in Ersch und Gruber.
L. Dukes, Rabbinische Blumenlese. Leipzig. 1844.
W. Robertson Smith, The Old Testament in the Jewish Church. Edinburgh.
  1881.
————— Lectures on the Old Testament. Edinburgh. 1884.
Dr. McCaul, Old Paths. London. 1854.
Barclay, The Talmud. London. 1878.
Allen, Modern Judaism. London. 1830.
Margoliouth, Modern Judaism. 1843.
Hershon, Talmudic Miscellany. London. 1880.
————— Genesis with a Talmudic Commentary. London. 1883.[1]

---

[1] My references to this book will not always exactly coincide with those
of the published volume, because I used an unpublished copy.

I I

Hershon, Treasures of the Talmud. London. 1882.
Etheridge, Hebrew Literature. London. 1856.
Deutsch, Lit. Remains. London. 1874.
C. Taylor, Sayings of the Jewish Fathers. Cambridge. 1877.
Edersheim, Temple Services. London. 1874.
Duschak, Flavius Josephus u. die Tradition. Wien. 1864.

BOOKS ON THE QABBALA.

Reuchlin, De Verbo Mirifico. Basle. 1494.
——— De Arte Cabbalistica. Hagenau. 1517.
Raymond Lully, De Auditu Cabbalistico. Strasb. 165̇1.
Kircher, Œdipus Ægyptiacus. Rome. 1635.
Jellinek, Beiträge zur Gesch. d. Kabbalah. Leipzig. 1852.
Franck, La Kabbale. Paris. 1843. Uebersetzt vom A. Jellinek. Leipzig. 1844.
Ginsburg, The Kabbalah, its Doctrines, Development, and Literature. London. 1865.
——— Coheleth, London. 1861.
Munk, Mélanges de Philos. Juive et Arabe. Paris. 1859.

LECTURE III.

Hody, De Bibl. Text. Originalibus. Oxon. 1715.
Frankel, Vorstudien zu d. Septuaginta. Leipzig. 1841.
Philonis Opera, ed. Richter. 1828-1830 [containing the Fragments discovered by Mai and Aucher].
Philonis Opera, ed. Mangey. 2 vols. London. 1742.
Tischendorf, Philonea Inedita. Leipzig. 1868.
Planck, De Principiis et Causis Interpretationis Philoniacæ Allegoricae. Göttingen. 1806.
Delaunay, Philon d'Alexandrie. Paris. 1867.
Grossmann, Quaestiones Philoneae. Leipzig. 1829.
Siegfried, Philo von Alexandria. Jena. 1875.
——— On Philo's use of the LXX. in Hilgenfeld's Zeitschrift. 1873.
Gfrörer, Philo und die Alexandr. Theosophie. Stuttgart. 1831.
Dähne, Gesch. Darstellung der Judisch-Alexandrinischen Religions-Philosophie. Halle. 1834.
Fürst, Bibl. Judaica. Leipzig. 1849-1863.
Bartolocci, Bibl. Rabbinica. Rome. 1693.
Munk, Palestine. Paris. No date.
Guericke, De Schola Alexandrina. Halae. 1824-1825.
Jowett, Epistles to the Thessalonians, &c., i. 363-417. London. 1855.
J. G. Müller, Des Juden Philo Buch von d. Weltschöpfung. Berlin. 1841.
Matter, Essai Historique sur l'École d'Alexandrie. Paris. 1820.
Drummond, Philo : Principles of the Jewish Alexandrian Philosophy. London. 1877.
Neander, Ch. History (E. T.), i. 65-93. Edinburgh. 1851.
Hausrath, Neutest Zeitg. Die Zeit d. Apostel, i. 123-171. Heidelberg. 1879.
Döllinger, Judenthum u. Heidenthum. Regensburg. 1857.
Lagarde, Anmerkungen zur Gr. Uebersetzung. Leipzig. 1863.
Wellhausen, Text der Bücher Samuel. Göttingen. 1871.

Hollenberg, Der Charakter d. Alex. Uebersetzung. Moers. 1876.
Döpke, Hermeneutik d. Neutest. Schriftst. Leipzig. 1829.
Reuss, Théologie Chrétienne. 3rd ed. Paris. 1864.
Grinfield, Apology for the Septuagint. London. 1850.
Herzog's Cyclopaedia, *s. vv.* Hellenism, Philo.
Lipsius, Alex. Religions-Philosophie. Schenkel, Bibel Lexicon, i. 87.
Dr. Deutsch, *s. v.* "Dispersion" in Kitto's Cyclopaedia.
Canon Westcott, Introduction to the Study of the Gospels. Revised edition. 1867.
Kuenen, Rel. of Israel. iii. 162-223. E. Tr. London. 1875.
Keim, Jesu von Nazara. i. 208-225. Zürich. 1867.
Jost, Gesch. d. Israeliten. iii. 174-181. Berlin. 1822.
———— Gesch. d. Judenthums und seiner Sekten. Leipzig. 1857. i. 368-402.
Grätz, Gesch. d. Juden, iii. 296-308. Leipzig. 1863.
Dähne in Ersch und Gruber, *s. v.* Philo.
Zöckler in Herzog, *s. v.* Philo.
Kingsley, Alexandria and her Schools. Cambridge. 1854.
Vacherot, Hist. de l'École d'Alexandrie. Paris. 1846.
Ueberweg, Hist. of Philos i. 222-231. E. Tr. 3rd ed. London. 1880.
Ewald, Gesch. d. Volkes Isr. vi. 257-312. Göttingen. 1868.
Olshausen, Ein Wort über tiefern Schriftsinn. Königsberg. 1824.

LECTURE IV.

For Patristic methods of interpretation, see

Origen, De Principiis. Lib. iv.
Adrianus, Εἰσαγωγὴ εἰς τὰς θείας γραφάς (Critici Sacri, viii. 11). Ed. Höschel. Wien. 1602.
Eucherius, Liber formularum. Bibl. Max. Patr., vi. 522.
Tichonius, De Septem Regulis. Bibl. Max. Patr., vi. 49. Gallandi, viii. 107.
Hieronymus, De Optimo Genere Interpretandi. Ep. 101, ad Pammach.
Augustinus, De Doctrina Christiana, iii. iv. Opp. Ed. Bened., t. iii.
Junilius, De Partibus Legis Divinae. Bibl. Max. Patr., x. 339. Ed. Kihn. Friburg. 1880.
Isidore of Pelusium, Epistolae de Interpret. Div. Script. Bibl. Max. Patr. vii.
Cassiodorus, De Institutione Div. Literarum. Opp. ii. 509 *sq.* Migne, lxx. 1105.
Whitby, Dissert de Sac. Script. Interpretatione. London. 1714.
Cave, Lives of the Fathers. Ed. Cary. Oxon. 1850.
J. G. Walch, Bibliotheca Patristica. Ed. Danz. 1834.
Flacius, Clavis Script. Sacr., pp. 134-145. Basle. 1609.
Böhringer, Die Kirche Christi und ihre Zeugen, 2te Auflage. Stuttgart. 1873.
Ewald, Gesch. d. Volkes Israel, vii. Göttingen. 3rd ed. 1868.
Huber, Die Philosophie der Kirchenväter. Munich. 1859.

---

[1] The literature on the subject of this Lecture is immense. I only indicate a few of the books and editions which will be found most useful.

Barbeyrac, Traité de la Morale des Pères. 1728.
Möhler, Patrologie, ed. Riethmayer. Regensb. 1840.
Bishop Kaye. Some Account of the Writings and Opinions of Clement of
    Alexandria. London. 1835.
Neander, Antignosticus, or Spirit of Tertullian. E. Tr. London. 1864.
Donaldson, The Apostolical Fathers. London. 1874.
F. Vogl, Die heilige Schriften u. ihre Interpretation durch die h. Väter.
    Augsb. 1836.
Cotelerius, Patres Apostolici. Amsterdam. 1724.
Lightfoot, Epistles of Clement. Cambridge. 1869-1877.
———Ignatius and Polycarp. London. 1885.
J. Temple Chevalier, Clement of Rome, &c., with Introduction. Cambridge.
    1833.
Philotheos Bryamios, τοῦ Κλήμεντος. Αἱ δύο πρὸς Κορινθίους ἐπιστολαί.
    Constant. 1875.
Irenaeus, ed. Stieren. Leipzig. 1853.
——— ed. Harvey. Cambridge. 1857.
Hilgenfeld, Hermae Pastor. Leipzig. 1881.
C. H. Hoole, The Shepherd of Hermas. London. 1870.
Otto, Corpus Apologetarum. Jena. 1847.
Semisch, Justin der Märtyrer. Breslau. 1842.
M. von Engelhardt, Das Christenthum Justins d. Märtyr. Erlangen. 1878.
Bishop Kaye, Some Account of the Writings and Opinions of Justin Martyr.
    Cambridge. 3rd edition. 1853.
Freppel, Des Apologistes Chrétiens du IIe Siècle. Paris. 1860.
E. de Pressensé, Hist. des trois premiers Siècles. Paris. 1870.
Renan, Les Évangiles. Paris. 1877.
——— L'Église Chrétienne. Paris. 1879.
Keim, Rom und das Christenthum. Berlin. 1881.
Origenis Opera ed. De La Rue. Paris. 1759.
——— ed. Huet. Rouen. 1668.
Huet, Origeniana. Colon. 1685.
Redepenning, Origenes. Bonn. 1846.
Ernesti, De Origene. Opusc., p. 288 *sq.* 1776.
Guericke, De Schola quae Alexandriae floruit Catechetica. Halle. 2 parts.
    1824-1825.
M. J. Denis, De la Philosophie d'Origène. Paris. 1884.
Tertulliani quae supersunt omnia. Ed. Oehler. Leipzig. 1853.
Hauck, Tertullian's Leben und Schriften. Erlangen. 1877.
Rönsch, Das Neue Testament Tertullians. Leipzig. 1871.
Bishop Kaye, Writings of Tertullian. 3rd edition. London. 1845.
H. Weiss, Die Grossen Kappadokier als Exegeten. Braunsberg. 1872.
Rupp, Gregorius von Nyssa. Leipzig. 1834.
Ullmann, Gregorius von Nazianz. Darmstadt. 1825.
F. Lücke, Quaestiones Didymianae. Göttingen. 1829.
Daillé, On the Right Use of the Fathers. E. Tr. London. 1841.
J. J. Blunt, The Right Use of the Early Fathers. London. 1857.
Smith and Wace, Dictionary of Christian Biography. London. 1877-1882.
Tillemont, Mémoires pour servir à l'Hist. Eccl. des Six Premiers Siècles.
    Paris. 1712.
R. Simon, Hist. Critique du Vieux Testament. Amsterdam. 1685.
——— Des Versions du N. Testament. Rotterdam. 1690.
——— Du Texte du N. Testament. Rotterdam. 1689.
——— Des Principaux Commentateurs du N. Testament. Rotterdam.
    1693.
——— Nouvelles Observations. Paris. 1695.
Baur, Church History. E. Tr. London. 1878.
Alb. de Broglie, L'Eglise et l'empire romain au 4me siècle. 4th ed. Paris.
    1868.

Schaff, History of the Christian Church. Edinburgh. 1884.
Hergenröther, Handb. d. allgem. Kirchengeschichte. Freiburg. 2nd edition. 1879.
D. Conybeare, Analyt. Exam. of the Writings of the Christian Fathers. Bampton Lectures. 1839.
Estlander, De Usu S.S. in Eccl. Cath. duobus primis post Christum Seculis. Helsingf. 1829.
Ebert, Gesch. d. Literat. d. lateinischen Mittelalters im Abendlande. Leipzig. 1874. Vol. ii. 1880.
H. A. Woodham, Tert. Liber Apologet. with Notes and Introduction. Cambridge. 1850.
Cypriani Opera, ed. Hartel. (Corpus Scrip. Eccles. Latin.)
Freppel, St. Cyprien. 2nd edition. Paris. 1873.
Clementis Alex. Opera, ed. Potter. Oxon. 1715.
Freppel, Clément d'Alexandrie. Paris. Revised edition. 1873.
Münter, De Schola Antiochena. 1814.
Hergenröther, Die Antioch. Schule. Würzburg. 1866.
Sieffert, Theod. Mopsuestenus Vet. Test. sobrie interpret. Vindex. Regensb. 1827.
H. B. Swete, Theod. Ep. Mops. in Epp. B. Pauli Commentarii. Cambridge. 1882.
Kihn, Die Bedeutung d. antioch. Schule. Weissenburg. 1856.
S. Chrysostomi Opera. Ed. Bern. de Montfaucon. Paris. 1718—1738.
Förster, Chrysostomus. Gotha. 1869.
W. A. Stephens, Life and Times of St. Chrysostom. London. 1872.
E. Binder, Études sur Théodoret. Geneva. 1844.
C. V. Lengerke, De Ephraemi Syri Arte Hermeneutica. Regiom. 1831.
Hieronymi Opera, ed. Vallarsi. Verona. 1734-1742.
Clericus, Quaest. Hieronymianae. Amstelod. 1700.
Engelstoft, Hieronymus Stridonensis. Havre. 1797.
Zöckler, Hieronymus. Gotha. 1865.
A. Thierry, St. Jérome. Paris. 1867.
Cutts, St. Jerome. London. 1877.
Trench, Augustine as an Interpr. of Scripture. The Sermon on the Mount. London. 1851.
Bindemann, Der Heilige Augustinus. Berlin. 1844-1869.
Nourisson, La Philos. de St. Augustin. 2nd ed. Paris. 1866.
Flottes, Études sur St. Augustin. Paris. 1861.

LECTURE V.

SOME ORIGINAL AUTHORITIES.

J. Scotus Erigena, De Divisione Naturae. Migne, t. 122.
Joh. Sarisburiensis, Opera. Migne, t. 199.
Rupertus Tuitensis, Praef. in Comment. in Joann. Opera. Venice, 1748-1750.
Hugo de Sto. Victore, Opera. Migne, tt. 175-177.
Bonaventurae Opera. Ed. Peltier. Paris. 1861.
St. Thomas Aquinas, Praef. in Psalmos, Praef. in Hiob.
———————— Summa. Cap. de Scripturis.
Petri Abaelardi, Sic et Non.
V. Cousin, Œuvres inédits d'Abélard. Paris. 1836.
Petr. Lombardi, ll. iv. Sententiarum. Migne, t. 192.

Bernardi Opera. Ed. Mabillon. Paris. 1719.
Nicolai Lyrani Prologi.
Gerson, Propositiones de Sensu Literali. Opera. Ed. Du Pin. Antwerp.
1706.
Herolt, Sermones et Exempla.
Vitalius a Furno, Speculum Morale. Lyons. 1513.
Badius Ascensius, Allegoriarum Bibliorum. 1520.
Coppenstein, Dispositio Sermonum ad Sens. Literalem et saepe Mysticum de
Aquinate et Bonaventura.
Whitaker, Disputation on Holy Scripture. Parker Society. 1849.
Goldast, Monarchia. Frankfort. 1640.

SOME GENERAL HISTORIES.

Brucker, Historia Crit. Philosophiæ, t. iii. Leipzig. 1743.
Ampère, Hist. Lit. de la France avant le Douzième Siècle. Paris. 1839.
Bouquet, Rerum Gallic. et Francic. Scriptores. Paris. 1752.
Herman Reuter, Gesch. der Rel. Aufklärung in Mittelalter. Berlin. 1875.
S. R. Maitland, The Dark Ages. London. 1844.
Hampden, Bampton Lectures. Oxford. 1832.
———— Life of Thomas Aquinas. Enc. Metropol. 1848.
Kaulich, Gesch. d. Scholast. Philosophie. Prag. 1853.
Stöckl, Gesch. d. Philos. d. Mittelalters. Mayence. 1866.
Prantl, Gesch. d. Logik. Leipzig. 1867.
Guizot, Hist. de la Civilisation en France.
Hauréau, De la Philos. Scolastique. Paris. 1850.
Léon Maitre, Les Écoles de l'Occident.
Hallam, Middle Ages. London. 1855.
———— Hist. of European Literature. London. 1856.
Saisset, Essais de la Philosophie Religieuse. 1859.
Sir J. Stephen, Lectures on the History of France. London. 1857.
R. A. Vaughan, Hours with the Mystics. London. 1680.
Werner, Die Scholastik d. Späteren Mittelalters. Wirn. 1881.
Ueberweg, Hist. of Philosophy. E. Tr. London. 1880.
F. D. Maurice, Mediaeval Philosophy. Encyclop. Metropolitana. 1857.
Colet on the Celestial Hierarchies of Dionysius. Ed. Lupton. London. 1869.
Figuier, Vie des Savants Illustres. Paris. 1867.
J. Bass Mullinger, The University of Cambridge. 1873.

SOME MONOGRAPHS.

Binder, De Schol. Theol. Tübingen. 1624.
Lud. Vives, De Causis Corrupt. Artium. Antwerp. 1531.
Thomasius, Theologia Scholastica et ejus Initium. Hist. Sap. et Stult., iii.
p. 225 *sq.* Halae. 1693.
Danaeus, Prolegom. in Lombardi Sent. Genevae. 1580.
Tribbechovius, De Doctoribus Scholasticis. Ed. Heumann. Jena. 1719.
Ittigius, De Bibliothecis et Catenis Patrum. Leipzig. 1708.
Noesselt, De Catenis Patrum Graecorum. Halae. 1762.
Elster, De Med. Aevi Theol. Exegetica. Göttingen. 1855.
De Launoy, De Varia Aristotelis Fortuna in Acad. Parisiensi. 1653.
Huber, Joannes Scotus Erigena. Munich. 1861.
Christlieb, Leben und Lehre d. J. Scotus. Gotha. 1860.
Hundeshagen, De Agobardi Vitâ et Scriptis. Giessen. 1831.
V. Cousin, Œuvres Inédits d'Abélard. Paris. 1836.
———— Cours de Philosophie. Paris. 1829.

Rémusat, Abélard. Paris. 1845.
Guizot, Lettres d'Abélard. Paris. 1839.
M. Deutsch, Peter Abälard, ein Kritischer Theolog. d. Zwölften Jahrhunderts. 1883.
Jourdain, Recherches sur: l'Age des Traductions Lat. d'Aristote. Paris. 1819.
———— La Philos. de Thomas d'Aquin.
Liebner, Hugo de Sto Victore. Leipzig. 1836.
Engelhardt, Richard v. St. Victor. Erlangen. 1838.
Hollenberg, Studien zu Bonaventura. Berlin. 1862.
Schaarschmidt, Johannes Sarisburiensis. Leipzig. 1862.
J. Cotter Morison, Life and Times of St. Bernard. London. 1863.
Renan, Averroes. Paris. 1851.
Munk, Mélanges de Philosophie Juive et Arabe. Paris. 1859.
F. C. Baur, Christliche Kirche des Mittelalters. Tübingen. 1861.
Görres, Die Christliche Mystik. Regensb. 1838-1842.
Vaughan, Life of St. Thomas Aquinas. London. 1871.
Tholuck, De Thoma Aq. et Abaelardo S.S. interpretibus. Halle. 1842.
R. Lane Poole. Illustrations of the History of Mediaeval Thought. London. 1884.
W. T. Townsend, The Great Schoolmen of the Middle Ages. London. 1881.
J. Owen, Evenings with the Sceptics. London. 1881.
J. B. Mullinger, The Schools of Charles the Great. London. 1877.

LECTURE VI.

SOME ORIGINAL AUTHORITIES.

Erasmus, Ratio seu Methodus perveniendi ad Ver. Theologiam. 1522.
Luther, Tractat. vom Dolmetschen. Werke, ed. Walch., iv. 170.
———— Sendbriefe vom Dolmetschen. Id. xxi. 309.
Melanchthon, Libri iii. de Rhetoricâ. 1519. Opera. Halle. 1834 ff.
———— Elementa Rhetorices, ii. 1536. Opera. Halle. 1834 ff.
Calvin, Works. Edinburgh. 1842-1853.
Matthias Flacius, Clavis Scripturae Sacrae. Basle. 1567.
Bellarminus, De Verbo Dei, ll. iv. Opera. Cologne. 1620.
J. Gerhard, De Legitima S.S. Interpretatione. Jena. 1610.
Canones et Decreta Conc. Trident. Sess. iv.
P. Melanchthon, Vita Martini Lutheri. Ed. Neander. Berlin. 1841.
J. Camerarius, Vita Philippi Melanchthonis. Ed. Neander. Berlin. 1841.
O. Myconius, Vita Huldrici Zwinglii. Ed. Neander. Berlin. 1841.
Theod. Beza, Vita Joh. Calvini. Ed. Neander. Berlin. 1841.
Luther, Werke. Ed. Walch. Halle. 1740-1752.
———— Erlangen ed. 1826-1855.
Corpus Reformatorum, ed. Bretschneider. Halle. 1834-1848.
Thuanus, Hist. Sui Temporis. London. 1723.
Grotius, Annales. 1658.

SOME GENERAL HISTORIES, &c.

Mayerhoff, J. Reuchlin und Seine Zeit. Berlin. 1830.
Fabricius, Loci Communes D. Mart. Luther. 1651.
Jortin, Life of Erasmus. London. 1806.
Drummond, Erasmus, his Life and Character. London. 1873.
Köstlin, Life of Luther. E. Tr. London. 1883.
———— Luther's Theologie. 2te Ausg. Stuttgart. 1883.
Paul Henry, Das Leben Joh. Calvins. Hamburg. 1835-1838.
A. Wratislaw, John Hus. London. 1882.
Thos. M'Crie, The Early Years of J. Calvin. London. 1880.
Ullmann, Die Reformatoren vor der Reformation. 1842. E. Tr. 1855.
Kurz, Hist. of the Christian Church from the Reformation. E. Tr. Edinburgh. 1864.
Hagenbach, Hist. of the Reformation. 2 vols. E. Tr. Edinburgh. 1878.
Merle d'Aubigné, Hist. de la Reformation.
Dorner, Hist. of Protestant Theology. 2 vols. E. Tr. Edinburgh. 1871.
Schaff, Creeds of Christendom.
Beard, Hibbert Lectures. London. 1883.
G. P. Fisher, Hist. of the Reformation. New York. 1873.
Döllinger, Die Reformation. 1848.
Seebohm, Oxford Reformers. London. 1869.
Tulloch, Leaders of the Reformation. Edinburgh. 1859.

SOME MONOGRAPHS.

Graf, Essai sur la Vie et les Écrits de Lefevre d'Étaples. Strasburg. 1842.
Geiger, Das Studium d. hebr. Sprache in 16ten Jahrhundert. Brussels. 1870.
Romberg, Die Lehre Luther's von der heiligen Schrift. Wittenb. 1868.
Preger, Flacius Illyricus und Seine Zeit. Erlangen. 1861.
Gerold, Luther Considéré comme Exégète. Strasbourg. 1866.
Thilo, Melanchthon im Dienste an heil. Schriften. Berlin. 1860.
Otto, De V. Strigelio Liberioris Mentis in Eccl. Luther. Vindice. Jena. 1843.
Tholuck, Die Verdienste Calvins als Ausleger. Vermischte Schriften, ii.
Aegid. Hunnius, Calvinus Judaisans. Vit. 1593.

LECTURE VII.

The Hermeneutic manuals of this epoch are very numerous and represent all the sects and schools of thought. For the names of many not here mentioned see Reuss, Gesch. d. Heil. Schrift, pp. 292-311 ; Diestel, Gesch. d. A. T., pp. 555-781 ; Kleinert, Abriss d. Einleit. zum A. T. 1878 ; Hertwig, Tabellen zur Einl. ins N. T. 1872. Winer.

SOME ORIGINAL AUTHORITIES.

Arminius, De Sensu et Interpr. S. Script. 1683.
Calixtus, Apparatus Theologicus. Helmstädt. 1628.
Calovius, Biblia Illustrata. Frankfort. 1672.
Quenstedt, Systema Theologicum. Wittenb. 1696.

J. Gerhard, De Legit. S.S. Interpretatione. Jena. 1610.
S. Glassius, Philologia Sacra. Amsterdam. 1694.
Spinoza, Tractatus Theologico-politicus. Hamb. 1670.
Sixtinus Amama, Anti-Barbarus. Amsterd. 1628.
Dannhauer, Hermeneutica Sacra. Strasburg. 1684.
Pfeiffer, Herm. Sacra. Enlarged by Carpzov. 1690.
Waterland, Scripture Vindicated.
L. Meyer, Philosophia Scripturae Interpres. 1666.
Bp. Wilkins, Ecclesiastes, p. 59. List of Works on the Interpret. of Scrip.
Franke, Manuductio ad Lectionem Sa. Scripturae. Halle. 1693.
Clericus, Praef. Comment. in Gen. Amsterdam. 1731.
Rambach, Instt. Hermen. Jena. 1723.
Beansobre, Remarques sur le N. T. La Haye. 1742.
Werenfels, Lectiones Hermeneuticae. Opera. Basle. 1782.
J. A. Bengel, Gnomon, Praefatio. Ed. 2. Tübingen. 1759.

SOME GENERAL HISTORIES.

T. H. Schuler, Gesch. d. Schrifterklärung. Tübingen. 1787.
Weismann, Introd. in Memorabilia Eccl. Hist. 1718.
Tholuck, Das Akad. Leben des 17 Jahrhunderts. Hamburg. 1854.
Heppe, Dogmatik des Deutschen Protestantismus. Marburg. 1857.
Pfaff, Introd. in Historiam Theol. Lit. Tübingen. 1724.
Lilienthal, Biblischer Archivarius. 1746.
Meyer, Gesch. der Schrifterklärung. Göttingen. 1802.
Dr. Cunningham, The Reformers and the Theology of the Reformation.
Kurz, History of the Christian Church. E. Tr. Edinburgh. 1864.
G. J. Plank, Gesch. d. Prot. Theol. Göttingen. 1831.
Dorner, History of Prot. Theology. E. Tr. Edinburgh. 1871.
S. Franck, Gesch. d. Protest. Theologie. 1862.
Kahnis, Gesch. d. Deutschen Protestantismus. E. Tr. Edinburgh. 1856.
Werner, Gesch. der Kath. Theol. seit dem Trienter Concil. München. 1866.
Pusey. Historical Enquiry. London. 1828.
Walch, Religionsstreit. innerhalb der Lutherischen Kirche. 1730-1739.

SOME MONOGRAPHS.

Henke, Georg Calixt und Seine Zeit. Halle. 1853.
Hossbach, Spener und Seine Zeit. 1853.
H. Schmid, Gesch. des Pietismus. Nördlingen. 1863.
Wächter, J. A. Bengel, Lebensabriss, Character, Briefe, und Aussprüche. 1865.
Bilfinger, De Spinosae Methodo Explicandi S. Scr. Jen. 1739.
Segaar, De Grotio N. T. Interprete. Traj. 1785.
Spangenberg, Idea Fidei Fratrum. Barby. 1782.
Glöckner, Interpretandi Ratio a J. J. Wetsteino adhibita. Leipzig. 1754.

LECTURE VIII.

The Hermeneutic and indirectly exegetic treatises of this epoch may be counted by scores. The following are only a few of them, chiefly bearing on theory.

SOME ORIGINAL AUTHORITIES.

Ernesti, Institutio Interpretis. Leipzig. 1761.
Semler, Vorbereitung zur Theol. Hermeneutik. Halle. 1760.
Wetstein, Libelli ad Crisin atque Interpret. N. T., ed. Semler. Halle. 1766.
Wolfenbüttler Fragmente. (Lessing, Beiträge, iii. iv.) 1774-1777.
J. E. Pfeiffer, Inst. Herm. Erlangen. 1771.
J. G. Carpzov, Introd. ad ll. canon. V. T. Leipzig. 1857.
J. A. Turretin, De S. S. Interpret. Utrecht. 1728.
Kant, Die Religion innerhalb der Grenzen d. blossen Vernunft. Königsberg. 1794.
Seiler, Bibl. Herm. Erlangen. 1800.
Herder, Theol. Werke. Weimar.
Jahn, Hermeneutica. Vienna. 1812.
De Wette, Einleitung. Berlin. 1819.
Hengstenberg, Pentateuch, &c. Berlin. 1831-1861.
Ewald, Gesch. d. Volkes Israel, &c. Göttingen. 1849-1868.
Baur, Dogmengeschichte. Tübingen. 1845-1853.
Töllner, Grundriss einer Hermeneutik. Frankfort. 1765.
Schleiermacher, Darstellung d. theol. Studiums. Berlin. 1811.
———— Glaubenslehre. 1821.
———— Hermeneutik. Lücke. 1838.
Lücke, Grundriss d. Neutest. Hermen. Bonn. 1817.
Olshausen, Ein Wort über tieferen Schriftsinn. Erlangen. 1824.
Stier, Andeutungen. Leipzig. 1828.
Strauss, Streitschriften. Tübingen. 1838.
Tholuck, Das A. T. im Neuen. 1836.
Klausen, Hermeneutik. Leipzig. 1841.
Coleridge, Confessions of an Enquiring Spirit.
Lutz, Bibl. Hermen. Berne. 1849.
Reuss, Die Gesch. d. heil. Schriften. Braunschweig. 1882.
Cellerier, Manuel d'Herméneutique. Genève. 1852.
J. P. Lange, Grundriss der Bibl. Hermeneutik. Heidelberg. 1878.
S. Davidson, Sacred Hermeneutics. Edinburgh. 1843.

SOME MONOGRAPHS.

J. V. Voorst, De J. A. Ernestio Interprete. Leyden. 1804.
Semler, Lebensbeschreibung. Halle. 1781.
Noesselt, De Semlero ejusque Ingenio. Rigae. 1792.
Strauss, H. S. Reimarus und Seine Schutz-schrift. Leipzig. 1861.
W. A. Teller, Ernesti's Verdienste um Theologie u. Religion. Leipzig. 1783.
A. C. Stauss, Utrum Philosophia Kantii Scripturae interpret. admitti possit ? Vit. 1795.

Stähelin, De Wette nach Seiner Theolog. Wirksamkeit. Basle. 1880.
Bachmann, Hengstenberg nach s. Leben u. Wirken. Gütersloh. 1879.
Renan, Œuvres. 1863-1883.
Hort's Essay on Coleridge. Camb. Essays. 1856.
Many other treatises will be referred to in the notes.

SOME GENERAL HISTORIES.

Dr. A. S. Farrar, Critical History of Free Thought. Bampton Lectures.
London. 1862.
Lecky, History of Rationalism. London. 1866.
Hagenbach, German Rationalism. E. Tr. Edinburgh. 1865.
Dorner, Hist. of Prot. Theology. E. Tr. Edinburgh. 1871.
Hundeshagen, Der Deutsche Protestantismus. Darmstadt. 1850.
Tholuck, Gesch. d. Rationalismus. Berlin. 1865: and Vermischte Schriften,
ii. Hamburg. 1839.
C. Schwarz, Zur Gesch. d. Neuesten Theologie. 1856. 4th edition. Leipzig.
1869.
Rosenmüller, Handbuch für die Litterat. d. Bibl. Kritik und Exegese.
Göttingen. 1800.
Mansel, Bampton Lectures. London. 1858.
F. C. Baur, Kirchengesch. d. 19ten Jahrh. Tübingen. 1853. E. Tr. London.
1879.

INDEX.

INDEX.

A.

ABÉLARD, his work and influence in scholastic exegesis, 259 ; by his *Sic et Non* he helped to break down the authority of tradition, 259 ; Rémusat's remark regarding, 259 *n.* ; he heads his sections boldly, 259 *n.* ; he writes like a man of genius, 260 ; his works, and authorities on them, 260 *ns.* ; the scholastic method of dialectics mainly due to him, 261 ; his motto, 266 *n.* ; retires into the monastery of St. Gildas de Rhuys, 301 ; his share in the origin of scholasticism, 467 ; account of the *Sic et Non* of, 468

Abravanel, his merits as a Jewish commentator, 464

Accommodation, the doctrine of the Alexandrian teachers as to, 187 and *n.*

Adrian, 115 *n.*

Adrian VI., 311 *n.*, 319 *n.*

Aeneas, 296 *n.*

Agobard of Lyons, Archbishop, an independent mediaeval thinker, 252 *n.*; he protests against the duel and ordeal, 252 *n.* ; and against silencing the Prophets, 369 and *n.*

Ahijah, writer of one of the lost sacred books, 7

Albam, 103

Albertus, his system of scholastic exegesis, 267 ; the extent of his works, and remarks on them, 267 *n.* ; his exegesis chiefly derived at third or fourth hand from the *Catenae* or glosses, 268 *n.* ; his self-denial, 301

Albo, Joseph, denies that Messianism is a Jewish doctrine, 67 *n.*

Alciati, 349

Algazel, 280 *n.*

Aleph and Beth, remarks on the Hebrew letters, 36

Alexander, what the worshippers of Apollo did when Tyre was besieged by, 8 ; the Jews pacify the wrath of, 54 ; effects of the conquests of, 114 ; benefit conferred on the world by the founding of Alexandria by, 114 ; authorities on the civilising mission of, 114 *n.*

Alexander, the Alabarch, wrote a book to prove that animals are endowed with reason, 138 *n.*

Alexander VI., Pope, 309, 312

Alexandria, fusion of Greek philosophy and Jewish religion took place in, 114 ; benefit conferred on the world by Alexander in founding, 114 : opinions of various authors on, 114 *n.*; position and commercial advantages of, 114 ; its literary and other attractions, 114, 115 ; number and influence of the Jews in, 115 ; grandeur of the Great Synagogue of, 115 and *n.* ; becomes the seat of the wealth and intellect of the East, 115 ; influence of Greek surroundings on the Jews of, 132 ; the exegetical school of, and its object, 182 ; its leading teachers—Clement of, 183-187 ; and Origen, 183-203

Alexandrian exegesis, nature and origin of, 11 ; period during which it lasted, 12 ; hermeneutic principles of, 22 ; influence of Philo in, 22 ; its influence on the Biblical studies of the Christian Church, 111 ; the writings of Philo its chief monument, 111 ; the rise, progress, and influence of, 111 *et seq.* ; the Septuagint and its influences, 116-128 ; its leading founders and expounders, 128-158 ;

K K

K K 2

L L

by some of the, 50 ; influence and teaching of the, 56 *et seq.* ; declared to be the successors of Moses, 60 ; the professed object of the, to exalt and glorify the law, 61 ; eulogy of the in the Targum, 60 *n.* ; teaching of the, deemed superior to that of Scripture, 62, 63 ; they substitute fiction for Scripture history, 63 ; and set aside the plain meaning of the laws they professed to deify, 64 ; their device for evading the Mosaic provision of the Sabbatic year, and of the law of the remission of debt, 64 *n.*

SCRIPTURE, threefold and fourfold sense of, 26 *n.* ; the Vulgate, the Septuagint, and the various Protestant versions teem with errors, 27 *n.* ; " Word of God " not applicable indiscriminately to all the books of, 28 ; when so applied is the deathblow to all honest interpretation of the, 28 ; testimony of a Scotch divine in reference to the interpretation of, 28 *n.* ; proof texts of, in common use, mistaken accommodations, 29 ; effects of the allegorical method as applied to various books of, 31, 32 ; on the importance of the true sense of, being made known, 38 *et seq.* ; the dreadful results of the misinterpretation of, 38-43 ; the greatest service that can be rendered to, is to free it from false dogma, 42, 43 ; testimony of various divines as to the spiritual value of the teaching of, 42, 43 ; teachings of the prophets as to the spirit of the, 49 *et seq.* ; division of the books of, in the days of Ezra, 59 ; the Mishna and the Gemara valued by the Rabbis above the, 62, 63 ; the Scribes substitute fictions for the teachings of, 63 ; Aqiba asserts that there is a mystical meaning in every letter of Scripture, 74-77 ; mistranslations and perversions of, in the Septuagint, 119 *et seq.* ; Aristobulus asserts Scripture is not to be literally understood, 130 ; explanation of the fact that the, has met with an infinitude of varying and opposite interpretations, 134 ; Philo's eclecticism, literalism, and rationalising results in a complete perversion of, 140-142 ; Philo's views on the inspiration of, 146, 147 ; extraordinary notion of Philo and others regarding, 148 and

n. ; what Scripture claims for itself, 161-163 ; Barnabas's views as to the teaching of the, 167 *et seq.* ; views of Theophilus of Antioch as to the, 171 ; of Justin Martyr, 172-174; of Irenaeus, 174-177 ; of Tertullian, 177 *et seq.* ; of Cyprian, 180-182 ; of Clement of Alexandria, 184-187 ; of Origen, 187-203 ; his views on the trivialities and immoralities of, 191, 192 ; Hippolytus's system of explaining, 201 *n.* ; Methodius's, 201 ; Hilary's, 203 ; St. Ambrose's, 205 ; Dionysius of Alexandria's, 206 ; Julius Africanus's, 207 ; on the mystical interpretation of, 210, 211 ; views of the founder and leading teachers of the school of Antioch as to the interpretation of, 210 *et seq.* ; St. Augustine's mode of interpreting, 236 *et seq.* ; the Venerable Bede's, 248 ; St. Bernard and the mediaeval mystics on, 255 *et seq.* ; an old Pope's remark on the, 258 *n.* ; views of Abelard and Peter Lombard on the, 259-263 ; of Albertus and of Thomas of Aquino, 267-272 ; of Bonaventura, 272 ; of Nicolas of Lyra, 274-278 ; views of Schoolmen generally on the, 278-300 ; services of Lorenzo Valla, of Jacques Le Fevre, of Reuchlin, and of Erasmus, to the, 312-322 ; above all, of Luther, 323 *et seq.* ; list of those who maintained the *single* sense of, in the 16th century, 328 *n.* ; views of Melanchthon and Zwingli, 341 ; of Calvin, 342 *et seq.* ; of some of the divines of the post-Reformation period, 367 *et seq.* ; of Rathmann of Lübeck, 372; of the Dutch divines, 379 ; of Spener, 380 ; of Calixtus, 382 ; of Spinoza, 383 ; of Böhme, 384 ; of Koch, 385 ; of Cappellus, 386 ; of Wetstein, 391 ; of Bengel, 392 ; of Lessing, 399 ; of Reimarus, 400 ; of Semler, 402 ; of Herder, 405 ; of Kant, 407 ; of Schleiermacher, 409 ; of Hegel, 412 ; of Strauss, 413 ; of Baur, 414 ; of Neander, 414 ; of divines of the English Church, 420 *et seq.* ; freedom of modern criticism of, 429 *et seq.*

SCRIPTURE, PASSAGES OF, QUOTED OR REFERRED TO :—

Acts i. 8	...	...	... 343*n*
— ii. 47	...	..	... 5*n*
— ii. 41	...	...	... 343*n*
— vii. 16	...	...	... 345*n*

N N

"Scripture, Analogy of," a nominally so-called, 26

"Scripture, perspicuity of," the so-called, 26, 27 n.

Seething a kid in its mother's milk, Rabbinical view of, 88 n.

Semler, marks an epoch in German exegetic study, 402 ; nature and influence of his work, 403

Septuagint, references to the, 3 n., 5 n. ; theological bias in the translators of, 5 ; its origin, and influence on the Jews and on Christianity, 116 ; list of authors and works treating of the, 116, 117 ns. ; fables regarding its origin, 117 ; use made of it by the writers of the New Testament, 117 ; defects of translations, 117 ; dislike of the Jews for the, 118 ; opposition of the Rabbis to the, 118, 119 ; their methods of interpretation for giving their own sense to the, 118, 119 ; faults of the, 119 and ns. ; traces of Jewish legendary lore found in the, 120 and ns. ; instances of mistranslations and perversions, 120 *et seq.* ; on traces of Alexandrian philosophy in the, 121 n. ; the translators of the, afraid of the word "ass," 121 and n. ; immense effect produced by the translation, 122 ; St. Augustine's veneration for the, 125 ; Theodore of Mopsuestia relies almost exclusively on the, 125 ; it shows no tendency to the method of allegory, 126 ; the object of Aristeas's letter the glorification of the, 128 ; the only Bible used by the Fathers was the, 165 ; Jerome's opinion of the, 224 ; Augustine believes in the inspiration of the, 235 n. ; Philo's use of, 452 ; account of the, 453, 455

Septuagint of the Greek Church teems with errors, 27 n.

Servetus, 235 ; on the burning of, 351 and n. ; the Abbé Glaire's remark on, 360 n. ; references to, 351 and n., 360 n.

Severianus, 115 n., 219 n.

Shabbath, extract from, on Ezekiel, 49 n. ; declares the most important law the one about fringes, 50

Shammai, Rabbi, the rival of Hillel, account of, 67

Shekhinah, Aqiba rebuked for appearing to render the, profane, 72 and n.

Shemaiah, writer of one of the lost sacred books, 6

Sic et Non of Abélard, account of the, 468

Sigismund, the Emperor, 310

Simeon ben Shetach, 19 n.

Simon the Just, the last member of the Great Synagogue, 57 n. ; the three things he asserts the world stands on, 61

Siphra, 18 n., 62 n.

Sirmium, 212

Sixtus Senensis, on the five methods of the Schoolmen, 291 n.

William Jessup University
Library
333 Sunset Blvd.
Rocklin, Ca 95765

twin brooks series BOOKS IN THE SERIES